Automotive Steering, Suspension, and Wheel Alignment

Classroom Manual

Third Edition

Chek-Chart

John F. Kershaw, Ed.D
Revision Author

James D. Halderman
Series Advisor

www.Tirerack.com
- shopping tools
- Tech center Diagram
- lowering Diagram

Extra Credit A

PEARSON
Prentice Hall

Upper Saddle River, New Jersey
Columbus, Ohio

Library of Congress Cataloging-in-Publication

Automotive steering, suspension, and wheel alignment / Chek-Chart; John F. Kershaw,
    revision author.—3rd ed.
        p; cm.
    [1] Classroom manual — [2] Shop manual.
    Includes index.
    ISBN 0-13-118481-4 — ISBN 0-13-118482-2
    1. Automobiles—Steering-gear. 2. Automobiles—Springs and suspension. 3.
Automobiles—Wheels—Alignment. I. Kershaw, John F. II. Chek-Chart Publications (Firm)

TL259.A96 2007
629.2'47—dc22   2005050937

Acquisitions Editor: Tim Peyton
Assistant Editor: Linda Cupp
Editorial Assistant: Nancy Kesterson
Production Coordination: Carlisle Editorial Services
Production Editor: Holly Shufeldt
Design Coordinator: Diane Ernsberger
Cover Designer: Jeff Vanik
Cover Art: Corel
Production Manager: Deidra Schwartz
Marketing Manager: Ben Leonard
Senior Marketing Coordinator: Liz Farrell
Marketing Assistant: Les Roberts

This book was set in Times by Carlisle Publishing Services. It was printed and bound by Bind-Rite Graphics. The cover was
printed by The Lehigh Press, Inc.

Portion of materials contained herein have been reprinted with permission of General Motors Corporation, Service and Parts
Operation. License Agreement #0410847.

10 9 8 7 6 5 4 3 2
0-13-118481-4

Introduction

Automotive Steering, Suspension, and Wheel Alignment is part of the Chek-Chart automotive series. The entire series is job-oriented and is designed especially for students who intend to work in the automotive service profession. The package for each course consists of two volumes, a *Classroom Manual* and a *Shop Manual.*

This third edition of *Automotive Steering, Suspension, and Wheel Alignment* has been revised to include in-depth coverage of the latest developments in automotive steering and suspension systems. Students will be able to use the knowledge gained from these books and from the instructor to diagnose and repair automotive steering, suspension, and wheel alignment systems used on today's automobiles.

This package retains the traditional thoroughness and readability of the Chek-Chart automotive series. Furthermore, both the *Classroom Manual* and the *Shop Manual,* as well as the *Instructor's Manual,* have been greatly enhanced.

CLASSROOM MANUAL

New features in the *Classroom Manual* include:

- A precise alignment between the *Classroom Manual* and the *Shop Manual.*
- New information on electric motor or electromagnetic device assisted power steering to include MAGNASTEER II®, four-wheel steering systems, such as, Quadrasteer™.
- Expanded coverage of the newer electronically controlled suspension systems.
- Increased coverage of computerized four-wheel alignment.

SHOP MANUAL

Each chapter of the revised *Shop Manual* correlates with the *Classroom Manual.* Like the *Classroom Manual,* the *Shop Manual* features an overhauled illustration program. It includes more than 75 new or revised figures and extensive photo sequences showing step-by-step repair procedures.

INSTRUCTOR'S MANUAL

The *Instructor's Manual* includes task sheets that cover many of the NATEF tasks for *Automotive Steering, Suspension, and Wheel Alignment.* Instructors may reproduce these task sheets for use by the students in the lab or during an internship. The *Instructor's Manual* also includes a test bank and answers to end-of-chapter questions in the *Classroom Manual.*

The *Instructor's Resource CD* that accompanies the *Instructor's Manual* includes Microsoft® PowerPoint® presentations and photographs that appear in the *Classroom Manual* and *Shop Manual.* These high-resolution photographs are suitable for projection or reproduction.

Because of the comprehensive material, hundreds of high-quality illustrations, and inclusion of the latest automotive technology, these books will keep their value over the years. In fact, *Automotive Steering, Suspension, and Wheel Alignment* will form the core of the master technician's professional library.

How to Use This Book

WHY ARE THERE TWO MANUALS?

This two-volume text—*Automotive Steering, Suspension, and Wheel Alignment*—is not like most other textbooks. It is actually two books, a *Classroom Manual* and *Shop Manual* that should be used together. The *Classroom Manual* teaches you what you need to know about how the automotive steering and suspension systems operate and why the relationship between engine components is so important. The *Shop Manual* will show you how to repair and adjust complete systems, and their individual components.

WHAT IS IN THESE MANUALS?

There are several aids in the *Classroom Manual* that will help you learn more.

- Each chapter is based upon detailed learning objectives, which are listed in the beginning of each chapter.
- Each chapter is divided into self-contained sections for easier understanding and review. This organization clearly shows which parts make up which system, and how various parts or systems that perform the same task differ or are the same.
- Most parts and processes are fully illustrated with drawings or photographs.
- A list of Key Terms is located at the beginning of each chapter. These terms are printed in **boldface type** in the text and defined in the glossary at the end of the manual. Use these words to build the vocabulary needed to understand the text.
- Review Questions follow each chapter. Use them to test your knowledge of the material covered.
- A brief summary at the end of each chapter helps you review for exams.

The *Shop Manual* has detailed instructions on test, service, and overhaul for automotive steering, suspension, and wheel alignment systems and their components. These are easy to understand and often include step-by-step explanations of the procedure. Key features of the *Shop Manual* include:

- Each chapter is based upon ASE/NATEF tasks, which are listed in the beginning of each chapter.
- Helpful information on the use and maintenance of shop tools and test equipment.
- Detailed safety precautions.
- Clear illustrations and diagrams to help you locate trouble spots while learning to read service literature.
- Test procedures and troubleshooting hints that help you work better and faster.
- Repair tips used by professionals, presented clearly and accurately.

WHERE SHOULD I BEGIN?

If you already know something about automotive steering, suspension, and wheel alignment systems and how to repair them, this book is a helpful review. If you are just starting in automotive repair, then the book will give you a solid foundation on which to develop professional-level skills.

Your instructor will design a course to take advantage of what you already know, and what facilities and equipment are available to work with. You may be asked to read certain chapters of these manuals out of order. That is fine; the important thing is to fully understand each subject before you move on to the next. Study the key terms and use the review questions to help you comprehend the material.

While reading the *Classroom Manual*, refer to your *Shop Manual* and relate the descriptive text to the service procedures. When working on actual automotive steering, suspension, and wheel alignment systems, look back to the *Classroom Manual* to keep basic information fresh in your mind. Working on such complicated modern steering and suspension systems isn't always easy. Take advantage of the information in the *Classroom Manual,* the procedures in the *Shop Manual,* and the knowledge of your instructor to help you.

Remember that the *Shop Manual* is a good book for work, not just a good workbook. Keep it on hand while you're working on a steering, suspension, or wheel alignment system. For ease of use, the *Shop Manual* will fold flat on the workbench or under the vehicle, and it can withstand quite a bit of rough handling.

When you perform actual test and repair procedures, you need a complete and accurate source of manufacturer specifications and procedures for the specific vehicle. As the source for these specifications, most automotive repair shops have the annual service information (on paper, CD, or Internet formats) from the vehicle manufacturer or an independent guide.

Acknowledgments

The publisher sincerely thanks the following vehicle manufacturers, industry suppliers, and individuals for supplying information and illustrations used in the Chek-Chart Series in Automotive Technology.

American Isuzu Motors, Inc.
American Racing Equipment
Balco, Snap-on Tools Corp.
Central County Occupational Center Program (CCOC/P), San Jose
CR Service, SKF Manufacturing Co.
DaimlerChrysler Corporation
Evergreen Valley College, San Jose, CA
Ford Motor Company
General Motors Corporation
Honda Motor Co. Inc.
Hunter Engineering Co.
Hyundai Corporation
Jaguar Cars, Ltd.
Laguna Seca Raceway

Mazda Motor Corp.
Mitsubishi Motors Corp.
Nissan North America, Inc.
OTC, a Division of SPX Corp.
Porsche Cars of North America, Inc.
Saab-Scania AB
Suzuki Motor Corp.
Tires Unlimited, San Jose
Toyota Motor Sales, U.S.A., Inc.
Volkswagen of America
Yokohama Tire Corp.

The publisher gratefully acknowledges the reviewers of this edition:

William Routley, Ferris State University
Vern Gagnon, Montana State University, Billings.

The publisher also thanks Series Advisor James D. Halderman.

Contents

1

The Automotive Chassis

OBJECTIVES

Upon completion and review of this chapter, you will be able to:

- Define the types of automotive suspensions.
- Explain the term *friction.*
- Identify terms, components, and definitions associated with steering and suspension systems.
- Define the terms used in automotive wheel alignment.

KEY TERMS

chassis	steering system
friction	suspension system

INTRODUCTION

This book describes and explains the work of the automotive **chassis.** The word *chassis* comes from an old French word meaning "frame," but in automotive technology the meaning of the term has expanded to include not only the frame but also the parts and systems that direct and support it. An automotive under vehicle specialist works on the steering and suspension systems and the wheels and tires. In addition, a chassis technician must also be able to perform repairs on systems and components that are not actually part of the chassis, but do interact with the wheels and suspension. These items can include the brake friction assemblies, axle shafts, and other driveline components.

To work professionally on chassis systems, a technician must understand how the assorted components and subsystems work and interact. This first chapter is an overview of the topics included in this *Classroom Manual.* The discussion begins with a look at the lubricants, bearings, and bushings that reduce friction between chassis components followed by a brief explanation of the basic physics involved in vehicle handling. The function and basic structure of the three major chassis systems are detailed next. These include the:

- Steering system
- Suspension system
- Wheels and tires

The chapter concludes with a discussion of wheel alignment. This overview serves as an introduction to the more detailed discussions in later chapters of this *Classroom Manual.*

REDUCING FRICTION

Chassis systems use parts that move in relation to each other to aim the wheels or to take up wheel travel, along with the wheels themselves that rotate on the axles. Whenever there is movement between facing surfaces, the surfaces create **friction**, which causes wear and generates heat. Because excessive friction-generated heat can cause parts to seize, engineers use lubricants, bushings, and bearings to reduce friction, limit wear, and minimize heat buildup.

The three main chassis lubricants are power steering fluid, gear oil, and wheel bearing or chassis grease (Figure 1-1). Power steering fluid is a relatively thin liquid used in power steering systems, both as a lubricant and as a means of transmitting hydraulic power. Gear oil, which is a thicker oil, is used in some manual steering gears and in the differential of rear-wheel drive (RWD)

vehicles. On many solid rear-axle designs, the differential gear oil serves as the rear-wheel bearing lubricant. Grease is a thick, oil-bearing lubricant placed in wheel bearings, ball joints, driveline joints, and other chassis pivot points.

Bushings, which can be made of metal, rubber, or synthetic plastics, have smooth facing surfaces

Figure 1-1. The lubricants that chassis technicians use the most are power steering fluid, gear oil, and grease.

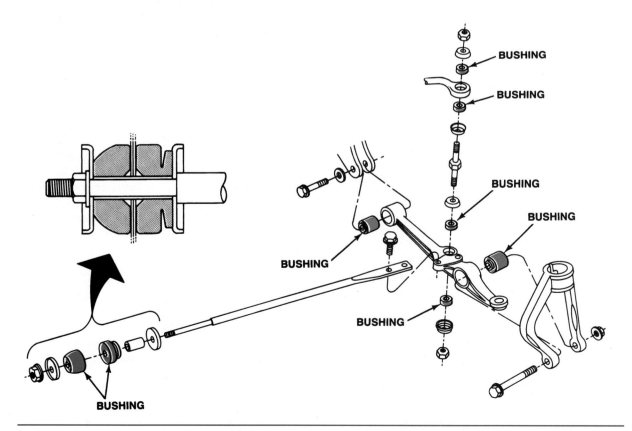

Figure 1-2. Bushings allow limited movement between parts. Metal bushings allow pivoting, while rubber bushings permit flexing and also cushion and isolate the body and passenger compartment from vibration and road shock.

to minimize friction and allow pivoting movement (Figure 1-2). The purpose of bushings is to isolate the vehicle body from the suspension in order to reduce the intrusion of road shock and vibration into the passenger compartment. Rubber bushings are flexible to take up movement and cushion shocks and vibrations. There are two types of bearings, as well. One type is a wear surface, such as inside a ball joint, where friction is allowed to wear down the softer bearing surface instead of the metal part. The other type is a ball-and-cage or a roller-and-cage construction that reduces friction by placing rolling parts between the facing surfaces.

HANDLING

A vehicle that is being driven is an object in motion, and certain laws of physics affect it. Exactly what effect they have is determined by the construction of the vehicle—where the wheels and tires are positioned, how much the vehicle weighs, and how the weight is distributed. In response to the forces of cornering, acceleration, deceleration, a vehicle body moves in three ways (Figure 1-3). These three basic types of body movement are:

- Roll
- Pitch
- Yaw

Body roll occurs during cornering, pitch is a response to acceleration or deceleration, and yaw is a result of sudden changes in direction. The effects of the airflow over, under, and around a moving vehicle—its aerodynamic qualities—also affect handling. Finally, the weight transfer that occurs whenever the vehicle changes speed or direction changes the amount of traction available at each tire.

THE STEERING SYSTEM

The **steering system** receives rotary, or circular, input from the driver at the steering wheel and changes it to lateral, or side-to-side, movement at the outer tie rod ends (Figure 1-4). The purpose of the steering system is to direct the wheels so the vehicle can change direction in response to commands from the driver.

All automotive steering systems consist of four basic parts, which are the:

- Steering wheel
- Steering shaft
- Steering gear
- Steering linkage

The steering wheel receives rotary input from the driver and transmits it to the steering shaft. The steering shaft operates the steering gear, which changes the rotary motion of the steering wheel into lateral movement of the steering linkage. The linkage pushes the steering knuckles to one side or the other, turning the wheels and tires to point the vehicle in a new direction.

Steering wheels and steering shafts are similar in all vehicles, but steering gear and steering linkage designs vary. The two most common types of steering gears are recirculating ball (Figure 1-5) and rack and pinion (Figure 1-6). Most late-model steering gears have a hydraulic power assist system. The most widely used steering linkage designs are the tie rods used with a rack and pinion gear, and the parallelogram linkage, which is the most common linkage used with a recirculating ball steering gear. A steering knuckle connects the linkage to the road wheel. A steering arm extends

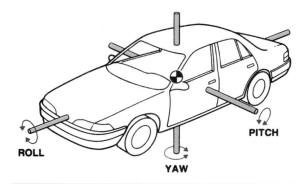

Figure 1-3. Sharp cornering causes roll, quick acceleration or deceleration causes pitch, and sudden changes in direction cause yaw.

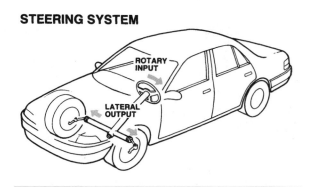

Figure 1-4. The steering system changes the rotary motion of the steering wheel into lateral movement of the steering linkage.

RECIRCULATING BALL STEERING GEAR

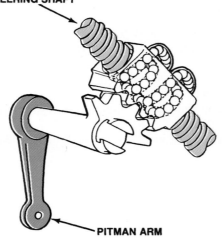

Figure 1-5. This cutaway view of a recirculating ball steering gear shows how the steering shaft operates a gear mechanism, with steel balls to reduce friction, that positions the steering linkage through the pitman arm.

RACK AND PINION STEERING GEAR

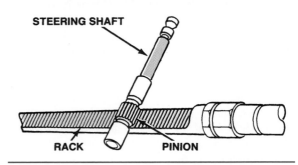

Figure 1-6. In a rack and pinion steering gear, a pinion gear turns with the steering shaft to move a rack and operate the steering linkage.

from the knuckle to the linkage, and when the linkage moves laterally, it pushes the steering arm to direct the wheels and tires (Figure 1-7).

In most vehicles, the steering system moves only the front wheels, but a few models have incorporated four-wheel steering (4WS) since the late 1980s.

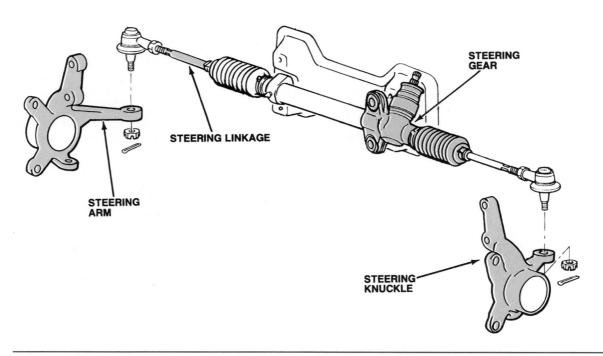

Figure 1-7. When the steering linkage moves side-to-side, it pushes the steering arm, which is an extension of the steering knuckle that connects to the steering linkage tie rods, to point the wheels in a new direction.

THE SUSPENSION

The **suspension system** consists of the components that support the vehicle body and transmit its weight to the wheels (Figure 1-8). An automotive suspension system serves two main purposes:

- Ensure vehicle control and stability by keeping the wheels in contact with the road
- Provide a comfortable ride

Suspension systems may be mounted on a solid axle, or be an independent design that allows each wheel to move vertically without directly affecting the wheel on the opposite side.

All suspensions use springs to cushion the frame and body, and shock absorbers to prevent excessive spring oscillation. Most also use control arms and other links to position the wheel. Ball joints and bushings allow the pivoting of suspension control arms and links relative to the car body and the wheel.

Except for a few heavy-duty trucks, nearly all production vehicles have independent front suspension. The solid front suspensions in use are beam axles, which use an axle tube, and I-beam suspensions, which use a steel axle beam. Some Ford Motor Company trucks use a twin I-beam independent front suspension. However, the three most common front suspensions are the following independent types:

- Short-long-arm (SLA)
- Strut
- Strut/short-long-arm (strut/SLA)

In general, SLA suspensions are more common on RWD vehicles and strut suspensions on front-wheel drive (FWD) models. The strut/SLA suspension, which is a more recent design, can be used with either drivetrain layout. An SLA suspension uses two control arms; a shorter upper arm and a longer lower arm (Figure 1-9). A strut suspension replaces the upper control arm with a strut (Figure 1-10). Strut/SLA suspensions use a strut with upper and lower control arms (Figure 1-11).

For rear suspensions, a greater variety of designs are in common use. These are classified into one of two main categories: those used with a solid rear axle and those used with independent suspensions. The most widely used solid rear suspensions are:

- Leaf spring
- Trailing arm
- Semi-trailing arm

Leaf springs attach to the frame ahead of and behind the axle and hold it in place (Figure 1-12). Trailing arms extend straight back from a frame crossmember to the axle (Figure 1-13). Semi-trailing arms run at an angle from a frame crossmember to the axle.

Independent rear suspensions are not as common as independent front suspensions, but more design variations are possible at the rear:

- Short-long-arm (SLA)
- Strut

SLA FRONT SUSPENSION

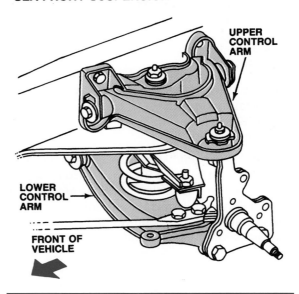

UPPER CONTROL ARM

LOWER CONTROL ARM

FRONT OF VEHICLE

SUSPENSION SYSTEM

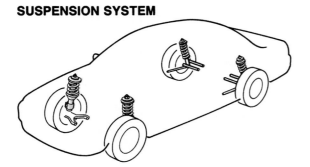

Figure 1-8. The suspension system controls wheel travel in order to keep the tires on the road and cushion the car body against shocks.

Figure 1-9. Once the most widely used front suspension design, the SLA suspension is now used mainly on trucks.

STRUT FRONT SUSPENSION

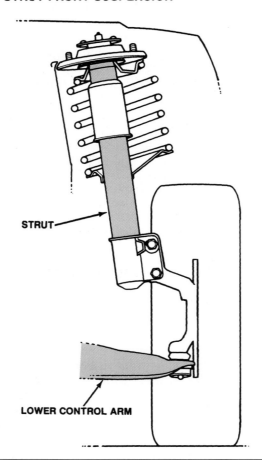

Figure 1-10. The strut front suspensions, which are more space-efficient and lighter than SLA suspensions, are common.

- Strut/short-long-arm (strut/SLA)
- Semi-trailing arm
- Multi-link
- Rear-engine

The SLA, strut, and strut/SLA designs are basically the same as those used in the front suspension. However, when these designs are used on the rear they usually include an additional trailing arm or trailing link. A semi-trailing arm independent suspension uses a control arm extending at an angle from a crossbeam to an independent wheel hub (Figure 1-14). A multi-link suspension is usually a unique design engineered specifically for an application where performance is a consideration (Figure 1-15). Rear-engine designs are not very numerous, but those that exist virtually always use an independent rear suspension. Finally,

STRUT/SLA FRONT SUSPENSION

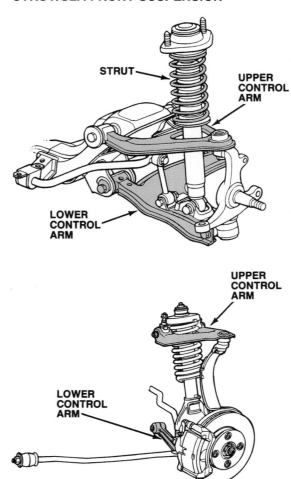

Figure 1-11. The strut/SLA suspension combines some of the characteristics of both strut and SLA suspensions.

LEAF SPRING REAR SUSPENSION

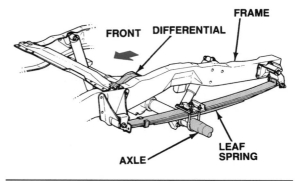

Figure 1-12. In a leaf spring suspension, the leaf spring links the axle to the frame.

TRAILING ARM REAR SUSPENSION

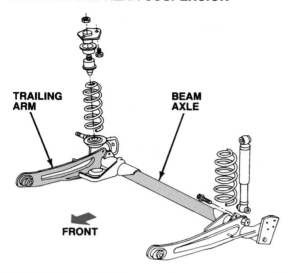

Figure 1-13. Trailing arms extend back from the frame to the axle.

SEMI-TRAILING ARM REAR SUSPENSION

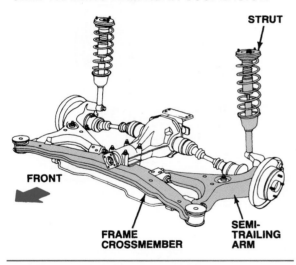

Figure 1-14. Semi-trailing arms pivot at an angle to the frame.

some FWD vehicles use a semi-independent suspension, in which a torsional beam is placed ahead of the wheels with trailing arms extending back to the knuckles (Figure 1-16).

Although universal joints (U-joints) and constant velocity (CV) joints are—strictly speaking—part of the drivetrain, rather than the suspension, chassis technicians often service them (Figure 1-17). Universal joints are commonly used on the driveshafts of RWD or four-wheel drive (4WD) vehicles to al-

MULTI-LINK REAR SUSPENSION

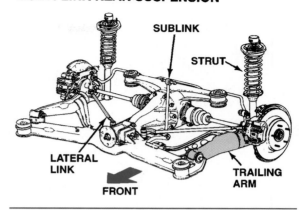

Figure 1-15. A multi-link rear suspension is often unique to the car in which it is installed.

SEMI-INDEPENDENT REAR SUSPENSIONS

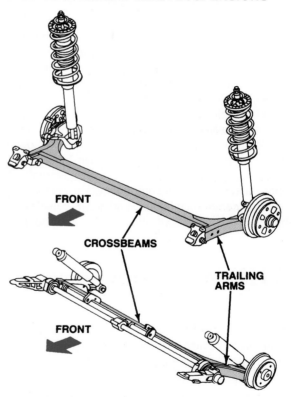

Figure 1-16. Semi-independent suspensions are used at the rear of many FWD vehicles.

low changes in angle between the transmission and differential. Constant velocity joints are commonly found on the axle shafts of FWD vehicles and are also used for RWD applications with independent rear suspension. A CV joint allows changes in angle

DRIVELINE JOINTS

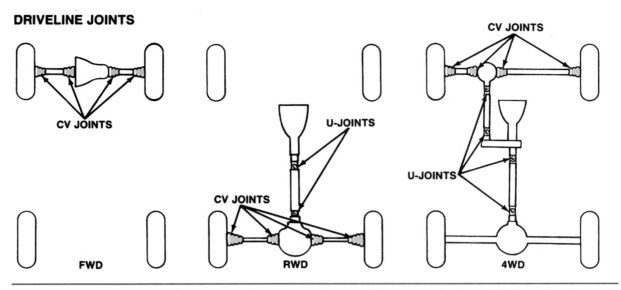

Figure 1-17. Chassis technicians often service driveline joints, which are usually either CV joints or U-joints.

between the transaxle or differential and the wheel. Some RWD vehicles also use CV joints on the driveshaft instead of U-joints, while a few vehicles use U-joints, rather than CV joints, on the drive axles.

A recent trend in suspension system design is to use electronic sensors and controls to offer varying response under differing conditions. Sensors monitor the driving conditions, and a computer determines the proper suspension response. Variable-rate shocks are the most commonly used electronically controlled suspension component. Variable-rate air springs are another option, and some vehicles use both electronically controlled springs and shocks.

THE WHEELS AND TIRES

The wheel and tire assemblies of a vehicle serve a number of purposes, including:

- Aiming the vehicle, through both steering system input and alignment angles
- Bearing the weight of the vehicle and transferring it to the ground
- Providing contact between the vehicle and the road
- Absorbing small road shocks
- Moving the vehicle by connecting to the drive axles

A wheel, which is usually made of steel or an aluminum alloy, consists of the disc and rim (Fig-

WHEEL

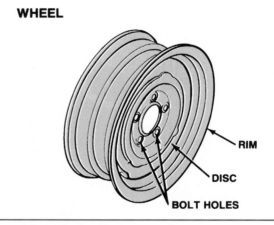

Figure 1-18. The wheel disc bolts to the axle and the rim holds the tire in place.

ure 1-18). Knowing the specifications of a wheel—measurements indicating its size and dimensions—is crucial to installing wheels that are safe for each vehicle. The wheel rotates through axle or wheel bearings, which reduce friction between the rotating and stationary parts.

A technician servicing the wheels and suspension must know how to safely remove and install the parts of the brake friction assembly found at each wheel. There are two types of brake friction assemblies in production. Drum brakes usually are found only on rear wheels, except in older vehicles. The front wheels nearly always have disc brakes, and often disc brakes are used on the rear wheels as well. Some rear disc brakes also have a

Early Adjustable Shock Absorbers

Early shock absorbers, which were originally called "stop-shock spring snubbers," were designed to reduce suspension spring oscillation, as are their modern-day successors. However, some early shocks used mechanical friction, rather than the hydraulic friction used on modern shock absorbers, to reduce spring oscillation.

One popular mechanical-friction variety, the Hartford shock absorber, used layers of hardwood sandwiched between metal disks and secured with an adjuster bolt. Arms extending from the metal disks attached to the vehicle frame and axle. To change shock stiffness, the car owner turned the adjuster bolt tighter to increase pressure on the hardwood disks, and thereby increase friction and the damping ability of the shock, or loosened the bolt for softer damping.

A later modification to the friction shock was the use of hydraulic pressure to adjust damping ability on the Andre Telecontrol system. This system used the Hartford friction shock but fitted it with a fluid-filled rubber chamber between the metal plates. When hydraulic pressure inside the rubber chamber increased, pressure on the friction disks increased as well. This had the same effect as tightening the adjuster bolt—damping ability was increased.

The car owner used a hand pump and pressure gauge, which were located in the passenger compartment, to adjust hydraulic pressure by applying pressure through hydraulic

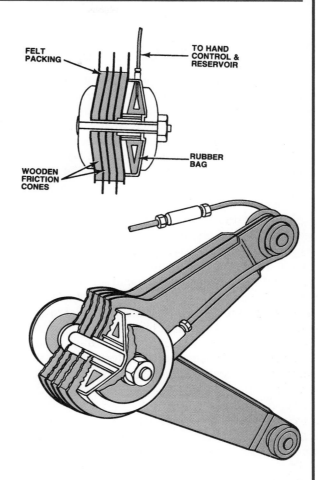

lines leading to the rubber chambers. There was just one fluid circuit, so pressure and damping at all four shocks was equal.

---

small drum brake assembly inside the rotor hub that is used as a parking brake.

The tire is constructed of three parts—the carcass, casing, and tread—that are bonded together (Figure 1-19). The air-filled rubber tire keeps the vehicle in contact with the road and cushions small road shocks. Because the tire beads fit into the wheel rim flanges, tire size must match wheel size, within a certain range. Just as with wheels, it is important for the sake of safety to install tires whose overall specifications match the needs of the wheels and vehicle.

There are a number of factors influencing the amount of adhesion, or grip, a tire has. These include, but are not limited to, the coefficient of

TIRE CONSTRUCTION

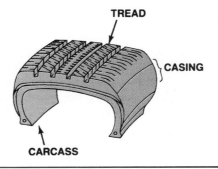

Figure 1-19. The air in the tire cushions the vehicle, and the rubber and tread design helps provide good traction under varying road conditions.

friction of the tire; the effects of acceleration, deceleration, and cornering; and the effects of pavement condition—whether wet or dry, and so on.

WHEEL ALIGNMENT

For the best handling characteristics and the least tire wear, wheels must be positioned correctly in relation to the suspension and body as the vehicle moves. This correct placement is what wheel alignment is all about. Incorrectly aligned wheels tend to go in a different direction than where the driver steers them. In addition, wheels that are out of alignment can cause tires to scuff, or drag, across the pavement as they roll, which accelerates tire wear.

Checking the wheels and tires for runout or lack of balance is an important preliminary step to wheel alignment. Like incorrect alignment, runout and balance problems affect handling and accelerate tire wear, and should be corrected when an alignment is performed. Runout and imbalance tend to make a wheel and tire assembly wobble or hop as it rolls (Figure 1-20).

The following five alignment angles are checked and corrected when performing a traditional front-wheel alignment:

- Camber
- Caster

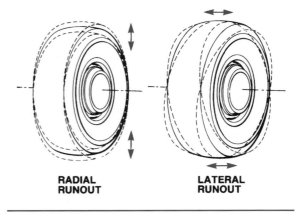

RADIAL RUNOUT   **LATERAL RUNOUT**

Figure 1-20. Runout and imbalance can make the wheel and tire wobble or hop, which accelerates tire wear and causes vibrations felt in the steering wheel and passenger compartment.

- Toe
- Steering axis inclination (SAI)
- Toe-out on turns

Camber, toe, and toe-out on turns are all tire wear angles, so if they are incorrect, the tires wear out more quickly. All traditional angles except toe are directional angles, meaning that they affect the direction the vehicle moves.

When performing a four-wheel alignment, check camber and toe at the rear wheels as well

Electromagnetic Suspensions of the Future?

As hydraulically or pneumatically actuated, computer-controlled suspension systems are becoming common on modern automobiles, advances in automotive technology may result in electromagnetic suspension systems for vehicles of the future.

Early developmental designs for electromagnetic struts appear similar to conventional hydraulic struts, and attach to the vehicle in a similar fashion as well. However, the housings for these new struts are permanent magnets, and, like all permanent magnets, they have positive and negative magnetic poles. A telescoping assembly, which would be the equivalent of the piston in a hydraulic strut, is an electromagnetic coil.

When current is applied to the coil, it produces a polarized magnetic field. The struts operate on the principle that magnetic poles that are alike repel each other, and those that are opposite attract each other.

Increasing the current passing through the coil also increases the magnetic repulsion between the strut housing and the coil, which makes the ride more controlled, or "stiff." Decreasing the current softens the ride. The amount of current delivered to the electromagnetic coil is controlled by an onboard computer that receives input from suspension system sensors, much like the computer controls on hydraulically actuated suspension systems.

The main advantage that electromagnetic suspensions have over hydraulically actuated suspensions is response time. Active hydraulic suspension response time is limited by the rate at which solenoid valves can open and apply pressurized fluid to the struts. Electromagnetic suspension response time is limited only by the amount of time it takes for electricity to energize the electromagnetic coils, and that is not very long at all!

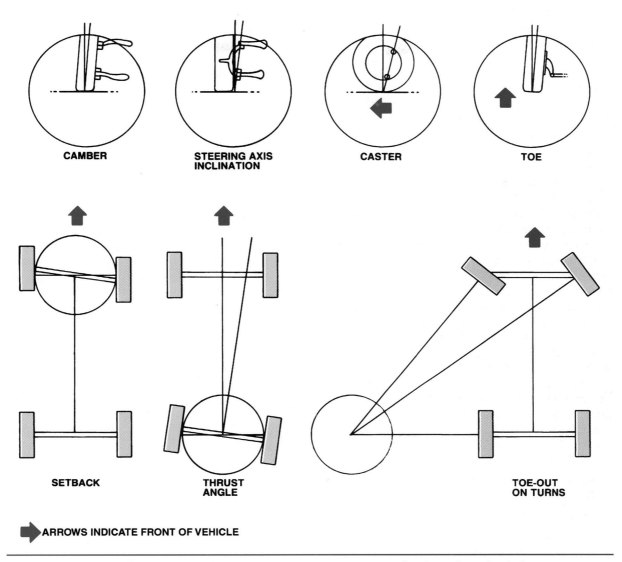

CAMBER

STEERING AXIS INCLINATION

CASTER

TOE

SETBACK

THRUST ANGLE

TOE-OUT ON TURNS

ARROWS INDICATE FRONT OF VEHICLE

Figure 1-21. Seven different angles are checked and corrected when performing a four-wheel alignment.

(Figure 1-21). In addition, the relationship of all four wheels to each other is also evaluated with the following two measurements:

- Thrust angle
- Setback

Camber is the tilt of the wheel from true vertical, as seen from the front. Zero camber, or a vertical wheel and tire, causes the least tire wear. When there is a camber angle, one side of the tire squirms on the pavement as the tire rolls, and that tire shoulder wears quickly.

Caster is the tilt of the steering axis from vertical, as seen from the side. Caster affects straight-ahead stability and steering wheel return. A great amount of positive caster makes the front wheels

"want" to go straight, so it gives stability and makes the steering wheel return to center after a turn. However, a great amount of positive caster also increases steering effort.

Toe is the direction, angle, or aiming of the wheels, as seen from above. Wheels that are aimed inward have toe-in, while those that are aimed outward have toe-out. Zero toe provides the least tire wear. During straight-ahead driving, a wheel and tire assembly that is toed in or out moves at an angle to the way it is aimed. This scuffs the tire along the pavement causing the tread to wear away very quickly.

Steering axis inclination (SAI) is the tilt of the steering axis from the vertical, as seen from the front. Like caster, SAI affects steering feel and stability. On a suspension design with a minimal amount of allowable caster, a high SAI can provide solid steering feel and stability.

Toe-out on turns occurs when the wheel at the outside of a turn does not turn as far as the wheel at the inside of the turn. Since the outside wheel has to drive in a wider curve than the inside one, it must be aimed differently. Otherwise, the outside tire would scuff as it tried to turn in a sharper curve than the cornering angle allows.

The thrust angle is the difference between the centerline of the vehicle and the direction in which the rear wheels are aimed. If the rear wheels point straight ahead, the thrust line is the same as the centerline and there is no thrust angle. When a vehicle is moving forward, the rear wheels "steer" it along the thrust line. Therefore, a zero thrust angle is ideal.

If one wheel on an axle is positioned farther back than the opposite wheel on the same axle, the rear-most wheel has setback. Setback is usually the result of a collision.

There are two basic types of wheel alignment procedures: two-wheel and four-wheel. A two-wheel alignment is an older procedure in which only the front wheels are aligned to the centerline of the vehicle. The newer, and preferred, alignment procedure is the four-wheel alignment. If possible, all four wheels are aligned with reference to the car centerline. If the rear wheels cannot be brought into correct alignment, a thrust line alignment is performed. A thrust line alignment sets the position of wheels in relation to the thrust line, rather than to the centerline of the vehicle.

SUMMARY

The automotive chassis consists of the vehicle frame and the parts and systems that direct and support it. Because the chassis includes moving parts, friction is a concern. Lubricants, bushings, and bearings reduce friction. The handling characteristics of a vehicle are the ways in which it responds to forces of motion. Roll, pitch, and yaw are the three ways that the body of a vehicle responds to cornering, acceleration, and deceleration forces. Aerodynamics and weight transfer also affect handling. The steering system, which consists of the steering wheel, steering shaft, steering gear, and steering linkage, directs the vehicle in response to driver input. The suspension system supports the vehicle body and transmits the body weight to the wheels. The suspension keeps the wheels in contact with the road and provides a comfortable ride. Although U-joints and CV joints are part of the drivetrain, they are often serviced as part of the chassis. Some suspension systems are electronically controlled to offer varying response under differing conditions. The wheel and tire assemblies aim the vehicle, bear its weight and transfer the weight to the ground, provide contact between the vehicle and the road, absorb small road shocks, and move the vehicle. Proper wheel alignment positions the wheel and tire assemblies correctly in relation to the suspension and body as the vehicle moves.

Review Questions

For each of the following questions, choose the letter that represents the best possible answer.

1. The automotive chassis includes the:
   a. Passenger compartment
   b. Engine and transmission
   c. Suspension system
   d. Exhaust system

2. Chassis lubricants are used to:
   a. Keep parts clean
   b. Reduce friction between parts
   c. Help parts adhere to each other
   d. All of the above

3. The handling characteristics of a vehicle are influenced by all of the following EXCEPT:
   a. Engine displacement
   b. Aerodynamics
   c. Wheel position
   d. Weight distribution

4. The steering system receives one type of input motion at the steering wheel and changes it to another type of output motion at the tie rod ends. These two types of motion are:
   a. Rotary and lateral
   b. Rotary and vertical
   c. Lateral and longitudinal
   d. Longitudinal and vertical

5. All suspension designs use some type of:
   a. Struts
   b. Upper control arm
   c. Trailing arm
   d. Spring

6. Nearly all production vehicles use:
   a. Short-long-arm suspensions
   b. MacPherson strut suspensions
   c. Independent front suspensions
   d. Independent rear suspensions

7. Universal joints are commonly used on the:
   a. Differential of a RWD vehicle
   b. Driveshaft of a RWD vehicle
   c. Axle shafts of a FWD vehicle
   d. Differential of a 4WD car

8. The most commonly used electronically controlled suspension component is the:
   a. Variable-rate spring
   b. Variable-rate shock
   c. Variable-rate bushing
   d. Variable-rate control arm

9. The wheel and tire assemblies do all of the following EXCEPT:
   a. Aim the vehicle
   b. Bear the vehicle weight
   c. Absorb small road shocks
   d. Reduce friction in the chassis

10. Technician A says that it is important to correct wheel runout and imbalance before performing a wheel alignment. Technician B says that it is important to correct toe-out on turns when performing a wheel alignment. Who is right?
    a. A only
    b. B only
    c. Both A and B
    d. Neither A nor B

11. Which of the following is a tire wear angle?
    a. Caster
    b. Camber
    c. SAI
    d. Setback

2

Lubricating, Sealing, and Reducing Friction

OBJECTIVES

Upon completion and review of this chapter, you will be able to:

- Define the term *lubricant.*

- Explain the terms *fluid, oil,* and *grease.*

- Identify the types and operation of seals used in automotive steering and suspension systems.

- Identify the types and operation of bushings and bearings used in automotive steering and suspension systems.

KEY TERMS

bearing	oil
bushing	play
consistency	pour point
dropping point	pour point depressants
fluid	power steering fluid
gear oil	soap
grease	viscosity

INTRODUCTION

Whenever two surfaces move against each other, they create friction, which generates heat. Most moving parts on a vehicle are made of metal, and friction-generated heat can damage metal parts. Therefore, engineers design lubricants to reduce friction and dissipate heat, seals to keep lubricants in place, and bushings and bearings to provide smooth or yielding surfaces that create minimal friction.

This chapter discusses the lubricants, seals, bushings, and bearings used in automotive chassis systems. Lubricants come in three basic types:

- Fluids
- Oils
- Greases

The chapter begins with a detailed explanation of the differences between the three lubricants and lists their various applications. This is followed by a look at how seals are designed to retain lubricants and provide an acceptable service life. The chapter concludes by detailing bushings and bearings, and discusses how they permit movement between two parts while minimizing friction.

FLUIDS, OILS, AND GREASES

All lubricants perform three tasks:

- Reduce friction between moving parts
- Dissipate heat caused by friction
- Prevent corrosion caused by oxidation

A lubricant that is also a hydraulic **fluid,** performs the additional—and usually most important—function of conveying pressure through a hydraulic system (Figure 2-1). Lubricants that do not apply hydraulic pressure are oil and grease. **Oil** is a thick, viscous, but still fluid and pourable lubricant (Figure 2-2) while **grease** is a thicker, non-pourable substance (Figure 2-3). Greases are usually oils that have been thickened by chemical agents.

It is *extremely important,* to use the exact lubricant specified by the vehicle manufacturer, or one certified as its equivalent by a reputable oil company, when lubricating or adding fluid to a component. Each individual type of lubricant contains additives and chemicals that are compatible with the parts and seals that it will come into contact with in use. Using the wrong lubricant can damage a part or system, and leave the technician liable for the damage. Read specifications and product labels carefully to avoid problems with misapplication.

The following paragraphs discuss the fluids, oils, and greases used in steering systems, suspension systems, and wheel bearings, specifically:

- Power steering fluid
- Gear oil
- Chassis, wheel bearing, and multipurpose grease

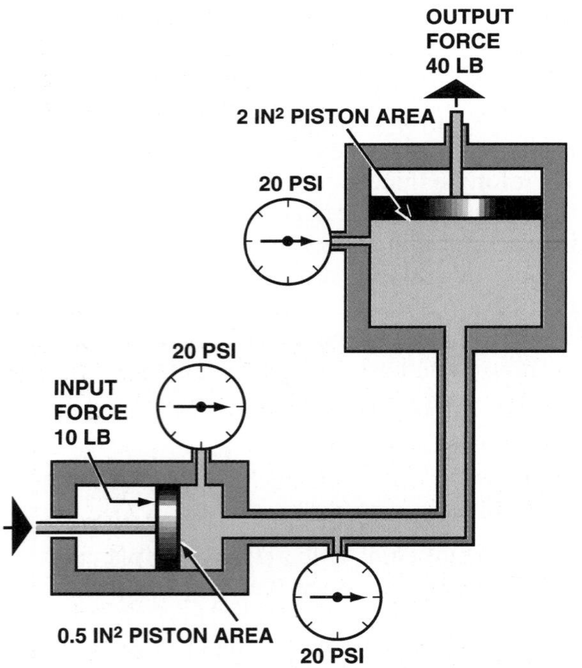

Figure 2-2.   Oil is thick, but it can still be poured into a reservoir or filler hole. Oil makes gear surfaces slick, to reduce friction, and helps dissipate heat.

Figure 2-1.   When force on a piston causes pressure to a fluid, the pressure exerted by the fluid is equal in all directions. If the piston surface the fluid affects is larger than the piston surface applying pressure, the force exerted increases.

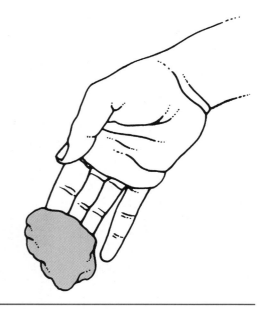

Figure 2-3.   Grease is a blend of oil and a thickening agent, or soap. The soap, which helps the grease cling to surfaces and stay in place, makes grease too thick to pour.

Power steering fluid is, of course, used in power steering systems. Gear oil is used to lubricate some manual steering gears and some rear-wheel bearings, and is also used in manual transmissions and differentials. Steering and suspension ball joints, constant velocity (CV) joints, universal joints (U-joints), some manual steering gears, and most wheel bearings are lubricated with grease.

Power Steering Fluid

Power steering fluid is an oil, usually petroleum-based, that contains additives to help it perform its task better (Figure 2-4). The chemical make-up of most power steering fluid is nearly identical to automatic transmission fluid (ATF). In fact, some manufacturers specify ATF in their power steering systems. However, never assume that you can substitute ATF for a specified power steering fluid—use ATF in a power steering system only if the manufacturer recommends it. Again, the chemical additives in different fluids are compatible with

Figure 2-4. Power steering fluid is both a hydraulic fluid and a lubricant for the power steering system. Use the fluid that the manufacturer specifies to avoid damaging system seals.

the parts and seals in the specific systems for which they are designed. The reason power steering systems and automatic transmissions use similar fluids is that the main function of the fluid in both applications is to transmit hydraulic power.

Fluid in a power steering system may by pressurized up to 1,500 psi (10,500 kPa) and

■ The Oldest Lubricant

Grease is the oldest lubricant known to mankind. Our English word *grease* comes from the Latin word *crassus,* meaning, "fat," but the use of grease as a lubricant in mechanical applications goes back to long before the Roman Empire (31 B.C. to A.D. 476). In fact, it probably predates the invention of the wheel. Drawings in opened Egyptian tombs show that workers used grease—most likely tallow rendered from mut-ton or beef—to reduce friction between sliding surfaces as early as 1400 B.C. Obviously, simple animal fat would not stand up to the demands of today's automotive requirements, but it was the best available lubricant at the time. Given that we still use fatty acids to produce grease, it seems it is only the details—not the basics—of lubrication technology that have changed over the course of 3,400 years.

EARLY
LUBRICATION
ENGINEER

ADDING THE
SPECIFIED
FLUID

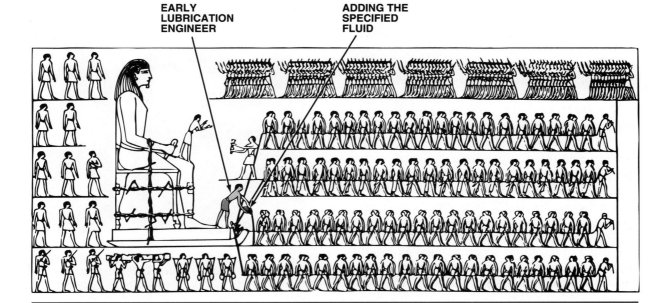

consequently may become as hot as 300°F (150°C). Power steering fluids, like brake fluids, have a very high boiling point, which helps prevent break down due to high temperatures. Excessively high temperatures cause the fluid to oxidize, which creates sludge and varnish in the fluid and damages seals. Antioxidant additives help prevent oxidation at high temperatures. Low temperatures also pose a problem. If the fluid becomes stiff when it is cold, the steering feels stiff in cold weather. To lower the **pour point,** the lowest temperature at which a fluid is liquid enough to flow, **pour point depressants** are added. To help preserve the proper **viscosity,** or the resistance to flow, over a wide range of temperatures, viscosity index improvers (VIIs) are blended into the power steering fluid.

A number of other additives are also included in the power steering formula to ensure adequate performance and a useful service life. These include rust and corrosion inhibitors, antiwear additives, and dispersants. Rust and corrosion inhibitors form a protective chemical film over iron and other metal surfaces that repels water and neutralizes corrosive acids. Foam inhibitors reduce surface tension in the fluid so that any bubbles that form can easily separate from the fluid. Antiwear additives also coat metals to reduce friction and heat between facing surfaces. Dispersants keep sludge and other particles suspended in the oil so they will not damage or clog hydraulic valves and fittings. In addition, some fluids have additives that cause system seals to swell slightly, to reduce the chance of fluid leaks.

All of the additives blended into a power steering fluid must be compatible with the seals and system components it comes into contact with. For example, a fluid that uses acid phosphates as an antiwear additive is not compatible with silicone and will damage seals. Although succinimide is an effective dispersant, using it in a system with fluoroelastomer seals causes seal failure. Therefore, fluid specifications must be matched to system seal requirements. Seal compatibility is one of the main reasons different fluids are recommended for different systems.

The OEM (original equipment manufacturer) specifies the type of power steering fluid that is compatible with the power steering system of their vehicles. Generally, they specify their own OEM brand of fluid as well as any acceptable aftermarket substitutes. Acceptable fluids are usually listed in the OEM repair manual and in the specification section of the vehicle owner's manual. Also, most vehicles have a label on or near the power steering filler cap that specifies the proper type of fluid for the system.

Gear Oil

Gear oil is a petroleum-based lubricant designed for use in gearboxes, such as differentials, manual transmissions, and manual steering gears (Figure 2-5). These lubricants cool the gears and coat them with a protective film to reduce wear. Some wheel bearings located in the axle housings of solid-rear-axle, rear-wheel drive (RWD) vehicles are lubricated by the gear oil specified for the rear differential. Also, gear oil is a common lubricant for manual steering gears.

The Society of Automotive Engineers (SAE) grades gear oils for viscosity using a numbering system similar to that for engine oils. These numbers refer only to oil viscosity. They do not rate the quality of the oil, or its suitability for use in any particular piece of machinery. The American Petroleum Institute (API), which classifies oils for different services, currently uses the designations GL-1, GL-4, and GL-5 for gear oils (Figure 2-6).

The additives in gear oils include rust inhibitors, copper-corrosion inhibitors, and foam suppressants. A GL-5 gear oil contains significant amounts of extreme-pressure (EP) additives, such as sulfur and phosphorous. These additives, which react chemically with the metal of the gear teeth under the heat and pressure of gear action, coat the gears and help reduce friction and wear. The EP additives in GL-5

Figure 2-5. Gear oil lubricates the gears in steering gear boxes and in differentials. Different additives determine which oil is suitable for a specific application.

gear oils can be harmful to some metals, such as bronze, which they corrode. In these cases, the manufacturer may specify GL-4, or even GL-1, gear oil that has a much smaller amount of EP additives.

There is no rule of thumb as to what service classification of gear oil manufacturers specify for their manual steering gears, if they specify gear oil. Daimler Chrysler generally specifies GL-5, while Hyundai, Mazda, and Mitsubishi usually specify GL-4. Specifications calling for GL-1 are less common, but not unheard of, so always check the appropriate service literature.

Chassis and Wheel Bearing Grease

As mentioned earlier, grease is oil that has been thickened with a chemical agent (Figure 2-7). Thickening agents help to keep the grease in place inside a ball joint, a CV joint, a wheel bearing, or a steering gear, and slowly release oil to the surfaces needing lubrication.

If a container of grease is stored for a long time, some of the oil may separate from the thickener. A slight amount of oil separation in a new container of grease is normal, the grease simply needs to be stirred to re-mix the oil and thickener. If there has been a great deal of separation, the grease may be old and not suitable for use. In general, grease has a shelf life of approximately two years if stored in a cool place. In hot climates, grease may last less than a year in storage.

The chemical thickener in most grease is called **soap.** A soap thickener is the product of a chemical reaction between a base, such as lithium, and a fatty acid. The base used for soap in automotive grease may be aluminum, calcium, lithium, or sodium (Figure 2-8). The most common source of fatty acid for soap is castor-bean oil. When the base and the fatty acid are combined, they undergo a chemical reaction and create a soap that can retain oil.

Like other lubricants, greases may contain additives for a number of purposes. Common grease additives are antioxidants, antiwear agents, and rust inhibitors. Grease may also contain dye. Some

Figure 2-7. Chassis grease is used to lubricate wheel bearings, CV joints, and ball joints, as well as some manual steering gears.

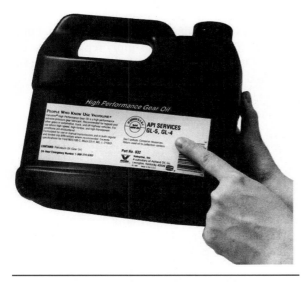

Figure 2-6. A gear oil label shows the API classification of the product. Be sure to select a lubricant that matches the specifications of the vehicle manufacturer.

Figure 2-8. The label on a chassis grease container shows the type of soap used to thicken the grease.

grease has an extreme-pressure (EP) additive such as sulfurized fatty oil or chlorine. If temperatures generated by moving metal parts become too high, the parts may melt together, or seize. Lamellar solids, such as graphite and molybdenum disulfide (moly), are anti-seize additives.

Of the different soap bases, lithium is the most common. Two-thirds of the grease made in North America has a lithium or lithium-complex base. Lithium grease offers high water resistance, to prevent rust and contamination in a component, and a high melting point, or dropping point, to prevent chemical breakdown at high temperatures. The **dropping point** of grease is the temperature at which the soap—having begun to melt and formed a drop on the grease—drops off of a heated grease sample.

Looking at other types of grease, aluminum greases have good water resistance and a high dropping point. Calcium grease is water resistant, but cannot be used at higher temperatures. Also, calcium grease tends to have a high soap content and therefore may harden sooner than other greases. Sodium grease is less water-resistant because sodium is water-soluble.

Greases with different soaps often are incompatible with each other, so it is important not to mix them. If mixed, the chemical reaction between the two can make both greases thinner, which causes leakage and leaves the component without lubricant. Always use the type of grease recommended by the manufacturer for a specific application.

The National Lubricating Grease Institute (NLGI) classifies greases according to their application and assigns them a number indicating their texture (Figure 2-9). The three most common automotive grease classifications are:

- Wheel bearing grease
- Chassis grease
- Multipurpose grease

Wheel bearing grease is formulated to reduce friction between rolling objects—namely, the balls and rollers in wheel bearings. Chassis grease is made to reduce friction between sliding or rotating parts, such as ball joints, tie rod ends, and kingpins. Multipurpose grease is suitable for both wheel bearing and chassis use.

Each type of grease is further categorized according to its quality. The three categories of wheel bearing grease are GA, GB, and GC. Chassis grease has two categories: LA and LB. Multipurpose grease may be categorized only with the type it is closer to—GC or LB—or it may have a combined categorization, GC–LB.

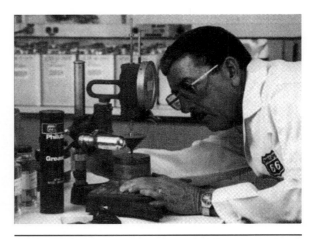

Figure 2-9. The National Lubricating Grease Institute (NLGI) tests greases to determine their consistency rating.

The NLGI also assigns a number to each grease that indicates **consistency,** meaning its firmness or texture. The NLGI numbers are: 000, 00, 0, 1, 2, 3, 4, 5, and 6, with 000 being the softest and 6 the hardest, or thickest. The most common automotive lubricating greases are NLGI #2. The NLGI number does not indicate anything except consistency—not melting point, nor compatibility with other greases, nor suitability for specific applications.

A final note about grease is that some advanced formulas are used in permanently sealed components, which do not have grease fittings. These greases are special formulations that should not be mixed with other greases. Never attempt to force lubricant into a permanently sealed component. These "Lubed-for-life" components may last as long as 200,000 miles (320,000 kilometers), but if they fail, the component is simply replaced, not repaired. Often, replacement parts do have grease fittings and require periodic lubrication.

SEALS

Once a fluid or lubricant is in place, a seal keeps it where it belongs. In addition to preventing leaks, seals protect the component from contamination from dirt or water. In the steering and suspension systems and the wheels, seals protect steering gears, power steering pumps, ball joints, and wheel bearings. They also protect CV joints. On CV joints, a rubber bellows type boot, which is held in place by metal band clamps at each end, seals the grease in place and prevents contamination from dirt and water.

Rubber seals are flexible and deform under pressure to fit tightly between the parts they seal, preventing leaks. Seals of materials such as Teflon®, plastic, or nylon are stronger than rubber, and since they do not deform, they can be used between parts which may move relative to each other.

Many manufacturers sell seal kits for various chassis components, such as the power steering pump, the steering gear, wheel bearings, and CV joints (Figure 2-10). When installing new seals, it is important not to stretch or twist them if they are rubber, and not to damage them in other ways. It is also important to install lip seals facing in the right direction.

Rubber Seals

Automotive parts that are described as being made of rubber are actually made of a synthetic rubber because natural rubber is not as strong or reliable as synthetics. A number of synthetic seal compounds, such as Buna-N (nitrile butadiene rubber), polyacrylic rubber, silicone rubber, and fluoroelastomer rubber, are derivatives of nitrile rubber used for automotive applications. Neoprene is another synthetic rubber material used for automotive seals.

Rubber seals are soft and can easily be damaged if mishandled, which makes the seal unusable. Special installation tools designed to install rubber seals without damage should always be used.

In addition to being made of different synthetics, rubber seals come in different shapes, including:

- O-rings
- Square-cut seals
- Lip seals
- Dust covers

Each shape has its own usefulness according to its application.

O-rings

One simple type of rubber seal is the O-ring, so named because its cross-section is O-shaped (Figure 2-11). When two parts fit together with an O-ring between them, the O-ring compresses to

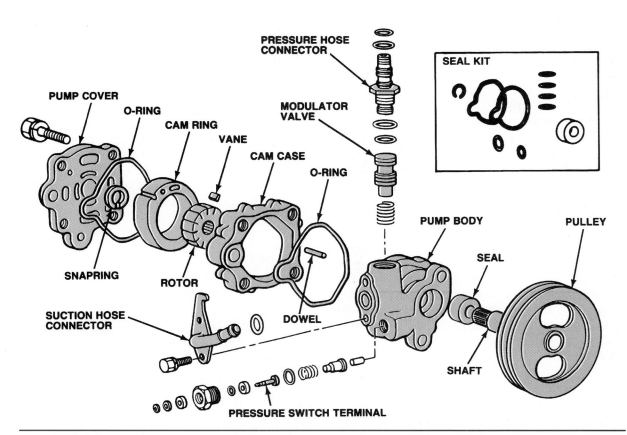

Figure 2-10. Complete seal kits, such as the one for this power steering pump, are available for servicing most steering pumps and gearboxes.

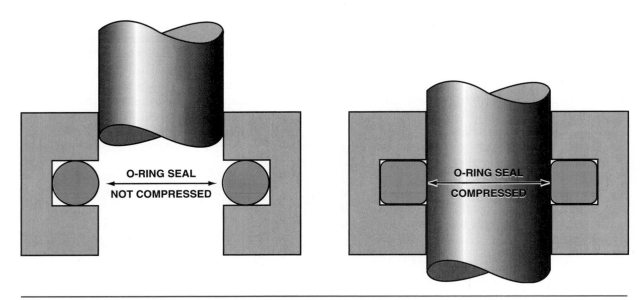

Figure 2-11.   An O-ring is a simple rubber seal that deforms to create a tight seal when it is compressed between two parts.

fill the space and seal the facing surfaces. O-rings work well between surfaces that do not move against each other, or that move very little. If there is too much movement between surfaces sealed by an O-ring, the O-ring may twist and lose its sealing ability. O-rings are used in many places throughout the steering system: in power steering pumps, fluid fittings, valves, and steering gears.

Square-Cut Seals

When two parts move against each other axially— that is, along the length of a shaft—a square-cut seal can maintain a better seal than an O-ring. Also known as a lathe-cut seal, a square-cut seal has a square cross-section (Figure 2-12). When the two surfaces sealed by a square-cut seal move axially, each side of the seal tends to move in the same direction as the surface it is contacting. This causes the square seal to distort between its inside diameter and its outside diameter (Figure 2-13). As long as the two sealing faces maintain contact with the moving surfaces, the seal is not broken. Because of the seal distortion, the amount of axial motion that a square-cut seal can deal with is limited. Square-cut seals are common in steering system applications.

Lip Seals

Lip seals are effective between two surfaces with rotational movement between them. The design of the lip seal varies according to which type of movement occurs between the surfaces it

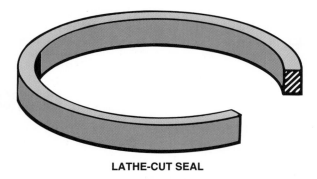

LATHE-CUT SEAL

Figure 2-12.   A rubber square-cut, or lathe-cut, seal allows limited axial movement, but cannot withstand rotational movement.

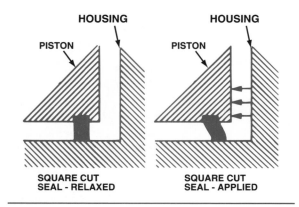

Figure 2-13.   The flex of this square-cut seal allows it to maintain contact with the housing as the piston moves.

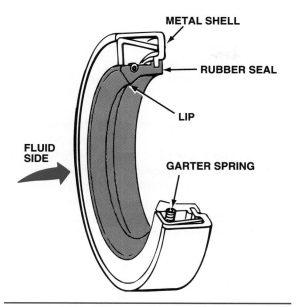

Figure 2-14. A lip seal allows rotational movement without leakage. The garter spring and hydraulic pressure keeps the seal tight around the rotating shaft.

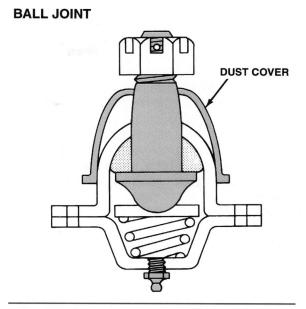

Figure 2-15. A dust cover on a ball joint prevents dirt or water from contaminating the grease and damaging the joint.

seals. It is called a "lip seal" because a thin, flexible lip touches and seals the moving surface. The small contact area between the seal and the moving surface reduces the amount of seal distortion, so a lip seal can handle more movement than an O-ring or square-cut seal. A lip seal is often bonded to a metal backing plate that is press fit into a recess machined into the surface that does not move. These metal-clad lip seals generally have a small internal spring, called a "garter spring," encircling the lip to keep it tightly positioned against the moving surface (Figure 2-14).

Lip seals are used where there is high rotational movement, such as wheel bearings, and where pressurized fluid must be retained, such as on a power steering pump. A lip seal is ideal for holding back pressurized fluid because the lip is formed so that fluid pressure against it pushes it more firmly against the surface to strengthen the seal.

Dust Covers

Rubber dust covers are used on grease-lubricated parts in which the lubricant is thick enough to stay in place without tight sealing, but a cover is needed to protect it from contamination. Suspension and steering linkage ball joints usually have a dome-shaped rubber dust cover to protect them from dirt or water (Figure 2-15). Service literature may refer to dust covers as "boots," but this book reserves the use of the term *boots* for the pleated covers on CV joints and rack and pinion steering gear tie rods.

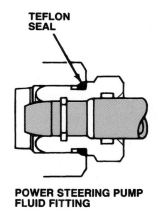

Figure 2-16. Teflon®, plastic, or nylon seals are stronger and more rigid than rubber seals, although they do not usually seal as tightly.

Other Seal Materials

Not all seals are rubber; seals can be made of other synthetic materials, such as Teflon®, plastic, or nylon, or soft metal, such as copper or brass. Seals of these materials provide more strength and rigidity than rubber seals, but they generally do not seal as tightly. Teflon® seals can be found in various places in power steering systems, such as at the input shaft opening of a rotary control valve or in a high-pressure fitting (Figure 2-16). Plastic and

■ **Time to Change the Oil—or Just Its Name?**

Most people have heard of Standard Oil and many are familiar with Exxon. However, few know how the name Exxon was derived from Standard Oil. The Standard Oil monopoly split into two companies in 1911: Standard Oil Company of New Jersey, also known as Jersey Standard, and the Standard Oil Company. Both companies saw potential difficulties in sharing a similar name in the same business, so Jersey Standard decided it was time to change its own name.

In the early 1930s, Jersey Standard on the East Coast became Esso, a sounding-out of the abbreviation S.O., for Standard Oil. But while Esso won rights to this version of the Standard Oil name on the East Coast, they had to compromise in other regions. Thus, Jersey Standard, now Esso, was called Enco on the West Coast and in most of the mid-western region. However, in Ohio and some of the neighboring states Esso was known as Humble Oil, after the Humble Oil and Refining division of Jersey Standard. Not surprisingly, this variety of names limited the ability of Jersey Standard to gain brand loyalty from consumers.

Jersey Standard decided to choose one easily recognizable name for the entire subsidiary, and was about to adopt Enco nationwide until its marketing experts discovered that the name had a hidden meaning. The term *enko* is part of a common Japanese phrase, "Kuruma ga enko shita," which translates to "the car has stalled!" Obviously, an oil company hoping to expand in the world economy did not want to base its reputation on a name with such a negative connotation. Instead, the company turned to the latest technology: a computer, which generated the name that in May of 1972 replaced Esso, Humble Oil, and Enco—a name chosen for its utter lack of meaning. That name is Exxon.

nylon seals are also used in power steering applications. These synthetic seals provide smooth sliding surfaces where sealing is needed between moving parts, such as on the rack assembly of a rack and pinion steering gear. Teflon®, plastic, and nylon seals can become scratched and damaged by contaminants relatively easily.

Soft-metal seals are commonly referred to as "sealing washers" and are used where there is no movement between the parts. Soft metal seals are also referred to as "crush washers," because they are designed to flatten and thin out as the fastener they install with is tightened. These seals, which actually function as a gasket, are often used to seal transmission and crankcase drain plugs, as well as to seal banjo fittings on power steering fluid lines. Like all other types of seal, sealing washers are one-time use items and must be replaced with new ones whenever they are removed.

Boots

A boot, which is sometimes called a "bellows boot," is the pleated rubber or plastic covering used at the inner tie rod end of a rack and pinion steering gear or to cover a CV joint (Figure 2-17). As described in Chapters 4 and 11 of this *Classroom Manual,* the pleats in the boot allow accordion-like movement, to accommodate lateral and axial movement of the part. A boot protects the tie rod end or CV joint from contaminants

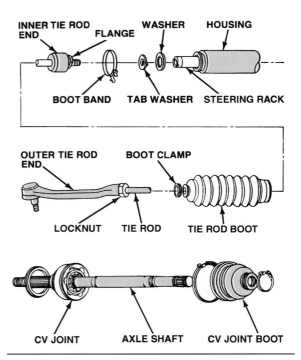

Figure 2-17. Pleated boots allow axial and lateral movement of tie rods and axle shafts while protecting the tie rod ends or CV joints.

and contains the lubricant for the part. Band clamps at each end of the boot hold it in place. Chapter 11 discusses CV joint boots in detail.

BUSHINGS AND BEARINGS

The steering and suspension systems use bushings and bearings where one part moves against another and the road wheels of a vehicle use bearings to reduce friction. Metal and rubber bushings are used at a variety of points of suspension and steering systems, and bearing surfaces permit low-friction movement inside of ball joints. Steering gears and power steering pumps use bushings, ball bearings, needle bearings, or roller bearings, wherever a shaft rotates in the housing. MacPherson and modified struts use bearings in the strut tower to allow rotation and the wheels use ball, roller, or tapered roller bearings in the hub.

Bushings

A **bushing** can serve as a pivot point, a cushion, or both. Bushings function as pivot points where they join suspension control arms and other links to the frame, to each other, and, in the rear, to the knuckle (Figure 2-18). In these applications, the bushing usually has metal inner and outer sleeves with rubber between the two. The metal allows sliding so the links can pivot, and the rubber absorbs shock and vibration.

Bushings also serve as cushions at the frame mounting points of components such as steering gear and antiroll bars (Figure 2-19). Cushioning bushings are usually solid rubber, but can be made of other compounds such as polyurethane. These bushings allow flexing rather than pivoting. The flexibility of the rubber helps absorb vibration that would otherwise be passed through the frame and into the passenger compartment.

While most suspension bushings are of a simple design, either rubber-filled metal sleeves or a rubber cushion, a few are a more complex hydraulic design. For example, both Mazda and Toyota use fluid-filled bushings on some of their performance models. These bushings, which are typically located on the strut rod ends, act as shock absorbers to damp vibrations or fore-and-aft suspension movement. There are several fluid chambers connected by orifices inside these rubber bushings

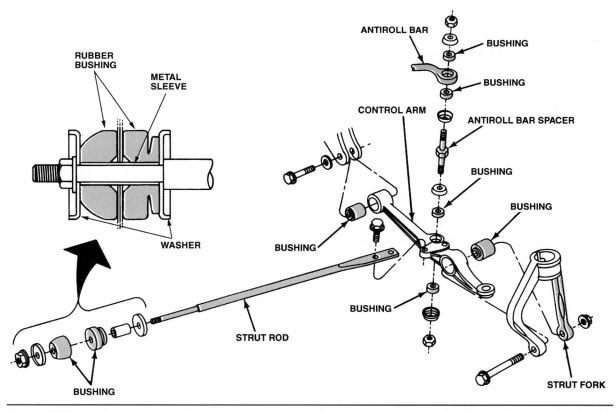

Figure 2-18. Bushings are used to mount a number of suspension components. Bushings with metal sleeves allow suspension links to pivot and flex.

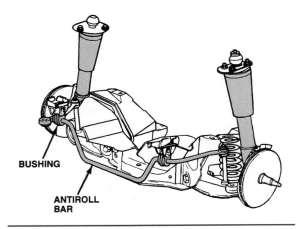

Figure 2-19. Solid rubber bushings, like those that mount this antiroll bar, absorb vibrations to prevent them from being transmitted to the frame and passenger compartment.

FLUID-FILLED BUSHINGS

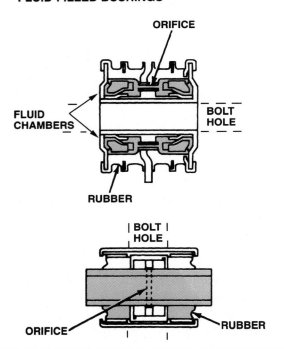

Figure 2-20. Fluid-filled, or hydraulic, bushings offer variable dampening of road shock by passing fluid through an orifice to increase their effectiveness.

(Figure 2-20). When road forces compress one side of the rubber, it pushes the fluid through the orifice into the opposite chamber.

Another variation on basic bushing design is to vary the hardness of the rubber within the bushing so that it deforms in predetermined ways un-

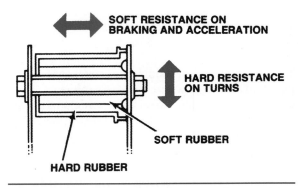

Figure 2-21. This bushing uses two different rubber compounds to provide variable dampening. The harder rubber resists turning forces, while the softer rubber gives way to provide a cushioning effect under braking and acceleration forces.

der compressing forces. Mazda is one of the most frequent users of this concept. A simple example is a bushing on the front lower control arm in the Mazda 929 (Figure 2-21). Here, harder rubber keeps up a stiff resistance to side-to-side forces, while softer rubber gives more easily to fore-and-aft forces. This provides more stable cornering with softer braking and acceleration.

Bearings

The term **bearing** refers either to a smooth metal or plastic surface that reduces the friction of one part moving relative to another, or to a ball-and-cage or roller-and-cage construction, generally used to reduce the friction of one part rotating within another. What both types have in common is their purpose—reducing friction between moving parts.

Bearing Surface

The bearing surface inside a ball-and-socket joint keeps the ball from rubbing against the socket and is often specially treated to retain grease (Figure 2-22). As explained in Chapters 5 and 8 of this *Classroom Manual,* the steering linkage uses small ball joints at its pivot points, and the suspension uses ball joints where the front suspension links join the steering knuckles. Ball joints are also occasionally used to join rear suspension links to the knuckles or to join small spacer links between a control arm and antiroll bar.

In addition to reducing friction, a bearing surface takes up space. When the surface wears down, there is more space between the ball and socket, which allows **play** in the joint. When there is too

■ **Lube Jobs Were Not Always Quick**

Today, one of the simplest tasks an automotive technician performs is to squeeze new grease into ball joints in the suspension and steering system using a grease gun. However, in 1909 the steering system ball joints (the suspension had no ball joints—only kingpins) did not even have dust covers to hold the grease in place.

In that year, the Charles C. Thompson Company of Chicago published a book titled *Automobile Troubles and How to Remedy Them*. The author, a Mr. Root, provided a handy procedure for fabricating joint covers that would protect the ball joints, keep grease inside them, and hold them together in the event that the ball came out of the socket.

First, the owner, a mechanic, or a blacksmith would acquire a quantity of "the best soft leather." As Mr. Root advised, "Such leather as is used for shoe uppers is very suitable." Next, a paper or cloth pattern was made for a cover that would fit the steering system. This pattern and the leather were taken to the local saddler, who cut and sewed the leather according to the pattern. Finally, the leather cover was installed onto the steering system and secured with "a couple of water-pipe clips."

In the same book, Mr. Root lamented the scant attention that was given to lubricating leaf springs.

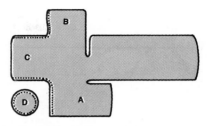

Figure 1. A is stitched to B along the dotted lines, and a circular piece, D, is inserted at the end, C, then sewn to close it up.

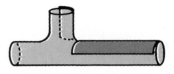

Figure 2. Cover shown stitched and adjusted to the arm and link, but without the holding links.

He advised to unload a leaf spring, pry apart the ends of the leaves with a sharp chisel, and apply grease between them "using a thin palette knife." Needless to say, there were no promises of a 10-minute lubrication service in those days.

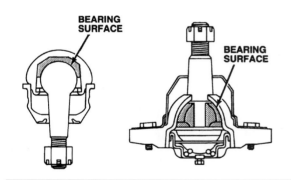

Figure 2-22. The bearing surfaces inside a ball joint allow smooth movement and also help feed grease to the sliding surfaces.

much play in a ball joint, it cannot hold parts in the proper relationship to each other. The parts move and slide around when they are not supposed to, creating instability in the steering and suspension systems. On a spring-loaded ball joint, a spring pushes the ball into the socket to take up play as the bearing surface wears. However, eventually even the spring cannot compensate for wear.

Some suspension ball joints have a wear indicator, often the shoulder of the grease fitting, that extends from the joint housing when the bearing surface is new. As the bearing surface wears down, the ball stud moves inward in the socket and pulls the wear indicator along with it (Figure 2-23). When the indicator is flush with or recessed into the housing, the bearing surface has worn down beyond allowable limits and the ball joint needs to be replaced.

Ball Bearings and Roller Bearings

Ball bearings and roller bearings are used wherever a shaft rotates inside another part and also where the wheel hub rotates on the spindle (Figure 2-24). Wheel bearings are described in detail in Chapter 13 of this *Classroom Manual*. Other common locations for bearings in the steering and suspension systems are where the top of a front MacPherson or modified strut moves against the strut tower during turns and where shafts rotate in the steering gear (Figure 2-25).

Ball or roller bearings consist of two races with facing surfaces against which the balls or rollers

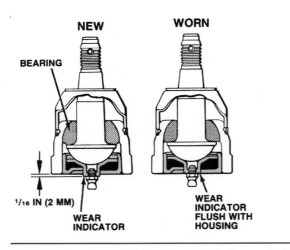

Figure 2-23. On a ball joint with a wear indicator, the indicator pulls inward as the bearing surface wears down. When the wear indicator is flush to the housing, the ball joint has excessive play and requires replacement.

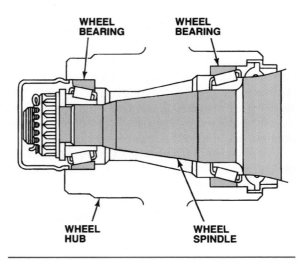

Figure 2-24. These tapered-roller wheel bearings reduce friction between the spindle and hub.

STEERING GEAR

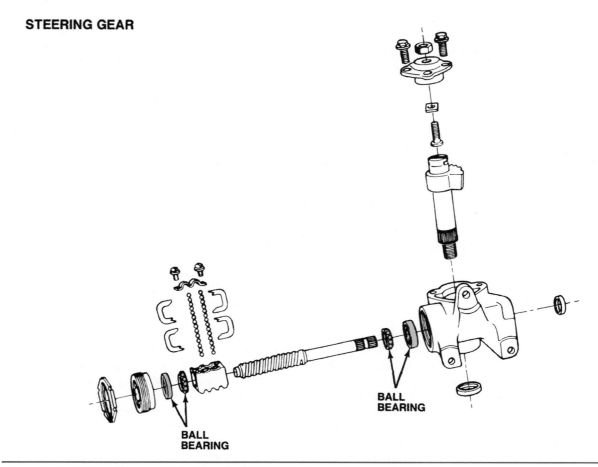

Figure 2-25. The caged ball bearings in this steering gear reduce friction between the shaft and the housing.

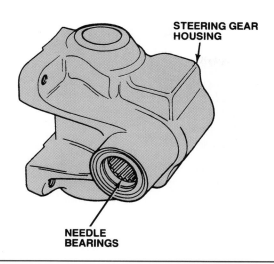

Figure 2-26.   Needle bearings, such as those used in this steering gear, use very thin rollers to reduce friction between a rotating shaft and a housing.

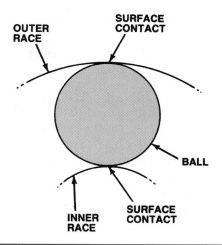

Figure 2-27.   Ball, or roller, bearings reduce friction because contact between the two moving surfaces occurs only at the small areas where the ball touches the races.

turn, a cage to keep the balls or rollers separated from each other, and the balls or rollers. Some wheel bearings have cone-shaped "tapered rollers." Some other bearing applications use small roller bearing called "needle bearings." Sometimes these have only one race and the needle rollers ride directly on a shaft (Figure 2-26).

Ball and roller bearings reduce friction by limiting the contact area between facing surfaces. If a shaft rotated directly against a housing, the rubbing of the two surfaces would generate enough heat that the surfaces would eventually melt and seize to each other. When a series of balls or rollers sits between the two surfaces, contact occurs only at two points on each ball or along two strips of each roller (Figure 2-27). Furthermore, the ball or roller turns whenever there is movement between the two surfaces, so the same part of it does not remain in contact for very long. Reduced friction means reduced heat and reduced wear. Also, the bearings are solidly packed with grease, which serves to dissipate any heat generated by friction.

SUMMARY

Wherever two parts move relative to each other, they create friction, and friction produces heat. Lubricants reduce friction and dissipate heat, seals keep lubricants in place, and bushings and bearings reduce friction between moving parts.

A fluid lubricant is usually a liquid used in a hydraulic system. Oil is a thick, viscous, but pourable lubricant, while grease is a thick, nonpourable lubricant consisting of oil with chemical thickeners added to it. The types of lubricants used in steering and suspension systems are: power steering fluid in power steering systems, gear oil in steering gears and differentials, and grease in steering and suspension ball joints, CV joints, U-joints, and some wheel bearings.

Seals keep lubricants in place. Rubber seals deform to fit into their place and form a tight seal. Rubber seals can be O-rings, square-cut seals, lip seals, or dust covers. Other seal materials include Teflon®, plastic, nylon, or soft metal. Pleated boots protect CV joints and the tie rod ends in a rack and pinion steering system.

Bushings and bearings allow relative movement between chassis parts. Bushings with a bolt running through a metal cylinder allow pivoting, while solid rubber bushings flex to absorb vibrations. Bearing surfaces provide a smooth face that reduces friction, and ball or roller bearings allow shaft rotation while reducing friction.

Review Questions

For each of the following questions, choose the letter that represents the best possible answer.

1. Automatic transmission fluid is sometimes used in:
   a. Power steering systems
   b. Manual steering gears
   c. Constant velocity joints
   d. All of the above

2. Fluid, when oxidized:
   a. Prevents excessively high temperatures
   b. Damages seals
   c. Has a lower pour point
   d. Has lower viscosity

3. The Society of Automotive Engineers (SAE) classifies gear oils by:
   a. Quality
   b. Viscosity
   c. Application
   d. All of the above

4. What classification of gear oil do most vehicle manufacturers specify for use in a differential?
   a. GL-1
   b. GL-2 or GL-3
   c. GL-4 or GL-5
   d. None of the above

5. The two components that commonly make up a soap thickener are:
   a. Graphite and molybdenum disulfide
   b. Sulfur and phosphorous
   c. Silicone and fluoroelastomer
   d. Lithium and fatty acid

6. The National Lubricating Grease Institute (NLGI) classifies grease according to:
   a. Thermal rating, application, and consistency
   b. Quality, viscosity, and suitability
   c. Application, quality, and consistency
   d. Application, viscosity, and thermal rating

7. Which of the four types of seals is designed to handle the most movement?
   a. O-rings
   b. Square-cut seals
   c. Lip seals
   d. Dust covers

8. Bushings and bearings may do any of the following, EXCEPT:
   a. Serve as pivot points
   b. Prevent lubricant leaks
   c. Reduce friction
   d. Absorb vibrations

9. A lubricant can perform any or all of the following tasks, EXCEPT:
   a. Reduce friction between moving parts
   b. Transmit hydraulic power
   c. Dissipate heat caused by friction
   d. Protect seals against distortion

10. Technician A says that permanently sealed ball joints can be serviced. Technician B says that replacement ball joints often have grease fittings. Who is right?
    a. A only
    b. B only
    c. Both A and B
    d. Neither A nor B

11. Which of the following statements about power steering fluid is NOT true?
    a. It serves as a lubricant
    b. It is interchangeable with automatic transmission fluid
    c. It is usually petroleum-based
    d. It withstands pressure of up to 1,500 psi (10,500 kPa)

12. All of the following are commonly found in gear oil, EXCEPT:
    a. Rust inhibitors
    b. Foam suppressants
    c. Particle dispersants
    d. Sulfur and phosphorous

13. Grease has a shelf-life of approximately:
    a. One month
    b. Six months
    c. Two years
    d. Six years

14. The chemical thickener in most grease is called:
    a. EP additive
    b. Soap
    c. Moly
    d. Lithium

15. Rubber dust covers are used on grease-lubricated parts to:
    a. Prevent lubricant contamination
    b. Hold moving parts in place
    c. Distribute the lubricant
    d. All of the above

16. For a tighter seal, a garter spring is often installed in:
    a. Square-cut seals
    b. O-rings
    c. Lip seals
    d. Dust covers

17. When serving as a chassis pivot point, the typical bearing surface is part of a:
    a. Ball-and-socket assembly
    b. Roller-and-cage assembly
    c. Ball-and-cage assembly
    d. All of the above

18. Spring-loaded ball joints are designed to:
    a. Show when they need replacing
    b. Provide even play within the joint
    c. Retain grease more effectively
    d. Compensate for wear

19. Seals in automotive applications can be made from all of the following materials, EXCEPT:
    a. Natural rubber
    b. Plastic
    c. Nylon
    d. Synthetic rubber

20. Combining greases that have different soaps can cause the grease mixture to:
    a. Harden due to high soap content
    b. Become thinner and leak
    c. Break down chemically
    d. Become less water resistant

3

Dynamics of Handling

OBJECTIVES

Upon completion and review of this chapter, you will be able to:

- Define the terms used in the dynamics of vehicle handling.

- Explain the term *aerodynamics*.

- Define the terms used in vehicle weight transfer and traction.

KEY TERMS

aerodynamics
axis
center of gravity (CG)
dive
downforce
electronic suspension control (ESC) system
ESC damper
ESC module
ESC position sensors
G
G-force
inertia
instant center
lateral horizontal axis
lift
longitudinal axis
oversteer
overturning moment
pitch
polar moment of inertia
roll
roll axis
roll center
squat
static weight distribution
track width
understeer
vertical axis
weight transfer
wheelbase
yaw

INTRODUCTION

This book covers in detail the buildup of steering and suspension systems, as well as the construction of wheels and tires. However, there is more to understanding the way these systems and parts work than simply knowing how they assemble. To correctly analyze vehicle handling characteristics when diagnosing problems, it is important to understand the forces that affect a vehicle in motion.

This chapter looks at some of the principles of chassis dynamics and explains terminology used to discuss this topic. This basic grounding in the subject enables you to begin analyzing the characteristics of specific chassis and suspension designs, and prepares you to continue expanding your knowledge as you gain experience.

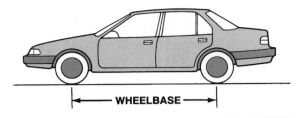

Figure 3-1. Wheelbase is the length from the center of the front wheels to the center of the back wheels.

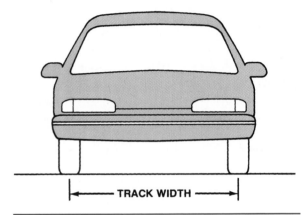

Figure 3-2. Track width is the distance between the centers of the contact patches of same-axle tires.

BASICS

The size and weight of a vehicle affect its handling in various ways. But, because handling is basically a function of the contact between the tires and the road, the aspects of size and weight that affect traction are the most important. The most critical dimension in relation to handling is the distance the wheels are from each other. The important weight considerations are the proportion of sprung to unsprung weight and the weight distribution, which determines the center of gravity.

Dimensions

The two tire-position dimensions that affect handling are:

- Wheelbase
- Track width

Wheelbase is the distance from the center of the front wheels to the center of the rear wheels (Figure 3-1) and **track width** is the distance between the centers of the contact patches of the two tires on the same axle (Figure 3-2). Track width is not always the same at the front and rear tires (Figure 3-3).

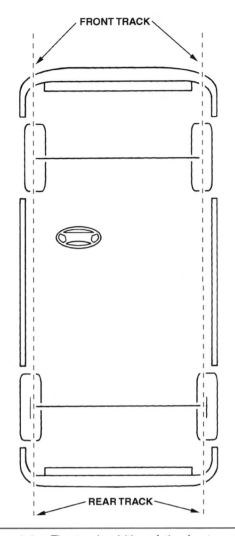

Figure 3-3. The track widths of the front and rear axles may be different.

Sprung and Unsprung Weight

The total weight of a vehicle can be divided into two parts:

- Sprung weight
- Unsprung weight

Sprung weight is all the weight that rests on the suspension springs, including the frame, body, and everything attached to them, including parts of the suspension. The unsprung weight is the weight of the suspension components on which the springs rest, or all the parts of the suspension that are not supported by the springs, such as the wheels and tires.

In a study of vehicle dynamics, an important fact is that sprung weight rotates around the axes of movement, which is discussed later in this chapter, while tire traction keeps the unsprung weight from moving relative to the rest of the car. If the unsprung weight does move around an axis of movement, such as the vertical axis, it is because the tires have broken loose from the pavement and the vehicle is out of control.

Chapter 8 of this *Classroom Manual* explains the functions of sprung and unsprung weight in terms of suspension action.

Center of Gravity

Another factor, besides the proportion of sprung to unsprung weight, that affects handling is the weight distribution around the **center of gravity (CG)**. The center of gravity could also be called the "weight center," since weight is simply a measure-ment of the force of gravity acting on an object. The center of gravity is where the vehicle weight is centered (Figure 3-4). Theoretically, if a vehicle were hung or balanced at its center of gravity, it would not teeter in any direction, assuming no force except gravity is acting on it. This is because the weight would be evenly distributed around the hanging or pivot point. The vehicle would hang motionless even if hung sideways or upside-down if the hanging point were the center of gravity.

Finding the center of gravity of a given vehicle requires knowing where the center of weight distri-bution is from front-to-rear and from side-to-side, as well as how high it is off the ground. If more weight is at the front, as is typical for FWD vehi-cles, the front-to-rear location of the center of grav-ity is closer to the front. If one side of the vehicle weighs more than the other, the center of gravity

---

■ The History of Suspensions

For an ancient driver touring Egypt or Persia in a chariot, the best way to smooth out the ride was to give way at the knees to absorb the jolts and bumps of a solid axle attached directly to the floor-boards of the vehicle. For millennia, this method worked for standing drivers, while heavy cushions and pads were the only protection sitting or re-clining passengers had against a jarring ride.

It was not until the 1500s that suspensions were invented. The term *suspension* comes from the designs in which the body of a carriage was suspended, or hung, from the frame by chains or by leather straps. This suspension made the pas-senger compartment sway instead of bump over rough road surfaces. In the 1600s, carriage mak-ers began mounting the suspension straps on metal springs that attached to the frame.

In 1805, it occurred to an English carriage builder to place fully elliptical springs between the axles and frame. Thus the "Elliot axle" was born, which greatly improved the ratio of sprung to unsprung weight, and consequently improved the ride.

The late 1800s saw automobile inventors struggling with the problems of suspensions for their engine-driven carriages. A wide variety of designs occurred in these days, as each inventor came up with a different idea. Most based their chassis designs on existing technology for horse-drawn carriages, with leaf springs, already widely available, being the popular choice. Most design-ers liked leaf springs because they located the axle as well as cushioned the frame.

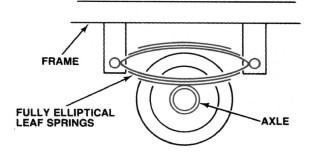

FRAME

FULLY ELLIPTICAL LEAF SPRINGS

AXLE

The 1930s finally saw the beginning of wide-spread use of independent front suspension. Most vehicles of that era were rear-wheel-drive (RWD), and the limitations and complexity of a system that allows independent travel for each drive axle kept most designers away from inde-pendent rear suspension. The post-World War II trend in Europe toward front-wheel drive (FWD) layouts was helped by the development of plung-ing constant velocity joints. Plunging joints allow the front axle shafts to compensate for indepen-dent suspension travel.

Now, with significant exceptions, most cars are FWD, and four-wheel independent suspension is common. Independent rear suspension is also now commonly found on RWD vehicles, espe-cially on performance models. Independent sus-pensions not only provide better ride quality, they also improve handling through increased tire trac-tion. Technology has come a long way since peo-ple first attached wheels to an axle.

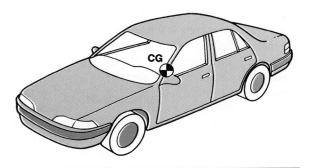

Figure 3-4. The center of gravity (CG) is the center point of the vehicle weight distribution. A vehicle suspended from its CG would hang motionless, without teetering in any direction.

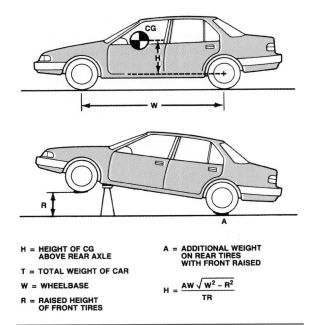

H = HEIGHT OF CG
ABOVE REAR AXLE

T = TOTAL WEIGHT OF CAR

W = WHEELBASE

R = RAISED HEIGHT
OF FRONT TIRES

A = ADDITIONAL WEIGHT
ON REAR TIRES
WITH FRONT RAISED

$$H = \frac{AW\sqrt{W^2 - R^2}}{TR}$$

Figure 3-6. To calculate CG height, measure the weight increase on the rear tires while raising the front of the vehicle. For more precision, drain all fluids beforehand so their shifting does not affect the weight readings.

moves toward the heavier side. Top-to-bottom weight distribution determines the height of the center of gravity. There are formulas for calculating the location of the center of gravity, using scales that can measure the weight on each wheel (Figures 3-5 and 3-6).

It should be clear that as soon as there is any load in the car—the driver, a passenger or two, some suitcases, or bags of groceries in the trunk—the location of the center of gravity changes. Similarly, when road forces place a load on a car, the center of gravity also moves. Since gravity is measured in terms of weight, a movement of the center of gravity is called "weight transfer." If the weight transfer is great enough, the sprung weight will move around one or more of the axes of movement.

AXES OF MOVEMENT

An **axis** is the line on which something spins. A vehicle driving down the road has three axes of movement that determine the movement of the sprung weight in relation to the unsprung weight (Figure 3-7). These are:

- Longitudinal
- Lateral horizontal
- Vertical

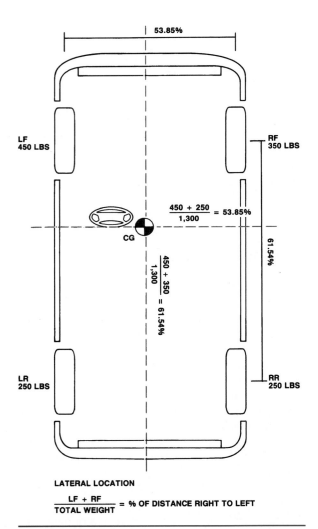

53.85%

LF
450 LBS

RF
350 LBS

$\dfrac{450 + 250}{1,300} = 53.85\%$

CG

$\dfrac{450 + 350}{1,300} = 61.54\%$

61.54%

LR
250 LBS

RR
250 LBS

LATERAL LOCATION

$\dfrac{LF + RF}{TOTAL\ WEIGHT}$ = % OF DISTANCE RIGHT TO LEFT

Figure 3-5. The more weight at the front of the vehicle, the further forward the center of gravity. The CG also is closer to the heavier side of the vehicle.

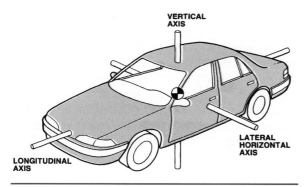

Figure 3-7. Forces of motion can make the sprung weight of a car rotate around the three axes of motion: longitudinal, lateral horizontal, or vertical.

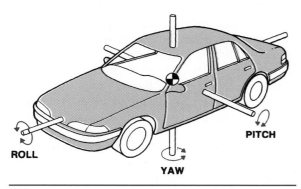

Figure 3-8. A vehicle rolls around its longitudinal axis, pitches around its lateral horizontal axis, and yaws around its vertical axis.

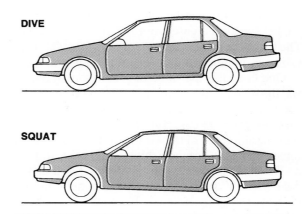

Figure 3-9. When a car pitches forward, the movement is called "dive." When it pitches toward the rear, it is called "squat."

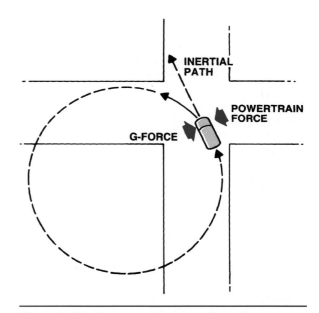

Figure 3-10. Because the force of gravity opposes changes in direction, it also opposes the force of the vehicle powertrain during cornering.

The unsprung weight can also rotate around an axis if the driver loses control of the vehicle, but most of the movement that the passengers feel—except road shocks caused by an uneven road surface—result from forces of motion trying to move the sprung weight of the chassis around one of these axes.

The **longitudinal axis**, also called the **roll axis**, runs from the center of the front suspension to the rear, and movement around this axis is called **roll** (Figure 3-8). Suspension design determines the location of the roll axis. The **lateral horizontal axis** runs horizontally from one side of the vehicle to the other, and movement around this axis is called **pitch** (Figure 3-8). When a vehicle pitches toward the front, it is called **dive**, and when it pitches toward the rear, it is called **squat** (Figure 3-9). The **vertical axis** is upright—through the floor and roof—and movement around this axis is called **yaw** (Figure 3-8). The locations of the lateral horizontal axis and the vertical axis are determined by the weight distribution of the vehicle.

Roll

When a vehicle corners, it is effectively driving around a circle, although most driving situations do not require or allow the vehicle to travel in a complete circle (Figure 3-10). An object that travels in a circle is continuously changing direction and therefore must overcome the force of gravity, which resists changes in speed and direction. As a vehicle is cornering, the force of gravity pushes any passengers or objects riding in it to one side because they resist the change of direction, while the steering system directs the force generated by the powertrain to move the vehicle around the circle. Higher speeds increase the gravitational resistance. The name for the force of gravity in this situation is **G-force,** and the unit of measurement is a **G.**

One G equals the force of gravity on an object and the hardest cornering most drivers do generates about 0.2 to 0.3 Gs. However, some performance cars can generate cornering forces of over 0.7 Gs. A cornering force of 0.2 Gs means that a sideways force equal to 0.2 of the vehicle weight is acting on it. The same force acts on the driver. So, a driver weighing 150 pounds in a vehicle generating 0.2 Gs feels a sideways force of 30 pounds. If a vehicle generated 1 G, the cornering force would equal the weight of the vehicle and driver. To skid out of control on a curve, a vehicle only needs to generate enough G-forces to make the tires lose traction. How much cornering force it takes to do this depends on the design of the vehicle and the tires.

It is common for automotive engineers to discuss cornering forces in terms of G-forces, but G-forces can also affect acceleration and deceleration. However, for some reason, the term is not as common in discussions of those topics, and is mainly used when talking about roll.

During cornering, G-forces effectively push the center of gravity outward (Figure 3-11). This lateral weight transfer has two effects. One, it creates body roll, based on the distance between the

center of gravity and the longitudinal axis. Second, it moves the vehicle toward its "overturning moment," which is based on the comparative measurements of the center of gravity height and the vehicle track width. Body roll is the movement of the sprung weight around the longitudinal axis, while the overturning moment is the tendency for the entire vehicle—sprung and unsprung weight—to roll on its longitudinal axis.

Body Roll

The amount of body roll on any given vehicle is determined by the distance of the center of gravity from the longitudinal axis. Each suspension, front and rear, has a **roll center,** around which that end of the vehicle rolls, and the longitudinal axis is a straight line that runs through the roll centers of the front and rear suspensions. The roll center is always on the vertical centerline of the vehicle when viewed from either the front or rear. However, the height of the roll center varies according to suspension design. In order to calculate the roll center of a vehicle, it is important to understand how it influences body roll.

A straight line drawn from the roll center of the front or rear suspension to the height of the vehicle center of gravity, would be the length of the "lever" that effectively causes body roll (Figure 3-11). When G-forces push the center of gravity to one side during cornering, the top of the lever moves outward, exerting force on the vehicle body and causing it to roll in relation to the wheels and tires. To complicate matters, the movement of the body pulls the suspension arms into new positions, changing their roll center locations as well.

The longer the lever between the center of gravity and roll center, the greater its effect, and the more body roll during turns. Therefore, one way to reduce body roll on turns is to lower the center of gravity of the vehicle, which brings it closer to the roll center. Unfortunately, production vehicles have certain design limitations that make it difficult to create a very low center of gravity, so designers turn to other methods of decreasing body roll, such as antiroll bars.

Another factor to consider when studying body roll is that the front and rear roll centers are seldom at the same height, so the longitudinal axis inclines up or down from the rear to the front (Figure 3-12). If the axis is lower at the rear, the distance between the roll center and the center of gravity is greater at the rear, which means the rear of the vehicle must roll through a greater angle than the front. However, the

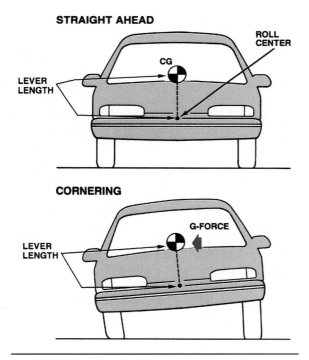

Figure 3-11. When G-forces push the CG outward, the vehicle body rolls on its longitudinal axis.

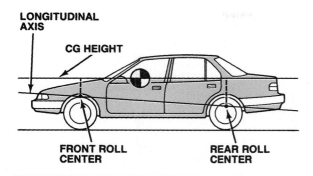

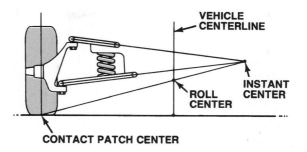

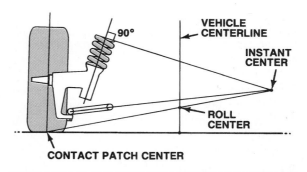

Figure 3-12. The front and rear roll centers may be at different heights, so the longitudinal axis is on an incline. Although this tends to create different amounts of roll front and rear, the stiffness of the vehicle body forces both ends to roll the same amount.

rigidity of the vehicle body makes the front roll nearly as much as the rear. This compresses the outer front suspension and spring and transfers more weight to the outer wheel than the center of gravity movement demands. In effect, the vehicle body acts as a torsion bar that conveys some of the roll force from the rear to the front. This forced weight transfer to the front tends to cause understeer. If the longitudinal axis is higher in the rear than the front, there is the same type of forced weight transfer from the front to the rear. This causes the vehicle to oversteer. The terms *understeer* and *oversteer* are discussed later in this chapter.

Keeping in mind what the roll centers do, look at how the suspension determines their location. The roll center is always on the vertical centerline of an axle, viewed from either the front or the side, but its height varies according to the angle of either the suspension control arms or the leaf spring installation and often varies between the front and rear axles.

Roll Center, Independent Suspension

To locate the roll center of an independent suspension, it is first necessary to locate the **instant center**, which is the point around which a wheel pivots during suspension travel (Figure 3-13). Draw a line from the instant center to the center of the tire contact patch, and the roll center is located where this line intersects the vertical centerline.

It is not difficult to locate the instant center in some independent suspensions. If an independent suspension uses only one arm at each wheel, the instant center is the pivot point of that arm. Examples of this are twin I-beam front suspensions and independent rear suspensions using one semi-trailing arm at each wheel. In a short-long-arm

Figure 3-13. A wheel pivots around the instant center as it moves up and down with suspension travel. The roll center is on the vehicle centerline between the instant center and the center of the tire contact patch.

(SLA) suspension, or in a strut/SLA suspension using only two lateral control arms, the instant center is where lines from each control arm intersect when viewed from the front (Figure 3-13). In a strut suspension in which the strut takes the place of the upper control arm, the instant center is where a line from the lower control arm intersects a line perpendicular to the strut.

Other independent suspension designs, particularly at the rear, can become more complex as more control arms are used and are positioned in different planes. Exactly how to calculate the roll center varies for each arrangement, and there are far too many designs to detail here. Simply remember that as the suspension compresses and rebounds, or as the wheel travels up and down, the knuckle effectively arcs around the instant center. Specific front and rear suspension designs are described in detail in Chapters 9 and 10 of this *Classroom Manual*.

Roll Center, Solid Axle

The three ways to find the roll center in a solid axle are according to the:

- Angles of the control arms
- Installation of a leaf spring
- Angle of the Panhard rod

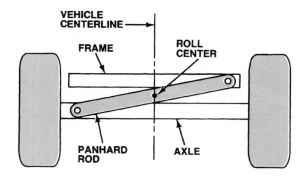

Figure 3-14. The roll center of a solid axle with a Panhard rod is where the Panhard rod intersects the vehicle centerline.

Unless a solid axle with coil springs has a Panhard rod, it generally has either semi-trailing arms or a number of trailing arms to position it front-to-rear. The angles of the arms determine a suspension pivot, or instant center, in front of the axle, which determines the roll center height. The angle of a semi-elliptical leaf spring installation determines the roll center height on some solid axles, and if the axle uses a Panhard rod, the roll center is located where the rod intersects the vehicle centerline (Figure 3-14). All three solid-axle suspension designs are described in Chapter 10 of this *Classroom Manual*.

Overturning Moment

The **overturning moment,** which is the tendency for a vehicle to overturn while cornering; is determined by center of gravity height, track width, car weight, and cornering force. As you recall, cornering force is determined by the speed and angle at which the vehicle is cornering. This force multiplied by the height of the center of gravity creates the overturning moment, which is the point where the vehicle becomes a rolling object moving sideways (Figure 3-15). The overturning moment is opposed by the weight of the vehicle multiplied by half the track width.

Given these factors, it is easy to see that the vehicle least likely to overturn during cornering is one with a:

- Low center of gravity
- Wide track width
- High overall weight

If a vehicle lacks these qualities, the driver must take care to reduce the risk of overturn by keeping the cornering force from becoming too great. In other words, the vehicle must corner at low speeds and wide angles.

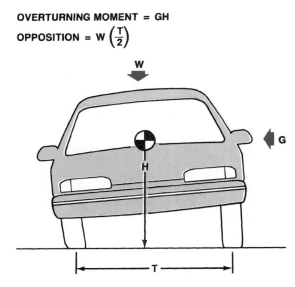

$$\text{OVERTURNING MOMENT} = \text{GH}$$
$$\text{OPPOSITION} = \text{W} \left(\frac{\text{T}}{2} \right)$$

W = WEIGHT

G = G-FORCE (CORNERING FORCE)

H = HEIGHT OF CG

T = TRACK WIDTH

Figure 3-15. The higher the center of gravity and the greater the cornering force, the more likely the vehicle is to roll over. The heavier it is and the wider its track width, the less likely it is to roll over.

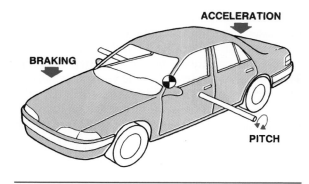

Figure 3-16. Pitch, which is movement around the lateral horizontal axis, is usually caused by the force of either braking or acceleration.

Pitch

Acceleration forces push the rear of the car down and braking pushes down on the front; both conditions move the vehicle body around its lateral horizontal axis (Figure 3-16). Pitch, as this movement is called, is considered one of the most disturbing motions to passengers who are prone to motion sickness. Therefore, chassis engineers take pains to keep pitch to a minimum.

■ Historical Steering

For thousands of years after the invention of the wheel, changing the direction the vehicle was moving in was accomplished by dragging the wheels into a new path. The axle of the wheels attached directly to the vehicle body, so wherever the wheels were dragged, the vehicle went.

The first refinement of this system was the invention of the kingpin. Originally a kingpin was a single pin at the center of a detached front axle; the kingpin joined the axle to the rest of the vehicle. With this system, the entire front angle could pivot under the vehicle frame, providing smoother cornering. Unfortunately, the front axle also tended to pivot in response to any road irregularities. If one wheel got stuck behind a stone, the front axle would begin to swing around that point. Nevertheless, this type of steering system, with the addition of a tiller and handle by which the driver could direct the front axle, made its way into some early automobiles.

The use of two kingpins and a steering linkage was the next step, and although this type of steering system was originally invented for horse-drawn carriages, the design is still used on some trucks today. With two kingpins, the wheels, rather than the whole axle, turned. A steering linkage design that allowed the outer wheel to turn wider than the inner wheel during cornering was patented by Rudolf Ackermann in 1818. The Ackermann design became the foundation on which all automotive steering linkages, up to the present day, are built.

Since the days of Ackermann and other innovators, kingpins have been replaced by ball joints,

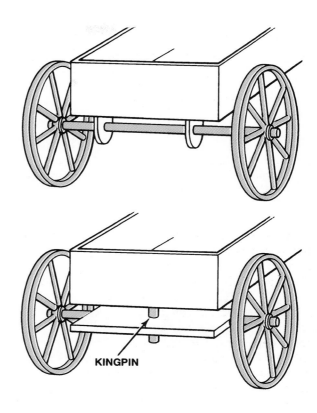

KINGPIN

and some ball joints have been replaced by struts. The evolution of steering system design, allowing more precise control of the vehicle, continues today, but the basic layout remains that of Rudolf Ackermann, an automotive pioneer.

As mentioned earlier, the lateral horizontal axis intersects the center of gravity, and front-to-rear weight distribution determines its location. The frequency with which pitch occurs is controlled by the wheelbase in relation to weight distribution and by the front and rear suspension spring rates.

A short wheelbase with some weight overhang at the front and the rear helps reduce pitch. The wheelbase of a vehicle is like a lever that uses the center of gravity where the lateral horizontal axis is located as a fulcrum (Figure 3-17). The distance from this fulcrum to the rear wheels is the length of the lever that acts to lift the weight at the front of the vehicle, and the distance from the fulcrum to the front wheels creates the lever that lifts the rear of the vehicle. Two things determine the lever effect: the length of the lever and the distance of the opposite weight from the fulcrum.

The shorter the lever, the less its effect. As for weight distribution, if the front weight is concentrated toward the fulcrum, the lever has a greater effect on the weight. This creates more pitch when acceleration exerts a downward force on the rear of the vehicle, which causes squat (Figure 3-18). If the weight is farther away from the fulcrum, the lever exerts less effect, and there is less pitch. The same principle applies for the concentration of rear weight and its effect on pitch.

Once pitching movement has started, it can develop a tendency to go back and forth repeatedly between the front and rear suspensions unless they are tuned to prevent this. Engineers vary the oscillation rate of the front and rear suspensions and springs to ensure that the suspension movements will cancel each other out instead of aggravating the pitch.

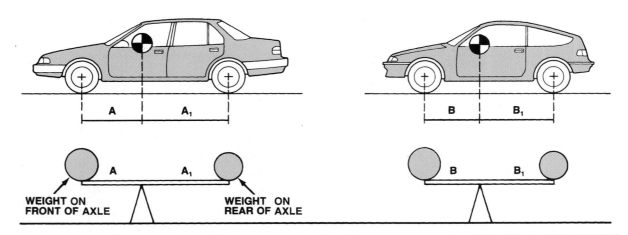

Figure 3-17. Lever A_1, which lifts the front of the larger vehicle, is longer than lever B_1, which lifts the front of the smaller vehicle. Therefore, lever A_1 has a greater effect than B_1, all other things being equal. The same is true of levers A and B and their effect on rear lift.

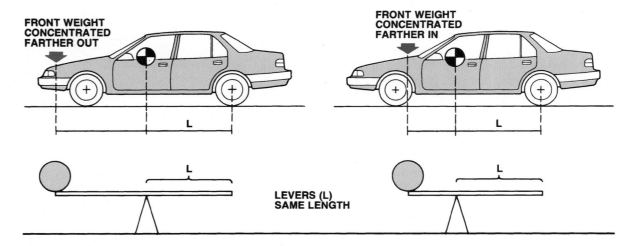

Figure 3-18. The length of the lever lifting the front is the same for both vehicles, but the distance from the fulcrum to the concentration of front weight differs. The vehicle on the right, with the weight concentrated closer to the CG, will pitch more, all other things being equal.

Yaw

Yaw occurs when the car body deviates from the straight-ahead and moves around its vertical axis (Figure 3-19). The same weight distribution that tends to reduce pitch—front and rear weight far away from the center of gravity—tends to prevent yaw by providing a high polar moment of inertia. But to attain this weight distribution requires a longer wheelbase.

The **polar moment of inertia** of a vehicle determines how easily it yaws, and the factor that influences this is weight distribution (Figure 3-20). **Inertia** is the tendency of an object to remain at rest if it is at rest and to remain in motion in the same direction if it is in motion. With a high po-

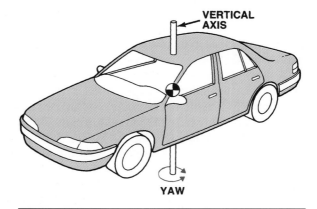

Figure 3-19. Changes in direction tend to cause yaw, or movement around the vertical axis of the vehicle.

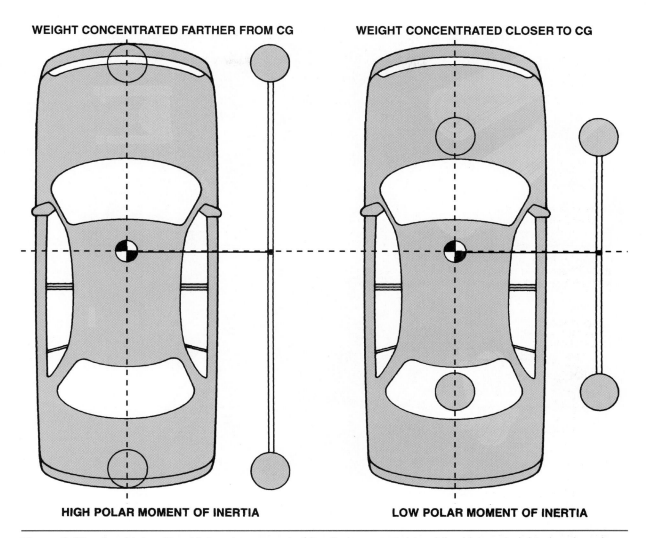

WEIGHT CONCENTRATED FARTHER FROM CG

WEIGHT CONCENTRATED CLOSER TO CG

HIGH POLAR MOMENT OF INERTIA

LOW POLAR MOMENT OF INERTIA

Figure 3-20. A vehicle with a high polar moment of inertia is more stable while driving straight ahead, and one with a low polar moment of inertia is less likely to spin out due to yawing movement.

lar moment of inertia, a vehicle tends to continue going straight when it is already going straight, while a vehicle with a low polar moment of inertia is deflected more easily from its current path.

The drawback to a high polar moment of inertia is that once an outside force—such as a strong G-force—causes the vehicle to move around its vertical axis, inertia tends to keep the vehicle moving this way. If the tires maintain traction, only the unsprung weight yaws, but if the tires reach the limit of adhesion and break loose, the entire vehicle spins out of control.

Vehicles with a low polar moment of inertia seem unstable to most drivers, but enthusiasts and professional race drivers think of this "instability" as "responsiveness." A vehicle with a low polar moment of inertia has less tendency to spin out. The weight on some vehicles, such as mid-engine sports cars or other performance cars, is concentrated near the center of gravity to provide a low polar moment of inertia and make the suspension and steering more responsive.

AERODYNAMICS

Aerodynamics is the study of the effect of airflow on a moving object. The aerodynamic "look" of many production vehicles is often more fancy than fact, but aerodynamics can become a factor in handling characteristics once vehicle speed exceeds approximately 50 mph (80 km/h).

To move, a vehicle must push air out of its way, and the resistance of that air along the body

Figure 3-21. Modern vehicles are designed with the aid of a wind tunnel to maximize the aerodynamic effect of the body design.

and undercarriage creates aerodynamic drag. The smoother the surface across which the air moves, the less drag is created. Protrusions, such as rear-view mirrors, body panel seams, door handles, suspension parts, and so on, increase drag. Drag is also influenced by the shape of the vehicle body. Designers concerned with reducing drag tend to specify a relatively small frontal area, with as much slope and smoothness as possible to direct the air over the length of the body (Figure 3-21).

Lift occurs when air pressure underneath the vehicle builds up enough to lift the chassis and relieve some of the vehicle weight from the wheels, which reduces tire traction. The theory behind front air dams and fender "skirts" is to prevent lift by not letting air flow under the chassis. This works for race cars, on which these air dams can reach very close to the ground. But driving on the street requires a certain amount of clearance and any air

flowing under a dam or skirt reduces its effectiveness. Rear spoilers, or "whale tails," on production cars usually are not large enough to actually create downforce, but they can slightly decrease lift to increase tire traction at high speeds. **Downforce** is the opposite of lift, occurring when air pressure builds on top of the vehicle and presses down to compress the chassis and load suspension.

WEIGHT TRANSFER AND TRACTION

When a vehicle is standing still, each tire bears a certain proportion of the total vehicle weight. Measuring the weight on each tire determines the **static weight distribution** (Figure 3-22). As mentioned earlier, road forces affect the center of gravity causing it to change position, which results in

STATIC WEIGHT DISTRIBUTION

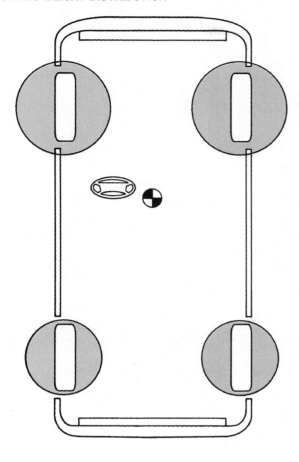

Figure 3-22. In a typical FWD design, the front tires have greater traction because they support more of the vehicle weight. The circles represent the amount of traction at each tire.

weight transfer. Whenever weight transfers, the weight distribution among the tires changes. Weight transfer decreases the total traction of the four tires, because the traction lost at the tires whose load is decreased is greater than the traction gained at the tires where the load increases.

Braking and acceleration cause longitudinal, or weight transfer from rear-to-front or from front-to-rear. Cornering causes lateral, or side-to-side, weight transfer. Four factors determine how much weight transfer occurs:

- Total vehicle weight
- Center of gravity height
- Strength of braking, acceleration, or cornering force
- Wheelbase and track width

Obviously, the more a vehicle weighs, the more weight can be transferred. The higher the center of gravity, the more easily road forces can move it, both longitudinally and laterally. The stronger the road force—braking, acceleration, or cornering—the greater its effect. Finally, the shorter the wheelbase and the narrower the track width, the more easily longitudinal or lateral weight transfer occurs. Aerodynamics become a contributing factor when lift decreases the load on the tires or when downforce increases tire load. However, aerodynamic effect is negligible for most production vehicles in most ordinary driving situations.

Longitudinal weight transfer is uncomplicated. During acceleration, the force of the acceleration pushes the center of gravity rearward, and weight is transferred from the front tires to the rear tires (Figure 3-23). During braking or deceleration, the opposite weight transfer occurs to load the front tires (Figure 3-24).

Lateral weight transfer is a little more complex because a vehicle that is cornering is usually either slowing or accelerating as well. A driver entering a turn tends to decelerate. Using a left turn as an example, you see that the deceleration tends to cause a forward weight transfer at the same time that the cornering force transfers weight from the left to the right side of the vehicle. The weight on both right tires increases, but the weight on the right front tire increases more (Figure 3-25). Also, the weight on both left tires decreases, but the weight on the left rear tire decreases more. As the driver accelerates out of the turn, more weight shifts to the rear (Figure 3-26).

In a hard corner with a lot of weight transfer, one of the tires, such as the outside front tire going into a turn, does most of the work of maintaining traction (Figure 3-25). Such a situation makes the vehicle unstable, so designers try to minimize weight transfer within the design limitations they are given. The driver can limit weight transfer by cornering at moderate speeds.

Oversteer and Understeer

Oversteer and *understeer* are popular terms among people discussing handling, but not everyone who uses them understands what they mean. A simple way to define these terms is according to the vehicle response to driver input at the steering wheel. If the vehicle turns more sharply than steering wheel input warrants, it has **oversteer** (Figure 3-27). However, **understeer** occurs when

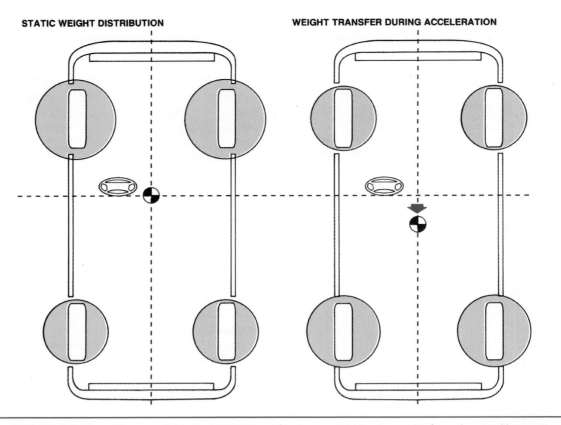

Figure 3-23. During acceleration, rearward weight transfer decreases traction at the front tires and increases it at the rear.

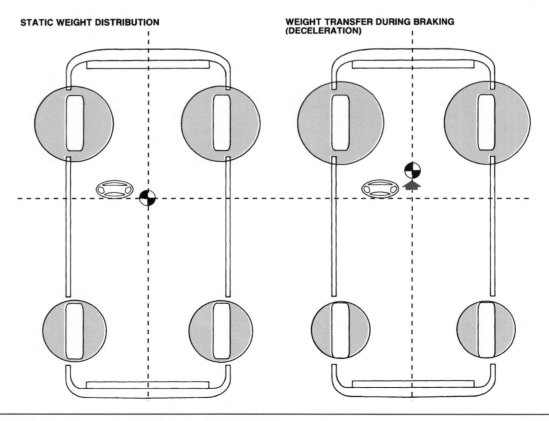

Figure 3-24. Braking or deceleration moves the CG forward, which causes a forward weight transfer increasing front tire traction and decreasing rear tire traction.

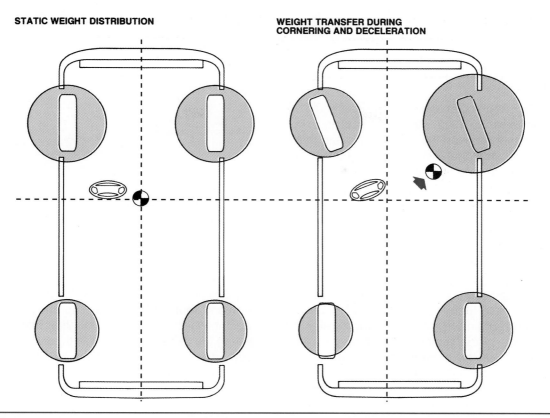

Figure 3-25. Cornering to the left while decelerating transfers weight to the right and front. In a FWD design, this places a great deal of weight on the right front tire, while the rear left tire loses much of its traction.

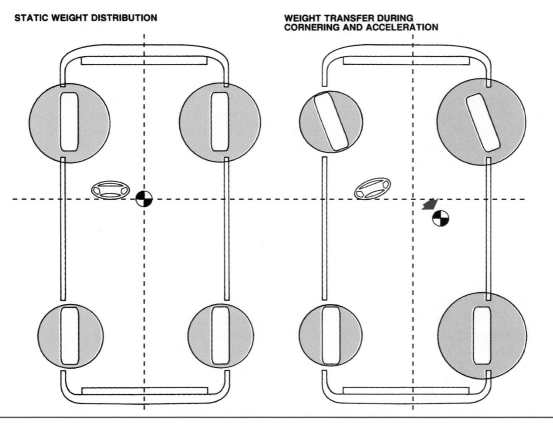

Figure 3-26. As a vehicle accelerates out of a left turn, weight transfers to the rear tires, especially the right rear one.

■ No Axles?

The chief selling point of a car produced and marketed in Japan in 1923 was that it had no axles. The designer believed the rough roads and many bridges in Japan demanded light-weight vehicles, and in order to save weight, he eliminated the differential and axle shafts. The front-engine, rear-wheel drive design of the Sekine mounted the engine and driveshaft at an angle to the vehicle centerline with the driveshaft connecting the engine directly to the right rear wheel. A bevel gear attached to the wheel was driven by the driveshaft through a pinion gear. A tube with flexible couplings at each end connected the two rear wheels to provide drive to the left wheel. To compensate for the powertrain weight being concentrated on the left side of the vehicle, other heavy components, such as the battery and fuel tank, were placed on the opposite side. All four wheels were

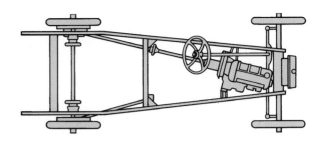

cushioned by transverse mounted multileaf springs. Therefore, in addition to saving weight, the Sekine design provided independent suspension and improved the ratio of sprung to unsprung weight, which produced a smoother ride, by eliminating the axles. However, this ingenious technology never caught on, and the axle-less chassis faded into oblivion.

---

a driver turns the steering wheel farther but the vehicle turns less sharply (Figure 3-27). Nearly all late-model production vehicles are designed to understeer to some degree.

A difference in slip angles at the front and rear tires causes oversteer or understeer. A slip angle, as described in Chapter 13 of this *Classroom Manual,* is the angle between the direction a tire is pointed and the direction that it actually moves. A slip angle opposes cornering because it results from the tendency of a tire to travel in a straight line. There is a greater slip angle at the rear tires than at the front tires on an oversteering vehicle. This causes the nose of the vehicle to point into the turn more than the angle of the front wheels. When understeering, the front tires have a greater slip angle and the nose of the vehicle does not point as far into the turn as the wheels (Figure 3-27). If front and rear slip angles are equal, the vehicle has neutral steer, but this is uncommon.

Changing speed during a turn aggravates both oversteer and understeer. This means that if the driver of an oversteering vehicle accelerates or decelerates in a turn, the vehicle turns its nose into the corner still more. To avoid losing control, the driver must turn the steering wheel out of the turn to compensate. If the driver of an understeering vehicle accelerates or decelerates in a turn, the tires offer more resistance to the tendency of the nose to turn into the corner, so the driver must turn the steering wheel more sharply into the corner to compensate.

The rear tires of an oversteering vehicle start to slip before the front ones. When this happens, the correct response is to turn the steering wheel in the opposite direction from the way the vehicle is cornering and continue accelerating. This increases traction at the rear tires. These are not instinctive actions for most drivers, particularly if they panic upon feeling that they are losing control. Drivers can, of course, learn these responses through experience and training.

However, the correct response to slipping at the front tires of an understeering car is to decelerate, which increases traction at the front tires. Because decelerating is an instinctive response in a panic situation, most drivers find understeering cars more predictable. Therefore, instead of asking *whether* a vehicle should understeer, vehicle designers and engineers ask themselves by *how much* should the vehicle understeer. Due to the large slip angles at the front tires, turning the steering wheel farther into the turn is not helpful. In some cases, counter-steering slightly can help the tires regain traction by decreasing the slip angle. However, as mentioned, this is not an instinctive response. Usually, the driver regains control by lifting off the accelerator, which causes a forward weight transfer and increases front-tire traction.

Oversteer was at one time considered an advantage for race cars because the need to accelerate in response to side-slip meant that oversteer would allow faster cornering as the vehicle approaches the limits of tire traction. Decelerating to maintain

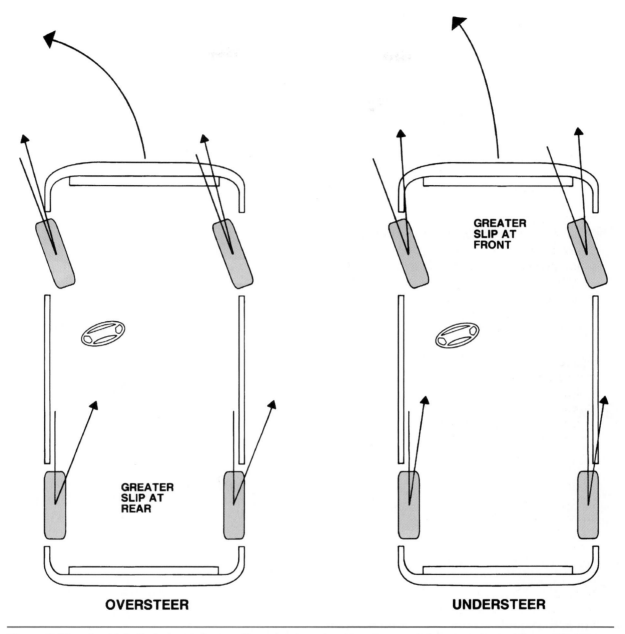

Figure 3-27. A vehicle that responds more than steering wheel input warrants has oversteer, while one that steers less sharply than the steering wheel is turned has understeer. Differing slip angles at the front and rear cause understeer and oversteer.

control, as required by an understeering vehicle, is the opposite of what a race driver wants to do. Today, thanks to advances in tire rubber technology, oversteer is less necessary, and neutral steering is preferred in a race car. With equal slip angles at all the tires, the driver can devote more tire traction to speed and less to side-slip. Since race car drivers are highly trained, they do not usually lose control of a neutral steering or oversteering car as a less skillful driver would.

Electronic Suspension Control Description and Operation

The **electronic suspension control (ESC) system** (Figure 3-28) consists of the following components:

- ESC module (3)
- Four dampers contained in the two front struts (5 and 6) and the two rear shock absorbers (1 and 9)

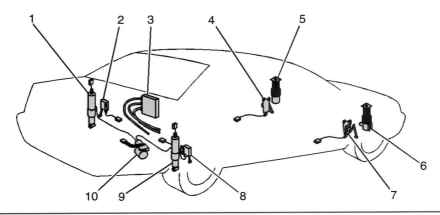

Figure 3-28. Electronic suspension control (ESC) system. (Courtesy of General Motors Corporation)

- Four position sensors (2, 4, 7, and 8)
- ALC air compressor module (10)
- ELC relay (not shown)

The ESC system with rear automatic level control (ALC) controls damping forces in the front struts and rear shock absorbers in response to various road and driving conditions. The rear ALC portion of the system maintains a proper vehicle trim height under various vehicle load conditions. For more information on the ALC, refer to *Automatic Level Control Description and Operation in Automatic Level Control.* The ESC module receives the following inputs: wheel-to-body position, vehicle speed, and lift/dive. The ESC module evaluates these inputs and controls actuators in each of the dampers independently to provide varied levels of suspension control.

Electronic Suspension Control (ESC) Module

The **ESC module** (Figure 3-29) is used to control how firm or soft each shock or strut should be to provide the best ride. The ESC module is also used to control the vehicle's rear height. The ESC module is located on the right side of the rear seat back and is accessed through the trunk.

Position Sensors

The **ESC position sensors** (Figure 3-30) are 0- to 5-volt DC output devices that are used to measure wheel-to-body movement/position. There are four position sensors on the vehicle, one per corner. Each position sensor is mounted between a suspension control arm and the body.

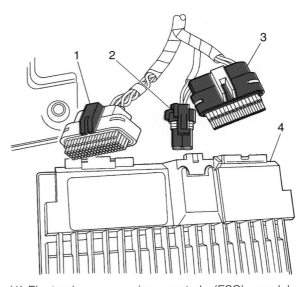

(1) Electronic suspension control (ESC) module connector C1
(2) Electronic suspension control (ESC) module connector C3
(3) Electronic suspension control (ESC) module connector C2
(4) Electronic suspension control (ESC) module

Figure 3-29. Electronic suspension control (ESC) module. (Courtesy of General Motors Corporation)

Shock Absorber or Strut

An **ESC damper** (Figure 3-31) is mounted at each corner of the vehicle. The four suspension dampers, two front struts and two rear shock absorbers, each contain an integral actuator that is controlled by the ESC module. The actuator provides a wide range of damping forces between soft and firm levels. Damping is controlled by the amount of current supplied to the actuator via pulse width modulation.

The ESC rear shock absorbers and front struts are mono tube types, which provide damping by increasing magnetic flux to magnetic particles to resist suspension movement. The ESC shock absorber or strut has the capability of providing multiple modes or values of damping forces, in both compression and rebound direction. Increasing or decreasing the magnetic flux to the shock absorbers or struts achieves the damping forces.

Vehicle Speed

The ESC module receives a vehicle speed input. It is obtained over the CLASS 2 serial communication bus. Vehicle speed is used to determine the amount of damper control necessary.

Lift/Dive

Lift/dive input is received from the PCM (powertrain control module). When the ESC module receives an active lift/dive input, it will command a firm damping level on all four corners. The lift signal is calculated in the PCM based on throttle position, transmission gear, vehicle speed, and brake switch status. The dive signal, also calculated in the PCM, is based upon the rate of change with the vehicle speed.

Warning Messages

The DIC (driver information center) displays two different warning messages that are set if there is an electronic suspension control system fault(s). The warning messages are as follows:

- SERVICE SUSPENSION SYS
- SPEED LIMITED TO XXX

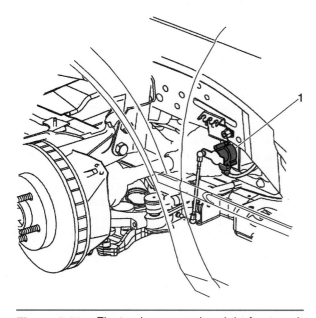

Figure 3-30. Electronic suspension right front position sensor. (Courtesy of General Motors Corporation)

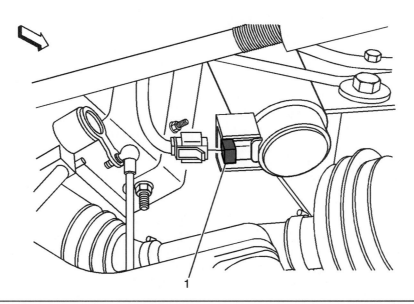

Figure 3-31. ESC damper. (Courtesy of General Motors Corporation)

The DIC will display one, both, or none, depending on the fault that was encountered. The warning message(s) will continue to be displayed, until the fault(s) has been corrected.

SUMMARY

Wheel and tire position along with weight distribution determine the handling characteristics of a vehicle. Important dimensions indicating tire position are wheelbase and track width. The proportion of sprung to unsprung weight and the location of the center of gravity are key factors of weight distribution.

Road forces can rotate the sprung weight of a vehicle around three axes of movement: the longitudinal axis, lateral horizontal axis, and vertical axis. Movement around the longitudinal axis is roll, around the lateral horizontal axis is pitch, and around the vertical axis is yaw.

The force of gravity that opposes changes in speed and direction is called G-force. Gs are the unit of measurement for G-force. Although G-forces also result from acceleration and deceleration, they are most often used to discuss cornering forces. G-force causes body roll. The front and rear ends of the vehicle body roll around their roll centers, which are determined by suspension design. The overturning moment is the point at which the entire vehicle—sprung and unsprung weight—overturns. The factors involved in determining the overturning moment are center of gravity height, track width, and overall vehicle weight.

Two factors determine how much a vehicle body pitches: wheelbase in relation to weight distribution, and front and rear suspension spring rates. Wheelbase and weight distribution are factors that determine the polar moment of inertia, which is an important factor in yaw.

Aerodynamics is the study of the effect of airflow on a moving object. Aerodynamics can contribute to handling, but generally this applies to race cars only.

Weight on the tires gives them traction. Weight transfer occurs during changes in speed and direction, and the weight transfer changes the amount of traction at each of the tires. Oversteer and understeer are the result of the tires on one axle having more traction than those on the other axle. The different traction causes different slip angles front and rear, and this results in oversteer or understeer.

The electronic suspension control system controls damping forces in the front struts and rear shock absorbers in response to various road and driving conditions. The rear automotive level control (ALC) portion of the system maintains a proper vehicle trim height under various vehicle load conditions. For more information on the ALC, refer to *Automatic Level Control Description and Operation in Automatic Level Control*. The ESC module receives the following inputs: wheel-to-body position, vehicle speed, and lift/dive. The ESC module evaluates these inputs and controls actuators in each of the dampers independently to provide varied levels of suspension control.

Review Questions

For each of the following questions, choose the letter that represents the best possible answer.

1. All of the following factors contribute to the handling dynamics of a vehicle, EXCEPT:
   a. Length of wheelbase
   b. Type of engine
   c. Proportion of unsprung weight
   d. Center of gravity

2. All of the following statements are true, EXCEPT:
   a. Track width at the front and rear axles does not have to be equal.
   b. The wheels and tires contribute to the vehicle unsprung weight.
   c. The center of gravity on a FWD layout is usually closer to the center of the vehicle.
   d. Extra weight inside a vehicle changes the location of its center of gravity.

3. Technician A says that pitch is the vehicle rotating around its lateral horizontal axis. Technician B says that the terms *dive* and *squat* refer to pitching movement. Who is right?
   a. Technician A only
   b. Technician B only
   c. Both A and B
   d. Neither A nor B

4. All of the following design factors reduce body roll, EXCEPT:
   a. A lower center of gravity
   b. An antiroll bar
   c. Front and rear roll centers at equal heights
   d. Small steering gear turning ratio

5. The point around which a wheel pivots during suspension travel is called the:
   a. Tire contact patch
   b. Instant center
   c. Roll angle
   d. Vehicle centerline

6. All of the following affect the location of the instant center on a solid axle, EXCEPT:
   a. The angle of the trailing or semi-trailing arms
   b. The angle of the leaf springs
   c. The angle of the Panhard rod
   d. The angle of the shock absorbers

7. Which of the following increases the tendency of a vehicle to overturn during cornering?
   a. Narrow track width
   b. Low center of gravity
   c. Cornering at low speeds
   d. Heavy vehicle weight

8. All of the following factors are important in determining the tendency of a vehicle to pitch, EXCEPT:
   a. Relation of tie rod position to wheel knuckle
   b. Front and rear weight distribution
   c. Relation of weight distribution to wheelbase
   d. Front and rear suspension spring rates

9. Technician A says that the distance of the front weight from the center of gravity on a vehicle affects its tendency to pitch. Technician B says that the farther the front weight is from the center of gravity, the more the vehicle will pitch. Who is right?
   a. Technician A only
   b. Technician B only
   c. Both A and B
   d. Neither A nor B

10. All of the following statements are true, EXCEPT:
    a. A vehicle with a high polar moment of inertia is not easily deflected from its straight-ahead path.
    b. A vehicle with a low polar moment of inertia is easily deflected from its straight-ahead path.
    c. A vehicle with a low polar moment of inertia is less likely to spin out while turning.
    d. A vehicle with a high polar moment of inertia is more prone to yaw than one with a low polar moment.

11. Lift does all of the following, EXCEPT:
    a. Reduce tire traction
    b. Occur when air pressure builds up under the vehicle
    c. Decrease with the use of air dams and fender skirts
    d. Increase with the use of spoilers, or "whale tails"

12. Technician A says that if a driver decelerates while making a left turn, the left front tire has the greatest increase in traction. Technician B says that in the same turn, traction decreases at the right rear tire. Who is right?
    a. Technician A only
    b. Technician B only
    c. Both A and B
    d. Neither A nor B

13. All of the following statements are true, EXCEPT:
    a. Most late-model vehicles have a slight amount of oversteer.
    b. Oversteer occurs when the slip angles at the rear tires are greater than the slip angles at the front tires.
    c. A correct response to oversteer is to continue accelerating.
    d. Counter-steering helps compensate for oversteer.

4

Steering Wheels, Steering Columns, and Manual Steering Gears

OBJECTIVES

Upon completion and review of this chapter, you will be able to:

- Identify the components of the steering wheel and explain their operation.

- Identify the components of the steering column and explain their operation.

- Identify the components of the different types of manual steering gears and explain their operation.

KEY TERMS

air bag	sector shaft endplay
air bag module	series circuit
axial play	shift lock actuator
ball nut	standard steering gear
cam and lever steering gear	steering column
clockspring contact	steering column locking motor
column cover	steering gear
column jacket	steering gear input shaft
end play	steering gear ratio
flexible coupling	steering ratio
gear lash	steering shaft
gear mesh preload	steering wheel
horn circuit	steering wheel freeplay
input gear	supplemental inflatatable restraint (SIR) system
kickback	
output gear	tilt mechanisms
passive restraint system	tolerance
pinion bearing preload	universal joint
pinion gear	variable steering ratio
pinion torque	worm and roller steering gear
preload	
rack	worm and sector steering gear
rack and pinion steering gear	worm bearing preload
recirculating ball steering gear	worm endplay
relay circuit	worm gear
sector gear	

INTRODUCTION

When the driver turns the steering wheel in a circle, or in a rotary motion, the steering linkage moves side-to-side, or in a lateral motion, to steer

55

the wheels. The three major parts of the steering system that transmit motion from the driver to the steering linkage are the:

- Steering wheel
- Steering column
- Steering gear

The steering wheel and steering column transmit rotary motion, while the steering gear changes rotary steering shaft motion into lateral steering linkage movement. This chapter examines the various designs of these steering system parts and explains how they work. Chapter 5 of this *Classroom Manual* covers steering linkages.

STEERING WHEELS

The **steering wheel** is the most familiar part of the steering system to most drivers. Although simple, it is important because it connects the driver to the steering system.

The steering wheel, which consists of a rigid rim and a number of spokes connecting the rim to a center hub, attaches to the top of the steering shaft at its center. Most steering wheel hubs have internal splines that fit over external splines on the steering shaft. A bolt or nut at the center of the hub secures the wheel to the shaft. The spokes must allow the driver a clear view of the instrument panel through the top of the steering wheel. The entire operation of the steering wheel consists of the turning input from the driver. In addition, the steering wheel may house some luxury controls, such as cruise control, as well as safety features, such as the horn and air bag.

Steering Wheel Buildup

The steering wheel used on older Dodge light trucks is a good example of a basic steering wheel design (Figure 4-1). Two spokes connect the rim of the steering wheel to the hub, which splines to the shaft. Three screws attach the steering column cover, which rotates along with the wheel, to the wheel. A horn cover snaps onto the steering wheel and is held in place by two metal clips. A single wire is used for the horn circuit and depressing the horn completes the ground circuit through a spring-loaded wiper switch. A retaining nut holds the steering wheel securely on the end of the steering shaft.

Horn Operation

In modern vehicles, horns are part of the electric **horn circuit.** One way to wire a horn is in a **series circuit** in which electricity has one path that it can

follow when the circuit is complete (Figure 4-2). A normally open switch in an electrical circuit is inside the horn button. As long as the horn button is in its normal position, there is no current through the circuit and the horn does not work. When the driver pushes the horn button, the contacts in the switch close, allowing electrical current through the circuit to operate the horn. A **relay circuit** is a more common method of wiring the horn (Figure 4-2). In a relay, closing a switch in a low-voltage series circuit triggers current through a separate, higher-voltage circuit that powers the horn.

Air Bags

U.S. Federal law requires a driver-side **passive restraint system** on all new passenger cars sold

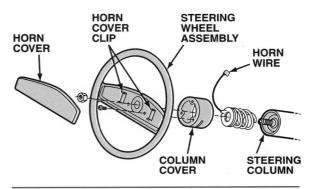

Figure 4-1. This steering wheel is a basic design: The only accessory in it is the horn.

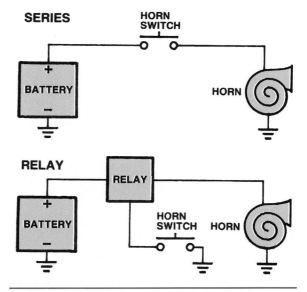

Figure 4-2. The horn button is a normally open switch. When the driver presses the horn button, the switch closes, allowing electrical current through the horn circuit to sound the horn.

in the domestic market since the 1990 model year. Because of this law, increasing numbers of cars are equipped with an **air bag,** sometimes referred to as a **supplemental inflatable restraint (SIR) system.** When used with shoulder and lap seat belts, air bags add an extra measure of safety in a head-on collision. Never attempt to remove an air bag module or service an air bag-equipped steering wheel without first consulting the factory service manual. The manual shows how to disarm the air bag system, which prevents accidental deployment and allows safe servicing of the steering wheel, steering column, and any other surrounding components.

An air bag is a large, mushroom-shaped device made of nylon cloth that is covered with neoprene. The air bag is folded and stored in the front center of the steering wheel. In a front-end collision, the air bag inflates in a fraction of a second to provide a cushion between the driver and the steering wheel and dashboard (Figure 4-3). The part of the steering wheel where the air bag is stored is called the **air bag module,** or the inflator module. The module also contains an ignitor, a canister of flammable gas, and a number of sodium azide pellets (Figure 4-4). Guidelines on how to service air bag-equipped steering wheels are in the accompanying *Shop Manual.* Always handle air bags with care to avoid accidentally deploying them.

The air bag module is part of an electrical circuit that includes a number of impact sensors. When the sensors detect vehicle deceleration so abrupt that it must be caused by a collision, a switch closes to send an electric current to the air bag module. At the module, the current sets off the air bag ignitor,

which ignites the gas canister and the sodium azide pellets. The sodium azide pellets burn quickly, and rapidly release nitrogen gas while they burn. The nitrogen gas fills the air bag. As it inflates, the air bag tears open the module cover and spreads out across the steering wheel, windshield, and dashboard. The entire process, from sensor reaction to full air bag deployment, takes 30–65 milliseconds. Within a second of inflating, the bag deflates partially as the nitrogen gas escapes through exhaust vents in the side of the bag. Once deployed, an air bag cannot be reused. The entire air bag module must be replaced, and collision repairs are needed as well.

Steering Wheel Buildup with Air Bag
The Infiniti Q45 provides a good example of a steering wheel with an air bag module; most other installations are similar (Figure 4-5).

In order to hold the air bag module, the column and the center of the steering wheel are larger than the same parts in vehicles without an air bag. The

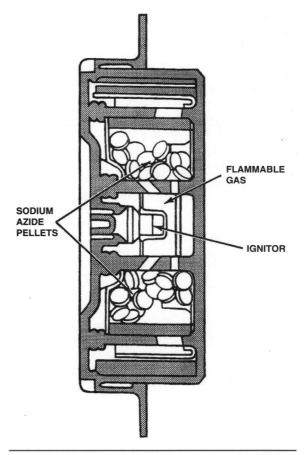

Figure 4-4. The flammable gas in this inflator module is boron potassium nitrate. When the gas burns and the flame reaches the sodium azide pellets, they burn and produce nitrogen gas to fill the air bag.

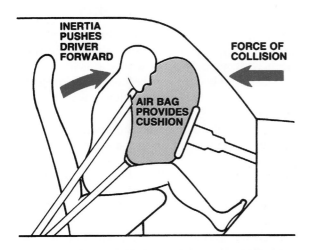

Figure 4-3. An air bag provides extra protection in a head-on collision when the steering wheel and dashboard could otherwise injure the driver.

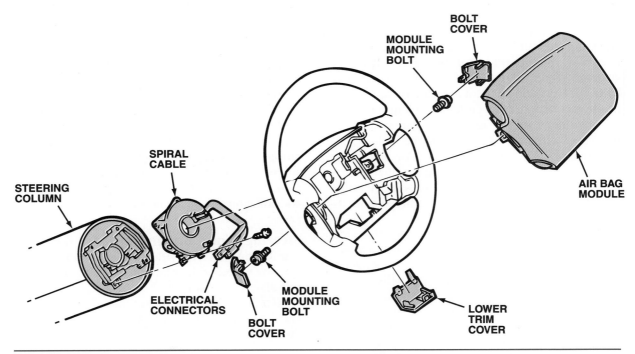

Figure 4-5. The air bag module bolts onto the steering wheel and is removed as a unit to service the steering wheel and column.

module fits in front of the nut that secures the steering wheel to the **steering shaft**. Two bolts at the back of the steering wheel fasten the air bag module to the steering wheel. Electrical current is provided to the air bag through the spiral cable, which is also known as a **clockspring contact**. The spiral cable connects to the air bag module with two wire leads. The spiral cable is a tightly coiled metal strip that allows steering wheel rotation while maintaining electrical continuity.

Heated Steering Wheel

The heated steering wheel system (Figure 4-6) consists of a heated steering wheel, a heated steering wheel switch, and a steering wheel heat module. The heated steering wheel includes a non-serviceable heating element and temperature sensor. The heating element and sensor are located in the rim of the steering wheel. The heated steering wheel switch is located in the steering wheel switch bezel. The steering wheel heat module is located on the backside of the steering wheel center hub. When the switch is pressed, a signal is sent to the controller and the heated steering wheel is turned on. The system then remains on until the customer turns it off. The wheel's normal operating temperature is 32°C (89.6°F). The wheel takes approximately

three to four minutes to reach the normal operating temperature. The wheel will take longer to heat up if the vehicle temperature is below −21°C (−5.8°F). The built-in temperature sensor provides input to the controller to limit the temperature to the normal operating temperature. The wheel will not operate if the vehicle temperature is at or above 32°C (89.6°F).

Steering Wheel Freeplay

Steering wheel freeplay is the distance the steering wheel can turn under light pressure before it meets resistance. In other words, it is the amount the steering wheel moves before the steering system responds. On vehicles with power steering, freeplay is checked with the engine running. The steering wheel freeplay measurement is a simple version of the gear mesh measurement described later in this chapter.

The amount of allowable steering wheel freeplay is typically specified by the vehicle manufacturer and can be found in the factory service manual. Although an extremely small amount of freeplay is allowable, it is preferable to have none. This is because freeplay causes a gap of time between when the driver moves the steering wheel and when the road wheels actually turn.

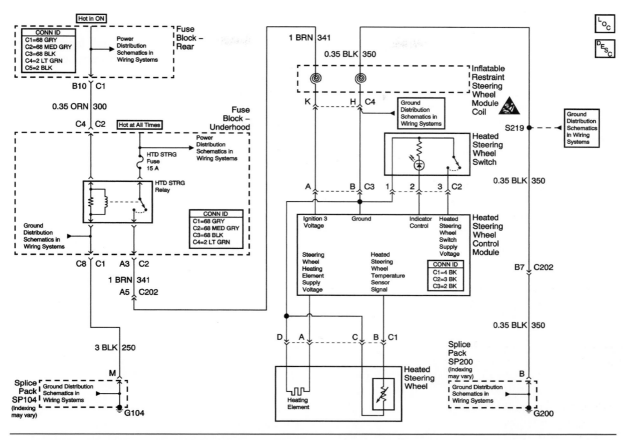

Figure 4-6. Heated steering wheel system. (Courtesy of General Motors Corporation)

Steering Ratio

The **steering ratio** is the number of degrees of rotation a steering wheel must move in order to move the road wheels one degree. So, if the steering ratio is 20:1, the steering wheel must move 20 degrees in order to move the wheels one degree (Figure 4-7). The designs of both the **steering gear** and the steering linkage determine the steering ratio, with steering gear design being the more significant factor.

Some steering gears provide a **variable steering ratio.** For example, the steering ratio may be 17:1 for the first 40 degrees of steering wheel movement, then begin to decrease, and drop to 14:1 by the end of steering wheel movement. This means that as the driver turns the steering wheel farther the wheels move one degree for only 14 degrees of steering wheel movement. In this way, a variable ratio increases maneuverability in sharp turns, but steering effort increases as the ratio drops. Variable ratio steering is explained in detail later in this chapter.

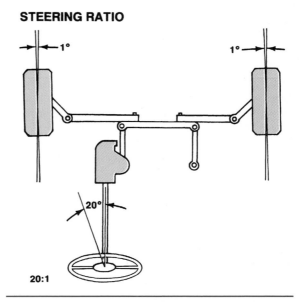

STEERING RATIO

Figure 4-7. Steering ratios are a compromise between a low ratio, which transmits steering input more directly, and a high ratio, which makes the wheel easier to turn. Low ratios give quick but stiff steering. High ratios, such as the 20:1 shown, provide slow but easy steering.

■ No Air Bags for Ferrari

In 1990, Ferrari Automobile of Modena, Italy, supplied the United States with its quickest, fastest—and most expensive—automobile, the F40. The F40, a true "supercar," featured a 478-horsepower, twin-turbocharged V8 engine, and a top speed of over 200 miles per hour.

To certify the $250,000-plus car for the U.S. market, Ferrari spent three years bringing it in line with National Highway Traffic Safety Administration (NHTSA) regulations. For the F40 to meet regulations, Ferrari had to lower tailpipe emissions, reinforce the bumpers, and install a passive restraint system—either an air bag or automatic shoulder belts.

Ferrari decided that they could not install an air bag on the F40 because its composite chassis and race-ready suspension were so stiff that normal driving and minor impacts might trigger the sensors and inadvertently deploy the air bag. Instead, the five-point restraint harnesses were removed, and automatic shoulder harnesses with manual lap belts were installed. An NHTSA official admitted, "Everybody recognizes that the Ferrari seat belt is a lot safer, but it requires hooking up. It is an active system, not a passive one."

In practice, meeting street-legal safety requirements may prove to be largely irrelevant. With investors offering prices as high as $1.4 million for the F40, the likelihood that many drivers will actually take one out on the road is slim.

A low steering ratio may be referred to as a "fast ratio" because the wheels turn faster in response to steering wheel movement. Similarly, higher ratios are called "slow ratios." Lower, faster ratios are more common on smaller vehicles, while larger vehicles tend to have higher, slower ratios. One reason for this general rule is that the faster the ratio, the more resistance the steering system offers to movement, and the stiffer the steering feels. Since the weight of a large vehicle already causes hard steering, decreasing the steering ratio and making the steering even stiffer are impractical.

STEERING COLUMNS

The **steering column** links the steering wheel to the steering gear and includes the:

- Steering shaft
- Column jacket
- Column cover

The steering shaft transmits rotary motion from the steering wheel to the steering gear, while the column jacket that encases it attaches to the vehicle body and offers a stationary mounting point for a number of switches and mechanisms (Figure 4-8). The column cover conceals the switches, wires, and mechanical linkages.

Steering Shaft

The **steering shaft** extends from the steering wheel to the steering gear. A bolt or nut secures the shaft to the steering wheel, and a flexible coupling joins it to the steering gear input shaft. The coupling can be a simple rubber or fabric insert, a universal joint (U-joint), or a pot joint. In addition to allowing a directional change of the shaft, a pot joint permits a limited amount of plunging motion (Figure 4-9).

Universal Joint

A **universal joint,** or U-joint, consists of two yokes with a steel crosspiece joining them to-

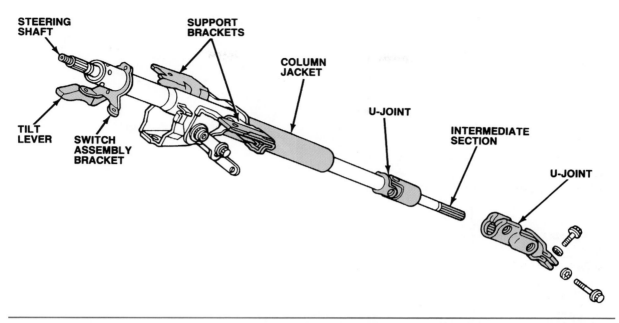

Figure 4-8. The steering shaft links the steering wheel to the steering gear while the column jacket, which surrounds part of the shaft, holds support brackets and switches. This steering shaft has a small intermediate section between the main section and the steering gear.

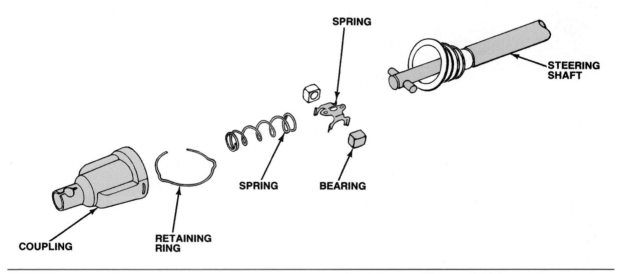

Figure 4-9. A pot joint is a flexible coupling used to join two shafts in a way that allows plunging motion.

gether (Figure 4-10). Universal joints allow changes in the angle between two rotating shafts. In a steering shaft, U-joints allow rotary motion transfer between the steering wheel and the steering gear even though the steering shaft meets the steering gear input shaft at an angle. On some models the steering shaft itself is assembled in sections that are connected by U-joints. This permits the steering shaft to bend around obstacles between the steering wheel and the steering gear.

Flexible Coupling

A **flexible coupling** is a simple device made of rubber, or rubber reinforced with fabric, that is placed between two shafts to allow for a change in angle between them (Figure 4-11). The rubber in a steering shaft flexible coupling absorbs vibrations and helps keep the steering wheel from shaking. A fail-safe connection between the steering shaft and the steering gear input shaft keeps the two shafts linked should the rubber coupling

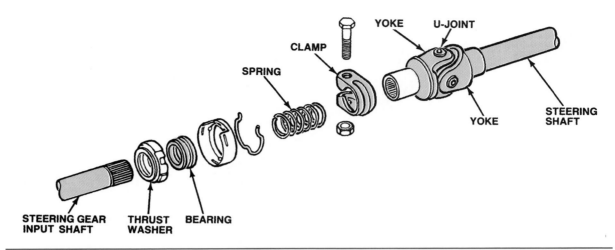

Figure 4-10. A U-joint has a crosspiece that links two yokes, one attached to the end of each shaft, together to connect the two shafts. The other parts shown—spring, bearing, thrust washer, and clamp—are designed for a particular model and this hardware will vary for different applications.

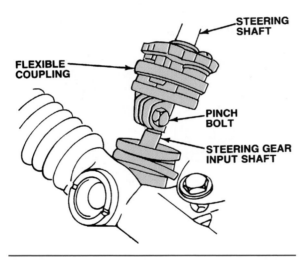

Figure 4-11. Flexible couplings are more prone to failure due to aging and wear than U-joints. To prevent the loss of steering control in the event of a failure, a flexible coupling contains a rigid fail-safe connector.

wear out or break. This allows the driver to maintain steering control, although the steering feels loose when this happens.

Flexible couplings are used on steering shafts less frequently than U-joints. DaimlerChrysler rear-wheel-drive (RWD) vans and General Motors (RWD) station wagons are among the few vehicles with flexible couplings on the steering shaft.

Column Jacket

The **column jacket** encases the steering shaft to protect it and provide a means of attaching it to the body (Figure 4-8). The jacket remains stationary while the steering shaft turns, so it can serve as the mounting point or seat of a number of items that need to be within reach of the driver, such as the ignition and turn signal switches. The jacket usually contains switches for a variety of electrical accessories, including cruise control, windshield wipers and washers, headlight dimmers, and hazard lights. If the vehicle has a column-mounted gear selector lever, the lever attaches to a shift tube that fits inside the column jacket and moves independently of it.

Column Cover

To keep the wiring from the jacket-mounted switches out of sight, the part of the steering column that extends into the passenger compartment is shrouded by the **column cover** (Figure 4-12). The column cover is usually at least two separate pieces, top and bottom. A knee bolster that mounts under the steering column is a safety feature designed to keep the driver from sliding forward during a collision. Knee bolsters are part of the passive restraint system required to meet U.S. Federal safety standards on certain vehicles.

Collapsible Column

Federal law requires that all vehicles sold in the United States have steering columns and shafts that collapse during a head-on collision to absorb some of the energy of the crash and lessen the danger of injury to the driver. The methods of meeting

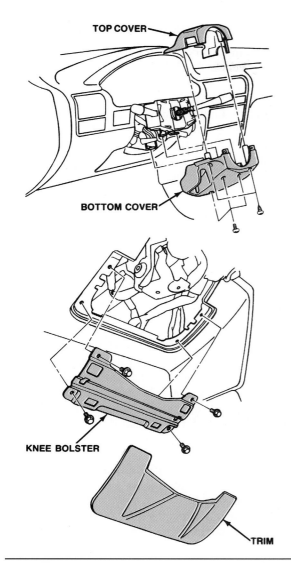

Figure 4-12. Steering column covers, which conceal the switches and mechanisms that are built onto the column jacket, are often part of the interior trim.

COLLAPSIBLE STEERING COLUMNS

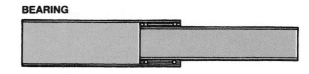

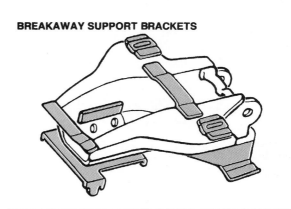

Figure 4-13. Collapsible steering column designs include mesh tubing that crushes easily, a bearing that allows one section of the column to slide into the other, and a breakaway device that separates the steering column from the vehicle's body parts that are being crushed and moving toward the driver.

this requirement vary among makes and models (Figure 4-13). One early method used a section of the steering column constructed out of mesh, which would collapse easily during a crash. Another method is to use a two-piece column. One section of the column has a smaller diameter so it fits inside the other and rides on a roller bearing. During a collision, the smaller section slides down into the larger one to collapse like a telescope. The DaimlerChrysler steering column described later in this chapter has two "breakaway capsules" built into the mounting bracket. With this design, the force of the driver moving forward during a collision pushes the bracket off of its attaching points

so that the column moves forward as well, instead of being pushed backward into the driver.

Tilt Mechanisms and Telescoping Columns

Many steering columns have **tilt mechanisms,** which allow the driver to adjust the angle of the steering wheel relative to the steering column. In a typical tilt-wheel steering column, the steering shaft has a short section at the top joined to the rest of the steering shaft either by a U-joint or gears. Most tilt mechanisms are some sort of ratchet device that enables the driver to lift the steering wheel and the top section of the steering shaft and place them in the desired position (Figure 4-14). Usually, spring tension locks the steering wheel in

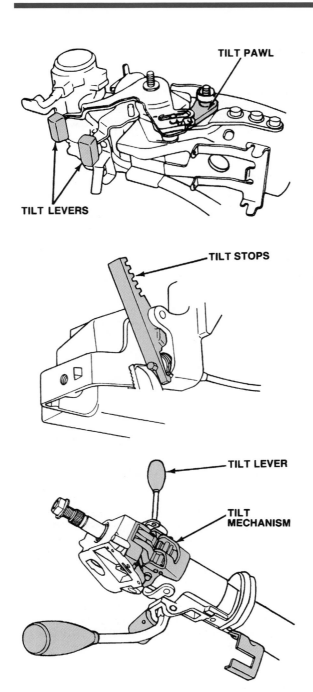

Figure 4-14. Although each manufacturer has a unique tilt mechanism design, most use a ratchet to position the top portion of the steering column. The location and method of the release devices vary.

place on the ratchet, and a release lever compresses the spring to allow tilt adjustment.

Some steering columns are designed to telescope. That is, when released, the top of the steering shaft and jacket can be pulled out toward the driver or pushed in toward the dashboard, and then locked into the new position.

Steering Column Buildup

The DaimlerChrysler steering column found in front-wheel drive (FWD) models will be used as an example of the buildup of a steering column (Figure 4-15). This particular example includes a column-mounted gear shift lever, but does not have a tilt mechanism. The steering wheel, not shown in the illustration, is air bag-equipped and therefore must be removed with care to avoid accidental deployment. Always follow the service manual instructions precisely to safely remove the air bag module and steering wheel.

The steering shaft is at the center of the steering column (Figure 4-16). The top end of the steering shaft splines to the center of the steering wheel, and a large nut fastens the steering wheel to the shaft. The lock housing, which contains the ignition lock cylinder, encases the top part of the steering shaft. The steering column jacket covers the shaft under the ignition lock housing, and the gear selector lever housing fits over a portion of the column jacket.

A number of components attach to the outside of the steering column jacket with spacers bracing them against each other to keep them in position. A ground clip provides a return circuit for the switches and other electrical devices in the column. A wiring trough holds and protects the electrical wires under the instrument panel. The lower section of the steering column jacket has two sets of flanges secured to mounting brackets under the instrument panel.

A U-joint connects the lower end of the steering shaft to a small intermediate shaft, which DaimlerChrysler calls the "stub shaft." Because this steering column includes a gear selector lever, the lower end of the column also incorporates an attachment point that connects the shift tube to the gearshift cable rod (Figure 4-17). The intermediate shaft extends through a hole in the floor where it is coupled to the steering gear input shaft by a U-joint.

A toe plate bolts to the floor of the passenger compartment to cover the shaft opening and to protect the interior from noise, drafts, and dirt (Figure 4-18). The toe plate has a tube for the intermediate shaft, and a seal and silencer fit on top of the tube.

Column-Mounted Controls and Switches

Two sections at the upper end of the steering column house the column-mounted controls (Figure 4-19). The lock housing, seated on top of the column jacket, is the topmost piece and contains the turn signal lever, hazard light control, and ignition

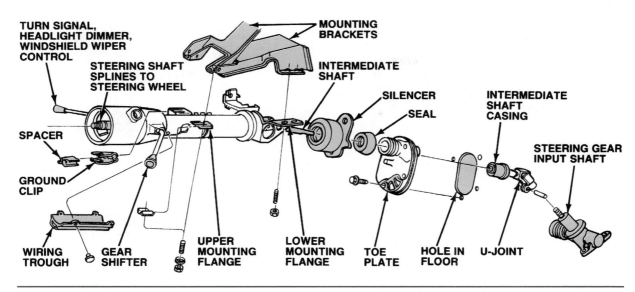

Figure 4-15. Due to all of the accessories attached to it, a modern steering column is a complex assembly.

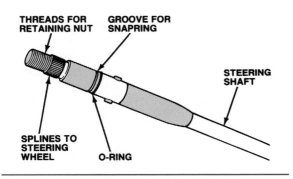

Figure 4-16. The steering shaft, which splines onto the steering wheel, transmits rotary motion from the steering wheel to the steering gear.

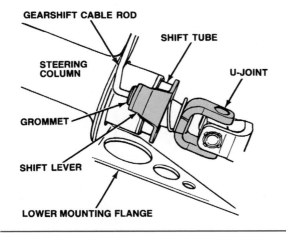

Figure 4-17. The shift tube turns when the gear selector lever on the steering shaft is moved, and controls the positioning of the manual valve in the automatic transmission by means of the gear shift cable rod.

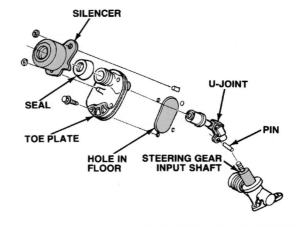

Figure 4-18. The toe plate seals the hole through which the steering shaft extends to the steering gear, the silencer reduces engine noise intrusion into the passenger compartment, and the seal keeps out dirt and moisture.

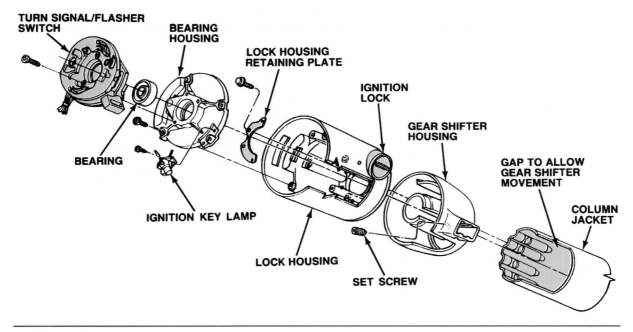

Figure 4-19. The upper section of the steering column includes the lock housing and the gear selector lever housing and contains switches and mechanisms.

Tilt Steering, 1920s-Style

One of the convenience options many modern drivers expect in their vehicles is a tilt steering wheel. A tilting wheel can adjust to a variety of positions to accommodate a number of different drivers and can also be flipped up and out of the way to make getting into and out of the front seat easier.

Truly adjustable steering wheels were a high-price luxury item in 1924, but for just a few dollars a driver could take advantage of the easier entry and exit available with a steering wheel that slid up and out of the way.

The Neville More-Room Steering Wheel kit replaced the stock steering wheel with another that mounted to a special bracket. The bracket attached to the top of the steering shaft by slots in the spokes instead of a bolt through the center. In the lower position it functioned just like a normal steering wheel, but pushing up on the wheel slid it up and out of the way for easier entry and exit. In addition, the steering wheel was constructed of aluminum and black walnut, which, advertisers boasted, "Adds as much to your car in value and appearance as it does in comfort!"

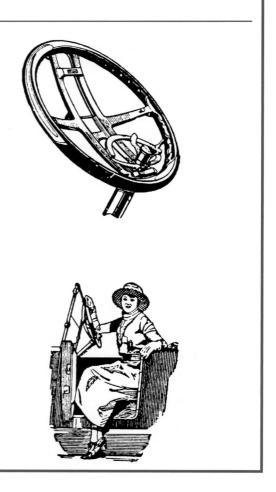

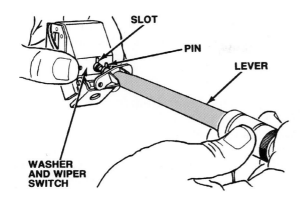

Figure 4-20. A single lever operates the turn signal, headlight dimmer, and windshield wiper and washer switches.

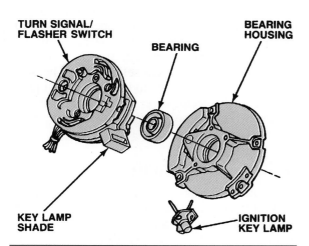

Figure 4-21. The turn signal and flasher switch fits onto the upper bearing housing.

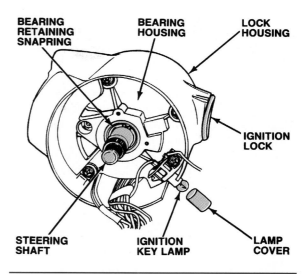

Figure 4-22. The bearing housing positions the bearing that holds the steering shaft in place and reduces turning friction. The bearing is secured on the shaft by a snapring.

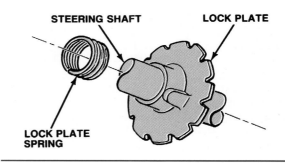

Figure 4-23. The lock plate engages an ignition lock pawl to keep the steering wheel in one position while the ignition is switched off.

lock. The gear selector lever and its housing are just below the lock housing, and the housing encases the top of the steering column jacket.

Lock Housing

The lock housing contains the ignition lock cylinder, several electrical switches, and a steering shaft bearing. Some of the switches have driver-operated controls on the outside of the lock housing.

The turn signal control lever operates the turn signals, the windshield wiper and washer switch, and the dimmer switch. Two screws and an alignment pin attach the lever to the switch, and the switch attaches to the turn signal switch (Figure 4-20). The turn signal switch is circular, with a hole in the middle through which the steering shaft extends (Figure 4-21). An actuating rod runs from a pocket on the windshield wiper switch

to the dimmer switch, which is farther down the column. The other two controls on the outside of the lock housing are the hazard light and the ignition lock, which controls the starting system.

Most steering shafts ride on at least two bearings, one near the top and one near the bottom of the shaft, to allow the shaft to rotate freely without affecting other parts of the steering column. In this steering column, the top steering shaft bearing is in a housing that bolts into the lock housing (Figure 4-22). A snapring at the center of the bearing housing rests in a groove on the steering shaft to secure the bearing, and an O-ring on the steering shaft keeps lubricant in the bearing.

Underneath the bearing and housing is a lock plate and coil spring that lock the steering shaft into position when the driver removes the ignition key (Figure 4-23). The ignition lock cylinder, which is under the lock plate, moves a bellcrank that in turn operates a spring and lever assembly linked to the ignition switch actuating rod (Figure 4-24). The rod extends through the bottom of the lock housing to the ignition switch (Figure 4-25). The shift lever gate on the bottom of the lock housing keeps the lever and spring assembly from triggering the ignition switch unless the automatic transmission is in park or neutral.

There are two more switches inside the lock housing, to which the driver does not have access.

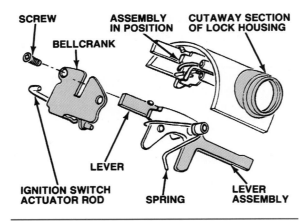

Figure 4-24. This bellcrank and lever system operate the ignition switch. The gear shift gate prevents engaging the ignition switch unless the gear selector lever is in the park or neutral position.

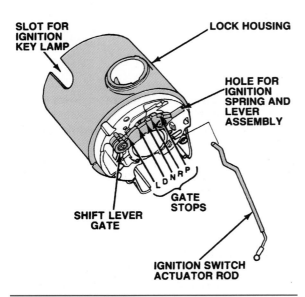

Figure 4-25. The end of the gear selector lever catches on each of these gate stops to keep the transmission in gear. The ignition switch actuator extends from inside the lock housing down the shaft to the ignition switch.

One switch turns on the ignition key lamp for a short time after the door closes so the driver can see where to put the key. The other switch sounds a buzzer or a chime if the key is in the ignition when the door is opened.

Gear Selector Lever Housing

The gear selector lever housing encases the steering column jacket under the lock housing (Figure 4-26). It is not linked to the lock housing, although the two parts make surface contact. The lock housing is a stationary part, while the gear selector lever housing can rotate.

The gear selector lever moves the housing and the shift tube (Figure 4-26). A pivot pin links the lever to the housing, and a spring pushes the inner end of the lever against the shift lever gate. A set screw secures the housing to the shift tube, so that one moves the other. The shift tube extends down the inside of the steering column jacket to the and is linked to the transmission through a cable rod.

On the back of the gear selector lever housing is a pointer that indicates to the driver what position the gear selector lever is in (Figure 4-27). A set screw secures the pointer to the housing.

Shift Lock Actuator

If the vehicle is equipped with an automatic transmission, it has a **shift lock actuator** (Figure 4-28) in the steering column as an added safety feature. The ignition lock cylinder control actuator system's purpose is to prevent putting the automatic transmission into gear without applying the service brakes.

The Chevrolet Corvette uses a **steering column locking motor** mechanism (Figure 4-29). The steering column lock control module (SCLCM) controls the steering wheel theft deterrent lock function, which allows the column to be electronically locked. The SCLCM controls the column lock motor using an internal lock relay, an internal unlock relay, and an internal lock enable relay. The lock and unlock relays provide a low input to the column lock motor. When the column needs to be locked the lock enable relay will energize the lock relay, which provides a high input to the lock side of the motor, energizing the motor to lock the steering column.

In order for the steering column to be locked, the SCLCM has to see three inputs. The first input the module needs to see is the vehicle in the park position (automatic transmission shift lever). When the shift lever is in the park position, the switch internal to the automatic transmission shift

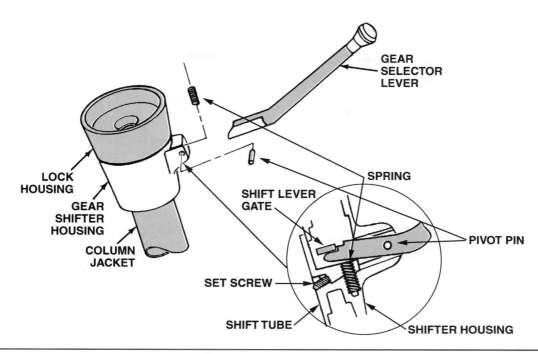

Figure 4-26. A pivot pin attaches the gear selector lever to the shifter housing, and the housing is connected to the shift tube by a set screw.

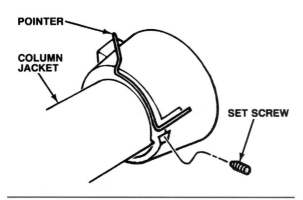

Figure 4-27. A pointer on the back of the shifter housing indicates the selected gear by pointing to an indicator plate attached to the column jacket.

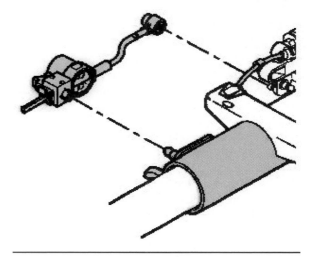

Figure 4-28. Automatic transmission shift lock actuator. (Courtesy of General Motors Corporation)

lever closes sending a high input to the SCLCM and the body control module (BCM). When this occurs the lock relay (internal to the SCLCM) is energized closing the lock relay switch.

The second input to the SCLCM is the ignition state. The remote control door lock receiver (RCDLR) and the BCM look at the power mode. When the ignition 1 input is in the off state or RAP mode, the RCDLR sends a class 2 message to the SCLCM indicating this state which will lock the column.

The third input the SCLCM receives comes from the BCM enable relay. When the BCM goes to the off power mode, the low input is sent to the SCLCM.

When the SCLCM receives this low input from the BCM, the internal lock enable relay is energized and provides a high input to a lock side of the column lock motor. The unlock side of the

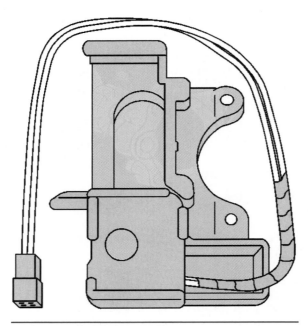

Figure 4-29. Corvette steering column locking mechanism. (Courtesy of General Motors Corporation)

column lock motor is grounded through the internal unlock relay within the SCLCM. The column lock motor will send an input back to the SCLCM indicating the motor is energized for the locked position. This results in the locking of the steering column. The SCLCM will unlock the steering column if the power mode is on and the SCLCM and RCDLR passwords match.

The SCLCM monitors the column lock system and will set DTC codes when the module detects malfunctions within the system. When a malfunction occurs, the driver information center (DIC) will display the Service Column Lock Now message indicating DTC codes are set within the SCLCM.

STEERING GEARS

The **steering gear** changes the rotary movement of the steering shaft into lateral movement of the steering linkage. A steering gear may be referred to as a "steering gearbox" because it contains a gear system. There are two types of steering gears:

- Standard
- Rack and pinion

All steering gears have an **input gear,** which transmits rotary movement from the steering

wheel into the steering gear, and an **output gear,** which causes the steering linkage to move laterally. For more information about steering linkages, see Chapter 5 of this *Classroom Manual.*

Standard Steering Gear Operation

The type of steering gear that is called "standard" is actually less frequently used today than a rack and pinion steering gear. The term **standard steering gear** came into use because this type of gearbox design was common at a time when rack and pinion steering was found only on European sports cars. As manufacturers downsized vehicles and focused on FWD platforms, the use of rack and pinion gears became more common. Today, rack and pinion steering applications have matched and even exceeded the use of standard steering gears. There are four standard steering gear designs:

- Worm and sector
- Cam and lever
- Worm and roller
- Recirculating ball

The worm and sector and cam and lever steering gears are early designs that are no longer in production, while worm and roller and recirculating ball steering gear designs are still in use. Primarily, both worm and roller and recirculating ball steering gears are used on trucks. However, some large, heavy sedans also have a recirculating ball steering gear.

Worm and Sector Operation
As the name implies, a **worm and sector steering gear** uses a **worm gear** and a **sector gear** (Figure 4-30). The worm gear, which wraps around a shaft, is the input gear, while the sector gear, which is a section of a gear, is the output gear. A worm gear changes the axis of rotation when it moves the sector gear. Because the sector gear never makes a complete rotation, only a section of a gear is needed. The center of the sector shaft is the axis of the sector gear. The semi-rotation of the sector shaft pivots the pitman arm to move its opposite end, along with the steering linkage, laterally.

Cam and Lever Operation
A **cam and lever steering gear** is similar to a worm and sector unit, except a cam is used in

WORM AND SECTOR STEERING GEAR

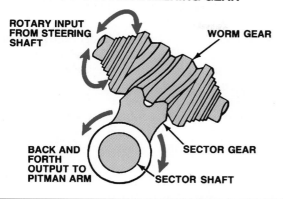

Figure 4-30. The worm and sector steering gear was one of the earliest steering gear designs.

CAM AND LEVER STEERING GEAR

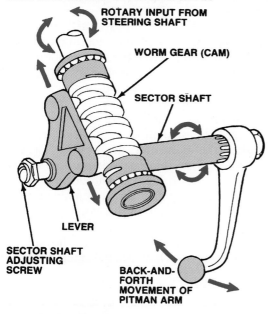

Figure 4-31. A variation on the worm and sector design, a cam and lever gearbox replaces the worm gear with a cam and the sector gear with a lever.

place of the worm gear and a lever replaces the sector gear (Figure 4-31). Although the cam gear looks like a worm gear, it is called a "cam" because the depth of its groove is not constant. The cam is at the end of the input shaft and the lever attaches to the sector, or output, shaft. A stud or studs on the sector shaft fit into the groove of the cam. As the stud slides up-and-down along the cam groove, the lever pivots back-and-forth, which turns the sector shaft and pivots the pitman arm to move the steering linkage laterally.

WORM AND ROLLER STEERING GEAR

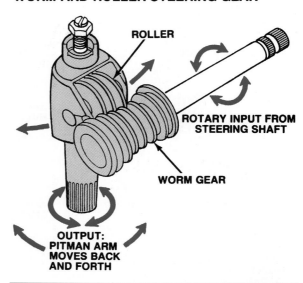

Figure 4-32. In a worm and roller design, the roller performs like a sector gear to pivot the pitman arm.

Worm and Roller Operation

A **worm and roller steering gear** uses a worm gear to turn a roller, which serves as a sector gear. Although older systems may use a roller with only one or two teeth, modern designs have three teeth in the roller (Figure 4-32). As the roller threads up-and-down along the worm gear, the sector shaft and pitman arm pivot so that the pitman arm moves the steering linkage from side-to-side.

Recirculating Ball Operation

The **recirculating ball steering gear** also uses a worm gear as an input gear. Rather than meshing with a gear, stud, or roller, a series of steel balls rides through the groove of the worm gear (Figure 4-33). A **ball nut** surrounds the worm gear and has a groove cut into it that corresponds to the worm gear groove. Steel balls roll through a tunnel formed between the worm gear and the ball nut. As the worm gear turns, the balls roll along the groove into the return guide, which is a small tube that runs across the outside of the ball nut to link the two ends of the groove. The balls rolling along the worm gear push the balls through the return guide, until they re-enter the groove from the other end of the guide. This design is so named because the balls constantly recirculate through the groove by way of the return guide.

Movement of the balls rolling through the tunnel formed by the worm gear and the ball nut

RECIRCULATING BALL STEERING GEAR

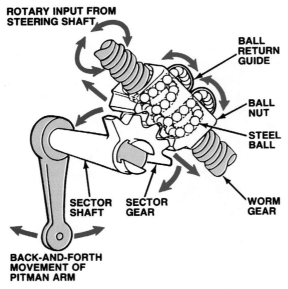

Figure 4-33. Although a recirculating ball steering gear looks more complicated than the other standard steering gear designs, its action is much the same. In effect, it is a worm and sector gearbox with the addition of a ball nut and steel balls to eliminate friction between the worm and sector.

causes the ball nut to travel back-and-forth along the length of the worm gear. Gear teeth on the outside of the ball nut mesh with teeth on the sector gear. As the ball nut moves along the worm gear, the external teeth pivot the sector gear back-and-forth, which causes the sector shaft and pitman arm to pivot as well and moves the steering linkage side-to-side.

Standard Steering Gear Buildup

As examples of how standard steering gears are constructed, this chapter details the buildup of a manual worm and roller steering gear and a manual recirculating ball steering gear. Studying manual steering gears allows a clear view of the steering gear, without confusing it with the power-assist system. Power-assisted steering gears are covered in detail in Chapter 6 of this *Classroom Manual*.

Worm and Roller Buildup

The Ross 504 steering gear, which is used on Ford F-600, F-700, and F-800 trucks with a 6,000-pound or 7,000-pound front axle and manual steering, is a fairly typical worm and roller design (Figure 4-34).

The **steering gear input shaft** splines to a U-joint at the base of the steering column or steering shaft to provide the rotary motion to the steering gear. The input shaft may be called the "worm shaft," because the worm gear and the input shaft are one assembly. The input shaft extends from the U-joint into the steering gear housing. An oil seal prevents lubricant from leaking where the shaft enters the housing. The worm gear is hourglass-shaped to keep it in mesh with the roller as the roller and shroud turn, but the depth of the worm gear thread remains the same along the entire length of the worm gear.

Two thrust bearings reduce friction between the worm gear and the steering gear housing. The upper bearing rides between the tapered top of the

■ **"It Makes a Funny Noise. . . "**

Automotive technicians have always had to stretch their vocabularies when describing the noises a vehicle can make. This note appeared in the Chek-Chart *Lubrication Bulletin* for March, 1936:

Steering Gear Chuckling
Steering gear "chuckles" may not always result from lack of lubrication. In a great many instances, chuckles can be eliminated, if all other factors are correct, by merely loosening the steering column to the dash bracket and retightening it after the column seeks its own alignment. Distortion of the column,

due to misalignment of the column caused by body settling, will cause a pronounced chuckle.

"Chuckling" was the notchy feel in the steering wheel caused by misaligned gear teeth being forced in and out of mesh. In modern applications, body-to-frame misalignment due to accident damage or incorrect assembly often results in scraping noises or binding as the steering shaft turns within the mast jacket. While the term is uncommon today, service manuals still occasionally warn automotive technicians about the causes and consequences of chuckling steering gears.

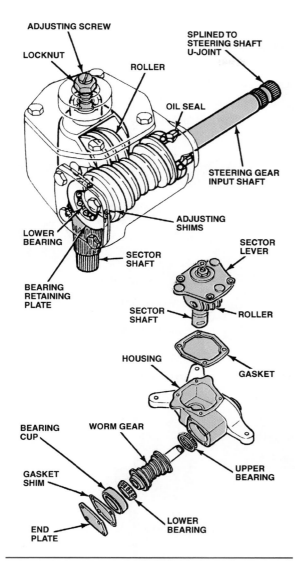

Figure 4-34. The Ross 504 steering gear is a worm and roller design that is used on medium-duty Ford trucks.

worm gear and the inside of the housing, and the lower bearing rides between the tapered bottom of the worm gear and the end plate.

In addition to reducing friction, the tight fit of the thrust bearings between the worm gear and housing keep the worm gear from moving up-and-down inside the housing. In other words, the thrust bearings help control **axial play**, which is up-and-down movement in line with the axis of a shaft. Axial play measured at the end of a shaft is commonly called **endplay**, and play at the end of the worm gear and shaft is called "worm endplay."

The end plate holds the bearings, worm gear, and shaft in place in the steering gear housing.

Four bolts secure the end plate to the housing, and a gasket between them provides a seal to prevent lubricant leakage.

The sector shaft, which splines to the pitman arm, moves the pitman arm to control the steering linkage. The top of the sector shaft forms a shroud to contain the roller. A pin runs through the shroud and roller from one side to the other and forms the axis on which the roller turns. Needle bearings between the roller and the pin reduce friction and allow the roller to move smoothly.

A small shaft extends into the sector cover at the top of the shroud, and a screw and lock nut secures the shaft to the cover. The screw serves three purposes:

- Attaches the sector shaft assembly to the sector cover
- Allows the sector shaft to pivot in response to roller movement
- Serves as the adjustment mechanism for sector lash

Sector lash, which is also called worm and roller mesh preload, is checked and adjusted at prescribed maintenance intervals. Sector lash adjustment is discussed later in this chapter.

With the sector shaft and roller secured to the sector cover, the entire assembly installs into the steering gear housing and is secured to it by the cover bolts. A gasket fits between the sector cover and housing to prevent fluid leakage. The sector shaft rides in either bearings or bushings, depending on the steering gear design, to reduce friction. One bearing or bushing installs into the housing at the bottom of the sector shaft, and the other installs into the cover at the top of the shaft. An oil seal prevents lubricant leakage where the sector shaft extends out of the housing.

Recirculating Ball Buildup

The manual steering gear used on Dodge light trucks serves as an example of a recirculating ball steering gear (Figure 4-35).

The end of the steering gear input shaft, or worm shaft, splines to the steering shaft U-joint and provides rotary input to the steering gear. An oil seal prevents fluid leakage where the input shaft enters the steering gear housing. At the top and the bottom of the worm gear are the upper and lower thrust bearings. The upper bearing cup seats in the housing, and the lower bearing cup seats in the adjuster plug. The thrust bearings reduce friction between the worm gear and the steering gear housing and control worm endplay.

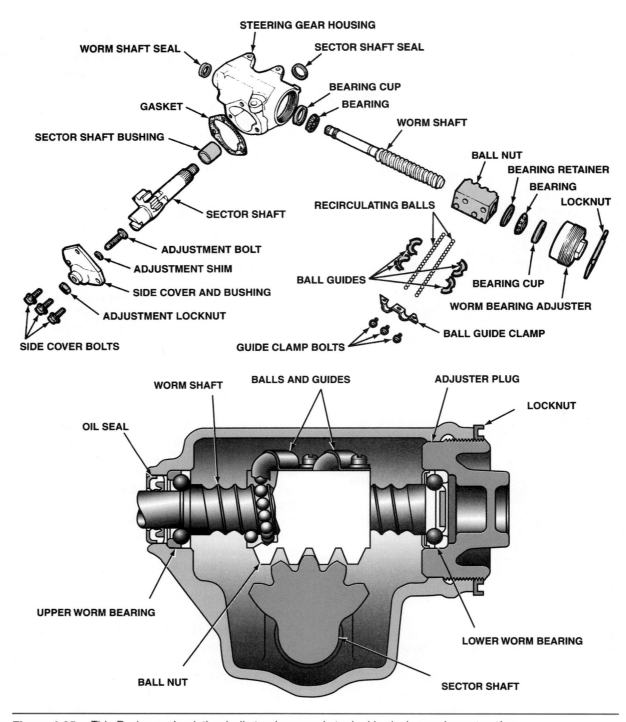

Figure 4-35. This Dodge recirculating ball steering gear is typical in design and construction.

The adjuster plug at the lower end of the worm gear holds the worm gear, shaft, and bearings inside the steering gear housing. The threads of the plug fit tightly into the housing so that a gasket is not required for sealing. In addition to supporting the worm shaft, the adjuster plug also provides a method of adjusting worm bearing preload, which is discussed later in this chapter. Once preload is adjusted, a lock nut keeps the plug in position.

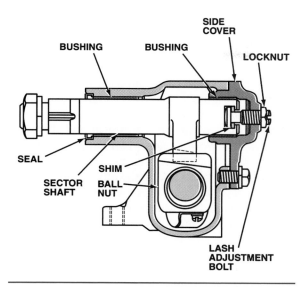

Figure 4-36. The sector shaft is supported by bushings, one in the housing and the other in the side cover assembly.

MANUAL STEERING GEAR MOUNTING

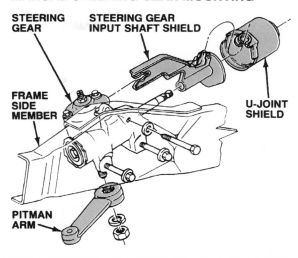

Figure 4-37. A typical steering gear bolts to a frame side member, the pitman arm connects it to the steering linkage, and splash shields protect the input shaft and steering shaft U-joint.

The ball nut, which has internal grooves that match the worm gear thread, fits over the worm gear. Steel balls roll through the tunnels formed by the ball nut grooves and the worm gear thread. Crescent-shaped ball return guides link the ends of the ball nut tunnels together, so the balls continuously circulate through the ball nut and worm gear, into the ball return guides, and back again. A clamp secured by screws holds the return guides in place on one side of the ball nut. Gear teeth that mesh with the teeth of the sector gear are machined into the outside of the ball nut on the side opposite the ball return guides.

The sector gear is an integral part of the sector shaft, which runs through the center of the sector gear, and forms the axis of the gear. One end of the sector shaft extends out of the steering gear housing and splines to the pitman arm. An oil seal prevents lubricant leakage where the sector shaft goes through the opening in the housing. To reduce friction, the sector shaft rides on two bushings. One bushing fits inside the housing and the other is part of the housing side cover (Figure 4-36).

The side cover bushing is not serviceable and the entire cover assembly must be replaced if the bushing is worn. A gasket fits between the side cover and housing to prevent fluid leakage, and three bolts attach the cover to the housing.

The head of an adjustment bolt fits into a slot machined into the end of the sector shaft. The threaded end of the bolt extends through an opening in the sector cover. Inside the sector cover, an adjustment shim fits between the cover and the bolt head. Turning the bolt or installing a different-size shim provides a method of adjusting sector lash, which is discussed in detail later in this chapter. Outside the cover, a lock nut secures the adjustment bolt into position.

Standard Steering Gear Installation

Standard steering gears are generally used in larger vehicles with a steel frame, and the steering gear typically bolts to the frame side member on the left side of the vehicle. Often, a splash shield installs over the exposed portion of the input shaft to protect it from dirt, flying stones, and other underbody hazards. A second protective shield fits around the U-joint that connects the gearbox to the steering shaft (Figure 4-37). The splined end of the sector shaft extends from the bottom of the steering gear housing and the pitman arm fits onto the sector shaft splines. A nut and washer secure the pitman arm to the shaft.

Standard Steering Gear Adjustments

For the steering gear to operate efficiently, the internal parts must be positioned correctly in relation to the housing and each other. As parts wear, clearances inside the housing and between parts increase, causing looseness and excessive play. The acceptable clearance between any two mechanical parts is called their **tolerance.** Insufficient tolerance causes binding between parts, increasing steering effort. Excessive tolerance causes delayed reaction to steering input and too much steering wheel freeplay.

To provide acceptable tolerances, standard steering gears require up to three adjustments:

* Worm bearing preload
* Gear mesh preload
* Sector shaft endplay

Almost all steering gears provide adjustment methods for worm bearing preload and gear mesh preload. Some also allow adjustment of sector shaft endplay.

Worm Bearing Preload

Worm bearing preload, also referred to as worm endplay, is a measurement of how much force is required to turn the steering gear input shaft against the force, or **preload,** that the thrust bearings apply to the worm gear and shaft. **Worm endplay,** which is the distance the worm gear can move end-to-end between the thrust bearings, is directly related to preload. The more tightly the bearings push against the worm gear, the less endplay there is, and the more force it takes to turn the input shaft and worm gear. Worm bearing preload is adjusted by one of two methods: turning an ad-

justment nut or screw, or installing selectively sized shims. Either adjustment method increases or decreases the worm endplay.

Although related, worm endplay and worm bearing preload are not technically the same measurements (Figure 4-38). Worm endplay is a linear measurement, made in fractions of inches or millimeters, of how far the worm gear and shaft can slide axially. Worm bearing preload is a measurement of how much force it takes to overcome bearing pressure in order to turn the input shaft. Preload is a torque, or turning force, measurement made in inch-pounds or Newton-meters. Because endplay and preload are related, one measurement indicates the other. When measuring and adjusting the worm bearing preload, a technician measures preload and adjusts endplay. The endplay is correct when the preload measurement is correct.

Gear Mesh Preload

Gear mesh preload is a measurement of how closely the teeth of the ball nut gear and sector gear, or the worm gear and roller, fit together. Gear mesh preload is related to another measurement, called "sector lash" or **gear lash.** Lash refers to a lack of mesh resulting in a lag between turning the steering wheel and engaging the gears to operate the steering linkage.

Gear mesh preload is a measurement of how much turning force must be applied to the input shaft to overcome the resistance of the sector gear and move it. Like worm bearing preload, gear

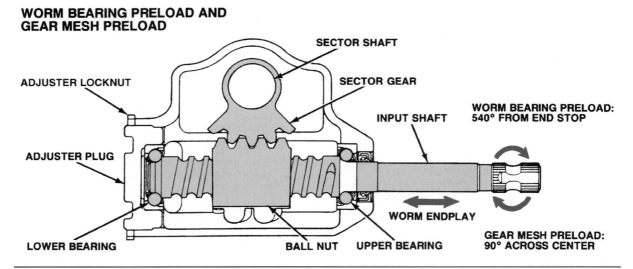

Figure 4-38. Worm bearing preload is a turning force measured in inch-pounds or Newton-meters, while worm endplay is axial movement, measured in inches or millimeters.

mesh preload is a turning force measured in inch-pounds or Newton-meters. However, worm bearing preload is typically measured across a turn and a half of the input shaft from the end stop of shaft movement, while gear mesh preload is usually measured in a 90-degree turn across the center of input shaft movement. Thus, gear mesh preload indicates how sensitive the steering gear is to small steering wheel movements during straight-ahead driving. Insufficient preload contributes to steering wander and the driver must constantly reposition the steering wheel to keep the vehicle moving in a straight path.

If there is too much gear lash, the steering becomes unresponsive because the steering gear does not transmit small steering wheel movements to the linkage. Instead, the driver must turn the steering wheel farther in order to make the wheels turn at all. However, insufficient lash makes the gears bind, offering too much resistance to steering wheel movement. In this case, the driver must exert a considerable amount of force to move the steering wheel.

With some steering gears, particularly worm and roller designs, a small amount of gear lash is normal. The decision whether to adjust gear mesh preload to eliminate the lash is based on driver preference. If lash is acceptable to the driver, adjustment is not necessary, but if the driver wants more responsive steering, the lash can be adjusted. In any event, lash must never exceed the allowable range specified by the manufacturer.

An acceptable gear mesh preload range is specified by the manufacturer. A specific procedure for measuring and adjusting preload is detailed in the service manual for the particular vehicle. Although exact procedures vary, gear mesh preload is usually adjusted by turning an adjustment bolt at the end of the sector shaft. Typically, the adjustment bolt is secured by a lock nut. The adjustment bolt moves the sector shaft along its axis. In a sense, this is a sector shaft endplay adjustment, except that the purpose of moving the sector shaft is to move the sector gear rather than to alter shaft position. Sector shaft endplay, as well as worm bearing endplay, should be adjusted to within specifications before a gear mesh preload adjustment is made.

Sector Shaft Endplay

Sector shaft endplay is a measurement of how much room the sector shaft has to slide axially (Figure 4-39). If provision is made to measure

sector shaft endplay, the measurement is taken in fractions of inches or millimeters. Some steering gears provide an external adjusting method, but it is more common for sector shaft endplay to be adjusted by internal shims, if it is adjustable.

Rack and Pinion Steering Gear Operation

The term *rack and pinion* is simply a description of the basic design of this type of steering gear. The **rack and pinion steering gear** is widely used on smaller FWD vehicles, where its compact size is an advantage. The input gear of a rack and pinion steering gear is a **pinion gear** that receives rotary input from the steering shaft. The **rack** is a rod with gear teeth machined into one side. The pinion gear teeth mesh with the teeth on the rack so that when the pinion gear turns, it pushes the rack from side-to-side (Figure 4-40). The rack connects directly to the tie rods in the steering linkage to move the linkage back-and-forth.

Rack and Pinion Buildup

Studying the buildup of a typical rack and pinion steering gear provides an example of how rack and pinion steering gears are constructed in general. Although many late-model rack and pinion steering gears are power assisted, the example shown here is a manual unit that is manufactured by Mitsubishi (Figure 4-41). Again, power-assist systems are covered in Chapter 6 of this *Classroom Manual*.

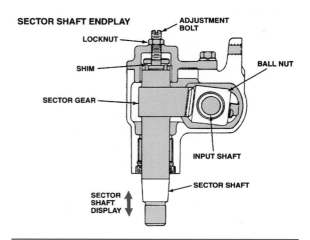

Figure 4-39. Sector shaft endplay, which is a measurement of how far the sector shaft can move axially, is taken in fractions of inches or millimeters.

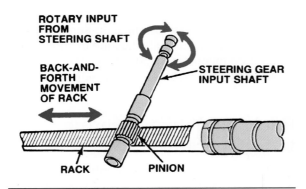

Figure 4-40. Rack and pinion steering gear operation is simple, direct, and generally more responsive than a standard steering gear.

The steering gear input shaft is splined to the steering shaft U-joint. At the end of the steering gear input shaft, which extends into the rack housing, is the pinion gear. Two ball bearings reduce friction between the shaft and the steering gear housing. The upper bearing is press fitted on the input shaft, and the lower bearing installs inside the housing at the bottom of the pinion gear. A cover, which fits around the shaft and threads into the housing, seats on top of the upper ball bearing to preload it and close the top of the steering gear housing. An oil seal between the top cover and the input shaft keeps lubricant from leaking out of the housing. A lock nut holds the top cover in position.

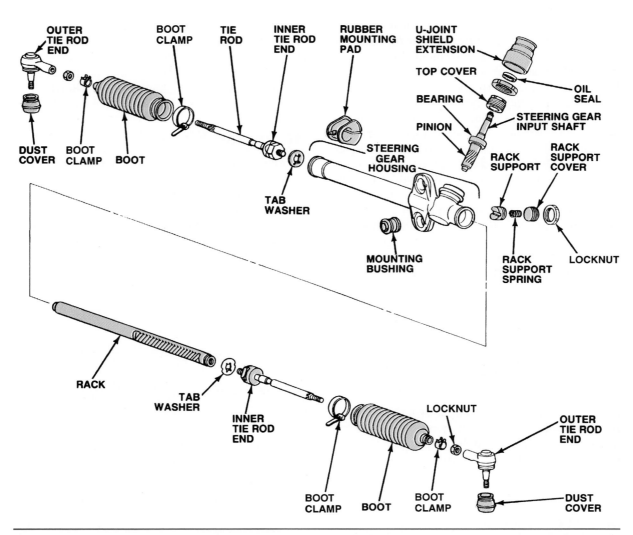

Figure 4-41. This Mitsubishi manual rack and pinion steering gear is a typical design for use in small FWD vehicles.

The teeth of the pinion gear mesh with the teeth of the rack. In this steering gear, the teeth are at one end of the rack and the pinion is offset to one side of the housing. However, on some rack and pinion steering gears, the pinion and the rack teeth are positioned at the center of the rack. These designs generally require additional U-joints to angle the steering shaft from the steering wheel to the center of the steering gear housing. It is more common for the pinion gear and the rack teeth to be offset, as on the Mitsubishi unit, to simplify the steering shaft design.

The rack is encased in the long, tubular steering gear housing with a mounting flange on the pinion end. Rubber bushings fit into the mounting flange bolt holes to absorb vibration and isolate the assembly from the frame. At the opposite end of the housing, a rubber mounting pad wraps around the housing tube to cushion and isolate it. A U-shaped bracket, not shown, fits over the mounting pad and bolts attach the bracket to the vehicle body.

A spring-loaded rack support and related hardware install through a hole at the back of the steering gear housing to position the rack (Figure 4-42). The face of the rack support curves to match the back of the rack, which rests on it and slides back-and-forth across it. A spring behind the rack support cushions the rack from vibration and shocks. A rack support cover threads into the housing to retain the rack support and spring. The rack support cover is also the adjustment mechanism for pinion torque, which is discussed later in this chapter. A lock nut holds the rack support cover in position.

While the rack support provides a sliding surface to reduce friction at the pinion end of the rack, the rack rides in a bushing pressed into the steering gear housing at the opposite end to reduce friction. One side of the bushing has a very small air passage between the back of the bushing and the housing (Figure 4-43). This air passage allows air from the tie rod boots to be displaced through the rack housing as the rack slides in and out of the housing. Other designs use a small metal tube running along the outside of the housing to connect the two boots and transfer air from one to the other. If there were no means for air displacement between the boots, they might collapse as they expanded or explode as they compressed.

Internal threads on each end of the rack allow attachment of the externally threaded tie rods. A tab washer fits between the tie rod and the rack to keep the tie rod end from working loose on the threads. Tabs on the inside diameter of the washer engage slots to secure the connection. Once assembled, tabs on the outside diameter of the washer are bent around the end of the tie rod to lock it in place (Figure 4-44).

A rubber boot at each side of the steering gear housing covers the end of the rack and the inner tie rod end to prevent dirt, water, and other contaminants from entering the assembly. Band clamps fasten the ends of the boots to the housing and tie rods. The tie rods move back-and-forth with the rack and connect it to the wheels through the steering linkage.

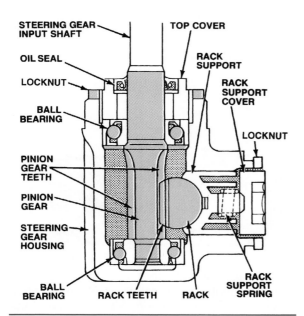

Figure 4-42. The spring-loaded rack support positions the rack to keep it from rubbing against the housing and establishes the pinion torque.

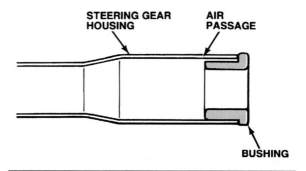

Figure 4-43. The small air passage between the bushing and the rack housing allows air transfer between the boots at each end of the housing as they compress and extend.

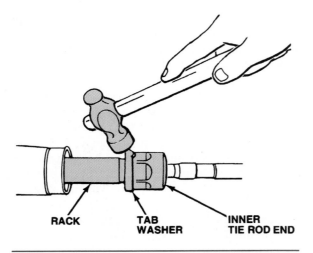

Figure 4-44. The outside diameter tabs of the washer are bent over the inner end of the tie rod to keep it secured to the rack.

Rack and Pinion Installation

Installation of a rack and pinion steering gear is fairly simple. The housing generally bolts to either a flange on the firewall or to the subframe or engine cradle. The Mitsubishi example bolts to a reinforced mounting flange on the firewall (Figure 4-45). The mounting points have rubber cushions to isolate the steering gear from shock and vibration. If the driver can feel vibration and road shocks through the steering wheel, the condition is called **kickback.** Some kickback is in-

evitable with a rack and pinion steering gear, but designers do what they can to minimize it.

A shield on top of the steering gear housing covers the steering gear input shaft and the steering shaft U-joint. The shield protects the shafts and U-joint from dirt, flying stones, and other underbody hazards that could damage them.

Rack and Pinion Adjustments

Just as with a standard steering gear, the parts inside a rack and pinion steering gear are set to specific tolerances to ensure proper operation. Two adjustments are possible in a rack and pinion steering gear:

- Pinion torque
- Pinion bearing preload

Pinion torque is adjustable on most rack and pinion steering gears, but not all designs provide a means to adjust pinion bearing preload.

Pinion Torque

Pinion torque is a measurement of how much turning force is needed at the input shaft for the pinion to overcome the resistance of the rack and move it (Figure 4-46). The measurement gives an indication of how closely meshed the pinion teeth and the rack teeth are. Like gear mesh preload in a standard steering gear, pinion torque indicates steering system responsiveness. The adjustment

■ **Heated Steering Wheels?**

It may seem eccentric today, but in 1914 one viable solution to the problem of providing driver comfort and weather protection was an exhaust-heated steering wheel. Open cars were the norm until the early 1920s, and the cold wind that chilled the hands of a driver encouraged experimentation.

This early heated steering wheel was made of hollow metal. A pipe picked up exhaust gases from the manifold and fed them into the steering wheel through a tube, where they flowed around inside the steering wheel rim and then out through another tube, to be dumped into the air beneath the floorboards. Both the inlet and outlet tubes ran through the floorboards alongside the steering column, and a foot-operated valve allowed the driver to control the entry of exhaust gases into the steering wheel.

This novel idea never caught on, perhaps because of the difficulty in making exhaust-tight

tubes that would still permit the steering wheel to turn through several rotations. No information is available about sealing, so presumably the tubes were flexible and simply coiled around the steering shaft as the wheel turned. Perhaps the possibility of an exhaust gas leak in the passenger compartment hurt the sales potential.

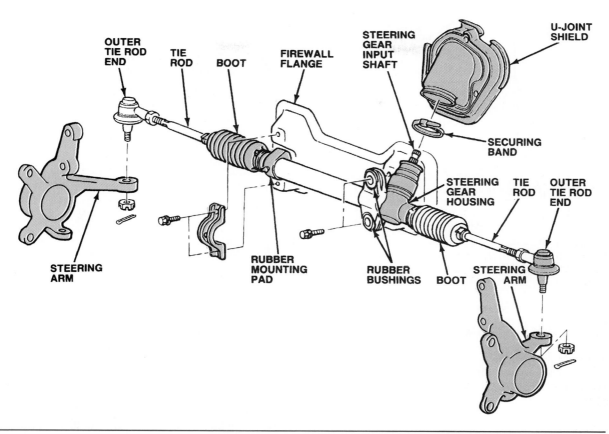

Figure 4-45. This Mitsubishi rack and pinion steering gear installs to the vehicle firewall. A major advantage of rack and pinion steering is that the steering gear and linkage take up a minimal amount space.

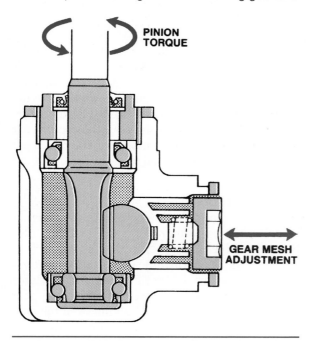

Figure 4-46. Pinion torque is a turning force measured in inch-pounds or Newton-meters. Tightening the rack support against the rack increases pinion torque, and loosening the rack support decreases it.

method is to thread the rack support cover farther into the steering gear housing to reduce gear lash, or thread it out to increase gear lash. Manufacturers specify an acceptable range of pinion torque in inch-pounds or Newton-meters. Because the middle teeth on the rack wear before the teeth at either end, pinion torque should be checked across the whole stroke of the rack. Otherwise, reducing gear lash to a very close tolerance in the middle may cause binding as the pinion travels toward the end of the rack.

Pinion Bearing Preload

Pinion bearing preload in a rack and pinion steering gear is the same concept as worm bearing preload in a standard steering gear. That is, it is a measurement of how much force is required to turn the steering gear input shaft against the force, or preload, that the bearings apply to the pinion gear and shaft (Figure 4-47). To provide adjustable pinion bearing preload, there may be a threaded adjustment mechanism or selectively sized shims that install behind a shim cover.

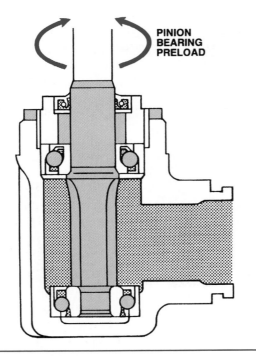

Figure 4-47. Pinion bearing preload is a measurement of the turning force required to overcome the resistance of the pinion shaft bearings, rather than the resistance of the rack.

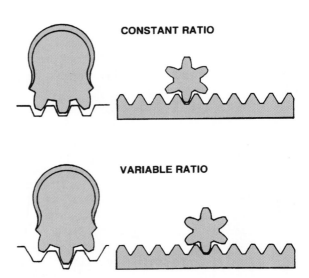

Figure 4-48. In a constant ratio steering gear, all of the gear teeth are the same size and shape. In a variable ratio steering gear, the gear teeth change size toward the ends, so that the gear ratio changes there as well.

To set pinion bearing preload, the rack may need to be removed or loosened to prevent false readings caused by the resistance of the gears. Therefore, pinion bearing preload, when adjustable, must be set before pinion torque is measured and adjusted.

Steering Gear Lubrication

All manual steering gears require lubrication and every manufacturer recommends the lubricant best suited to a particular steering gear. The most frequent recommendations are for gear oil or lithium grease. These lubricants are discussed in Chapter 2 of this *Classroom Manual*.

As a general rule, manual steering gears do not require periodic lubrication or fluid changes. However, most manufacturers recommend periodically checking the fluid level and inspecting the steering gear for signs of leakage. Under normal circumstances, manual steering gears require lubrication service only when they are disassembled for repair.

Steering Gear Ratios

The **steering gear ratio** is the major determining factor of overall steering ratio. The steering gear ratio is the number of degrees the input gear must turn for the output gear to turn one degree. The steering gear ratio may be constant or variable, and consequently the overall steering ratio can be constant or variable as well (Figure 4-48).

Constant Ratio

A constant steering ratio is one that remains the same no matter how far to the left or right the driver turns the steering wheel. The wheels that are being turned move at the same rate throughout the turn. Resistance to movement also stays the same. In a constant ratio steering gear, the sector gear and ball nut teeth or the pinion gear and rack teeth are the same size from end to end.

Variable Ratio

A variable steering ratio changes as the steering wheel is turned further to the left or right. This helps the driver maneuver in tight spots, such as parking lots. The farther the driver turns the steering wheel, the faster the wheels turn. In a variable ratio steering gear, the spaces between the gear teeth of the sector gear and ball nut or of the rack increase in size toward the ends, where the steering nears the maximum turning angle.

The advantage of a variable steering ratio is increased maneuverability, because the wheels turn more quickly as the turning angle becomes sharper. In some power-assisted steering designs, variable power assist offsets the increasingly stiff steering as the steering ratio becomes faster.

SUMMARY

Three parts of the steering system transmit movement from the driver to the steering linkage: the steering wheel, steering column, and steering gear. The driver turns the steering wheel, and it turns the steering shaft. Many steering wheels include an electrically operated horn, and many late-model steering wheels contain an air bag. Steering wheel freeplay indicates how responsive the steering system is to steering wheel movement, and the steering ratio indicates the relation between how far the steering wheel turns and how far the wheels turn in response. Some steering systems have a variable steering ratio.

The steering column links the steering wheel to the steering gear and uses three main parts: the steering shaft, column jacket, and column cover. The steering shaft is the direct mechanical link, the column jacket protects the shaft and is the mounting surface for driver-operated accessories, and the column cover encases the part of the steering column that extends into the passenger compartment. Federal law requires that all steering columns be collapsible. Many columns have a tilt mechanism, and some can be telescoped.

The steering gear receives rotary input motion from the steering shaft and in response moves the steering linkage laterally. There are two basic types of steering gears: standard and rack and pinion.

Four similar designs of standard steering gears have been used: worm and sector, cam and lever, worm and roller, and recirculating ball. The two designs still in common use are the worm and roller and the recirculating ball. Standard steering gears typically bolt to a frame side member. Three measurements, which may be adjustable, are important to standard steering gear operation: worm bearing preload, gear mesh preload, and sector shaft endplay.

There is one basic rack and pinion design. Rack and pinion steering gears typically bolt to the firewall or to the subframe. Two measurements, which may be adjustable, that are important indicators of rack and pinion operation are pinion torque and pinion bearing preload.

The typical lubricant in a manual steering gear is gear oil or lithium grease. The steering gear ratio is the major determining factor of overall steering ratio. Steering gears may have a constant or a variable ratio.

The heated steering wheel includes a heating element and temperature sensor. The heating element and sensor are located in the rim of the steering wheel. The heated steering wheel switch is located in the steering wheel switch bezel. The steering wheel heat module is located on the backside of the steering wheel center hub. When the switch is pressed, a signal is sent to the controller and the heated steering wheel is turned on.

If the vehicle is equipped with an automatic transmission, it has a shift lock actuator in the steering column to prevent putting the automatic transmission into gear without applying the service brakes. The Chevrolet Corvette uses a steering column locking motor mechanism, which allows the column to be electronically locked or unlocked.

Review Questions

For each of the following questions, choose the letter that represents the best possible answer.

1. In modern automobiles, when the driver presses the horn button, the horn circuit is completed by:
   a. Activating a transducer in the clockspring
   b. Closing contacts in a switch or relay
   c. Energizing a vacuum motor, which operates the horn
   d. Triggering an ignitor, which releases the air to blow the horn

2. In the passive restraint system, air bags are inflated when impact sensors send signals to:
   a. An electric air pump on the right front fender well
   b. A cylinder of compressed nitrogen
   c. An ignitor containing flammable gas and gas-producing pellets
   d. A container of liquid nitrogen, which is released as gaseous nitrogen

3. The clockspring contact:
   a. Operates the vehicle's clock when the ignition is off
   b. Pushes the air bag forward when the impact sensors send signals to it
   c. Maintains electrical contact between a wiring harness in the steering column and electrical components on the steering wheel
   d. Keeps column-mounted accessories secured to the column jacket

4. Technician A says that all new cars since 1990 are required to have air bags. Technician B says that an air bag that has been deployed once cannot be reused. Who is correct?
   a. Technician A only
   b. Technician B only
   c. Both A and B
   d. Neither A nor B

5. To check the steering wheel freeplay on a vehicle with power steering, it is important to:
   a. Leave the engine running
   b. Disconnect the tie rods
   c. Drain the power steering fluid
   d. Start and stop the engine one time

6. Which one of the following is the most common device used to connect the steering shaft to the steering gear input shaft?
   a. Universal joint
   b. Flexible coupling
   c. Pot joint
   d. CV joint

7. Which of the following is NOT a type of standard steering gear?
   a. Worm and sector
   b. Worm and cam
   c. Cam and lever
   d. Recirculating ball

8. Excessive worm endplay in a worm and roller steering gear is likely to be caused by:
   a. Worn thrust bearings at either end of the worm gear
   b. Worn splines at the steering shaft U-joint
   c. An over-tightened housing end plate
   d. Too many shims between the lower bearing and the worm gear

9. Technician A says that bearing preload in a worm and roller steering gear can be adjusted by placing shims between the lower bearing and the end plate. Technician B says sector lash can be adjusted by turning the adjusting screw at the top of the steering gear housing. Who is correct?
   a. Technician A only
   b. Technician B only
   c. Both A and B
   d. Neither A nor B

10. Kickback is most common with a:
    a. Worm and sector steering gear
    b. Recirculating ball steering gear
    c. Rack and pinion steering gear
    d. Manual steering system

11. Technician A says that changing internal shims is a common method of adjusting sector shaft endplay. Technician B says that shims are the *only* method used for adjusting gear mesh preload. Who is correct?
    a. Technician A only
    b. Technician B only
    c. Both A and B
    d. Neither A nor B

12. Which of the following is often NOT adjustable on a standard steering gear?
    a. Worm bearing preload
    b. Gear mesh preload
    c. Sector shaft endplay
    d. All of the above

13. Excessive gear lash that causes a loss of steering response on a vehicle with a recirculating ball steering gear can generally be eliminated by adjusting:
    a. Worm bearing preload
    b. Gear mesh preload
    c. Sector shaft endplay
    d. None of the above

14. On standard steering gear systems, adjustments should be made in the following order:
    a. Worm bearing preload, then gear mesh preload
    b. Gear mesh preload, then sector shaft endplay
    c. Gear mesh preload, then worm bearing preload
    d. Worm bearing preload, then pinion torque

15. A standard steering gear transfers motion to the pitman arm, while a rack and pinion steering gear transfers motion from the rack to the:
    a. Pinion
    b. Tie rods
    c. Steering gear housing
    d. Steering shaft

16. In a rack and pinion system, the gear teeth that are most likely to wear first are located at the:
    a. Center of the rack
    b. Driver's side of the rack
    c. Passenger's side of the rack
    d. None (the teeth wear evenly)

17. On a rack and pinion steering system, tightening or loosening the rack support cover adjusts:
    a. Pinion torque
    b. Pinion bearing preload
    c. Both a and b
    d. Neither a nor b

18. Technician A says tightening the rack cover is a possible method of adjusting pinion bearing preload. Technician B says that using shims and turning an adjuster screw are possible methods of adjusting pinion bearing preload. Who is correct?
    a. Technician A only
    b. Technician B only
    c. Both A and B
    d. Neither A nor B

19. On a rack and pinion steering system, if the center teeth on the rack are narrow and the outer teeth on the rack are wide, the steering system:
    a. Provides a constant steering ratio
    b. Is worn and must be replaced
    c. Was installed upside-down
    d. Provides a variable steering ratio

20. Technician A says that manual steering gears generally do NOT require periodic lubrication or fluid changes. Technician B says that gear oil is a commonly specified lubricant for manual steering gears. Who is correct?
    a. Technician A only
    b. Technician B only
    c. Both A and B
    d. Neither A nor B

5

Steering Linkages

OBJECTIVE

Upon completion and review of this chapter, you will be able to:

- Identify the components of the steering linkage and explain their operation.

KEY TERMS

Ackermann angle
Ackermann effect
ball joints
boot
bump steer
center link
center point steering linkage
cross steering linkage
drag link
Haltenberger steering linkage
idler arm
long-and-short-arm
memory steer
parallelism

parallelogram steering linkage
pitman arm
rack and pinion steering linkage
rubber-bonded socket (RBS) tie rod end
single-tie-rod steering linkage
standard ball joint
steering arm
steering axis
steering damper
steering linkage
tie rod

INTRODUCTION

The **steering linkage** is the assembly of components that transmits movement from the steering gear to the wheels. With the exception of a single-tie-rod linkage, most steering linkages are designed for use with independent suspensions. To allow for suspension travel, **ball joints** connect most steering linkage parts to each other and to the steering arms at the wheel.

Parallelogram linkage is the type of linkage used most often with standard steering gears, while a simpler linkage is used with a rack and pinion steering gear. These two linkage configurations are the most widely applied designs in late-model vehicles (Figure 5-1). However, some trucks, such as the 4WD Dodge pickup with a solid-front axle, use a single-tie-rod linkage, and older-model cars, such as the original Volkswagen Type I sedan, may have long-and-short-arm steering or some other linkage configuration.

Technically, the steering linkage ends at the outer tie rod ends, which attach to the steering arms. However, the steering arm and steering knuckle work with the linkage as the last pieces

PARALLELOGRAM

RACK AND PINION

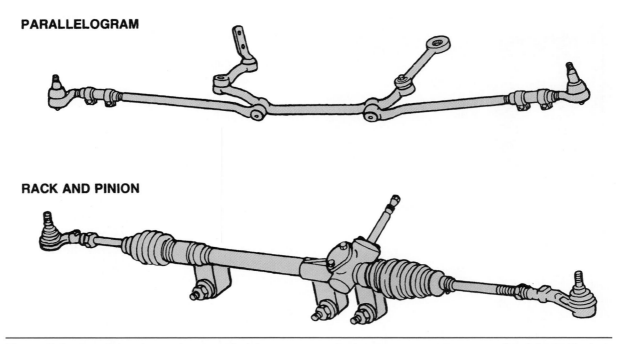

Figure 5-1. Parallelogram and rack and pinion are currently the two most common steering linkage designs in production.

involved in transmitting steering motion to the wheels. The steering knuckle also serves an important function in the suspension, as explained in Chapter 8 of this *Classroom Manual.*

STEERING LINKAGE BALL JOINTS

Steering linkages use ball joints to join components to each other and to join the linkage to the steering arms. Most modern ball joints are a standard type, consisting of a steel ball and socket that can slide against each other, but some Ford Motor Company vehicles use rubber bonded socket (RBS) ball joints. Also, the ball joints on the inner tie rod ends of a rack and pinion steering gear are slightly different from both standard steering linkage ball joints and RBS ball joints. This chapter begins with a look at these three types of ball joints used in steering linkages, then continues with a discussion of overall steering linkage design.

A ball joint (Figure 5-2) connects the steering knuckle to the control arm, allowing it to pivot on the control arm during steering. Ball joints also permit up-and-down movement of the control arm as the suspension reacts to road conditions. The ball joint stud protrudes from its socket through a rubber seal that keeps lubricating grease (when used) in the housing and keeps dirt out. Some ball

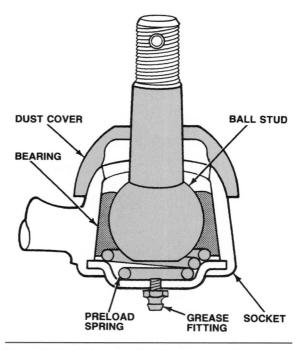

Figure 5-2. This typical ball joint is seated in an outer tie rod end and the stud connects it to the steering arm. Although this joint has a grease fitting, some have a removable plug while others provide no means of adding lubricant.

joints require periodic lubrication, while most do not. These maintenance-free ball joints move in a prelubricated nylon bearing. Ball joints are either load carrying or are followers. A load-carrying ball joint supports the car's weight and is generally in the control arm that holds or seats the spring. Load-carrying joints can be called tension-loaded or compression-loaded ball joints.

Newer vehicles have a ball joint that uses a highly polished steel ball and a single- or two-piece ball seat of the hard plastic polyacetal that has rigidity, high load durability, and elasticity. Older vehicles use a steel-on-steel (high friction) design and require periodic lubrication. The newer vehicles using the low-friction type ball joint may or may not require periodic lubrication. Always consult the original equipment manufacturer's (OEM) service information for proper maintenance instructions. Ball joints will be covered in more detail in Chapter 8 of this *Classroom Manual*. Chapter 8 of the *Shop Manual* will cover the service and maintenance of ball joints.

Standard Ball Joints

A **standard ball joint** used in the steering linkage typically is made up of the following (Figure 5-2):

- Ball stud
- Socket
- Wear surface, or bearing
- Preload spring
- Dust cover, or seal

Standard ball joints require lubrication to reduce friction and wear. Many vehicles are equipped with ball joints that are lubricated when manufactured and then permanently sealed. These ball joints do not require service and, in fact, are impossible to lubricate. The principle behind their use is to replace them when they wear out, rather than to preserve them by regular maintenance. However, some ball joints do have a grease plug or fitting through which new lubricant can regularly be added to prolong their service life. The greases used to lubricate steering linkages are discussed in Chapter 2 of this *Classroom Manual*.

A ball stud is made of steel machined into a ball, with a stud extending from it. The stud is threaded for installation of a castle nut, and it has a hole near the end of the stud for a cotter pin. The shank of the stud is machined to a close tolerance to provide an interference fit with the bore it installs into the linkage. The ball seats inside the socket, which is integral to a linkage component such as a tie rod or center link.

The movement between the ball and socket requires a metal or nylon wear surface, or bearing, to reduce friction between them. This bearing is a wear item that is not replaceable. When the bear-

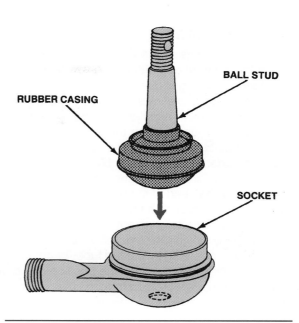

Figure 5-3. The ball stud of an RBS joint fits tightly into the socket. The hole in the socket allows air displacement as the ball stud is installed.

ing surface wears to the extent that it causes sloppy ball joint movement, the joint must be replaced.

A preload spring at the base of the ball stud keeps the ball seated in the socket. The spring can give way under pressure of linkage movement from road shock, but its force keeps the ball seated. This allows the parts linked by the ball joint to maintain their position in relation to each other. Spring force also helps take up additional clearance caused by bearing surface wear.

A rubber dust cover, or seal, fits tightly onto a standard ball joint. This dust cover, which requires no bands or clamps to hold it in place, protects the ball joint by keeping lubricant inside and contaminants outside.

Rubber-Bonded Socket Joints

Ford Motor Company introduced the **rubber-bonded socket (RBS) tie rod end** on the 1983 Ranger. Use of RBS joints has expanded since then to include other light trucks as well as passenger cars. The RBS ball joint is a simple device consisting of two parts, the ball stud and the socket (Figure 5-3). The joint requires no lubrication.

The ball section of the stud, which is shaped like a hemisphere, is encased by a rubber compound that forms a bushing around it. The coated ball is then press-fitted into the metal housing, or socket. A lip on the top edge of the housing is bent

■ Early Ball Joints

While the ball joints on modern steering linkages vary in detail, the basic pattern is the same for all: a stud with a ball-shaped end, fitting into a cup-shaped bearing, and enclosed in a cover. Not very many years ago, steering linkages used a differently designed ball joint that could be disassembled for inspection and lubrication, and sometimes could be adjusted to compensate for wear or to alter wheel alignment.

This unit was a true ball-and-socket joint. Of the two components that the ball joint connected, one was forged with a round ball on the end and the other was fitted with a hollow tube. The ball was inserted through a slot in the side of the tube. A spring-loaded, concave bearing supported one side of the ball, and a threaded bearing assembly supported the other.

To install the joint, the technician packed the tube with grease and inserted the spring and inner bearing. Next, the ball-end of the other component was pushed through the slot in the tube, and threaded onto the outer bearing until the tension was correct—sometimes described as when the outer plug was flush with the tube. A cotter pin kept the plug from backing out.

Adjustable ball joints came with identical inner and outer concave bearings. The threaded plug simply held the outer bearing inside the tube. To adjust the joint, shims were switched from the back of one bearing to the other, which moved the position of the ball inside the tube without altering the spring force. Adjustable ball joints were common in steering linkages through the 1950s.

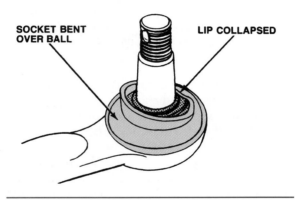

Figure 5-4. When the ball stud is in place, the socket is crimped over the ball so that part of the socket lip retains the stud.

over the ball and this portion of the lip collapses during assembly and holds the ball in the socket (Figure 5-4). Instead of sliding inside the socket, the ball stud moves by stretching or bending the rubber that is bonded to it. This lack of movement between the ball and socket eliminates the need for a bearing, lubricant, spring, and seal. Furthermore, eliminating the moving parts in an RBS ball joint allows use of a higher grade of steel to construct the stud. The steel used for other ball joints is softer, since it must be ground and case hardened to provide a bearing surface. In addition, the rubber compound helps absorb vibration, which reduces feedback to the steering wheel.

Because the rubber is elastic and firmly positioned in the socket, an RBS ball stud resists movement and tends to stay in position. When the force

of road shock overcomes its resistance, the ball stud moves, but returns to its normal position as soon as the force is removed. This torsional quality of the rubber eliminates the need for a preload spring.

The strong torsion of RBS ball joints means that it is important for the steering linkage to be straight and the steering wheel centered before the stud is secured to the linkage. If the RBS joints are installed with the steering system aimed for even a slight turn, the rubber keeps trying to return the stud to that position, causing the vehicle to pull toward one side. This problem is called **memory steer**, as if the ball stud "remembered" its original position and returned there. There are other causes of "memory steer," such as unequal length FWD drive shafts and binding strut bearings on a strut suspension.

Rack and Pinion Inner Tie Rod Ends

The inner tie rod end used with a rack and pinion steering gear usually is a ball joint with the same internal parts as a standard ball joint, but in a slightly different configuration. Instead of using linkage with an integral socket and a separate ball stud, the ball is formed from the end of the tie rod and installed into a separate socket on this type of joint (Figure 5-5). The open end of the socket threads onto the end of the steering rack and is anchored to it.

There are several methods of attaching the socket to the rack, and the following are common:

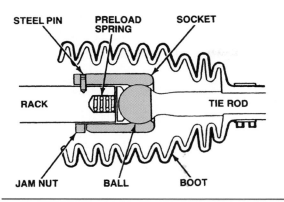

Figure 5-5. On rack and pinion steering the end of the inner tie rod forms the ball and a separate socket fits over the ball and anchors the tie rod to the rack.

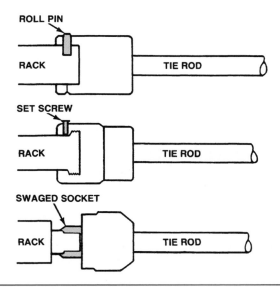

Figure 5-6. The inner tie rod socket, which threads onto the rack, may be secured in a number of ways.

- Steel pin
- Roll pin
- Set screw
- Swaged socket
- Tab washer and threads

A steel pin is a solid rod driven a short distance into the rack between the socket and a lock nut, a set screw threads through the socket and jams against the end of the rack, and a swaged socket is bent around the end of the rack (Figure 5-6). Roll pins are installed similar to steel pins, but they are not solid and require a special pin punch. A roll pin punch has a small ball tip that centers the end of the punch over the end of the roll pin. Two

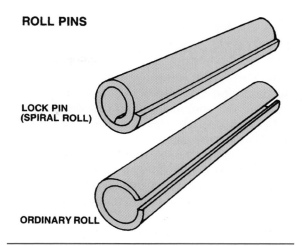

Figure 5-7. A spiral roll pin, also called a lock pin, must be drilled out to remove it, while an ordinary roll pin is readily removed with a punch and hammer.

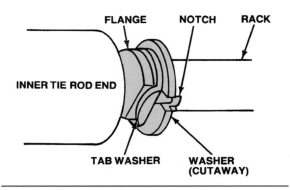

Figure 5-8. Tab washers use a notch and tooth method of attaching the inner tie rod to the rack. This is one of many design variations.

TAB WASHERS

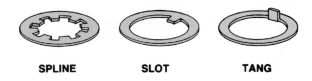

Figure 5-9. Tab washers used to secure the inner tie rod end to the rack come in a number of designs.

types of roll pin are used: ordinary and spiral roll (Figure 5-7). A tab washer has internal tabs that fit into slots on the end of the rack. Typically, when the washer is installed, two sides of it are bent over flats on the tie rod flange to secure it (Figure 5-8). A number of tab washer designs are used (Figure 5-9).

PARALLELOGRAM LINKAGES

A **parallelogram steering linkage** is used with a standard, non-rack and pinion, steering gear. At one time, this combination was the norm, but rack and pinion steering gears and linkages have become more prevalent with the trend toward smaller, compact vehicle designs. Today, standard steering gears combined with parallelogram linkages are used mainly on some trucks and certain heavy, relatively large sedans and station wagons.

If a parallelogram steering linkage is viewed from above, the **pitman arm**, **idler arm**, and the **center link** form three sides of a parallelogram (Figure 5-10). The entire parallelogram steering linkage consists of:

- One pitman arm
- One idler arm
- One center link
- Two tie rods

As mentioned previously, ball joints are used to link these parts together and to connect the **tie rods** to the steering arms.

Parallelogram Operation

The sector shaft in the steering gear pivots one end of the pitman arm, which causes the other end of the arm to move right or left. A ball joint attaches this end of the pitman arm to the center link, so the center link moves in the same direction as the arm and the center link moves the tie rods. The tie rods push the steering arms right or left to move the wheels. The idler arm serves no active purpose in the linkage; it merely supports and aligns one end of the center link to maintain parallelism.

Parallelogram Buildup

Station wagons are one type of vehicle still likely to use a typical parallelogram steering linkage (Figure 5-11). At one time, every passenger car built in the United States had this type of linkage.

Pitman Arm

Internal splines on the pitman arm fit onto the matching splines of the sector shaft at the steering gear, and the opposite end of the arm extends to the center link of the steering linkage (Figure 5-12). A nut and washer secure the pitman arm to the sector

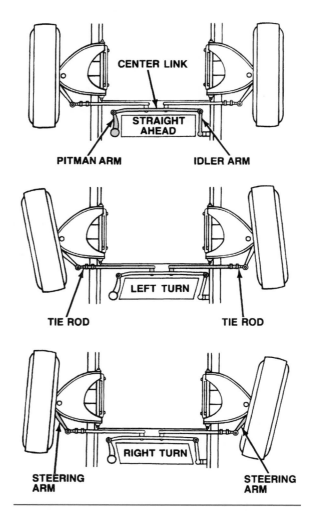

Figure 5-10. The sides of a parallelogram are always equal length and parallel, regardless of the angle at which they intersect. The pitman arm, idler arm, center link, and an imaginary line form a parallelogram steering linkage.

shaft and a ball joint connects the arm to one end of the center link. The ball joint socket is on the center link, and the stud fits through a machined hole in the pitman arm. The ball stud installs into the pitman arm with an interference fit, that is, the stud is slightly larger than the bore. Tightening the ball joint nut draws the stud into the hole to seat it, and a cotter pin secures the castle nut. A seal between the pitman arm and center link protects the ball joint.

Idler Arm

The idler arm is similar to the pitman arm in that it is joined to the center link by a ball joint at one end, and the other end pivots on a shaft (Figure 5-13). However, the idler arm is simply a pivot point and does not provide any input mo-

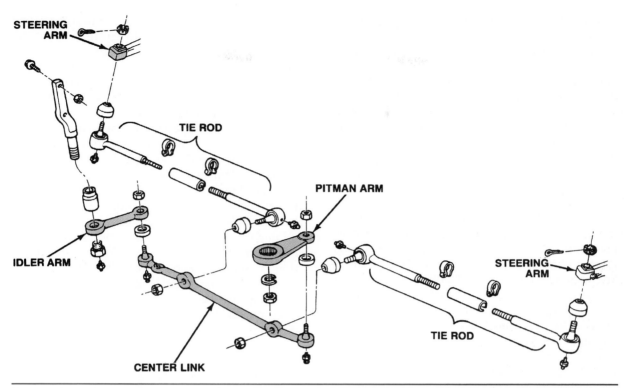

Figure 5-11. Although no longer universal, parallelogram steering linkages are still used on some large sedans, station wagons, and trucks.

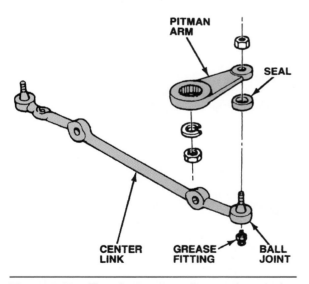

Figure 5-12. The pitman arm splines to the steering gear sector shaft so when the sector shaft pivots, the opposite end of the pitman arm pushes the center link to operate the steering linkage.

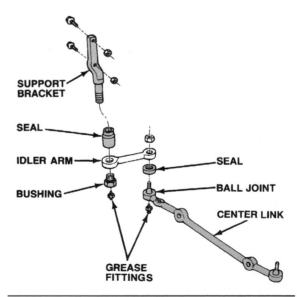

Figure 5-13. The idler arm is similar to the pitman arm, one end attaches to the center link with a ball joint, but the other end pivots on a support bracket, rather than the steering gear.

tion to the steering linkage. An idler arm mimics the movement of a pitman arm as the pitman arm moves the center link. The purpose of the idler arm is to support one end of the center link to keep

it at the same height as the pitman arm without interfering with steering linkage movement. This keeps the steering linkage in proper alignment both when steering straight ahead and during turns.

The ball joint at the idler arm is identical to the ball joint at the pitman arm, with a castle nut and cotter pin to secure it to the idler arm. The other end of the idler arm fits onto a shaft that is part of a support bracket. The bracket bolts to the vehicle frame so that the shaft remains stationary while the idler arm pivots with steering linkage movement. A bushing between the idler arm and the shaft helps reduce friction. Idler arm bushings generally have a fitting for adding lubricant and a seal on top of the idler arm to keep the lubricant from leaking out.

Center Link

The center link is a heavy rod that links all the other parts of the steering linkage together (Figure 5-14). It is sometimes called the "relay rod" because it relays input from one side to the other. There are two ball joints in the center link that connect it to the pitman and idler arms, as described earlier. In each of these, the ball is anchored in the center link, and the stud extends through the arm and is secured by a nut. Toward the middle of the center link, two ball studs anchored in the inner tie rod ends join to the link at right, or 90-degree, angles to the pitman and idler arm joints. Each stud extends through the center link and is secured by a nut.

Tie Rods

Each **tie rod** transmits motion from the center link to a steering arm, which changes the position of the wheel. There are two tie rods, one connected to each wheel, in every parallelogram steering linkage. A typical tie rod is made of three pieces: inner tie rod end, outer tie rod end, and adjuster sleeve (Figure 5-15).

Each tie rod end consists of a section of rod and a ball joint. The ball joint stud from the outer tie rod end extends through the steering arm and the ball joint stud from the inner tie rod end extends through the center link. Both studs are secured with a nut, as described earlier. The ball joints in the tie rod ends are protected by dust covers and are generally equipped with grease fittings.

The two sections of tie rod are joined together by the internally threaded adjuster sleeve. The adjuster sleeve has female threads and each tie rod section has male threads. The threads on one tie rod are left-hand threads, and those on the other tie rod are right-hand threads. When both are in the adjuster sleeve, turning the sleeve one direction causes both rods to thread out of the sleeve, and turning the other direction causes both ends to thread further in. This design allows the tie rod length to be changed without detaching the tie rods from the rest of the linkage for making toe adjustments. The adjuster sleeve is open down one side, so it will be loose enough for easy adjustment. When the tie rods are not being adjusted, two clamps hold each sleeve in place. Wheel toe is discussed in more detail in Chapter 14 of this *Classroom Manual,* and specific toe adjustment procedures are described in the *Shop Manual.*

On some tie rods, the two tie rod ends have female threaded connections and are connected by a threaded adjuster rod instead of an adjuster sleeve (Figure 5-16). These tie rod ends also have left-hand threads in one and right-hand in the other, so turning the adjuster rod one way lengthens the tie rod and turning it the other way shortens it. A lock nut secures the adjuster rod in position. In an al-

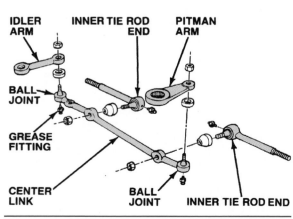

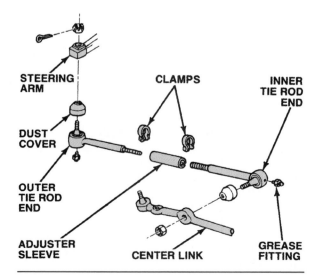

Figure 5-14. The center link lives up to its name, being the central piece that joins the rest of the steering linkage parts together.

Figure 5-15. A typical tie rod consists of two end pieces joined by an adjuster sleeve and transmits motion from the center link to one of the steering arms.

ternative design, some tie rods are made of two pieces instead of three. The female end of the outer tie rod threads onto the male end of the inner tie rod, and a lock nut secures them. These cannot be adjusted without separating one of the ball studs.

Parallelogram Linkage Variants

There a number of parallelogram steering linkage design variations that still use a pitman arm, idler arm, center link, and tie rods, but have added

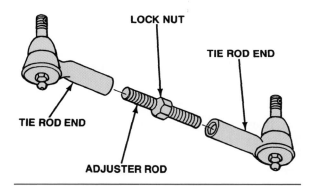

Figure 5-16. On some tie rod designs, an externally threaded adjusting rod works on the same principle as an adjusting sleeve.

parts, such as a **drag link,** or other modifications as well.

On a steering linkage, a drag link is a rod that extends from the pitman arm to another linkage part so that the pitman arm is connected to the rest of the linkage indirectly. Drag links extend horizontally from the steering gear to the steering linkage, and it is important that this position not be changed. Raising the frame and suspension of a vehicle higher than the linkage design allows can misalign the steering wheel. This results in the steering wheel being turned slightly when the tires are pointing straight ahead, and can also cause the vehicle to turn more widely in one direction than the other.

Variations on the parallelogram linkage design can be simple or complex (Figure 5-17). One common variation attaches the inner tie rod ends to extensions on the pitman arm and idler arm, instead of to the center link. The pitman pivots at the sector shaft and the idler arms pivots at the frame mount in the first example shown in Figure 5-17. Other linkage variants can be somewhat unorthodox and complex arrangements. In the second example shown, the pitman arm operates the center link indirectly through a drag link that attaches to a bellcrank, which provides the input motion to the linkage. Viewed from above, the bellcrank is shaped like the

VARIANTS OF PARALLELOGRAM STEERING LINKAGE

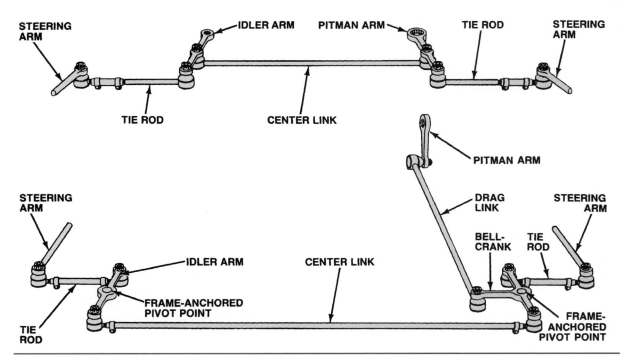

Figure 5-17. These variations on the parallelogram steering linkage use many of the same parts and operate in basically the same way as the more typical parallelogram linkage.

letter "T." A ball joint attaches the drag link to the base of the "T," and two ball joints, one at each end of the cross piece, attach the bellcrank to the center link and to a tie rod. Centered on the cross of the bellcrank is a frame-mounted pivot. The idler arm mimics the bellcrank cross piece. It has a ball joint at each end, attaching it to the center link and a tie rod, and a frame-mounted pivot at its center. The outer tie rod ends attach to the steering arms. The pitman and idler arms pivot at their center points. Linkage arrangements such as this are used to maintain **parallelism** when the chassis design does not allow the steering gear to mount close to the linkage.

Parallelism

Parallelism is the condition of parallelogram steering linkages when the center link is parallel to a level ground surface (Figure 5-18). In

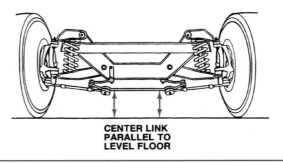

PARALLELISM

**CENTER LINK
PARALLEL TO
LEVEL FLOOR**

Figure 5-18. On linkages with a flat surfaces machined under the pitman and idler arms, parallelism is checked by measuring the distance from these surfaces to the ground. Otherwise, measure from the inner tie rod end to the upper control arm mounting bolt on each side of the vehicle.

some vehicles, the center link has two flat surfaces on the bottom to permit accurate measurements from the ground to the linkage. Parallelism helps ensure even steering. If one side of the center link is lower than the other, the inner tie rod end on that side is also lower than the other inner tie rod end. Since the tie rods determine the position of the steering arms, a lack of parallelism positions the arms differently from side to side. This results in unequal turning radii for left and right turns. Bump steer, described later in this chapter, can be another result of a lack of parallelism.

RACK AND PINION LINKAGES

For many years, rack and pinion steering was used only on European sports cars, and the 1971 Ford Pinto was the first domestic car with rack and pinion steering. By that time, 10 out of 21 import platforms were already using it. Rack and pinion steering is more compact than a standard steering gear with a parallelogram linkage, so it is better suited for use in smaller and lighter vehicles. Just as the rack and pinion steering gear design is simpler than the design of a standard steering gear, so the linkage used with it is simpler than a parallelogram linkage (Figure 5-19). There is no descriptive name for the linkage itself because it consists of only two tie rods, but it is commonly referred to as **rack and pinion steering linkage.** Because of its relative simplicity, rack and pinion steering has fewer wear points within the steering gear and linkage than other system designs.

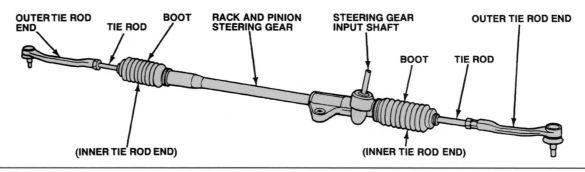

Figure 5-19. The linkage used with a rack and pinion steering gear consists simply of two tie rods; the steering gear along with its linkage are often treated as a single unit.

Rack and Pinion Linkage Tie Rods

The tie rods form a direct link from the steering gear rack to the steering arms. When the rack moves back and forth, the tie rods transmit the motion to the steering arms and reposition the wheels.

Each tie rod has an inner end attached to the rack and an outer end attached to the steering arm (Figure 5-20). Most inner tie rod ends are linked to the end of the rack by a ball joint, as described earlier. The inner tie rod ends attach to the center of the rack on some designs, such as that of the Audi V8 Quattro, Eagle Premier, Volkswagen Fox, and several General Motors models (Figure 5-21). These inner tie rod ends are not ball joints, but pivots, with bushings installed in the bolt holes. The outer tie rod ends are always ball joints that connect to the steering arms.

The two tie rod sections may be joined together indirectly, through an adjusting sleeve or rod, as described earlier, or they may be joined directly to each other and secured with a lock nut (Figure 5-22). Either design allows for adjusting the length of the tie rod without removing it from the rack or steering arm.

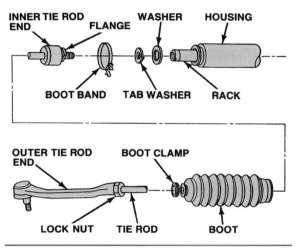

Figure 5-20. The tie rod extends directly from the steering gear rack to the steering arm.

Boots

A rack and pinion steering gear **boot** seals each opening of the gear housing where the rack and an inner tie rod end are joined together. Most boots have a wide end and a narrow end (Figure 5-23). The wide end fits over the end of the gear housing, and a boot band holds it in place. The narrow end fits over the tie rod, and a clamp holds it in place.

The boot must compress when the rack pulls the tie rod into the gear housing and extend when the rack pushes the tie rod out of the housing. Therefore, boots are made with pleats, so they can fold and unfold like a bellows. In fact, some

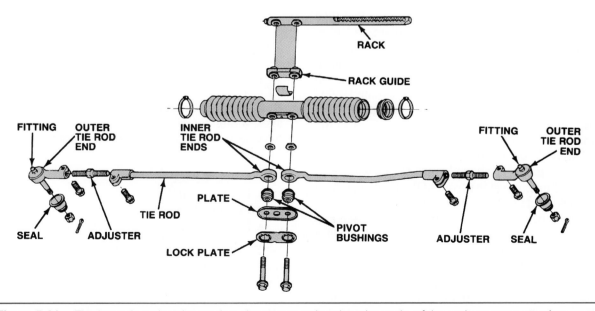

Figure 5-21. The inner tie rod ends attach to the center, rather than the ends, of the rack on some steering gears, but the steering linkage still consists of only the two tie rods.

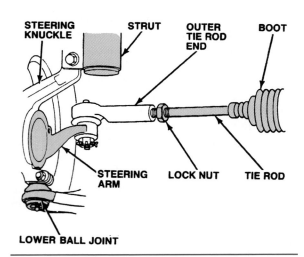

Figure 5-22. With the lock nut loose, the tie rod can be threaded in and out of the outer tie rod end to adjust its length and set wheel toe.

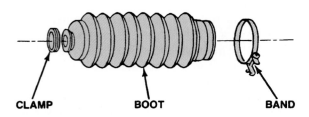

Figure 5-23. The boot covers the connection between the rack and the inner tie rod; one end clamps to the rack housing and the other clamps around the tie rod shaft.

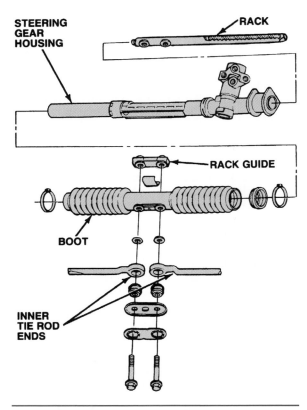

Figure 5-24. This boot covers the opening in the steering gear housing and has holes for the bolts that attach the tie rods to the center of the rack.

service literature uses the term *bellows* rather than boots. Boots must have a means to displace air between them to prevent them from ballooning and collapsing during compression and extension. In manual steering gears, the air transfers through the steering gear housing. In power-assisted steering gears, the power steering fluid chambers seal the housing, so a tube runs from one boot to the other to provide an air transfer passage.

On assemblies with the tie rods bolted to the middle of the rack, a large boot with two wide ends seals the opening at the front of the housing where the rack guide slides back and forth (Figure 5-24). The boot fits over the gear housing, and each end of the boot is anchored by a band clamp. Both sides of the boot are pleated to allow compression and extension as the rack and guide slide side-to-side.

Rack and pinion boots may be made of soft natural rubber, rubber compounds, soft plastic, or hard plastic. Because they protect the steering gear, it is important that boots stay in good repair. It is easier

and more economical to replace a recently damaged boot than a steering gear damaged by fluid loss or contamination that results from a torn boot.

OTHER STEERING LINKAGES

Besides parallelogram and rack and pinion linkages, a number of other steering linkage designs have seen common use in the past. Some of these include:

- Single-tie-rod
- Center point
- Long-and-short-arm
- Haltenberger

While less common today than parallelogram or rack and pinion linkages, these steering linkage designs are not so rare as to be unfamiliar. Most technicians will encounter one or another of them at some time, most likely on older vehicles and trucks. The word *arm* in some of the descriptive names for these linkages refers to the tie rods, which are steering linkage components. Do not confuse them with the suspension arms described later in this *Classroom Manual.*

Single Tie Rod

The simple **single-tie-rod steering linkage** consists of:

- One pitman arm
- One drag link
- One tie rod

This linkage is used only on solid-axle front suspensions (Figure 5-25). The only late-model vehicles with a solid front axle are some heavy-duty trucks and four-wheel-drive (4WD) vehicles. The tie rod runs across the vehicle, from one steering arm to the other, while a drag link extends from the pitman arm to one of the steering arms. When the drag link reaches to a steering arm on the opposite side of the vehicle, the linkage design is called **cross steering linkage.** The Suzuki Samurai uses a cross steering linkage.

Center Point

A center point, or equal arm, steering linkage uses two tie rods joined at the center of the linkage to an intermediate steering arm (Figure 5-26). This link-

age is sometimes called equal arm linkage because both tie rods are the same length. Volkswagen used **center point steering linkage** on the Type II van.

Since the pitman arm and steering gear are off to one side of the chassis, the pitman arm operates the intermediate steering arm at the center of the vehicle through either a drag link and bellcrank or a drag link only. An extension from the intermediate steering arm attaches the linkage to a frame crossmember. This connection is a pivot point that supports the arm without interfering with steering linkage movement.

Long-and-Short-Arm

In a **long-and-short-arm,** also known as compensated pitman, steering linkage, both tie rods are joined directly to the pitman arm (Figure 5-27). The Volkswagen Type I sedan, or Beetle, used a long-and-short-arm linkage design. Because the pitman arm is located to one side of the chassis, the tie rod from the opposite steering arm is longer than the one from the steering arm on the same side. The inner tie rod ends attach separately to the pitman arm at different distances from its pivot, so that the inner end of the shorter tie rod swings through a tighter arc than the inner end of the longer tie rod. These different arcs counter the opposite tendency that results from unequal-length tie rods in order to move the wheels in unison. This

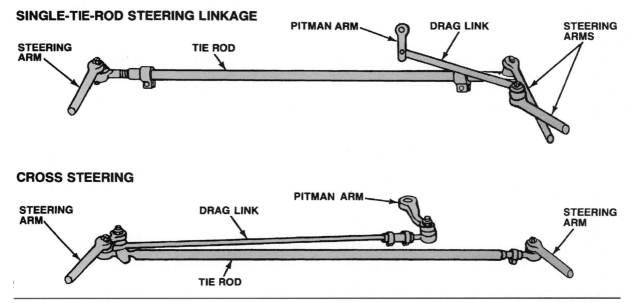

SINGLE-TIE-ROD STEERING LINKAGE

STEERING ARM   TIE ROD   PITMAN ARM   DRAG LINK   STEERING ARMS

CROSS STEERING

STEERING ARM   DRAG LINK   PITMAN ARM   STEERING ARM   TIE ROD

Figure 5-25. The single-tie-rod steering linkage is used with a solid front axle, and the cross steering linkage is a variation on the same design.

CENTERPOINT STEERING LINKAGES

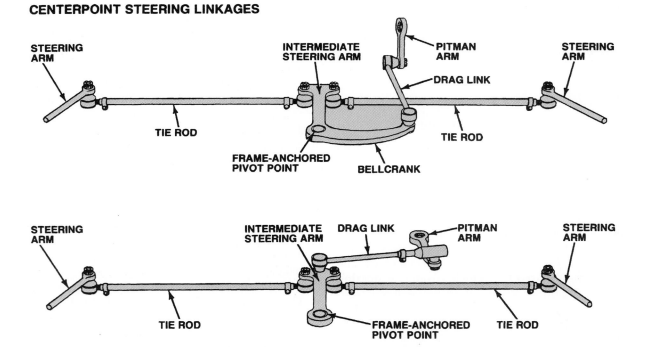

Figure 5-26. With a center point configuration, the linkage moves from the center of the chassis instead of from one side.

LONG-AND-SHORT-ARM STEERING LINKAGE

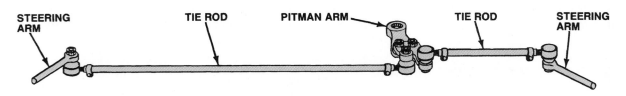

Figure 5-27. The long-and-short-arm design is simple: two tie rods and a pitman arm. However, the tie rods must connect to the pitman arm in such a way as to compensate for the difference in their lengths.

linkage is sometimes called "compensated pitman" because the pitman arm design compensates for the unequal lengths of the tie rods.

Haltenberger

The **Haltenberger steering linkage** uses one long drag link and one tie rod (Figure 5-28). The drag link extends from the pitman arm to the opposite steering arm. At the center point of the linkage, the tie rod attaches to the drag link. The pitman arm operates the drag link and the drag link operates one steering arm and the tie rod that attaches to the other steering arm. The Ford Ranger and Bronco II are examples of late-model vehicles with Haltenberger steering linkage.

HALTENBERGER STEERING LINKAGE

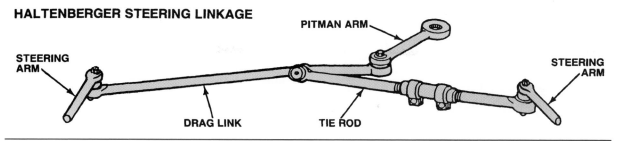

Figure 5-28. Haltenberger linkages, which have a pitman arm, one drag link, and one tie rod, are used in Ford trucks with twin I-beam suspensions.

■ **Steam Engine Steering Linkage**

Many steam engines of the late 1800s used a gear-driven crossbeam and a chain as the steering linkage. The way this system works is quite simple. The front axle pivots at the center, and each end of the axle is connected to one end of the chain. The length of the chain is wrapped around the crossbeam. When the operator turns the steering wheel, the worm gear turns the crossbeam. As the crossbeam rotates, one end of the chain winds more tightly around the beam, while the other end receives more slack. The tightening end pulls one side of the axle back, turning the front wheels to one side. When the turn is complete and the operator straightens the steering wheel, the crossbeam winds the chain so that each end is equally taut.

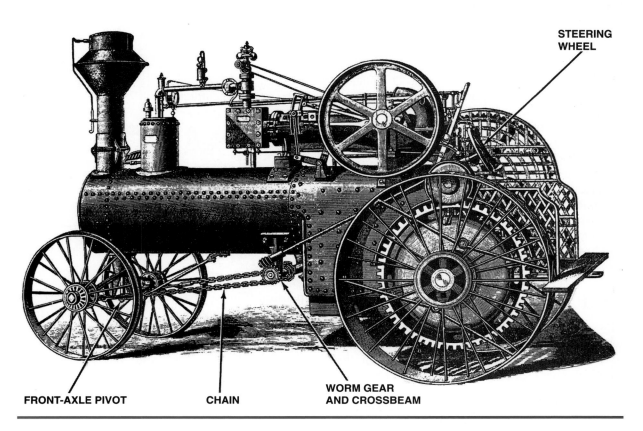

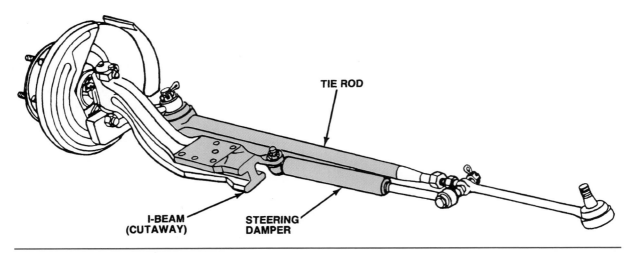

Figure 5-29. The steering damper is a shock absorber installed on the steering linkage to decrease kickback and shimmy.

STEERING DAMPER

A **steering damper** is a shock absorber that cushions road feedback to the steering wheel—just like the shocks described in Chapter 8 of this *Classroom Manual* except that a steering damper damps steering linkage movement instead of suspension movement. Steering dampers are typically found on 4WD trucks, but are also used on some Cadillac models and other 2WD vehicles. Exact installations vary, but one end of the steering damper is always attached to the frame or axle and the other to some part of the steering linkage.

A typical steering damper has a mounting stud extending from either end (Figure 5-29). A nut secures one end to a small extension on the I-beam axle, and a castle nut and cotter pin secure the other end to the tie rod. As the tie rod moves from side to side, the shock absorber damps any uneven motion, reducing kickback and shimmy, and keeping bumps from affecting steering.

STEERING ARMS

The **steering arm** is part of the steering knuckle, which is a suspension component that helps support the wheel. The suspension aspects of the steering knuckle are explained in Chapter 8 of this *Classroom Manual*. The steering arm can be either an integral part of the steering knuckle or a separate piece that bolts to the knuckle.

The steering knuckle serves two purposes; to support the wheel and to link the wheel to the sus-

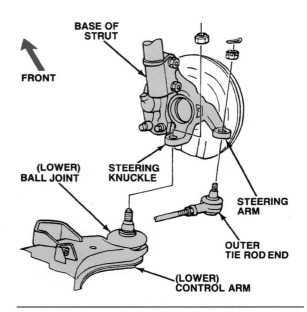

Figure 5-30. This steering knuckle, in which the steering arm is an integral part of the knuckle, is typical of a MacPherson strut suspension.

pension (Figure 5-30). The steering arm extends from the steering knuckle. Although most steering arms extend from the knuckle toward the rear of the vehicle, some vehicles have steering arms that extend toward the front. When the steering linkage, which is joined to the steering arm by the outer tie rod end, pulls or pushes the steering arm, the entire steering knuckle pivots on the suspension ball joints so that the wheel changes direction. The axis on which the steering knuckle pivots is called the **steering axis** (Figure 5-31).

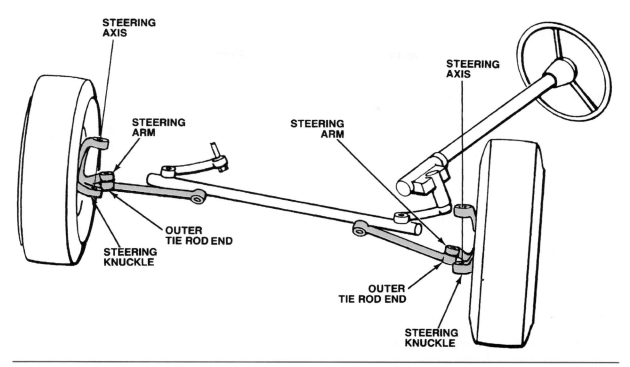

Figure 5-31. The steering knuckle pivots on the steering axis, which intersects the upper and lower ball joints, in order to direct the wheels.

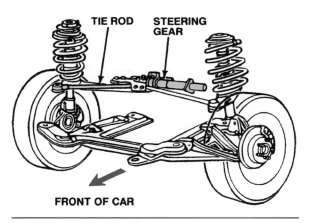

Figure 5-32. The steering arms on some chassis are located much higher than usual and connect to the struts instead of the knuckles. This arrangement allows the steering gear to be mounted higher on the firewall.

Most steering arms extend forward or back at about the same level as the wheel hub. On some designs, the steering arm is located just underneath the coil spring support on the strut where it attaches to a flange on the strut tube (Figure 5-32). The lower end of the strut assembly attaches to the steering knuckle. On these designs, the tie rod moves the steering arm and pivots the strut, which in turn moves the steering knuckle.

Bump Steer

When designing a steering linkage, engineers must consider that the linkage joins the suspension at the steering arm, which presents a dilemma. The purpose of the suspension is to protect the rest of the vehicle from road shock, so it moves up and down with the wheels over bumps. However, the purpose of the steering linkage is to turn the wheels, so it is intended to move laterally. To ensure proper operation, the steering and suspension must be designed in such a manner to provide the same range of travel for both the outer tie rod end and the end of the steering arm.

When the wheel and tire go over a bump, the steering knuckle and arm travel vertically, following a slight arc. The outer tie rod end should be able to follow the same arc. If the tie rod end cannot travel freely in this arc, it resists the steering arm movement at some point of its travel. This causes the steering linkage to bind and jerk the steering arm, suddenly pulling it inward or pushing it outward—in effect, the wheels steer in a direction not intended by the driver. This problem is referred to as **bump steer** because it is a result of the wheel riding over a bump. When discussed in the context of wheel alignment angles, bump steer is called "toe change" because the toe angle changes as the wheel is deflected. Three factors affect bump steer:

- Tie rod length
- Relative heights of the inner and outer tie rod ends
- Steering arm length

Methods of measuring toe change are discussed in Chapter 14 of this *Classroom Manual,* and procedures for correcting it are given in the *Shop Manual.*

The Ackermann Angle

Ackermann steering geometry helps prevent tire scuffing during turns. In the perfect application of the **Ackermann angle,** imaginary lines drawn through the steering arms form a "V" whose point intersects the center point of the rear axle of the vehicle (Figure 5-33). The Ackermann angle is built into most steering arms, even those that extend toward the front of the car.

The Ackermann angle affects the alignment angle called the turning radius, or toe-out on turns. In order for a vehicle to negotiate a turn, the wheel at the outside must travel in a wider arc than the one at the inside. Ackermann geometry has the effect of causing the outside wheel to track this wider arc correctly by making both front wheels arc around the same turning center (Figure 5-34). Without the **Ackermann effect,** the outside wheel would try to turn around a separate turning center and the weight and direction of the vehicle would force the outside wheel to arc more widely. As a result, the tire scuffs the road during the turn because the wheel is not aimed into this arc.

ACKERMANN ANGLE

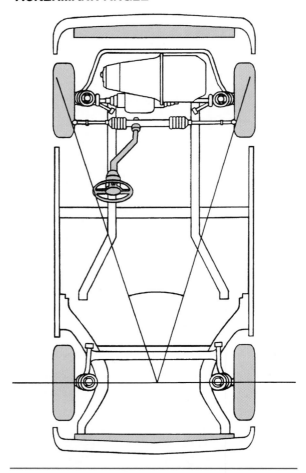

Figure 5-33. The Ackermann angle is formed by the imaginary meeting point of the steering arms at the center of the rear axle.

Since the Ackermann effect makes the wheels toe-out—the front edges of the wheel are farther apart than the rear edges—during turns, the turning radius is often called "toe-out on turns." Turning radius is discussed further in Chapter 14 of this *Classroom Manual.*

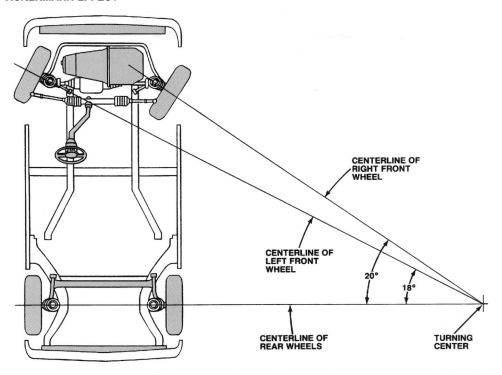

ACKERMANN EFFECT

CENTERLINE OF
RIGHT FRONT
WHEEL

CENTERLINE OF
LEFT FRONT
WHEEL

20°

18°

CENTERLINE OF
REAR WHEELS

TURNING
CENTER

Figure 5-34. The Ackermann effect, or the result of Ackermann steering geometry, allows the front wheels to travel along different arcs to reduce tire scuffing during turns.

SUMMARY

The steering linkage is the assembly that transmits movement from the steering gear to the wheels. Ball joints hold the steering linkage parts together. The two most common linkage designs are parallelogram and rack and pinion steering linkages, but a number of others exist as well.

Three different types of ball joints may be used in a steering linkage. The most common type is referred to in this chapter as a "standard ball joint." Two other types are rubber-bonded socket (RBS) joints, which Ford uses at the tie rod ends of some of their vehicles, and the ball joints that link inner tie rod ends to the rack of a rack and pinion steering gear.

A parallelogram steering linkage is used with a standard, non–rack and pinion steering gear and for many years was the most widely used linkage design. A parallelogram linkage transmits movement from the steering gear sector shaft through the pitman arm, center link, and tie rods. An idler arm supports the center link on the side of the chassis opposite the steering gear. Some vehicles use steering linkages that are basically a parallelogram

design, but have a few additional parts or features. Parallelogram linkages are said to have parallelism when the center link is parallel to a level surface.

Two tie rods make up the simple steering linkage used with a rack and pinion steering gear. The tie rods connect the steering rack directly to the steering knuckles.

Other steering linkage design variations include: single-tie-rod, center point, long-and-short-arm, and Haltenberger. Center point is also known as equal arm linkage, while long-and-short-arm may be referred to as compensated pitman arm linkage.

Some steering linkages include a steering damper, which is a shock absorber connected to the steering linkage and frame. These devices damp linkage movement to lessen the effects of road shocks on the steering wheel and to reduce shimmy and kickback.

The tie rod is linked to the steering arm, which extends either forward or backward from the steering knuckle, and attaches the steering linkage to the wheel. If the outer tie rod end and the steering arm do not have the same range of travel, they interfere with each other and cause a condition known as "bump steer."

Ackermann steering geometry uses the Ackermann angle, which is formed by the steering arms and the center point of the rear axle. The Ackermann angle allows the front wheels to travel in different arcs and reduces tire scuffing on turns. The effect this angle has on steering is called the "Ackermann effect."

Review Questions

For each of the following questions, choose the letter that represents the best possible answer.

1. Which part of a standard ball joint keeps the ball seated in the socket and takes up clearance as the ball joint wears?
   a. Dust cover
   b. Grease plug
   c. Preload spring
   d. Ball stud

2. Technician A says that the Rubber Bonded Socket (RBS) joints used on Ford trucks must be lubricated every 100,000 miles. Technician B says that the RBS joints have memory steer, and therefore must be secured only when the steering wheel and linkage are centered. Who is correct?
   a. A only
   b. B only
   c. Both A and B
   d. Neither A nor B

3. Which of the following parts is NOT found in a parallelogram steering linkage?
   a. Center link
   b. Drag link
   c. Bellcrank
   d. Rack

4. On a standard steering gear with parallelogram steering linkage, the pitman arm splines to and is driven by which of the following?
   a. Steering rack
   b. Sector shaft
   c. Worm shaft
   d. Center link

5. Technician A says that to adjust the wheel toe alignment angle with rack and pinion steering, the outer tie rod end must be removed from the steering knuckle and shimmed. Technician B says that the wheel toe alignment angle can be adjusted on most vehicles without disassembling the steering linkage by loosening a lock nut on a tie rod and turning an adjuster sleeve. Who is correct?
   a. A only
   b. B only
   c. Both A and B
   d. Neither A nor B

6. Technician A says that in parallelogram steering linkages, a drag link can be used to connect the pitman arm to the rest of the linkage. Technician B says that the pitman arm can be connected directly to the center link in a parallelogram linkage. Who is correct?
   a. A only
   b. B only
   c. Both A and B
   d. Neither A nor B

7. On a vehicle with parallelogram steering linkage, the steering linkage lacks parallelism when the:
   a. Tie rods are not parallel to the ground
   b. Center link is not parallel to the ground
   c. Pitman arm is not parallel to the idler arm
   d. Tie rods are of two different lengths

8. On a rack and pinion steering gear, the inner tie rod end may be secured to the rack by all of the following EXCEPT:
   a. Castle nut and cotter pin
   b. Swaged socket
   c. Set screw
   d. Roll pin

9. The steering linkage on a rack and pinion steering system consists of:
   a. Two tie rods
   b. A center link, pitman arm, drag link, and two tie rods
   c. A bellcrank and two tie rods
   d. A center link and unequal-length tie rods

10. In a rack and pinion steering system, which of the following are used to connect the end of the rack to the tie rod?
    a. Ball joint
    b. Pivot bushing
    c. Either a or b
    d. Neither a nor b

11. In long-and-short-arm steering linkages, the effects of unequal tie rod lengths are compensated for by a specially designed:
    a. Center link
    b. Pitman arm
    c. Drag link
    d. Steering damper

12. Parallelogram steering linkage variants may use all of the following components EXCEPT:
    a. A frame anchored bellcrank
    b. A drag link
    c. A center-pivoting idler arm
    d. An intermediate steering arm

13. Which of the following steering linkages uses a center link?
    a. Haltenberger
    b. Center point
    c. Long-and-short-arm
    d. Parallelogram

14. A steering damper performs all of the following functions EXCEPT:
    a. Reduce kickback
    b. Reduce shimmy
    c. Keep road bumps from affecting steering
    d. Maintain parallelism

15. Compensated pitman arm steering linkage is also known as:
    a. Center point steering linkage
    b. Long-and-short-arm steering linkage
    c. Single tie rod steering linkage
    d. Haltenberger steering linkage

16. Technician A says that some steering arms are a cast part of the steering knuckle. Technician B says that some steering arms are bolt-on items. Who is correct?
    a. A only
    b. B only
    c. Both A and B
    d. Neither A nor B

17. The steering knuckle pivots on the:
    a. Steering axis
    b. Knuckle axis
    c. Steering radius
    d. Ackermann angle

18. Which of the following factors affect bump steer?
    a. Tie rod length
    b. Steering arm length
    c. Both a and b
    d. Neither a nor b

19. Bump steer is caused by:
    a. Worn shock absorbers that contact the pitman arm and deflect the steering linkage as the wheel travels over a bump
    b. An outer tie rod end that does not travel the same arc as the steering knuckle and steering arm when the wheel rides over a bump
    c. Ball joint or steering damper wear that results in excessive steering linkage movement as the wheel travels over a bump
    d. Worn steering column U-joints that create excessive steering freeplay that makes the steering wheel bump slightly before the wheels begin to turn

20. The most likely cause of a "toe-out on turns" measurement being out of specification would be a:
    a. Bent tie rod
    b. Bent steering arm
    c. Loose center link
    d. Loose drag link

6

Power-Assisted Steering

OBJECTIVES

Upon completion and review of this chapter, you will be able to:

- Identify the fundamental laws of hydraulics and explain how they apply to the operation of automotive power steering.
- Identify the components of a power steering pump and explain how the pump operates.
- Identify the components of a non-rack and pinion steering gear and explain its operation.
- Identify the components of a rack and pinion steering gear and explain its operation.

KEY TERMS

check ball
control valve
electric power steering (EPS)
EPS motor
flow control valve
force
gear pump
Hydraulics
integral power steering system
integral reservoir
MAGNASTEER II®
magnetic rotary actuator
modulator valve
orifice
Pascal's Law
power-assisted steering
power piston
power steering control module (PSCM)
powertrain control module (PCM)

pressure
pressure hose
pressure relief valve
pressure switch
remote reservoir
return hose
roller pump
rotary control valve
sensor
serpentine belt
slipper pump
solenoid
spool control valve
spool valve
steering limit valve
steering wheel position sensor
torque sensor
V-belt
vane pump
variable-assist power steering system
variable effort steering (VES)

INTRODUCTION

Power-assisted steering hydraulically boosts the mechanical steering gear operation, so the driver can turn the steering wheel with less effort for the same response. Hydraulic power steering has been available since the 1950s, and many late-model systems are enhanced by electronic controls. Over the years, engineers have designed electronically controlled and operated power-assist systems, which eliminated hydraulics, but these have seen only limited production. This chapter begins by examining general hydraulic principles, continues with a study of hydraulic power steering systems and their components, then concludes with a discussion of electronic controls used with hydraulic systems.

POWER STEERING HYDRAULIC SYSTEMS

Hydraulics is the study of liquids and their use to transmit force and motion. The term "hydraulics" is derived from the Greek word "hydor," which means water. The principles that govern the behavior of water apply to all liquids. Several automotive systems use hydraulics, including automatic transmissions, brake systems, and power steering systems. While all hydraulic systems use liquids, the specific fluid each uses varies. Power steering systems use power steering fluid or, in some cases, automatic transmission fluid. Power steering fluid is discussed in Chapter 2 of this *Classroom Manual.*

Hydraulic Principles

Hydraulic systems transmit force and motion through the use of fluid pressure. **Force** is a push or pull acting on an object and is usually measured in pounds or newtons. **Pressure** is force applied to a specific area. Pressure is usually measured in force per unit of area, such as pounds per square inch (psi), or kilopascals (kPa). One psi is equal to 6.895 kPa.

The pascal is a unit of measure named after the French scientist Blaise Pascal (1623–1662), who studied the behavior of fluids in closed systems. One of his discoveries, known as **Pascal's Law,** was that pressure on a confined fluid is transmitted equally in all directions and acts with equal force on equal areas.

Hydraulic systems can transmit force and motion through liquids because, for all practical purposes, a liquid cannot be compressed. No matter how much pressure is placed on a liquid, its volume remains the same. This allows a liquid to transmit force much like a mechanical lever (Figure 6-1). The advantage of a liquid over a mechanical lever is that a liquid has volume but does not have a fixed shape. Because it assumes the shape of its container, a liquid can transfer force around obstacles or through pipes and passages of any shape. As explained by Pascal's Law, a liquid

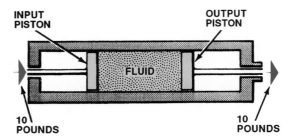

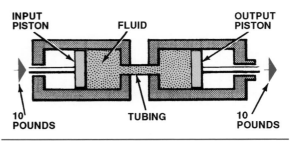

Figure 6-1. Hydraulic fluid transmits the same force whether it passes through a single chamber or two chambers joined by a narrow passage.

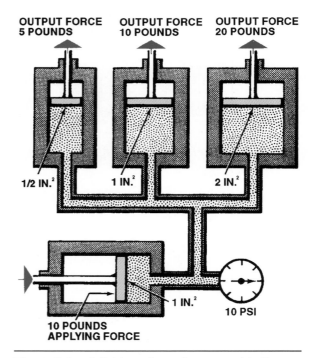

Figure 6-2. A fluid applies a force equal to the applied force on a surface that is equal in size to the applying surface. On a surface that is half the size of the applying surface, the fluid exerts half the force; on one twice as large, it exerts twice as much force.

can also decrease or increase the force it transmits depending on the area of the output surface to which the force is applied (Figure 6-2).

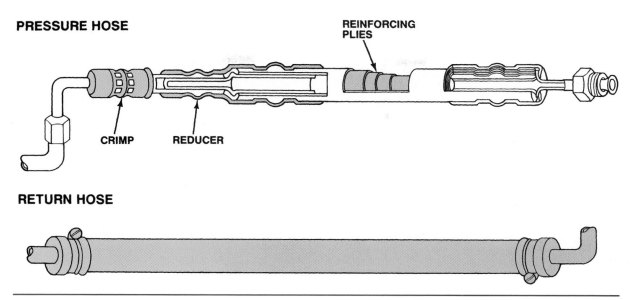

Figure 6-3. Both the pressure hose and the return hose are made of reinforced synthetic rubber, but the pressure hose is stronger and uses special fluid-tight fittings to withstand high pressures. Special fittings, called "reducers," may join hoses with different diameters.

In addition to its primary purpose of transmitting force, power steering fluid performs the secondary task of lubricating the gears and bearings inside the steering gear housing.

System Components

Hydraulically operated power steering systems use the following components:

- Hoses and fittings
- Pump and reservoir
- Power piston, or power cylinder
- Control valve

The hoses and fittings link the parts of a power steering system together. The pump pushes power steering fluid under pressure through the system, and the reservoir stores fluid until the pump draws it out. The pump and reservoir may be either one single assembly or two separate parts. Fluid pushed against the power piston in the steering gear provides the hydraulic assist that helps reposition the wheels. The control valve directs fluid to one side of the power piston or the other, depending on which way the steering wheel is turned.

There are two basic hydraulic power steering system designs: integral and linkage. On an integral power steering system the power piston and control valve are incorporated into the construction of the steering gear. On a linkage power

steering system the power cylinder, which is used in place of a power piston, and control valve are separate from the steering gear. Integral systems are more common, but linkage systems were used in some 1980 and older Ford models and on some early 1960s Chevrolet models.

Hoses and Fittings

All hydraulic systems use two types of power steering hose (Figure 6-3):

- Pressure hose
- Return hose

The **pressure hose** brings fluid from the pump to the steering gear, while the **return hose** routes fluid from the steering gear back to the reservoir. An additional suction hose is installed between the reservoir and pump on systems with a remote reservoir. Power steering hoses are made of reinforced synthetic rubber, but pressure hoses are of stronger construction to withstand the high fluid pressures produced by the power steering system.

The high pressure of fluid as it leaves the pump and assists in the steering gear creates high temperatures. The fluid in a power steering system may become as hot as 300°F (150°C). Some systems route the return fluid through a cooling circuit to reduce its temperature before it flows back into the reservoir. The cooling circuit is usually a simple set of pipes running behind the radiator.

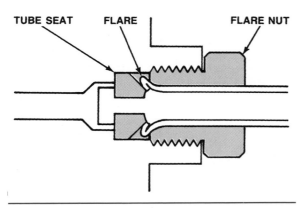

Figure 6-4. In a flared fitting, the flare nut pushes the flared end of the tube against the tube seat.

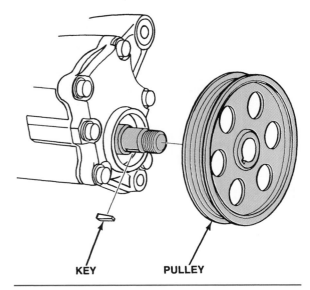

Figure 6-5. The pulley is keyed to the driveshaft on this power steering pump, a nut threads on the end of the shaft to hold the pulley in place.

However, some cooling circuits, such as that of the Chevrolet Corvette, use a separate, radiator-like cooler for the power steering system. Using a cooling circuit keeps the fluid from deteriorating and prolongs its service life.

Simple hose clamps can secure fittings to the ends of low-pressure return and suction hoses, but the fittings on a pressure hose are crimped to the hose to keep them secure in spite of the high pressure in the hose. The fittings in a power steering system are steel tubes with flares that connect them to the steering gear, pump, or reservoir (Figure 6-4).

POWER STEERING PUMP AND RESERVOIR

The power steering pump draws fluid from the reservoir, pressurizes it, and delivers it to the power steering system. A power steering pump produces a high-pressure stream of fluid, typically in the 1,500 psi (10,500 kPa) range. The fluid reservoir may be either integral to, or built into, the pump or remotely mounted and connected to the pump by a hose. There are several power steering pump designs, including:

- Vane
- Slipper
- Roller
- Gear

Design characteristics of vane, slipper, and roller pumps are similar, and they all operate on the same principles. A gear pump is a unique design that operates differently from the other three types. All four power steering pump designs are belt

driven by the engine crankshaft, and may use either an integral or remote fluid reservoir.

Pulley and Belt

A pulley on the front of the power steering pump is belt driven by the engine crankshaft. The pulley attaches to the pump driveshaft, which connects it to the operating parts inside the pump. Some pump pulleys are press-fit onto the shaft, while others use a key to prevent them from turning on the shaft (Figure 6-5). A large retaining nut or bolt secures a keyed pulley to the shaft.

The engine crankshaft runs a number of accessory pulleys and may be linked to them in one of two basic patterns (Figure 6-6). One way is to use one V-belt for every one or two accessories. The other way is to use a single **serpentine belt** for all the accessories. A **V-belt** is so called because its cross-sectional shape forms a "V." A serpentine belt, also known as a "V-ribbed" or "poly-V" belt, is so named because it snakes around all of the accessory pulleys. The bottom, or inner edge, of a V-belt may be either solid or notched, while a serpentine belt has a number of V-shaped ribs along its inner circumference (Figure 6-7).

Belt Tension
Correct drive belt tension is important for proper operation of the power steering system. If the belt linking the pump to the crankshaft is too tight, it places a severe load on the pump bearings that support the

V-BELTS

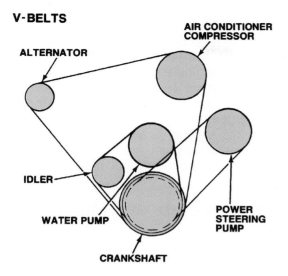

SERPENTINE BELT

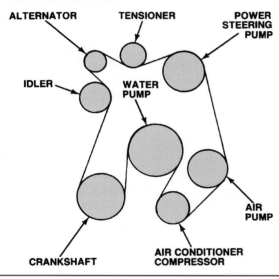

Figure 6-6. A V-belt drives one or two accessories off the crankshaft, while a serpentine belt is a single belt that powers all, or most, of the engine-driven accessories.

pulley shaft. A tight belt causes bearing failure and premature pump wear. If the belt is too loose, it slips and the pump may not operate efficiently.

Belt tension can be measured with a strand tension gauge, or estimated using a deflection test. Manufacturers provide belt tension specifications in pounds or kilograms, or in allowable inches or millimeters of deflection. Most serpentine-belt pulley systems have a belt tensioner that automatically keeps the belt properly tensioned. Adjustments to V-belt tension are generally made in one of two ways (Figure 6-8):

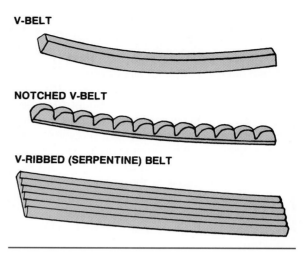

Figure 6-7. The inner edge of a V-belt may be either solid or notched; notches help to curve the belt around small pulleys. The number of ribs on a serpentine belt varies according to the number and types of accessories the belt drives.

MOVING AN IDLER PULLEY

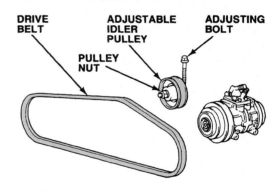

REPOSITIONING THE PUMP

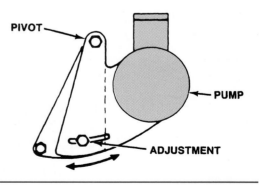

Figure 6-8. Typical methods of adjusting belt tension include moving an idler pulley or repositioning the pump.

- Moving an idler pulley
- Repositioning the pump

Both of these methods are described in detail in the *Shop Manual*.

Pump Installation

In order to align the pump pulley with the crankshaft pulley, the pump must be installed at the front of a longitudinally mounted engine or the side of a transverse engine. The pump bolts into support brackets on the engine (Figure 6-9). If belt tension is adjusted by repositioning the pump, the support brackets have slotted bolt holes, so that the pump can be moved inside the bracket for adjustment (Figure 6-10).

Pump Buildup and Operation

This section provides some general information about power steering fluid reservoirs and a detailed discussion on the construction of a vane pump and a gear pump. Roller and slipper pumps, which are virtually the same as a vane pump, are briefly discussed as well.

Power Steering Fluid Reservoirs

The power steering fluid reservoir is usually made of either plastic or stamped metal, and it includes the fluid filler neck, cap, and dipstick. It can be integral to or remote from the pump. An

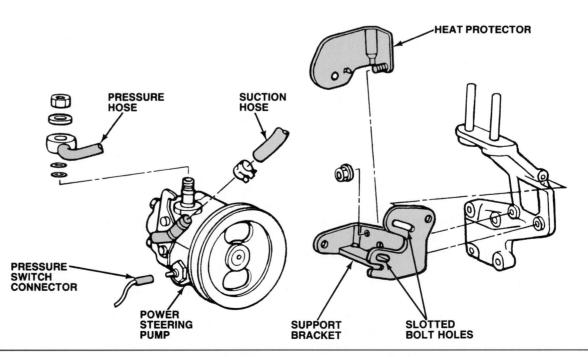

Figure 6-9.   A power steering pump installs into a bracket that bolts to the front of the engine.

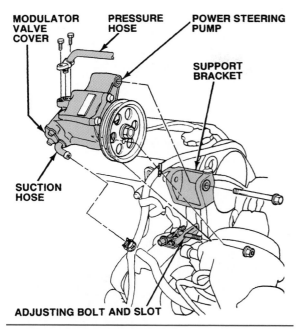

Figure 6-10. Slotted pump mounting holes on this support bracket allow the pump to swing back and forth in the bracket for drive belt adjustment.

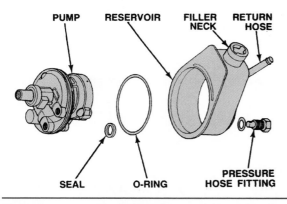

Figure 6-11. In this typical steering pump with an integral reservoir, the pump draws fluid directly from the reservoir in which it operates.

integral reservoir is part of the pump, and the pump itself operates submerged in power steering fluid (Figure 6-11). Although once common, steering pumps with an integral reservoir have given way to those with a remote reservoir on the majority of current production vehicles. This is because the remote reservoir allows for a smaller, more compact pump assembly that is better suited to the cramped engine compartment of a modern vehicle. The operation of the pump itself remains the same, no matter which type of reservoir it uses.

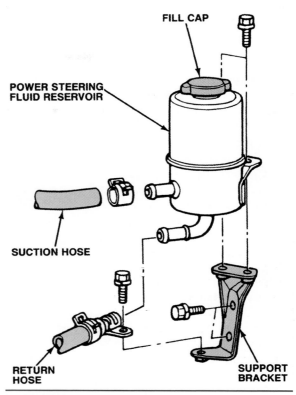

Figure 6-12. The pump draws fluid from this remote reservoir through the suction hose, and the return hose brings fluid back from the steering gear.

A **remote reservoir** is a separate assembly from the pump and provides fluid to it through a suction hose (Figure 6-12). The remote reservoir has become increasingly popular because it can fit more easily into the restricted engine compartment of a FWD vehicle. Since the reservoir need not be placed close to the pump, designers have more options in using the available engine compartment space.

Vane Pump

Although the details of **vane pump** assembly vary among manufacturers, all vane pumps operate the same. The DaimlerChrysler pump detailed here is a typical example of how a vane-type power steering pump operates (Figure 6-13).

The DaimlerChrysler pump can be broken down into three subassemblies:

- Pump body
- Cam case
- Pump cover

The pump body contains the fluid inlet and outlet ports, the modulator valve, and the pressure switch

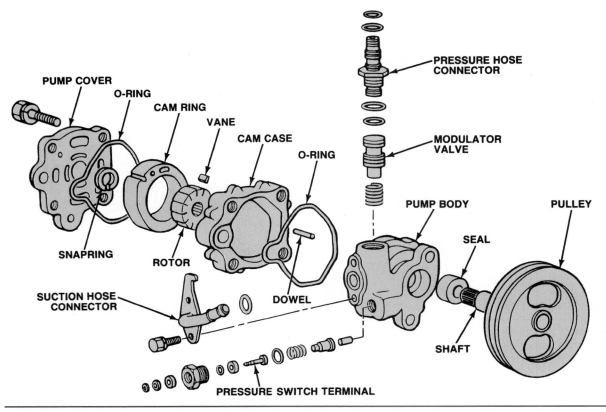

Figure 6-13. Exploded view of a DaimlerChrysler vane-type power steering pump.

terminal. In addition, the pulley shaft enters the pump through the pump body. The cam case houses the working parts of the pump, and the pump cover closes off the back of the pump. Two O-rings, one between the pump body and cam case and the other between the cam case and cover, prevent fluid leakage. There are three working parts in the cam case:

* Rotor
* Vanes
* Cam ring

Together, these parts draw fluid into the pump and deliver it to the power steering system under pressure.

Pump Body

The pulley is press-fit onto the pump shaft, and the pulley and shaft install into the pump body as a unit (Figure 6-14). A seal installs into the opening where the pulley shaft enters the pump body to keep fluid from leaking out of the pump.

A suction hose feeds fluid from a remote reservoir into the inlet port, which bolts onto the pump body (Figure 6-15). An O-ring seals the suction hose fitting to the pump body to prevent fluid

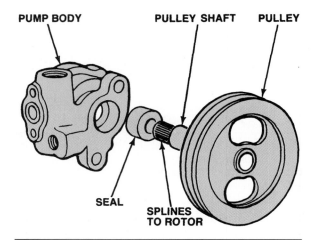

Figure 6-14. The pulley and shaft install as a unit into the pump body and a seal keeps fluid from leaking out of the pump at the pulley shaft opening.

leakage. Passages in the pump body bring the fluid from the inlet to the fluid chambers in the cam case, and other passages bring pressurized fluid from the fluid chambers to the outlet port.

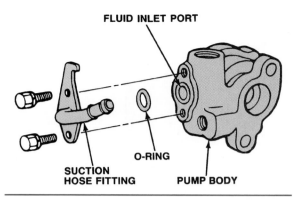

Figure 6-15. The fitting that connects the suction hose to the pump bolts to the pump body and seals with an O-ring.

The pressure hose connects to a fitting that threads into the outlet port of the pump body. A **modulator valve,** commonly called a **flow control valve,** installs in the same bore as the hose fitting (Figure 6-16). The modulator valve is a spring-loaded pressure-relief device that bleeds off excess pressure to prevent system damage. When pump output is more than the power steering system requires, the excess pressure overcomes spring force and moves the valve down in its bore. This uncovers an **orifice** through which the fluid can flow back into the inlet passages. An orifice is a small opening that regulates fluid pressure and flow. It can be a restriction in a fluid line or a hole between two fluid chambers. This particular opening is called a "variable orifice" because the size of the opening varies with the amount of pressure applied to the valve. When fluid pressure is not excessive, spring force keeps the valve seated so that all of the pressurized fluid flows through the outlet port and into the pressure hose.

Because the engine drives the pump, the power steering pump places a load on the engine whenever the engine is running. Under certain conditions, such as when the steering is turned to or near full stop for more than a few seconds, pressure builds in the system and the pump must work harder to keep up with the demand. As a result, the pump draws more power from the engine. If the engine is running at idle, the extra load can cause it to stall. A **pressure switch,** known as the power steering pressure (PSP) switch, transmits an electronic signal to the powertrain control module (PCM) when the pressure in the system is high enough to increase the load on the engine (Figure 6-17). In response to the PSP switch signal, the PCM increases the engine idle speed to prevent stalling. Some ve-

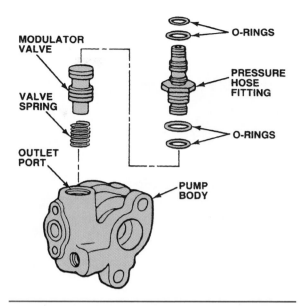

Figure 6-16. The modulator valve and the pressure hose fitting occupy the same bore in the pump body. The modulator valve is a pressure-relief device that keeps system pressure from becoming too high.

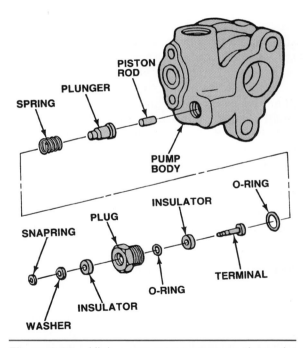

Figure 6-17. High pump output pressure closes the contacts in the power steering pump switch to transmit an electronic signal to the PCM; in response, the PCM increases engine rpm to prevent stalling.

hicles use a pressure relief valve, rather than a switch, to prevent stalling due to heavy pump loading. The relief valve bleeds off pressurized fluid to the pump inlet to reduce the load.

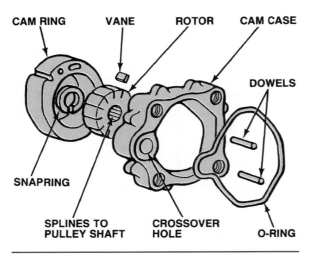

Figure 6-18. The cam case houses the rotor, vanes, and cam ring, which are the working parts of the pump. A snapring secures the rotor to the pulley shaft and dowels position the cam ring in the case.

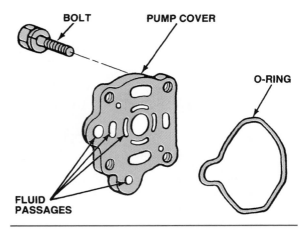

Figure 6-19. Passages in the pump cover route pressurized fluid to the insides of the vanes to hold their sealing edges tight against the cam ring.

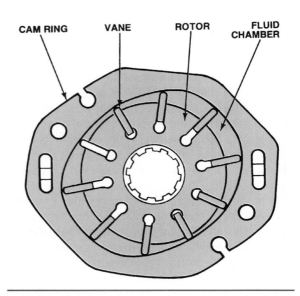

Figure 6-20. The vanes slide in and out of the rotor to create fluid chambers of varying sizes as the rotor spins inside the eccentric bore of the cam ring.

Cam Case and Pump Cover

The cam case, which bolts between the pump cover and pump body, houses the cam ring (Figure 6-18). The vanes install in the rotor, which installs and rotates in the center of the cam ring. A crossover passage in the case allows fluid to flow between the pump cover and pump body.

In addition to sealing the back of the pump, the pump cover contains fluid passages that bring a small amount of pressurized fluid from the fluid chambers to the inside of the vane slots in the rotor (Figure 6-19). Because this force acts on the underside of the vanes, it is sometimes referred to as "under-vane pressure." This under-vane pressure forces the vanes out against the cam ring to form a more positive seal. Excess fluid from the pump cover is routed back into the pump body.

Rotor, Vanes, and Cam Ring

The rotor, vanes, and cam ring, which are the working parts of the pump, operate virtually the same in every vane-type pump (Figure 6-20). The pulley shaft extends through the pump body and splines to the inside of the rotor. The outside of the rotor has slots into which the thin, rectangular vanes fit. The outer edges of the vanes are slightly rounded, or chamfered, to avoid scraping the surface of the cam ring where they make contact. The cam ring fits inside the cam case and is held in a stationary position on the pump body by dowels. The internal bore of the cam ring is an eccentric that allows the vanes to create variable-sized fluid chambers.

As the pulley shaft spins the rotor inside the cam ring, centrifugal force and under-vane fluid pressure force the edges of the vanes against the inner surface of the cam ring. The outside of the rotor, the inside of the cam ring, and the vanes create a number of enclosed spaces that act as fluid chambers. Because the inside of the cam ring is eccentric, not circular, each fluid chamber changes size as the rotor spins and the vanes slide in and out of their slots to maintain contact with the cam ring. This change in chamber size is the key to pump operation.

When the size of a fluid chamber increases, something has to fill the space. Therefore, as the volume of the fluid chamber increases, the pressure of the fluid decreases to form a low-pressure area. The low-pressure area draws power steering fluid into the chamber from the pump body, as the rotor continues to turn and the chamber gets smaller. Since there is nowhere for the fluid to escape, the same amount of fluid must be contained in the smaller area and fluid pressure increases as a result. By the time the chamber reaches the outlet port passages in the pump body the chamber is at its smallest and the fluid is highly pressurized. The outlet port passages route the pressurized fluid through the modulator valve and fitting into the pressure hose. As this happens to one chamber after another in rapid succession, the pump provides a constant stream of pressurized fluid to the system.

The fact that the cam ring has two lobes, opposite each other, means that whenever the pump is running, the process of fluid intake and output occurs simultaneously on both sides of the rotor. The fluid passages in the pump body bring intake fluid from the pump inlet to two sections of the rotor and take pressurized fluid from the two sections to the pump outlet. This cam ring design maintains equal pressure on both sides of the rotor to keep the rotor centered in the cam ring.

Roller Pump and Slipper Pump

Roller pumps and slipper pumps both operate according to the same principles as a vane pump. However, instead of vanes, a **roller pump** uses rollers while a **slipper pump** uses spring-loaded slippers to pressurize the fluid (Figure 6-21). Roller pumps are used infrequently, but a number of Ford vehicles use a slipper-type pump.

Gear Pump

The **gear pump** used on certain Honda and Acura models is a relatively uncommon design for a power steering pump (Figure 6-22). Three parts make up the pump housing:

- Pump cover
- Pump body
- Port housing

The pump cover seals the end of the pump while allowing an opening for the pulley shaft, which operates two gears inside the pump body. The action of the two gears draws fluid into the pump and forces it out into the power steering system under pressure. The port housing contains the fluid inlet and outlet ports, the modulator valve, and the pressure relief valve.

Mechanical Power Steering

Modern power steering systems operate hydraulically, but occasionally a designer has tried to buck the trend. One of these unsung individualists developed the Studebaker Mechanical Power Steering as an option for the top-of-the-line 1953 Commander and Land Cruiser models.

The Studebaker system used three main components: a power steering unit that mounted on the conventional steering gear, a pulley and bracket assembly that bolted to the front of the engine, and a short, exposed drive shaft that connected the two together. The belt-driven pulley turned the shaft, which transmitted power from the crankshaft pulley to the power steering unit.

Inside the power unit, two ring gears constantly revolved in opposite directions at one-quarter crankshaft speed. Each ring gear assembly had a multiple-disc clutch pack. When the driver turned the steering wheel to the left, the upper clutch pack engaged its ring gear and transmitted power to the conventional steering

gear to turn the linkage to the left. When the wheel was turned to the right, the lower clutch pack engaged its ring gear and applied force to rotate the steering gear in the opposite direction and turn the wheels to the right.

The clutches were spring-loaded, so they did not contact the spinning ring gears unless the driver applied a force of two pounds to the steering wheel rim. Because the steering gear and linkage were otherwise conventional, a power steering failure simply returned the car to non-assisted steering.

Mechanical power steering impressed the Studebaker marketing staff enough that they advertised it early in the model year. However, the unit never made it into production. While the idea was novel and elegantly designed, the $134 price was considerable in 1953 and the more affordable ordinary hydraulic power steering was offered instead.

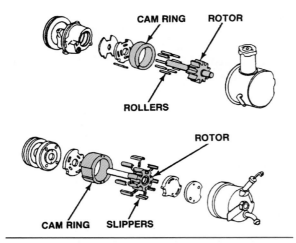

Figure 6-21. A roller pump and slipper pump work according to the same principles as a vane pump.

Pump Cover

The pump cover bolts to the pump body to enclose and secure the internal components (Figure 6-23). The pulley shaft extends through a seal in the pump cover, and a nut secures the pulley to the shaft. The underside of the pump cover has two seals. One is the plunger seal, which seals the tops of the gear plungers in the pump body. The other is an O-ring that seals the pump cover and body together.

Pump Body

The port housing routes fluid into the pump body where the two gears mesh (Figure 6-24). The drive gear is part of the pulley shaft, which forms its axis. The drive gear meshes with and powers the driven gear (Figure 6-25). Fluid enters the pump body through a port housing inlet where

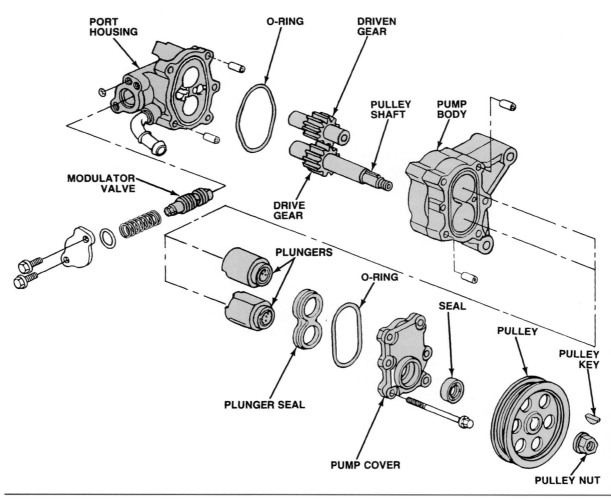

Figure 6-22. This Honda gear pump uses two gears inside cylindrical chambers instead of a rotor, vanes, and a cam ring.

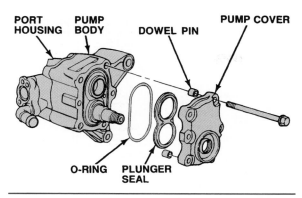

Figure 6-23. The port housing, pump body, and pump cover bolt together to encase the gear pump.

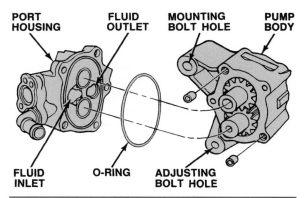

Figure 6-24. The pump inlet and outlet ports are in the port housing, while gears are in the pump body.

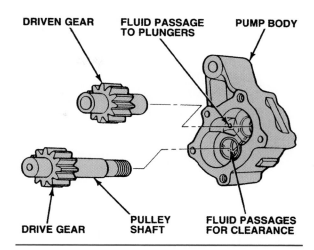

Figure 6-25. The drive gear turns the driven gear, and the action of the gear teeth draws in, pressurizes, and pumps out fluid.

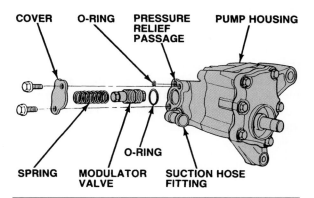

Figure 6-26. The suction hose fitting connects the pump to the reservoir and the modulator valve modulates the pressure leaving the pump.

the mesh of the gear teeth opens up as the gears rotate. As the gear mesh opens, a low-pressure area is created, just as the fluid chambers in a vane pump do, to draw fluid into the pump body. The ends of the rotating gear teeth contact the internal bore of the pump body, which traps and seals off a small amount of fluid. The teeth push this fluid around the inside of the housing to the point where the gears again begin to mesh. As the teeth mesh, they squeeze the fluid between them to pressurize it, then expel the pressurized fluid through passages in the port housing. From here, the stream of pressurized fluid is routed through the outlet port and into the pressure hose.

Between the gears and the pump cover, one plunger fits onto the pulley shaft and another one onto the driven gear shaft. These plungers are notched and fit together to keep them from rotating with the shafts. However, the plungers can move axially, up and down, on the shaft. A fluid passage in the pump body allows pressurized fluid to flow behind the plungers, which also contain fluid passages. The plunger fluid passages route

fluid between the plungers and the gear shafts in order to reduce friction and maintain clearance between them. A plunger seal, located between the tops of the plungers and the pump cover, prevents fluid leakage. The fluid in the plungers flows down to the bottom of the plungers, where it maintains clearance between the plungers and the gears. As the gears expand from the heat of operation, the oil maintains this clearance by pushing the plungers up on the gear shafts.

Port Housing
Passages inside the port housing allow fluid to flow from the inlet to the pump gears and from the gears to the outlet. A fitting attaches the suction hose from the remote power steering reservoir to the port housing inlet (Figure 6-26). The pressure hose and fitting bolt onto the housing outlet.

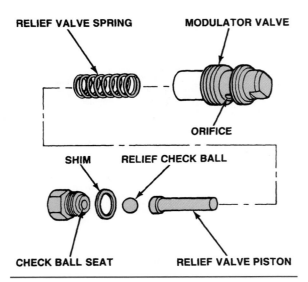

Figure 6-27. The pressure relief valve piston, inside the modulator valve, actuates when the modulator valve reaches the limit of its travel.

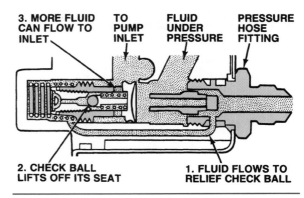

Figure 6-28. A pressure relief valve, rather than a PSP switch, keeps the pump from lugging down the engine.

The fluid passages in the housing also lead to the modulator valve bore, which installs behind a cover plate and seals with an O-ring. This valve bleeds off excessive fluid pressure to prevent power steering system damage. The modulator valve assembly includes:

- An O-ring
- A relief spring
- A valve

The O-ring installs at the top of the bore to prevent leaks at the cover. The spring seats the valve until fluid pressure in the outlet passage becomes high enough to overcome spring force and move the valve in its bore. Valve movement opens a variable orifice through which fluid flows back into the pump inlet passage.

On occasion, pressure may become too high even for the modulator valve to regulate it. This usually happens when the steering wheel is turned to its full stop in either direction. To handle the excess pressure, a pressure relief passage runs from a point near the pressure hose fitting to the spring end of the modulator valve. Inside the passage is a **pressure relief valve.** The spring end of the modulator valve forms a seat for the pressure relief **check ball.** Under normal circumstances, the check ball remains seated. The parts of the pressure relief valve (Figure 6-27), are the:

- Spring
- Valve piston
- Check ball
- Seat

A shim installs on the check ball seat to adjust the pressure, at which the check ball unseats to open the pressure relief valve. Normally, the spring force holds the piston against the check ball to keep it in its seat. When pressure becomes excessive in the pressure relief passage, the check ball rises off its seat to allow fluid to flow through the relief passage and out through an orifice in the modulator valve (Figure 6-28). As a result, pressure at the pressure hose fitting is reduced. When power steering systems are pushed to the limit, most will make a chattering or squealing noise until the pressure is reduced.

INTEGRAL POWER STEERING

In an **integral power steering system,** the control valve and the power piston are incorporated into the steering gear construction. Today, this is the only type of power steering system in production. The **control valve** regulates the application of pressurized fluid against the **power piston,** and the power piston helps move the output member of the steering gear when pressure is applied to one side of it. Whether used on a standard steering gear or a rack and pinion steering gear, there are only two types of control valve:

- Spool valve
- Rotary valve

On a standard steering gear, the ball nut is adapted to function as the power piston. The piston is a separate part that is added to the construction of the gearbox rack on a power rack and pinion steering gear. For descriptions of the parts and operating

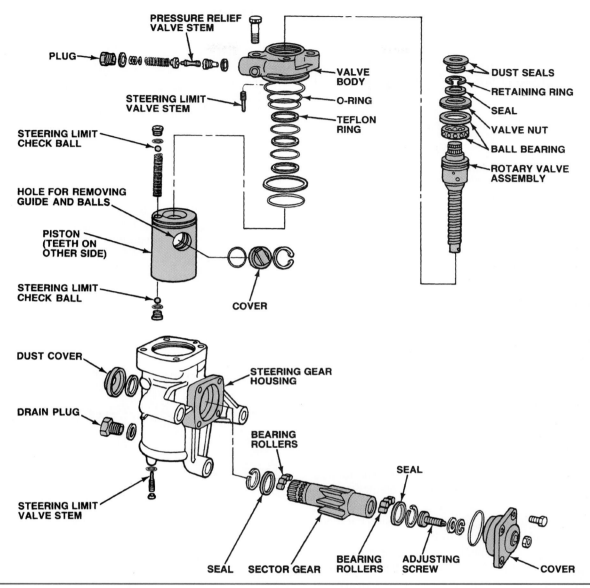

Figure 6-29. This integral standard steering gear with a rotary control valve has all the elements of a manual steering gear—the gear housing, worm gear, ball nut, and sector gear—plus added parts to allow for hydraulic assist.

principles of standard and rack and pinion steering gears, see Chapter 4 of this *Classroom Manual.*

Integral Standard Steering Gear

Most standard steering gears with power assist are the recirculating ball type, and the ball nut functions as the power piston. Hydraulic pressure from the steering gear control valve is applied directly against the ball nut to help it move through the housing. The ball nut in this type of power steering gear is called the "power piston" because hydraulic pressure moves it as if it were a piston traveling in a cylinder.

Rotary Control Valve

A **rotary control valve** is a two-piece assembly that operates by rotating an inner valve within an outer valve. A steering gear with a rotary control valve is also called a "torsion bar steering gear" because a small torsion bar is used to control valve movement. The steering gear used on heavy-duty Ford trucks serves as an example of a unit that uses a rotary control valve (Figure 6-29).

The rotary control valve consists of two cylindrical elements: the inner valve element and outer valve element. The inner valve element is secured to the steering gear input shaft and the torsion bar. In the Ford valve, the inner element and the input

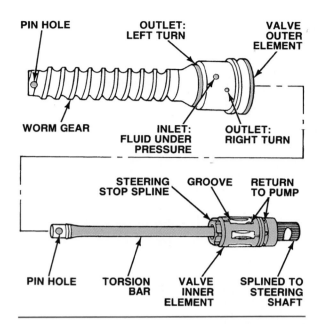

Figure 6-30. The rotary valve consists of inner and outer elements. The worm gear is part of the outer element, and the torsion bar is part of the inner element. A pin attaches the worm gear to the bottom of the torsion bar to join the two elements together.

shaft are one piece, and the torsion bar attaches to them (Figure 6-30). The inner element assembly fits inside the outer valve element, and is also secured to the torsion bar by a pin. The outer valve element is also the steering worm gear. The torsion bar acts as a spring between the two elements to allow movement between them when the steering shaft turns. The spring force of the torsion bar tends to pull the elements back to their neutral positions when the steering wheel is released or returned to center. The strength of the torsion bar determines steering feel. A weak torsion bar moves easily and provides soft steering, while a strong bar resists movement and makes steering feel firm.

The facing surfaces of the inner and outer elements have grooves machined into them through which fluid can flow. Passages carry fluid from some of the inner element grooves to the center of the element, where it travels through the return line to the pump reservoir. The outer element has three sets of fluid passages that connect the outside of the element to a groove at the inside. One set of passages carries fluid into the element from the pressure hose fitting, the second set carries fluid to and from the left-turn side of the power piston, and the third to and from the right-turn side.

When the steering wheel is aimed straight-ahead, the valve is in its neutral position. Fluid enters the

STRAIGHT-AHEAD

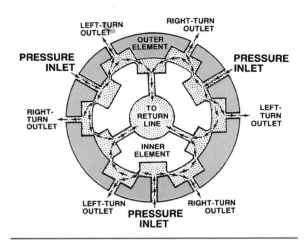

Figure 6-31. When the steering wheel is straight-ahead, all the ports in a rotary control valve are open equally to the pressure and return circuits.

LEFT TURN

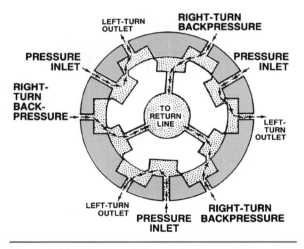

Figure 6-32. During a left turn, the inner element turns so that only the left-turn outlets are open to pressure and the right-turn outlets are open to the return circuit.

valve and flows equally to both sides of the steering gear piston and to the return line (Figure 6-31).

When the steering wheel and steering shaft turn to the left, the inner element twists on the torsion bar and repositions the valve ports. In this left-turn position, pressurized fluid flowing into the valve can only exit through the left-turn ports (Figure 6-32). Meanwhile, the right-turn ports align with the return-line ports to bleed off residual pressure from the opposite side of the power piston. Pressurized fluid flowing through the left-turn ports is directed

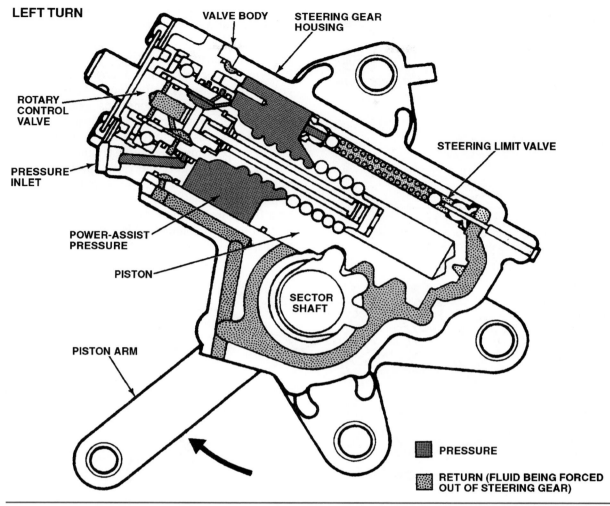

LEFT TURN

VALVE BODY

STEERING GEAR HOUSING

ROTARY CONTROL VALVE

STEERING LIMIT VALVE

PRESSURE INLET

POWER-ASSIST PRESSURE

PISTON

SECTOR SHAFT

PISTON ARM

■ PRESSURE

▦ RETURN (FLUID BEING FORCED OUT OF STEERING GEAR)

Figure 6-33. The high-pressure fluid helps to push the piston along the worm gear, which reduces the manual effort needed to move the sector shaft and pitman arm to effect a left turn through the steering linkage.

into the steering gear where it applies force to the power piston and reduces the effort needed to turn the steering linkage to the left (Figure 6-33). As the piston moves, it forces fluid out of the right-turn side, and that fluid returns through the control valve to the pump reservoir. Exactly the opposite flow occurs during a right-hand turn: The right-turn ports are opened and the left-turn ports exhaust to the return line (Figure 6-34). Hydraulic pressure moves the piston up the housing bore during a right-hand turn (Figure 6-35).

When the steering wheel is released, the spring force of the torsion bar returns the two elements to their neutral positions. Fluid pressure equalizes throughout the steering gear and re-centers the piston in the middle of the steering gear.

Steering Limit Valve

This Ford steering gear uses a **steering limit valve** to reduce power assist as the steering wheel is turned farther toward its complete stop. The steering limit valve bore is in the steering gear piston. A check ball is seated at each end of the bore and a spring is placed between the two check balls. Two valve stems line up with holes in the ball seats. One stem is anchored in the valve body and the other mounts in the steering gear housing. When the piston is in its neutral position, neither stem enters the valve. As the piston moves to the extreme of either direction, it pushes the steering limit valve onto one of the valve stems to unseat the check ball. This allows fluid to pass through the valve from the pressure side to the return side,

RIGHT TURN

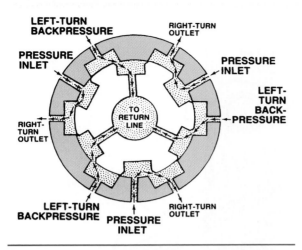

Figure 6-34. During a right turn, the inner element turns so that only the right-turn outlets are open to pressure and the left-turn outlets are open to the return circuit.

which reduces the amount of pressure on the piston and limits power assist.

Pressure Relief Valve

Like power steering pumps, many power steering gears have pressure relief valves. The relief valve on the Ford rotary valve steering gear is located near the inlet on the same valve body as the control valve. A fluid passage runs from the pressure inlet port to the pressure relief valve (Figure 6-36). Under normal conditions, the valve spring holds the relief valve closed. If fluid pressure increases to a point that exceeds spring force, the valve opens to vent fluid through the valve from the pressure inlet to the return channel. This lowers the pressure until spring force can close the valve again.

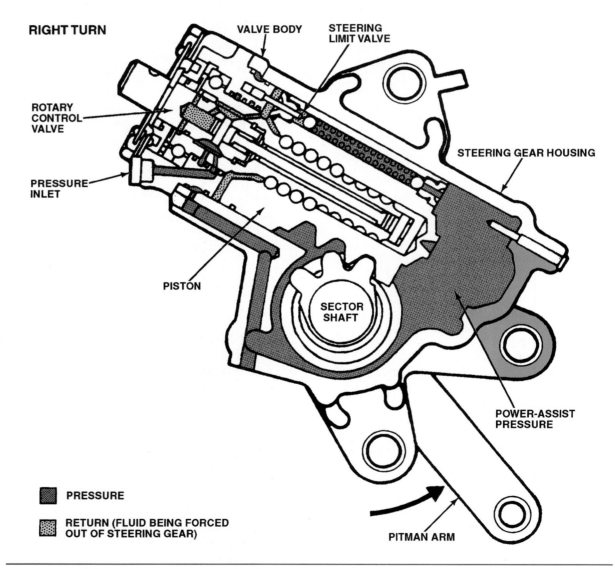

Figure 6-35. The high-pressure fluid pushes the piston up the worm gear, moving the sector shaft and pitman arm to provide assist during a right turn.

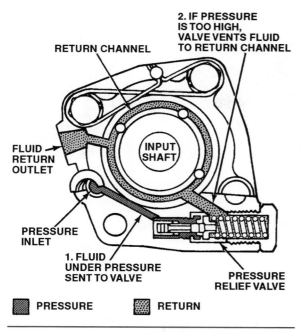

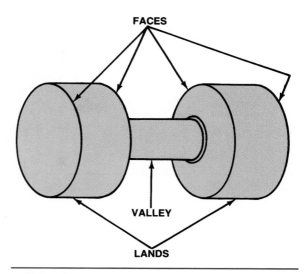

Figure 6-37. A spool valve moves in a machined bore when fluid pressure or spring force is applied to one of the valve faces.

Figure 6-36. If fluid pressure coming into the steering gear becomes high enough to move the pressure relief valve, some fluid is directed to the return channel to lower pressure in the steering gear.

This pressure relief valve is not a back-up device in case the relief valve in the pump fails. It is set to open at a lower pressure than the pump relief valve, so it activates before the pump valve. This relief valve keeps pressure in the steering gear below a predetermined maximum.

Spool Control Valve

Some steering gears use a **spool control valve,** rather than a rotary valve, to regulate pressure. A **spool valve,** so named because it looks somewhat like a spool for thread, acts as a hydraulic piston when it slides back and forth in a machined bore (Figure 6-37). The sections of the valve that contact the sides of the bore are called "lands," and the surfaces that fluid pressure act upon are called "faces." The machined slots that leave an open space between the faces are called "valleys."

The spool valve power steering gear featured in the following discussion is a DaimlerChrysler unit used on rear-wheel-drive vans. The valve body containing the control valve bolts to the steering gear housing. The valve body contains the:

- Control valve
- Fluid pressure inlet
- Return fluid outlet
- Pressure relief valve

Three valleys are machined into the spool valve for directing fluid flow (Figure 6-38). The center valley is under the fluid pressure inlet, which is at the top of the valve body. The return outlet is at the end of the valve body, and the pressure relief piston is inside the outlet passage. O-rings seal the valve body passages to prevent leaks wherever two parts join together.

Depending on valve position, pressurized fluid can flow through the center valley of the control valve and into one of two fluid passages in the steering gear body. One passage is open during a left turn and the other is open when the steering wheel is turned to the right. A pivot lever extending from the input shaft thrust bearing to a notch in the control valve determines valve position. As the thrust bearing moves, it moves the lower end of the lever as well. This causes the lever to pivot so that the opposite end repositions the control valve. The distance from the lever pivot to the control valve is about four times greater than the distance from the pivot to the bearing, and valve movement is about four times that of thrust bearing movement as well.

Turning the steering wheel causes the thrust bearing to move forward or backward, as the steering shaft threads into or out of the thrust bearing. With the steering wheel aimed straight-ahead, the thrust bearing is centered so that the pivot lever is upright. In this position, the control valve directs pressurized fluid equally to each side of the steering gear piston, and through the outlet to the reservoir.

When the steering wheel is turned to the left, the input shaft threads into the thrust bearing, which pushes the bearing forward (Figure 6-39). As the thrust bearing moves, it pulls the bottom of

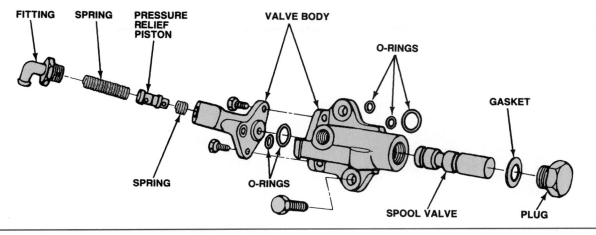

Figure 6-38. An exploded view of this DaimlerChrysler control valve body shows the three valleys machined on the spool valve and the pressure relief piston that assembles in the outlet fluid fitting.

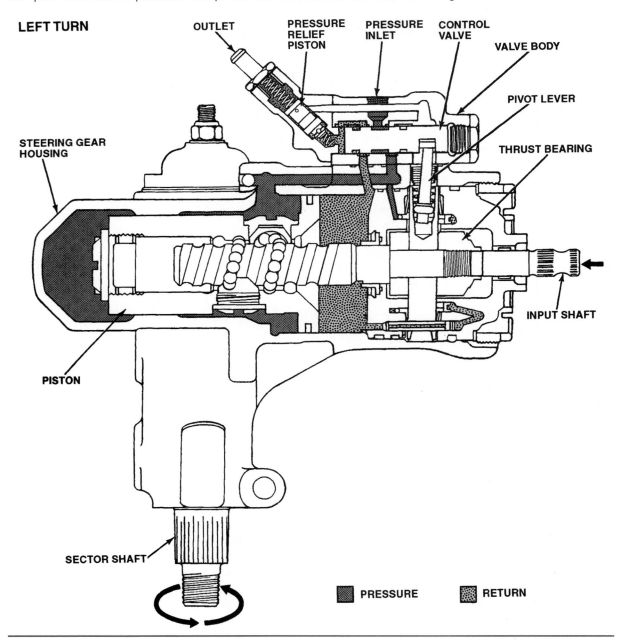

Figure 6-39. During a left turn, the spool valve routes fluid to the left-turn side of the power piston to provide hydraulic assist.

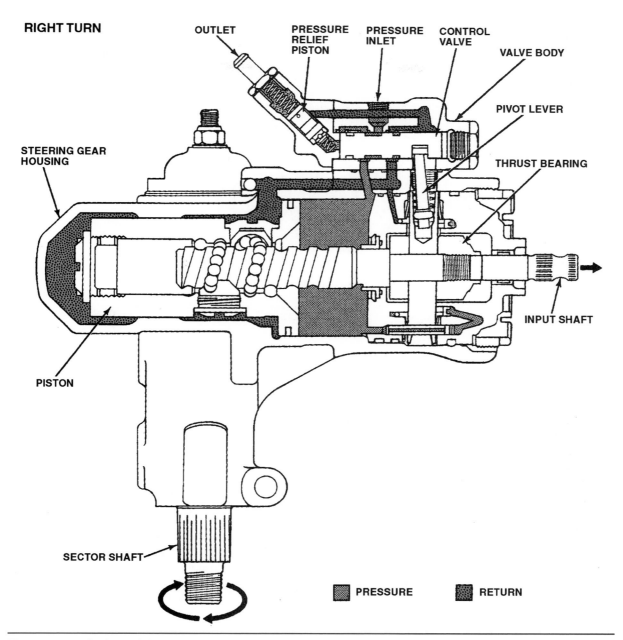

RIGHT TURN

OUTLET

PRESSURE RELIEF PISTON

PRESSURE INLET

CONTROL VALVE

VALVE BODY

PIVOT LEVER

STEERING GEAR HOUSING

THRUST BEARING

INPUT SHAFT

PISTON

SECTOR SHAFT

PRESSURE RETURN

Figure 6-40. During a right turn, the spool valve routes fluid to the right-turn side of the power piston to help move the piston down the worm gear.

the pivot lever along with it causing the control valve to move in its bore in the opposite direction. In this position, the valve channels pressurized fluid to the front of the piston, where it assists in moving the piston up the worm shaft. As the piston moves up the worm shaft, the sector shaft pivots to turn the steering linkage to the left. The piston forces any fluid behind it through exhaust passages leading to the outlet. During a right-hand turn, the steering gear component actions are the same, but in the opposite direction (Figure 6-40).

Integral Rack and Pinion Steering Gear

Although a few rack and pinion power steering gears, such as those used on certain Honda and Acura models, use a spool control valve to direct hydraulic fluid flow, most use a rotary control valve. The majority of power rack and pinion steering gears with a rotary control valve are similar in design and operation to the Ford unit described in the following text.

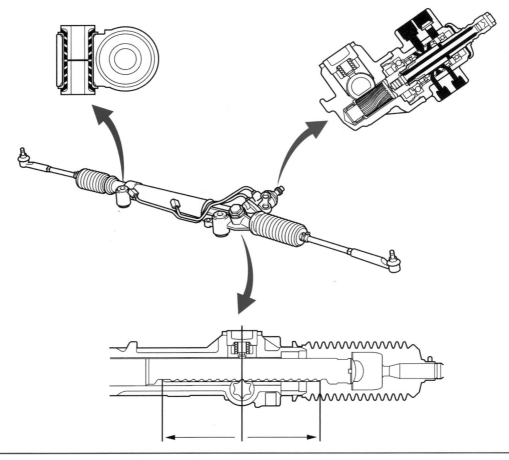

Figure 6-41.   Rack and pinion steering gear. (Provided courtesy of Toyota Motor Sales U.S.A., Inc.)

Rotary Control Valve

The steering gear used on the Toyota Camry is typical of those with a rotary control valve (Figure 6-41). The rotary control valve is located between the steering gear input shaft and the pinion gear (Figure 6-42). Fluid discharged by the valve travels through external steel lines to either side of the power piston. A steel air-transfer tube allows air displacement between the boots as they compress and expand, since the power piston prevents air from passing through the rack housing. The rotary valve in this rack and pinion gearbox operates in the same manner as the one previously described for a standard steering gear. During a left-hand turn, the control valve directs fluid flow into the left-turn steel line, which routes it to the right-hand side of the power piston in order to move the rack to the left (Figure 6-43). As this happens, fluid on the opposite side of the power piston is forced out through the right-turn steel line and back to the control valve where it is exhausted to the return circuit. When the steering wheel is turned to the right, fluid flow is reversed so the power piston moves to the right and fluid in the left-turn chamber is exhausted to the return circuit (Figure 6-44).

Spool Control Valve

The Honda Accord power rack and pinion steering gear serves as an example of a system with a spool control valve (Figure 6-45). The control valve is in a valve body located underneath the steering gear housing, and the power piston is built onto the rack. A pin links the pinion holder and the control valve to transfer pinion movement to the valve, and the valve directs pressurized fluid to the appropriate side of the piston (Figure 6-46). The pinion holder surrounds and moves with the pinion. However, the pin is not concentric with the pinion gear. The pin is located at the

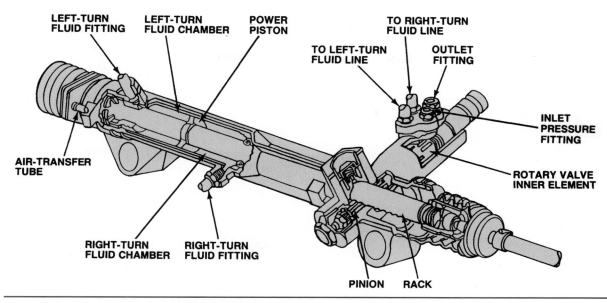

Figure 6-42. The power piston is built into the rack, with a fluid chamber on either side of it. Pressurized fluid from the rotary control valve flows through one of the external fluid lines, not shown, into the appropriate fluid chamber where it pushes the power piston to assist in moving the rack.

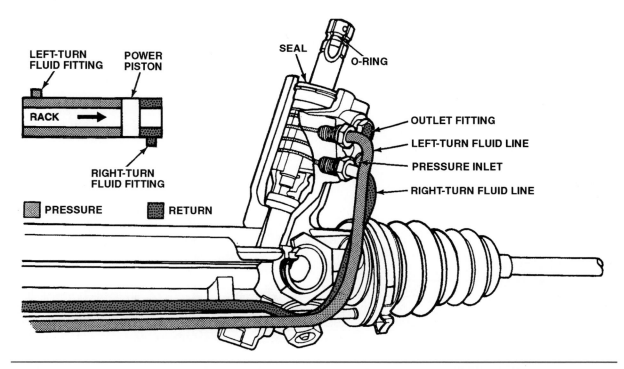

Figure 6-43. During a left turn, the control valve directs pressure into the left-turn fluid line and the rack moves left (inset), with the pressure at the piston assisting. Fluid pushed out of the right-turn fluid chamber travels back through the right-turn fluid line and control valve to the return circuit.

edge of the pinion holder farthest from the pinion center. As the pinion rotates to move the rack, the pinion holder rotates slightly with it, which causes the pin and the control valve to move

slightly as well. Two stops in the steering gear housing limit the amount that the pinion holder can rotate, and consequently limit the amount of valve movement. Movement of the control valve

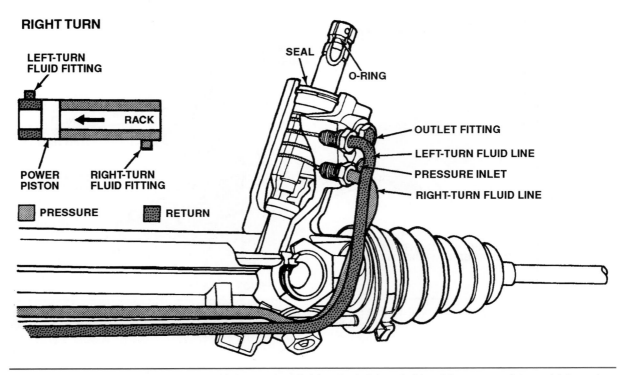

RIGHT TURN

LEFT-TURN
FLUID FITTING

RACK

SEAL

O-RING

POWER
PISTON

RIGHT-TURN
FLUID FITTING

OUTLET FITTING

LEFT-TURN FLUID LINE

PRESSURE INLET

RIGHT-TURN FLUID LINE

PRESSURE   RETURN

Figure 6-44. The control valve routes high-pressure fluid to the left-hand side of the power piston, which pushes the piston and assists in moving the rack toward the right when the steering wheel is turned right.

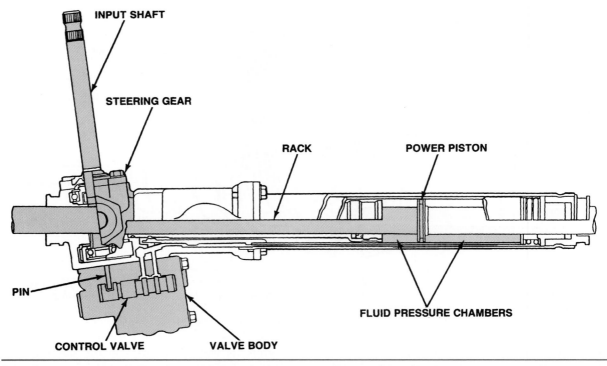

INPUT SHAFT

STEERING GEAR

RACK

POWER PISTON

PIN

CONTROL VALVE

VALVE BODY

FLUID PRESSURE CHAMBERS

Figure 6-45. In this Honda power rack and pinion steering gear, the spool control valve is in a separate valve body and the fluid lines to the power piston fluid chambers are inside the steering gear housing.

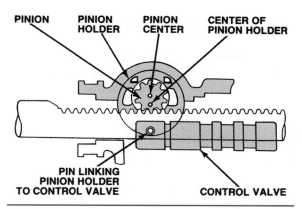

Figure 6-46. The pinion holder moves slightly as the pinion rotates and a pin that extends from the pinion holder to the control valve moves the valve in response to pinion movement.

LEFT TURN

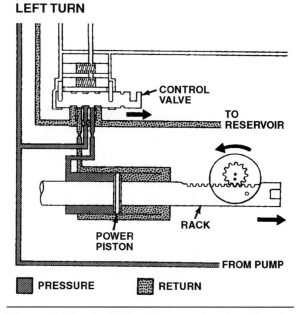

Figure 6-47. During a left turn, the control valve moves to direct pressurized fluid to the left side of the power piston to assist in moving the rack.

opens passages that direct pressurized fluid to either the right or left side of the power piston and allow fluid on the opposite side of the piston to return to the reservoir (Figure 6-47). Turning the steering wheel in the opposite direction reverses the flow of pressurized fluid (Figure 6-48).

At the limits of steering wheel movement, the hydraulic assist is cut off. When the pinion comes to the end of the rack, it "walks" up the end of the rack and repositions the pinion holder (Figure 6-49). This also repositions the pin, which allows the control

RIGHT TURN

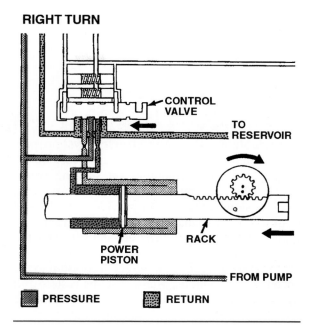

Figure 6-48. The steering arms extend toward the rear of the chassis, so in this steering gear, as in most rack and pinion units, the rack moves left in order to turn the wheels right.

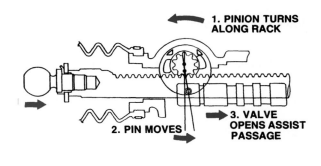

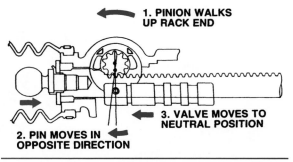

Figure 6-49. The pinion holder usually turns only slightly before being held against its stops. As the pinion climbs the end of the rack, it lifts the pinion holder along with it to return the pin and control valve to their neutral positions.

valve to move back to its neutral position where it sends equal pressure to both sides of the piston.

VARIABLE-ASSIST POWER STEERING

A **variable-assist power steering system** provides different levels of power assist based on vehicle speed, and sometimes on steering wheel angle. When the engine is idling or the vehicle is moving slowly, the system provides a high level of power assist to make sharp cornering easier. At higher speeds, sharp turns are unusual and too much assist detracts from road feel. Therefore, the power assist is reduced in direct proportion to the speed of the vehicle. Many systems restore full assist at any speed if the driver quickly turns the steering wheel, as in an emergency maneuver.

There are two basic types of variable-assist power steering:

- Hydraulically controlled
- Electronically controlled

Both are designed around a conventional power steering hydraulic system that includes the following components:

- Reservoir
- Pump, with modulator and pressure relief valves

- Control valve
- Power piston

Additionally, these systems use hydraulic or electronic components to regulate hydraulic pressure and provide the variable assist.

Hydraulically Controlled Systems

The variable-assist power steering of the Acura Integra serves as an example of a hydraulically controlled system in the following discussion (Figure 6-50). A typical design, this system uses a "speed sensor," which is actually a fluid pump, to provide hydraulic pressure that varies in response to speed (Figure 6-51). In addition to the conventional power steering components described earlier in this chapter, the Acura hydraulic system uses the following devices to vary the level of hydraulic assist:

- Pressure control valve
- Speed sensor orifice
- Speed sensor, with one-way and relief valves
- Gain control valve
- Reaction chambers

The pressure control valve, gain control valve, reaction chambers, and speed sensor orifice are located in the valve body along with the conventional

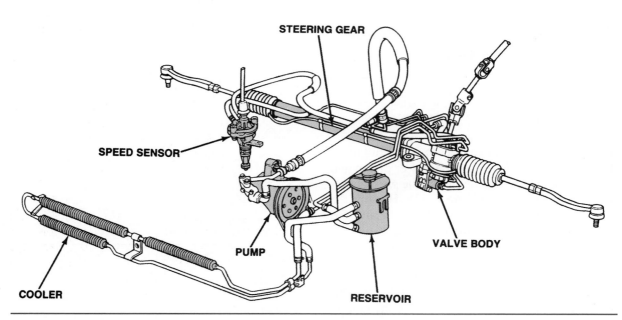

Figure 6-50. The variable-assist power steering system of the Acura Integra uses hydraulic controls to regulate boost pressure.

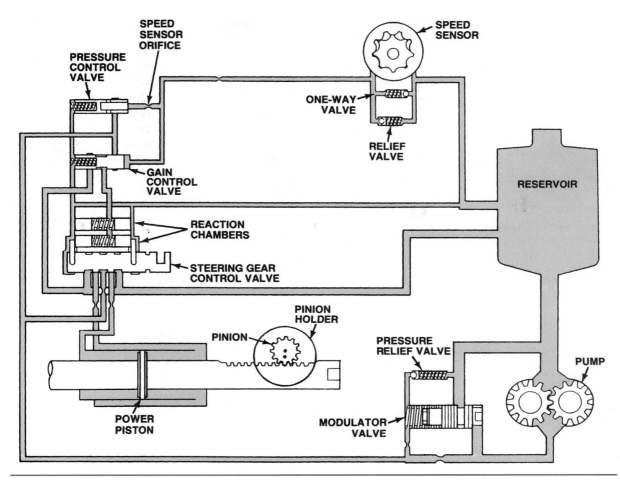

Figure 6-51. The speed sensor is a fluid pump that regulates pressure in the passages downstream of the speed sensor orifice to position the gain control valve.

steering gear control valve (Figure 6-52). The valve body assembly attaches to the bottom of the steering gear. The speed sensor is a separate assembly that installs on the transaxle case and is driven off the differential by the speedometer gear. Two check-ball valves, a one-way valve and a relief valve, assemble in the speed sensor to prevent excess pressure buildup (Figure 6-53).

Pressure Control Valve and Speed Sensor Orifice

The pressure control valve modulates pressure received from the pump and sends a constant pressure through the speed sensor orifice to the speed sensor (Figure 6-54). Everything downstream of the sensor orifice, which includes the gain control valve, is affected by the pressure changes generated by the speed sensor.

Speed Sensor

Although the name "sensor" makes it sound like an electronic component, the speed sensor is actu-

ally a rotor-type hydraulic pump. A rotor pump consists of an inner rotor, the drive member, whose lobes are in mesh with the lobes of the outer rotor, and the driven member. The inner rotor is mounted off-center within the outer rotor, so the lobes mesh tightly on one side of the assembly and just touch to create fluid chambers on the opposite side (Figure 6-55). As with other pump designs, low-pressure areas are created as the tightly meshed lobes open up to form fluid chambers. These low-pressure areas draw fluid from the hydraulic system into the speed sensor through an elongated inlet port. As the fluid travels around the center of the assembly, the chambers become smaller to pressurize the fluid. An outlet port on the side of the pump opposite the inlet delivers a stream of pressurized fluid to the system. Drive for the inner rotor of the speed sensor is taken off of a gear in the differential. Since the differential also drives the wheels, the speed of the pump varies in direct proportion to the speed of the vehicle. So the faster the vehicle moves, the faster

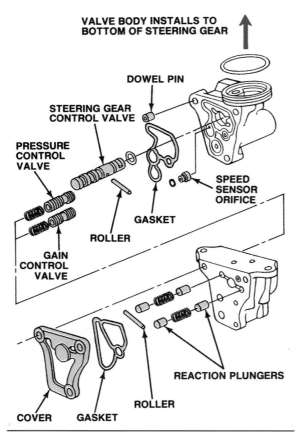

Figure 6-52. The valve body, which attaches to the steering gear housing, houses the spool valves that control hydraulic pressure in the system to provide the variable assist.

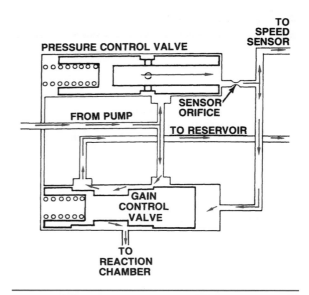

Figure 6-54. The pressure control valve modulates system pressure to provide a constant pressure to the speed sensor through a restricted orifice.

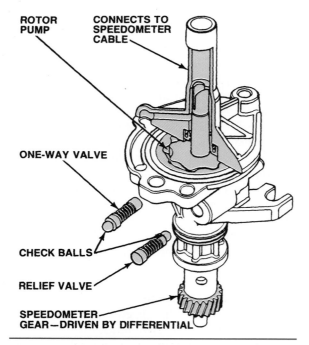

Figure 6-53. The speed sensor is powered by the speedometer driven gear and contains two check-ball valves to prevent excess system pressure.

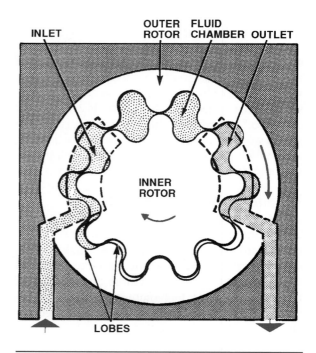

Figure 6-55. The spinning lobes of a rotor pump create varying-sized fluid chambers that draw fluid in, pressurize it, and force it out.

the pump turns and more fluid flows through the speed sensor.

The speed sensor actually draws fluid out of the system to reduce pressure. Fluid is fed into the speed sensor through passages located downstream of the sensor orifice. When the speed sensor pumps fluid out of these passages, hydraulic pressure in them decreases. Since this decreased pressure is applied to the gain control valve, the speed sensor affects gain control valve operation (Figure 6-51).

One-Way and Relief Valves

The valves in the speed sensor both use a spring, seat, and check ball to permit fluid flow in one direction only. At high speeds, the sensor may pump out more fluid than the system can supply. To compensate, the one-way valve allows fluid to flow from the pump outlet back to the inlet in order to feed the sensor when demand is high. When the vehicle is moving in reverse, the speed sensor operation is reversed as well. This causes the sensor to pump fluid from the reservoir into the power steering system. To prevent excessive system pressure, the relief valve drains off some of the fluid from the speed sensor inlet and returns it to the outlet.

Gain Control Valve and Reaction Chambers

The gain control valve directs fluid flow to the two reaction chambers, which provide a variable pressure to the control valve. Pressure applied to the pressure control valve changes in response to speed sensor operation. The steering gear control valve provides hydraulic assist at the power piston independently of the gain control valve boost. The variation is in the amount the gain control valve adds to that assist.

Two forces oppose each other to operate the gain control valve. Spring force acts on one end of the valve, and hydraulic pressure affected by the speed sensor is applied to the other end. Fluid from the pump flows through the center of the valve where it is directed to either the reaction chambers or to the reservoir. The position of the valve determines how the fluid is routed.

The reaction chambers are simply a bore with a plunger at each end and a spring separating the two plungers. Boost pressure from the gain control valve, which is used to strengthen the assist at the control valve, flows past the outside of each reaction plunger, while system pressure from the steering system pump fills the cavity between the plungers. When pressure decreases inside the reaction chamber, the plungers move closer to-

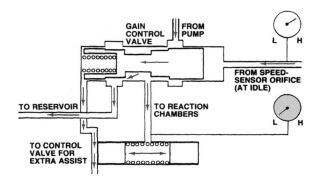

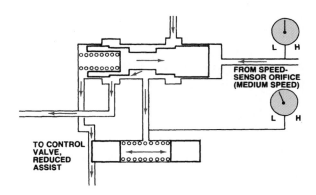

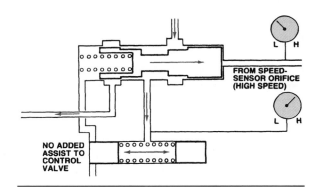

Figure 6-56. Pressure from the speed sensor operates the gain control valve, and it controls the reaction chambers and plungers. At idle, the plungers are close together and allow a strong pressure flow to the control valve providing a high assist. At medium speed, the plungers move out to reduce flow to the control valve and limit assist. At high speed, the plungers are forced all the way out and steering assist is minimal.

gether and more fluid can flow past the ends for a stronger assist. As pressure in the chamber increases, the plungers move away from each other to restrict flow and reduce boost.

The interaction of the gain control valve and the reaction chambers is speed dependent (Figure 6-56). At idle, the speed sensor is not drawing

Electronic Power Steering

Using electronics to run the power steering system potentially has a number of advantages over the use of hydraulics. While leaks, damaged seals, and split hoses are common problems with hydraulic power steering, a completely electronically actuated system would have no fluid-related failures. Powering the system from the battery instead of the engine saves fuel and ensures power assist, even if the engine stalled. However, developing a workable system has not been a trouble-free process.

Several problems confronted the early designers of electronic power steering systems. One was providing sufficient amperage to the system for all turning conditions. During a sharp turn, as much as 75 amps of power are needed to provide adequate assist. Fortunately, advances in microchip technology have provided circuitry that can handle high-amp current. Where to locate the power steering motor presented another design consideration. The motor must be positioned in such a way as to allow the driver to operate the steering manually in the event of a power steering system failure. Placing motors on the steering gear input shaft and below the steering gear housing failed to solve this problem.

In 1981, a TRW engineer patented an electronically operated steering gear with the motor mounted on the rack. The rack passes through a hollow armature in the center of the motor. Five years later, TRW unveiled its Powertronic rack and pinion power steering system. The part of the rack that the motor operates has a spiral track, and the motor uses a ball nut and ball bearings to move the rack—a concept similar to a recirculating ball steering gear. Conventional rack teeth mate with the pinion gear to provide manual steering if needed.

At a 1986 demonstration of the Powertronic unit, TRW officials predicted that by 1988 they would be supplying 30,000 of them for production cars, and that by 1992 more than three million would be needed. In short, they predicted a power steering revolution. As it turns out, automobile manufacturers have opted for evolution instead of revolution, and the Powertronic was shelved. While electronic controls have become more prevalent for power steering systems, most of these are integrated with hydraulic systems, rather than completely replacing hydraulics. It was not until 1991 that the TRW electronic power steering system was applied to a production vehicle, and this was in the limited production Acura NSX. It is not always easy to start a revolution, particularly in the automotive industry.

fluid out of the hydraulic system, so high pressure forces the valve against the spring. In this position, the valve directs most of the fluid flowing through it to the reservoir. Pressure is low in the reaction chamber, and fluid can flow unobstructed around the ends of the plungers to boost control valve operation. As vehicle speed increases, the speed sensor starts pumping fluid out of the system to lower the pressure at the gain control valve. Now, spring force is slightly greater than the force of the low pressure applied to the valve and the valve moves to open up the fluid passage leading to the reaction chamber. This increases pressure in the reaction chamber and forces the plungers out, which reduces fluid flow to the control valve. At high speed, the speed sensor pumps a high volume of fluid out of the system, which allows spring force to overcome fluid pressure. Spring force seats the valve against the opposite end of the bore. In this position, the gain control valve directs most of the fluid flowing through it into the reaction chamber. The high pressure in the chamber forces the plungers out to seal off the passage to the control valve so that no boost is added to the hydraulic assist.

VARIABLE-ASSIST SYSTEMS

In addition to the conventional parts of a power steering system described earlier in this chapter, electronically controlled variable-assist systems use:

- Electronic sensors
- Electronic control module
- Solenoid, motor, or another electrically actuated device

Mazda Electronic Controlled Power Steering

A **sensor** is an input device that provides an electronic signal to the **powertrain control module (PCM).** Sensor signals provide information to the PCM about vehicle operating conditions, such as speed. The two most commonly used input sensors for operating a variable-assist steering system are the vehicle speed sensor (VSS) and the steering wheel angle sensor. Some systems also process the input signals from an engine speed (RPM) sensor or a sensor that indicates how quickly the steering wheel is being turned. Sensors are discussed in more detail in Chapter 12 of this *Classroom Manual.*

The PCM is a computer that processes the information received from the sensors, then transmits an output signal to the **solenoid** to "tell" it how to respond to the driving conditions (Figure 6-57). A solenoid is an electromagnet, whose magnetic field pulls a rod or shuttle into the solenoid. When the magnetic field is weak, a spring pushes the rod or shuttle out of the solenoid. In this way, a solenoid changes an electric signal into a mechanical action. The shuttle opens and closes a port to regulate how much fluid is allowed to flow through it. In a variable-assist power steering system, the solenoid is frequently designed to interfere with pump flow in some way. That is, its action either decreases fluid pressure from the pump for less assist, or allows full flow for higher assist.

The actuating device in a variable-assist system is not always a solenoid. Some systems, such as those on the Ford Thunderbird and Mercury Cougar, use an electronically actuated valve in place of a solenoid. A small electric motor moves the valve to vary the size of an orifice, thus varying the amount of fluid pressure available for assist. Although the type of device and its exact method of operation varies among systems, the device that responds to the control unit signal always has the same purpose, which is to regulate the amount of hydraulic assist.

Electronic Sensors and Control Unit

The system used on the Mazda 929 serves as an example of an electronically controlled variable-assist power steering system. First introduced in 1988, this Mazda system regulates assist based on the input of three electronic sensors. These sensors transmit signals that reflect:

- Steering wheel angle
- Vehicle speed
- Engine speed

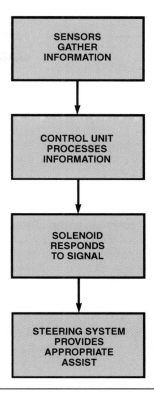

Figure 6-57. In an electronically controlled variable-assist power steering system, the sensors gather information, the powertrain control unit processes the information to determine how much assist is needed, and the solenoid adjusts hydraulic pressure to create the needed level of assist.

The steering wheel angle and VSS signals provide the data the PCM needs to determine the correct assist level. In the event of a VSS failure, the PCM regulates assist based on engine, rather than vehicle, speed. The PCM is powered through the ignition, so it operates only when the engine is running. Based on the input signals, the PCM varies the amperage applied to the solenoid to control pressure (Figure 6-58). At low vehicle speeds and small steering wheel angles, the PCM applies high-amperage to the solenoid. As speed and steering wheel angle increase, the applied amperage is reduced.

Solenoid

The solenoid attaches to a valve body, which also contains a control valve and a pressure switch. The solenoid actuates a rod that varies the size of one of the valve orifices. Although Mazda refers to this valve as a "control valve," it will be referred to as the "power-reducing valve" in this discussion to avoid confusing it with the control valve in the steering gear. In addition to controlling the

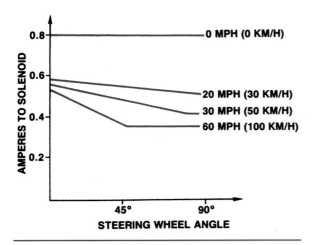

Figure 6-58. The amperage the PCM applies to the solenoid decreases as vehicle speed and steering wheel angle increase.

LOW SPEED
SMALL STEERING WHEEL ANGLE —
HIGH ASSIST

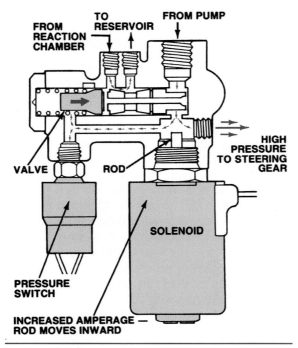

Figure 6-59. When the PCM applies high amperage to the solenoid, the magnetic field is strong and the rod is retracted to allow a strong fluid flow and provide a high level of power assist.

pressure sent to the steering gear control valve, the solenoid and power-reducing valve control fluid flow to a reaction chamber that opposes input shaft motion to provide a stiffer steering feel.

HIGH SPEED
LARGE STEERING WHEEL ANGLE —
LOW ASSIST

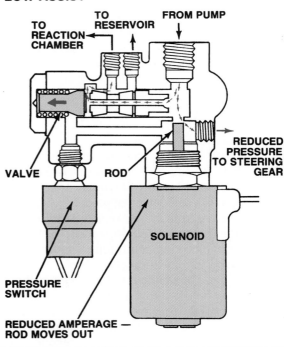

Figure 6-60. When amperage to the solenoid decreases, spring force inside the solenoid overcomes the magnetic field and the rod moves out to restrict fluid flow through the orifice and reduce the level of power assist.

The solenoid rod is positioned near an orifice through which fluid flows out of the power-reducing valve on its way to the steering gear. When both vehicle speed and steering wheel angle are low, the PCM applies high amperage to the solenoid. This pulls the rod inward so full fluid flow is allowed through the orifice (Figure 6-59). High-pressure fluid from the pump flows past the end of the valve, through the orifice, to the steering gear control valve. Some of the fluid from the orifice is directed to the spring end of the valve to augment the spring force holding the valve in position. In this position, a valley between two valve lands opens a passage between the reaction chamber fluid line and a return line to the reservoir. At this point, with fluid flowing full-force to the control valve and the reaction chamber draining, the power-assist level is high.

In response to increased speed and steering wheel angle, the PCM reduces the amperage applied to the solenoid so that spring force moves the rod out toward the orifice (Figure 6-60). With the rod extended, fluid flow through the orifice is restricted. Several conditions result from this.

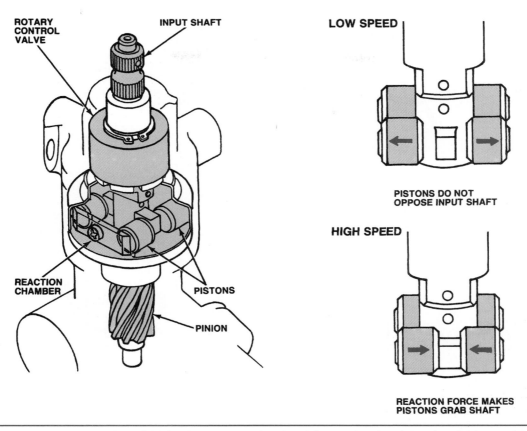

Figure 6-61. When pressurized fluid fills the reaction chamber it forces the pistons against the base of the shaft, which results in a harder steering feel. As the chamber drains, the pistons retract from the input shaft, producing a softer steering feel.

First, fluid flow to the steering gear control valve is reduced, which reduces assist pressure as well. Second, the fluid flow to the spring end of the power-reducing valve decreases, while pressure at the orifice end increases. This causes the valve to move in its bore and compress the spring. In this new position, a valve land blocks the return passage from the reaction chamber to the reservoir. Third, a passage through the center of the valve is now opened to a channel in the valve body to permit fluid flow through it. A valve valley directs pressurized fluid to flow from this channel into the line leading to the reaction chamber.

Fluid directed to the reaction chamber, which is located near the base of the steering gear input shaft, acts on two flat surfaces to move two pairs of pistons (Figure 6-61). When hydraulic pressure is sent to the reaction chamber, it forces the pistons together so they clamp around an extension of the steering gear input shaft. This force opposes input shaft movement to increase the effort required to turn the steering wheel.

System Operation

If the steering wheel is turned while the vehicle is traveling at low speed, high pressure fluid flows to the steering gear control valve to boost the amount of power assist (Figure 6-62). As there is no fluid flow to the reaction chamber under these conditions, the pistons are not applied to oppose input shaft motion. These two factors, high boost pressure and no input shaft resistance, reduce the effort needed to turn the steering wheel and make the vehicle easy to maneuver.

Turning the steering wheel while the vehicle is traveling at a higher rate of speed produces a different result. At higher speeds, some fluid still flows to the control valve, but the pressure level is considerably lower. In addition, pressurized fluid flows to the reaction chambers where it forces the pistons together in order to oppose input shaft motion (Figure 6-63). These two factors, low boost pressure and high input shaft resistance, combine to increase the required steering effort, making it more difficult for the driver to turn the steering wheel.

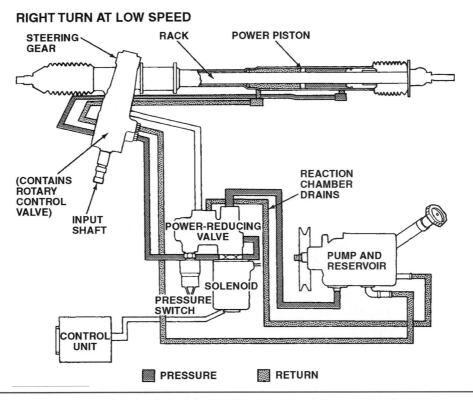

Figure 6-62. Fluid flow through the Mazda variable-assist power steering system during a low-speed right turn.

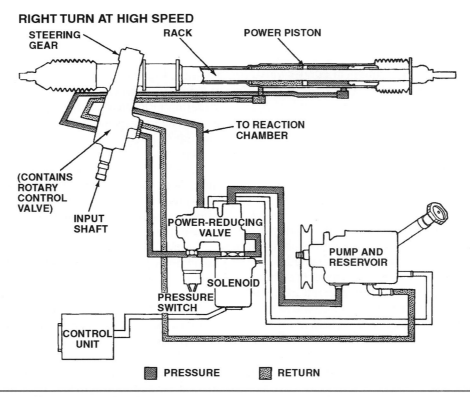

Figure 6-63. Fluid flow through the Mazda variable-assist power steering system during a high-speed right turn.

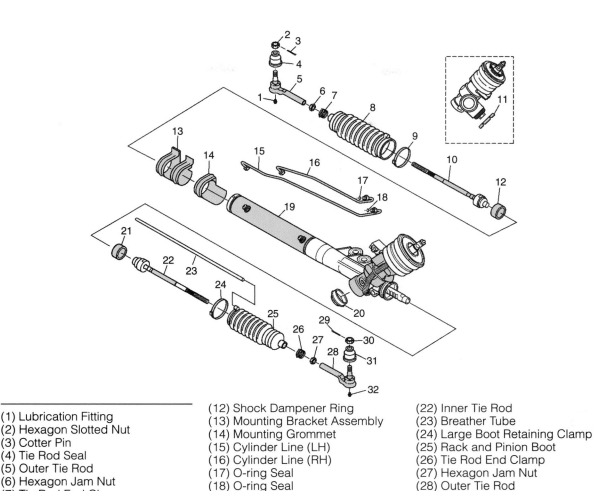

Figure 6-64. MAGNASTEER II® steering gear exploded view. (Courtesy of General Motors Corporation)

(1) Lubrication Fitting
(2) Hexagon Slotted Nut
(3) Cotter Pin
(4) Tie Rod Seal
(5) Outer Tie Rod
(6) Hexagon Jam Nut
(7) Tie Rod End Clamp
(8) Rack and Pinion Boot
(9) Large Boot Retaining Clamp
(10) Inner Tie Rod
(11) Adjuster Plug Lock Nut

(12) Shock Dampener Ring
(13) Mounting Bracket Assembly
(14) Mounting Grommet
(15) Cylinder Line (LH)
(16) Cylinder Line (RH)
(17) O-ring Seal
(18) O-ring Seal
(19) Rack and Pinion Gear
     Assembly (Partial)
(20) Dust Cover
(21) Shock Dampener Ring

(22) Inner Tie Rod
(23) Breather Tube
(24) Large Boot Retaining Clamp
(25) Rack and Pinion Boot
(26) Tie Rod End Clamp
(27) Hexagon Jam Nut
(28) Outer Tie Rod
(29) Cotter Pin
(30) Hexagon Slotted Nut
(31) Tie Rod Seal
(32) Lubrication Fitting

MAGNASTEER II® Variable Effort Steering (VES)

The **variable effort steering (VES)** system, or **MAGNASTEER II®** (Figure 6-64), varies the amount of effort required to steer the vehicle as vehicle speed changes or lateral acceleration occurs. At low speeds, the system provides minimal steering effort for easy turning and parking maneuvers. At high speeds, the system provides firmer steering (road feel) and directional stability. When the system senses lateral acceleration, steering becomes firmer to reduce oversteering.

The electronic brake control module (EBCM), as shown in (Figure 6-65), controls a bi-directional **magnetic rotary actuator** located in the steering rack and pinion shown in (Figure 6-66) and also on the schematic in Figure 6-65. The EBCM varies the steering assist by adjusting the current flow through the magnetic rotary actuator. The actuator adjusts the amount of power steering assist to achieve a given level of effort to steer the vehicle. The VES system accomplishes this by adding or subtracting torque on the input shaft to the rack and pinion. The main component of the system is an electromagnetic actuator, which consists of a multiple-pole ring-style permanent magnet, a pole piece, and an electromagnetic coil assembly. The VES system uses the antilock brake system (ABS) wheel speed sensor inputs to determine vehicle speed (Figure 6-67). When the EBCM senses vehicle

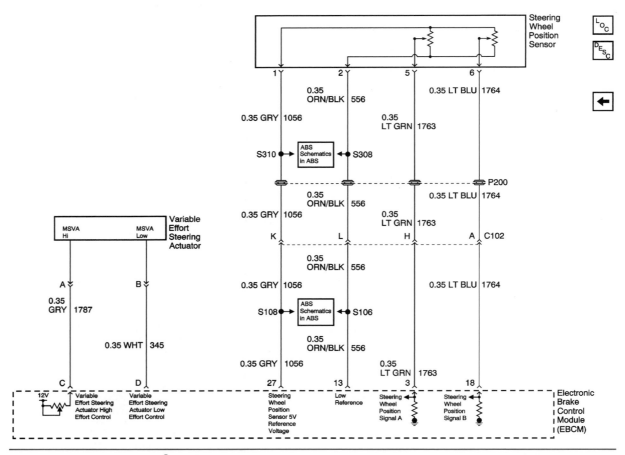

Figure 6-65. Magnasteer II® steering electrical schematic. (Courtesy of General Motors Corporation)

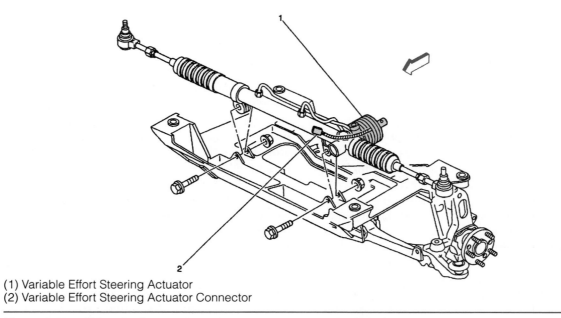

(1) Variable Effort Steering Actuator
(2) Variable Effort Steering Actuator Connector

Figure 6-66. Chevrolet Corvette lower steering. (Courtesy of General Motors Corporation)

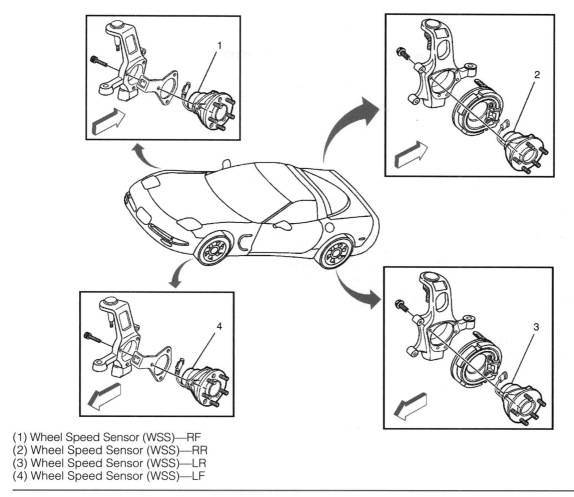

(1) Wheel Speed Sensor (WSS)—RF
(2) Wheel Speed Sensor (WSS)—RR
(3) Wheel Speed Sensor (WSS)—LR
(4) Wheel Speed Sensor (WSS)—LF

Figure 6-67. Corvette ABS wheel sensors. (Courtesy of General Motors Corporation)

speed, it commands a current to the actuator that is most appropriate for each speed.

The system also uses inputs such as handwheel position from the **steering wheel position sensor** shown in Figure 6-68, wheelbase, understeer coefficient, and steering ratio to calculate lateral acceleration. The EBCM commands current from negative two amps to positive three amps to the actuator, which is polarized. At low speeds, a negative current is commanded, which assists steering. At medium speeds, no current is commanded and steering is assisted by hydraulics only. At high speeds, a positive current is commanded, which creates steering resistance. Ignition voltage and ground are provided through the EBCM. The EBCM has the ability to detect malfunctions in the actuator or the circuitry to the actuator. Any malfunctions detected will cause the system to ramp to zero amps and steering will be assisted by hydraulics only.

Saturn Vue Electric Power Steering (EPS)

The **electric power steering (EPS)** system (Figure 6-69) on the GM Saturn Vue reduces the amount of effort needed to steer the vehicle. The system uses the under hood fuse block (UHFB), instrument panel fuse block (IPFB), **power steering control module (PSCM)** shown in Figure 6-69, torque sensor, discrete battery voltage supply circuit, EPS motor, class 2 serial data circuit, and the instrument panel cluster (IPC) to perform the system functions. The PSCM, torque sensor, and EPS motor are serviced as an assembly and part of the steering column. Any EPS components diagnosed to be malfunctioning require replacement of the complete steering column assembly, also known as the EPS assembly, shown as number "6" in Figure 6-70.

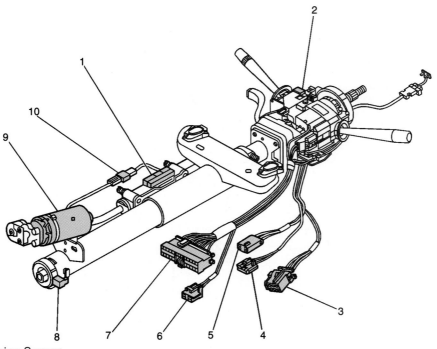

(1) Telescoping Sensor
(2) Steering Column Lock
(8) Steering Wheel Position Sensor
(9) Telescoping Drive Motor

Figure 6-68. Corvette MAGNASTEER® steering column steering wheel position sensor. (Courtesy of General Motors Corporation)

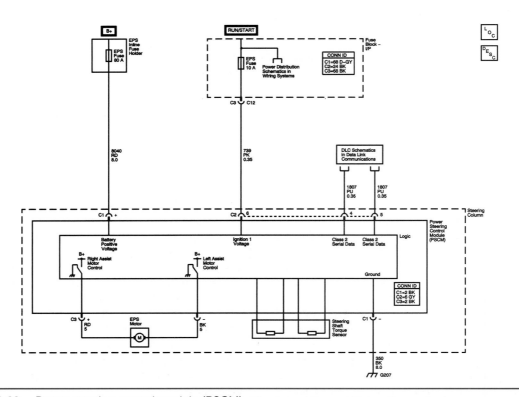

Figure 6-69. Power steering control module (PSCM). (Courtesy of General Motors Corporation)

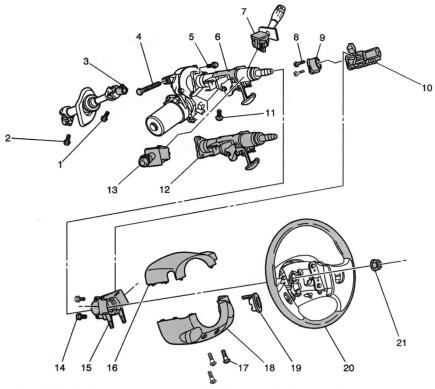

(1) Upper Intermediate Shaft Bolt
(2) Lower Intermediate Shaft Bolt
(3) Intermediate Shaft Assembly
(4) Lower Steering Column Support Bracket Bolt
(5) Lower Steering Column Jacket Bolt
(6) Steering Column Assembly
(7) Wiper/Washer Switch Assembly
(8) Ignition Start Switch Screw
(9) Ignition Start Switch Assembly
(10) Ignition Start Switch Housing Assembly
(11) Upper Steering Column Support Bracket Bolt

(12) Steering Column Jacket Assembly
(13) Headlamp/Dimmer/Park/Turn Signal Switch Assembly
(14) Ignition Start Switch Bracket Bolt
(15) Wiper/Washer Switch and Headlamp/Dimmer/Park/Turn Signal Switch Bracket
(16) Steering Column Shroud Assembly
(17) Lower Steering Column Shroud Screw
(18) Steering Column Shroud
(19) Ignition Start Switch Bezel
(20) Steering Wheel Assembly
(21) Steering Wheel Nut

Figure 6-70. Saturn Vue steering column with EPS. (Courtesy of General Motors Corporation)

Torque Sensor

The PSCM uses a **torque sensor** (Figure 6-69) schematic as its main input for determining the amount of steering assists. It is part of the EPS assembly and not serviced separately. The steering column has an input shaft, from the steering wheel to the torque sensor, and an output shaft, from the torque sensor to the steering shaft coupler. The input and output shafts are separated by a torsion bar, where the torque sensor is located. The sensor consists of a compensation coil, detecting coil, and three detecting rings. These detecting rings have toothed edges that face each other. Detecting ring 1 is fixed to the output shaft, while detecting rings 2 and 3 are fixed to the input shaft. The detecting coil is positioned around the toothed edges of detecting rings 1 and 2. As torque is applied to the steering column shaft, the alignment of the teeth between detecting rings 1 and 2 changes, which causes the detecting coil signal voltage to change. The PSCM recognizes this change in signal voltage as steering column shaft torque. The compensation coil is used to compensate for changes in electrical circuit impedance due to circuit temperature changes from electrical current and voltage levels as well as ambient temperatures for accurate torque detection.

EPS Motor

The **EPS motor** (Figure 6-71) is a 12-volt brushed DC reversible motor with a 58 amp rating. The motor assists steering through a worm shaft and reduction gear located in the steering column housing.

Power Steering Control Module (PSCM)

The power steering control module (PSCM) that is part of the EPS assembly (Figure 6-69) schematic, uses a combination of torque sensor inputs—vehicle speed, calculated system temperature, and the turning profile—to determine the amount of steering assist. When the steering wheel is turned, the PSCM uses signal voltage from the torque sensor to detect the amount of torque being applied to the steering column shaft and the amount of current to command to the EPS motor. The PSCM receives a class 2-vehicle speed message from the engine control module (ECM) to determine vehicle speed. At low speeds more assist is provided for easy turning during parking maneuvers. At high speeds, less assist is provided for improved road feel and directional stability. Neither the PSCM nor the EPS motor is designed to handle 65 amps continuously. The PSCM will go into overload protection mode to avoid system thermal damage. In this mode the PSCM will limit the amount of current commanded to the EPS motor, which reduces steering assist levels. The PSCM must be programmed with the proper turning profile using the Saturn Service Stall whenever it's replaced. The turning profiles are different in relation to the vehicle configuration—FWD, AWD, V6, and so on. The PSCM has the ability to detect malfunctions within the EPS system. Any malfunction detected will cause the IPC to display the SERVICE VEHICLE SOON warning message.

Lexus Variable Gear Ratio Steering (VGRS) System

Figure 6-72 shows a Lexus electronic variable power steering system. The electronically controlled steering column uses an electric motor to provide steering power assist. It does not use a hydraulic system. In addition to the steering assist the Lexus variable gear ratio steering (VGRS) system uses a lock mechanism to engage a gear reduction transmission to vary the steering ratio.

Electronic rack and pinion steering uses an electric motor to provide steering power assist. It does not use a hydraulic system (Figure 6-73). In the case of the TRW system, instead of using a flat rack with straight teeth as in a standard rack, this type of system uses a helical-gear rack driven by a fast-acting electric motor. A torque sensor mounted on the pinion shaft measures input steering torque. As torque is applied, a signal is sent to the powertrain control module (PCM). The PCM sends a signal to the electric motor, which provides the power assist.

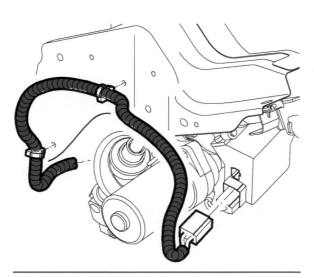

Figure 6-71. Saturn Vue EPS motor and EPS controller connector. (Courtesy of General Motors Corporation)

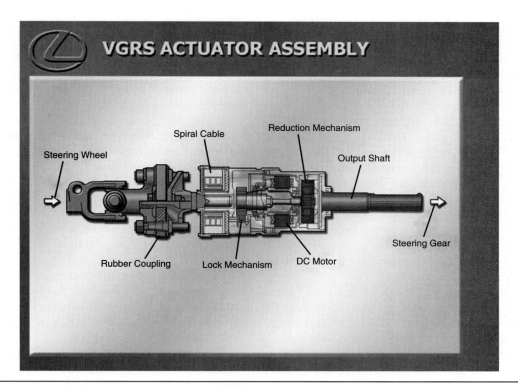

Figure 6-72. Lexus variable gear ratio steering. (Courtesy of Toyota Motor Sales, Inc.)

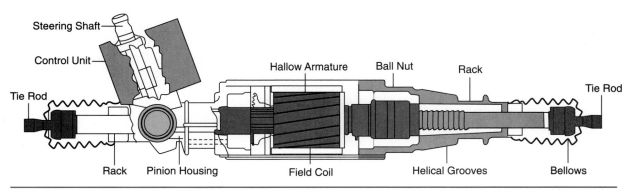

Figure 6-73. TRW electronic rack and pinion steering gear. (Courtesy of TRW, Inc.)

SUMMARY

Power-assisted steering adds a hydraulic boost to the mechanical operation of the steering system so the driver can use less effort to turn the steering wheel. The main components of a power steering system are: hoses, fittings, pump, reservoir, power piston, and control valve. The two basic kinds of power steering systems are integral and linkage.

The pump draws fluid from the reservoir and delivers it under pressure to the power steering system. Four types of power steering pump are used: vane, slipper, roller, and gear. The pump bolts into support brackets on the engine and is belt-driven by the crankshaft. The reservoir, which stores power steering fluid, may be integral to the pump or remotely mounted.

The three operative parts of a vane pump are the rotor, vanes, and cam ring. A modulator, or flow control, valve regulates fluid flow from the pump. Roller pumps and slipper pumps are similar in design and operation to a vane pump. Gear pumps use two meshing gears inside the pump body to pressurize the fluid.

In an integral power steering system, the control valve and the power piston are incorporated into the steering gear. The control valve regulates the application of pressurized fluid against the power piston, and the power piston assists in moving the output member of the steering gear when pressure is applied to one side of it. For both standard and rack and pinion steering gears, there are two kinds of control valves: spool and rotary.

Ford and Chevrolet once used linkage power steering systems that integrated the control valve and the power cylinder into the steering linkage instead of the steering gear.

A variable-assist power steering system provides different levels of assist based on vehicle speed and sometimes steering wheel angle. Electronically controlled systems use input sensors, a control module, and an actuator, such as a solenoid.

The GM variable effort steering (VES) system, or MAGNASTEER II®, varies the amount of effort required to steer the vehicle as vehicle speed changes or lateral acceleration occurs. At low speeds, the system provides minimal steering effort for easy turning and parking maneuvers. At high speeds, the system provides firmer steering (road feel) and directional stability. When the system senses lateral acceleration, steering becomes firmer to reduce oversteering.

The electric power steering (EPS) system used on the GM Saturn Vue reduces the amount of effort needed to steer the vehicle. The system uses the under hood fuse block (UHFB), instrument panel fuse block (IPFB), power steering control module (PSCM), torque sensor, discrete battery voltage supply circuit, EPS motor, class 2 serial data circuit, and the instrument panel cluster (IPC) to perform the system functions. The PSCM, torque sensor, and EPS motor are serviced as an assembly and part of the steering column.

Review Questions

For each of the following questions, choose the letter that represents the best possible answer.

1. To make turning the wheels easier, power steering systems use:
   a. Mechanical friction
   b. Pressurized gas
   c. Pressurized fluid
   d. Electric motors

2. Power steering fluid performs all of the following functions, EXCEPT:
   a. Transmit force to turn the wheels
   b. Lubricate the gears and bearings inside the steering gear housing
   c. Reduce system operating temperature
   d. Develop hydraulic pressure

3. Technician A says that some power steering systems use automatic transmission fluid instead of power steering fluid. Technician B says that it is allowable to replace high-pressure fittings with strong hose clamps. Who is correct?
   a. A only
   b. B only
   c. Both A and B
   d. Neither A nor B

4. Technician A says that heat can break down power steering fluid. Technician B says that power steering fluid is sometimes routed through a cooling circuit. Who is correct?
   a. A only
   b. B only
   c. Both A and B
   d. Neither A nor B

5. The power steering pump delivers fluid to the system under high pressure; this high pressure also raises the fluid:
   a. Temperature
   b. Viscosity
   c. Weight
   d. Volume

6. The high-pressure lines of power steering systems normally are made of:
   a. Reinforced rubber with crimped fittings
   b. Polyurethane tubing with snap-lock fittings
   c. Reinforced rubber with hose clamp fittings
   d. Steel tubing with flare-nut fittings

7. Which of the following is NOT a type of power steering pump?
   a. Vane
   b. Shoe
   c. Roller
   d. Gear

8. The power steering pump is driven by:
   a. Electricity
   b. Engine oil pressure
   c. The engine
   d. The differential

9. Technician A says that most compact FWD vehicles use a remote power steering fluid reservoir rather than one that is integral to the pump. Technician B says that power steering pumps with integral reservoirs produce a higher volume of pressurized fluid than pumps with remote reservoirs. Who is correct?
   a. A only
   b. B only
   c. Both A and B
   d. Neither A nor B

10. Which of the following devices routes excess pressurized fluid back into the pump inlet passages when the power steering pump puts out more pressurized fluid than is needed by the power steering system?
    a. Rotary control valve
    b. Flow control valve
    c. Spool control valve
    d. Gain control valve

11. On most vehicles with electronic engine controls, an electronic signal is transmitted to the powertrain control unit when the power steering pump places an excessive load on the engine by the:
    a. Throttle switch
    b. Speed sensor
    c. Pressure switch
    d. Solenoid

12. If the vanes of a vane-type power steering pump do not seal tightly against the cam ring, the result will be:
    a. High fluid pressure at the pump outlet
    b. Low fluid pressure at the pump outlet
    c. Power steering fluid leakage at the pump housing
    d. Fluid breakdown due to high temperature

13. Most standard, non-rack and pinion, power steering gears are which type?
    a. Recirculating ball
    b. Worm and cam
    c. Worm and sector
    d. Cam and lever

14. In a power steering system with a rotary control valve, steering feel is determined by the:
    a. Pressure relief valve
    b. Orifice size
    c. Pump output
    d. Torsion bar

15. Technician A says that most power rack and pinion steering gears have external fluid lines. Technician B says that most power rack and pinion steering gears use a rotary control valve. Who is correct?
    a. A only
    b. B only
    c. Both A and B
    d. Neither A nor B

16. In a linkage power steering system, hydraulic pressure is applied to the power cylinder to help move the:
    a. Rack and tie rods
    b. Centerlink
    c. Ball nut
    d. Piston

17. Technician A says that some variable-assist power steering systems respond to steering wheel angle. Technician B says that on a variable-assist power steering system the amount of assist increases at low speeds and decreases at high speeds. Who is correct?
    a. A only
    b. B only
    c. Both A and B
    d. Neither A nor B

18. On the Honda hydraulically controlled, variable-assist steering system, the function of the speed sensor is to:
    a. Monitor steering assist as it changes
    b. Pump fluid out of the power steering system
    c. Transmit an electronic signal if system pressure increases
    d. Increase fluid pressure during high-speed operation

19. In the event of a vehicle speed sensor failure, the powertrain control module of the Mazda electronic variable-assist system regulates boost pressure based on:
    a. Throttle position
    b. Steering wheel angle
    c. Engine speed
    d. Differential speed

20. In addition to a vehicle speed sensor, some electronically controlled, variable-assist power steering systems regulate the amount of boost based on an input signal from the:
    a. Steering knuckle angle sensor
    b. Power steering fluid temperature sensor
    c. Power steering fluid pressure sensor
    d. Steering wheel angle sensor

7

Four-Wheel Steering

OBJECTIVE

Upon completion and review of this chapter, you will be able to:

- Identify the components of an electronically controlled four-wheel power steering system and explain the system operation.

KEY TERMS

bevel gears
fail-safe system
four-wheel steering (4WS)
internal gear
opposite-phase operation
phase-reverse operation
Quadrasteer™
rear power cylinder
rear steering gear
rear-wheel position sensor
rear-wheel steering control module
rear-wheel steering mode switch
rear-wheel steering motor
same-phase operation
slip yoke
steering wheel position sensor (SWPS)
stepper motor
two-wheel steering (2WS)

INTRODUCTION

Four-wheel steering (4WS) is one of the most significant steering innovations in many years. It changes the way a vehicle handles by steering the rear wheels as well as the front wheels during turns. Four-wheel steering adds a steering unit and linkage to the rear axle, requiring rear wheels equipped with steering arms, and some type of connection between the front steering gear and the rear unit.

Four-wheel steering first became available on mass-market automobiles in the late 1980s, and by 1990 three manufacturers offered 4WS on one or more of their models. Those three were Honda Motor Company, Mazda Motor Corporation, and Nissan Motor Company. In 1991, Mitsubishi also introduced a 4WS system on the 3000GT VR-4, which was also available on the Dodge Stealth R/T Turbo. The Mitsubishi system is similar to the Nissan system. This chapter focuses on the Honda, Mazda, and Nissan systems.

To provide rear-wheel steering, a 4WS system needs some means of transferring the input from the steering wheel to the **rear steering gear** (Figure 7–1). The original Honda 4WS system transfers movement front to rear using a completely mechanical system. Mazda and Nissan both use

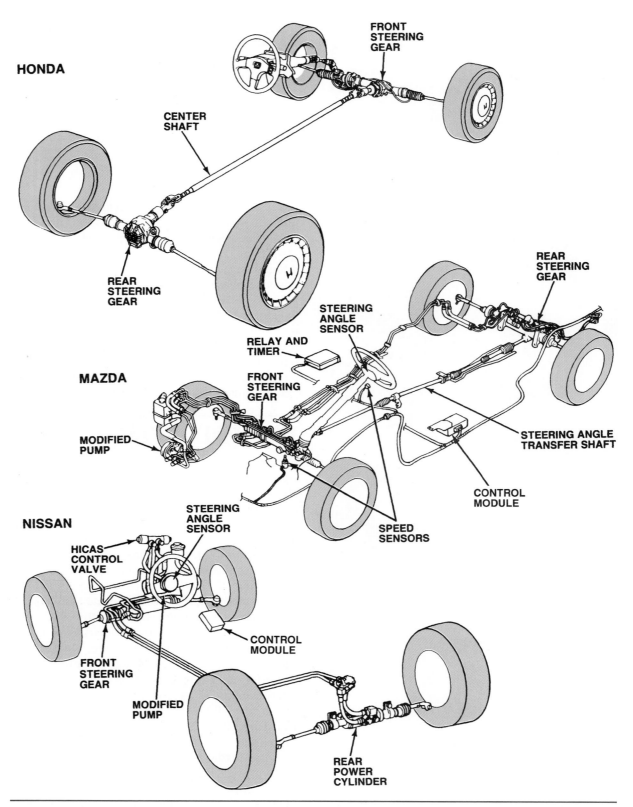

HONDA

FRONT STEERING GEAR

CENTER SHAFT

REAR STEERING GEAR

MAZDA

STEERING ANGLE SENSOR

RELAY AND TIMER

FRONT STEERING GEAR

MODIFIED PUMP

REAR STEERING GEAR

STEERING ANGLE TRANSFER SHAFT

CONTROL MODULE

SPEED SENSORS

NISSAN

STEERING ANGLE SENSOR

HICAS CONTROL VALVE

CONTROL MODULE

FRONT STEERING GEAR

MODIFIED PUMP

REAR POWER CYLINDER

Figure 7-1. The first Honda 4WS system operates mechanically, and the original Mazda system uses a combination of mechanical and electronic controls and a hydraulic actuator, while the Nissan system is electronically controlled and hydraulically operated.

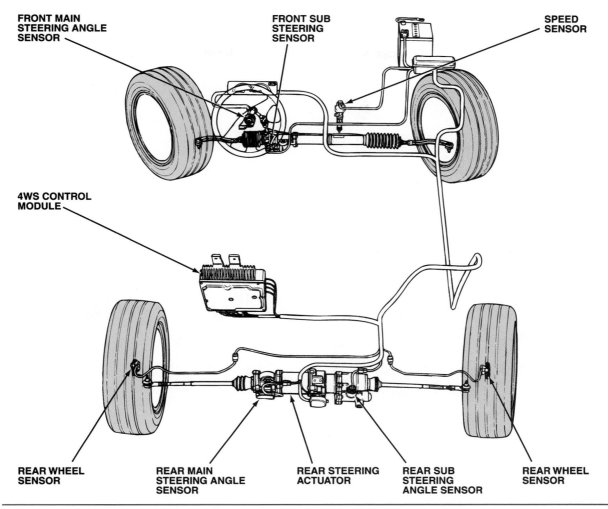

FRONT MAIN STEERING ANGLE SENSOR

FRONT SUB STEERING SENSOR

SPEED SENSOR

4WS CONTROL MODULE

REAR WHEEL SENSOR

REAR MAIN STEERING ANGLE SENSOR

REAR STEERING ACTUATOR

REAR SUB STEERING ANGLE SENSOR

REAR WHEEL SENSOR

Figure 7-2. The Honda electronic 4WS system uses computer-controlled electric motors to steer the rear wheels; the turning angle is determined by a number of input sensors.

hydraulically actuated, electronically controlled systems, but the designs for each differ considerably. Of these three systems, the more recent Mitsubishi system is most similar to the Nissan design because it uses electronic controls to operate the system hydraulically, but the Mitsubishi design does not provide the phase-reverse operation, which is described later in this chapter, of the Nissan system. Beginning with the 1992 model year, Honda switched to an electronic steering box to steer the rear wheels. On this system, there is no mechanical or hydraulic link between the front and rear wheels; the rear wheels are steered by an electric motor inside the rear steering actuator (Figure 7-2).

The following sections explain how 4WS systems transfer movement from the front steering gear to the rear wheels and how rear steering operates, but do not discuss the operation of the front-wheel steering system except as it relates to the front-to-rear transfer. For more information about front-steering systems, refer to Chapters 4 through 6 of this *Classroom Manual*.

FOUR-WHEEL STEERING OPERATIONAL MODES

There are three methods of 4WS operation:

- Opposite-phase
- Same-phase
- Phase-reverse

During **opposite-phase operation,** the rear wheels steer in the opposite direction of the front

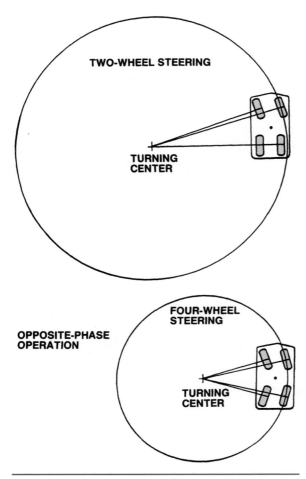

Figure 7-3. Opposite-phase 4WS operation, which provides a smaller turning circle than 2WS, is particularly useful in parking maneuvers.

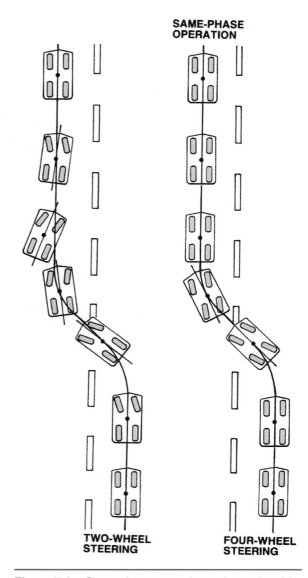

Figure 7-4. Same-phase operation reduces the side-slip that occurs with 2WS during high-speed maneuvers.

wheels (Figure 7-3). In **same-phase operation,** the rear wheels steer in the same direction as the front wheels (Figure 7-4). Both the Honda mechanical and electronic systems, as well as the Mazda 4WS system, operate in the opposite phase at low speeds and for sharp turns, and in the same phase at higher speeds and for wider turns or lane changes.

Phase-reverse operation, used exclusively on the Nissan system, is really a combination of the other two operational modes. In phase reverse, the rear wheels momentarily steer opposite the front wheels, then quickly change to steer in the same direction as the front wheels (Figure 7-5). The Nissan 4WS system uses phase-reverse operation at lower speeds and during sharper, quicker turns, and it operates in the same phase at high speeds and for wider, more gradual turns.

Each operational mode provides a unique advantage over conventional **two-wheel steering (2WS).**

Opposite-phase operation occurs during sharp turns and at low vehicle speeds. This mode allows

tighter turns than when only the front wheels steer. Opposite phase improves maneuverability during sharp, slow turns—for example, during parking. Honda, Mazda, and Mitsubishi use this mode, but Nissan does not.

Same-phase operation is used for smaller directional changes and at higher speeds, such as during lane changes. It provides better handling and stability when changing direction at high speed by reducing the tire side-slip angle. As a result, rear axle yaw is reduced, both in angle and time, when compared to the same vehicle with 2WS. The Honda, Mazda, Mitsubishi, and Nissan 4WS systems all use this mode.

Only the Nissan 4WS system uses phase-reverse operation, which helps the rear wheels track the front wheels during cornering. The vehicle starts its

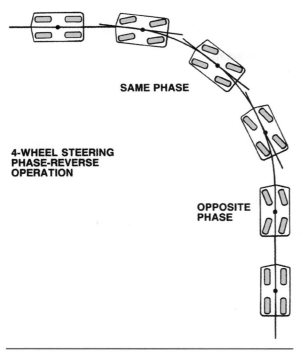

4-WHEEL STEERING PHASE-REVERSE OPERATION

SAME PHASE

OPPOSITE PHASE

Figure 7-5. The Nissan system phase-reverse 4WS operation switches from opposite- to same-phase operation as the vehicle steers through a curve during cornering.

turn more quickly than with 2WS, so the steering feels more responsive to the driver. This initial opposite phase occurs only at relatively low speeds and sharp turning angles. At very low speeds, the rear wheels of the Nissan system do not steer at all.

MECHANICAL FOUR-WHEEL STEERING

As mentioned earlier, the original Honda 4WS system uses mechanical means to steer the rear wheels, although the front steering gear is equipped with hydraulic power steering assist. This Honda design is the simplest of the all the systems available.

Honda Mechanical System

Honda introduced its mechanical 4WS system on the 1988 Prelude to provide more responsive handling at high speeds and greater maneuverability at low speeds. There are three main system components (Figure 7-6):

- Front steering gear
- Center shaft
- Rear steering gear

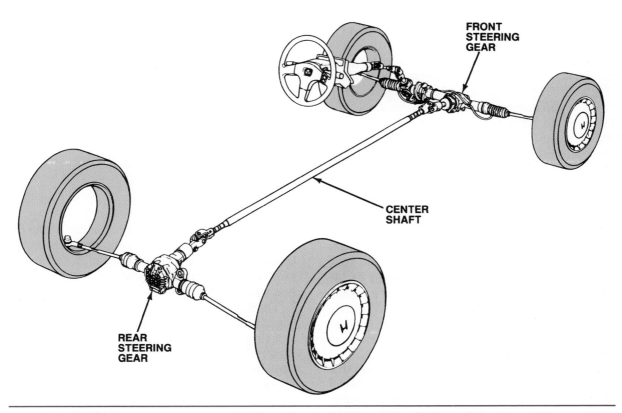

FRONT STEERING GEAR

CENTER SHAFT

REAR STEERING GEAR

Figure 7-6. The main components of the Honda mechanical 4WS system—front steering gear, rear steering gear, and center shaft—transfer steering movement directly to the rear.

HONDA 4-WHEEL STEERING OPERATION

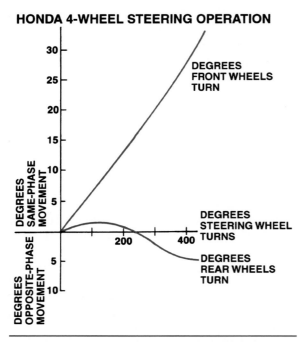

Figure 7-7. In the Honda mechanical system, steering wheel angle alone determines the direction and degree that the rear wheels steer.

In addition, tie rods form the rear steering linkage. For information about Honda power-assisted front steering gears, see Chapter 6 of this *Classroom Manual*.

When the driver turns the steering wheel slightly, the Honda 4WS operates in the same-phase mode (Figure 7-7). As the steering wheel is turned farther, the rear wheels come back to neutral, then move in the direction opposite the front wheels—opposite-phase operation. The farthest the rear wheels can steer in either direction is five degrees.

Front Steering Gear

The front steering gear is a power-assisted rack and pinion unit modified to drive the center shaft (Figure 7-8). The rack has two sets of gear teeth: one set is driven by the steering shaft pinion gear, and the second set, located to the right of the power piston, drives the center shaft pinion gear. The steering gear housing is modified to contain the driven pinion and the parts related to it.

Driven Pinion and Related Parts

The axis of the driven pinion is a short shaft that splines to the front center shaft universal joint (U-joint) (Figure 7-9). A ball bearing on the pinion shaft reduces friction between the shaft and the driven pinion holder. A collar positions the pinion

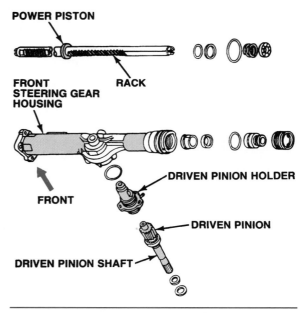

Figure 7-8. The front steering gear rack has an additional set of gear teeth that drive the center shaft pinion gear and relay steering wheel movement to the rear steering.

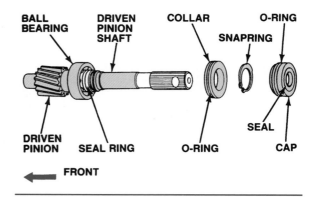

Figure 7-9. The driven pinion shaft splines to the front center shaft U-joint and is supported by a ball bearing.

in the holder, and a snapring secures the collar. Finally, a cap and seal keep contamination from entering the front steering gear through the driven pinion and holder. O-rings at the cap and collar help prevent fluid leaks.

The driven pinion holder positions the pinion and shaft in the steering gear housing (Figure 7-9). A lock ring secures the driven pinion, the shaft, and the parts riding on the shaft in the holder. When the driven pinion holder is installed into the steering gear housing, an opening in the holder allows the pinion gear to mesh with the rack teeth. An O-ring under the holder flange helps prevent fluid leaks. Bolts secure the flange and a washer to the gear housing, and

Passive Four-Wheel Steering

Four-wheel steering as a response to driver action is the latest in automotive technology. However, a design concept called "passive" 4WS has been around on production cars since the 1978 introduction of the Porsche 928. The front wheels of the Porsche 928 steer conventionally, but the rear axle—called the Weissach axle, after the place where the idea was developed—provides passive steering. Passive steering does not activate when the steering wheel is turned; rather, the system responds to road forces simply by virtue of its design.

The Weissach axle uses a flexible front mount on the lower control arms of the rear suspension. During deceleration from throttle lift or braking, rear wheels naturally tend to toe out, which creates oversteer. However, the flexible mount causes the rear wheels to toe in under these circumstances. The result is a consistent, slight toe-in under all driving conditions. Today, a

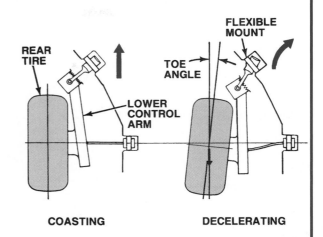

number of manufacturers use some type of passive four-wheel steering in performance-oriented multi-link rear suspension designs, such as the "tri-axial floating" hub used at the rear of the Mazda RX-7.

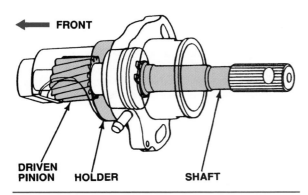

Figure 7-10. The driven pinion holder, which positions the pinion in the steering gear, has an open area that allows the pinion teeth to mesh with the teeth on the rack.

a small rod on the flange provides a hand-hold for adjusting preload (Figure 7-10). A dust cover slides over the driven pinion shaft to seal and protect the assembly and is secured with a band clamp.

Center Shaft

The center shaft, which connects the front steering gear to the rear steering gear, has U-joints at each end. The U-joints attach the center shaft to short shafts extending from each steering gear. Universal joints, as explained in Chapter 4 of this *Classroom Manual,* permit changes in angles be-

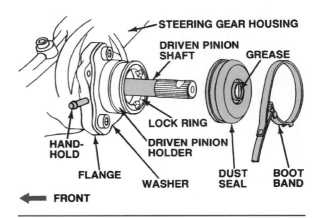

Figure 7-11. A lock ring secures the moving parts in the pinion holder, the hand-hold is used for adjusting preload, and the assembly is protected by a dust cover.

tween two shafts while still allowing them to transfer rotary motion.

The front U-joint connects the center shaft to the driven pinion shaft, and the rear U-joint connects it to the offset shaft in the rear steering gear. Dust covers protect both U-joints from dirt and debris. When the front steering gear rack turns the driven pinion, the pinion shaft turns the center shaft (Figure 7-11). The center shaft in turn rotates the offset shaft of the rear steering gear.

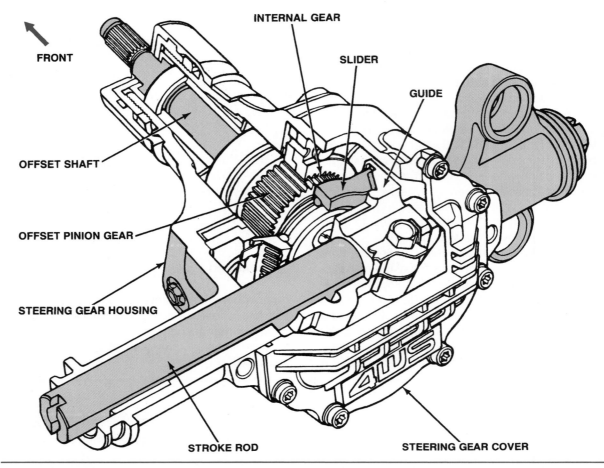

FRONT

INTERNAL GEAR

SLIDER

GUIDE

OFFSET SHAFT

OFFSET PINION GEAR

STEERING GEAR HOUSING

STROKE ROD

STEERING GEAR COVER

Figure 7-12. Inside the rear steering gear housing, the rotary steering input of the offset shaft is converted to lateral movement of the stroke rod by the offset pinion gear, internal gear, and slider and guide mechanism.

Rear Steering Gear

The working parts of the rear steering gear are encased in the rear steering gear housing, and the action of these parts changes the rotary input from the center shaft into lateral motion at the rear wheels (Figure 7-12). The main components of the rear steering gear are the:

- Offset shaft and pinion gear
- Internal gear
- Slider and guide mechanism
- Stroke rod

Inside the rear steering gear, the offset shaft is machined with a disc face and a short shaft that extends from the disc into the center of the pinion gear. The offset shaft is so named because the axis of the short shaft that the pinion gear mounts to is offset from the input shaft axis. As the offset shaft rotates, it drives the pinion gear around the inner circumference of the **internal gear** (Figure 7-13). As the pinion gear travels in a circle around the offset shaft axis, its teeth walk around the internal

gear, and the pinion spins on its own axis due to the offset. This type of gear drive is also known as a "planetary gearset" because the pinion gear circles a center point of the internal gear while rotating on its own axis at the same time.

The trailing end of the pinion gear also ends with a disc face and a short offset shaft. This shaft extends from the pinion into the slider and guide mechanism. As the pinion rotates, the offset shaft causes the slider and guide to follow its movement. When the pinion gear transmits vertical, or up-and-down, movement to the slider, the slider moves vertically in tracks on the guide, but the guide does not move up-and-down. However, the slider does not slide horizontally, so when the pinion transmits horizontal, or side-to-side, movement to the slider, the guide also moves side-to-side.

The slider and guide mechanism works because moving in a circle involves both vertical and lateral motion. When the disc follows the circular path of the offset pinion, it transmits both vertical and lateral motion to the slider. The slider moves verti-

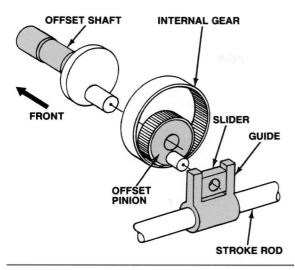

Figure 7-13. As the pinion gear on the offset shaft turns, it walks around the internal gear to move the slider and guide mechanism. The guide moves the stroke rod, and thus the tie rods and rear wheels, side-to-side.

cally, in the guide tracks, and laterally, but transmits only the lateral movement to the guide. The bottom of the guide attaches to the stroke rod, so lateral movement of the guide transfers to the stroke rod as well. The outer ends of the stroke rod attach to the rear tie rods, so as the stroke rod moves, the tie rods move along with it to steer the rear wheels.

Stroke Rod Movement
When the steering wheel is turned slightly, the rear steering gear system turns the rear wheels in the same direction as the front wheels. When the steering wheel is turned further, the rear steering gear turns the rear wheels in the opposite direction of the front wheels. To understand this, picture the face of the offset pinion as the face of a clock. As the shaft to the slider progresses from six o'clock to nine o'clock, the lateral movement is toward the left, and when the shaft moves from nine to twelve o'clock, its lateral movement is toward the right (Figure 7-14). Thus, when the slider and guide mechanism transmits lateral movement to the stroke rod, it moves the rod first completely to one side, then brings it back and moves it completely to the opposite side. So, as the driver turns the steering wheel slightly, the wheels move in the same direction as the front wheels. As the driver continues turning the steering wheel farther, the offset shaft of the pinion gear travels past center and the slider and guide begin moving in the opposite direction, which causes the rear wheels to steer opposite the front wheels.

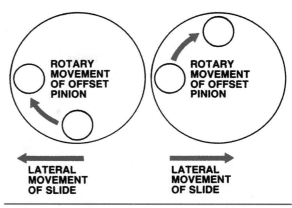

Figure 7-14. Only the lateral portion of the rotary movement of the slider is transferred to the guide. As the slider shaft rotates past center, the result of a sharp steering wheel turning angle, the guide moves in the opposite direction of the offset shaft.

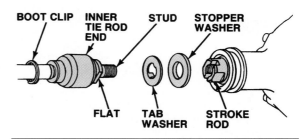

Figure 7-15. Similar to the front steering gear, threads on the inner end of the rear tie rod connect it to the stroke rod and a tab washer secures the assembly.

Rear Steering Linkage
The rear steering linkage consists of two tie rods, one at each end of the steering gear stroke rod. The tie rods install onto the ends of the stroke rod, in the same way that front tie rods install onto the ends of a steering gear rack (Figure 7-15). The end of the stroke rod is notched and has female threads. A boot protects each inner tie rod end and is secured to the steering gear and tie rod by band clamps. The outer tie rod end stud fits through the end of the steering arm, and a nut threads onto the top of the stud to hold the two parts together.

ELECTRONICALLY CONTROLLED FOUR-WHEEL STEERING

Mazda, Mitsubishi, and Nissan use electronically controlled hydraulic devices to steer the rear wheels in their 4WS systems. Mazda uses mechanical means to transfer the steering wheel

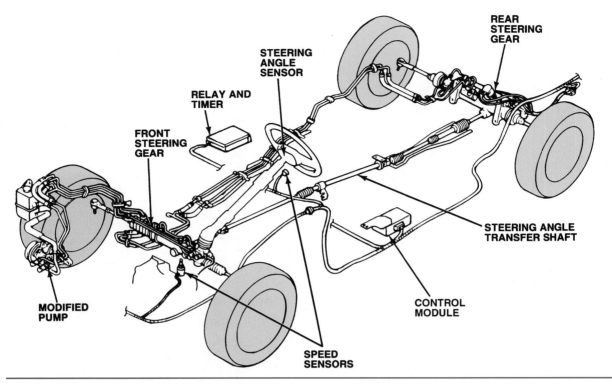

Figure 7-16. The steering angle transfer shaft provides a direct mechanical link between the front and rear steering gears on the Mazda 4WS system. The rear hydraulic system is controlled by an electronic system that reacts to steering wheel angle and vehicle speed.

angle to the rear steering gear and electronic controls to provide vehicle speed input. A hydraulic control valve turns the rear wheels. Mitsubishi and Nissan systems have no mechanical link between the front and rear steering gears. The rear-unit controls are all electronic, and a rear hydraulic system actuates the rear wheels. All of these 4WS designs are hybrid electronic systems. That is, although the angle at which the rear wheels are turned is determined by electronic input signals, some other means, either hydraulic or mechanic, are used to actually steer the rear wheels. The only true electronic 4WS system is the one used from 1992 through 1996 on the Honda Prelude. The Honda system steers the rear wheels with an electric motor.

Mazda System

Mazda introduced their 4WS system on the 1988 626 to provide improved handling on the highway and sharper steering response in city driving. A steering angle transfer shaft connects the front and rear steering gears, but the actual turning

force applied to the rear wheels is provided by hydraulic pressure (Figure 7-16). The Mazda system saw limited production and was discontinued after the 1990 model year. The main components of the system are the:

- Front steering gear
- Steering angle transfer shaft
- Electronic sensors and control unit
- Modified pump
- Rear steering gear

In the Mazda 4WS system, the front and rear steering gears are served by separate hydraulic systems, which required some modifications to the pump (Figure 7-17). Two tie rods compose the rear steering linkage. A **fail-safe system** centers the rear wheels in the event of an electronic or hydraulic failure. During fail-safe operation, only the front wheels are steered.

At speeds below 22 mph (35 km/h), the rear wheels of the Mazda 4WS system turn in the opposite direction of the front wheels, where as at speeds above 22 mph (35 km/h), the rear wheels turn in the same direction as the front wheels

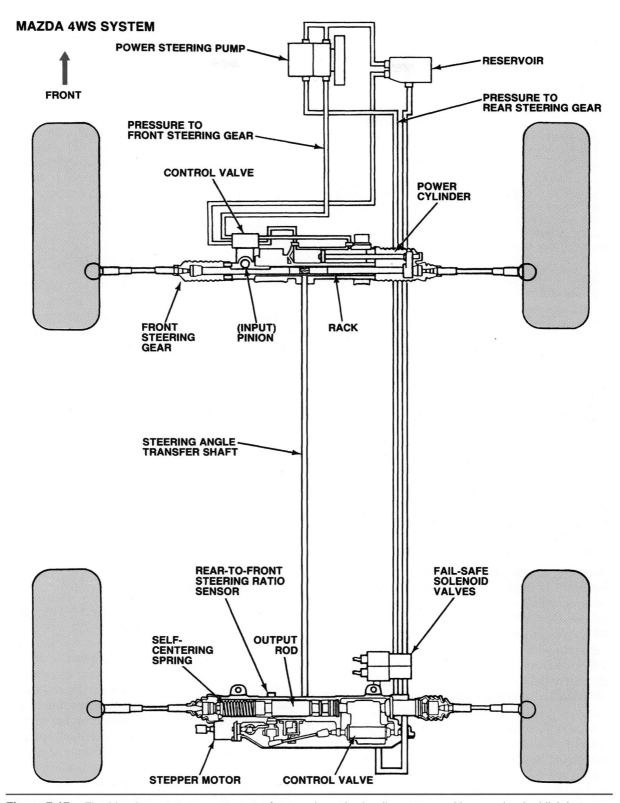

MAZDA 4WS SYSTEM

FRONT

POWER STEERING PUMP

RESERVOIR

PRESSURE TO
REAR STEERING GEAR

PRESSURE TO
FRONT STEERING GEAR

CONTROL VALVE

POWER
CYLINDER

FRONT
STEERING
GEAR

(INPUT)
PINION

RACK

STEERING ANGLE
TRANSFER SHAFT

REAR-TO-FRONT
STEERING RATIO
SENSOR

FAIL-SAFE
SOLENOID
VALVES

SELF-
CENTERING
SPRING

OUTPUT
ROD

STEPPER MOTOR

CONTROL VALVE

Figure 7-17.   The Mazda system uses separate front and rear hydraulic systems with a mechanical link between the two steering gears. Note that the design of the front rack and pinion steering gear is unusual in that the power cylinder is separate from the rack.

MAZDA 4-WHEEL STEERING OPERATION

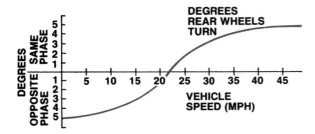

Figure 7-18. Mazda 4WS operates in the opposite-phase mode when vehicle speed is below 22 mph (35 km/h) and in the same-phase mode at higher road speeds. Steering wheel angle affects how many degrees the rear wheels steer.

(Figure 7-18). Although steering wheel angle does not determine whether the rear wheels operate in same-phase or opposite-phase, it does affect how many degrees the rear wheels turn in either direction. Maximum allowable rear wheel steering angle is limited to five degrees.

Front Steering Gear

The front steering gear is a power-assisted rack and pinion unit, similar to those in 2WS systems. Again, for precise information about 2WS power-assisted steering gears, refer to Chapter 6 of this *Classroom Manual.* As in the Honda 4WS system, the Mazda front steering gear has a modified rack to transmit mechanical motion to the rear steering gear. The "steering angle transfer shaft" links the two gearboxes.

Steering Angle Transfer Shaft

The steering angle transfer shaft transfers rotary movement from front to rear in much the same manner that a driveshaft transfers torque in a RWD powertrain. The transfer shaft is a three-piece unit with U-joint connections (Figure 7-19). A U-joint connects the front section of the transfer shaft to the front steering gear output shaft, and a U-joint and **slip yoke** attach the rear section of the shaft to the rear steering gear input shaft. Pleated rubber boots seal and protect the U-joints and slip yoke. Two brackets secure the center section of the transfer shaft to the underside of the chassis and a two-piece cover installs over the rear section of the transfer shaft to protect it.

Electronic Sensors and Control Module

The electronic control module (ECM) is a small computer that receives and sends electronic sig-

nals to operate the 4WS system. The ECM processes input signals from three sensors:

- Speed sensor at the speedometer
- Speed sensor at the transaxle
- Rear-to-front steering ratio sensor, at the rear steering gear

A slide switch on the ECM permits manual adjustment of steering feel (Figure 7-20). The difference between the high and low switch settings is approximately 10 percent at 6.2 mph (10 km/h). This switching capability is a characteristic of Mazda electronically controlled power steering systems, both two-wheel and four-wheel, and is not specific to the 4WS system.

Speed Sensors

The transaxle speed sensor is used as a backup in the event of an instrument panel speed sensor failure (Figure 7-21). Both speed sensors detect speedometer cable rotation and transmit a variable-frequency voltage signal that corresponds to vehicle speed. In response to speed sensor input, the ECM outputs a variable current to the stepper motor at the rear steering gear, which operates the control yoke. The effect of control yoke angle on the rear steering gear will be discussed in detail later.

Rear-to-Front Steering Ratio Sensor

The rear-to-front steering ratio sensor, which monitors stepper motor operation, consists of a:

- Power supply wire and ground wire
- Control yoke pivot shaft
- Brush and brush attachment panel
- Resistance plate
- Conduction plate
- Output signal wire

These components are housed in a casing mounted on the rear steering gear (Figure 7-22). The shaft, which is the pivotal axis of the control yoke, rides on a bearing to reduce friction between it and the casing. The power supply and ground wires send a voltage signal through the sensor. The resistance plate is positioned between the power source and the conduction plate, and the output signal wire attaches to the conduction plate. The shaft operates the brush and brush attachment panel, which affect the level of resistance in the resistance plate. The higher the resistance, the less voltage can travel through the conduction plate to the output wire and back to the ECM. Thus, the strength of the voltage signal from the rear-to-front steering ratio sensor provides an electronic reference of control yoke angle. Based on this signal, the ECM

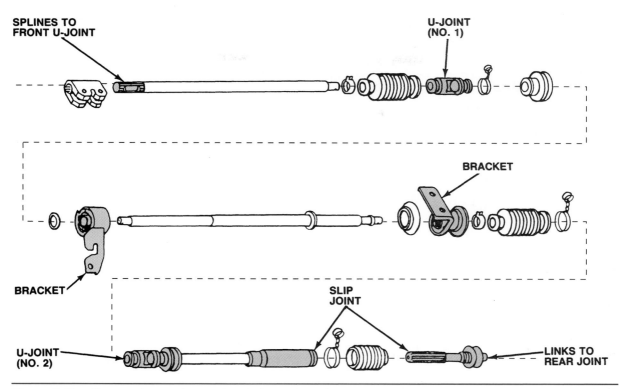

Figure 7-19. The steering angle transfer shaft consists of several sections connected by U-joints. The brackets on the center section bolt to the underside of the chassis.

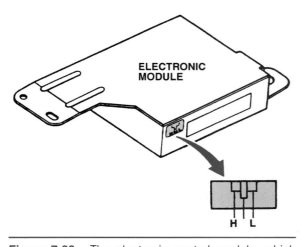

Figure 7-20. The electronic control module, which dictates steering hydraulic system response to driving conditions, can be manually set at "high" for harder steering or "low" for easier steering.

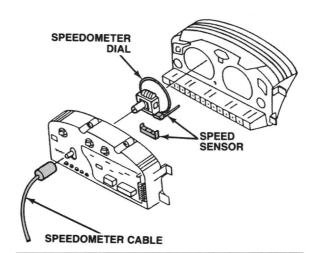

Figure 7-21. The speed sensor located behind the instrument cluster provides the primary vehicle speed signal to the ECM based on speedometer cable rotation.

regulates voltage to the stepper motor to produce the correct turning angle for operating conditions.

Modified pump

The power steering pump on the Mazda 4WS system is essentially two pumps driven by one shaft

and lodged in one housing (Figure 7-23). One suction hose from the remote reservoir splits to feed two inlet ports on the pump housing. Each rotor and vane assembly takes in power steering fluid and forces it out under pressure into separate pressure lines. A separate flow control valve modulates fluid flow on each side. Pressure to the front

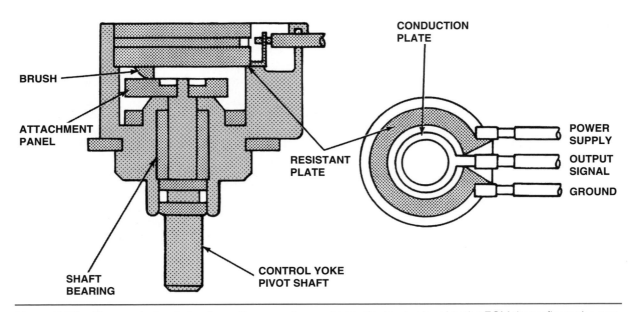

Figure 7-22. The rear-to-front steering ratio sensor transmits an electronic signal to the ECM that reflects the control yoke angle.

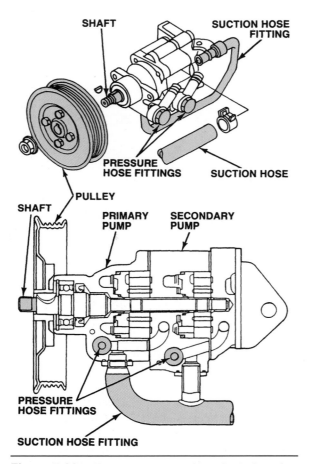

Figure 7-23. Two vane pumps in a single housing provide pressure to the front and rear hydraulic systems.

hydraulic system is about 140 psi (980 kPa) higher than the pressure sent to the rear control valve.

Rear Steering Gear

The Mazda rear steering gear is electronically operated by the stepper motor, mechanically operated by the steering angle transfer shaft, and hydraulically operated by the control valve. The main working parts inside the rear steering gear are the:

- Control yoke
- Swing arm
- Main and small bevel gears
- Control rod and valve input rod
- Control valve
- Output rod

Together, these parts operate the rear steering linkage to provide the proper direction and degree of turn for the rear wheels. Mazda refers to this assembly as a "phase control system," rather than a steering gear (Figure 7-24).

Control Yoke and Swing Arm

The control yoke regulates the position of the swing arm. The **stepper motor** moves the control yoke through a gear system, according to the signal it receives from the ECM.

The stepper motor, which is mounted on one side of the assembly, rotates a worm shaft through

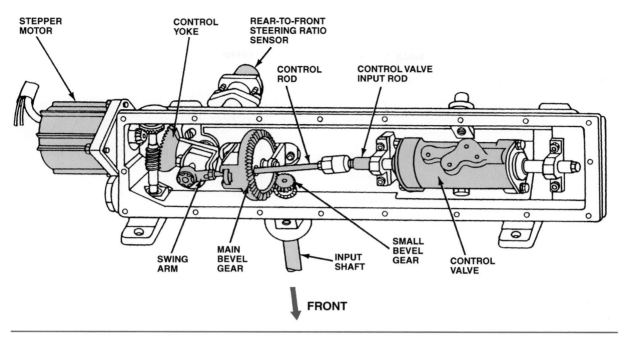

Figure 7-24. The rear steering gear, or phase control system, uses the stepper motor, the input shaft, and hydraulic pressure to control steering gear operation. This view is from underneath the steering gear with the oil pan removed.

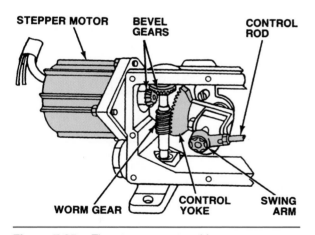

Figure 7-25. The stepper motor drives a worm gear through a set of bevel gears to position the control yoke. Control yoke position determines in what direction the swing arm travels when the control rod moves it.

a set of **bevel gears.** An electronic signal from the ECM determines how far, and in which direction, the stepper motor bevel gear rotates (Figure 7-25). The worm gear meshes with teeth on the control yoke. The stepper motor responds to the speed-based signal from the ECM and turns the first bevel gear either clockwise or counterclockwise. In turn, the second bevel gear rotates the worm gear, so that the control yoke climbs up or down the worm gear thread. When the vehicle is travel-

ling at 22 mph (35 km/h), the worm gear centers the control yoke in a neutral position. At speeds below 22 mph (35 km/h), the worm gear moves the yoke downward, and when speed exceeds 22 mph (35 km/h), the yoke moves upward.

The control yolk provides the anchor point for one end of the swing arm, and the other end of the swing arm attaches to the control rod. The anchor point of the swing arm to the control yoke corresponds to the pivot point of the control yoke, so repositioning the control yoke does not move the swing arm. Rather, when the swing arm does move, the position of the control yoke determines in what direction it moves. This means that the position of the control yoke determines in which direction the rear wheels turn. However, repositioning the control yoke does not actually turn the rear wheels. Input from the steering angle transfer shaft is needed for that.

Main and Small Bevel Gears
The rear steering gear input shaft extends from the rear U-joint of the steering angle transfer shaft into the rear steering gear. The small bevel gear located at the end of the input shaft meshes with and drives the main bevel gear (Figure 7-26). The control rod, which runs from the swing arm to the control valve input rod, passes through an opening in the main bevel gear.

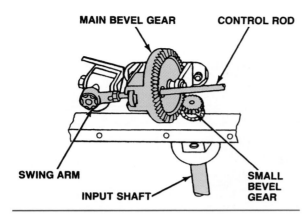

Figure 7-26. The small and main bevel gears transmit motion from the transfer shaft to the control rod, which is linked to the swing arm.

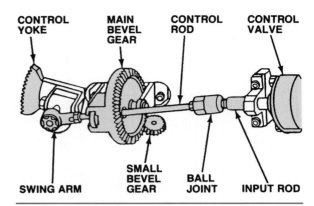

Figure 7-27. The main bevel gear moves the control rod in a path determined by the control yoke and swing arm. Control rod movement operates the input rod, which in turn positions the control valve.

Steering wheel movement transfers through the steering shaft, front steering gear, steering angle transfer shaft, rear steering gear input shaft, and small bevel gear to move the main bevel gear. When this gear moves, it pulls one end of the control rod with it. How far this end of the control rod moves depends on how far the steering wheel is turned. However, the direction it moves depends on the position of the swing arm and control yoke, and thus on vehicle speed.

In summary, the combination of the control yoke position and the position of the main bevel gear determines the travel path of the control rod. Thus, both vehicle speed and steering wheel angle are factors in positioning the rear wheels for a turn.

Control Rod and Valve Input Rod

The control rod extends from the swing arm through the main bevel gear and attaches to the input rod with a small ball joint (Figure 7-27). The input rod moves the steering gear control spool valve in its bore to determine the path of the hydraulic pressure that controls the position of the rear wheels. If the input rod pushes the valve inward in its bore, the rear wheels steer left, and the wheels steer right if the rod pulls the valve outward.

Because the control yoke and swing arm vary their position in relation to road speed, the travel path of the control rod varies too. At speeds below 22 mph (35 km/h), the control rod travels away from the control valve and pulls the input rod with it (Figure 7-28). This moves the spool valve outward in its bore and causes the rear wheels to steer right in opposite-phase operation. At 22 mph

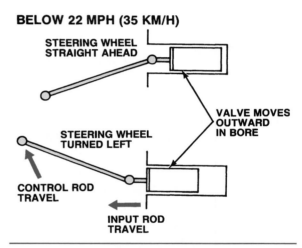

Figure 7-28. At low speeds, below 22 mph (35 km/h), the swing arm guides the control rod so that when the main bevel gear moves the rod, it pulls away from the control.

(35 km/h), the control rod pivots on the ball joint and does not affect the input rod or spool valve, so the rear wheels remain straight (Figure 7-29). At speeds above 22 mph (35 km/h), the control yoke and swing arm make the control rod move toward the valve, pushing the input rod and moving the valve inward in its bore (Figure 7-30). This directs hydraulic pressure to steer the rear wheels left and provide same-phase operation.

Control Valve

In its neutral position, the control valve spool directs pressurized fluid flowing into the rear steering gear equally to both sides of the actuator, or

AT 22 MPH (35 KM/H)

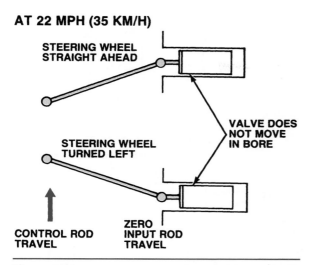

Figure 7-29. At 22 mph (35 km/h), the rear wheels remain in a neutral, straight-ahead position.

ABOVE 22 MPH (35 KM/H)

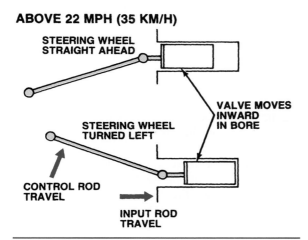

Figure 7-30. At higher speeds, above 22 mph (35 km/h), the control rod pushes the input valve inward to provide same-phase operation of the 4WS system.

power piston, on the output rod (Figure 7-31). An equal amount of fluid is also returned to the reservoir from both sides of the actuator. With this fluid flow, the rear wheels are aimed straight-ahead.

If the input rod pushes the valve inward in its bore, the spool valve directs more pressurized fluid to the left side of the output rod actuator and restricts the return flow of fluid from that side to the reservoir. At the same time, the valve closes the inlet port to restrict the flow of pressurized fluid to the right-side chamber, and opens the return port to route fluid in the right chamber back to the reservoir. If the input rod pulls the valve outward in its bore, the fluid flow is reversed.

Output Rod

The output rod in the Mazda rear steering gear serves the same purpose as the rack in a rack and pinion gear, which is to move the tie rods to reposition the wheels. The actuator on the output rod functions as the power piston on a power-assisted rack. When fluid pressure is greater on the left side of the actuator than the right, the pressure pushes the output rod toward the right. This movement repositions the tie rods and steers the rear wheels to the left. If pressure is greater on the right side of the actuator, the opposite occurs and the rear wheels steer to the right.

One thing to keep in mind about this rear steering gear operation is that the output rod is hydraulically, not mechanically, operated with a hydraulic assist like most front rack and pinion units. If the hydraulic system fails, the rear steering gear cannot operate manually. This is permissible for a rear steering gear because it is not crucial to retaining control of the vehicle, while the front steering gear is.

Rear Steering Linkage

The linkage between the rear steering gear and the rear-wheel steering arms consists of two tie rods, one at each end of the steering gear output rod (Figure 7-32). Each inner tie rod stud installs into an end of the output rod, and the inner tie rod end is protected by pleated boots. The outer tie rod end is a ball joint whose stud fits through the rear steering arm and is secured by a castle nut and cotter pin. A lock nut on each outer tie rod end allows toe adjustment.

Fail-Safe System

The fail-safe system mechanically straightens the rear wheels in the event of a hydraulic or electrical failure to disable rear-wheel steering (Figure 7–33). The components of the fail-safe system are:

- Self-centering spring
- Two solenoid valves
- Two dashboard warning lamps

The self-centering spring coils around a section of the output rod. Whenever hydraulic pressure pushes the output rod right or left, the hydraulic pressure is stronger than the spring force. The fail-safe system activates any time pressure in the hydraulic system drops to the point that it is not strong enough to overcome spring force. When this happens, the spring centers the output shaft to keep the rear wheels pointed straight-ahead. If the problem is a hydraulic

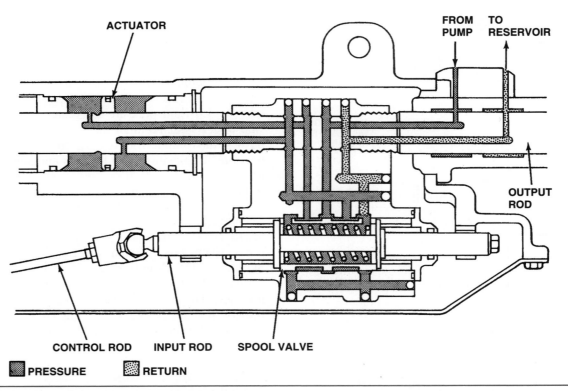

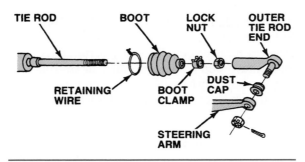

Figure 7-31. The control valve, shown in neutral position, operates the output rod using hydraulic pressure.

Figure 7-32. The rear steering linkage is similar to the front, using two tie rods.

system leak, a fluid level sensor in the reservoir illuminates a warning light on the dashboard to alert the driver.

The ECM, as explained earlier, monitors electrical signals from several sensors. If one or more of the signals fails or if there is some other form of electrical failure, the ECM operates the solenoid valves to drain the rear hydraulic system. Again, the self-centering spring holds the rear wheels straight and a dashboard warning lamp illuminates to alert the driver.

Two solenoid valves are used so that there is a backup should one of them fail. Normally, the solenoid rod in each valve holds the spool valve so

that no fluid flows through the valve. Spring force opposes the rod, but as long as the solenoid receives current it overcomes the spring force so the rod positions the valve. If power to the solenoid is lost, the rod cannot oppose the spring force, so the spring repositions the spool valve. This opens a drain passage from the rear steering gear to bleed off pressure and return the fluid to the reservoir.

Nissan System

Nissan introduced the Super High Capacity Actively Controlled Suspension (Super HICAS), a system that incorporates 4WS with active suspension control, in 1990. The system uses electronic controls to hydraulically steer the rear wheels (Figure 7-34). Super HICAS was available on the Nissan 300ZX through 1996 and on the Infiniti Q45 through 1994. Both vehicles use the same system, but some of the components, such as the ECM and control valve, are in different locations on the vehicle. Exact specifications, such as alignment angles, also differ. Main components of the Nissan 4WS system include the:

- Front steering gear
- Electronic sensors and control unit

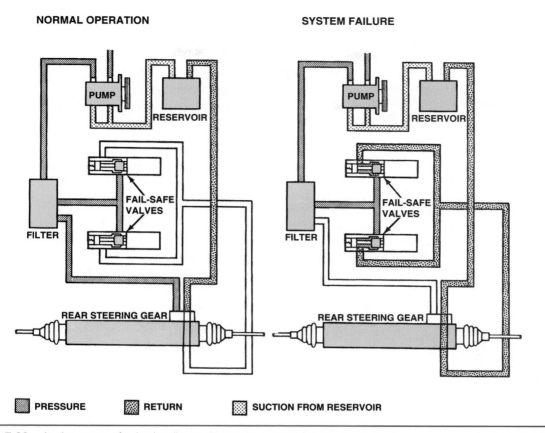

NORMAL OPERATION

SYSTEM FAILURE

PUMP
RESERVOIR
FAIL-SAFE VALVES
FILTER
REAR STEERING GEAR

PUMP
RESERVOIR
FAIL-SAFE VALVES
FILTER
REAR STEERING GEAR

PRESSURE   RETURN   SUCTION FROM RESERVOIR

Figure 7-33. In the event of a hydraulic or electronic system failure, the fail-safe valves open to drain fluid from the rear hydraulic system.

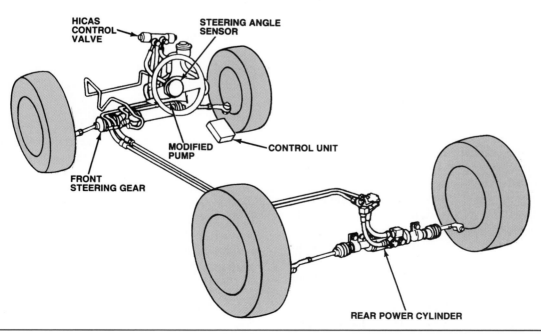

HICAS CONTROL VALVE
STEERING ANGLE SENSOR
MODIFIED PUMP
CONTROL UNIT
FRONT STEERING GEAR
REAR POWER CYLINDER

Figure 7-34. The rear power cylinder of the Nissan 4WS system is hydraulically operated and electronically controlled, but there is no mechanical connection from front to rear.

- Modified pump
- HICAS control valve
- Rear power cylinder

The Nissan 4WS system has separate front and rear hydraulic systems, similar to the Mazda system, which required some modifications to the pump (Figure 7-35). Unlike the Mazda system, there is no mechanical link between the front steering gear and the rear power cylinder on the Nissan system. The rear steering linkage of the Super HICAS system consists of two links connecting the rear power cylinder to the rear steering arms. A fail-safe system centers the rear wheels in the event of an electronic or hydraulic failure. In fail-safe mode, only the front wheels are steered.

When vehicle speed is below 20 mph (32 km/h), the rear wheels in the Nissan 4WS system do not respond to steering wheel movement. With the 4WS system active, at speeds above 20 mph (32 km/h), three factors affect rear-wheel movement:

- Vehicle speed
- Steering wheel angle
- Rate of steering wheel movement

A large steering wheel angle and quick steering wheel movement when the vehicle is traveling at low speeds produce phase-reverse operation. That is, the rear wheels momentarily turn opposite the front wheels, then quickly turn in the same direction. When traveling at higher speeds, slowly moving the steering wheel in a small angle produces same-phase operation mode. That is done to steer the rear wheels in the same direction as the front wheels.

Steering wheel position and rate of turn determine whether the 4WS system operates in the same-phase mode only or in the phase-reverse mode. Vehicle speed affects the turning angle of the rear wheels (Figure 7-36). During high-speed driving, the rear wheels turn most sharply in the same direction as the front wheels. The rear wheels turn slightly in the opposite direction and then less sharply in the same direction if the vehicle is traveling at medium speeds. At low vehicle speeds, the rear wheels turn the most sharply in the opposite direction and only slightly in the same direction.

A mechanical link between the front and rear steering gears in the Nissan 4WS system is impractical because the rear-wheel response to steering wheel angle is variable, while the front wheels operate in direct response to steering wheel angle. The rear steering unit is hydraulically actuated, but it is completely electronically controlled.

Electronic controls provide quicker, more exact response to driver input and vehicle conditions than either mechanical or hydraulic controls.

Front Steering Gear

Nissan uses virtually the same front steering gear for 4WS as the one used for similar models with conventional steering. This is possible because there is no transfer shaft, or any other direct link, between this steering gear and the rear power cylinder. With Super HICAS, the front steering gear controls only the front wheels.

Electronic Sensors and Control Module

Two sensors provide the primary inputs that the 4WS electronic control module uses to regulate rear-wheel steering. These two sensors are the:

- Vehicle speed sensor
- Steering angle sensor

Super HICAS relies on the signal of the same vehicle speed sensor (VSS), located in the instrument panel, used for the electronic speedometer and engine management system. The VSS transmits a variable-frequency signal to the ECM. The steering angle sensor, which is mounted in the steering column, provides information on how far the steering wheel is turned and how quickly it is moving (Figure 7-37). Based on the signals of these two sensors, the ECM determines whether, how far, and in what direction the rear wheels should turn. To implement rear-wheel steering, the ECM outputs a signal to operate the HICAS control valve, which applies the appropriate hydraulic pressure to the rear power cylinder.

Modified Pump

In effect, the Nissan 4WS system has a second rear-system power steering pump built into the same housing and driven by the same shaft as the front-system pump (Figure 7-38). Both units are vane-type pumps. Fluid from the front pump flows to the front steering gear to provide hydraulic assist, while the rear pump directs pressurized fluid to the HICAS control valve, which controls fluid pressure application to the rear power cylinder.

HICAS Control Valve

Also known as the "HICAS solenoid valve," the HICAS control valve uses two solenoids, left-hand and right-hand, to apply hydraulic pressure to the

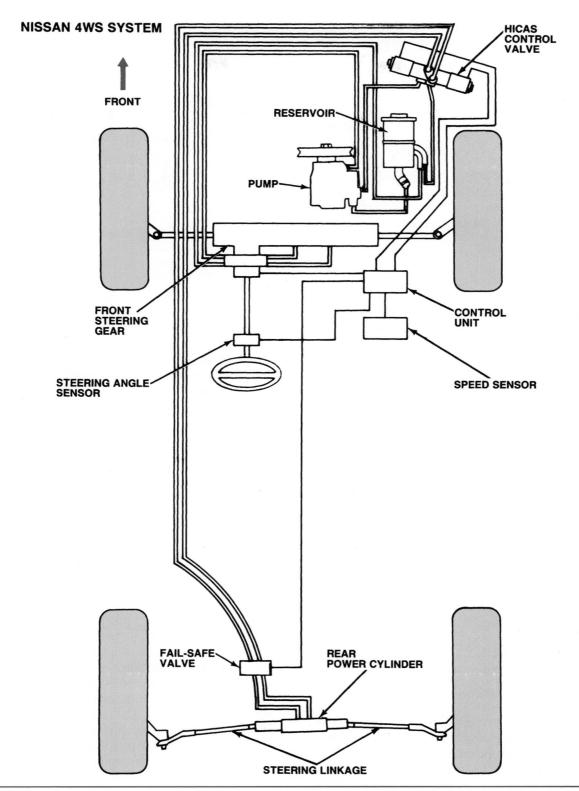

NISSAN 4WS SYSTEM

FRONT

HICAS CONTROL VALVE

RESERVOIR

PUMP

FRONT STEERING GEAR

STEERING ANGLE SENSOR

CONTROL UNIT

SPEED SENSOR

FAIL-SAFE VALVE

REAR POWER CYLINDER

STEERING LINKAGE

Figure 7-35.   There is no mechanical link between the front and rear steering gears on the Nissan Super HICAS system; the ECM controls the rear hydraulic system in response to steering wheel position and vehicle speed.

173

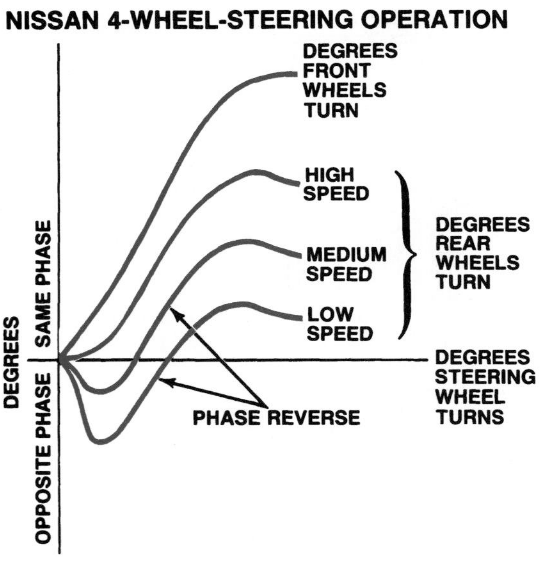

NISSAN 4-WHEEL-STEERING OPERATION

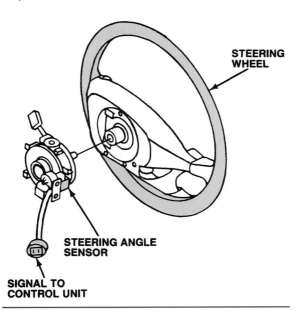

Figure 7-36. Depending on vehicle speed, the same steering wheel angle and rate of turn produce different responses at the rear wheels.

Figure 7-37. The steering angle sensor is located in the steering column behind the steering wheel and monitors both how far and how quickly the steering wheel turns.

rear power cylinder (Figure 7-39). Depending on which solenoid the ECM activates, the HICAS control valve routes pressurized fluid from the power steering pump to either the right or left side of the rear power cylinder to turn the rear wheels. The output signal from the ECM also determines the amount of pressure the valve relays to the power cylinder, which in turn determines how far

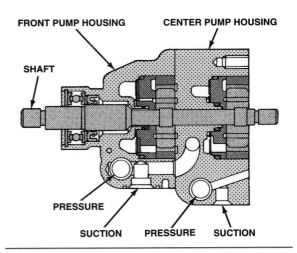

Figure 7-38. A dual-stage, vane-type pump routes pressurized fluid to the front steering gear and the rear power cylinder.

the rear wheels turn. To provide phase-reverse operation, the control module first activates one solenoid, then the other, to change the direction of the rear wheels during low-speed cornering.

Rear Power Cylinder

The **rear power cylinder** is not a true steering gear, because it uses hydraulic pressure, rather than gears, to operate the rear wheels (Figure 7-40). Power steering fluid travels through two fluid lines from the right-hand and left-hand sides of the HICAS control valve into the power cylinder. Hydraulic pressure on one side or the other inside the cylinder applies force to move the cylinder rod to reposition the rear wheels.

To operate the rear power cylinder, the hydraulic pressure must be strong enough to overcome the force of the centering spring located inside the cylinder. As explained later, this spring is part of the 4WS fail-safe system.

Rear Steering Linkage

The rear steering linkage is simple. Two links, similar to tie rods, join the power cylinder rod to the rear steering arms. The inner end of each link attaches to the power cylinder with a ball joint, while the outer end is a pivot secured to the steering arm by a nut and cotter pin.

Fail-Safe System

The fail-safe system positions the rear wheels straight-ahead in the event of a hydraulic or electrical failure. The fail-safe components are the

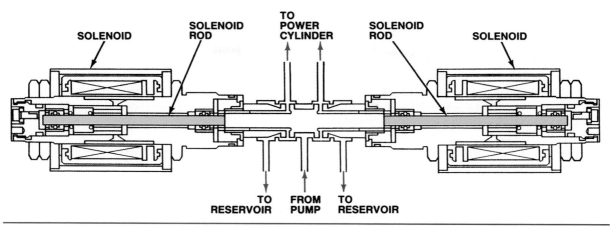

Figure 7-39. The HICAS control valve contains two solenoids that direct the flow of pressurized hydraulic fluid to the appropriate chambers of the rear power cylinder.

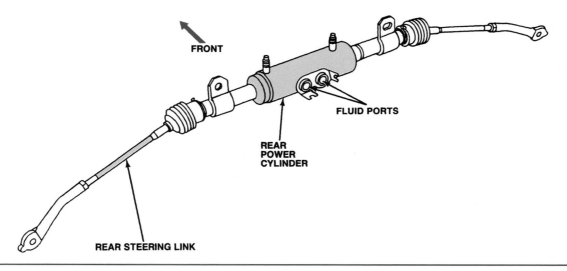

Figure 7-40. Hydraulic pressure, not gearing, operates the rear power cylinder to move the steering links and reposition the rear wheels.

rear cylinder centering spring and a solenoid-operated fail-safe valve.

The centering spring straightens the rear wheels by spring force if hydraulic pressure drops, as from a leak, pump failure, or broken drive belt, below spring force. During normal 4WS operation, the fluid pressure that pushes and pulls the rod in the power cylinder is strong enough to overcome spring force.

Fluid from the HICAS control valve passes through the fail-safe valve on its way to the power cylinder (Figure 7-41). Normally, the fail-safe valve does not interfere with pressure applied to or returning from the power cylinder. However, if a failure occurs, the ECM commands the fail-safe solenoid to equalize the fluid pressure on both sides of the power cylinder to center the cylinder rod.

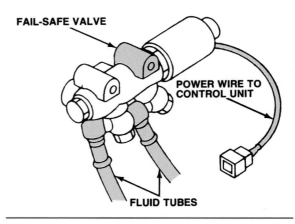

Figure 7-41. The fail-safe valve equalizes pressure in the rear power cylinder so that spring force can hold the rear wheels in a straight-ahead position should a system failure occur.

Honda Electronic System

The 4WS system available on the Honda Prelude from 1992 through 1996 is the only system that is completely electronic. On this system, a conventional power-assisted rack and pinion steering gear is used to turn the front wheels, while an electronic steering actuator is used to steer the rear wheels. There is no direct link, mechanical or hydraulic, between the front steering gear and the rear steering actuator. However, the two are indirectly linked by the wiring harnesses that relays input signals from the input sensors to the 4WS control module, which transmits output signals to the rear steering actuator (Figure 7-42).

Operational modes of the electronic system are similar to those of the mechanical system used on earlier Prelude models and discussed previously in this chapter. At low vehicle speeds, the rear wheels operate in opposite phase and at higher speeds the rear wheels steer in the same direction as the front wheels. Two factors, steering wheel angle and the rate of steering wheel movement, determine the steering angle of the rear wheels.

Input Devices

Information on vehicle speed is provided to the ECM by the speed sensor. This device, which is actually a hydraulic pump, is the same unit used to provide vehicle speed information for the variable-assist power steering system. Operation of the speed sensor was detailed when discussing the variable-assist power steering system of the Acura Integra and will not be repeated here. Refer to the appropriate section in Chapter 6 of this *Classroom Manual* for speed sensor information.

Two sensors, the front main steering angle sensor and the front sub steering angle sensor, provide steering wheel movement information to the ECM. The front main steering angle sensor, which is mounted on the steering column, transmits an electrical signal that reflects both steering wheel angle and rotation speed (Figure 7-43). The front sub angle sensor, which is located on the steering gear, transmits a signal that reflects how far and in what direction the front wheels are turned (Figure 7-44).

Two additional sensors, the rear main steering angle sensor and the rear sub steering angle sen-

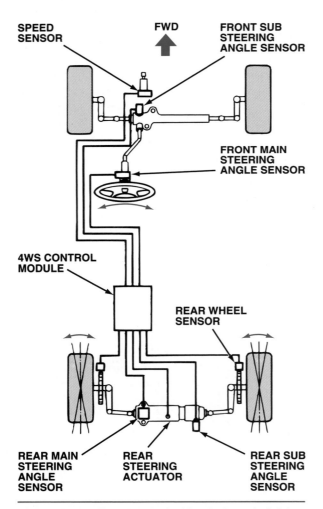

Figure 7-42. The electrical wiring is the only link between the front steering gear and the rear steering actuator on the Honda electronic system.

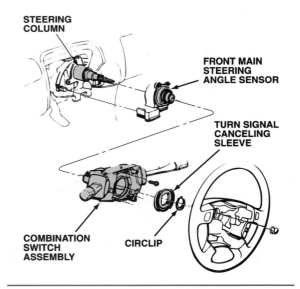

Figure 7-43. The front main steering angle sensor mounts on the steering column below the combination switch and steering wheel.

sor, provide feedback information to the ECM. Signals from these sensors, both of which are mounted on the rear steering actuator, allow the ECM to determine if and how well the rear steering actuator is responding to output commands. The rear main steering angle sensor signal corresponds to the turning angle and direction of the rear wheels, while the rear sub steering angle sensor signal provides information on the position of the rear wheels.

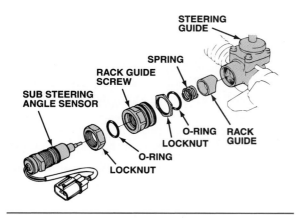

Figure 7-44. The front sub steering angle sensor installs on the steering gear along with the rack guide assembly.

Rear Steering Actuator

The rear steering actuator contains a permanent-magnet electric motor and a recirculating-ball drive mechanism (Figure 7-45). However, the recirculating ball mechanism operates differently than those used in a standard steering gear. On the actuator, the motor and steering shaft, which contains the worm gear, are on the same axis and the shaft runs through the center of the motor. The motor drives the ball nut, rather than the worm gear. The ball nut is held in a fixed position so it can rotate but cannot move laterally. The steering shaft moves instead when current is applied to the motor.

When the ECM applies current to the motor, the motor turns the ball nut, which moves the shaft laterally in one direction. Reversing the polarity of the current applied to a motor also reverses the rotational direction of the motor. So, to move the steering shaft in the opposite direction, the ECM simply reverses the polarity of the motor current. Two return springs, one at each end of the steering shaft, exert force to center the shaft when no current is applied to the motor.

The rear steering actuator assembly, which is a non-serviceable unit, bolts to the underside of the chassis. Tie rods connect each end of the steering shaft to the steering arms of the rear wheels. The

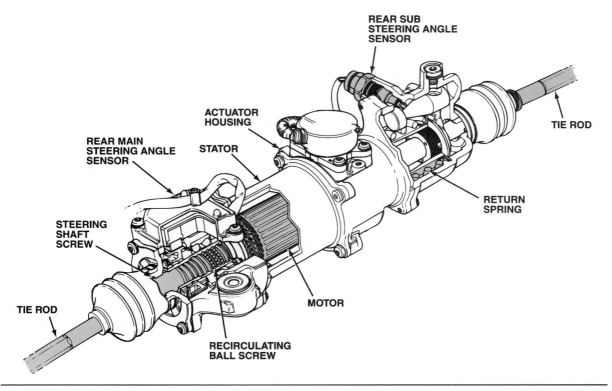

Figure 7-45. The rear steering actuator uses an electric motor and a recirculating ball gearbox to steer the rear wheels.

steering arms extend to the rear of the knuckles, so the rear wheels steer in the opposite direction of shaft movement.

GM REAR-WHEEL STEERING DESCRIPTION AND OPERATION

Quadrasteer™ is a four-wheel steering system that dramatically enhances low-speed maneuverability, high-speed stability, and towing capability. The system is an electrically powered rear-wheel steering system comprised of the following components:

- A steerable, solid rear axle
- A heavy duty wiring harness and fuse
- A programmable control module
- A power relay in the control module
- A rack and pinion style steering actuator mounted on the rear differential cover
- An electric motor assembly on top of the rear steering actuator
- Three Hall-effect switches in the motor assembly
- A shorting relay in the motor assembly
- A rear-wheel position sensor located under a cover on the bottom of the actuator, below the motor assembly
- A steering wheel position sensor located at the base of the steering column
- A mode select switch on the dash

The rear-wheel steering control module has these inputs:

- Battery voltage
- Switched battery voltage
- Class 2 serial data
- Steering wheel position sensor analog signal, via class 2 message from the BCM
- Steering wheel position sensor phase A
- Steering wheel position sensor phase B
- Steering wheel position sensor marker pulse
- Rear-wheel position sensor position 1
- Rear-wheel position sensor position 2
- Rear-wheel steering motor hall sensor hall A
- Rear-wheel steering motor hall sensor hall B
- Rear-wheel steering motor hall sensor hall C

- Vehicle speed signal from the IPC
- Rear-wheel steering mode switch signal

The rear-wheel steering control module has these outputs:

- Rear-wheel steering module class 2 serial data
- Rear-wheel steering motor phase A control
- Rear-wheel steering motor phase B control
- Rear-wheel steering motor phase C control
- Rear-wheel steering motor shorting relay voltage
- Rear-wheel steering mode select switch supply voltage
- Two-wheel steer mode indicator control
- Four-wheel steer mode indicator control
- Four-wheel steer tow mode indicator control
- Rear-wheel position sensor 5-volt reference
- Rear-wheel steering motor hall sensor 12-volt reference
- Steering wheel position sensor Phase A, Phase B, and marker pulse 12-volt reference

Separate connectors to the rear-wheel steering control module are provided for the following four capacities:

- Vehicle battery power
- The vehicle class 2, steering wheel position, mode select switch, speed sensor signals
- The motor phase power leads
- The motor hall sensors, shorting relay, and rear-wheel position sensor signals

Steering Modes

The system operates in three principal modes, as follows.

Two-Wheel Steer Mode
Normal steering operation, where the rear wheels are held in a centered position. Rear-wheel steering is disabled while in this mode.

Four-Wheel Steer Mode
The four-wheel steering mode provides three principal phases of steering: negative phase, neutral phase, and positive phase. Negative phase occurs at low speeds and the rear wheels turn opposite of the front wheels. In the neutral phase, the rear wheels are centered and do not turn. Positive

---

IMPORTANT: Beginning with the 2003 model year, the rear-wheel steering control module supports flash programming. Beginning with the 2004 model year, the combination yaw rate/lateral accelerometer sensor has been removed.

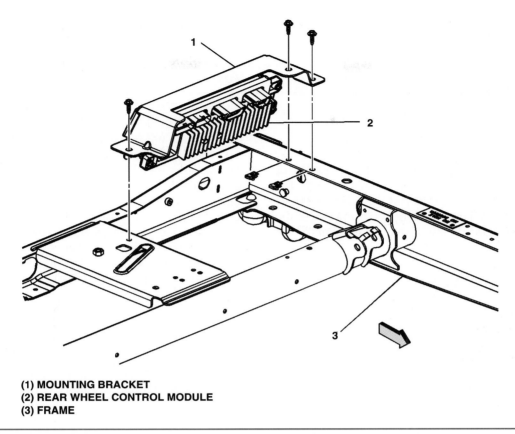

(1) MOUNTING BRACKET
(2) REAR WHEEL CONTROL MODULE
(3) FRAME

Figure 7-46. Rear-wheel steering control module. (Courtesy of General Motors Corporation)

phase occurs at higher speeds and the rear wheels turn in the same direction as the front wheels.

NOTE: Crossover speed is the speed at which the control module transitions from negative phase steering to positive phase steering. In four-wheel steer mode, this transition occurs when the vehicle obtains a speed of 65 km/h (40 mph).

Four-Wheel Steer Tow Mode
The four-wheel steer tow mode provides more positive phase steering than the normal four-wheel steering at high speed. During low speed driving, the four-wheel steer tow mode provides similar negative phase steering as it does in the normal four-wheel steering mode. The crossover speed in the four-wheel steer tow mode occurs at 40 km/h (25 mph).

Rear-Wheel Steering Control Module

The **rear-wheel steering control module** (Figure 7-46) controls all functions of the rear-wheel steering system. The module has a dedicated power feed line from an under hood fuse holder, via a 125-amp mega fuse. The module is located in the rear of the vehicle on the underbody. The module uses the previously listed inputs to determine when and how far to turn the rear wheels. The module uses the hall switches in the motor assembly, a shorting relay, and a motor control relay to monitor and control the direction and speed of the motor. The module also controls the duty cycle of the phase leads to the motor. The motor control relay is part of the rear-wheel steering control module and is not serviceable. The module uses both a class 2 and a discrete vehicle speed signal. The two vehicle speed signals are used for comparison purposes. The system will not function without a discrete vehicle speed sensor signal. The module uses digital inputs from the steering wheel position sensor to determine steering wheel position and rate of change. The BCM sends a class 2 message for the analog portion of the signal from the steering wheel position sensor. The rear-wheel position sensor signals provide the module with rear-wheel position data. The module will send out a class 2 message to the IPC to turn on and off the service four-wheel steering message. The rear-wheel steering control module

IMPORTANT: The rear-wheel steering control module may shut down if the system is operated under very extreme conditions and becomes overheated. The service four-wheel steering message will not be displayed. Once the temperature decreases back to operating range, the rear-wheel steering system will resume normal operation upon the next ignition cycle.

also controls the ground circuits for the mode indicator lamps in the mode select switch.

The control module allows the vehicle's rear wheels to turn a maximum of 12 degrees left or right. When the vehicle is operated in reverse, the maximum rear-wheel steering angle is 5 degrees left or right. When the vehicle is sitting still in the test mode the system will move a maximum of 5 degrees left or right.

Rear-Wheel Steering Mode Switch

The **rear-wheel steering mode switch** (Figure 7-47) located in the instrument panel allows the driver the option of selecting two-wheel steering, four-wheel steering, or four-wheel steering tow modes of operation. The mode switch has indicators that show which mode the rear-wheel steering system is in. When all indicators are lit the rear-wheel steering control module has lost its memory settings and the scan tool must be used to recalibrate the rear-wheel steering control module. During a mode change, the indicator for the selected mode will flash until the mode change is complete. The rear-wheel steering control module will wait for the steering wheel to pass the center position before entering the selected mode. The indicators on the mode switch are LEDs; the switch is also backlit.

Rear-Wheel Steering Motor Assembly

The **rear-wheel steering motor** (Figure 7-48) assembly is a three-phase, six-pole, and brushless DC motor. The motor assembly is located on the

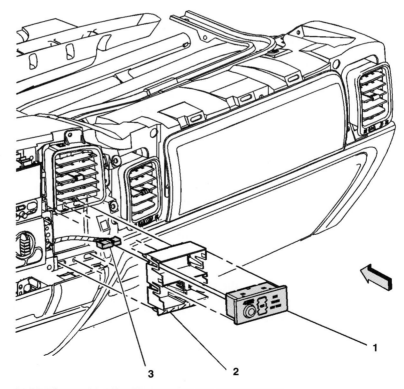

(1) REAR WHEEL STEERING MODE SELECT SWITCH
(2) SWITCH HOUSING
(3) SWITCH ELECTRICAL CONNECTOR

Figure 7-47.   Rear-wheel steering mode switch. (Courtesy of General Motors Corporation)

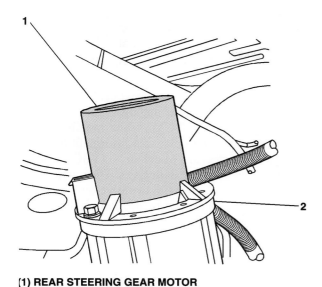

(1) REAR STEERING GEAR MOTOR
(2) STEERING GEAR ASSEMBLY

Figure 7-48. Rear-wheel steering motor assembly. (Courtesy of General Motors Corporation)

top of the rear steering actuator, and transmits its power through a planetary gear set inside the actuator. There are three hall switches inside the assembly: Hall "A," Hall "B," and Hall "C." The rear-wheel steering control modules use the hall switch inputs to monitor the position, speed, and direction of the motor. There is a motor phase shorting relay located inside the motor assembly. The hall switches and shorting relay are part of the motor assembly and cannot be serviced separately. The motor leads are not to be repaired or spliced in any fashion. If there is damage to the motor wiring, the motor assembly must be replaced, as any damage to the wiring could permit water intrusion into the actuator. The motor assembly can be serviced separately from the actuator.

Steering Wheel Position Sensor

The **steering wheel position sensor (SWPS),** as shown in Figure 7-49, provides one analog signal and three digital signals. The digital signals, Phase A, Phase B, and marker pulse, are direct inputs to the rear-wheel steering control module. The analog signal is input to the BCM and is sent

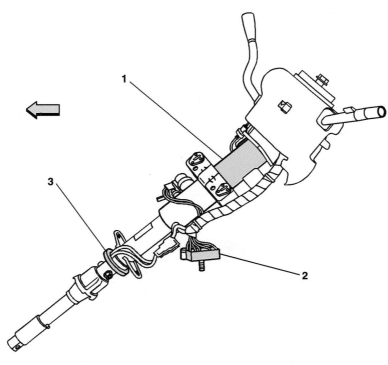

(1) STEERING COLUMN
(2) C201
(3) STEERING WHEEL SPEED/POSITION SENSOR

Figure 7-49. Steering wheel position sensor. (Courtesy of General Motors Corporation)

via a class 2 message to the rear-wheel steering control module. Battery voltage is supplied to the sensor from the cruise fuse to operate the digital portion of the sensor. A 12 V reference is provided by the rear-wheel steering control module to the Phase A, Phase B, and marker pulse circuits of the SWPS. The module monitors each circuit as it either remains high or is pulled low by the SWPS. The scan tool displays the Phase A and Phase B data parameters as either HIGH or LOW when the steering wheel is being rotated. Each change from HIGH to LOW, or LOW to HIGH, represents one degree of steering wheel rotation. When observing the Phase A and Phase B data with the scan tool, the parameters will not always display the same value at the same time. The marker pulse is a digital pulse signal that is displayed as HIGH by the scan tool with the steering wheel angle between $+10°$ and $-10°$. At greater than $10°$ steering wheel angle in either direction, the marker pulse data will be displayed as LOW. The BCM (body computer module) provides the 5-volt reference and low reference for the analog portion of the SWPS. The BCM reads the SWPS analog signal in voltage, which is typically 2.5 volts with the steering wheel on center.

The voltage ranges from .25 volts at approximately one full turn left to 4.75 volts at approximately one full turn right. The voltage will then remain at that level for the remainder of steering wheel travel. This voltage can be monitored in BCM data display. The rear-wheel steering control module receives the analog signal via a class 2 message from the BCM. When monitoring the rear-wheel steering data, this information is displayed in the steering wheel angle (TBC) data parameter, and is shown in degrees. The range of the display is $+/- 225°$, with negative numbers representing steering input to the left, and positive numbers representing input to the right. The sensor may also be utilized by other optional systems.

Rear-Wheel Position Sensor

The **rear-wheel position sensor** (Figure 7-50) has two signal circuits: position 1 and position 2. Position 1 is a linear measurement of voltage per degree. The voltage range for position 1 is from 0.25 to 4.75 volts, and the angular measurement range is from $-620°$ to $+620°$. At 0.25 volts the steering wheel has been rotated $-600°$ past cen-

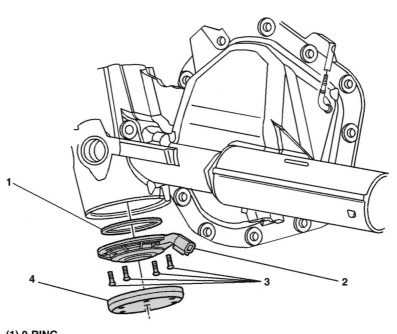

(1) O-RING
(2) REAR WHEEL POSITION SENSOR
(3) RETAINING BOLTS
(4) SENSOR COVER

Figure 7-50. Rear-wheel position sensor. (Courtesy of General Motors Corporation)

ter. At 4.75 volts the steering wheel has been rotated $+600°$ past center. Position 2 circuit is a linear measurement of voltage per degree. The voltage for position 2 increases or decreases from 0.25 to 4.75 volts every $180°$. When the steering wheel is $0°$ or at center, position 1 and position 2 output signals measure 2.5 volts, respectively.

Steerable Rear Axle

The steerable rear axle (2), as shown in Figure 7-51, has a rack and pinion style actuator mounted to the differential cover (1) specially designed axle shafts, and movable hub and bearing assemblies mounted by upper and lower ball joints. The actuator housing is part of the differential cover. In the event of a system malfunction, the actuator returns the rear wheels to the center position through internal springs. The actuator has specially designed inner and outer tie rod ends. There are inner tie rod boots to prevent contaminants from entering the actuator. Long-term exposure to moisture due to a damaged boot or components can result in an internal malfunction or damage.

The actuator has the rear-wheel steering motor assembly attached to the upper housing. There are shields and a skid plate on the rear axle to protect the actuator. There are no internal adjustments to the actuator. It is mandatory to perform a four-wheel alignment if any hard parts, such as tie rods, ball joints, or wheel bearings, are serviced. The axle shafts are a heavy-duty design with a specially designed CV joint and boot at the wheel end of the axle to provide up to $15°$ of movement. The axle

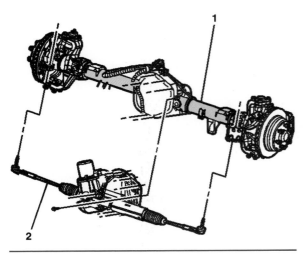

Figure 7-51. Steerable rear axle. (Courtesy of General Motors Corporation)

assembly is a heavier duty version of the standard rear axle used on a non-rear-wheel steer truck.

SUMMARY

Four-wheel steering uses the rear wheels as well as the front ones to steer the vehicle. The first systems became available in 1988 on the Honda Prelude and Mazda 626. The Nissan 4WS system was released in 1990, and Mitsubishi introduced a 4WS system in 1991. Most manufacturers abandoned 4WS by the mid-1990s, and the Mitsubishi is the only manufacturer still producing a 4WS system.

Four-wheel-steering systems can operate in opposite-phase, same-phase, and phase-reverse modes. The Honda, Mazda, and Mitsubishi 4WS systems use opposite-phase and same-phase operation. Phase-reverse operation is a unique characteristic of the Nissan Super HICAS system.

The original Honda design is a completely mechanical 4WS system, in which the front steering gear operates a center shaft, which in turn operates the rear steering gear. The rear steering gear uses a planetary gearset to transmit rotary motion to a slider and guide mechanism that directs the rear wheels through a stroke rod and tie rods.

The Mazda 4WS system is both mechanically and hydraulically operated and uses electronic controls. The front steering gear operates a steering angle transfer shaft, which provides input motion to the rear steering gear. An electronic control module sends a speed-based signal to a stepper motor at the rear steering gear and monitors steering gear operation. Inside the rear steering gear, a complex system of gears and rods responds to transfer shaft movement and stepper motor input to operate a control valve. The control valve hydraulically actuates an output rod that moves the tie rods to steer the rear wheels.

The Nissan Super HICAS is an electronically controlled, hydraulically operated 4WS system. The electronic control module monitors vehicle speed and steering wheel movement through sensors, and controls the hydraulic system accordingly. The signal from the control module operates one of two solenoids in a control valve to apply hydraulic pressure to one side or the other of the rear power cylinder. The rear cylinder operates the rear steering linkage to steer the rear wheels. The Mitsubishi system is similar to the Nissan system, but does not offer phase-reverse operation.

Honda introduced a completely electronic 4WS system on the 1992 Prelude. This system uses electronic sensors to determine steering wheel angle and turning rate and front wheel position. Based on these conditions, an ECM applies current to drive a motor in the rear steering actuator. The motor-driven steering actuator operates the steering linkage to steer the rear wheels.

GM Quadrasteer™ is a four-wheel steering system that dramatically enhances low-speed maneuverability, high-speed stability, and towing capability. The system is an electrically powered rear-wheel steering system. The system operates in three principal modes: two-wheel steer mode, four-wheel steer mode, and four-wheel tow mode. The two-wheel mode is normal steering operation where the rear wheels are held in a centered position and rear-wheel steering is disabled while in this mode. The four-wheel steering mode provides three principal phases of steering: negative phase, neutral phase, and positive phase. Negative phase occurs at low speeds and the rear wheels turn opposite of the front wheels. In the neutral phase, the rear wheels are centered and do not turn. Positive phase occurs at higher speeds and the rear wheels turn in the same direction as the front wheels. The four-wheel steer tow mode provides more positive phase steering than the normal four-wheel steering at high speed. During low-speed driving, the four-wheel steer tow mode provides similar negative phase steering as it does in the normal four-wheel steering mode. The crossover speed in the four-wheel steer tow mode occurs at 40 km/h (25 mph).

Review Questions

For each of the following questions, choose the letter that represents the best possible answer.

1. Which phrase does NOT describe a four-wheel steering (4WS) mode of operation?
   a. Opposite-phase
   b. Phase-forward
   c. Phase-reverse
   d. Same-phase

2. During high-speed directional changes, which operational mode is used on the Honda, Mazda, and Nissan 4WS systems to reduce rear-end yaw?
   a. Opposite-phase
   b. Phase-forward
   c. Phase-reverse
   d. Same-phase

3. The 4WS mode that is unique to the Nissan HICAS system is:
   a. Opposite-phase
   b. Phase-forward
   c. Phase-reverse
   d. Same-phase

4. Which mode of 4WS operation momentarily turns the rear wheels in the opposite direction of the front wheels, and then quickly turns them in the same direction as the front wheels?
   a. Opposite-phase
   b. Phase-forward
   c. Phase-reverse
   d. Same-phase

5. Which component of the Honda mechanical 4WS system is driven by a pinion on the front steering gear to transmit motion from the front steering gear to the rear steering gear?
   a. Center shaft
   b. Stroke rod
   c. Steering angle transfer shaft
   d. Control yoke

6. At the rear wheels of the Honda mechanical 4WS system, the stroke rod is connected to the rear steering arms by:
   a. U-joints
   b. Tie rods
   c. Control rods
   d. Link arms

7. What type of joint is used on the Honda mechanical 4WS system to allow angle changes between the three sections of the center shaft while still allowing them to transfer rotary motion?
   a. CV joints
   b. U-joints
   c. Pivot joints
   d. Slip yokes

8. In the Honda mechanical 4WS system, rotary motion is converted to lateral motion in the rear steering gearbox using:
   a. A control yoke and swing arm
   b. A control valve and output rod
   c. A slider and guide mechanism
   d. Bevel gears and a swing arm

9. Technician A says that in the Mazda 4WS system, the front and rear hydraulic systems are separate, and are driven by essentially two pumps enclosed in the same housing. Technician B says that in the Nissan 4WS system, there is one hydraulic system for both the front and rear, and a single, high-capacity pump is used. Who is correct?
   a. A only
   b. B only
   c. Both A and B
   d. Neither A nor B

10. Technician A says that the rear steering gear in the Mazda 4WS system has electrical input from a stepper motor, and mechanical input from the steering angle transfer shaft. Technician B says that the rear steering gear in the Mazda 4WS system uses a hydraulic control valve to direct pressure. Who is correct?
    a. A only
    b. B only
    c. Both A and B
    d. Neither A nor B

11. The Mazda 4WS fail-safe system disables the rear steering mechanism if there are hydraulic or electrical problems. The hydraulic fluid is drained from the rear steering system by:
    a. Solenoids
    b. Orifices
    c. Control valves
    d. Over-centering springs

12. In the Mazda 4WS fail-safe system, the rear steering mechanism positions the rear wheels straight-ahead using:
    a. Actuator current
    b. Spool valves
    c. Spring force
    d. Hydraulic pressure

13. Which one of the following factors does NOT affect 4WS in the Nissan system?
    a. Vehicle speed
    b. Steering wheel angle
    c. How quickly the steering wheel is turned
    d. Front power assist

14. In the Nissan 4WS system, the rear wheels are controlled:
    a. Hydraulically
    b. Mechanically
    c. Electronically
    d. Pneumatically

15. In which 4WS system is the rear-wheel steering system mechanically linked to the front-wheel steering system?
    a. Honda mechanical
    b. Nissan Super HICAS
    c. Mitsubishi
    d. Honda electronic

16. Technician A says that in the Nissan 4WS rear steering linkage, the inner end of the link is a pivot. Technician B says that a ball joint connects the link to the wheel in the Nissan 4WS rear steering linkage. Who is correct?
    a. A only
    b. B only
    c. Both A and B
    d. Neither A nor B

17. Which 4WS system uses a modified front rack and pinion steering gear to provide steering input to the rear steering gear?
    a. Honda mechanical
    b. Nissan Super HICAS
    c. Mitsubishi
    d. Honda electronic

18. Technician A says the Nissan Super HICAS combines a 4WS system with an electronic active suspension system. Technician B says that there is no mechanical link between the front steering gear and the rear power cylinder on the Nissan 4WS system. Who is correct?
    a. A only
    b. B only
    c. Both A and B
    d. Neither A nor B

19. On the Honda electronic 4WS system, which input sensor is mounted on the steering column?
    a. Rear main steering angle
    b. Rear sub steering angle
    c. Front main steering angle
    d. Front sub steering angle

20. Which of the following sensors used on the Honda electronic 4WS system provides feedback information to the ECM?
    a. Rear main steering angle
    b. Vehicle speed sensor
    c. Rear steering actuator
    d. Front sub steering angle

8

Suspension Components

OBJECTIVES

Upon completion and review of this chapter, you will be able to:

- Define the terms "jounce," "rebound," and "bounce."
- Identify the types of automotive vehicle frames and body types and define their use.
- Identify the types of automotive drive axles and define their use.
- Identify the types of automotive suspension ball joints and bushings, and define their use.
- Identify the types of automotive suspension links and define their use.
- Identify the types of automotive suspension cushioning devices (springs, struts, air devices, and shock absorbers) and explain their operation.
- Define the term "steering knuckle."

KEY TERMS

air shock absorber
air spring
antiroll bar
axle
ball joint
bar mount
bayonet mount
bounce
bump stop
clearance
coil spring
coil-over shock absorber
compression-loaded
  ball joint
constant-rate spring
control arm
crossmember
damping force
dead axle
direct-acting shock
  absorber
drive axle
flat ride tuning
frame
gas-filled shock
  absorber
heavy-duty shock
  absorber

hydraulic shock
  absorber
independent
  suspension
integral-stud
  mount
interleaf friction
jounce
kingpin
knuckle
leaf spring
lever arms
lever shock
  absorber
link
live axle
load-carrying ball
  joint
MacPherson strut
modified strut
monoleaf spring
monotube shock
  absorber
natural frequency
non-load-carrying
  ball joint
pig-tail spring end
pivot-base strut

187

platform
rebound
resilience
ring mount
semi-elliptical leaf
  spring
shock absorber
shock absorber ratio
side member
solid axle
spring
spring frequency
spring rate
sprung weight
square spring end
static load
steering knuckle

stiffness
stress raiser
strut
stub axle
sub-frame
tangential spring end
tapered-end spring
tension-loaded ball
  joint
torsion bar
uncompressed length
unit-body construction
unsprung weight
variable shock
  absorber
variable-rate spring
wheel rate

BOUNCE CYCLE

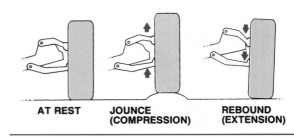

Figure 8-1. Suspension compression, or "jounce," occurs as the wheel rises, while "rebound," or extension, occurs when the force of compression is removed. Jounce and rebound are the two phases in a suspension "bounce."

INTRODUCTION

The suspension is the system of components that supports the vehicle and transmits its weight to the wheels. The suspension serves two main purposes:

- Ensure vehicle control and stability
- Provide a comfortable ride

When a freely rolling wheel hits a bump, its natural tendency is to lift off the pavement and land with a thump. If the wheels of a vehicle did this, not only would the ride be uncomfortable, but it would also be nearly impossible to keep the vehicle under control. The suspension prevents these problems by keeping the wheels in contact with the road and cushioning the passenger compartment from road shocks.

The suspension also serves several secondary purposes. First, it alters the positions of the wheels to increase traction when the load transfers during cornering. Second, it resists changes in wheel positions during cornering that would decrease traction. Third, by cushioning against road shocks, the suspension helps the metal brackets, wiring harnesses, and structural components throughout the vehicle last longer. Excessive vibration causes fatigue in these parts, so without the suspension they would wear out more quickly.

One word best summarizes how the suspension does its job: "compression." When a wheel rides

over a bump, the suspension compresses to absorb the energy of the jolt instead of transmitting it to the frame. Compression of the suspension is known as **jounce.** The opposite of jounce is **rebound,** which occurs when the force compressing the suspension is removed and the suspension extends. During rebound, the suspension usually extends beyond its at-rest position before settling at normal ride height. The term **bounce** describes the complete cycle of suspension jounce and rebound, or compression and extension (Figure 8-1).

This chapter discusses the parts used to construct suspension systems and also studies suspension-related components, such as frames, axles, and knuckles. The actual suspension parts examined can be classified into three broad categories: ball joints and bushings, suspension links, and cushioning devices (Figure 8-2). The overall organization of the items addressed in this chapter progresses from the frame outward toward the wheels in the following order:

- Frames
- Axles
- Ball joints and bushings
- Suspension links
- Cushioning devices
- Wheel knuckles

How these components work together in various suspension designs is discussed in later chapters of this *Classroom Manual*.

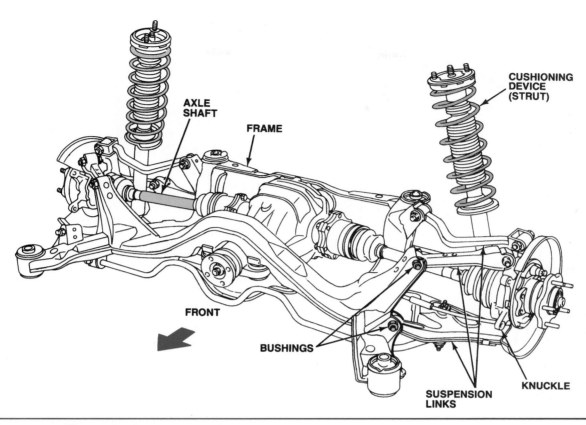

Figure 8-2. The suspension starts at the frame where bushings and bearings attach the suspension links. Bushings and bearings also connect the links to the knuckles, and cushioning devices absorb vertical suspension movement.

FRAMES

The **frame** supports the vehicle body, engine, drivetrain, and exhaust system, while the suspension supports the frame. The frame can be separate from the vehicle body or integral to some of the body panels. Whether the frame is separate or integral, the term **side member** describes any structural rail running longitudinally, or lengthwise, along the side of the vehicle, and the term **crossmember** describes a transverse rail, or one that runs from side-to-side.

Ladder Frame

In the early days of automobile construction, the frame was a separate, wooden structure consisting of two side members and as many crossmembers as the length of the chassis required. The body was constructed of hand-formed, aluminum panels that were supported by this "ladder frame." In the early 1900s, the invention of the sheet metal press made steel body panels easy to make, and eventually the frame was made of steel, too (Figure 8-3). By the 1930s, steel frames and bodies had become standard in the automobile industry.

Building frames and bodies separately and joining them together on the assembly line remained a common practice among European manufacturers until World War II, and in American production as late as the 1980s (Figure 8-4).

Conventional Body-Over-Frame Ladder Frame Construction

In the conventional body-over-frame construction, the frame is the vehicle's foundation. The

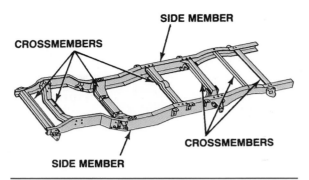

Figure 8-3. This truck frame is a good example of a ladder-type frame that is separate from the body. The two side members are connected by a number of crossmembers.

LADDER FRAME

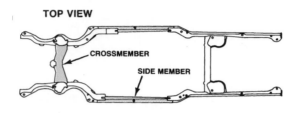

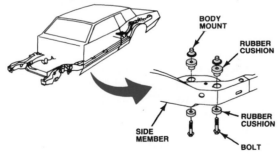

Figure 8-4. Through the early 1980s, many domestic vehicles used a separate frame and body. Rubber cushions at the body-to-frame mounting bolts act as insulators to keep unwanted vibration out of the passenger compartment.

body and all major parts of a vehicle are attached to the frame. It must provide the support and strength needed by the assemblies and parts attached to it. In other words, the frame is an independent, separate component because it is not welded to any of the major units of the body shell. General Motors referred to this design as body-on-frame and last used it in their "B" body Chevrolet Caprice, Cadillac Fleetwood Brougham,

UNIT-BODY CONSTRUCTION

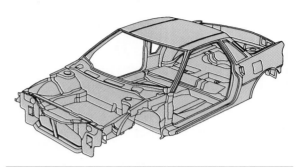

Figure 8-5. With unit-body construction, welded metal pieces form a platform that integrates the body with the frame.

and Oldsmobile "D" series until 1996. Until the 1990s, GM built virtually all of its vehicles using this body-on-frame design. Trucks still use the body-over-frame ladder frame design.

Unit-Body

In a unit-body, or integral body, the frame and part of the body form a single assembly (Figure 8-5). General Motors of Germany became the first manufacturer to use an integral body design when they released the 1935 Opel Olympia. Following World War II, the use of integral bodies, called **unit-body construction,** became common in Europe. In the industry, "unit-body" is commonly referred to as "uni-body" construction.

Although GM was a pioneer of unit-body construction in Europe, this design concept was not widely applied to United States production until the 1960s. American consumers preferred large, heavy, comfortable riding vehicles for traveling vast expanses of highways. This, coupled with readily available, inexpensive steel, allowed U.S. manufacturers to continue producing separate-frame vehicles longer than their European counterparts. However, when fuel economy became a concern, American manufacturers began shifting production toward lighter-weight, unit-body designs.

Although a unit-body automobile has no frame, as such, a separate **sub-frame** is often used to support the engine, and sometimes an additional sub-frame supports the rear differential. A unit-body is constructed on a **platform** made of sheet-metal sections that are pressed, fitted, and welded together to form the bottom and lower sides of the vehicle. Since there is no frame to support the weight, it is important to use the proper lift points when raising a unit-body on a hoist or lifting it with a jack. Failure to do so can result in damage to the chassis.

Early unit-body designs were constructed on a relatively heavy platform, with side members incorporated into the door sills and a structurally reinforced transmission tunnel running front-to-rear. Late-model designs are a lightweight assembly that is reinforced only where necessary, a result of stress tests performed on a prototype. Many late-model versions are partially constructed of lighter metals, such as aluminum. In fact, the unit-body of some Audi models is constructed entirely of aluminum. Other weight-saving practices on late-model vehicles include a unit-body floor pan that supports composite plastic body panels.

There has been a tradeoff in the switch from heavy frames to light platforms. Designers must choose between strength and rigidity on the one hand, and fuel efficiency, reduced emissions, and inexpensive construction on the other. The choice engineers make also has implications for safety. Steel frames obviously can resist impact better than sheet metal, although an integral body has an advantage in minor collisions because it can crush to absorb some of the crash energy.

AXLES

Traditionally, an **axle** is a rod on which one or more wheels rotate. On an independent suspension that uses stub axles, the axle is an imaginary line that connects the axes of two wheels. Although stub axles provide no mechanical link between the two wheels, the term "axle" is used when discussing the two wheels as a unit.

With the exception of some heavy-duty vehicles, vehicles use two axles—front and rear—with two wheels on each axle. There are three general categories of vehicle axles (Figure 8-6):

- Dead axles
- Stub axles
- Drive axles

Axles may be solid or part of an **independent suspension.** A **solid axle** acts as a unit, as far as suspension travel goes. If one wheel goes over a bump, the whole axle responds to the shock. In an independent suspension, the suspension travel of one wheel has no direct effect on the wheel at the opposite end of the axle.

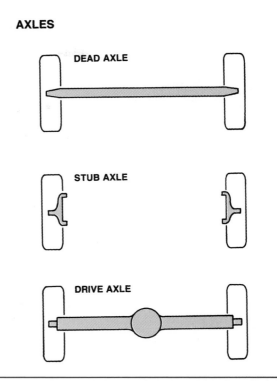

Figure 8-6. A dead axle does not drive the wheels, stub axles do not provide a direct connection between the two wheels, and a drive axle connects the wheels to the differential gears.

The term **dead axle** describes a solid, non-drive axle (Figure 8-7). The most common dead axle is a beam axle at the rear of front-wheel drive (FWD) vehicles. Beam axles can also be used at the front of rear-wheel drive (RWD) vehicles, but it is more common for solid front axles to be an I-beam design.

Stub axles may be thought of as the two ends of a beam axle with the center portion of the beam missing. Each **stub axle** consists simply of the wheel spindle that extends from the knuckle or a suspension arm (Figure 8-8). Independent and semi-independent, non-drive suspensions with coil springs, torsion bars, or struts use stub axles.

A **drive axle** is the axle that transmits driving power from the differential gearing to the wheels. A solid, rear-wheel drive (RWD) axle may also be referred to as a **live axle.**

Drive axles use two axle shafts. The axle shafts may be part of a solid, rear-axle housing, or they may operate with an independent suspension (Figure 8-9). All front-wheel drive (FWD) axles use independent suspensions, but rear axles can be either solid or independent. In a solid drive axle, one end of each axle shaft splines directly to

DEAD AXLES

REAR BEAM AXLE

FRONT I-BEAM AXLE

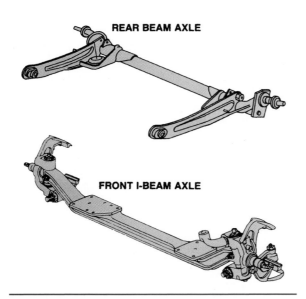

Figure 8-7. The two most common dead axle designs are the beam axle used at the rear of a FWD (front-wheel drive) vehicle and the I-beam axle used on the front of RWD (rear-wheel drive) trucks.

STUB AXLE

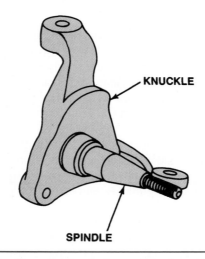

KNUCKLE

SPINDLE

Figure 8-8. The wheel spindle and the knuckle or mounting flange form a stub axle, which connects the wheel to the suspension.

the side gears of the differential and the opposite end attaches to the wheel. With an independent suspension, the axle shafts use a joint—either a constant velocity (CV) joint or a universal joint (U-joint)—at each end to allow for changes in angle that result from wheel travel (Figure 8-10). For

DRIVE AXLES

SOLID AXLE

DIFFERENTIAL

AXLE SHAFT

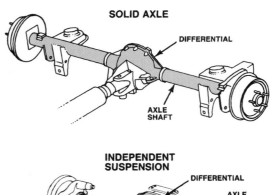

INDEPENDENT SUSPENSION

DIFFERENTIAL

AXLE SHAFT

FRONT

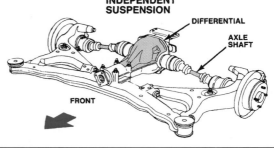

Figure 8-9. Axle shafts may be part of either a solid rear axle or an independent suspension.

DRIVELINE JOINTS

CONSTANT VELOCITY (CV) JOINT

UNIVERSAL JOINT (U-JOINT)

Figure 8-10. To allow one side of the suspension to move without affecting the opposite side, CV-joints or U-joints are used at both ends of the drive axles on an independent suspension.

additional information on CV joints and U-joints, see Chapter 11 of this *Classroom Manual*.

Axle shafts used on a FWD vehicle are frequently of two different lengths because the transaxle is offset to one side of the chassis. However, unequal length drive shafts result in unequal torque transfer between the transaxle and the two driven wheels. To compensate, an intermediate shaft may be installed between the transaxle and one of the axle shafts to help equalize torque transfer (Figure 8-11).

■ Henry's Rough Rider

In 1909, Henry Ford made automotive history with the introduction of his Model T—a mass-produced car specifically designed to be simple, inexpensive, and easy-to-repair. The Ford "three-point" design for the Model T suspension was itself a model of simplicity. Both the front and the rear axles were sprung with transverse multileaf springs. The springs attached with shackles at both ends of the axles and rigidly bolted to the chassis at the center. Radius rods, which ran from the ends of the axles to the centerline of the chassis, kept the axles aligned with the frame while allowing the suspension to compress and the axles to twist.

The radius arms and axle-mounted transverse spring formed a triangle in the front and the rear suspensions of the Model T, proof that Ford understood the basics of suspension design. Many modern suspension designs—such as short-long-arm (SLA) suspensions, sometimes called "double-wishbone"—still use a triangle as the basic suspension unit. Triangulation is particularly common on front suspensions because it allows the front wheels to turn for steering, while bracing them against side-to-side and front-to-rear road forces.

Although the Ford design was sound, it lacked some refinements modern drivers take for granted. Most notably, the Model T used no shock absorbers, leading some owners to christen their cars "Theodore," after Teddy Roosevelt and his famous Rough Riders. On the plus side, the suspension was simple, lightweight, and economical to manufacture. In fact, the Model T kept essentially the same suspension until its demise in 1927—over 14 million units later.

FRONT

BALL JOINTS AND BUSHINGS

Apart from the cushioning devices, the suspension consists of a number of links and the couplings that join them together. For the suspension to compress, the couplings must allow some movement between the links (Figure 8-12). Parts held rigidly together cannot absorb movement; they can only pass it along. The two types of couplings used to allow suspension compression are:

• Ball joints
• Bushings

Independent suspensions, especially on the front axle, generally use one or more ball joints at the knuckle. A **ball joint** is a ball and socket that allow continuous angle changes in different directions between the parts that the joint couples. It connects the steering knuckle to the control arm, allowing it to pivot on the control arm during steering. Ball joints also permit up-and-down movement of the control arm as the suspension reacts to road conditions. The ball joint stud protrudes from its socket through a rubber seal that keeps lubricating grease (when used) in the housing and keeps dirt out. Some ball joints require periodic lubrication, while most do not. These

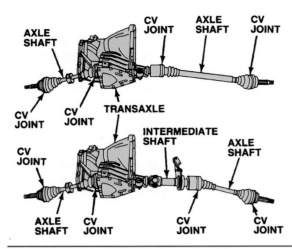

Figure 8-11. Axle shafts in a FWD powertrain transfer torque from a transaxle to the wheels. Some designs use two different length (top) axles, while others use equal-length axles with an intermediate shaft on one side (bottom).

SUSPENSION COUPLINGS

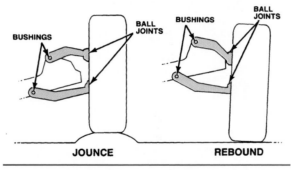

Figure 8-12. To permit compression and extension, bushings and ball joints allow suspension links to move in relation to each other, the frame, and the wheels.

maintenance-free ball joints move in a prelubricated nylon bearing. Ball joints are either load carrying or are followers. A load-carrying ball joint supports the car's weight and is generally in the control arm that holds or seats the spring. Load-carrying joints can be called tension-loaded or compression-loaded ball joints.

Newer vehicles use a low-friction ball joint that uses a highly polished steel ball and a single or two-piece ball seat of a high-strength polymer hard plastic polyacetal that has rigidity, high-load durability, and elasticity. Older vehicles use a steel-on-steel (high-friction) design and requires periodic lubrication. Low-friction ball joints provide precise low-friction movement of the ball socket in the ball joint. Compared to conventional steel-on-steel

ball joints, two-thirds of the internal friction is eliminated in a low-friction ball joint. The smooth ball socket movement in a low-friction ball joint provides improved steering performance, better steering wheel return, and longer ball joint life. The newer vehicles using the low-friction type ball joint may or may not require periodic lubrication. Always consult the original equipment manufacturer's (OEM) service information for proper maintenance instructions. When used to connect the knuckle to the suspension arms, ball joints permit the knuckle to tilt as the wheel travels over an irregular road surface. The ball joint also absorbs some of the wheel movement so that it is not entirely transmitted to the suspension. Additionally, ball joints allow a steered knuckle to pivot in response to steering system operation.

Ball joints are most often used at the knuckles of independent suspensions. Some suspension designs use small ball joints to connect parts such as the antiroll bar and spacer bar, but using rubber or metal bushings to link these suspension parts to each other and to the frame is more common. Bushings allow some degree of pivoting or twisting movement between parts, but they cannot move as freely as ball joints. Independent rear suspension designs frequently use bushings, rather than ball joints, at the knuckle connections. Bushings provide adequate flexibility in these situations since the knuckle does not need to pivot on a vertical steering axis.

Ball Joint Use

Suspension ball joints link steering knuckles to control arms in virtually all independent front suspensions and in some independent rear suspensions (Figure 8-13). Short-long-arm (SLA) and strut/short-long-arm (strut/SLA) front suspensions generally use two ball joints at each knuckle—upper and lower—while MacPherson strut and modified strut suspensions use a single—lower—ball joint. These front suspensions are described in detail in Chapter 9 of this *Classroom Manual*.

In a suspension ball joint, the ball stud and its socket are mounted to the control arm, and the stud extends through the mounting bore in the knuckle. A castle nut threads onto the stud to seat it in the knuckle and a cotter pin secures the nut. There are two basic types of suspension ball joints:

- Non-load-carrying
- Load-carrying

Ultimately, the wheels and tires bear the entire weight of the vehicle, and the suspension trans-

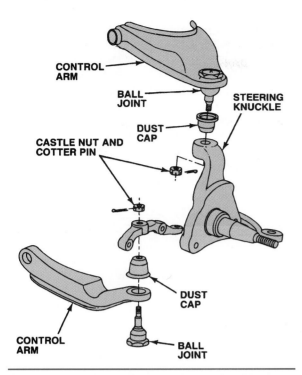

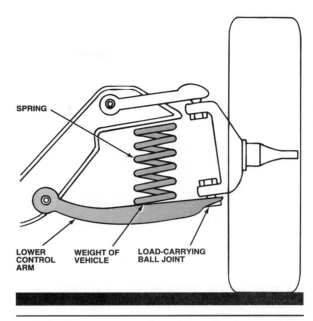

Figure 8-13. Suspension ball joints, which allow both up-and-down wheel travel and the pivoting movement of wheels that steer the vehicle, are used to join control arms to steering knuckles.

Figure 8-14. Because the spring transfers the weight of the frame, body, and some of the suspension parts to the lower control arm, the ball joint linking this arm to the steering knuckle—the lower ball joint—is the load-carrying ball joint.

fers this weight from the frame to them. As the link between the suspension and wheels, the ball joints or the ball joint and strut must support and control this weight. The weight is not evenly split between the two couplings. In SLA, strut/SLA, and modified strut suspensions, the load-carrying ball joint bears the sprung weight, which is most of the weight, of the vehicle. The non-load-carrying ball joint or the modified strut merely helps position the wheel. On a MacPherson strut suspension, the strut bears the sprung weight and transfers it directly to the knuckle, while the lower ball joint is non-load-carrying. Sprung weight is discussed later in this chapter. An easy way to identify the load-carrying ball joint is to locate the suspension spring. The component on which the spring rests is the weight-bearing component. If the weight-bearing part is a control arm linked to the knuckle by a ball joint, that is the load-carrying ball joint (Figure 8-14).

Non-Load-Carrying

A **non-load-carrying ball joint** may also be referred to as a "follower joint" because it works together with the other, load-carrying, ball joint or the strut. Although it does not support the weight

of the vehicle, a non-load-carrying ball joint allows the wheel to compress the suspension and to pivot in response to steering system operation, while keeping the wheel in a controlled position under the vehicle. A preload spring keeps the ball seated in the socket to minimize clearance in the joint (Figure 8-15). However, excessive preload in a steering knuckle ball joint eliminates all clearance and causes the joint to resist the pivoting action of the steering knuckle.

Load-Carrying

A **load-carrying ball joint** serves the same purpose as the non-load-carrying one in respect to positioning the wheel. However, a load-carrying joint also transfers the vehicle weight from the suspension to the knuckle and wheel. Load-carrying ball joints usually have some initial **clearance,** or play, which the weight of the vehicle eliminates.

There are two types of load-carrying ball joints, and the way in which the vehicle weight loads the joint determines if the ball joint is:

- Tension-loaded
- Compression-loaded

As the names imply, a tension-loaded ball joint is extended, or pulled tight, to reduce clearance, and

NON-LOAD-CARRYING BALL JOINT

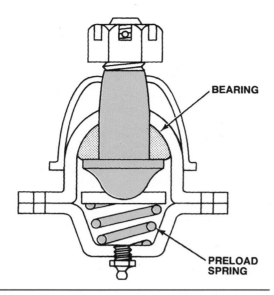

Figure 8-15. A non-load-carrying ball joint uses a preload spring to eliminate excessive clearance in the ball and socket assembly.

a compression-loaded ball joint is compressed, or pushed, to take up play. With either type of ball joint, a bearing provides a wear surface where the ball contacts the socket (Figure 8-16).

Tension-Loaded
The control arm of a **tension-loaded ball joint** is located below the knuckle mount (Figure 8-17). The weight of the vehicle pushes the arm down, which pulls it away from the knuckle. At the same time, the wheel resting on the ground pushes the knuckle upward and away from the arm. Because the ball joint holds the arm and knuckle together, the opposing forces applied to the ball joint pull the ball against its seat in the socket, so that tension provides the preload. Therefore, this is a tension-loaded ball joint.

Compression-Loaded
The control arm of a **compression-loaded ball joint** is located above the knuckle mount (Figure 8-18). Both the weight of the vehicle and the resistance of the wheel resting on the ground push the ball into the socket. Since the forces applied to the ball joint compress it, this design is known as a compression-loaded ball joint.

Ball Joint Wear Indicators
Some ball joints have wear indicators. As the joint wears, the grease fitting of the joint recedes into

LOAD-CARRYING BALL JOINTS

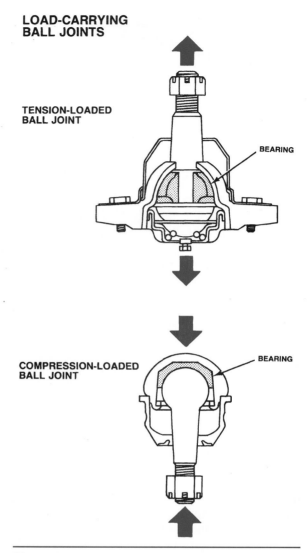

Figure 8-16. All ball joints, whether tension or compression loaded, have a bearing surface between the ball stud and socket to reduce friction.

the housing. When the shoulder of the fitting is flush with the housing, the joint needs to be replaced. Ball joint service will be covered in detail in Chapter 9 of this *Shop Manual.*

Bushings

Bushings are couplings that allow the parts they join to pivot or twist in relation to each other (Figure 8-19). Suspension bushings may be rubber or metal. In a metal bushing, facing metal surfaces that slide against each other provide the pivoting action. Rubber bushings twist, rather than slide, to allow pivoting or twisting. Rubber also helps absorb vibrations.

TENSION LOADING

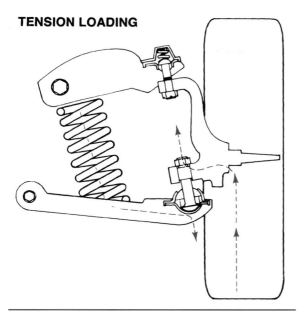

Figure 8-17. In a tension-loaded ball joint, the forces acting on the ball joint pull the parts of the joint away from each other to reduce clearance and keep the joint under tension.

COMPRESSION LOADING

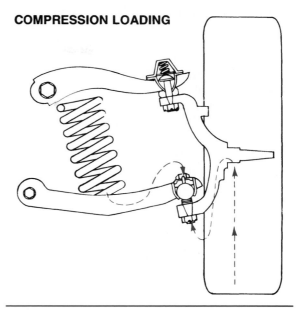

Figure 8-18. In a compression-loaded ball joint, the forces acting on the ball joint push the ball and socket toward each other to reduce clearance by compressing the joint.

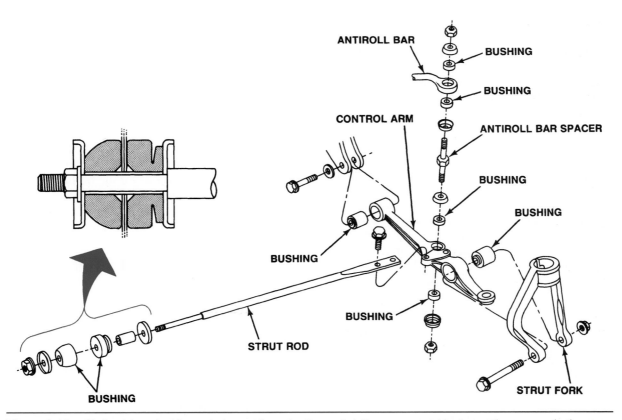

Figure 8-19. Six bushings in this control arm allow pivoting or twisting movement between the arm and other suspension components.

197

Bushing action differs from ball joint action in that the sliding of a ball in a socket allows the ball joint to pivot on a variety of axes, while a bushing pivots on a fixed axis. This is particularly true of rigid, metal bushings. Rubber bushings offer more play because rubber is softer and more pliable. Sometimes manufacturers use rubber bushings for their "sloppiness," to economize in situations where a ball joint might actually be a better solution.

Bushings and their general characteristics are discussed in Chapter 2 of this *Classroom Manual*.

SUSPENSION LINKS

The word **link** applies to any of the metal rods or arms that are used to connect the suspension to the frame and the wheels, or to other suspension components. Most suspension links are steel, although some high-performance vehicles, such as the Chevrolet Corvette, use aluminum suspension components to save weight.

When discussing suspension components, the words "link," "arm," and "rod," are often interchanged when describing the same part. This book uses and defines the most common terms for specific types of suspension links and presents other frequently used terms as well. Be aware that other service literature may use different terms for the same parts and systems, and that the terminology used for similar components often differs between manufacturers.

Electronically Adjusted Shock Absorbers

Electronically adjusted shock absorbers are one step above manually adjustable shocks. They are basically remote control shocks that allow the driver to select a soft, medium, or firm ride by pressing a button on the instrument panel. When activated, variable shock damping is accomplished by varying the size of the metering orifices inside the shock absorber. This is done by rotating a control rod inside the shock using a small electric actuator motor mounted on the tip of the shock. This control rod varies the size of the metering orifices, which, in turn, changes the shock rate from firm to medium to soft. The speed at which this occurs is usually less than half a second. This type of electronically controlled shock can be used alone as a driver-controlled device or it can be part of a computer-controlled suspension system. In a computer-controlled system, the shock is activated based on input from

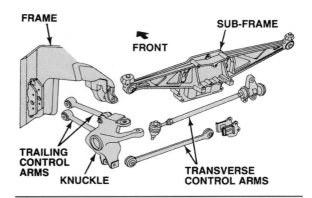

Figure 8-20. The transverse control arms in this suspension pivot on bushings at the frame end, while the outer ends attach to the knuckle with either a bushing or ball joint.

various vehicle sensors. Computer-controlled suspensions are discussed later in this chapter.

Control Arms

A **control arm** is a suspension link that connects a knuckle or wheel flange to the frame. One end of a control arm attaches to the knuckle or wheel flange, generally with either a ball joint or bushing. The opposite end of the arm, which attaches to a frame member, usually pivots on a bushing (Figure 8-20). The end attached to the frame must pivot to allow the axle or knuckle to travel vertically. Whether a ball joint or a bushing is used at the end attached to the knuckle depends upon what type of movement is required. Some rear control arms are integral to, or part of, the knuckle. Control arms may be the upper and lower arms of SLA or strut/SLA suspensions, the lower arms of MacPherson strut or modified strut suspensions, or the trailing arms or semi-trailing arms of multi-link rear suspensions. These suspension systems are discussed in Chapters 9 and 10 of this *Classroom Manual*.

Other Suspension Links

Many minor suspension links that brace or position another component have no specific name, but descriptive terms, such as "lateral link," "transverse link," or "control link," are used to describe them. Some links are common enough to have widely accepted names, and among these are:

- Strut rods
- Radius arms
- Panhard rods
- Antiroll bars

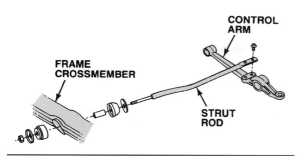

Figure 8-21. A strut rod braces a control arm against the frame to prevent the control arm from pitching or shifting under the forces of braking and acceleration.

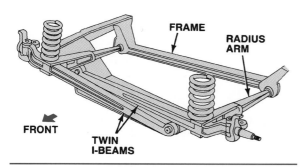

Figure 8-22. On a twin I-beam suspension, a radius arm braces the outer end of the axle beam against the frame to stabilize it.

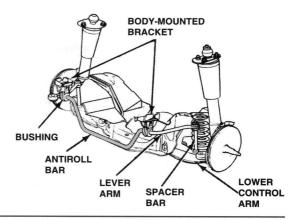

Figure 8-23. The center section of this front-axle antiroll bar is supported by bushings where it attaches to the body and the ends of the bar are bent to form lever arms. Spacer bars connect the lever arms to the lower control arms.

Short-long-arm (SLA), strut/SLA, MacPherson strut, and modified strut suspensions use strut rods to position the control arm (Figure 8-21). Twin I-beam suspensions and some front drive axles use radius arms to locate the axle (Figure 8-22). Chapter 9 of this *Classroom Manual* describes these systems used on front suspensions in detail, and Chapter 10 provides information on their rear suspension applications. The Panhard rod, which is a frequently used element on solid rear suspension designs, is discussed in Chapter 10 as well.

Most independent suspensions—front or rear— use an **antiroll bar** to reduce body roll on turns. This component is often referred to as a "stabilizer bar," "anti-sway bar," or simply a "sway bar." Although these bars go by a number of names, the term "antiroll" most accurately describes their purpose. Body roll, discussed in Chapter 3 of this *Classroom Manual,* occurs as vehicle weight shifts outward during cornering. Body roll pushes down on the outer side of the vehicle as it rounds a corner, which causes the body to lean. To help equalize the weight distribution during cornering, an antiroll bar transfers some of the load back to the inner wheel so that the body does not lean as far.

An antiroll bar runs across the chassis from one side to the other. On a typical front-axle installation, the antiroll bar attaches to spacer bars that extend upward from each lower control arm. Bushings connect the spacers at each end to the antiroll bar and the control arm. Two rubber bushings anchor the middle section of the antiroll bar to the frame. These bushings surround the bar and a U-shaped metal clamp fits over each bushing to attach the assembly to the frame (Figure 8-23). In the installation shown, the bar bends so that when viewed from the top it has two short sections, called **lever arms,** at each end and one long middle section. The lever arms extend forward and inward from the spacer bars. This is a common antiroll bar design, but the actual shape and installation can vary considerably in different applications.

The disadvantage of an antiroll bar is that it tends to make the suspension react like a solid axle or semi-independent suspension. That is, it transfers the action of one wheel to the other, similar to a beam axle. However, an antiroll bar is usually not as strong or stiff as a beam axle or the rod of a semi-independent suspension. Therefore, an antiroll bar twists when one side of it moves, much like the torsion bars described later in this chapter, to absorb some movement and limit the amount of motion it transfers to the other side.

Antiroll bars vary in strength according to their length and diameter, as well as by the length and angle of the lever arms. The stronger, or stiffer, the antiroll bar is, the more it detracts from the

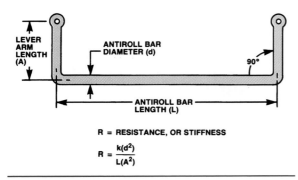

$$R = \frac{k(d^2)}{L(A^2)}$$

R = RESISTANCE, OR STIFFNESS

Figure 8-24. In the formula for calculating antiroll bar stiffness, the "k" is a constant based on the characteristics of the metal and differs slightly for each bar. Changes in the angle between the lever arms and bar also affect overall stiffness.

action of an independent suspension. Manufacturers make antiroll bars stiffer by:

- Increasing the diameter
- Decreasing the total length
- Decreasing the length of the lever arm
- Using stiffer spring metal

The stiffness of an antiroll bar can be calculated using equations (Figure 8-24). Even without making any calculations, looking at the equation shows that increasing the diameter of an antiroll bar stiffens it much more than shortening the length of the lever arm the same amount. Decreasing the length of the lever arm is also much more effective than decreasing the overall length of the bar the same amount. Obviously, the easiest way to make an antiroll bar stiffer is to make it thicker, but designers can also adjust the bar length and shape to change stiffness. In a chassis where clearance problems dictate the shape and length of the antiroll bar, the designers can still get the stiffness needed by changing the diameter of the bar.

CUSHIONING DEVICES

The cushioning devices that absorb the force of road shock and keep the frame from bouncing are the springs and shock absorbers. Although these two components are always used at each wheel, their design varies—especially spring design—and so does their installation. This section examines the various types of springs and shock absorbers

used on vehicles and how they work together to improve ride quality and handling.

In addition to springs and shock absorbers, a small but important cushioning device is the **bump stop.** Bump stops prevent metal-to-metal contact between components when the suspension compresses. When installed on a suspension arm or frame member, a bump stop is usually a rubber cone that provides increasing resistance as it compresses, (Figure 8-25). Some bump stops are located inside the shock absorber or on the strut assembly. Bump stops prevent the suspension from compressing too much, which stresses the spring. If left unchecked, excessive compression can eventually break the spring, especially a leaf spring.

Springs

A suspension **spring** serves two purposes. First, it acts as a buffer between the suspension and frame to absorb vertical wheel and suspension movement without passing it on to the frame. Second, each spring transfers part of the vehicle weight to the suspension component it rests on, which transfers it to the wheels.

The basic method by which springs absorb road shocks varies according to the type of spring. Simply stated, leaf springs flatten, coil springs and air springs compress, and torsion bars twist. What all springs have in common is that they somehow give way to absorb the vertical force of the moving wheel during jounce, then release that force during rebound as they return to their original shape and position.

Spring Materials

Most springs are made of a tempered steel alloy known as spring steel. Tempering is a process of heating and cooling metal under controlled conditions, which increases the **resilience** of the metal. Resilience is the ability of the metal to return to, or spring back to, its original shape after being twisted or compressed.

Tempering is a technique calling for special training and expertise. Incorrectly applying high-temperature heat to a spring can actually damage the metal, rather than improve its resilience. *Never heat springs—or any other suspension component—in an attempt to change its characteristics;* it is extremely dangerous. The part can be severely weakened and give way under normal dri-

CUSHIONING DEVICES

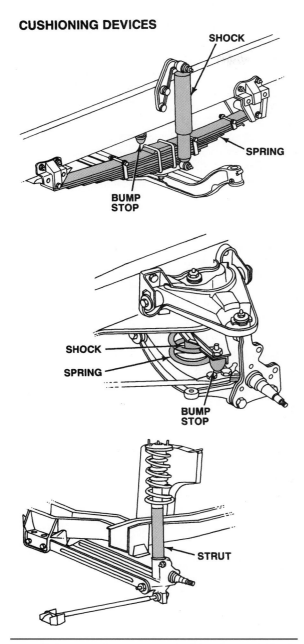

Figure 8-25. Suspension cushioning devices include springs, shock absorbers, struts, and bump stops.

ving forces. Heating spring metal and allowing it to cool too slowly makes the metal soft, so it bends and sags easily. If the metal cools too quickly, it becomes brittle and may snap instead of bending.

Some leaf springs are made of a plastic composite reinforced by graphite or fiberglass, rather than spring steel. Most plastic-composite leaf springs are a monoleaf design. Buick, Chevrolet, and Oldsmobile all use a plastic-composite leaf spring at the rear axle of one or more of their models, as

do some imports. The Chevrolet Corvette uses this type of leaf spring at both the front and rear.

A few applications use springs made of rubber. Air springs, as described later in this chapter, are essentially rubber sleeves, closed off at the top and bottom to encase the air inside.

Spring Characteristics

Although spring designs vary, any given suspension spring has certain characteristics. Every spring has a spring rate and frequency and carries a certain amount of sprung weight. These characteristics, along with the particular installation, affect the wheel rate of the spring and the natural frequency of the suspension. This section describes these aspects of spring design and application.

Spring Rate

Also known as "deflection rate," **spring rate** is a value that reflects how much weight it takes to compress a spring a certain amount. Generally, spring rate is specified in pounds per inch, which is the weight in pounds it takes to compress the spring one inch. In other words, if a 100-pound weight causes a spring to compress one inch, the spring has a spring rate of 100 pounds. Methods for calculating spring rate, which varies for each type of spring, are detailed later in this chapter when discussing the different types of springs.

A **constant-rate spring** continues to compress at the same rate throughout its complete range of deflection. For example, if a constant-rate spring compresses one inch under a 100-pound load, it will compress two inches under a 200-pound load, and so on (Figure 8-26). Many automotive suspension springs, both coil and leaf, compress at a variable rate. That is, they become stiffer and exert more force the farther they compress. For example, a **variable-rate spring** may compress one inch under a 100-pound load, but only compress an additional half an inch under a 200-pound load. Variable-rate springs offer a soft, comfortable ride under normal circumstances but will not bottom out as quickly when adverse road conditions compress them farther.

There are several methods of designing springs to provide a variable rate. Making the steel wire of a coil spring progressively thicker toward one end provides a variable rate, as does winding the coils successively further apart. Another method is to wind the coils in progressively larger diameter loops to create a cone-shaped spring (Figure 8-27). With a leaf spring, using

CONSTANT-RATE SPRING

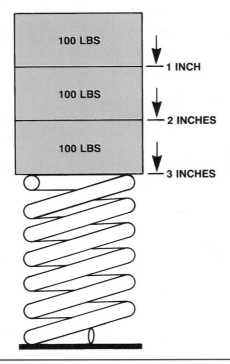

Figure 8-26. A constant-rate spring compresses at the same rate, no matter how much weight is placed on it.

leaves of different thickness provides a variable rate of compression. Some manufacturers add a second leaf spring, called an "overload spring," to increase overall spring rate and provide a variable compression rate. The overload spring does not begin to compress until after the regular leaf spring compresses a certain amount. Electronic controls are used to provide a variable rate for air springs. Manufacturers specify the rate for a variable-rate spring as an average rate.

Before a spring is installed on a vehicle or any load is placed on it, it is at its **uncompressed length,** or free length. Once installed, the weight of the corner of the vehicle resting on the spring is called its static load. The **static load** constantly compresses the spring to some extent. Therefore, the uncompressed length and the spring rate must be such that the spring has room to compress and keep the vehicle at the correct ride height *after* the static load is applied to it (Figure 8-28).

Spring Frequency
Spring frequency is a value that reflects the speed at which a spring oscillates, or bounces, after it is released from compression or extension.

VARIABLE-RATE SPRINGS

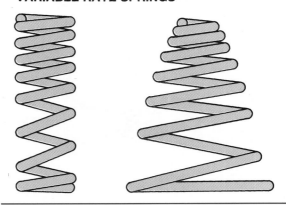

Figure 8-27. Variable-rate springs compress more slowly as more weight is placed on them. Progressively wider-spaced coils and coils of increasing diameter are two methods of providing a variable spring rate; both increase resistance as the spring compresses.

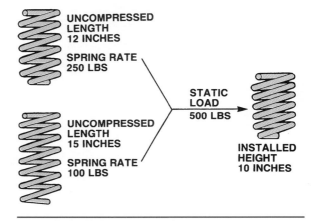

Figure 8-28. Although both of these springs provide the same ride height when installed, the higher-rate spring is stiffer and also has a higher frequency.

Frequency is typically measured in cycles per second (CPS) of extension and compression (Figure 8-29). There is a direct correlation between spring rate and spring frequency: the higher the spring rate, the higher the spring frequency. This means that stiffer springs bounce at a higher frequency, while softer springs bounce more slowly.

Sprung Weight
Out of the total weight of a vehicle, the weight that the suspension springs support is the **sprung weight.** The sprung weight of a vehicle includes the frame and everything mounted on it, such as the body, engine, and transmission. Sprung weight may also include some parts of the sus-

SPRING FREQUENCY

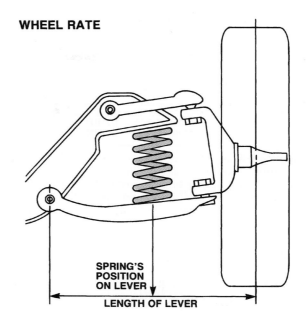

Figure 8-29. Stiffer springs bounce at a higher rate—that is, more often within the same amount of time—while softer springs bounce at a lower rate.

pension, if they are supported by the springs. The remaining weight—the rest of the suspension parts, including some portion of the springs themselves, and of the wheels—is the **unsprung weight** of the vehicle.

As a general rule, the greater the proportion of sprung weight to unsprung weight, the smoother the ride. When the wheel travels over a bump and transfers that motion to the suspension, the unsprung weight creates an upward force. If the vehicle has a lot of unsprung weight, this force may be more than the suspension can handle, which causes the frame and body to bounce as well. If the upward force of the unsprung weight is great enough, it can lift some of the vehicle weight off of the tire, which decreases traction. In extreme cases, the force of the unsprung weight can even lift the tire off of the road.

Wheel Rate

Depending on the suspension design, springs are installed a certain distance away from the wheel, which determines the ratio of wheel travel to spring travel (Figure 8-30). For example, if a coil spring is mounted on the midpoint of a control arm, or half-way between the center of the wheel

WHEEL RATE

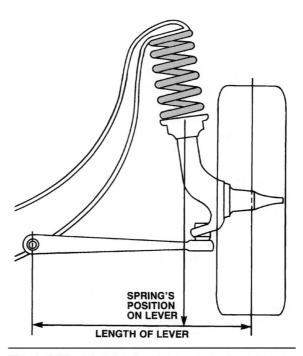

Figure 8-30. The wheel and arm act as a lever to compress the spring. The lever length is the distance from the arm mount to the middle of the wheel, and the fulcrum is the inner pivoting mount of the arm. The spring in the top picture is at the center of the lever, while the spring in the MacPherson strut is closer to the end.

and the arm pivot points, it compresses approximately one inch when the wheel travels vertically two inches (Figure 8-31). On a MacPherson strut suspension, the coil spring has a more direct ratio

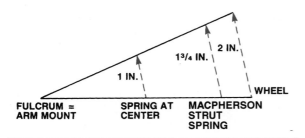

Figure 8-31. The closer the spring is to the fulcrum, or arm pivot point, the greater the exertion the leverage places on the spring, and the further the spring is from the fulcrum, the more it compresses with the same amount of wheel travel.

because it is closer to the wheel. Therefore, when the wheel of a MacPherson strut travels vertically two inches, the spring compresses nearly two inches as well (Figure 8-31).

The distance of the spring from the wheel also determines how much weight the spring must be able to support. In the first example, the length between the spring and the center of the wheel acts as a lever to increase the force exerted by the wheel resting on level ground. If the sprung weight at this corner of the vehicle is 350 pounds, the ground is exerting 350 pounds of resistant force against the wheel. Since the spring in the example is at the midpoint between the fulcrum and the end of the lever, the lever doubles the 350-pound resistant force. Thus, a 700-pound load is applied to the spring without any vertical wheel movement. Therefore, this spring must be able to support a 700-pound static load in order to keep the vehicle at its proper ride height. With the same 350-pound sprung weight applied to the MacPherson strut shown in the illustration, the coil spring does not need to support much more than the original 350 pounds because it is much closer to the end of the lever.

Because the same-rate spring will have different effects if placed in a different position on a suspension, a second method of rating a spring for a particular application is needed. This second rating is the **wheel rate.** Spring rate defines the spring action at the spring, while wheel rate defines spring action in relation to vertical wheel movement. The greater the wheel travel in relation to spring compression, the lower the wheel rate. The SLA spring of the first example has a lower wheel rate than the MacPherson strut spring in the second example.

Natural Frequency
Natural frequency is the rate at which the frame and body of a vehicle would bounce if there were

no shock absorbers on the suspension. Like spring frequency, natural frequency is measured in cycles per second (CPS). One CPS is a typical natural frequency for a passenger car suspension. A natural frequency of any more than two CPS would make the ride uncomfortable. The two factors affecting natural frequency are spring frequency and sprung weight. Natural frequency may also be referred to as "suspension frequency" or "wheel frequency."

Engineers often design front suspensions to have about a 20 percent slower natural frequency than the rear suspension. When a vehicle travels over a bump, the front wheels hit it first, and then the rear wheels. If the front and rear suspensions have the same natural frequency, their jounce and rebound cycles can become opposed. That is, when the front suspension is moving down, or extending, the rear suspension is moving up, or compressing; then the opposite occurs. This rolling motion, which is called "pitch," is discussed in Chapter 3 of this *Classroom Manual.* Pitch can become particularly unpleasant when the vehicle is driven over repeated, regular bumps, such as road expansion joints. However, if the front natural frequency differs from the rear, the two frequencies tend to cancel each other (Figure 8-32). Because the front and rear suspensions bounce more evenly, the vehicle has less of a tendency to pitch. Designers call this approach **flat ride tuning** because the frame and body remain more level as the vehicle travels over bumps.

Types of Springs
Although suspension springs all serve the same purpose and have certain characteristics in common, actual spring designs vary widely. Four types of springs are currently in use in automotive suspensions:

- Leaf springs
- Coil springs
- Torsion bars
- Air springs

The less external friction a spring creates, the more efficiently it operates. During their operation, leaf springs create external friction, which interferes with their movement. Coil springs create virtually no external friction, while torsion bars create a small amount at their pivot point. External friction is not a problem with air springs because they do not use moving metal parts.

NATURAL FREQUENCY

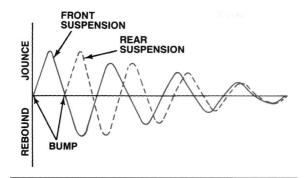

Figure 8-32. If the front suspension bounces at a lower rate than the rear, the jounce and rebound cycles go from being nearly opposed to being nearly synchronized.

All springs create some degree of internal friction because the materials they are made of resist compression. Internal friction makes springs eventually stop oscillating and also causes them to generate heat during extended oscillation. However, internal friction is not a problem that designers try to overcome; it is merely a part of how springs work.

Leaf Springs

In the early days of automobile construction, leaf springs were popular because they were easily and cheaply produced by a blacksmith, and were readily available since they were already widely used on horse-drawn carriages. Today, the use of leaf springs is limited mainly to the rear axles of some trucks and heavy passenger cars.

A typical **leaf spring** is assembled from a number of long, thin strips—or leaves—of spring-steel alloy. Each leaf is longer than the next, up to the longest one, which is the main leaf (Figure 8-33). The leaf spring is slightly curved when uncompressed and absorbs the force of road shocks by straightening out. The rate at which it compresses, or its spring rate, varies according to the number, width, and thickness of the leaves, as well as the material from which the spring is made. Although calculating spring rates can be complicated, a basic equation is used to determine the spring rate of a constant-rate leaf spring (Figure 8-34). In general, a leaf spring can be made stiffer by:

- Adding more leaves
- Making the leaves thicker or wider
- Making the leaves shorter
- Using stiffer spring metal

Of these, making the leaves thicker or making them shorter has the greatest effect. Simply doubling the number or the width of the leaves doubles the spring rate. However, doubling the thickness of the spring leaves or cutting their length in half makes the spring eight times as stiff. This is why the leaf springs on heavy trucks are often constructed of many thick, short leaves. However, a leaf spring designed for a lightweight vehicle generally has only a few leaves that are long, slender, and fairly thin.

The **semi-elliptical leaf spring** is the most common automotive configuration. On a semi-elliptical design, the length of the spring is parallel to the side of the vehicle. Each end of the main leaf attaches to the frame and U-bolts secure the center of the spring assembly to the beam axle or axle housing. The U-bolts allow the leaves to slide as the spring compresses. One end attachment is solid, but the other end of the spring attaches to a shackle that hangs from a bracket connected to the frame. Bushings are used to attach both ends of the shackle, which pivots to allow for the increase in spring length as the spring compresses (Figure 8-35).

Semi-elliptical leaf springs are used on the rear axle of many late-model trucks, and can also be found on the rear axle of a number of heavy, RWD sedans and wagons. Some heavy-duty trucks use an I-beam front axle with semi-elliptical leaf springs. When an axle has semi-elliptical leaf springs, it does not need control arms to locate it front-to-rear.

Leaf springs can also be mounted transversely, with one end at each end of the axle (Figure 8-36). Most transversely installed leaf springs are plastic-composite, monoleaf springs. A **monoleaf spring,** as the name implies, has only one leaf. As mentioned earlier, a number of vehicles use this type of leaf spring at the rear suspension, and a few models have them at the front. Usually, each end of a transverse, monoleaf spring attaches to a lower control arm. Rubber mounting pads and insulators protect the chassis from spring vibrations, and spring retainers, which bolt around the end of the spring, hold it in place (Figure 8-37).

Fiber Composite Monoleaf Springs

While most leaf springs are still made of steel, recent years have shown the fiber composite types increasing in popularity. Some automotive people call them plastic springs in spite of the fact that the springs contain no plastic at all. They are made of fiberglass, laminated, and bonded together by tough polyester resins. The long strands

LEAF SPRING

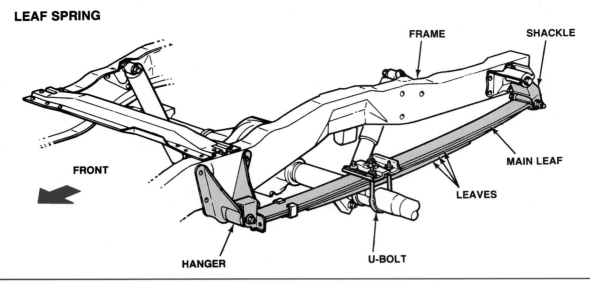

Figure 8-33. This semi-elliptical installation is a typical leaf spring consisting of a number of metal leaves. The longest of these, the main leaf, attaches to the frame through a shackle and hanger.

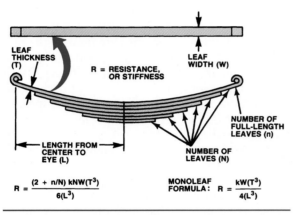

$$R = \frac{(2 + n/N)\, kNW(T^3)}{6(L^3)} \qquad \text{MONOLEAF FORMULA:} \quad R = \frac{kW(T^3)}{4(L^3)}$$

Figure 8-34. Calculating the strength of a multileaf spring is considerably more complicated than figuring the stiffness of a monoleaf spring because each leaf is a different length, which affects its stiffness.

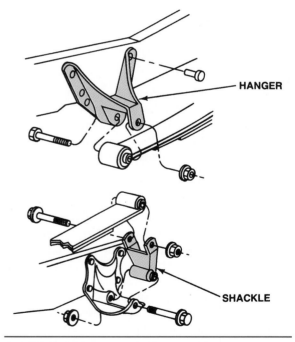

Figure 8-35. One end of a leaf spring rigidly attaches to a hanger and the other end is mounted to the frame with a shackle. Bushings allow the shackle to pivot so that the end of the spring can move backward and forward as the spring compresses and extends.

of fiberglass are saturated with resin and bundled together by wrapping (a process called filament winding) or squeezed together under pressure (compression molding). The Chevrolet Corvette uses this type of monoleaf spring.

Fiber composite leaf springs are incredibly lightweight and possess some unique ride control characteristics. Conventional monoleaf steel springs are real heavyweights, tipping the scale at anywhere from 25 to 45 pounds (11 to 20 kg) apiece. Some multiple-leaf springs can weigh almost twice as much. A fiber composite leaf spring

is a featherweight by comparison, weighing a mere 8 to 10 pounds (3.6 to 4.5 kg). As every performance enthusiast knows, springs are dead weight. Reducing the weight of the suspension

TRANSVERSE LEAF SPRING

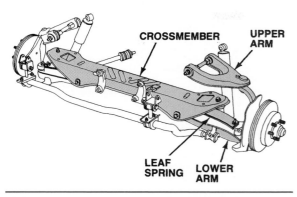

Figure 8-36. A transverse, monoleaf spring, which runs from one side of the vehicle to the other, usually bolts to the lower control arm of an SLA or strut system.

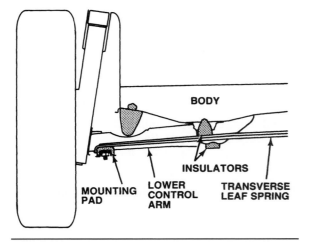

Figure 8-37. Rubber insulators protect the body from spring vibration in a transverse leaf spring installation.

not only reduces the overall weight of the vehicle but also reduces the sprung mass of the suspension itself. This reduces the spring effort and amount of shock control that is required to keep the wheels in contact with the road. The result is a smoother riding, better handling, and faster responding suspension, which is exactly the sort of thing every performance enthusiast wants. Other advantages of using fiber composite springs include the following attributes:

- **Quieter ride.** A fiber composite spring does not resonate or transmit sound like a steel spring. In fact, it actually dampens noise.
- **Smoother ride.** Because fiber composite springs use a one-piece monoleaf design, there is no rubbing friction like there is be-

tween the leaves in a multiple-leaf steel spring.
- **No spring sag.** All steel springs sag with age, whether leaves or coils. Spring sag affects ride height, which in turn alters wheel alignment, handling, steering, and braking. A weak spring can load the suspension unevenly, allowing the wheel under the weak spring to lose traction when accelerating or braking. According to the manufacturers of fiber composite springs, there is no sag with age.
- **Less body roll.** In applications where the leaf springs are mounted sideways (transversely), the spring also acts like a sway bar to limit body sway and roll when cornering. This load transfer characteristic also permits softer-than-normal spring rates to be used for a smoother ride.

With fiber composite leaf springs, there is little or no danger of the spring suddenly snapping. The laminated layers create a built-in fail-safe mechanism for keeping the spring intact should a problem arise.

When operating smoothly, leaf springs provide a good ride, but multileaf springs are prone to a problem called **interleaf friction.** As the leaves bend and straighten, they slide against one another. This friction generates heat that results in wear, which can eventually cause the leaves to bind and stick together. To reduce this problem, the spring may be assembled with insulating pads of low-friction material, such as plastic or zinc, placed between the leaves. An alternative is to fit rubber spring pads at the ends of the leaves to reduce friction. Both types of pads act as spacers to prevent contact between the leaves.

The main reason leaf springs are less popular than they used to be is because they take up more space and are heavier than other types of springs. This makes them impractical for the relatively small, lightweight vehicles that now dominate the market. Also, because most of the weight of a semi-elliptical leaf spring rests directly on the axle, it contributes to the unsprung weight of the vehicle. However, leaf springs are still common on trucks because it is easy to build them with a high overall spring rate while maintaining a soft initial rate.

Coil Springs

The **coil spring,** which is a length of steel alloy wire formed into a coil, is the most commonly used type of suspension spring. Coils springs are used with solid axles and independent suspensions, and

COIL SPRING

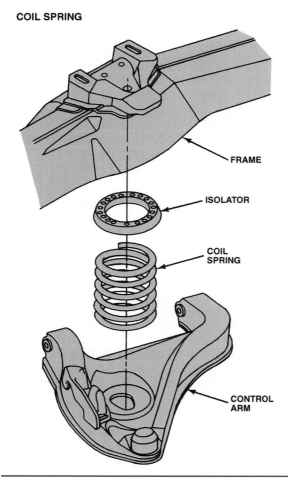

FRAME

ISOLATOR

COIL
SPRING

CONTROL
ARM

Figure 8-38. A coil spring, which fits firmly between its upper and lower seats, does not require any mounting hardware because the force of the frame pushing down on the spring and the resistance of the control arm pushing up keep the spring in place.

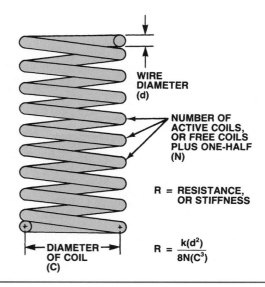

WIRE
DIAMETER
(d)

NUMBER OF
ACTIVE COILS,
OR FREE COILS
PLUS ONE-HALF
(N)

R = RESISTANCE,
OR STIFFNESS

DIAMETER
OF COIL
(C)

$$R = \frac{k(d^2)}{8N(C^3)}$$

Figure 8-39. When dealing with a constant-rate coil spring, figuring the spring rate is fairly straightforward; the constant, "k", varies according to the material the spring is made of.

on both front and rear suspensions. Compared with leaf springs, coil springs are lighter, take up less space, and operate with less external friction. Unlike leaf springs or torsion bars, coil springs do not require space around them in which to operate. Because they do not have a pivoting attachment point, there is nowhere for external friction to develop in coil springs. In addition, coil springs are relatively easy to remove and install.

A coil spring fits between a suspension component and the frame (Figure 8-38). The spring seat, on which the spring rests, may be on a beam axle, an axle housing, the base of a strut, or a control arm. When force is applied to the coil spring and it compresses, the coils move closer together. The diameter of the spring wire, the number of coils, the diameter of the coil, and the material from which the spring is made all affect the rate at

which a coil spring compresses, or its spring rate. To make a coil spring stiffer, manufacturers can:

- Increase the wire diameter
- Decrease the coil diameter
- Decrease the number of coils
- Use stiffer spring metal

The equation shows that the most important factor for increasing the stiffness of a fixed-rate coil is the wire diameter (Figure 8-39). Doubling the wire diameter multiplies the spring rate *16 times!* Decreasing the coil diameter is also effective, but not as much—decreasing the coil diameter by one-half stiffens the spring by a factor of eight. Spring stiffness goes up and down in inverse proportion to the number of coils in the spring. Twice as many coils makes a spring half as stiff.

At each end of a coil spring, the spring wire is cut off and shaped to fit a particular application (Figure 8-40). On a **tapered-end spring** the ends of the wire are ground flat to fit the seat. If the wire is cut off mid-coil, leaving the end in the coil shape, the spring has a **tangential spring end.** If there is a smaller, tighter coil at the end, it is called a **pig-tail spring end.** Another method is to bend the end of the wire square to the coil, which produces a **square spring end.** Each of these different ends requires a matching seat, or pocket, at the suspension or frame. A spring may have two different end shapes, in which case it has a top and bottom end and can be installed in only one way.

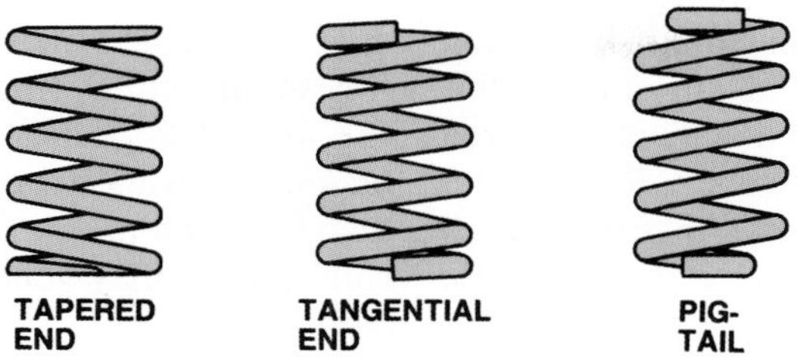

COIL SPRING ENDS

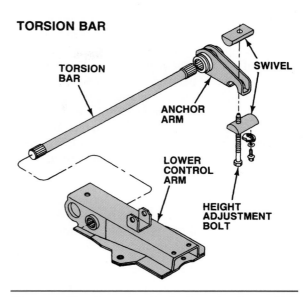

TAPERED
END

TANGENTIAL
END

PIG-
TAIL

Figure 8-40. These are a few of the ways that the end of a coil spring can be shaped. A tapered-end spring has flat seating surfaces, the tangential end retains the coil shape, and a pig-tail end has a tighter coil.

When coil springs age, they tend to sag. Sagging springs bring the frame and body below their proper ride height, which causes handling problems, prevents proper alignment, and accelerates tire wear. The only cure for sagging springs is to replace them. If the cost of replacing the springs is more than the vehicle is worth, an alternative is to either place a thick rubber "doughnut" under the spring or install rubber spacers between some of the coils. Either method temporarily brings the frame to the correct ride height. However, these are both stop-gap measures. Rubber doughnuts gradually compress under the weight of the vehicle and force of the spring, while spacers keep the coils they separate from compressing normally. With spacers, the other coils must compress farther to compensate, which places those coils under greater stress and concentrates the bending load at one spot. In addition, the spacers frequently fall out of the spring when it extends.

Coil springs generally do not break unless they are damaged in some way. As mentioned earlier, heating a spring can make it either soft or brittle and cause it to sag or break. Another form of damage that can eventually break a coil spring is a scratch or nick in the metal. The term **stress raiser** describes a small flaw like this, because the metal will bend more easily at this point and place extra stress at the bend. When metal is repeatedly bent at one point, it eventually breaks. Many springs are coated with paint or epoxy to prevent stress raisers, but it is still a good idea to handle them carefully to avoid accidental damage. Severe rust pits can also act as stress raisers.

Torsion Bars

A **torsion bar** is a length of steel alloy that takes up movement between the frame and suspension by twisting. In a typical longitudinal application, the torsion bar is attached to a control arm at one end,

TORSION BAR

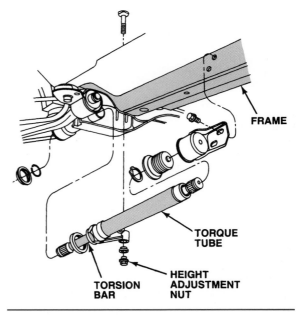

Figure 8-41. On a longitudinal torsion bar, which runs parallel to a frame side member, one end attaches to the control arm and the other to a swiveling anchor arm on the frame.

Figure 8-42. On this now obsolete Honda design, a torque tube encloses the torsion bar and the cap of the torque tube replaces the anchor arm.

and to an anchor arm that extends from the frame at the other end (Figure 8-41). Some torsion bars, such as those on older Honda and Acura models, fit inside a torque tube that attaches to the frame (Figure 8-42). Torsion bars may also be mounted transversely, or across the chassis. The ends of some transverse torsion bars, especially on rear suspensions, attach to the suspension arms on either side of the vehicle and anchor to the frame in the middle (Figure 8-43).

The length and diameter of the bar and the length of its anchor arm determine the rate at which a torsion bar twists to allow suspension compression, or its spring rate. Calculating the spring rate of a torsion bar is similar to determining the stiffness of an antiroll bar. In fact, both calculations use the same formula with different constants (Figure 8-44). As with an antiroll bar, a torsion bar can be made stiffer by:

- Increasing the diameter
- Decreasing the total length
- Decreasing the length of the anchor arm
- Using stiffer spring metal

As with an antiroll bar, the simplest way to make a torsion bar stiffer is to make it thicker.

TRANSVERSE TORSION BARS

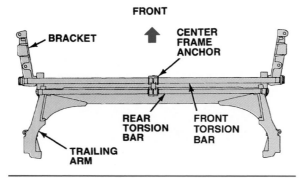

Figure 8-43. The transverse torsion bar installation on this rear axle features two torsion bars that attach to the suspension arms at either end and are secured to the frame at the centerline of the chassis.

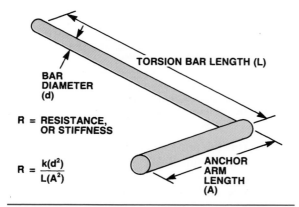

Figure 8-44. The same formula used for determining antiroll bar stiffness is used to calculate the strength of a torsion bar. A torsion bar has only one anchor arm, rather than the two lever arms of an antiroll bar.

Like a coil spring, a torsion bar tends to sag after extended service. Most torsion bars have an adjustment nut or bolt, which can tighten the bar to take up some of the sag. Also, like coil springs, torsion bars can break due to a stress raiser if damaged. Replacement torsion bars usually have marks that indicate whether they belong on the left or right side of the vehicle, since they generally are not interchangeable.

Although a torsion bar is as effective and light-weight as a coil spring, and is more space-efficient than a leaf spring, it is not frequently used for automotive suspensions.

Early DaimlerChrysler models used a transverse torsion bar front suspension on its RWD models (Figure 8-45). By 1990, the use of torsion bar front suspensions was primarily limited to trucks. However, a few European manufacturers, such as Porsche, still use transverse torsion bars on some of their limited-production models.

There are two reasons for this decline in torsion bar use. First, most late-model vehicles are a unit-body construction, which does not provide a strong frame side member to which the torsion bar can be anchored. Second, the widespread use of MacPherson struts, which include coil springs, at the front axle eliminates the need. The advantage of a MacPherson strut over a torsion bar is that the strut compresses straight down while a torsion bar needs space around it to twist when taking up wheel movement. The limited engine compartment space of a FWD vehicle makes the use of torsion bars impractical.

The most frequent front-axle application for torsion bars is on RWD and 4WD trucks, which do have the strong frame and the space needed for a torsion bar suspension. Chevrolet, Daimler-Chrysler, GMC, Isuzu, Mazda, Mitsubishi, Nissan,

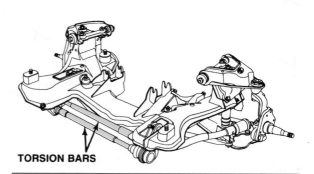

Figure 8-45. Transverse, L-shaped torsion bars on the front axle, running from the lower control arm to an opposite-side bracket, were a DaimlerChrysler trademark from the mid-1970s to the late 1980s.

and Toyota all use torsion bar front suspensions on some or all of their truck models. Most truck applications have longitudinally mounted bars, secured to a frame member through a swiveling anchor arm, and equipped with a height-adjusting nut or bolt.

Air Springs

Some electronically controlled suspension systems use air springs. A basic **air spring** consists of a rubber air chamber, generally closed at the bottom by a piston fitted into a control arm, or by a strut shock absorber (Figure 8-46). On top, a cap assembly that includes an air valve seals the chamber. A line attaches to the valve to feed air pressure from a compressor into the air chamber. A solenoid or another type of electrically operated actuator controls the air valve. An onboard computer determines how much pressure the air spring needs and signals the solenoid accordingly, thus determining the spring rate. Electronically controlled suspension systems that use air springs as the only springs are available on some DaimlerChrysler and Ford models.

Some air springs are in effect auxiliary springs inside a coil-spring strut. In these designs, the coil spring supports the weight of the vehicle, while the air spring raises or lowers the body to adjust ride height according to load (Figure 8-47). Mitsubishi uses this type of air spring in its electronically controlled suspension. Electronically

controlled suspensions are covered in Chapter 12 of this *Classroom Manual*.

Shock Absorbers

The ideal spring creates little or no friction because friction interferes with spring movement. However, the less friction within a spring, the longer it continues to oscillate after it compresses and extends—again, because nothing interferes with its movement. On a vehicle suspension, a **shock absorber** provides the friction needed to control and quickly stop spring oscillation. In Europe, shock absorbers are known as "dampers," which is actually a more accurate name, since the springs actually absorb road shocks while shock absorbers damp the spring action. Some Japanese

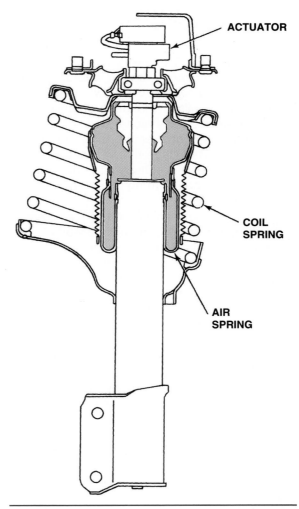

Figure 8-47. Some air springs are auxiliary units to the coil spring and are used only to control ride height, while the coil spring is the weight-bearing component.

AIR SPRING

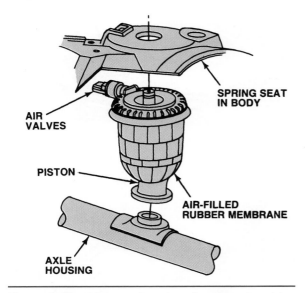

Figure 8-46. Like a coil spring, the air spring rides between the axle or a control arm and the frame. Air valves allow the control system to increase or decrease air pressure in the spring, which makes it stiffer or softer.

manufacturers refer to shock absorbers as "dampeners."

Automotive shock absorbers use hydraulic friction, rather than mechanical, or surface-to-surface, friction to control spring oscillation. Like mechanical friction, hydraulic friction generates heat by resisting movement. However, unlike mechanical friction, hydraulic friction is created without surface-to-surface contact between the moving parts. Therefore, a hydraulic shock absorber has a much longer service life than a mechanical device designed to perform the same task. The movement a shock absorber resists is suspension movement, since one end of the shock mounts to the frame and the other end attaches to a suspension member. The heat created by the internal hydraulic resistance of the shock absorber dissipates into the air surrounding the shock.

In addition to damping spring oscillation, shock absorbers used with coil springs frequently serve a second purpose of limiting suspension travel. To achieve this second purpose, a rubber bump stop is installed on the shock absorber piston rod, either inside or outside the shock cylinder. Be aware, removing a shock absorber that limits downward suspension travel allows the suspension to drop unless it is properly supported. For the same reason, it is dangerous to drive a vehicle with the shocks removed because the coil springs can fall out if the suspension extends too far.

Shock Absorber Mounts

There are four common types of mounts used to attach a shock absorber to the frame and suspension (Figure 8-48). These are the:

Shocking the Model T

The Ford Model T made history by providing average Americans with an affordable personal car. To keep the price low, Ford left out unnecessary frills and luxuries whenever possible. However, many Model T owners felt that ride quality was one feature that should have been left in. The stiff front and rear transverse leaf springs had no shock absorbers of any kind, and the bone-jarring ride of the Model T was legendary.

Aftermarket manufacturers quickly stepped in with many designs of shock absorbers that softened the ride of the stock leaf springs. Most of these were not dampers as we know them today, but rather bolt-on attachments that gave a dual spring rate to the existing leaves.

One of the most sophisticated designs was that used in the "Genuine H. & D. Shock Absorbers," which came as a set for all four wheels. When installed, these items provided an additional pivoting link between the axle and the spring shackle. A lever arm that attached to the link was tensioned by a coil spring bolted to the frame.

As the suspension began to compress, the extra link pivoted to absorb the first few inches of wheel travel by stretching the softer coil spring. Only after the "shock absorber" completed its full travel did the stiffer leaf spring begin to absorb the rest of the bump.

The results were the same as installing a dual-rate spring. The soft initial spring rate from the coil spring cushioned slight road irregularities and uneven pavement, and the stiff spring rate from the original-equipment leaf spring absorbed heavier shocks from potholes and rocks.

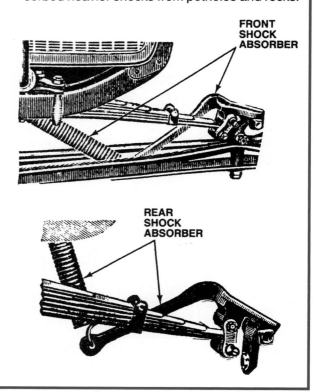

FRONT SHOCK ABSORBER

REAR SHOCK ABSORBER

SHOCK ABSORBER MOUNTS

BAYONET MOUNTING   **BAR MOUNTING**   **RING MOUNTING**   **INTEGRAL-STUD MOUNTING**

Figure 8-48. A bayonet mount extends straight through the mounting point, a bar mount hangs the shock between two attachment points, and ring and integral-stud mounts allow the shock to be connected at a right angle to a component.

- Bayonet
- Bar
- Ring
- Integral-stud

Some shock absorbers use the same type of mount on both ends, while the top and bottom mounts are two different types on others.

A **bayonet mount** is a stud that extends straight out of the end of the shock absorber. A rubber bushing fits onto the bayonet stud, the stud is inserted through a mounting hole on the frame or suspension member, then another rubber bushing installs onto the stud. A washer at each bushing distributes the pressure across the bushing, and a nut fits onto the threaded stud to secure the assembly to the chassis.

With a **bar mount,** the end of the shock is formed into a ring and a rubber bushing is fitted to the inside of the ring. A bar with flat, slotted arms on each end is located at the center of the bushing. The bushing and bar are part of the shock absorber and are not serviced in the field. Either bolts or studs and nuts fit through the slots on the bar ends to attach the shock to the chassis. Bar mounts are often used on applications where the shock fits between the two arms of an A-shaped control arm.

On a **ring mount,** the end of the shock is shaped similar to one with a bar mount, and the ring also houses a rubber bushing. However, there is no bar installed into the bushing. Instead, a cylindrical metal bushing is installed at the center of the rubber bushing. The bushing assembly on some ring mount shocks is removable, while others are factory-installed and not serviceable. A bolt or stud fits through a metal bushing to attach the shock to the frame or a suspension member.

An **integral-stud mount** is similar to a ring mount, except the mounting stud is part of the bushing assembly instead of being a separate part. Integral-stud mounts are not serviceable and the shock absorber must be replaced if the bushing is worn.

Shock Absorber Characteristics

A hydraulic shock absorber has two main performance characteristics: ratio and damping force. **Shock absorber ratio** indicates the relationship between the resistance of the shock during jounce and the resistance during rebound. Damping force, also referred to as stiffness, is the total resistance level of a shock absorber. In general, only the engineers who design and build the shocks know the actual numbers involved—how many pounds or kilograms of resistance for a particular shock. However, since these characteristics affect performance and handling, it is important to understand them.

Shock Absorber Ratio

A shock absorber ratio indicates the proportion of resistance during compression and extension. In other words, some shocks offer greater resistance during compression than extension, and others resist movement more during extension. The shock absorber ratio is a comparison between the two rates, given as resistance to extension, followed by a slash, then resistance to compression. For example, a 70/30 shock absorber applies 70 percent of its resistance against extension and only 30 percent against compression. This 70/30 ratio is quite typical for shocks designed for road-going vehicles. A 50/50 shock resists movement equally in both directions. The shock absorber ratio compares resistance rates, but does not indicate how strong the total resistance is.

Lever Shock Absorber

A modern hydraulic shock is called a **direct-acting shock absorber,** as opposed to some older designs that were lever-operated. One end of a **lever shock absorber** attaches to the frame, but the other end connects the suspension indirectly through a lever and connecting rod. Once popular with British manufacturers, the use of lever, or "knee-action," shocks as original equipment was discontinued in the 1970s. All modern production vehicles use direct-acting shocks that attach directly to both the frame and the suspension.

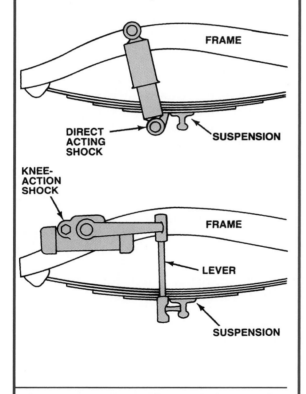

Contemporary direct-acting shock absorbers fasten directly to the frame and suspension, while some older vehicles used lever shocks, which indirectly link to the suspension.

Damping Force

Damping force, which is the total resistance of a shock absorber, may also be called the "control force," but is more commonly referred to as **stiffness.** The greater the damping, or control, force, the stiffer the shock, while less damping force means softer shocks. Depending on overall suspension design, vehicle weight, the intended use of the vehicle, and other factors, design engineers determine a range of acceptable damping force for the shocks on a given vehicle. Usually, a number of shocks can fit within this range, and manufacturers specify them as acceptable for use on a particular model. When replacing shocks, stiffer or softer shocks can be selected from within the range to satisfy the individual tastes and driving habits of the vehicle owner.

Soft shocks offer less resistance to suspension travel. The benefit of soft shocks is that they allow the suspension to compress and extend easily and therefore to absorb more of the energy as the wheel travels over a bump. The drawback is that this lack of resistance also applies to spring oscillation, body roll, and brake dive. A vehicle with softer shocks bounces longer after driving over a bump, leans more during turns, and dives more during braking. The advantage of stiffer shock absorbers is that they resist bounce, roll, and dive, but as a drawback a stiff shock also resists ordinary suspension travel. Stiffer shocks make the suspension more rigid and allow more road shock and vibration to be passed through the frame and body, which results in a harsh ride.

The choice of soft versus stiff shocks for a particular vehicle depends mainly on the preference and driving habits of the owner. Drivers who tend to accelerate rapidly, brake quickly, and corner hard are likely to appreciate the characteristics of stiffer shocks. However, a comfortable ride is more important than improved handling to a more conservative driver, and softer shocks would be a better alternative. For trucks and off-road vehicles, an important factor in selecting replacement shocks is the intended use of the vehicle. A truck that is frequently used to haul heavy loads would benefit from stiffer—even heavy-duty—shocks. However, softer shocks would be the logical choice for the same model truck used primarily as a passenger vehicle.

Hydraulic Shocks

Actually, all modern shocks are hydraulic shocks in that they use hydraulic friction to damp suspension movement. However, the term **hydraulic shock absorber** is generally used to indicate the most basic shock design (Figure 8-49). That is, one that is *not* gas charged or does *not* have an air chamber or any other device that enhances the hydraulic action of the shock. Other types of shock absorbers, such as gas-charged shocks, air shocks, and coil-over shocks, are variations of this basic design.

HYDRAULIC SHOCK ABSORBER

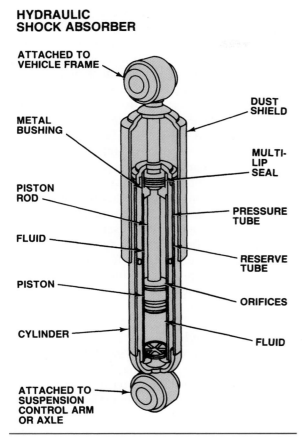

ATTACHED TO VEHICLE FRAME

DUST SHIELD

METAL BUSHING

MULTI-LIP SEAL

PISTON ROD

PRESSURE TUBE

FLUID

RESERVE TUBE

PISTON

ORIFICES

CYLINDER

FLUID

ATTACHED TO SUSPENSION CONTROL ARM OR AXLE

Figure 8-49. Fluid fills the pressure tube and escapes through valves into the reserve tube in a typical hydraulic shock absorber. The top of the piston rod attaches to the frame, and the bottom of the cylinder mounts to the suspension.

The three major parts of a hydraulic shock absorber are the:

- Cylinder
- Piston
- Piston rod

The top of the cylinder contains a metal bushing and a seal with several lips at its inner circumference that allow the piston rod to slide through it. There are two tubes in the cylinder: the pressure tube and the reserve tube. The pressure tube is inside the reserve tube. The bottom of the cylinder attaches to a suspension member by one of the mounting methods described earlier. The piston fits into the pressure tube and onto the lower end of the piston rod. Often, the piston has one or more bands, or sealing rings, around it to maintain good contact with the pressure tube. The upper end of the piston rod attaches to the frame. A dust cover usually attaches just below the mounting point of

COMPRESSION

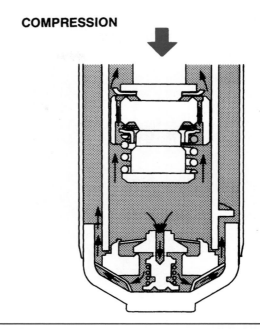

Figure 8-50. During suspension compression, the shock absorber piston moves down through the pressure tube, and the valves in the piston allow a restricted fluid flow up past the piston to create resistance. Valves in the bottom of the shock allow some fluid to escape into the reserve tube.

the piston rod and extends part-way down the outside of the cylinder.

When the wheel rides over a bump, the suspension compresses and the cylinder moves upward. As the cylinder moves up, the piston slides along the inside of the pressure tube, which is filled with hydraulic fluid. The hydraulic fluid generates the resistance that provides the damping effect of the shock absorber. Although there are orifices and valves in the piston through which fluid can flow, the fluid still resists piston movement. There is also a small valve system at the bottom of the pressure tube that fluid passes through. When the piston pushes down on the liquid, some liquid is forced out of the pressure tube, through these lower valves, and into the reserve tube (Figures 8-50).

When the suspension extends, the cylinder moves downward causing the piston to move up inside the pressure tube. Hydraulic fluid above the piston is now forced through the valves to the chamber below the piston and fluid is also drawn from the reserve chamber through the valves at the bottom of the shock (Figure 8-51). An orifice or a small valve is located just below the seal at the top of the pressure tube to allow some fluid to bleed into the reserve tube if necessary. This orifice or valve also transfers

EXTENSION

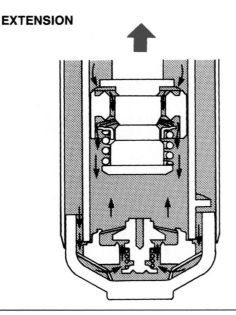

Figure 8-51. When the suspension extends, the shock absorber piston moves up in the pressure tube causing fluid to flow down through the piston valves as the lower valves allow fluid to be drawn into the pressure tube from the reserve tube.

air from the reserve tube to the pressure tube when there is no upward pressure from the piston.

The valves in the piston and at the top and bottom of the pressure tube work in stages. Orifices allow immediate fluid flow, and other valves allow increased fluid flow as pressure increases. Each time a new valve or set of valves opens, the shock absorber begins a new stage of operation. This valving ensures that the piston does not move so slowly through the liquid as to interfere with suspension movement. Bump stops, installed either on the piston rod or elsewhere in the suspension, limit piston travel to protect the valves. Without bump stops, the piston would hammer against the delicate valves and destroy them.

The use of hydraulic friction to damp spring oscillation is useful for several reasons. As explained in Chapter 6 of this *Classroom Manual,* a liquid cannot be compressed. Therefore, it offers firm resistance when suspension movement forces the piston against it. The faster the suspension moves the piston, the greater the resistance because the resistance of a liquid flowing through an orifice increases as the rate of flow increases. Therefore, the shock naturally becomes stiffer on sharp bumps. The valve system keeps resistance from becoming too great. Finally, hydraulic friction wears parts down far more slowly than mechanical

friction, so the shock can extend and compress many times without wearing out.

The hydraulic fluid in a shock absorber can become aerated—mixed with air—if the agitation of repeated compression and extension mixes air into the fluid or if the heat of operation causes the fluid to boil. To prevent air from being drawn into the pressure tube during extension, the shock must be mounted upright or nearly upright. Aerated liquid reduces damping ability because, unlike liquid, air can be compressed and so offers less resistance to piston movement.

To help prevent liquid aeration, some shock absorbers have a spiral groove machined in the cylinder wall outside the reserve tube. Other shocks use a baffle spring that surrounds the outside of the reserve tube to reduce aeration. Both of these methods prevent aeration by breaking up air bubbles in the reserve tube.

Gas-Filled Shocks

The air in the reserve tube of a **gas-filled shock absorber** is replaced by pressurized gas, generally nitrogen. The pressure of the gas on the hydraulic fluid helps keep the fluid from boiling. The nitrogen in a gas-charged shock is usually charged to between 100 and 150 psi (690 and 1,030 kPa) of pressure, and the seal at the top of the cylinder must be strong enough to contain this extra pressure. The pressure in a gas shock tends to make the piston extend.

Monotube Shocks

A **monotube shock absorber** is a gas-charged unit with a cylinder that consists of a single tube, the pressure tube (Figure 8-52). However, a monotube shock contains two pistons: a working piston and a dividing piston. The working piston is on the piston rod and contains all the shock absorber valving. The dividing piston is located near the bottom of the cylinder and separates the pressurized gas from the fluid. The dividing piston shifts up or down slightly in response to the amount of fluid the piston rod displaces as it moves in the cylinder.

An advantage of the monotube design is that the pressure tube is in direct contact with the outside air, so the fluid is cooled more efficiently when it heats up due to extended operation. However, the disadvantage of having only one tube is that even a small dent in the cylinder can make the shock less effective or even non-usable. External damage can cause either of the pistons to loose contact with the inside of the pressure tube, or interfere with piston travel.

MONOTUBE SHOCK ABSORBER

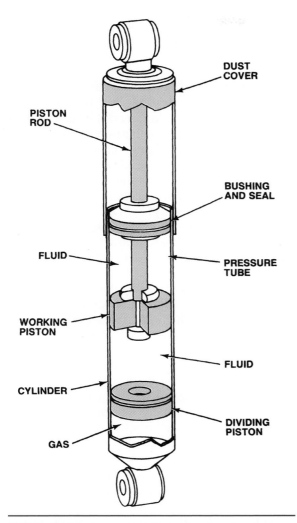

DUST COVER

PISTON ROD

BUSHING AND SEAL

FLUID

PRESSURE TUBE

WORKING PISTON

FLUID

CYLINDER

DIVIDING PISTON

GAS

Figure 8-52. A monotube shock absorber uses a second piston, the dividing piston, in place of a reserve tube. The dividing piston moves slightly to compress the gas charge and allow some fluid displacement.

Because the dividing piston keeps the gas charge in place, a monotube shock can be mounted upside-down, with the pressure tube on top and the piston rod below. Some engineers prefer this method because it makes the heavier part of the shock part of the sprung weight of the vehicle.

Heavy-Duty Shocks

A **heavy-duty shock absorber** is an extra-stiff shock that helps damp spring oscillation. It contains a dividing piston in the lower chamber. The area below this piston is pressurized with nitrogen

gas to 360 psi (2,482 kPa). Hydraulic oil is in the chamber above the dividing piston. Heavy-duty shocks are used to maintain proper ride height on vehicles that frequently carry heavy loads. These shocks may be used at the front or the rear. Manufacturers prohibit the use of certain aftermarket heavy-duty shocks, or load-leveling devices, on some vehicles because they can interfere with the operation of a height-sensing brake proportioning valve. On these vehicles, too much shock damping can cause the height sensor to signal a light load to the brake system, even though the vehicle is heavily loaded. This causes the brake system to supply inadequate pressure to the rear brake circuits.

A number of vehicle factors limit the capability of a shock absorber. For instance, if shocks capable of supporting 1,000 pounds (455 kg) are installed onto mounting studs designed to support only 800 pounds (365 kg), the maximum load is 800 pounds. Loading the vehicle to the rating of the shocks can break the mounts. The maximum load the tires can bear is another important consideration.

Some heavy-duty shocks are simply ordinary hydraulic or gas-charged units with a large-diameter piston and pressure tube. A typical shock piston is about 1 3/16 inches (30 mm) in diameter, while the piston of a heavy-duty shock may have a diameter of 1 3/8 inches (35 mm) or 1 3/4 inches (45 mm).

Other heavy-duty shocks, such as coil-over shocks and air shocks, are modifications of the basic shock absorber design.

Coil-Over Shocks

A **coil-over shock absorber** uses the force of an external coil spring to boost the performance of the basic shock absorber (Figure 8-53). The spring usually extends from the upper shock mount to a seat on the lower portion of the cylinder. The spring rate added to the hydraulic resistance makes the shock stiffer. Some models are also adjustable.

Air Shocks

A typical **air shock absorber** has a rubber tube attached to the inside top of the dust cover and the outside top of the cylinder, which creates an air chamber (Figure 8-54). The tube is long enough to fold into a thin U-shape that lies along the side of the cylinder when the shock is compressed. An air valve on the side of the dust cover allows for increasing or decreasing the air pressure inside the chamber. The higher the air pressure in the chamber, the stiffer the shock.

Manually charged air shocks usually have a tube leading from the valves on the shock chambers to a

COIL-OVER SHOCK ABSORBER

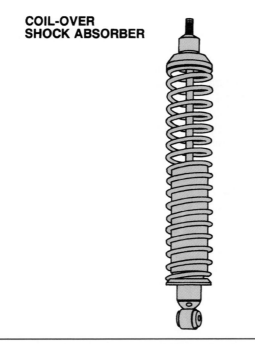

Figure 8-53. A coil-over shock is a basic hydraulic shock absorber with a coil spring wrapped around it to increase its stiffness.

AIR SHOCK ABSORBER

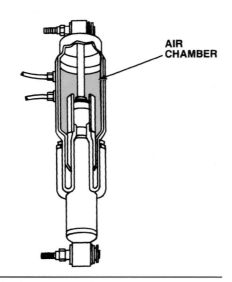

AIR CHAMBER

Figure 8-54. A rubber tube forms an inflatable air chamber at the top of an air shock. The higher the air pressure in the chamber, the stiffer the shock.

service valve, which is used to add or bleed air. The air shocks on some vehicles are part of an electronic leveling system. The air chambers on these shocks have an air tube that leads to an onboard air com-

pressor. The compressor is computer-controlled and activates to increase or decrease pressure in the shocks in response to changes in ride height. A small amount of air pressure is kept in the chamber at all times to prevent it from collapsing during extension.

Electronic Variable Shock Absorbers

A **variable shock absorber** can be adjusted to make it stiffer or softer. Aftermarket variable shocks are usually adjusted by rotating a collar on the shock itself. While original equipment manufacturer (OEM) units are either manually adjusted through a driver-controlled switch or automatically adjusted by a computer-controlled electronic control system, variable shocks generally have two or three settings: stiff and soft, or stiff, medium, and soft. The settings may have different names, such as "sport" for a stiff setting and "luxury" for a soft setting. Some systems use a combination control system that allows the driver to override the computer-determined setting. Electronically adjusted shock absorbers are one step above manually adjustable shocks.

Adjusting a variable shock changes the stiffness of the damping by altering the operation of the valves in the piston. A control rod inside the piston regulates the valves, usually by rotating in one direction or another. The actuator that moves the control rod is usually located on top of the shock or strut unit, and may be manually or electronically operated (Figure 8-55). This control rod varies the size of the metering orifices, which, in turn, changes the shock rate from firm to medium to soft. The speed at which this occurs is usually less than half a second. At a soft setting, the control rod opens more orifices so the piston moves more easily through the fluid. Stiffer settings close off some of the orifices to restrict fluid flow and increase resistance to piston movement. This type of electronically controlled shock can be used alone as a driver-controlled device or it can be part of a computer-controlled suspension system. In computer-controlled systems, the shock is activated based on input from various vehicle sensors. Electronically controlled shock absorbers are covered in detail in Chapter 12 of this *Classroom Manual*.

Struts

A **strut** is a sturdy shock absorber that is also a structural component of the suspension (Figure 8-56). A conventional shock absorber is in effect an add-on

VARIABLE SHOCK ABSORBERS

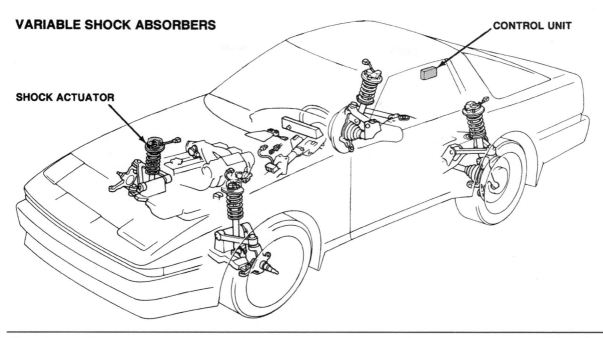

Figure 8-55. An electronic actuator located on top of these variable struts responds to commands from an on-board computer to adjust shock valving.

device that completes the suspension design. Without conventional shock absorbers, the suspension would bounce more, but it would still be structurally complete. In contrast, a strut is a suspension link as well as a shock absorber. Therefore, the casing of a strut must be strong and rigid to function as a suspension link. The shock absorber assembles inside the casing of a strut, and may be either a removable cartridge or an integral part of the strut.

Struts are used on three suspension designs:

- MacPherson strut
- Modified strut
- Strut/short-long-arm (strut/SLA)

On all three suspensions, the top of the strut mounts to the body of the vehicle. With MacPherson and modified struts, the strut is part of the steering axis. A bearing on the top of the strut allows it to rotate on the vertical steering axis while the top mounting remains stationary. The base of both MacPherson and modified struts rigidly mounts to the top of the wheel knuckle, which links it to the platform. The base of a strut used in a strut/SLA suspension mounts to a pivot bushing located on a suspension component.

The top mount of a front strut is accessible from above, rather than from underneath the vehicle. The front struts generally attach to a strut tower that extends into the engine compartment, while the rear strut towers are over the wheel-wells and are accessed through the trunk or hatchback compartment, or by removing the parcel shelf trim.

MacPherson Struts

The **MacPherson strut,** which is named after Earle S. MacPherson, who developed the suspension design in the late 1940s and patented it in 1953, is the most commonly used type. A MacPherson strut includes the suspension spring—a coil spring that surrounds the strut casing—so that it transfers the weight of the body to the wheel. Although the coil spring around a MacPherson strut resembles a large coil-over shock, its function is quite different. For one thing, a coil-over shock is neither a structural nor a load-bearing part of the suspension, while a MacPherson strut is both. Also, the spring of a coil-over shock is used in addition to the suspension spring, while the coil spring of a MacPherson strut is the main, load-carrying suspension spring.

In addition to the shock absorber and coil spring, a MacPherson strut typically incorporates an upper and a lower spring seat, a shock absorber mount and dust cap, a dust cover for the piston rod, and a bump stop. The upper mount secures the upper spring seat to the strut tower. A rubber

MACPHERSON STRUT

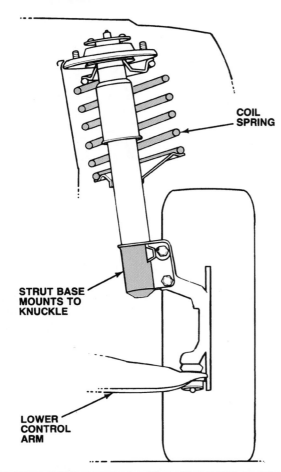

**COIL
SPRING**

**STRUT BASE
MOUNTS TO
KNUCKLE**

**LOWER
CONTROL
ARM**

Figure 8-56. A strut is a structural part of the suspension that helps support the frame. This MacPherson strut also includes the suspension spring.

MODIFIED STRUT

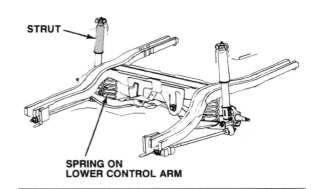

STRUT

**SPRING ON
LOWER CONTROL ARM**

Figure 8-57. Typically used on the rear suspension, a modified strut attaches to the knuckle and the body, but does not include a coil spring.

Chapman Strut

The first designer to put MacPherson-type struts in a rear suspension was an Englishman, Colin Chapman. For this reason, a rear strut suspension is often referred to as a Chapman strut suspension by European manufacturers and engineers. In the United States, any integral-spring strut rigidly mounted to the wheel knuckle is commonly termed a "MacPherson strut," regardless of whether it is at the front or rear axle. For the sake of simplicity, this text follows the U.S. custom and uses "MacPherson strut" to define an integral spring assembly, and "modified strut" when discussing struts without integral springs.

Modified Struts

Since MacPherson struts were the first struts used in automobiles, they were considered conventional when the next strut design appeared. This later design became known as the **modified strut** because it was a modification of the original MacPherson design.

Unlike a MacPherson unit, a modified strut does not include a spring as part of the assembly. Although a few vehicles have modified struts at the front, this type of strut is usually found on the rear suspension (Figure 8-57). Most modified strut rear suspensions use coil springs mounted on the lower control arm. A few vehicles, such as the Oldsmobile Toronado, use a transverse, monoleaf spring with modified struts. The bottom of a modified strut mounts on the wheel knuckle or axle and the top attaches to the body.

bushing at the top of the strut absorbs vibrations. The bayonet mount of the shock absorber extends through the center of the spring seat and the strut tower and is secured by a nut and covered by a dust cap. A bearing on a front-wheel strut allows it to rotate on the vertical steering axis without rubbing against the strut tower when the steering knuckle turns. The lower spring seat is attached to the strut casing. The piston rod dust cover is similar to the dust cover on a conventional shock absorber and a bump stop at the top of the piston rod keeps the strut from bottoming out during suspension jounce. Many struts also have an internal bump stop to keep the strut from overextending during rebound.

■ Who Was MacPherson?

Earle S. MacPherson is best known as the inventor of the MacPherson strut, but the man behind the invention has been an obscure figure. MacPherson began his automotive career in 1915 at Chalmers Motors and worked briefly for both the Liberty Motor Company and Hupmobile before arriving at General Motors in 1934. As chief engineer of the light-car program at GM, MacPherson was deeply involved in developing lighter, simpler suspension systems. It was probably during this period that MacPherson came across the idea of the automotive strut suspension, an obscure design dating from the turn of the century.

MacPherson joined Ford Motor Company in 1947, where he refined and developed his strut suspension, finally patenting it in 1953. Compared to the short-long-arm front suspensions common at the time, the MacPherson strut eliminated a ball joint and the upper control arm. Two 1951 British Ford models, the Consul and Zephyr, were the first production vehicles equipped with MacPherson struts.

The MacPherson strut got its real test a year later on the new Lincoln Capri. Meant to compete against Oldsmobile rather than Cadillac, the Capri was moderately sized by American standards of the time, but still much larger than the Consul or Zephyr. Although critics praised the handling, they said the new front suspension system would never last under the weight of the Lincoln.

The Capri silenced its critics by winning the stock car class of Carrera Panamericana in 1952, then repeating the win in 1953 and 1954. The Carrera was a tough, grueling, flat-out road race across the 2,000-mile Mexican section of the new Pan American highway. Beginning at the southern tip of Mexico, the highway led through tropical jungle, crossed long desert flats, and rose to 10,000 feet in mountain passes. Fewer than half the field ever finished the race.

Sadly, the father of the most popular front suspension system in the world did not live to see the worldwide acceptance of the strut that bears his name. MacPherson retired from Ford in 1958 and passed away two years later.

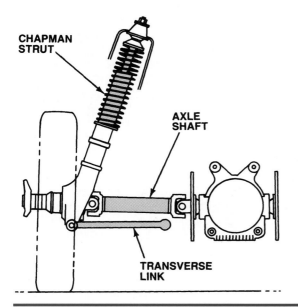

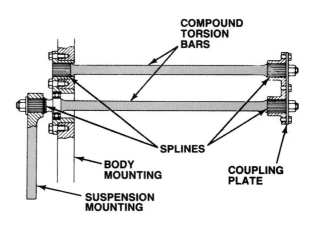

Except for the lack of a spring and spring seats, the construction and function of a modified strut are basically the same as those of a MacPherson strut. When used on the front suspension, a modified strut also rotates on the steering axis when the wheels turn.

Pivot-Base Struts

A more recent innovation in strut design is the **pivot-base strut** used in strut/SLA suspension systems. Pivot-base struts include the suspension spring and resemble a MacPherson strut in appearance. However, the location and design of

PIVOT-BASE STRUT

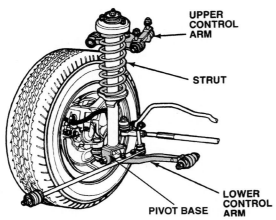

Figure 8-58. The pivot-base strut in a strut/SLA system typically mounts to, and pivots on, the lower control arm.

the lower mount on a pivot-base strut differs from those of a MacPherson strut (Figure 8-58). Rather than solidly attaching to the knuckle, these struts mount on a pivot, which is usually located on the lower control arm. Also, while the other types of struts are used *instead of* an upper control arm and ball joint, a pivot-base strut is used *in addition to* these components. Because it does not mount onto the knuckle, a pivot-base strut used on the front suspension is not generally part of the steering axis. Although some Nissan and Toyota models have pivot-base struts mounted on the rear suspension knuckles, the rear wheels usually do not rotate on a steering axis. On Nissan models with four-wheel-steering (4WS), the rear pivot-base strut *is* affected by the turning of the steering knuckle. However, since the rear-wheel turning angle never exceeds one degree, the strut does not need a ball bearing in the top mount—a bushing supplies enough flexibility.

KNUCKLES

A **knuckle** is hard to classify either as part of the suspension or as part of the wheel. A knuckle serves two purposes: to join the suspension to the wheel and to provide pivot points between the suspension and wheel. Knuckles are not the only way to join suspensions to the wheels. Solid rear suspensions do not use a knuckle because they do not need pivots between the suspension and wheel. However, an independent suspension requires pivots that al-

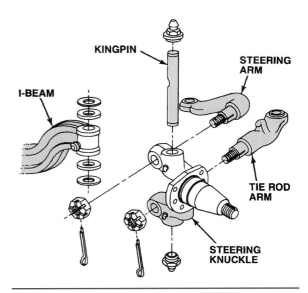

Figure 8-59. A kingpin is a steel shaft or pin that joins the steering knuckle to the suspension and allows the steering knuckle to pivot.

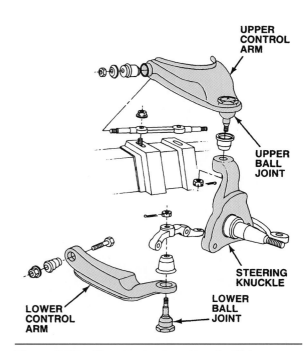

Figure 8-60. The steering knuckle of a SLA suspension or a strut/SLA suspension has two ball joints, an upper one and a lower one.

low up-and-down movement of the wheel without passing it on to the suspension. In addition, the rear wheels, as well as the front wheels of a 4WS system, must be able to rotate on a vertical axis—the steering axis—to move left and right. Therefore, knuckles are used with independent suspensions

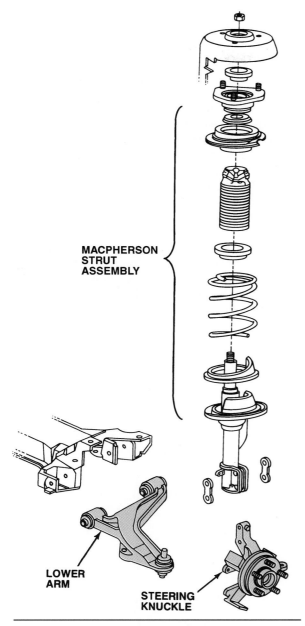

Figure 8-61. The knuckle used with a MacPherson or modified strut has one ball joint or pivot and a mounting point for the base of the strut.

and at the wheels that steer the vehicle. When used to steer the vehicle, the knuckle includes a steering arm and is called a **steering knuckle.**

Four types of connection are used between a knuckle and the suspension:

- Kingpin
- Ball joint
- Strut base
- Pivot bushing

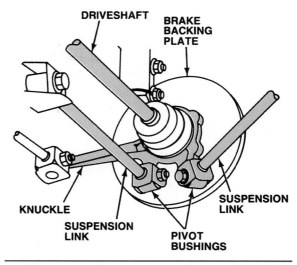

Figure 8-62. Pivots can link suspension parts to the knuckle of a non-steering axle.

The only knuckle that uses a **kingpin** is a steering knuckle on an I-beam or twin I-beam front suspension (Figure 8-59). A kingpin steering knuckle keeps the wheel rigid in relation to the I-beam during up-and-down wheel movement, but rotates around the steering axis to turn the wheels left and right. The steering axis is the vertical center of the kingpin.

The use of ball joints with steering knuckles is discussed earlier in this chapter. Ball joints allow the angle between the suspension and wheel to change during up-and-down wheel movement, and also allow the steering knuckle to steer the wheels left and right. An imaginary line drawn through the two ball joints defines the steering axis. Short-long-arm (SLA) and strut/SLA suspensions use upper and lower ball joints (Figure 8-60).

A strut base is a solid connection to the strut and is used with MacPherson and modified struts to replace the upper ball joint (Figure 8-61). The shock, and the coil spring of a MacPherson strut, takes up vertical movement. When used in a steering knuckle, the strut rotates on the steering axis along with the knuckle. An imaginary line drawn through the top of the strut and the lower ball joint shows the steering axis location.

A pivot bushing allows up-and-down movement of the wheel but cannot rotate on a vertical steering axis. Rear-wheel knuckles commonly use pivot bushings (Figure 8-62).

At non-drive axles, the knuckle includes a spindle on which the wheel rotates. A knuckle at a drive axle has a bore at its center that the axle shaft fits through.

SUMMARY

The two main functions of the automotive suspension are to keep the tires in contact with the road and to isolate the passenger compartment from road shocks. The suspension also keeps tire traction at the best levels and protects all the vehicle components from excessive vibration. Basically, the suspension works by compressing to take up vertical wheel movement and then extending, or rebounding, to its original position.

The suspension directly supports the frame, which in turn is the supporting structure of the rest of the vehicle. Frames may be separate structures or integral to the body. The wheels rotate on an axle. Axles may be solid or part of an independent suspension.

Ball joints and bushings are the couplings that hold suspension parts together and link them to the frame and wheels. These couplings are designed to allow suspension movement. Suspension parts are generally called "links," and some have more specific names, according to their purposes.

The main cushioning devices in a suspension are the springs and shock absorbers. Bump stops are small cushions that prevent excessive compression and extension of the suspension. The types of springs used in suspensions vary in their appearance and design, but they all absorb vertical movement and then return the suspension to its normal height.

Shock absorbers damp spring oscillation. Struts are a combination of a shock absorber and a suspension link. MacPherson struts and pivot-base struts also include the suspension spring.

The knuckle joins the suspension to the wheels in an independent suspension, or to the wheels that steer in a solid suspension. A steering knuckle is used at the steering axle and includes a steering arm to join it to the steering linkage.

Review Questions

For each of the following questions, choose the letter that represents the best possible answer.

1. Technician A says that suspension extension is also known as "bounce." Technician B says that suspension compression is sometimes called "jounce." Who is correct?
   a. Technician A only
   b. Technician B only
   c. Both A and B
   d. Neither A nor B

2. Which type of frame construction is used on most current-production vehicles?
   a. Ladder
   b. Space
   c. Unit-body
   d. Monocoque

3. An independent suspension uses which of the following?
   a. Stub axle
   b. Tube axle
   c. I-beam axle
   d. Solid axle

4. Technician A says that ball joints are suspension couplings that allow the suspension to compress. Technician B says that bushings are suspension couplings that allow the suspension to compress. Who is correct?
   a. Technician A only
   b. Technician B only
   c. Both A and B
   d. Neither A nor B

5. The two basic types of automotive suspension ball joints are:
   a. Extension and compression
   b. Compression and decompression
   c. Strut and non-strut
   d. Load carrying and non-load-carrying

6. The two ends of a control arm attach to a:
   a. Panhard rod and a frame bushing or strut rod
   b. Frame member and the knuckle or wheel flange
   c. An idler arm and a ball joint or bushing
   d. A stub axle or radius rod and an antiroll bar

7. The primary purpose of an antiroll bar is to:
   a. Help support the sprung weight
   b. Control jounce and rebound
   c. Transfer cornering load back to the inner wheel
   d. Maintain ride height when the vehicle is loaded

8. The most important dimension for determining the stiffness of an antiroll bar is:
   a. Bar diameter
   b. Overall bar length
   c. Lever arm length
   d. Bar shape

9. Other than steel alloy, suspension springs can be made of:
   a. Aluminum
   b. Plastic composite
   c. Copper
   d. Cast iron

10. How much weight it takes to compress a spring a certain amount is called:
    a. Spring rate
    b. Spring compression
    c. Spring deflection
    d. Spring frequency

11. Technician A says that a high proportion of unsprung weight-to-sprung weight results in a poor ride quality and handling. Technician B says that the vehicle unsprung weight is the total weight of the frame and body. Who is correct?
    a. Technician A only
    b. Technician B only
    c. Both A and B
    d. Neither A nor B

12. All of the following are characteristics of leaf springs EXCEPT:
    a. They are inexpensive to manufacture
    b. They have high external friction
    c. They are the earliest type of automotive spring
    d. They are lightweight and space efficient

13. Which type of suspension spring is comparatively heavy and requires the most amount of space to operate?
    a. Leaf spring
    b. Coil spring
    c. Torsion bar
    d. Air spring

14. Technician A says that shock absorbers improve ride quality by damping spring action. Technician B says that some shock absorbers provide means of limiting suspension travel. Who is correct?
    a. Technician A only
    b. Technician B only
    c. Both A and B
    d. Neither A nor B

15. The shock absorber ratio is a comparison of the internal resistance during:
    a. Compression and proportion
    b. Jounce and frequency
    c. Compression and extension
    d. Deflection and extension

16. The purpose of the pressurized gas in a gas shock is to:
    a. Increase shock deflection
    b. Replace the fluid in the pressure tube
    c. Replace the air in the reserve tube
    d. Increase piston resistance

17. In a hydraulic shock, fluid friction resists the movement of which part?
    a. The piston rod
    b. The cylinder
    c. The actuator
    d. The piston

18. What changes when an electronically variable shock is switched to its soft or "luxury" setting?
    a. Additional fluid orifices are closed
    b. Additional fluid orifices are opened
    c. Gas pressure is increased in the shock
    d. Gas pressure is reduced in the shock

19. Technician A says that unlike a conventional shock absorber, a MacPherson strut is a load-bearing part of the suspension. Technician B says that a modified strut is similar to a MacPherson strut because it is also a load-bearing part of the suspension. Who is correct?
    a. Technician A only
    b. Technician B only
    c. Both A and B
    d. Neither A nor B

20. The purpose of a knuckle is to:
    a. Attach the shock absorber to the frame
    b. Join the suspension to the wheel
    c. Attach the Panhard rod to the axle
    d. Join the shock absorber to the suspension

9

Front Suspension Designs

OBJECTIVES

Upon completion and review of this chapter, you will be able to:

- Identify the types of automotive solid front suspension axles and explain their use.

- Identify the types of automotive independent front suspension axles, including short-long arm (SLA), strut, modified strut, strut/SLA, and multi-link, and explain their use.

KEY TERMS

A-arm suspension
beam axle
camber change
compression rod
double-wishbone
  suspension
equal-arm suspension
I-beam
I-beam suspension
lower control arm
MacPherson strut
  suspension
modified strut
  suspensions
radius arm
short-long-arm
  (SLA) suspension

strut rod
strut/short-long-arm
  (strut/SLA)
  suspension
strut suspension
tension rod
torsion
triangulation
twin I-beam axle
twin I-beam front
  suspension
unequal-arm
  suspension
upper control arm

INTRODUCTION

This chapter examines common front suspension designs on rear-wheel drive (RWD) and front-wheel drive (FWD) vehicles. As mentioned in Chapter 8 of this *Classroom Manual,* the two main purposes of any suspension—front or rear—are to keep the tires in contact with the road and to provide a comfortable ride. When an engineer designs the suspension for a specific vehicle there are a number of factors that must be taken into consideration. The suspension must be able to compress and extend within the space available on the chassis. Longitudinal links must be able to brace the suspension against braking and acceleration forces without interfering with vertical suspension movement. A suspension must also be designed to provide the best ride and handling characteristics for a particular vehicle. This task includes achieving the most appropriate alignment angles and roll center height.

While the above items apply to any suspension—front or rear—additional criteria must be considered in the design of a front suspension. First, the front suspension must be able to work together with the steering system. The suspension must allow the wheels to move up and down, while the steering pivots them left or right on a vertical steering axis. As discussed in Chapter 8, ball joints at the steering knuckle permit this movement. Adequate space for the suspension components to move is critical in a front suspension. With the trend toward smaller, FWD vehicles, space in the engine compartment for suspension parts has decreased. As a result, front suspension systems must be compact, yet still perform adequately. In the interests of ride and handling, virtually all production vehicles, except some trucks, have independent front suspensions. On a FWD platform the engine effectively rests on the front axle, so independent front suspension is needed to keep the engine from being severely jolted.

Six basic designs achieve the various engineering goals for late-model front suspensions:

- Beam axle
- I-beam
- Twin I-beam
- Short-long-arm (SLA)
- Strut
- Strut/short-long-arm (strut/SLA)

Typically, use of a solid beam axle or I-beam suspension is limited to heavy-duty vehicles. Twin I-beams provide a sturdy but independent suspension on some Ford trucks. Used primarily on RWD vehicles, short-long-arm (SLA) suspensions were the nearly universal front suspension for many years. Strut suspensions took over most of the market in the 1980s with the advent of the compact FWD platform. Strut/short-long-arm (strut/SLA) suspensions, which combine some characteristics of SLA and strut suspensions, first appeared in the late 1980s and their use has expanded in recent years.

SOLID FRONT SUSPENSIONS

Today, the use of solid front suspensions is limited because the design cannot provide the smooth ride and precise handling of an independent suspension. However, a solid front suspen-sion is used on a number of current off-road and heavy-duty vehicles where function and dependability are more important than ride and handling. On these vehicles, solid front suspensions are practical because they are simple, inexpensive to manufacture, easy to service, and strong.

Solid Suspension Characteristics

In spite of its merits—simplicity, economy, and strength—the drawbacks of a solid front suspension outweigh the benefits as a general rule. A rough ride results when a vehicle with a solid suspension is driven over uneven roads because the design tends to cause wheel tramp and shimmy. As one wheel on a solid axle travels over a bump, the entire axle tilts to shift more weight to the opposite side, which compresses the tire. The compressed tire rebounds, or tramps, when the axle straightens. The solid axle transmits the force of the rebound to the opposite wheel, and both wheels bounce back-and-forth, or shimmy, as a result.

The tires have a less secure grip on the road with a solid axle than on an independent suspension. Anytime a solid axle tilts, whether caused by one wheel riding over a bump or simply turning a corner, the opposite wheel must tilt as well. This tilt results in positive camber on the opposite wheel and also causes the contact patch of the tire to slide sideways, or scuff (Figure 9-1). Scuffing wears out tires quickly.

Solid axles are large and cumbersome, so they require a considerable amount of space. The engine in a solid-front-axle vehicle must be positioned behind the axle, requiring a long front end. A related problem is the additional

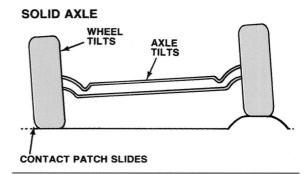

Figure 9-1. When one wheel on a solid front axle rides over a bump, the axle tilts causing positive camber and tire scuff on the opposite wheel, which produces a rough ride and accelerates tire wear.

weight of a large steel tube running across the chassis. While large, weighty parts may be suitable for heavy-duty vehicles, they are impractical for applications where fuel economy is a concern.

Beam Axle Suspensions

A **beam axle** is a tube that runs between the two front wheels. Some designs have an antiroll bar inside the axle tube. Beam axles usually provide some amount of twisting action, or **torsion,** to help reduce the amount of tilt transferred from one wheel to the other. However, a beam axle is still a solid suspension and transmits a noticeable amount of motion from wheel to wheel.

A recent application of a beam axle front suspension on a production vehicle was the RWD version of the Jeep Cherokee, which was available through 1996 (Figure 9-2). Other older two-wheel drive Jeep models used the beam axle as well. The main components of the Jeep front suspension are the:

- Axle tube
- Coil springs
- Shock absorbers
- Antiroll bar

The axle tube has a C-shaped extension at each end, but does not contain an internal antiroll bar. The extensions of the axle tube connect it to the steering knuckles through ball joints, and to this extent they function as upper and lower control arms. Four mounting brackets are used to secure the axle beam to the chassis. The two vertical brackets attach the axle tube to the frame, while the two brackets extending toward the rear secure the tube to the front sub-frame and also provide a location for the lower shock absorber mounts. The coil springs rest on spring perches located on top of the beam near the end of the axle (Figure 9-3). Two additional brackets on the front of the axle tube provide mounting points for an antiroll bar.

I-Beam Suspensions

Some heavy-duty trucks use an **I-beam** as the front beam axle. It is so named because it is constructed from a solid metal piece whose cross-section looks like the capital letter "I" (Figure 9-4). The beam reaches from one steering knuckle to the other, and kingpins secure it to the knuckles while allowing the steering knuckles to turn. Leaf springs position and attach the I-beam to the frame. An I-beam is considerably heavier than a beam axle because it is a solid metal bar. Since the I-beam is solid, it provides virtually no torsional action and transmits suspension travel directly from one wheel to the other.

The only mass-market vehicles that use I-beam suspensions are heavy-duty trucks. Ford F-Series

BEAM AXLE SUSPENSION

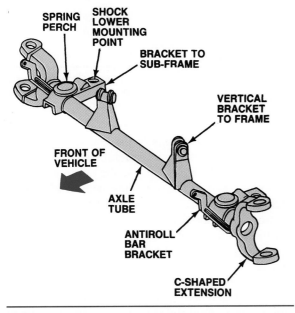

Figure 9-2. Older, two-wheel-drive Jeep models have a solid front suspension featuring an axle tube that attaches to the wheel knuckles with ball joints.

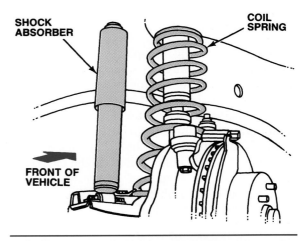

Figure 9-3. In the front suspension of the RWD Jeep, the shock absorber attaches to a bracket on the sub-frame and the coil spring seats on a perch on top of the axle tube.

I-BEAM AXLE

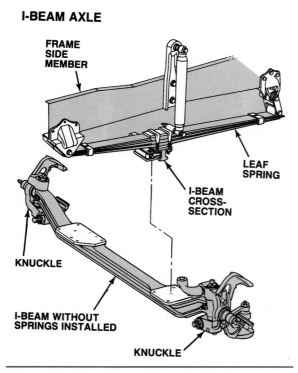

Figure 9-4. An I-beam axle, which is built on a beam whose cross-section resembles the letter "I," is a large assembly suitable for truck and off-road use.

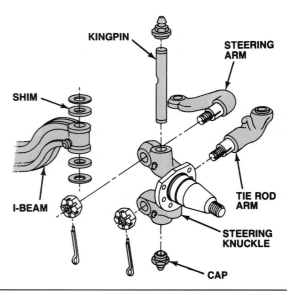

Figure 9-5. Kingpins attach the steering knuckles to the I-beam and provide a pivot for the steered wheels.

I-BEAM SUSPENSION

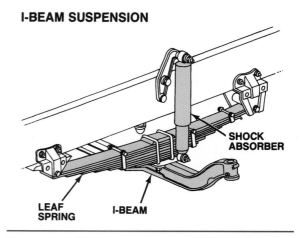

Figure 9-6. The entire weight of the solid steel I-beam is unsprung because the leaf spring rests on top of the beam and does not cushion its movement.

and C-Series trucks with a gross vehicle weight rating (GVWR) over 6,000 pounds and Chevrolet P-Model trucks with an optional heavy-duty front suspension use an I-beam front axle.

An **I-beam suspension** is a simple design consisting of only three main parts:

- I-beam
- Leaf springs
- Shock absorbers

The I-beam is a solid, one-piece crossbar. At each end, a kingpin fits through a machined bore to attach the I-beam to the steering knuckle (Figure 9-5). Spindle caps at the top and bottom of the knuckle secure the kingpin to the knuckle and I-beam. The spindle caps may thread into the knuckle, such as on the Ford suspension, or be held in place with a retaining plate and bolt, such as on the Chevrolet design. Both the Ford and Chevrolet steering knuckles have removable steering arms.

The semi-elliptical leaf springs rest on flat spring perches on top of the I-beam and are secured with U-bolts. Spacers between the bolts and the spring perch isolate the spring to reduce road shock transmission into the chassis. Brackets and

shackles attach the ends of the leaf springs to the bottom of a frame side member. The I-beam hangs below the leaf spring so the entire weight of the axle is part of the unsprung weight of the vehicle (Figure 9-6). The suspension bump stops are located on the bottom of the frame side members to limit spring compression.

The top of each shock absorber mounts to a bracket attached to the outside of the frame side member, and the bottom mounts to a bracket on the I-beam located next to the spring perch. Some versions of the Chevrolet suspension have an antiroll bar, which connects to spacer bars that are fastened to the spring perches. Rubber-insulated brackets fasten the middle section of the antiroll bar to the bottom of the frame side members. See Chapter 9 of the *Shop Manual* for front suspension service.

INDEPENDENT FRONT SUSPENSIONS

Most production vehicles have an independent front suspension, which provides better ride quality and more precise handling than a solid front axle. There are more designs for independent front suspensions than solid ones because more types of vehicles use them. Independent suspension designs range from the relatively large, heavy twin I-beam to the lightweight, compact MacPherson strut.

Independent Suspension Characteristics

Independent front suspensions offer a number of advantages over solid axles including:

- A smoother ride over uneven roads
- Less wheel shimmy and tramp
- More efficient use of space
- Lower weight

When one wheel in an independent suspension travels over a bump, it can move vertically without affecting the opposite wheel (Figure 9-7). Since there is no axle beam to transfer motion from one wheel to the other, independent front suspensions do not have the problems with wheel shimmy and tramp that plague solid suspensions. Designers can use engine compartment space more efficiently with most independent suspensions because there is no axle beam to intrude into the engine compartment. In addition, most independent suspensions are smaller and weigh less than a solid axle.

All independent suspensions are similar in the fact that each wheel rises and falls in a curve around an imaginary axis. This imaginary axis, or pivot point, which is known as the "instant center," is determined by the angles of the control arms on SLA suspensions (Figure 9-8). The instant center of a strut suspension is the intersection of lines drawn through the lower control arm and across the top mount of the strut, which usually leans inward to some degree.

As explained in Chapter 3 of this *Classroom Manual,* the position of the instant center deter-

INDEPENDENT SUSPENSION

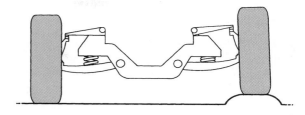

Figure 9-7. When one wheel of an independent front suspension rides over a bump, the wheel on the opposite end of the axle is unaffected.

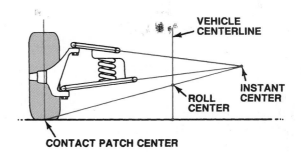

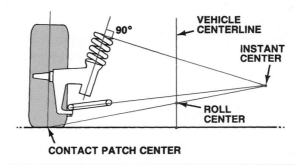

Figure 9-8. The instant center, which is determined by the angle of the control arms, is the pivot point for each side of the suspension. If a line was drawn from the instant center to the middle of the tire contact patch, the point where this line intersects the vertical centerline of the vehicle is the roll center of the front suspension.

mines the height of the suspension roll center, which is an important handling factor. Thus, the angle at which the control arms are installed influences how the car handles. The length of the arms and their relative position to each other determine the caster, camber, and steering axis inclination alignment angles. Given one type of independent suspension, engineers can vary the details—arm or strut length, angle, and position—to provide the most suitable handling characteristics for a specific model.

The Hudson Axleflex

While most automotive suspensions use links at each wheel that are joined to a solid frame member in the center of the chassis, the Hudson Axleflex—manufactured in 1934–35—used a different approach. On the Axleflex, upper and lower links at the center of the front axle connect to solid beams at each wheel. In effect, the front axle of the Axleflex is an I-beam with the center cut out and replaced by two center links that pivot on metal bushings at each end. Outboard of the center links, elliptical leaf springs cushioned the axle and positioned it under the frame.

When new, the Axleflex was an effective semi-independent front suspension. The design did have some quirks, such as twisting leaf springs. In addition, when one front wheel hit a bump, one end of the axle would move in an arc relative to the rest of the axle, which produced a tug on the steering arm because the steering linkage consisted of a single tie rod. However, in the early 1930s, independent front suspension was so rare that this semi-independent axle favorably impressed buyers, and even remained a drawing card when Hudson models equipped with the Axleflex were sold second-hand.

Unfortunately, the axle bushings used small plugs instead of grease fittings and Hudson failed to stress the lubrication of these critical points as a maintenance procedure, so most owners simply did not grease them. As a result, the bearings tended to rust, often to the point of turning solid and causing the formerly flexible axles to seize in strange-looking positions. As years went by, restoration technicians who had encountered these stiff, twisted axles spoke of them with such contempt that the Axleflex obtained a worse reputation than it deserved. After all, the engineers had come up with a design that worked. Their real mistake was in not specifying or providing adequate means for regular maintenance. To keep the Axleflex functioning as designed, an ounce of prevention—in this case, a few ounces of chassis grease—would have been worth a pound of cure.

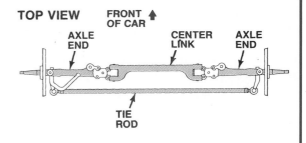

TOP VIEW   FRONT OF CAR ↑

AXLE END   CENTER LINK   AXLE END

TIE ROD

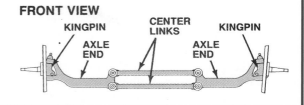

FRONT VIEW

KINGPIN   CENTER LINKS   KINGPIN

AXLE END   AXLE END

Twin I-Beam Suspensions

A **twin I-beam axle** consists of two I-beams, one for each wheel (Figure 9-9). Each I-beam is separate from the other and consequently allows independent wheel travel. The wheel end of each I-beam attaches to the steering knuckle with either a pair of ball joints or a kingpin. From the wheel, the I-beam progressively narrows as it extends across the chassis to where it attaches to a frame crossmember. Whether attached directly to the frame or indirectly through a bracket, this end of the I-beam pivots on a bushing to allow vertical movement of the wheel. This bushing at the frame mount allows some torsional action in response to vertical travel of the I-beam. However,

a **radius arm** near the outboard end of each I-beam braces it against the frame to limit fore and aft movement and make it more stable.

Ford used the **twin I-beam front suspension** extensively on pickup trucks, sport utility vehicles, and RWD vans through the 1997 model year (Figure 9-10). However, the design was abandoned in favor of a SLA suspension for 1998 models. The Ford truck suspension consists of:

• Twin I-beams
• Radius arms
• Coil springs
• Shock absorbers

On pickup and sport utility applications, ball joints link the twin I-beams to the steering knuck-

TWIN I-BEAM AXLE

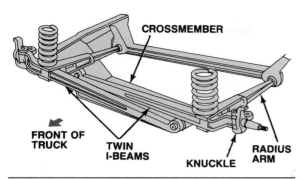

Figure 9-9. Twin I-beams provide independent wheel movement because a separate beam is used for each wheel. One end of the beam attaches to a steering knuckle and is braced by a radius arm, while the other end pivots at the suspension crossmember.

TWIN I-BEAM SUSPENSION

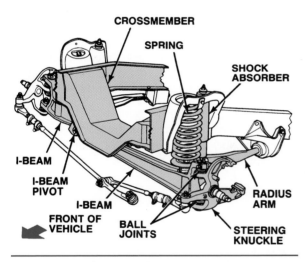

Figure 9-10. The twin I-beam suspension used on Ford trucks offers a compromise between the strength of an I-beam suspension and the superior ride quality of an independent suspension.

les, while kingpins were used on the Econoline vans. An antiroll bar was included on the Bronco II front suspension.

All of these truck models have a frame crossmember running between the front wheelwells that bends downward toward the middle to accommodate the engine. Brackets extend down from the underside of this crossmember to mount and provide a pivot point for the inner ends of the twin I-beams. Trailing ends of the radius arms, which extend toward the rear of the chassis from the outer ends of the I-beams, anchor to brackets attached to the frame side

SHORT-LONG-ARM (SLA) SUSPENSION

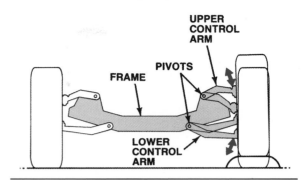

Figure 9-11. The upper control arm is shorter than the lower control arm on a short-long-arm, or SLA, suspension.

members. The coil springs seat between perches on top of the twin I-beams and the wheelwells. The shock absorbers mount next to the springs and attach to the radius arms and the wheelwells.

Twin I-Beam Characteristics

Twin I-beam front suspensions combine some of the strength and sturdiness of an I-beam with some of the benefits of independent suspensions. However, they differ from other types of independent front suspensions in a few aspects. The angle of the wheel in relation to the control arm is rigid because each wheel attaches to a single arm—the I-beam. Therefore, design engineers cannot easily vary the wheel alignment angles to suit different models. Another drawback of twin I-beams is that they produce a jacking effect. That is, if the wheel tilts for any reason, the opposite end of the I-beam lifts up or pulls down the side of the chassis to which it is anchored. Also, because the springs rest on top of the I-beams, all the weight of the beams is unsprung weight, which detracts from ride quality.

Short-Long-Arm Suspensions

The two main links in a **short-long-arm (SLA) suspension** are the **upper control arm** and **lower control arm**. The upper control arm is shorter than the lower one (Figure 9-11). This type of suspension system goes by a variety of names, including **unequal-arm suspension, double-wishbone suspension,** or **A-arm suspension.** Unequal arm refers to the fact that the two arms are of different length, while double-wishbone and A-arm derive

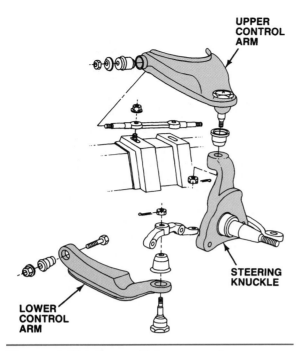

Figure 9-12. Some SLA suspensions use a straight—two-point—lower control arm rather than a wishbone or A-shaped—three-point—arm.

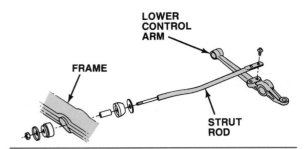

Figure 9-13. A strut rod braces a two-point lower control arm against the frame to form a triangular link, which resists braking and acceleration forces.

from the shape of the arms, which are frequently triangular with one mounting point at the knuckle and two at the frame. However, the control arms, especially the lower one, are not always triangular (Figure 9-12). When an SLA suspension uses a straight, two-point lower control arm, there is nearly always another link, called a **strut rod,** that braces the lower arm against the frame (Figure 9-13). The strut rod can attach to the frame at a point either forward or to the rear of the control arm. A strut rod that extends forward from the lower control arm may be called a **tension rod** or a "trailing strut rod," while one that extends rearward from the control arm may be called a **compression rod** or a "leading strut rod." Note that the terms "trailing" and "leading" refer to the position of the control arm in relation to the frame anchor point, not the direction the strut rod extends from the control arm.

A strut rod is similar to a radius arm in that they both brace another part of the suspension to resist the forces of braking and acceleration. In addition, both mount to the frame with rubber bushings to allow some torsional action in response to vertical movement. In fact, technical literature may interchange the terms "strut rod" and "radius arm," or use the term "radius rod" to define either or both devices. In addition, some repair manuals refer to these suspension links as

"reaction rods" because they provide a reaction to the braking and acceleration forces acting on the axle. However, in this textbook the term "strut rod" is used in reference to rods used with lower control arms and "radius arm" applies to the arms used with twin I-beams.

Using a strut rod provides **triangulation** between the wheel and frame. Triangulation is necessary in front suspensions because a three-point brace resists forces from every direction, while still allowing the wheels to pivot on the steering axis.

A typical SLA suspension consists of the:

- Upper control arm
- Lower control arm, sometimes with a strut rod
- Coil spring, torsion bar, or transverse leaf spring
- Shock absorber
- Antiroll bar

At one time, from the 1950s through the 1970s, the SLA front suspension was nearly universal. However, as manufacturers switched their focus to compact FWD platforms, the design gave way to lighter, more space-efficient strut suspensions. Although a few large RWD sedans and wagons still use a SLA front suspension, this arrangement is more commonly found on trucks. Chevrolet, DaimlerChrysler, Ford, Isuzu, Mazda, Mitsubishi, Nissan, and Toyota are among those using SLA front suspensions in one or more of their truck models.

A number of different SLA front suspension designs are currently in production, or have been recently used in production. The main difference between one SLA suspension design and another is the location and type of suspension spring. A SLA suspension may use:

- Coil springs on the lower control arms
- Coil springs on the upper control arms

- Longitudinal torsion bars
- Transverse torsion bars
- A single, transverse leaf spring

In general, only coil springs are used on either the upper or lower control arm, while torsion bars and leaf springs nearly always mount on the lower control arms.

Coil Springs on Lower Control Arms

Locating the coil spring on the lower control arm is a popular SLA design that was used by a number of manufacturers, including DaimlerChrysler, Ford, General Motors, Jaguar, Mitsubishi, and Mercedes-Benz, over the years. The front suspension of the 1998 Dodge RWD Ram Truck serves as an example of the design in the following discussion (Figure 9-14).

The upper control arm is A-shaped, with two mounting points at the frame side member and one at the steering knuckle. The inboard ends of the arm attach to a pivot bar that is rigidly bolted to the frame, and the outboard end connects to the steering knuckle with a ball joint. Bushings between the inner arm mounts and the pivot bar allow the arm to swing vertically. The lower control arm is also A-shaped with two inboard pivot mounts and a ball joint connection at the knuckle. Bolts attach the inboard ends of the lower arm to brackets that extend from the bottom of the frame crossmember. Bushings on the inboard mounts allow the arm to pivot vertically.

The coil springs seat between the lower control arm and a bracket below the frame side member. The shock absorber installs alongside the coil spring and attaches to the lower control arm and the frame side member. An antiroll bar is connected to the lower control arm through vertical links with bushings at either end. Rubber-insulated brackets attach the middle of the antiroll bar to the frame side members.

Coil Springs on Upper Control Arms

In a typical coil spring on the upper control arm design a portion of the unit-body wheelwells is reinforced to withstand spring force and act as the upper spring seats (Figure 9-15). Originally, placing the spring on the upper control arm was a method of getting it out of the way to accommodate the axle shafts in a FWD vehicle. Most FWD vehicles now use MacPherson struts, rather than a SLA suspension. One of the last production vehicles featuring a coil spring on the upper control

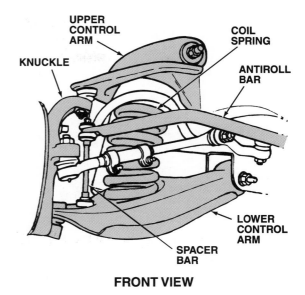

FRONT VIEW

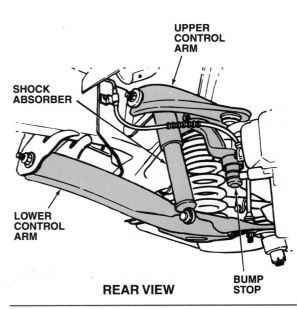

REAR VIEW

Figure 9-14. On this Dodge truck SLA front suspension the coil spring rests on the lower control arm, which makes the upper arm and the frame member it attaches to part of the sprung weight of the vehicle.

arms was the 1993 SAAB 900. Current model SAAB 900s use a MacPherson strut design.

On the older Saab suspension, the coil spring seats between the upper control arm and the wheelwell. Both the upper and lower control arms are wishbone-shaped. The inboard ends of the control arms mount to the underbody through brackets and pivot on bushings. The bushings fit onto the ends of a bar that connects the two

SLA SUSPENSION — COIL SPRING ON UPPER ARM

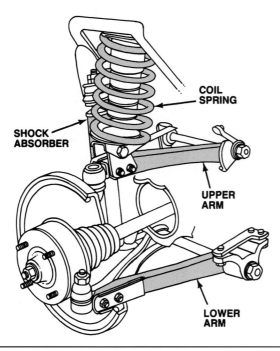

Figure 9-15. Placing the coil spring on the upper control arm leaves room for the drive axles of a FWD powertrain and retains the handling characteristics of a SLA suspension.

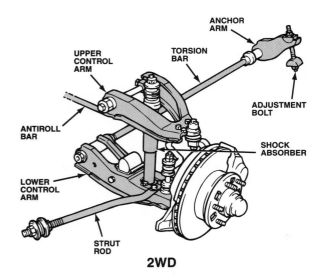

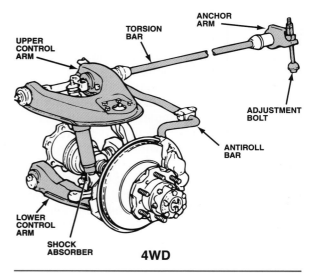

Figure 9-16. Longitudinal torsion bars take up less vertical space than coil springs, but they use more front-to-rear space. Toyota uses this arrangement for both RWD and 4WD versions of the T1000 because the position of the torsion bars does not interfere with the front axle shafts of a 4WD model.

branches of the arm and serves as the pivot axis. A flanged ball joint assembly fits into a slot on the outboard end of each control arm. Two bolts attach the ball-joint flange to the control arm, while the ball stud fits through a machined bore in the steering knuckle and is secured by a self-locking nut. The shock absorbers mount between the body and the lower control arms.

Longitudinal Torsion Bars

Longitudinal torsion bars, which run parallel to the frame side members, have been used on a number of the front suspension designs. Although Honda and Acura used a longitudinal torsion bar front suspension on select models through 1987, for the most part they are found in trucks. This is because the design requires a sturdy frame for support and considerable space to operate in. A number of import manufacturers use a longitudinal torsion bar front suspension in their pickup trucks and sport utility vehicles. Recent applications include the Isuzu Amigo, Trooper, and Trooper II; Mazda B2200 and B2600; Mitsubishi

Montero and the Toyota truck line. The front suspension of the Toyota T100 2WD pickup serves as an example of a longitudinal torsion bar arrangement in the following discussion (Figure 9-16).

Toyota uses wishbone-type upper and lower control arms that connect to the frame and pivot on bushings. The primary difference between 2WD and 4WD versions is that the torsion rod bolts to the lower control arm on 2WD applications and to the upper control arm on 4WD models. The lower control arm of the 2WD version pivots on a single bushing assembly that spans the

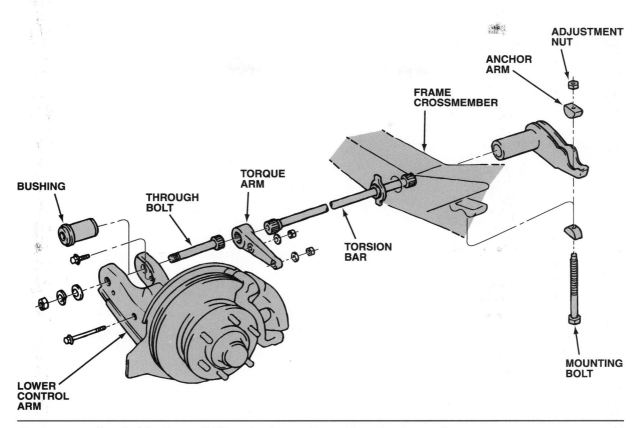

Figure 9-17.   Detail of the Toyota 2WD torsion bar and lower control arm mounting.

gap between the two inboard ends of the control arm and is secured by a through bolt: External splines on the head of the through bolt mate to internal splines on the torque arm, which bolts to the rear face of the control arm. A strut rod bolts to the top of the lower control arm and extends forward to mount in a bracket on the frame. The strut rod helps position the lower control arm and resists fore and aft movement that results from braking and acceleration forces.

The forward end of the torsion bar has external splines and shares the splined socket of the torque arm with the control arm through bolt. Because the torque arm is rigidly bolted to the control arm, motion transfers to the torsion bar whenever the control arm pivots. The torsion bar extends rearward from the control arm and connects to an anchor arm that attaches to a frame crossmember. The torsion bar splines to the anchor arm and the anchor arm is secured to the frame by a bolt and adjusting nut. The adjusting nut varies the spring force of the torsion bar to establish the ride height of the vehicle (Figure 9-17). A bar mount attaches the bottom of the shock absorber to the lower control arm and a bayonet mount at the top connects

the shock to the body. An antiroll bar, secured at the ends to spacer bars and attached to the frame by rubber cushions and brackets, connects the two lower control arms.

Transverse Torsion Bars

DaimlerChrysler used a transverse torsion bar front suspension design on a number of RWD vehicles produced from the mid-1950s through 1989. The last version of this suspension was used on the DaimlerChrysler Fifth Avenue and Newport, Dodge Diplomat, and Plymouth Caravelle Salon and Gran Fury. The front suspension of these vehicles assembled on a removable crossmember, called an "isolated crossmember," so named because rubber cushions installed between the crossmember and the front sub-frame isolate the suspension from the body (Figure 9-18). Some DaimlerChrysler service manuals refer to this crossmember as the "H-member" because of its shape.

The upper control arm in this suspension is A-shaped and pivots on a bar that bolts to the isolated crossmember. The lower arm is straight and pivots on a single bolt at the crossmember.

SLA SUSPENSION — TRANSVERSE TORSION BAR

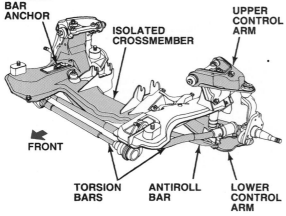

Figure 9-18. These L-shaped, transverse torsion bars were a DaimlerChrysler trademark for many years. The entire suspension mounts on an isolated crossmember to reduce the intrusion of road shock into the passenger compartment.

However, the design of the torsion bars eliminates the need for a strut rod to brace the lower arm. The two torsion bars are somewhat L-shaped. A bushing and flange at the end of the shorter section bolt to the lower control arm. From the control arm, the bar extends forward and slightly inward, then bends into the long, transverse section. At the bend, a bushing called the "pivot cushion bushing" links the bar to the underside of the crossmember through a bolt-on bracket. An anchor arm and swivel secure the opposite end of the torsion bar to the crossmember. An adjusting stud on the anchor arm provides a means of setting ride height.

An antiroll bar is used to control body roll during cornering. The ends of the antiroll bar are secured to brackets attached to the torsion bars just forward of the lower control arms. Two links and bushings, one on either side, secure the middle section of the antiroll bar to the isolated crossmember. The shock absorber mounts between the lower control arm and an extension of the front sub-frame.

Transverse Leaf Springs

Since 1984, the Chevrolet Corvette has used a rather unique SLA front suspension featuring a transverse, fiberglass monoleaf spring. Although a number of vehicles use a transverse monoleaf rear spring, the Corvette is the only model to successfully apply this technology to the front suspension.

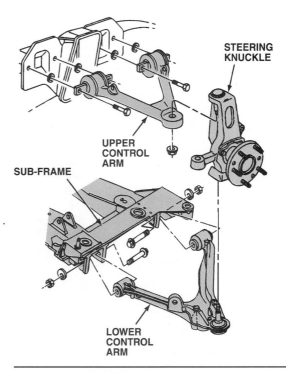

Figure 9-19. The Chevrolet Corvette has lightweight, aluminum control arms that pivot in the frame on integral bushings and attach to the steering knuckle with ball joints.

Each end of the transverse leaf spring contains a spring adjuster bolt assembly that is used to establish ride height. The lower portion of the adjuster is a cushion that fits onto a spring perch on top of the lower control arm. Retainer brackets and isolator cushions attach the central portion of the spring to the sub-frame on either side of the chassis (Figure 9-19). A special spring compressor is required to remove and install the transverse leaf spring.

On the latest version of the Corvette front suspension, both the upper and lower control arms are wishbone-shaped and pivot on integral bushings (Figure 9-20). The bushings of the forged aluminum upper control arms contain a mounting bar, similar to those used on shock absorbers, that bolts to the frame. The upper ball joint is part of the steering knuckle assembly, and the ball stud fits through a machined bore on the outboard end of the control arm. The bushings on the inboard ends of the cast aluminum lower control arms install into brackets on the front sub-frame and are secured by a through bolt. An integral ball joint on the outboard end of the lower control arm installs into a machined bore on the steering knuckle and is secured by a lock nut. A bar mount secures the bottom of the shock absorber to the lower control arm and a bayonet mount at-

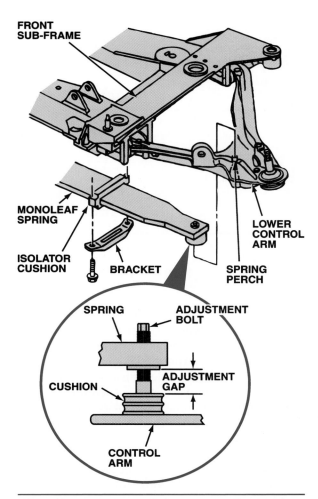

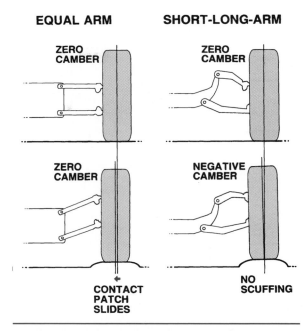

Figure 9-21. An equal-arm suspension maintains zero camber, but causes tire scuffing when a wheel rides over a bump. A wheel traveling over a bump on a SLA suspension produces negative camber, which reduces tire scuffing.

Figure 9-20. The adjustment bolt assembly seats the Corvette transverse, monoleaf spring on the lower control arm and an isolator cushion and bracket secure the spring to the front sub-frame.

taches the top of the shock to an extension of the frame. An antiroll bar attaches to the lower control arms through spacer bars and is secured to the sub-frame by brackets and rubber cushions.

Short-Long-Arm Characteristics

Before SLA suspensions came into general use, the typical independent front suspension was an **equal-arm suspension** design sometimes called a "parallelogram suspension." Like the SLA suspension, the equal-arm suspension used upper and lower control arms, but both arms were the same length. When a wheel in an equal arm suspension travels vertically, its camber angle remains the same throughout the travel. As explained in Chapter 14 of this *Classroom Manual,* with positive camber the top of the wheel tilts outward, with negative camber it tilts inward, and with zero camber it remains vertical.

Zero camber is considered ideal for straight-ahead driving because it gives the best handling and causes the least tire wear. However, zero camber is *not* the best angle for a wheel traveling over a bump. As two equal-length arms pivot, their angle changes and pulls the wheel inward, which causes the tire contact patch to scrub across the road surface (Figure 9-21). Tire scrub decreases traction and quickly wears out the tires.

In the 1940s, engineers eliminated the trade-off between the benefits of zero camber for straight-ahead driving and the drawback of tire scuff over bumps by designing the SLA suspension. During straight-ahead driving the wheel maintains zero camber, but as the wheel travels over a bump, the shorter upper arm pulls the top of the wheel in farther than the lower arm pulls the bottom. This causes the wheel to tilt inward at the top—negative camber—so that the tire contact patch is not pulled as far inward across the road (Figure 9-21). Creating negative camber over a bump is called **camber change,** and engineers design SLA suspensions to provide the best camber change for a particular vehicle or to achieve a desired handling effect.

Another aspect of handling related to control arm length and camber is the scrub radius of the tire, which is the distance between the center of the

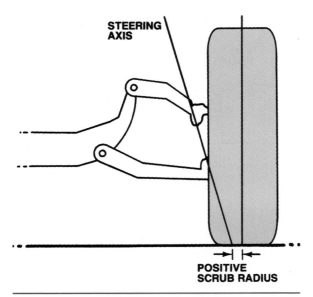

Figure 9-22. The friction between the tire contact patch and the road causes a wheel with positive scrub radius to toe out during straight-ahead driving. To compensate, manufacturers generally specify aligning the wheels with a slight amount of toe-in to obtain zero toe while driving.

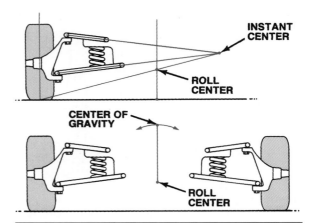

Figure 9-23. The angle at which the control arms are installed affects how much the vehicle leans during cornering. The vertical line between the roll center and the center of gravity acts like a lever to create body roll.

tire contact point and the point at which the steering axis line intersects the ground (Figure 9-22). Most SLA front suspensions provide a positive scrub radius. That is, the scrub radius is toward the inside of the tire contact patch. A positive scrub radius causes the wheels to toe out slightly during straight-ahead driving. If braking forces are uneven on a vehicle with a positive scrub radius, the chassis pulls toward the side with the stronger braking force when the brakes are applied. Scrub radius and its effects are discussed in more detail in Chapter 14 of this *Classroom Manual.*

The positioning, rather than the length, of the control arms indirectly affects the amount of body roll a vehicle exhibits during cornering. As explained in Chapter 3 of this *Classroom Manual,* the distance between the height of the roll axis—the line between the front and rear roll centers—and the center of gravity is effectively a lever that creates roll during turns. The angle of the control arms affects the height of the roll center (Figure 9-23). The antiroll bar is another influencing factor of body roll.

Within the basic SLA design, engineers have enough variables to work with—arm length and angle, the camber and steering axis angles—to tailor the handling characteristics of a front suspension to a variety of models. Of course, a number of other factors, such as vehicle weight, and engine and drivetrain position, influence handling as well. The

relative ease with which designers can vary certain details of suspension design is a major advantage of a SLA suspension. Aftermarket chassis modifications are also more feasible with a SLA suspension than with, for example, a strut suspension.

The primary problem with SLA front suspensions is not their performance but their size. An engine compartment containing a transverse-mounted engine, a transaxle, and two axle shafts has much less room to spare for the front suspension. Large, A-shaped control arms simply do not fit into the available space. Also, unit-body construction does not provide a sturdy frame attachment point for the control arms, and either a sub-frame or extensive reinforcement is required to accommodate a SLA suspension.

Strut Suspensions

A **strut suspension** consists of a strut and a lower control arm. The base of the strut rigidly mounts to the steering knuckle and the top of the strut attaches to the body and forms one point on the steering axis. Strut suspensions, especially MacPherson strut, are the most widely used front suspension design in current production. The use of modified struts in the front is less common, but there are a few models with that layout.

MacPherson Struts

So many models use a **MacPherson strut suspension** that to list them all would be cumbersome. Regardless of the model application, MacPherson strut front suspensions do not vary in their basic design, which includes:

- A strut with integral coil spring
- A lower control arm
- An antiroll bar

In addition, many, but not all, MacPherson strut front suspensions use a strut rod to limit fore and aft movement of the lower control arm. Some designs, such as that of the Lexus ES 250, also have a "performance rod," which is basically a second antiroll bar that connects the tops of the two struts. Sometimes, the design of the antiroll bar combines the function of a strut rod, which eliminates the need for a separate strut rod.

The DaimlerChrysler MacPherson strut front suspension serves as an example in the following discussion. All DaimlerChrysler FWD suspensions are similar to the example shown in Figure 9-24. However, the exact shape of the components, attachment points, and strut mounting does vary by year and model.

The top of the strut bolts into the strut tower, which is molded into the front fender, and the base bolts to the steering knuckle. The lower control arm has two pivoting attachment points to a frame crossmember, so there is no need for a strut rod to stabilize it. A bracket clamps each end of the antiroll bar to the underside of the control arm, and a rubber bushing around the end provides torsional action. Another pair of bushings and clamps secures the center section of the bar to the underside of the crossmember.

Modified Strut Suspension

Modified strut suspensions do not use an integral spring. Although the use of a modified strut suspension in the front is fairly unusual, the Chevrolet Camero, Ford Mustang, Geo Tracker, Pontiac Firebird, and Suzuki Sidekick do use this design. In this configuration, the coil spring is seated on the lower control arm instead of being integral to the strut. A modified strut front suspension includes the:

- Strut
- Coil spring
- Lower control arm
- Antiroll bar

The front suspension used on the 1998 Ford Mustang serves as an example of a modified strut design (Figure 9-25). The top of the strut bolts to a reinforced section of the fender apron, and the

MACPHERSON STRUT SUSPENSION

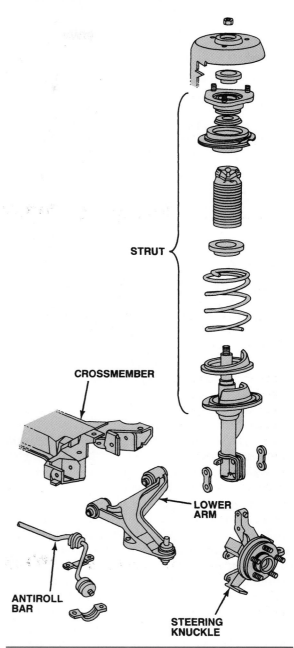

Figure 9-24. A MacPherson strut suspension always includes a strut with integral spring that is rigidly mounted to the knuckle, a lower control arm, and an antiroll bar.

base bolts to the steering knuckle. The A-shaped control arm pivots on bushings and is secured to a frame crossmember by through bolts. The coil spring seats between the lower control arm and the underside of the crossmember. A nut fastens each end of the antiroll bar to a spacer bar and the

MODIFIED STRUT SUSPENSION

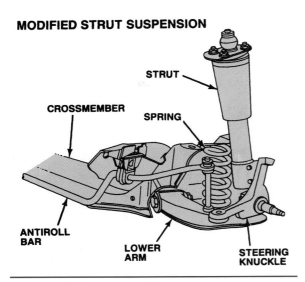

Figure 9-25. The modified strut suspension is similar to a MacPherson strut suspension except that the coil spring, which is seated on the lower control arm, is not integral to the strut.

spacer bars attach to the lower control arms. Two rubber-insulated U-bolts attach the center section of the antiroll bar to frame-mounted brackets.

Strut Characteristics

The overall steering geometry of a strut suspension is similar to that of a SLA design. The strut angles inward from the knuckle to the top fender mount. As the strut compresses when the wheel travels over a bump, the top of the wheel moves inward, which creates negative camber to minimize tire scrub (Figure 9-26). With the strut at an angle, the weight of the vehicle places a side load on the strut, so the strut body is strongly constructed to compensate. The spring of a MacPherson strut is generally mounted off-center to the strut, which further reduces the strain of the side loading (Figure 9-27).

The side load and the high mounting point of the top of the strut combine to create a problem during cornering. Centrifugal force causes the body to lean outward during a turn. Because the top mounting point of a strut is near the top of the body, the effect of body roll on a strut is greater than it would be on a SLA suspension, where the upper control arm mounts much lower on the chassis (Figure 9-28). Body roll tends to push the top of the strut outward to induce positive camber. Since a vehicle tends to pull toward the side where the front wheel has more positive camber, the positive camber on the outside wheel opposes the steering wheel input during cornering.

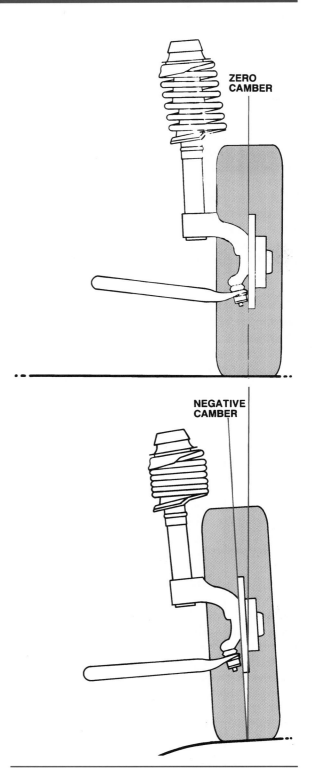

Figure 9-26. Like SLA suspensions, strut suspensions create negative camber during suspension compression to prevent tire scuffing.

Most strut suspensions produce a negative scrub radius, which in a FWD vehicle can provide extra braking stability (Figure 9-29). If braking forces are greater at one front wheel than the other,

MACPHERSON STRUT

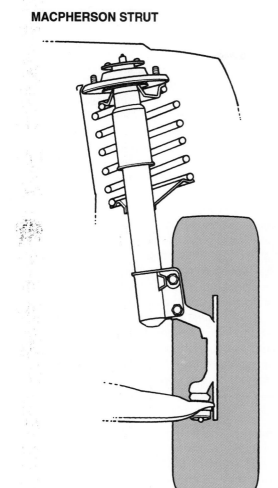

Figure 9-27. The spring on a MacPherson strut is mounted off-center to help alleviate the side load on the strut body.

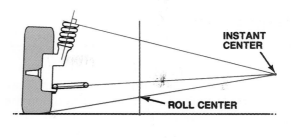

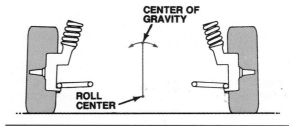

Figure 9-28. The angle of the strut and the lower control arm determine the roll center. The resulting lever between the roll center and the center of gravity creates body roll that tilts the top of the strut outward.

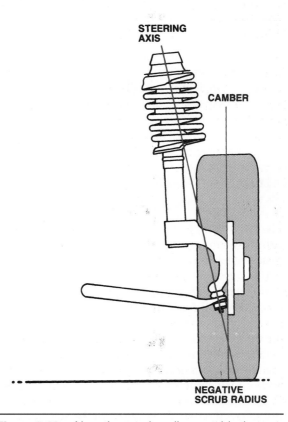

Figure 9-29. Negative scrub radius, outside the center of the tire contact patch, on a strut suspension tends to make the wheels toe in during driving. However, on a FWD vehicle, the weight of powertrain helps counteract the inward-turning force of the wheels.

a negative scrub radius makes the wheel with the greater braking force tend to turn inward. Because the front drivetrain makes the front of the car heavy, the forward force of the engine and transaxle counteract the action of the wheel, and the vehicle keeps moving straight-ahead. This handling characteristic also helps to keep the vehicle stable in the event of a front tire blowout.

When working with a strut suspension, engineers do not have as much flexibility in choosing alignment angles as with a SLA suspension. The angle of strut installation is limited by several strut characteristics, including that the top of it is in effect anchored to the body and its base is rigidly attached to the steering knuckle. The strut is also part of the suspension structure. There are only so many degrees that the strut mountings can be moved without redesigning the sheet metal, the

---

"In the Weeds"

The vehicle customizing business is subject to the whims of fashion, but one enduringly popular modification is lowering the body on the suspension—whether dropping a '32 Ford "into the weeds" or "slamming" a late-model mini-truck. Owners sometimes drop the body to emulate the low center of gravity of a race car, but more often, the purpose is simply to make it look unique.

Lowering the body makes the suspension perform differently from the way the designers intended, and the change is not always for the better. With front-wheel drive, lowering the front end forces the drive axles inward on the transaxle, which can cause premature axle bearing and seal failure. In addition, certain methods of modifying suspensions are unsafe. Heating springs until they sag or cutting a coil or two off the springs is *not* a hot tip for a reliable, safe ride height modification. To safely lower the body, install shorter, stiffer coil springs

or dropped front wheel spindles, or use lowering blocks for rear axles with leaf springs.

Changing the body height always requires reworking the wheel alignment. Lowering the front usually decreases caster. In fact, dropping the front ride height by an inch can change caster by almost half a degree. Installing shorter springs on short-long-arm or MacPherson strut suspensions decreases camber, as does lowering the rear end on vehicles with independent rear suspensions. Because shorter springs in the front suspension change the tie rod geometry, they can also cause the wheels to toe in or out excessively, depending on the particular configuration. In addition, surprising toe changes can occur as the suspension compresses and extends.

Before lowering a body, make sure you understand the changes it will cause. Also, keep in mind that it is all too easy to put the wheels so far out of alignment that the normal means of adjustment cannot correct it.

---

steering knuckle, and the method of weight distribution. This limits the variations allowable in the camber change and the roll center.

Overall, strut types of front suspensions are sturdy, compact, and inexpensive systems that generally provide good ride and handling in FWD applications.

Strut/Short-Long-Arm (Multi-Link) Suspensions

The **strut/short-long-arm (strut/SLA) suspension** is a combination of a SLA suspension and a strut suspension (Figure 9-30). The design came into widespread use in the North American market during the 1980s. European manufacturers, including BMW and Jaguar, used a pivot-base strut suspension on some of their models, but Honda was the first manufacturer to apply the technology to a mainstream vehicle. By the early 1990s, the list of models using a strut/SLA front suspension had grown to include the Acura Integra and Legend, Ford Thunderbird, Honda Accord and Prelude, Infiniti Q45, Lexus LS 400, Mazda Miata, Mercury Cougar, Nissan 300 ZX, and Toyota Supra.

All variations of this type of suspension are referred to as a "strut/short-long-arm suspension" in this book, but manufacturers call them by differ-

ent names. The design may be called a "double-wishbone suspension," "multi-link suspension," or "long spindle, short-long-arm suspension" in various service publications. The term "double-wishbone" is a confusing term for two reasons: The arms are not always wishbone-shaped, and the name is already commonly used in reference to a SLA suspension. The term "multi-link" suspension is a generic term for suspensions that have no other simple descriptive name. It usually applies to rear suspensions. The term "multi-link" is somewhat vague and also already used to refer to a number of older rear suspension designs. The Ford "long spindle, short-long-arm suspension" descriptive term is not useful for the general discussion purposes of this book because not all strut/SLA suspensions have a long spindle, which is an alternate term for a wheel knuckle.

Although they look dissimilar, all strut/SLA suspensions share a few common features, such as:

- Upper control arm
- Lower control arm
- Integral-spring strut with a pivot bushing base
- Antiroll bar

Some designs use a strut rod, while others do not. The pivot-base strut is significantly different from both MacPherson and modified struts. MacPherson

STRUT/SLA SUSPENSION

MAZDA

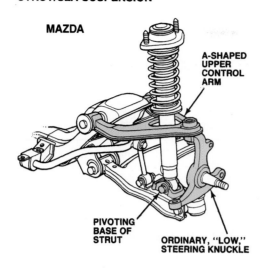

A-SHAPED
UPPER
CONTROL
ARM

PIVOTING
BASE OF
STRUT

ORDINARY, "LOW,"
STEERING KNUCKLE

HONDA

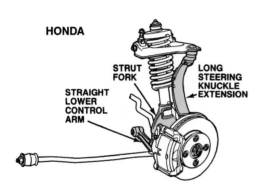

STRUT
FORK

LONG
STEERING
KNUCKLE
EXTENSION

STRAIGHT
LOWER
CONTROL
ARM

NISSAN

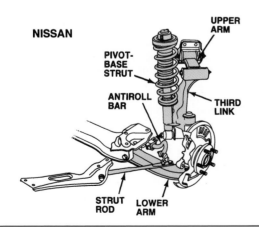

UPPER
ARM

PIVOT-
BASE
STRUT

ANTIROLL
BAR

THIRD
LINK

STRUT
ROD

LOWER
ARM

Figure 9-30. The Mazda Miata suspension has a low knuckle, meaning that the control arms are positioned similar to a SLA suspension. The Honda Accord suspension has a long knuckle that places the upper control arm higher than in a SLA suspension. The Nissan suspension uses a third link to connect the pivot base of the strut and the knuckle to the upper arm.

and modified struts both rigidly mount to the knuckle and rotate on the steering axis when used in the front suspension, while a pivot base strut does neither. A suspension can use pivot-base struts only if the strut is *not* part of the steering axis. Usually, the strut pivot is installed on the lower control arm, but it can also be on the knuckle. In the Nissan design, the strut bushing installs onto a stud that extends from the upper control arm next to where the arm joins the knuckle.

The front-axle applications of this suspension vary in some details. If the upper control arm is placed at a high location, near the top of the strut, the knuckle has a long arm that extends up to the upper ball joint. However, some upper arms are positioned lower, which eliminates this feature. Nissan uses two upper links, joined by a pivot, that in effect form a two-piece upper control arm. The pivot-base strut may extend upward between the two branches of the upper control arm, or the upper control arm may be positioned behind the strut. Rear-axle applications, which are described in Chapter 10 of this *Classroom Manual,* use other variations.

For the purposes of this chapter, front-axle versions of the strut/SLA suspension are grouped into three categories, depending on which of the following parts they use:

- Low knuckle
- Long knuckle
- Third link

What is referred to as a "low knuckle" is the type of knuckle typical in a SLA suspension, with the upper and lower arms at heights similar to those in a SLA system (Figure 9-30). A "long knuckle" is one with an extension reaching to an upper arm that is placed higher than the top of the tire (Figure 9-30). The "third link" describes the Nissan configuration that links the upper arm to the knuckle in a way unique enough not to be easily grouped with the other strut/SLA suspension designs.

Low Knuckle

The Lexus LS 400, Mazda Miata, and Toyota Supra all use a strut/SLA front suspension with a low knuckle. Although the three designs are similar, the following discussion is based on the Toyota Supra suspension (Figure 9-31).

A low knuckle strut/SLA design uses upper and lower control arms that mount to the frame in a similar position as those of a conventional SLA suspension. Each control arm has two frame pivot points and attaches to the steering knuckle with a ball joint. The pivot-base of the strut, which is a

STRUT/SLA SUSPENSION — LOW KNUCKLE

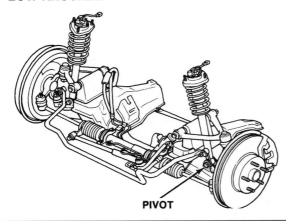

Figure 9-31. Except for the pivot-base struts with integral coil springs, the front suspension components of the Toyota Supra resemble those of a conventional SLA front suspension.

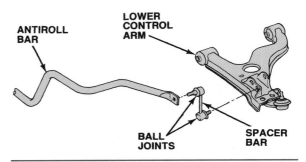

Figure 9-32. Using ball joints to connect the spacer bars to the antiroll bar and the lower control arms provides greater flexibility than bushings.

ring mount with a bushing, fits into a bracket on top of the lower control arm and is secured by a through bolt. From the base, the strut extends up through the open center of the upper control arm and attaches to a strut tower in the engine compartment. The strut is a support member of the suspension and incorporates a coil spring. Spacer bars with ball joints at either end link the antiroll bar to the lower control arms (Figure 9-32).

Long Knuckle

The upper ball joint of a long knuckle design is positioned higher than the top of the tire, which limits the inward tilt of the steering axis as the wheel rides over a bump. A number of manufacturers, including Acura, Ford, Honda, and Toyota, use a strut/SLA front suspension with a long knuckle. The front suspension of the Ford Thunderbird and Mercury Cougar, used from 1989 through 1997, serves as an example of a long knuckle design in the following discussion. Designs from other manufacturers differ from the Ford system in minor ways. For example, in the Honda and Acura suspensions, the base of the strut installs into a fork whose two prongs attach to the pivot bushing on the lower control arm, and the axle shaft extends through the fork. Like the Toyota Supra, the Lexus uses ball joints at the spacer bar between the antiroll bar and the lower control arm.

The upper control arm of the Ford suspension is wishbone-shaped and pivots on two bushings that

STRUT/SLA SUSPENSION — LONG KNUCKLE

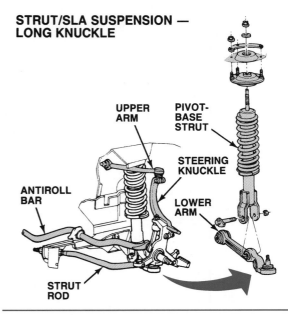

Figure 9-33. This Ford front suspension is typical of strut/SLA front suspensions with long knuckles. A unique feature of the Ford design is the antiroll bar spacer bar attachment at the top of the steering knuckle rather than on the lower control arm.

attach to mounts in the wheelwell (Figure 9-33). A ball joint on the outboard end of the upper control arm connects it to a long extension arm that rises off of the steering knuckle. The top of the strut bolts to the wheelwell, while the mount at the base of the strut is open and straddles the lower control arm to fit over the pivot bushing, which installs directly into the lower control arm. The lower control arm is a straight link that attaches to the front sub-frame and pivots on a bushing. A strut rod extends forward from the lower control arm and attaches to the sub-frame to brace the arm against fore and aft movement.

Volkswagen Semi-Independent Suspension

The original Volkswagen used a rather unique front suspension that combined features of a beam axle and torsion bars to produce a semi-independent suspension. This enduring design, used on air-cooled, rear-engine Volkswagen and Porsche models, was in production from the 1930s through the 1970s. During that time, the only significant change occurred in the early 1960s when ball joints replaced the kingpin connection at the steering knuckles.

The suspension is built on two cross-beams, which are actually transverse torsion bars, running across the front of the chassis with one directly above the other. These torsion bars are not the usual solid rods of spring steel but consist of 10 flat leaves stacked inside the tubes of the beam. Torsion arms attach at each end of the beam axle to connect it to the steering knuckle. The torsion bar leaves fit internal bores on the arms and the arms pivot on bushings at the ends of the beam tubes. There are four torsion arms in all, an upper and a lower one at each wheel. An antiroll bar connects two lower arms to reduce body roll.

Brackets running from the upper torsion bar to the lower one provide mounting points to attach the axle to the frame. The steering gear mounts directly onto the upper torsion bar. Toward each end of the upper bars, a vertical tube links them, then extends upward and bends outward to serve as the upper mounting point of the shock absorber. The lower shock mount is an extension from the steering knuckle.

TRAILING ARM SUSPENSION

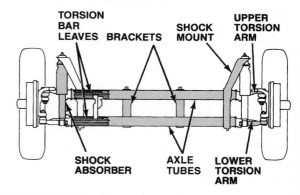

The ends of the antiroll bar connect to spacer bars that attach to the top of steering knuckles.

Third Link

A third link connects the pivot base of the strut to the upper control arm on the Nissan strut/SLA front suspension design. This front suspension with an extra link was used from 1990 through 1996 on both the Nissan 300 ZX and the Infiniti Q45 (Figure 9-34). The lower control arm, which is straight, pivots on a bushing at the frame and attaches to the steering knuckle with a ball joint. To provide rigidity, a strut rod extends forward from the lower control arm to an underbody bracket. An antiroll bar also attaches to the lower control arm. The antiroll bar runs in front of the suspension on the 300 ZX and behind the suspension on the Q45.

Unique aspects of this strut/SLA suspension are the construction of the upper arm, the third link, the use of a kingpin, and the position of the strut (Figure 9-35). The short, straight upper arm is positioned horizontally and contains a pivot bushing at either end. The inboard end of the arm pivots in a bracket in the wheel-well located above the top of the tire,

**STRUT/SLA SUSPENSION —
NISSAN'S THIRD LINK**

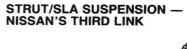

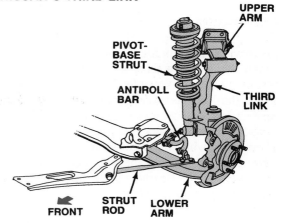

Figure 9-34. The Nissan strut/SLA suspension is unique in the fact that it uses an extra "third link" to connect the pivot base of the strut and the knuckle to the upper control arm.

while the outboard end connects to the third link. The third link runs vertically from the upper arm to the steering knuckle. At the base of the third link, a

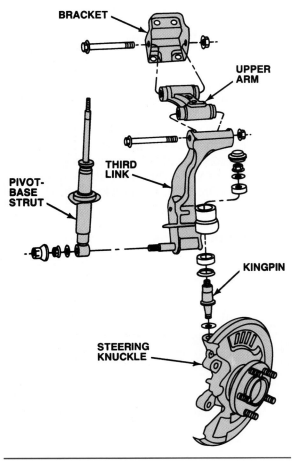

Figure 9-35. The pivot-base strut of the Nissan strut/SLA front suspension mounts on the third link and a kingpin is used in place of an upper ball joint to connect this third link to the steering knuckle.

stud provides a mount for the pivot base of the strut and a machined bore accepts the kingpin that connects the link to the knuckle. Together, the kingpin and the third link provide the range of movement usually allowed by an upper ball joint. The kingpin allows the steering knuckle to rotate on the vertical steering axis, while the pivot joining the third link to the upper arm permits the wheel and upper arm to move vertically. Bearings at the top and bottom of the kingpin reduce friction.

Strut/Short-Long-Arm Characteristics

A strut/short-long-arm (strut/SLA) suspension combines the space-saving characteristics of a MacPherson strut suspension with some of the preferable handling characteristics of a conventional SLA suspension. The manufacturers using this type of suspension tend to classify it *as* a SLA suspension because it uses a shorter upper control

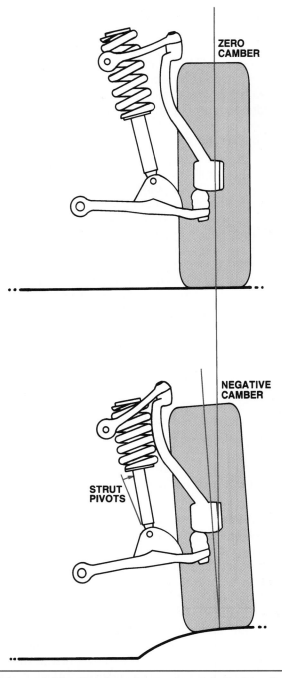

Figure 9-36. Camber change is not limited by the strut position on a strut/SLA suspension because the strut base pivots on a bushing, but the strut does not pivot on the vertical steering axis.

arm and a longer lower arm. However, as described earlier, these arms are different from the conventional SLA arms.

The camber change for the strut/SLA suspension is similar to that of the strut and SLA suspension designs (Figure 9-36). As with other struts, the possible angles at which the strut in this suspension can be installed are limited by the function of the strut as a weight-bearing component. However, the pivot-base strut in a strut/SLA suspension does not determine wheel alignment angles, for two reasons. First, an upper arm connects to the knuckle through a ball joint, or kingpin, and together with the lower arm determines wheel alignment. Second, the bottom of the strut is usually attached to the lower control arm instead of the knuckle and pivots instead of being rigidly mounted. When vertical wheel travel moves the control arms up, the base of the strut pivots so that the whole suspension does not have to compress in the direction that the strut is installed. Another benefit of a pivot-base strut is that it does not change the wheel camber as body roll pushes the top of the strut outward when the vehicle corners.

The scrub radius in strut/SLA suspensions is a compromise between the negative scrub radius in strut suspensions and the positive scrub radius in SLA suspensions. In FWD models that switched from strut suspensions to strut/SLA systems, the steering axis inclination (SAI) generally decreased by as much as four or five degrees, while the camber angle remained the same. Rear-wheel drive models switching from modified struts to strut/SLA suspensions also had smaller SAI angles, as well as decreased camber. Both of these changes tend to create a positive scrub radius in strut/SLA suspensions, as opposed to the negative scrub radius of strut systems with a rigid base mount. However, the positive scrub radius in a strut/SLA suspension is generally smaller than that in an SLA suspension, especially when the strut/SLA suspension uses a long knuckle or a third link (Figure 9-37). A small positive scrub radius has minimal effect on wheel toe during driving.

Another noticeable tendency among RWD cars using a strut/SLA front suspension is a large positive caster angle. As explained in Chapter 14 of this *Classroom Manual,* greater positive caster increases the straight-ahead stability of the vehicle and makes the steering wheel return to center more quickly after a turn. A caster angle increase of three degrees or more is possible by replacing the conventional strut front suspension with a strut/SLA front suspension on the same RWD chassis (Figure 9-38). All RWD models using strut/SLA front suspensions have caster angles of at least four degrees, and some are as large as nine degrees or more. It is not unusual for RWD cars

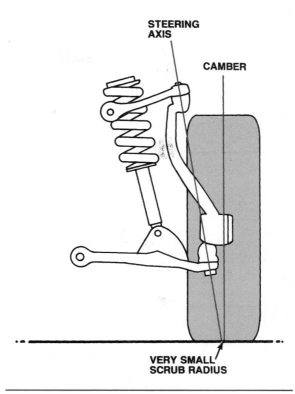

Figure 9-37. A typical strut/SLA front suspension has a positive scrub radius, like a SLA suspension, but the scrub radius is much smaller in a strut/SLA suspension.

to have caster angles in the four-to-six degree range or even in the seven-to-eight degree range—especially BMW and Mercedes models. However, the SLA suspensions that usually provide these large caster angles are large, require a higher hoodline, and also have a larger positive scrub radius. Only a strut/short-long-arm suspension is able to provide high caster for straight-ahead stability while taking up relatively little space.

The details of a strut/SLA front suspension are quite variable, as a look at the different systems in use demonstrates. Therefore, engineers can vary front wheel alignment and steering geometry to suit a particular model. Strut/short-long-arm suspensions fit equally well in the front of a FWD or RWD vehicle. Because the strut has an integral spring and a relatively small pivoting mount that attaches the base of it to the lower control arm or knuckle, smaller control arms can be used to save space and weight. The compact design of a strut/SLA suspension easily fits under a low-profile hood, yet allows engineers the option of tuning the suspension for optimal handling.

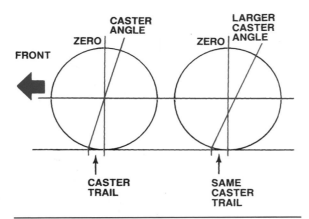

Figure 9-38. Strut/SLA front suspensions used in RWD applications permit a larger caster angle because the caster line can be placed behind the wheel center since the strut does not pivot on the steering axis.

SUMMARY

Front suspension systems must provide tire adhesion and a smooth ride, as well as work with the steering system. Some front suspensions also must work around a front drivetrain.

Not many vehicles use solid front suspensions because they provide a rough ride over uneven surfaces and they transfer shocks from wheel to wheel. The use of solid front axles is limited to beam axles in a few off-road, heavy-duty, and 4WD vehicles and I-beams in heavy-duty trucks.

Compared with solid front suspensions, independent front suspensions provide a number of benefits, including a smoother ride over uneven surfaces, less shimmy and wheel tramp, and, usually, smaller size and less weight.

Some Ford trucks use a twin I-beam suspension, which combines the strength of a solid I-beam with some of the benefits of independent suspension.

Short-long-arm (SLA) suspensions offer good handling and for years were the most commonly used front suspension design. However, their size and weight make them impractical for use in a modern, compact FWD platform. Currently, SLA front suspensions are used only on trucks and a few large, RWD sedans and wagons. Short-long-arm suspensions can use coil springs on the lower control arms, coil springs on the upper control arms, longitudinal torsion bars, transverse torsion bars, or a transverse leaf spring.

The majority of late-model FWD vehicles use strut suspensions in front. By far, the most common front suspension is the MacPherson strut design, in which the strut has an integral spring. A modified strut front suspension, with the spring on the lower control arm, is used on a few FWD applications. Strut suspensions offer acceptable ride and handling, although certain aspects of the design limit the range of wheel geometry angles designers may choose. The height of the struts can aggravate body roll during turns. Strut front suspensions are convenient in FWD vehicles because they are more space-efficient than a SLA suspension.

A number of manufacturers, including Ford, Honda, Nissan, and Toyota, offer models with a strut/short-long-arm (strut/SLA) front suspension. This design combines control arms with struts, to obtain some of the preferable SLA handling characteristics without taking up as much space. The strut in a strut/SLA suspension is not rigidly anchored to the steering knuckle, as in a MacPherson or modified strut suspension. Instead, the strut base mounts on a pivot, usually on the lower control arm. Strut/short-long-arm suspensions vary from one another in a number of details, and this allows the engineers to tailor the exact configuration to suit a specific model.

Review Questions

For each of the following questions, choose the letter that represents the best possible answer.

1. Compared to other front suspension designs, a solid axle provides superior:
   a. Ride quality
   b. Strength
   c. Handling
   d. Space efficiency

2. On late-model vehicles, the most common front suspension is the:
   a. Beam axle
   b. Strut
   c. SLA
   d. I-beam

3. Which of the following statements is *NOT* true of a twin I-beam front suspension?
   a. Provides some of the advantages of beam axles and independent front suspension
   b. Can produce a jacking effect
   c. Has relatively high unsprung weight
   d. The heavy twin I-beams add to the sprung weight of the vehicle

4. Older 2WD Jeep models used which type of front suspension?
   a. Twin I-beam
   b. Beam axle
   c. Longitudinal torsion bar
   d. Short-long arm

5. Technician A says that the coil spring on most SLA front suspensions is seated on the lower control arm. Technician B says that the coil spring on some SLA front suspension seats between the upper control arm and the unit-body. Who is correct?
   a. A only
   b. B only
   c. Both A and B
   d. Neither A nor B

6. Torsion bars may be used in place of coil springs on which type of suspension?
   a. SLA
   b. I-beam
   c. MacPherson strut
   d. Twin I-beam

7. The wheels of an independent suspension travel in a curve around an imaginary pivot point called the:
   a. Instant center
   b. Imaginary center
   c. Dead center
   d. Pivot center

8. What is the basic drawback to equal-arm suspension?
   a. Weight
   b. Size
   c. Tire scrub
   d. Excessive negative camber

9. Technician A says that a strut/SLA suspension creates positive camber when it is compressed. Technician B says that a SLA suspension creates negative camber when it is compressed. Who is correct?
   a. A only
   b. B only
   c. Both A and B
   d. Neither A nor B

10. A transverse torsion bar front suspension was used for many years by which manufacturer?
    a. Honda
    b. Ford
    c. DaimlerChrysler
    d. Saab

11. A SLA suspension reduces tire scuffing as a wheel travels over a bump by producing:
    a. Zero camber
    b. Positive camber
    c. Negative camber
    d. No camber change

12. The basic parts of a strut suspension are the strut and:
    a. Semi-elliptical leaf spring
    b. Upper control arm
    c. Longitudinal torsion bar
    d. Lower control arm

13. A monoleaf SLA front suspension is unique to the:
    a. Chevrolet Corvette
    b. Saab 900
    c. Toyota T100 pickup
    d. Honda Accord

14. A modified strut suspension differs from a MacPherson strut suspension in which of the following ways?
    a. It has no antiroll bar
    b. It uses torsion bars
    c. The coil spring is not integral with the strut
    d. The strut does not attach to the body or frame

15. Most strut front suspensions provide:
    a. Positive scrub radius
    b. Negative scrub radius
    c. Neutral scrub radius
    d. No scrub radius

16. Under braking, a strut suspension has an advantage over a SLA suspension because it has:
    a. Greater stability
    b. Neutral camber change
    c. Greater camber
    d. Less camber

17. In which of the following ways does a strut/SLA suspension differ from a MacPherson strut suspension?
    a. It uses torsion bars
    b. The coil spring is not integral with the strut
    c. The base of the strut has a pivot
    d. The top of the strut has a pivot

18. The control arms of most strut/SLA suspensions connect to the knuckle through:
    a. Antiroll bars
    b. Ball joints
    c. Metal bushings
    d. Strut rods

19. Strut/SLA suspensions on a RWD vehicle usually have a:
    a. Small positive caster angle
    b. Large positive caster angle
    c. Small negative caster angle
    d. Large negative caster angle

20. A drawback to the high mounting point of the top of the strut on a strut suspension is:
    a. Increased body roll
    b. Positive scrub radius
    c. Less stability under braking
    d. Positive camber change

10

Rear Suspension Designs

OBJECTIVES

Upon completion and review of this chapter, you will be able to:

- Identify the types of automotive solid axle rear suspension axles and explain their use.

- Identify the types of automotive trailing and semi-trailing arm rear suspension axles and explain their use.

- Identify the types of automotive independent rear suspension axles, including short-long-arm (SLA), strut, modified strut, strut/SLA, multi-link, and explain their use.

KEY TERMS

axle windup
Chapman strut
 suspension
compliance steer
full-floating axle
Hotchkiss drive
leaf spring suspension
multi-link suspension
Panhard rod
semi-floating axle
semi-independent
 suspension
semi-trailing arm

semi-trailing arm
 suspension
three-quarter-floating
 axle
torque arm
track rod
tracking
trail angle
trailing
trailing arm
trailing arm
 suspension

INTRODUCTION

All suspensions have two basic jobs: keeping the tires on the ground and providing a smooth ride. Some of the principles of front suspensions discussed in Chapter 9 of this *Classroom Manual,* such as the effects of camber change during bounce and the general performance differences between solid and independent designs, apply to rear suspensions as well. Keep this in mind while studying the rear suspensions presented in this chapter.

A secondary purpose for any suspension is to position the wheels for maximum tire traction and minimum tire wear. Wheel position and tire wear concerns relate to wheel alignment. Since rear wheels do not usually steer the vehicle, directional control angles—steering axis inclination, caster, and toe-out on turns—are generally not a concern. The two suspension angles that *are* important for rear wheels are camber and toe (Figure 10-1). These are discussed in detail in Chapter 14 of this *Classroom Manual.*

In addition to normal suspension functions, a rear suspension has the unique task of keeping the rear wheels following in the tracks of, or **tracking,** the front wheels. A difference between the directions the front and rear wheels are aimed is called a "thrust angle." With a large thrust angle, the front and rear wheels oppose each other and the vehicle moves at an angle to its centerline— a condition called "dog-tracking." Rear-wheel toe is an important aspect of tracking. Tracking,

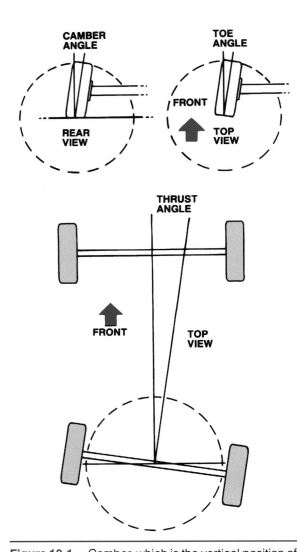

Figure 10-1. Camber, which is the vertical position of the wheel, and toe, which is the direction the wheels point when the steering is aimed straight ahead, are the two most important alignment angles for rear wheels. The thrust angle indicates whether the rear wheels track the front wheels.

dog-tracking, and thrust angles are discussed more completely in Chapter 14 of this *Classroom Manual.*

During turns, the rear wheels cannot exactly track the front wheels, which rotate on the steering axis up to 20 degrees or more. Most rear wheels do not turn at all, and even in a 4WS system turn only 1 to 5 degrees. However, the rear suspension and wheels do respond to cornering forces, and that response affects overall handling and traction. Chassis engineers must decide exactly how they want the rear suspension to respond to cornering forces. For example, some engineers try to keep the rear wheels at zero toe—straight ahead in relation to the vehicle centerline— throughout a turn, while others prefer the outer rear wheel to toe-in slightly during cornering to provide compliance steer.

Before studying specific rear suspensions, it is important to be aware of a few significant differences between front and rear suspensions in general. As mentioned in Chapter 9, a front suspension generally uses a triangulated design. That is, the suspension links form a three-point connection between the frame and wheels, so that the wheels are firmly braced but can also pivot on the steering axis. Many rear suspensions also use triangulated designs, with extra links to prevent rear toe changes. However, since the rear suspension has little or no steering axis, four or more linkage connection points between the frame and wheel may be used. Many rear suspensions use some other design instead of triangulation. A greater number of links prevents any directional change at the rear wheels, or allows only small, carefully controlled toe change. The suspension links usually have either pivot bushings or solid attachments to the frame and wheel, although a few rear suspensions use ball joint attachments. There is a greater variety of rear, compared to front, suspension designs because of the greater number of links allowable. Another difference is that there are many more solid axles, both driven and non-driven, at the rear than at the front. Independent rear suspension (IRS) is not at all unusual, but it is not close to universal, the way independent front suspension is.

Overall, most rear suspension designs fit into one of three broad categories:

• Solid rear axle
• Independent rear suspension
• Semi-independent rear suspension

Both solid and independent rear suspensions can be used on either a driven or non-driven axle, while semi-independent suspensions are used only on a non-driven rear axle. See Chapter 10 of the *Shop Manual* for Rear Suspension Service.

SOLID REAR AXLES

A solid axle can be used at the rear of either a rear-wheel drive (RWD) or front-wheel drive (FWD) vehicle (Figure 10-2). On a RWD vehicle, a solid rear axle consists of the differential gears and axle shafts inside a solid housing. On a FWD model, a solid axle is usually a simple U-shaped or tubular beam that may contain a torsion bar, rod, or tube to allow some twisting action. Solid, driven rear axles are usually found in trucks or relatively large sedans and wagons, while FWD models ranging from minivans to sub-compacts use solid, non-driven rear axles.

Certain characteristics apply to any solid rear axle, while other characteristics vary by the type of suspension used to attach the axle to the frame. Three common methods of attaching a solid rear axle are:

- Leaf spring suspension
- Trailing arm suspension
- Semi-trailing arm suspension

Solid rear axles do have good qualities. They are simple and strong, the technology involved in designing them is established and familiar, and their handling characteristics are adequate for the vehicles that use them.

Solid Rear Axle Characteristics

While simple, easy, and inexpensive to manufacture, solid axles have some handling characteristics that are inferior to those of an independent suspension. Disadvantages of a solid axle include:

- Increased proportion of unsprung weight
- Side-to-side road shock transference
- Poorer tire adhesion

Increasing the proportion of unsprung weight decreases ride quality, transferring road shock from side-to-side causes wheel tramp and shimmy, and poor tire adhesion accelerates tire wear (Figure 10-3).

The sprung weight of the frame and body must be heavy to oppose the unsprung weight of a solid axle, especially on a driven axle. Unsprung weight, wheel tramp, and shimmy all reduce tire adhesion. The effects of these problems are more noticeable in RWD vehicles due to the weight of the rear axle and differential assembly. On a typical

SOLID REAR AXLES

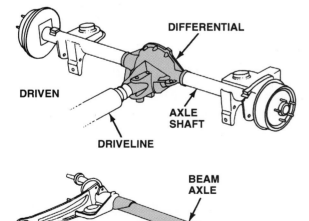

Figure 10-2. When used on a RWD vehicle, a solid rear axle combines the differential gearing and the axle shafts into a solid housing, while a simple beam-type solid axle is all that is required on the rear of a FWD vehicle.

SOLID AXLES

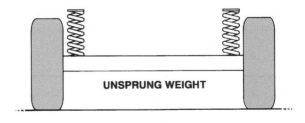

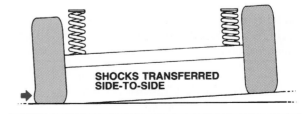

Figure 10-3. A solid axle supports the springs, so the axle and suspension components are unsprung weight. When one wheel rides over a bump, the shock transfers through the solid axle to compress the tire on the opposite side, which causes shimmy and tramp as the suspension rebounds.

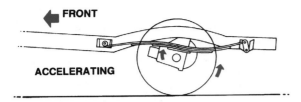

AXLE WINDUP

FRONT

ACCELERATING

Figure 10-4. When the axle housing reacts against the force of axle shaft rotation, it has a tendency to lift the front of the vehicle, which is a condition called "axle windup."

FWD vehicle, the simple axle beam is not heavy enough to impair ride quality or cause extreme tire wear. In fact, the rear tires of a FWD model always wear more slowly than the front tires because the rear axle is so much lighter than the powertrain. Also, the rear wheels do not slip or spin during acceleration and are not subject to camber changes and other forces applied during steering.

There are two matters that relate only to solid, driven axles. The first is a problem called "**axle windup,**" and the second is the method used to connect the wheels to the differential gears. How the differential gears and wheels are connected determines what part of the axle bears the weight of the wheel.

Axle Windup

Axle windup is a product of the law of physics: every action produces an equal and opposite reaction. As the axle shafts rotate in one direction to drive the wheels, the axle housing attempts to rotate in the opposite direction. The force of this reaction tends to lift the front end of the vehicle during acceleration (Figure 10-4). Axle windup is a particular problem with a solid, driven rear axle because the axle housing concentrates the reacting force. Under extreme acceleration, the reacting force can actually tilt the driveshaft upward and lift the front wheels off the ground. Leaf springs, control arms, and torque arms all are means of controlling axle windup.

Solid, Drive Axle Classifications

Depending upon what part of the axle bears the weight of the wheel, a solid RWD axle fits into one of three categories:

- Full-floating
- Three-quarter-floating
- Semi-floating

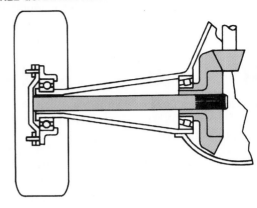

THREE-QUARTER-FLOATING

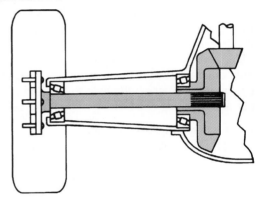

SEMI-FLOATING

Figure 10-5. Rear axle shafts may be full-floating, three-quarter-floating, or semi-floating, depending on whether the shafts or the axle housing supports the wheels.

These terms indicate whether the axle shafts or the axle housing supports the wheel (Figure 10-5). Which category an axle belongs in is determined by how the wheel and wheel bearing mount to the axle or housing.

Full-Floating Axle

On a **full-floating axle,** the bearings are mounted and retained in the hub of the brake drum or rotor. The hub and bearings mount onto the axle housing, and a bearing retainer or adjustment nuts and safety locks hold them in place. The flanged end of the drive axle is attached to the hub by bolts or nuts. The inner end of the axle splines into the differential side gears. The wheel mounts onto the hub, and lug bolts or nuts retain it. Most three-quarter-ton pickups, all heavy-duty truck tractors, and trailers use full-floating axles.

In this design, the axle shafts "float" in the axle housing and drive the wheels without supporting their weight. Because the axle shafts do not retain the wheel, the axle shafts can usually be removed from the vehicle while it is standing on the wheels.

Three-Quarter-Floating Axle

The bearings in a **three-quarter-floating axle** are mounted and retained in the brake drum or rotor hub, which mounts onto the axle housing. The outer extension of the hub fits onto the end of the axle, which is usually splined and tapered, and a nut and cotter pin secure the hub to the axle. The axle shaft splines to the side gears inside the differential. The wheels are mounted on the hub and retained by lug bolts or nuts. As in the full-floating axle, the axle housing and bearings in the hub support the weight in a three-quarter-floating axle. Because of the construction of a three-quarter-floating axle, the wheel must be removed before removing the axle shaft from the vehicle.

Semi-Floating Axle

The wheel bearings in a **semi-floating axle** either press onto the axle shaft or are installed in the outer end of the axle housing. A retainer plate at the outer end of the axle shaft or a C-clip inside the differential at the inner end keeps the axle shaft in the housing. The brake drum or rotor fits onto the end of the axle, and lug bolts or nuts fasten the wheel to the drum or rotor and to the axle. These axles are called "semi-floating" because only the inboard end of the axle shaft "floats" in the housing. The outboard end of the shaft retains the wheel and transmits the weight of the wheel to the housing. Most solid-axle RWD cars and light trucks use a semi-floating type of axle.

Leaf Spring Suspensions

A **leaf spring suspension** is a simple system because it does not require control arms to brace and position the axle. The leaf springs link the axle to the frame and effectively serve two purposes: absorbing road shock and locating the axle under the vehicle. Leaf springs are used only with solid axles, which can be either driven or non-driven.

Leaf Springs With Driven Axle

Most RWD trucks use a solid rear axle with semi-elliptical multi-leaf springs in an arrangement called a **Hotchkiss drive** (Figure 10-6). Some light-duty trucks, such as the Chevrolet Astro,

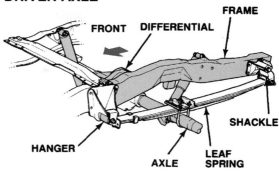

LEAF SPRING SUSPENSION— DRIVEN AXLE

Figure 10-6. The typical rear suspension for a RWD truck, known as a "Hotchkiss drive," uses a semi-elliptical leaf spring to support the axle.

have semi-elliptical monoleaf springs, rather than multi-leaf springs. Leaf springs on a driven axle control axle windup by transferring force from the axle housing to the frame. The front portion of the leaf spring, from the axle housing to the frame mount, acts like a trailing control arm. However, if the front section of the leaf spring is too flexible, it may not control axle windup as well. To compensate, some manufacturers make the front section of the spring shorter—therefore less flexible—than the rear section.

Leaf Springs With Non-Driven Axle

Leaf springs are not common on small FWD vehicles, but a few larger FWD vehicles, such as the DaimlerChrysler minivans, use them. The rear beam axle of the DaimlerChrysler FWD van is a tube with a cast flange and spring seat attached to each end (Figure 10-7). The wheel spindles bolt to the flanges, the center of the leaf springs rest on the seats, and U-bolts secure the springs to the axle. A shackle attaches the rear of each spring to the unit-body frame, while the front of each spring pivots on a through bolt and bushing connected to a hanger that bolts to the body. The shock absorbers attach between the axle and frame side rails, and extend forward at a slight angle.

The spring hanger also houses the brake proportioning valve, which adjusts braking force between the front and rear wheels depending on load. Be aware, aftermarket load-leveling devices impair the performance of this type of brake-proportioning valve, and are illegal to install. Should some device lift the rear of the vehicle that is carrying a heavy load, the proportioning

LEAF SPRING SUSPENSION— BEAM AXLE

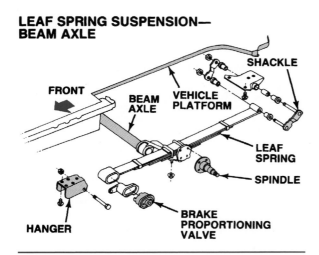

Figure 10-7. An exploded view of the beam axle with multi-leaf springs on the DaimlerChrysler FWD van. Note that the front section of the spring is shorter to reduce axle windup and the rear mounts with a shackle to allow for spring compression.

valve interprets the raised height as an indication of a light load and directs less braking force to the rear wheels. This is an example of why it is important to check the factory service manual for warnings and prohibitions before installing any type of load-leveling mechanism.

Trailing Arm Suspensions

A **trailing arm** extends from a frame crossmember located ahead of the rear axle back to the axle housing or a wheel knuckle. Trailing arms run parallel to the centerline of the chassis (Figure 10-8). A trailing arm mounts to the frame with bushings, which allows the arm to pivot as the wheel rides over bumps. Some rear suspensions use two sets of trailing arms, one set positioned higher in the chassis than the other. Although the arms in this type of arrangement are commonly referred to as the "upper control arms" and "lower control arms," they are simply called trailing arms in this text to avoid confusion with short-long-arm (SLA) and strut/short-long-arm (strut/SLA) suspension arms. Remember, the word **trailing** applies to any link that extends back from the frame to the member it supports. That is, the supported member trails the arm.

Trailing arms may be used to brace either a driven or non-driven solid rear axle against front-to-rear forces, but they do not provide much resistance to side-to-side, or lateral, forces. The axle itself is one means of locating the wheels side-to-side, and solid rear suspensions fre-

TRAILING ARM

TOP VIEW

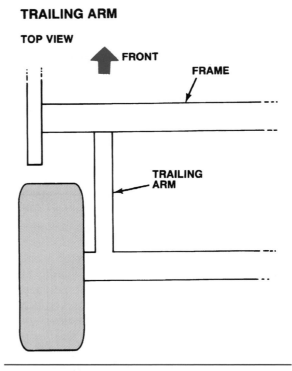

Figure 10-8. Trailing arms extend back, parallel to the vehicle centerline, from a frame mounting point to the axle or a wheel knuckle.

PANHARD ROD

REAR VIEW

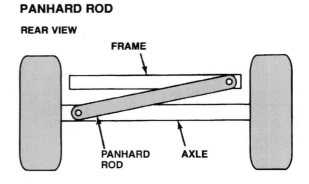

Figure 10-9. A Panhard rod helps brace a solid rear axle against side-to-side motion.

quently use a **Panhard rod** to provide additional support. A Panhard rod is a transverse link joined to the frame at one end and the beam axle or axle housing at the other end (Figure 10-9). Both attachments are pivots that allow the rod to compress and take up vertical movement. While a Panhard rod solves one handling problem—side-to-side sway—it creates another. The rear roll center tends to be at one height during left-hand turns and at a different height during right-hand turns because the axle anchor point of the rod is

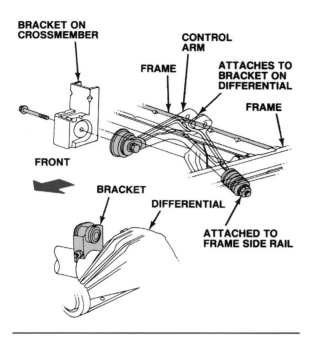

Figure 10-10. Nissan uses two sets of trailing arms to control fore-and-aft movement and a Panhard rod to brace the axle side-to-side on the Pathfinder's rear suspension.

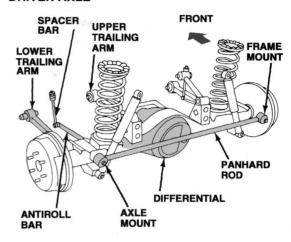

Figure 10-11. The rear suspension of the Ford Aerostar uses a control arm at the center of a frame crossmember to brace the rear axle against side-to-side movement.

lower than its frame anchor point. Although this is a problem during high-speed maneuvers, most chassis engineers consider the handling of a suspension with a Panhard rod adequate for normal driving conditions. The Panhard rod, which may also be called a **track rod,** is popular because it is a simple, lightweight device that adds stability to the suspension.

In general, a **trailing arm suspension** system typically uses a:

• Trailing arm
• Coil spring or strut
• Panhard rod or central control arm

Trailing arm suspensions work equally well for driven and non-driven rear axles. A trailing arm suspension is commonly found on a solid axle, although trailing arms often serve as a part of an independent rear suspension as well.

Panhard Rod

The Nissan Pathfinder's rear suspension is an example of a trailing arm suspension using a Panhard rod at the driven axle (Figure 10-10). This suspension uses two pairs of trailing arms at different heights. The lower trailing arm is positioned further outboard on the axle than the upper arm. The lower arm attaches to a bracket on the

axle housing and pivots on bushing. The **upper trailing arm,** which is positioned closer to the differential, attaches to a bracket on top of the axle housing and also pivots on a bushing. The coil springs rest in seats located on top of the axle housing. One end of the Panhard rod, which runs parallel to the axle, attaches to the rear of the axle housing, while the other end connects to the frame on the opposite side of the chassis. Both ends of the Panhard rod mount with pivot bushings. Spacer bars link the antiroll bar to the underbody, and rubber-insulated brackets fasten it to the front of the axle housing.

Trailing Arms With Driven Axles

Trailing arms transfer axle windup force to the frame and control front-to-rear axle movement. Additional links may also be used to control axle movement. As mentioned, a Panhard rod can be used to control side-to-side movement, but other suspension links can also be used for the same purpose. For example, the Ford Aerostar van uses a control arm to prevent side-to-side movement of the rear axle (Figure 10-11). On a few models, especially those with a high-performance suspension, a torque arm provides additional resistance to axle windup. The following paragraphs detail two different trailing arm suspension configurations used on rear driven axles—one with a Panhard rod and one with a torque arm.

Torque Arm

As mentioned earlier, axle windup becomes more severe under extreme acceleration. For this reason, two RWD General Motors performance models—the Chevrolet Camaro and the Pontiac Firebird—have a **torque arm** on the rear axle (Figure 10-12). Built on the same platform, these two vehicles have virtually the same rear suspension, including trailing arms, a Panhard rod with a brace, and a torque arm. The Panhard rod brace keeps the Panhard rod in a more horizontal position to reduce the side-to-side difference in roll center.

The torque arm extends parallel to the driveshaft between the rear axle and the transmission. One end of the torque arm is rigidly bolted to the differential housing, while the other end attaches to the transmission through a cushioned bracket to allow some flex. A torque arm transfers the force of axle windup along its length more effectively than a trailing arm because it is larger, heavier, and longer.

Trailing Arms With Non-Driven Axles

A trailing arm rear suspension on a non-driven solid axle virtually always includes a Panhard

TRAILING ARM SUSPENSION—DRIVEN AXLE

Figure 10-12. The Camaro and Firebird rear suspension uses a torque arm to control axle windup. Cushioned brackets attach the front of the torque arm to the transmission and bolts rigidly secure the rear of the arm to the differential.

Watts Linkage

The Watts linkage is a clever lateral suspension linkage for solid rear axles that solves some of the handling problems posed by the more common Panhard rod.

A Panhard rod creates a different roll center height in left and right turns because it is asymmetrical. With a Panhard rod attached to the frame on the right side of the chassis, the roll center rises as the vehicle rolls to the left during a right turn. This causes more load transfer to the left tire when accelerating out of the turn than to the right tire when turning in the opposite direction. The only way to avoid this problem is to keep the Panhard rod perfectly horizontal—a solution that suspension travel makes impossible.

The Watts linkage keeps the roll center in a fixed location through the use of a center bellcrank, usually attached to the differential, and two parallel links running in opposite directions from each end of the bellcrank to the frame. Although Watts linkages are popular for racing,

use on production vehicles is limited. For a long time, the first-generation Mazda RX-7, produced from 1979 to 1985, was the only United States market production vehicle to use a Watts linkage. However, a redesigned rear suspension that incorporates a Watts linkage debuted on the Ford Crown Victoria and Mercury Grand Marquis for the 1998 model year. Also, since 1997 the Japanese market Honda Accord features a Watts linkage, as do some of the Toyota off-road vehicles available only in Japan.

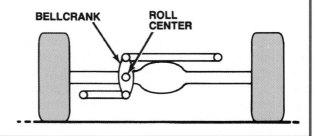

TRAILING ARM SUSPENSION— BEAM AXLE

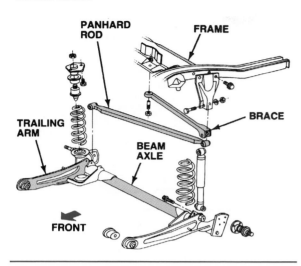

Figure 10-13. This DaimlerChrysler FWD beam axle rear suspension uses trailing arms and coil springs along with a Panhard rod, which limits side-to-side axle movement.

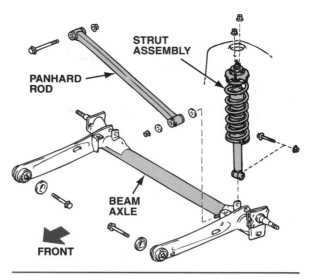

Figure 10-14. The Toyota Tercel rear suspension features a beam axle with pivot-base struts and a Panhard rod.

rod. The suspension may use either coil springs or struts as the cushioning devices.

Coil Spring

A number of manufacturers, including Daimler-Chrysler, General Motors, Hyundai, Saab, and Toyota, have recently produced models with a rear beam axle and coil springs. However, this rear axle design has been abandoned in favor of a strut suspension on the non-driven axle of most current production vehicles. The DaimlerChrysler rear axle used through the 1994 model year serves as an example of a beam axle with coil spring suspension (Figure 10-13). With the exception of the minivan, which has leaf springs, all domestically produced DaimlerChrysler FWD models with a transverse engine used this arrangement at one time.

The DaimlerChrysler rear axle is a U-shaped steel beam that is open on the bottom. Flat metal axle end plates, to which the wheel spindles bolt, are attached to each end of the beam. A torsion tube or rod fits inside the beam and is welded to the axle end plates.

Trailing arms extend from the outboard ends of the axle forward to mounting brackets on the frame side rails. The trailing arms, which DaimlerChrysler calls "blade-type" trailing arms because they are made of flat steel plates, are welded to the axle beam and pivot on a bushing in the frame bracket.

The lower coil spring seats are formed of steel plates welded in place at the corner where the trailing arms attach to the axle beam. The upper spring is a reinforced area of the unit-body. Shock absorbers extend from brackets on top of the axle to mounting brackets in the wheelwells.

A Panhard rod, which is called a "track bar" in DaimlerChrysler service manuals, attaches to a bracket on the right-hand (passenger) end of the axle beam, extends across the chassis, and connects to a bracket on the left (driver) side frame rail along with a diagonal brace. The brace runs from the bracket to a frame-mounting point on the crossmember near the vehicle centerline. The bracket and brace keep the right side of the Panhard rod lower, so the rod is more horizontal.

Strut

Until recently, a beam axle with struts was a popular rear suspension design used by American, Asian, and European manufacturers for FWD applications. However, this arrangement has been replaced by an independent rear suspension on most current production vehicles. The few vehicles that still use a rear beam axle with struts are generally compact, light-weight, entry-level models, such as the Nissan Sentra and Toyota Tercel. The rear suspension of the Toyota Tercel serves as an example of this design in the following discussion (Figure 10-14).

The Tercel beam axle is a hollow tube located by two trailing arms. Both ends of the axle tube

SEMI-TRAILING ARM

TOP VIEW

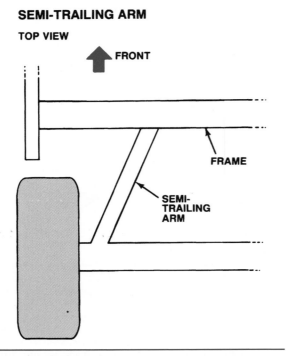

Figure 10-15. Semi-trailing arms extend from a frame mount back to the axle at an angle to the vehicle centerline.

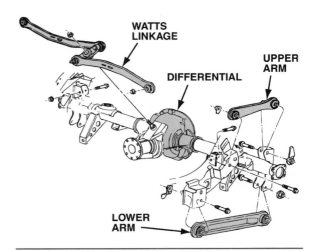

Figure 10-16. This Ford suspension uses upper and lower semi-trailing arms to mount the rear axle and a Watts linkage to control side-to-side motion.

are capped with a flange that includes the wheel spindle. The trailing arms, which are welded to the outboard ends of the axle, extend forward and attach to the frame with pivot bushing mounts. A bracket on top of the beam axle locates the ring-type lower strut mount, and the upper strut mount attaches to a reinforced area of the wheelwell. One end of the Panhard rod, called the "lateral control rod" in the Toyota repair manual, attaches to a stud that projects toward the front at one end of the axle. The Panhard rod extends across the chassis and bolts to a bracket on the frame. Both ends of the Panhard rod pivot on bushings.

Semi-Trailing Arm Suspensions

A **semi-trailing arm** is similar to a trailing arm in that it extends back from a frame member to the axle. However, a trailing arm is parallel to the vehicle centerline while a semi-trailing arm pivots at an angle to the vehicle centerline (Figure 10-15). Semi-trailing arms have an advantage over trailing arms because they control both side-to-side and front-to-rear motion. Typically, a **semi-trailing**

arm suspension uses coil springs, air springs, or pivot-base struts.

A semi-trailing arm suspension may be used with either a solid axle or an independent suspension. The following discussion applies to solid axle applications. Semi trailing arms used with an independent rear suspension are described later in this chapter. The rear suspension of the Ford Crown Victoria, Lincoln Town Car, and Mercury Grand Marquis provides an example of a solid axle with semi-trailing arms. A unique feature of this Ford suspension is the use of a Watts linkage, rather than a Panhard rod, to control side-to-side motion of the axle.

The Ford suspension uses two pairs, upper and lower, of semi-trailing arms and the Watts linkage to locate the driven rear axle (Figure 10-16). Brackets welded to the rear of the axle housing near each of the outboard ends provide a mounting point for the semi-trailing arms. The arms attach to the brackets with through bolts and pivot on bushings. Both the upper and lower arms extend forward of the axle, attach to brackets on the frame, and pivot on bushings. The arms are unequal in length, with shorter upper arms and longer lower arms. The slight inward angle of the arms helps stabilize the axle, while the Watts linkage provides additional side-to-side control.

The pivot bar of the Watts linkage installs onto a stud on the front of the differential housing. Two lateral arms extend outward from the pivot bar, one in each direction. The lower lateral arm bolts to a bracket on the axle housing and the upper arm attaches to a bracket on the frame. All of the Watts linkage connections—pivot bar-to-differential, pivot bar-to-lateral arm, lateral arm-to-axle, and lateral arm-to-frame—are pivot bushings.

Coil springs, which fit between seats on top of the axle housing and the frame, cushion the assembly. An antiroll bar completes the suspension. The antiroll bar is positioned below the axle and attaches to the housing with insolation brackets. Spacer bars attach the ends of the antiroll bar to brackets on the frame.

INDEPENDENT REAR SUSPENSIONS

Once found only on performance-oriented models, the use of independent rear suspensions (IRS) has grown dramatically over the past several decades to the point where they are now fairly common, especially on FWD vehicles. Although rarely used on trucks, a number of RWD vehicles do feature an independent rear suspension. On a RWD platform, an IRS makes the process of building the rear drivetrain and suspension more complicated—and more expensive. Therefore, IRS application is generally limited to higher-priced performance or luxury models. However, making the rear suspension independent on a FWD platform is not as complex, and a vast number of economy models have IRS. A third, and extremely rare, type of rear axle to use an independent suspension is on a rear-engine or mid-engine layout, where IRS is almost a necessity.

There is a greater variety among independent suspension systems used at the rear than among those at the front. Designs used at the rear axle include:

- Short-long-arm suspensions
- Strut suspensions
- Strut/short-long-arm suspensions
- Semi-trailing arm suspensions
- Multi-link suspensions

All IRS systems share some common characteristics, and there are some unique handling characteristics to each individual design as well. The IRS systems used on rear-engine and mid-engine platforms will not be addressed in this text due to their limited applications.

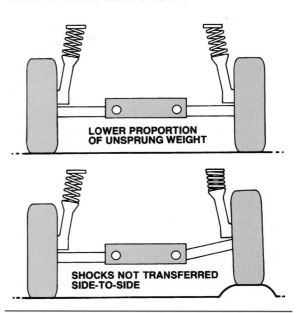

Figure 10-17. The frame and many parts of the suspension are sprung weight with an independent suspension because they are supported by the springs. Also, when one wheel rides over a bump, the wheel on the opposite side of the axle is not affected.

Independent Rear Suspension Characteristics

Independent rear suspensions provide a number of benefits over solid axles, including:

- Lower proportion of unsprung weight, for better ride quality
- Reduced transference of shock side-to-side, for less tramp and shimmy
- Better tire traction, for less tire wear
- Increased control, for better handling

The reduction in unsprung weight is particularly noticeable for driven axles, which are constructed to transfer the weight of the differential and axles to the frame. The reduction in tramp and shimmy, tire slippage, and unsprung weight all combine to help an independent suspension perform its primary task—keeping the tires on the road (Figure 10-17). This overall result is more control. When a vehicle has independent rear suspension, the rear tires are less likely to break loose during cornering or other maneuvers.

Short-Long-Arm Suspensions

At the front wheels, short-long-arm (SLA) suspensions are generally used only if the front axle is non-driven, because a typical FWD powertrain does not provide enough space for the large control arms of the SLA design. However, the area occupied by the rear axle is less crowded, even when the rear axle is driven, so a SLA suspension may be used at the rear of a RWD vehicle. In fact, SLA rear suspensions are usually found only on a RWD platform because these are the only vehicles built with a frame strong enough to support the control arms. In theory, a SLA suspension could be used on a FWD platform, but a large, heavy sub-frame would be required to support the suspension arms. In general, some other type of IRS is more practical for a unit-body FWD platform.

A popular application of a rear SLA system was on the RWD Ford Thunderbird and Mercury Cougar, which ran through the 1997 model year (Figure 10-18). The main components of this Ford design are the:

- Lower control arm
- Coil spring
- Upper control arm
- Compensator link
- Antiroll bar

The differential carrier bolts to the rear sub-frame, which bears the weight of the axle. Equal-length axle shafts with constant-velocity (CV) joints at either end connect the differential to the rear wheels, and allow the wheels to move independently of each other. Bushings are used at the differential mounts to limit the intrusion of drive-line vibration into the chassis.

The lower control arm, called an "H-arm," uses two pivot bushings at the sub-frame and two at the knuckle. A four-point mounting is possible since the wheels do not need to pivot on a steering axis. The coil springs seat between a perch on top of the lower control arm and the body. One end of the small compensator link attaches alongside the inboard front lower control arm mount, and the other end of the link installs in a bracket on the front face of the arm. This compensator link, sometimes referred to as a "toe control link," helps control wheel toe-out during braking. The upper control arm is a straight, two-point link with one pivot bushing at the sub-frame and a second one at the knuckle.

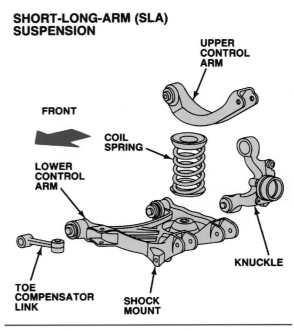

SHORT-LONG-ARM (SLA) SUSPENSION

Figure 10-18. The Ford Thunderbird short-long-arm independent rear suspension can use four-point lower control arms because the rear wheels do not need to pivot on a steering axis. The compensator link controls toe-out under braking.

A flange on the front of the lower control arm near the outboard end provides an attachment point for the bottom ring mount of the shock absorber. At the top, a bayonet mount attaches the shock absorber to the body. The shock absorbers contain internal rebound stops, so if they are disconnected from the lower arms, the arms will drop unless supported. An antiroll bar, which attaches to the rear of the lower control arms through small spacer bars, completes the suspension.

Short-Long-Arm Characteristics

Most performance characteristics of SLA suspensions are discussed in detail in Chapter 9 of this *Classroom Manual,* and are reviewed only briefly here. The main benefit of a SLA suspension is the camber change, which reduces tire scrub and improves traction. The positioning of the control arms determines the suspension roll center location. In general, the lower the roll center, the less body roll. Using a four-point lower control arm in the rear suspension, instead of the three-point mounting necessary in a front suspension, helps minimize toe changes during acceleration and braking.

Strut Suspensions

Unit-body, FWD vehicles frequently use strut suspensions at the rear axle. Typically, the strut mounts to the knuckle and replaces the upper control arm. Like front strut suspensions, rear strut designs fit into one of two categories:

- MacPherson strut
- Modified strut

The first designer to put MacPherson-type struts in a rear suspension was an Englishman, Colin Chapman. For this reason, a rear strut suspension is often referred to as a **Chapman strut suspension** by European manufacturers and engineers. In the United States, any integral-spring strut rigidly mounted to the wheel knuckle is commonly termed a "MacPherson strut," regardless of whether it is at the front or rear axle. For the sake of simplicity, this text follows the U.S. custom and uses "MacPherson strut" to define an integral spring assembly, and "modified strut" when discussing struts without integral springs.

MacPherson Strut

The MacPherson strut system is the most popular independent rear suspension for late-model FWD vehicles. Most manufacturers, including Daimler-Chryster, Ford, General Motors, Mazda, Nissan, and Toyota, use a MacPherson strut rear suspension on at least one of their FWD models. Although they differ in detail, all of these rear MacPherson strut systems use the same basic parts:

- MacPherson strut
- Two parallel lower control arms
- Trailing arm or trailing strut rod

The suspension of the Hyundai Elantra serves as an example of an IRS with MacPherson struts (Figure 10-19). A coil spring is integral to the strut and the strut base mounts rigidly to the wheel knuckle, while the top of the strut attaches to a reinforced area of the unit-body. Two parallel, transverse lower control arms connect the knuckle to the rear frame crossmember to control lateral movement of the wheels. The control arms install with pivot bushings at both ends to allow the wheel to move vertically. A trailing arm, also mounted with bushings, extends from a bracket on the frame back to the knuckle to control fore and aft movement. An antiroll bar,

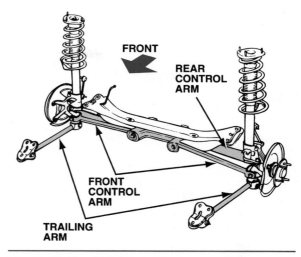

Figure 10-19. This Hyundai rear suspension uses a MacPherson strut, two parallel lower control arms, and a trailing arm to locate each knuckle and allow independent movement of the wheels.

which attaches with spacer bars to brackets on the rear of the struts, reduces body roll.

Modified Strut

Although not as popular as MacPherson struts, modified strut rear suspensions are found on a variety of FWD models from a number of different manufacturers. General Motors uses them the most frequently. Modified struts typically use coil springs on the lower control arms, but several GM models use a transverse monoleaf spring instead. The typical rear modified strut system uses:

- Struts
- Lower control arms
- Coil springs or transverse leaf spring

Lower control arm design varies by application. Some models use a single A-shaped or H-shaped control arm on each side, while others use two parallel lower control arms at each wheel. Some systems also use a trailing arm to help stabilize the suspension. Following are two examples of a modified strut suspension: one with coil springs and one with a transverse leaf spring.

Coil Spring

General Motors has two modified strut rear suspensions that use a coil spring on the lower control arm. One system—found on large FWD models such as the Buick LeSabre and Park Avenue;

**MODIFIED STRUT SUSPENSION—
COIL SPRING**

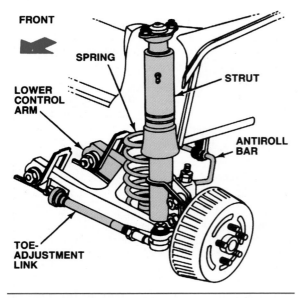

Figure 10-20. This General Motors modified strut suspension uses a three-point lower control arm. The strut is rigidly mounted to the knuckle, and the coil spring seats on the lower control arm.

Cadillac DeVille and Fleetwood; Oldsmobile Eighty-Eight and Ninety-Eight; and Pontiac Bonneville—is referred to in the following discussion as the GM system. The other system, found on the sub-compact Geo Metro and Suzuki Swift, is manufactured by Suzuki and is referred to as the Suzuki system. On both systems, the rear struts rigidly mount to the knuckle, the coil springs seat on the lower control arms, and an antiroll bar connects the two lower arms.

On the GM system, an A-shaped lower control arm attaches to the frame with two pivot bushings and to the knuckle with a ball joint (Figure 10-20). The pivot axis of the control arm is parallel to the centerline of the vehicle. A toe-adjustment link, which resembles a tie rod, runs from the front of the lower control arm to a forward attachment point on the knuckle. A ball stud joins the link to the knuckle.

The Suzuki system lower control arm also has three mounting points and attaches to the frame with pivot bushings. However, the knuckle attachment is also a pivot bushing, rater than a ball joint. Another difference between the two systems is that the axis of the frame pivots on the Suzuki lower control arm is at an angle to the centerline of the vehicle (Figure 10-21). An additional link, the

**MODIFIED STRUT SUSPENSION—
COIL SPRING**

TOP VIEW

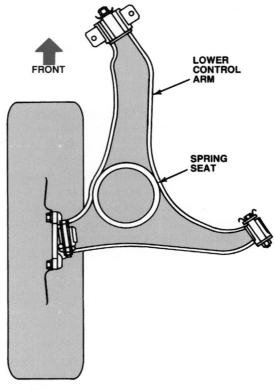

Figure 10-21. This Suzuki three-point lower control arm has a pivot axis that is at an angle to the centerline of the vehicle.

toe-control rod, connects the knuckle to the frame at the rear of each control arm (Figure 10-22).

Transverse Leaf Spring

At one time, General Motors produced two different rear modified strut systems with transverse leaf springs. As with the coil spring systems, the primary difference between the two systems was the lower control arm configuration (Figure 10-23). The upper system in Figure 10-23 was used on the GM E & K series (SEVILLE-ELDORADO-RIVIERA), the lower system (Figure 10-23) is used on current and past model "W" series vehicles (Impala-GRAND-PRIX, Century). This is a "TRI-LINK SUSPENSION," which consits of two parallel transverse lower links and a trailing arm. Both designs have been abandoned in favor of coil springs or MacPherson struts on later models. A transverse leaf spring is also used on the Chevrolet

Swing-Arm Rear Suspensions

Swing-arm suspensions were never widely popular, but they were used in several mass production vehicles, most notably the Volkswagen Type I and the Chevrolet Corvair. The success of the Volkswagen had proven that a swing arm suspension was an inexpensive and acceptable match to a rear engine, RWD layout, so Chevrolet adopted the same configuration when introducing the Corvair in 1960. The rear-engine Corvair with a swing arm rear suspension was produced for four model years.

In a swing-arm suspension, or swing axle, the inboard ends of the axle shafts connect to the differential with a U-joint, but rigidly attach to wheels at a right angle to the wheel hub. Trailing, or semi-trailing, arms take up braking forces. The weakness of this design is that the rear wheels "tuck in" and develop extreme positive camber during cornering. Lift a vehicle with a swing axle on a rack and the rear wheels tilt in at the bottom. This characteristic was not a problem for the light weight Volkswagen, but the heavier Corvair suffered for it.

Almost immediately after its introduction in 1960, reports circulated of Corvair drivers losing control when cornering or during tire blow-outs. Research into the accidents determined that owners were not maintaining the correct air pressures in the rear tires and the underinflated tire gave way to the forces between the tire bead and rim during cornering.

The result was an instantaneous loss of tire pressure that sent the steel rim into the pavement at high speed with an extreme positive camber angle, which caused the vehicle to slide or spin out of control.

For 1964 a transverse leaf spring was added to the rear of the Corvair to limit the amount of suspension travel. Chevrolet completely redesigned the Corvair for 1965 and the new model featured a four-link semi-independent rear suspension. Unfortunately for Corvair sales, Ralph Nader lambasted the Corvair swing-axle problems in his book *Unsafe At Any Speed,* which was published the same year. This negative publicity, along with "horsepower wars" and the beginning of federal emissions regulations, forced General Motors to abandon the Corvair in 1969.

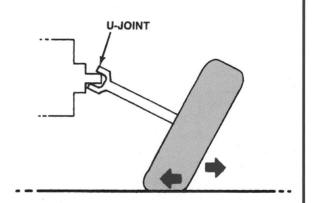

Corvette, but the Corvette uses a multi-link rear suspension, which is discussed later in this chapter.

Strut Characteristics

Most of the characteristics of strut suspensions are discussed in detail in Chapter 9 of this *Classroom Manual.* The camber change of a strut suspension as the wheels travel over bumps, which is similar to that of a SLA suspension, helps prevent tire scuffing. As in front strut suspensions, the angle of the control arm and the strut determine the rear suspension roll center.

The purpose for using two parallel links or an H-shaped lower control arm is to prevent toe changes

during braking and acceleration (Figure 10-24). When an A-shaped lower control arm is used, an additional transverse link—such as the GM adjustment link or the Suzuki control rod—is required to brace the knuckle and prevent toe changes. Trailing arms keep the knuckle located front-to-rear.

Strut/Short-Long-Arm Suspensions

Although manufacturers often classify any strut/short-long-arm (strut/SLA) suspensions as a "double-wishbone" design, a strut/SLA rear suspension system tends to be more sophisticated than those used

MODIFIED STRUT SUSPENSION— COIL SPRING

REAR VIEW

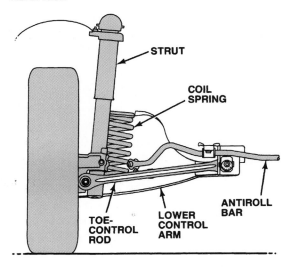

Figure 10-22. The toe-control rod, which mounts on pivot bushings, provides an extra brace against toe changes during braking or acceleration.

on the front axle. Originally found only on European luxury and performance models, the strut/SLA rear suspension has been gaining in popularity across the model range spectrum. Honda was the first manufacturer to apply the technology to a mass-market vehicle with the debut of the 1986 Accord. Currently, all Honda models use a strut/SLA rear suspension. Other Japanese manufacturers, such as Mazda, Nissan, and Toyota, use various strut/SLA rear suspension designs on a number of sport and luxury models.

A strut/SLA suspension is extremely adaptable and can be used with either a driven or non-driven rear axle (Figure 10-25). As explained in Chapter 9 of this *Classroom Manual,* all strut/SLA suspensions share certain common characteristics. Although specific applications vary considerably, all strut/SLA systems use the following:

- Upper control arm
- Lower control arm
- Pivot-base strut

In addition, other transverse links and trailing arms are used on some designs. Usually, the strut pivot mounts to a lower control arm, but it attaches to the knuckle on some applications. Strut/short-long-arm suspensions differ more from one another than SLA or strut suspensions do, so it is more difficult to use one system as an example.

MODIFIED STRUT SUSPENSION— TRANSVERSE LEAF SPRING

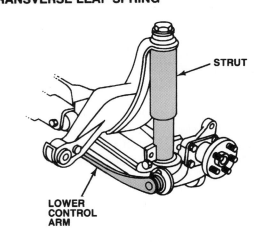

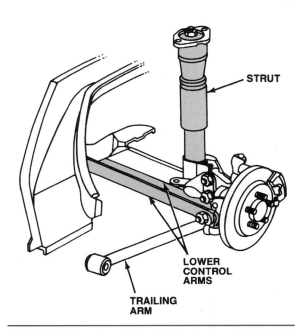

Figure 10-23. One General Motors transverse leaf spring modified strut rear suspension uses an "H-shaped" lower control arm, while the other uses two parallel lower links and a trailing arm.

Therefore, several systems are discussed individually in the following sections. These are broken down into two categories: those used on a driven axle and those used on a non-driven axle.

Strut/Short-Long-Arm Systems With Driven Axles

Mazda, Toyota, and Nissan use a strut/SLA rear suspension with RWD powertrains. Mazda has

FOUR-POINT CONNECTION
TOP VIEW

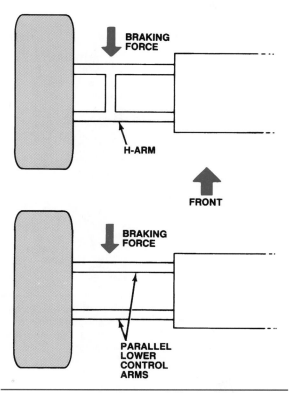

Figure 10-24. On a strut suspension, an H-shaped lower control arm or two parallel lower control arms help prevent toe changes during braking.

two rear strut/SLA suspensions, one a relatively simple design found on the Miata and the other a more complex design used on the 929 and Millenia known as the "E-link suspension." Toyota has one basic strut/SLA rear suspension design that was used on the Cressida through 1992 and is currently used on the Supra and the Lexus LS 400. Nissan also uses one design, which is currently used on the 240SX and the Infiniti Q45, and was also applied to the 300ZX through 1996.

Mazda
The rear strut/SLA suspension of the Mazda MX-5 Miata is similar to a SLA suspension and uses the following:

- Pivot-base strut
- Lower control arm
- Upper control arm
- Antiroll bar

The lower control arm, which is a four-point brace to keep the wheel positioned, has two pivots at the

STRUT/SLA SUSPENSION

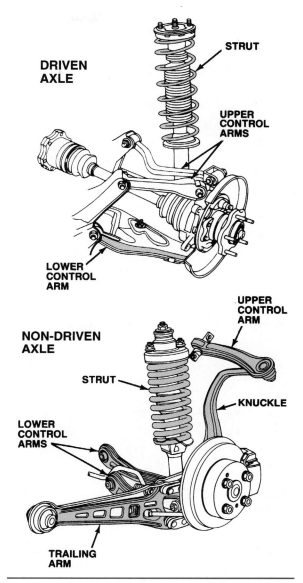

Figure 10-25. Variations on the strut/SLA suspension design allow it to be used with both driven and non-driven rear axles.

frame and two at the knuckle (Figure 10-26). The pivot-base strut mounts on the lower control arm. The upper control arm has a three-point connection: two pivots at the frame and one at the knuckle. Spacer bars link the antiroll bar to the lower control arms.

To support the rear axle, the Miata differential case has two lateral extensions extending from the top that attach to the rear sub-frame (Figure 10-27). The assembly mounts to the frame through isolation

STRUT/SLA SUSPENSION— MAZDA

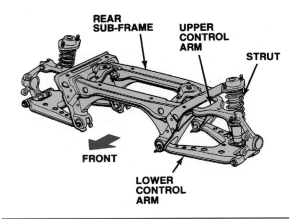

Figure 10-26. The Mazda Miata rear strut/SLA suspension is very similar to a SLA suspension, except that it uses a pivot base strut on the lower control arm instead of a separate coil spring and shock.

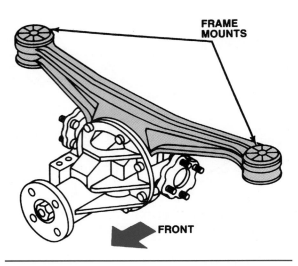

Figure 10-27. The Miata rear differential mounts to the rear sub-frame through two extensions and is isolated by bushings.

bushings to prevent vibrations from transferring into the body.

The Mazda Millenia and 929 also use a strut/SLA rear suspension, but the design is a bit more complex (Figure 10-28). To support the differential, the back of the differential case bolts to a rear sub-frame crossmember and the front bolts to another crossmember. The system, which Mazda calls an "E-link suspension," uses the following components:

- Pivot-base strut
- Trailing arm

STRUT/SLA SUSPENSION— MAZDA E-LINK

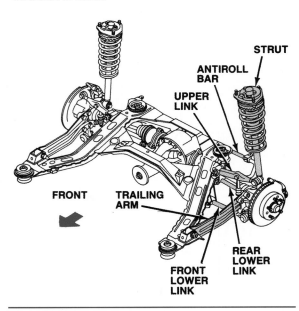

Figure 10-28. The rear suspension of the Mazda Millenia and 929 uses an E-link, consisting of three transverse arms—two lower links and one upper link—and a trailing arm to position the knuckle.

- Upper link
- Front lower link
- Rear lower link
- Antiroll bar

The trailing arm pivots in a bracket on the sub-frame side member and extends straight back to where it rigidly attaches to the wheel knuckle. Three transverse links—one upper and two lower—form the "E" of the E-link suspension when viewed from above (Figure 10-29). The front lower link, which is farthest forward of the three, is the shortest link and the rear lower link is the longest. The upper link is placed between the two lower arms, offset slightly toward the front. Each of these three links, or arms, attaches to the sub-frame with a pivot bushing and to the knuckle with a ball joint. The rubber in the bushing for the front lower link is softer than that of the rear-link bushing. This allows compliance steer, which is discussed later in this chapter. The antiroll bar attaches to the upper link through spacer bars and the pivot-base strut mounts on the steering knuckle.

Toyota

The Toyota Supra and Cressida and the Lexus LS 400 all use basically the same strut/SLA system, although there are slight variations between the

E-LINK SUSPENSION

REAR VIEW

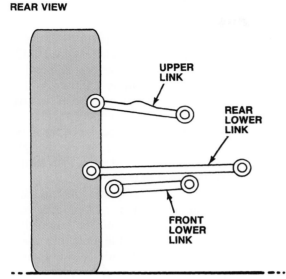

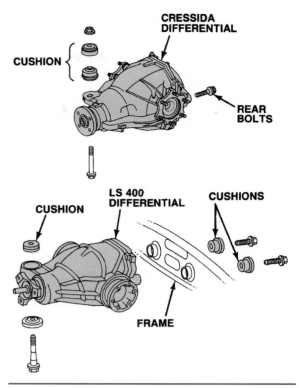

Figure 10-30. Rubber cushions at one or more of the differential mounts help keep vibrations from being transmitted to the frame.

TOP VIEW

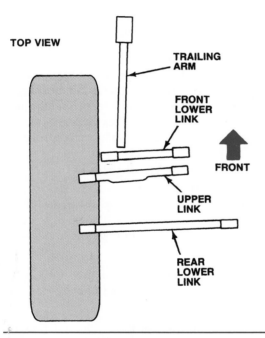

Figure 10-29. Three transverse links form the Mazda "E-link" rear suspension. The toe adjustment cam is located on the rear lower link.

three models: particularly, the method by which the differential is secured to the rear sub-frame. The Supra differential is secured to the subframe by mounting bolts and nuts, the Cressida differential is attached by bolts at the rear and a single rubber-cushioned mount at the front of the case, while the LS 400 differential installs with three rubber-cushioned mounts (Figure 10-30). The rub-

ber cushioning helps keep vibrations out of the passenger compartment.

Although the three rear suspensions are similar, that of the Lexus LS 400 serves as an example in the following discussion (Figure 10-31). The Lexus rear suspension components are the:

- Pivot-base strut
- Upper control arm
- Front (No. 1) lower control arm
- Rear (No. 2) lower control arm
- Strut rod

The upper control arm attaches to the sub-frame by two pivots and to the knuckle with a ball joint. The pivots are placed with their axis at an angle to the vehicle centerline—the front bushing is further outboard than the rear one. Toyota calls this a "reverse angle" in their service literature.

The front (No. 1) lower control arm, is the shorter of the two. Both lower arms attach with pivot bushings to the sub-frame. A ball joint attaches the front (No. 1) lower arm to the knuckle, while a pivot bushing provides the knuckle connection for the rear (No. 2) lower arm. Although the shape and layout of these two lower arms is

STRUT/SLA SUSPENSION—TOYOTA

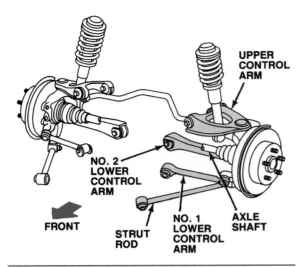

Figure 10-31. The Lexus LS 400 rear strut/SLA suspension is shown here. Toyota uses a similar system on the Supra and Cressida.

similar to that of the Mazda E-link suspension—the front arm being shorter than the rear—the Lexus's lower arms are not parallel. Also, the Mazda suspension allows compliance steer under certain conditions, but the Lexus design resists it. Compliance steer is discussed more fully later in this chapter. The strut rod, which mounts with pivot bushings at both ends, extends forward at an angle from the knuckle to the sub-frame. The pivot-base strut mounts on the knuckle. The antiroll bar attaches to the rear (No. 2) lower arm at either side through spacer bars with ball joint connections.

Nissan

The Nissan 300ZX and 240SX, and the Infiniti Q45, have a strut/SLA system with a rear drivetrain. The front and rear of the differential are secured to the crossmembers of a rear sub-frame. Nissan refers to the entire sub-frame assembly as the "rear crossmember." Rubber cushions isolate the rear crossmember from the body to prevent suspension vibrations from intruding into the passenger compartment. The Nissan rear-crossmember mounting is similar to the DaimlerChrysler isolated crossmember front suspension described in Chapter 9 of this *Classroom Manual*.

The three Nissan suspensions differ from one another in certain details, but all use the following:

- Pivot-base strut
- Front upper link
- Rear upper link
- Lower control arm
- Lateral link

Each upper link attaches with pivot bushings to the crossmember and the knuckle (Figure 10-32). On the 300ZX and 240SX, the rear upper link opens into a circle in the middle and narrows to a single rod at each end. The pivot-base of the strut attaches to the knuckle. From the knuckle, the strut extends through the open center of the upper link to the upper mount on the body. On the Q45, the rear upper link is a solid arm that simply curves around the front of the strut.

The lateral link, called a "lower link" in some Nissan service literature, also has a pivot at each end. Positioned behind the strut, the lateral link attaches lower on the knuckle than the upper links. This lateral link resists side-to-side forces.

The lower control arm mounts with two pivot bushings at the crossmember and a ball joint at the knuckle. The axis of the lower control arm pivots at an angle to the vehicle centerline, similarly to the Toyota upper arm described earlier. To allow compliance steer in this suspension, the lower control arm bushings have less resistance to side-to-side forces than the lateral link bushings.

The strut pivots on the knuckle, behind the axle shaft. A small spacer bar attaches the end of the antiroll bar to the underside of the lower control arm.

Strut/Short-Long-Arm Systems With Non-Driven Axles

Honda uses three strut/SLA suspension designs at the rear of their FWD models. The three systems can be divided up according to the models in which they are used:

- Honda Civic and Acura Integra
- Honda Accord and Acura Legend
- Honda Prelude

The first system, used in the Civic and Integra, uses a low wheel knuckle, like those in the systems used at the front axle of some RWD powertrains. The other two systems use high knuckles similar to those described for front strut/SLA systems in Chapter 9 of this *Classroom Manual*.

Civic and Integra

Honda Civic models, including the CRX and wagon, and the Acura Integra, use a strut/SLA system with a low wheel knuckle. The components at each wheel are:

- Pivot-base strut
- Trailing arm

**STRUT/SLA SUSPENSION—
NISSAN**

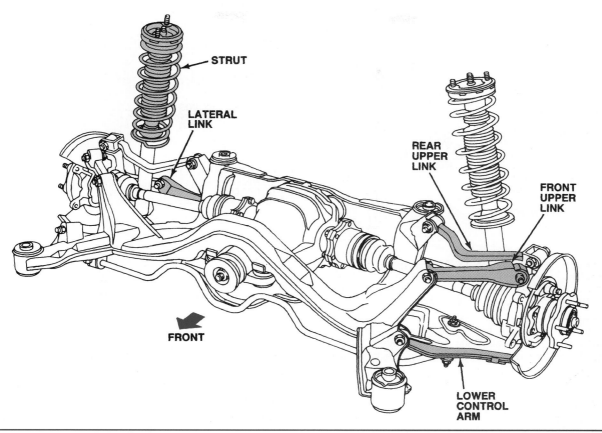

STRUT

LATERAL
LINK

REAR
UPPER
LINK

FRONT
UPPER
LINK

FRONT

LOWER
CONTROL
ARM

Figure 10-32. The Infiniti Q45 rear suspension has a diagonal lower control arm, two upper control arms, and a lateral link. Similar rear suspensions are used on the Nissan 300ZX and 240SX.

- Compensator arm
- Upper control arm
- Lower control arm
- Antiroll bar

The trailing arm is the largest suspension part and the rear of the arm serves as the knuckle. The wheel spindle bolts onto knuckle. The pivot bushing attaching the trailing arm to the frame is not at the front end of the arm—part of the arm extends further forward than the bushing mount (Figure 10-33). The compensator arm, which is a lateral link that extends from a frame-mounted bracket to the front end of the trailing arm, regulates how far the trailing arm can pivot. The upper and lower control arms each use one pivot bushing at a frame bracket and another at the knuckle portion of the trailing arm. The pivot-base strut attaches to the lower arm with a bushing, and a small spacer bar connects the antiroll bar to the lower arm.

Accord and Legend
The Acura Legend and Honda Accord use a strut/SLA suspension with a long knuckle. The components of this suspension are:

- Pivot-base strut
- Trailing arm
- Upper control arm
- Lower control arm A
- Lower control arm B
- Antiroll bar

Lower control arm A is toward the front and lower control arm B is toward the rear (Figure 10-34). The trailing arm extends back from a pivot bushing at a frame-mounted bracket to the steering knuckle, to which it bolts solidly. The upper control arm uses a pivot bushing at the frame and a ball joint at the knuckle. Lower arm A is the shorter of the two control arms. Both control arms

STRUT/SLA SUSPENSION—
HONDA CIVIC

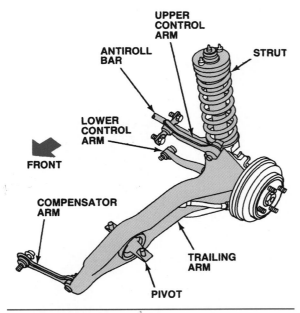

Figure 10-33. The trailing arm pivots near its mid-section on this Honda Civic rear suspension and the compensator arm regulates how far the trailing arm can pivot.

use pivot bushing connections at the frame and at the knuckle.

Prelude

The Honda Prelude's rear suspension is a long knuckle design that uses the following components:

- Pivot-base strut
- Strut rod
- One or two lower control arms
- Upper control arm
- Antiroll bar

When four-wheel-steering (4WS) versions of the Prelude were available they used a similar rear suspension, but the 4WS version has only one lower control arm rather than two (Figure 10-35). The main difference between the Prelude rear suspension design and the one in the Accord and Legend is the use of a strut rod that solidly mounts to the frame instead of a trailing arm that mounts with a pivot bushing. The strut rod bushings do allow some torsional, or twisting, action.

The pivot-base strut mounts to the front lower control arm, and a strut rod, or radius rod, braces that arm. Both ends of the front lower arm pivot on bushings. The rear lower arm, or "lower arm B,"

STRUT/SLA SUSPENSION—
HONDA ACCORD

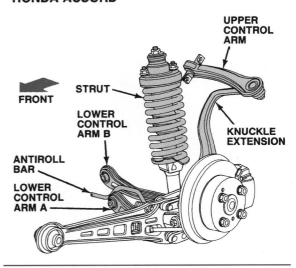

Figure 10-34. This Honda Accord rear suspension is a long knuckle design, that is, the upper control arm joins the knuckle at a point outboard of the wheel.

STRUT/SLA SUSPENSION—
HONDA PRELUDE

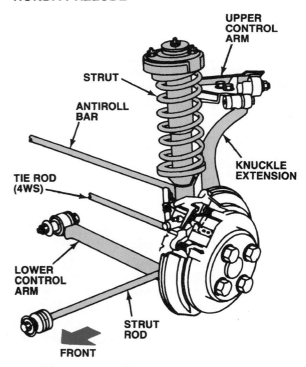

Figure 10-35. The rear suspension of the 4WS Honda Prelude had only one lower control arm. Because the long knuckle extension to the upper control arm bends out over the wheel, the steering axis tilts outward at the top.

pivots in a bushing at the frame and attaches to the knuckle with a ball joint. The upper control arm connects to the frame with two pivot bushings and attaches to the knuckle with a ball joint. A spacer bar links each end of the antiroll bar to the strut rod near the lower control arm.

Strut/Short-Long-Arm Characteristics

Strut/short-long-arm suspensions resemble SLA suspensions in that they use a shorter upper arm and a longer lower arm to provide a camber change as a wheel rides over a bump. Of the rear strut/SLA systems previously described, the Mazda Miata two-arm system, which uses just one upper and one lower control arm, is the design most similar to a SLA suspension. The Honda systems are also similar, although they all use trailing arms or, in the case of the Prelude, a strut rod. Two lower control arms are used with the trailing member, a common rear strut suspension arrangement, on the Honda Accord and 2WS Prelude and the Acura Legend. As mentioned earlier in this chapter, a benefit of using two links where a front suspension would use one A-shaped arm is that the two links work together to resist toe changes during braking, acceleration, cornering, and traveling over bumps.

Some strut/SLA suspensions use other methods to control rear wheel toe. Because strut/SLA suspensions are individually designed, they differ from each other in significant ways. Consequently, the ways in which they control rear wheel toe also differ.

As one wheel travels over a bump on the Mazda E-link suspension, the shorter lower arm draws the knuckle further inward than the longer lower arm does, which tends to create *toe-in*. However, when the trailing arm pivots, both lower links move forward, so they tend to swing outward. The shorter front link swings further outward, which tends to create *toe-out* (Figure 10-36). These opposing forces minimize toe change. Braking forces tend to pull the wheel toward the rear (Figure 10-37). Again, the shorter front link has a sharper arc than the longer rear one, which tends to create toe-in. To prevent excessive toe-in, a soft bushing at the inner end of the front link gives or deforms more than the firmer bushing at the outer end, which reduces toe-in. The inner bushing at the rear link is stiffer than the outer bushing, which offers resistance to excessive toe-in. In combination, these forces create a slight toe-in during braking.

MAZDA E-LINK SUSPENSION

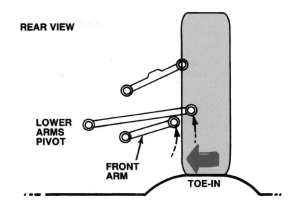

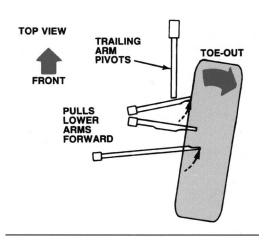

Figure 10-36. In the Mazda E-link rear suspension, the shorter front lower control arm pulls the front of the wheel inward to create toe-in during jounce, while the trailing arm pulls the front arm forward to create toe-out as a counterforce.

On the Toyota rear strut/SLA suspension, the upper control arm regulates toe change through its "reverse angle" of installation. As one wheel rides over a bump, the shorter front (No. 1) and longer rear (No. 2) lower control arms tend to create toe-in, but the upper control arm pivots on a different axis than the lower arms to counteract the toe change (Figure 10-38). During braking, the different stiffness of the control arm bushings regulate toe-in and toe-out in a similar manner to those of the Mazda E-link suspension (Figure 10-39). The Toyota rear suspension design also resists toe changes during cornering because the wheel center is located exactly between the front and rear mounting points at the rear sub-frame (Figure 10-40). This arrangement

MAZDA E-LINK SUSPENSION

TOP VIEW

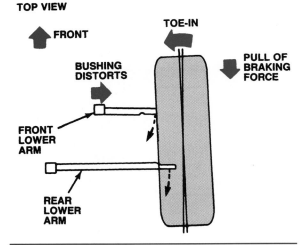

Figure 10-37. When braking force pushes the two lower control arms of the Mazda E-link suspension toward the rear, the soft bushing at the frame mount of the shorter front arm allows the front of the wheel to move outward to prevent excessive toe-in.

LEXUS LS 400 SUSPENSION

TOP VIEW

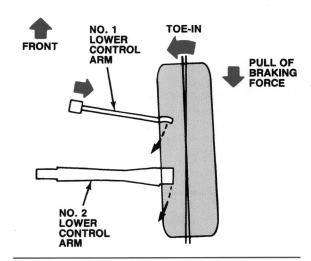

Figure 10-39. To control rear wheel toe during braking, the shorter front (No. 1) lower control arm of the Toyota arcs more sharply than the rear (No. 2) arm, but a softer frame bushing allows braking force to pull the arm outward.

LEXUS LS 400 SUSPENSION

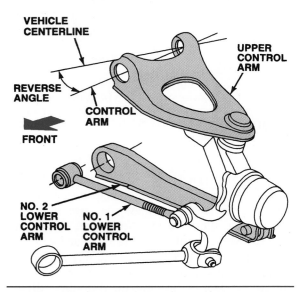

Figure 10-38. The reverse angle of the Toyota upper control arm axis, which is not parallel to the vehicle centerline, counteracts the tendency of the wheels to toe-in when the suspension compresses.

LEXUS LS 400 SUSPENSION

TOP VIEW

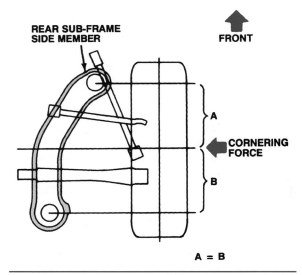

Figure 10-40. With the Toyota design, cornering force, which is lateral, is the same on the front and rear of the wheel because the sub-frame mounting points are an equal distance from the center of the wheel. Therefore, the wheel does not pivot during turns, so there is no toe change.

equalizes lateral forces on the front and rear of the wheel during turns, so there is no toe change.

Both the Mazda E-link and Nissan strut/SLA rear suspensions allow some toe change during cornering, which is known as compliance steer.

Compliance Steer

The word "compliance" means giving way, and when the toe angle of a wheel changes, it effectively "steers" in a new direction. **Compliance steer** is a toe change that results from suspension links and bushings giving way to cornering force. Some suspensions are designed to toe-in at the outer rear wheel during cornering so the rear tires more closely track the front ones.

Mazda and Nissan have designed compliance steer into their strut/SLA rear suspensions (Figure 10-41). A softer bushing at the front lower link of the Mazda E-link suspension compresses from cornering force on the outside of the wheel, so the front of the wheel tends to move inward. At the same time, a stiffer bushing on the rear lower link resists compression, so inward movement at the rear of the wheel is limited. Therefore, the two bushings work together so the wheel toes in slightly while cornering. Nissan uses soft bushings to mount the A-shaped lower control arm and firm bushings on the lateral link. Since the lower arm attaches farther forward on the knuckle than the lateral link, the soft bushings allow the front of the wheel to move in farther when cornering creates a lateral load, so the wheel toes in.

Semi-Trailing Arm Suspensions

Independent semi-trailing arm suspensions were popular with European manufacturers, such as BMW, and were used extensively through the early 1990s. Some Japanese manufacturers produced models with semi-trailing arm rear suspensions as well. However, most of these semi-trailing arm designs have been replaced by a multi-link IRS system on current production models. The semi-trailing arm rear suspension of the short lived Infiniti M30 provides a straightforward example of this design used with a RWD powertrain (Figure 10-42). The major components of the Infiniti semi-trailing arm IRS system are:

- Semi-trailing arm
- Pivot-base strut
- Antiroll bar

The rear differential of the Infiniti M30 is suspended from a mounting bracket that bolts to the

COMPLIANCE STEER

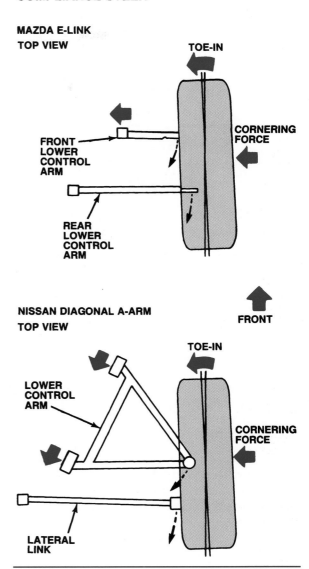

Figure 10-41. Mazda and Nissan rear strut/SLA suspensions use bushing technology to provide compliance steer. Softer front bushings compress more than the firmer rear bushings under the lateral load of cornering force causing the outer wheel to toe in.

underbody at the rear of the unit, while a frame crossmember supports the front of the differential. This crossmember curves so the center, where the differential housing attaches, is further back in the chassis than the two outboard ends. The ends of the crossmember share a frame attachment point with the semi-trailing arms. The crossmember and semi-trailing arms install to the frame with pivot bushings. The front inboard ends of the semi-trailing arms attach to brackets on the

**SEMI-TRAILING ARM—
INDEPENDENT SUSPENSION**

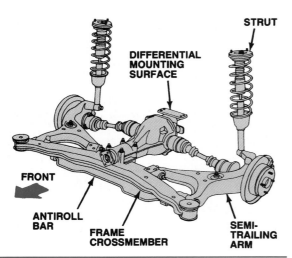

Figure 10-42. The semi-trailing arm mounts with bushings to the frame crossmember on the Infiniti M30 independent rear suspension.

SEMI-TRAILING ARM—CAMBER CHANGE

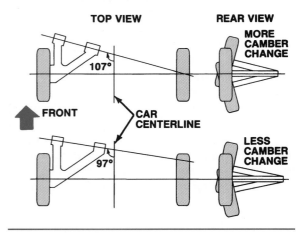

Figure 10-43. Increasing the trail angle of a semi-trailing arm of an independent suspension increases camber change during bounce, while reducing the angle results in less camber change.

crossmember with pivot bushings. The wheel knuckle is an integral part of the rear section of the semi-trailing arm, and the pivot-base strut mounts on an arm that extends from the rear of the knuckle assembly. An antiroll bar, which attaches to the semi-trailing arms and is secured to the crossmember by rubber-cushioned bushings, reduces body roll.

Semi-Trailing Arm Characteristics
Semi-trailing arms used with an independent suspension have different effects than those used with a solid driven axle. With a solid axle, the semi-trailing arms respond to the up-and-down movement of the whole axle unit, but on an IRS system each arm responds to the travel of a single wheel. Also, while the wheels stay perpendicular to a solid axle, the motion of an independent axle shaft moves the wheel in an arc. There are some similarities between the two applications: In both cases, semi-trailing arms brace the axle or axle shafts against both front-to-rear and side-to-side forces.

The pivot axis of the semi-trailing arm bushings determines wheel travel during jounce and rebound. The angle at which this axis intersects the vehicle centerline—or the **trail angle**—determines camber change (Figure 10-43). The closer this angle is to 90 degrees, the less camber change occurs during bounce. The angle of the axis to the ground determines toe change during bounce (Figure 10-44). When the front of the axis is lower, the wheel tends to toe in during jounce and toe out during rebound.

If the front of the axis is higher, the toe change is the opposite.

Multi-Link Suspensions

The term **multi-link suspension** is a generic term for suspensions that have no other simple, descriptive name. This term is usually applied to independent rear suspensions used in RWD performance models, because engineers generally design a suspension unique to one specific application. The popularity of multi-link rear suspensions has grown dramatically over recent years with American, European, and Japanese manufacturers. Although the arrangement and number of links used varies for each application, all multi-link suspensions do share some common characteristics. The rear suspensions of the Chevrolet Corvette, Mazda RX-7, and Cadillac XLR serve as examples of multi-link suspension designs in the following discussion.

Corvette and Cadillac XLR Five-Link
On the Chevrolet Corvette five-link system, a carrier assembly supports the differential and also serves as the back cover of the differential. Two arms extend from the sides of the carrier and attach to brackets on the side rails of the rear sub-frame (Figure 10-45). A driveline support, which parallels the driveshaft, attaches to the rear of the transmission and the front of the differential housing to help

■ The de Dion Axle

A French company formed by Count Albert de Dion and George Bouton invented the de Dion axle in 1894 and used it extensively on de Dion-Bouton vehicles until 1914. The de Dion axle was a compromise between early independent rear suspensions—which were swing axles—and solid axles. The swing axle provided superior handling to solid axles in many ways, but it allowed too much camber change through the range of suspension travel, which greatly reduced traction. Under certain conditions, a swing axle produces a jacking effect that lifts the back of the chassis causing the axle shafts to angle toward the ground. With the rear tires at extreme positive camber angles and riding only on the outside edges, the vehicle would usually spin out of control.

The original de Dion axle was basically a swing axle with a large, rigid tube added to it. This "de Dion" tube bolted to each rear wheel to keep them vertical and parallel. As a compromise between independent rear suspension and a solid axle, the de Dion axle provided the relatively low unsprung weight of an independent suspension, but ride quality was only slightly better than that of a solid axle.

The de Dion axle was never used by American manufacturers, but was popular in European production and racing applications during the 1940s through the 1960s. With the development of sophisticated independent rear suspensions, the de Dion axle has faded nearly into oblivion. However, a de Dion axle was used on the Aston Martin Virage—a rare, quarter-million-dollar sports car—as late as 1991.

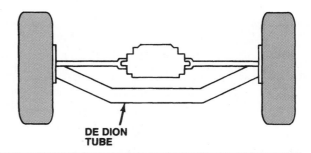

DE DION TUBE

transfer axle windup toward the front of the chassis. The five links of the Corvette rear suspension are:

- Axle shaft
- Spindle rod
- Axle outer socket
- Upper control rod
- Lower control rod

The axle shaft is considered part of the suspension because it attaches with U-joints, rather than CV joints, at each end. As explained in Chapter 11 of this *Classroom Manual,* U-joints do not allow any plunging action of the axle shafts at the differential. As a result, the arc of the axle shaft and the arc of the rest of the suspension components must match each other as the wheel travels vertically.

The spindle rod extends outward from a bracket on the differential carrier to the wheel knuckle. Chevrolet calls the knuckle a "spindle," so this link is named the "spindle rod." The axle outer socket is also a transverse link that resembles the tie rod in a steering system. The outboard end of the axle outer socket attaches to an arm on the knuckle with a ball joint, while the inboard end of the link attaches to a bracket at the center of the differential carrier. The upper and lower control rods are trailing arms.

The transverse monoleaf spring extends from one wheel knuckle to the other (Figure 10-46). A bolt and insulators attach each end of the spring to the knuckle and isolation brackets mount the center of the spring to the differential carrier. A shock absorber is mounted between the front of the knuckle and the frame on each side.

Mazda Multi-Link Semi-Trailing

The Mazda RX-7 uses a rear differential carrier that serves as the differential case and has two arms that extend toward either side (Figure 10-47). Bolts, cushioned by large rubber insulators, secure the differential carrier to the underbody. A wide crossbeam, which serves as a one-piece rear sub-frame, supports the front of the differential and provides anchoring points for some of the suspension links. The suspension components are:

- Pivot-base strut
- Trailing arm
- Control link
- Lateral link
- Sublink
- Antiroll bar

In effect, the trailing arm assembly is actually two arms: one trailing and one semi-trailing. Mazda service literature calls the unit a "trailing arm" but refers to the overall suspension as a "semi-trailing" design.

**SEMI-TRAILING ARM—
TOE CHANGE**

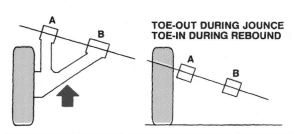

Figure 10-44. The angle of the arm pivot in relation to the ground determines toe change during bounce on a semi-trailing arm independent suspension.

The trailing and semi-trailing arms merge together and join into the structure of the knuckle to which the wheel hub mounts. The trailing arm pivots at the crossbeam on a large bushing. The semi-trailing part of the arm indirectly joins the crossbeam through the small, vertical control link (Figure 10-48). Another semi-trailing member, the lateral link, extends from the crossbeam to the wheel knuckle and attaches with ball joints at each end. At the front left side of the differential, a vertical link, called the "sublink," installs with pivot bushings to the side of the differential and the underbody. Spacer bars connect to the antiroll bar with ball joints and attach to the knuckles with pivot bushings. A pivot-base strut mounts

MULTI-LINK SUSPENSION— CORVETTE

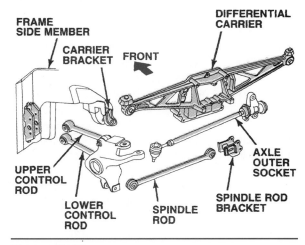

Figure 10-45. On the "five-link" Corvette rear suspension, the axle outer socket and the spindle rod are transverse links, the upper and lower control rods are trailing members, and the axle shaft is the fifth link.

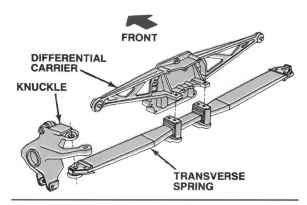

Figure 10-46. The Corvette Cadillac XLR rear suspension uses a transverse monoleaf spring that attaches to the wheel knuckles at each end and is anchored to the differential carrier in the center.

between the knuckle and body to cushion suspension movement.

Multi-Link Characteristics

Chassis engineers can vary the characteristics of a multi-link suspension design to meet the specific needs of a particular vehicle. The Corvette

MULTI-LINK SUSPENSION-MAZDA RX-7

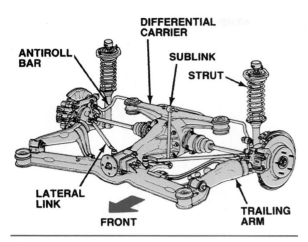

Figure 10-47. The second generation Mazda RX-7 uses a multi-link IRS, which Mazda simply calls a "semi-trailing arm" suspension.

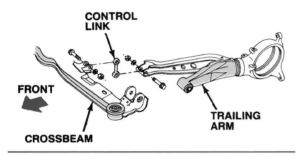

Figure 10-48. The control link joins the semi-trailing section of the trailing arm to a frame crossbeam on the RX-7 rear suspension.

provides a stiff suspension to keep the wheels on the road, while the RX-7 provides compliance steer under certain circumstances.

The suspension design of the Corvette minimizes camber and toe changes to keep the tires firmly planted for greater control (Figure 10-49). The transverse links—axle shaft, spindle rod, and axle outer socket—control the wheel alignment angles during vertical wheel travel. The spindle rod keeps camber under control by managing the movement of the bottom of the wheel, while the axle outer socket restricts movement at the back of the wheel to regulate toe. The longitudinal upper and lower control rods locate the wheel front-to-rear and transfer braking force from the wheel to the frame.

CORVETTE—CAMBER AND TOE CHANGE

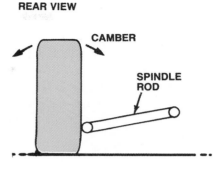

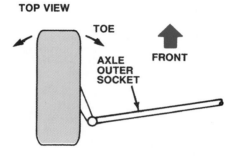

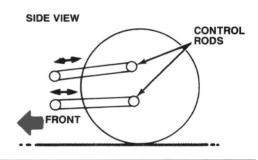

Figure 10-49. On the Corvette five-link rear suspension, the spindle rod controls camber change, the axle outer socket regulates toe, and the control rods manage fore and aft forces.

The Mazda RX-7 is designed for a variety of compliance steer characteristics: toe-in during braking, toe-out under low cornering force loads, and zero toe that changes to toe-in under high cornering force loads. The bushings joining the trailing arm to the wheel hub deform in controlled ways to create the toe changes (Figure 10-50). The semi-trailing members determine camber, and keep it nearly constant under most conditions.

MAZDA RX-7—COMPLIANCE STEER

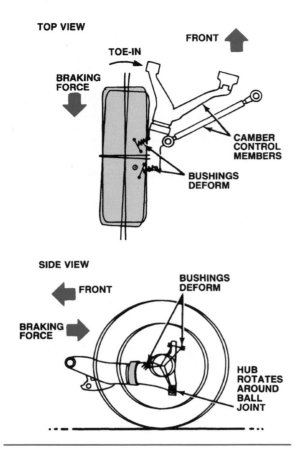

Figure 10-50. The bushings of the Mazda RX-7 multi-link rear suspension deform under braking forces to provide a slight amount of toe-in.

SEMI-INDEPENDENT REAR SUSPENSIONS

A **semi-independent suspension** is used only at a non-driven rear axle. The semi-independent design is based on a crossbeam that is similar to the beam axle of a solid, non-driven rear suspension. However, on a semi-independent design the crossbeam is placed ahead, rather than at the centerline, of the wheels (Figure 10-51). Trailing arms extend rearward from the crossbeam to the wheels. The name semi-independent points out that, although an axle does not directly link the wheels, the wheels are not completely independent of each other because they are indirectly connected through the crossbeam.

A number of semi-independent rear suspension designs are used, but all share some common

SEMI-INDEPENDENT SUSPENSIONS

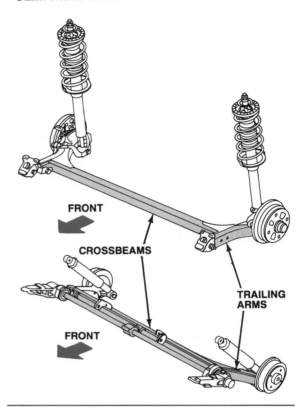

Figure 10-51. The crossbeam connects the two sides of a semi-independent rear suspension forward of the knuckles toward the pivot point of the trailing arms, so motion does not transfer directly from side to side.

characteristics. Semi-independent configurations can be categorized by the type of spring used in the suspension. These can be:

• Coil spring suspensions
• Strut suspensions
• Transverse torsion bar suspensions

Semi-Independent Rear Suspension Characteristics

The characteristics of a semi-independent rear suspension are similar to those of a trailing arm beam-axle suspension. The main difference is that one wheel can travel further vertically without affecting the opposite wheel, because the beam is at the pivot point of the trailing arm rather than at the end. How far back the crossbeam is in relation to the trailing arms determines the characteristics of the rear suspension. The effect of crossbeam position is simi-

TOP VIEWS

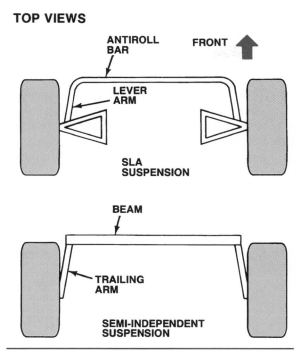

Figure 10-52. The function of a semi-independent suspension is similar to that of an antiroll bar, with the trailing arms acting like lever arms.

lar to that of the length of the lever arms on an antiroll bar—the shorter the length of the trailing arm from the wheel to the crossbeam, the stiffer the suspension, all other things being equal. Other similarities between a semi-independent layout and an antiroll bar are also valid (Figure 10-52). For example, making the crossbeam thicker also makes the suspension stiffer, in the same way that increasing the diameter of an antiroll bar makes it stiffer.

Coil Spring Suspensions

Over the years, a number of models from various manufacturers have used a semi-independent rear suspension with coil springs. A partial list includes the Buick Skylark; Chevrolet Cavalier, Corsica, and Beretta; Dodge Colt Vista; Hyundai Excel; Isuzu I-Mark; Mitsubishi Precis; and Pontiac Grand Am, LeMans, and Sunbird. The suspension of the Hyundai Excel, which is the same as that of the Mitsubishi Precis, Dodge Colt Vista, and Eagle Vista wagon, serves as an example of the design. The Hyundai semi-independent suspension consists of:

- Crossbeam
- Trailing arm

SEMI-INDEPENDENT SUSPENSION— COIL SPRING

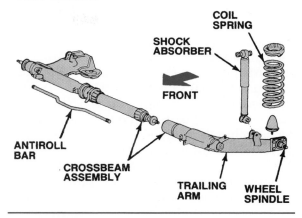

Figure 10-53. This Hyundai semi-independent rear suspension used with coil springs is a typical example of this fairly simple design.

- Coil spring
- Antiroll bar

The crossbeam is a two-piece assembly in which the right piece extends across the width of the chassis and the sleeve-like left piece fits over the right section (Figure 10-53). An antiroll bar connects one side of the crossbeam to the other. Each trailing arm is an integral part of one of the crossbeam sections. Brackets at each end of the crossbeam secure the entire assembly to the underbody. The wheel spindle attaches to the rear of the trailing arm, and the coil spring sits on a seat just inboard of the spindle. The shock absorber base mounts to a bracket on top of the trailing arm.

SUMMARY

Like front suspensions, rear suspensions must keep the tires on the road and smooth out road shocks. A rear suspension must also enable the rear wheels to track the front wheels during straight-ahead driving, and control rear-wheel compliance during turns. Because the rear wheels do not steer, more links can be installed between the wheels and frame to keep the wheels rigidly in place. Solid axles—both driven and non-driven—are more common at the rear than at the front, although there are also many independent rear suspensions. Semi-independent rear suspensions are only used with a non-driven axle.

Solid rear axles are inexpensive and strong, but provide poor handling compared to an independent suspension. One common problem with a solid driven rear axle is axle windup. Solid driven axles can be classified as full-floating, three-quarter-floating, or semi-floating. Whether driven or non-driven, three main types of suspensions are used with a solid rear axle: leaf spring, trailing arm, and semi-trailing arm. Leaf springs act both as locating members and suspension cushions. Trailing arms locate an axle front-to-rear, and trailing arm suspensions include some type of lateral member, usually a Panhard rod, to control side-to-side movement. Semi-trailing arms can control both front-to-rear and side-to-side movement.

Independent rear suspensions provide better handling, traction, and control. Rear SLA and strut suspensions have similar characteristics to the same types of front suspensions. The strut/ SLA suspension system combines the characteristics of SLA and strut suspensions. The links of a rear strut/SLA suspension are often designed to oppose each other to prevent alignment changes during cornering and braking. Some designs use controlled bushing distortion to provide compliance steer. In a semi-trailing arm, independent rear suspension, the angle at which the arms are installed determines camber and toe change during vertical wheel movement. A multi-link suspension is a unique design for a specific vehicle application, and handling characteristics vary according to the design.

Finally, a semi-independent rear suspension provides a compromise between the characteristics of an independent suspension and a solid axle.

Review Questions

For each of the following questions, choose the letter that represents the best possible answer.

1. The important rear suspension angles are:
   a. Caster and camber
   b. Caster and toe
   c. Camber and toe
   d. Caster, camber, and toe

2. A difference in the directions the front and rear wheels are aimed is called the:
   a. Axis angle
   b. Steering angle
   c. Suspension angle
   d. Thrust angle

3. All of the following characteristics apply to a solid rear axle EXCEPT:
   a. Inexpensive to manufacture
   b. Simple design
   c. Strong and reliable
   d. Low unsprung weight

4. The wheel bearings in a full-floating axle ride on the:
   a. Axle housing
   b. Axle shafts
   c. Pinion gear
   d. Wheel hub

5. Multi-leaf springs are used with:
   a. Independent rear suspensions
   b. Semi-independent rear suspensions
   c. Solid rear axles
   d. Swing axles

6. How many control arms are used on a typical rear suspension with leaf springs?
   a. None
   b. 1 transverse
   c. 2 lateral
   d. 2 sets of 2

7. A transverse link that connects to the frame at one end and the beam axle or axle housing at the other end is called:
   a. A Watts linkage
   b. A Panhard rod
   c. A MacPherson strut
   d. A trailing arm

8. Another name for a lower trailing arm is a:
   a. Panhard rod
   b. Torque arm

   c. Track rod
   d. Lateral link

9. A Panhard rod is most always used with which type of rear suspension?
   a. Semi-trailing arm
   b. Torsion bar
   c. Trailing arm
   d. Semi-independent

10. Which of the following is a characteristic of an independent rear suspension?
    a. Increased unsprung weight
    b. Lower cost of manufacture
    c. Reduced tramp and shimmy
    d. Unusual handling qualities

11. A short-long arm (SLA) suspension is typically used:
    a. On a driven front axle
    b. On a driven rear axle
    c. On compact unit-body vehicles
    d. With a rear beam axle

12. A MacPherson strut-type suspension, when used at the rear of a vehicle, is sometimes called a:
    a. Chapman strut
    b. Panhard strut
    c. de Dion strut
    d. Watts linkage

13. The camber change of a strut suspension over bumps is similar to that of:
    a. SLA suspensions
    b. Leaf spring suspensions
    c. Trailing arm suspensions
    d. Semi-trailing arm suspensions

14. A strut/short-long-arm suspension does NOT use:
    a. A lower control arm
    b. A monoleaf spring
    c. A pivot-base strut
    d. An upper control arm

15. A predictable toe change that results from suspension links and bushings deforming under cornering force is called:
    a. Bump steer
    b. Compliance steer
    c. Oversteer
    d. Understeer

16. Camber changes during bounce are lower the closer the trail angle is to:
    a. 30 degrees
    b. 45 degrees
    c. 65 degrees
    d. 90 degrees

17. In rear strut suspensions, the angle of the control arm and the strut determine which characteristic of the suspension?
    a. Coefficient of compliance
    b. Roll center
    c. Thrust angle
    d. Trail angle

18. The purpose for using two parallel links or an H-arm as the lower control arm of a rear suspension is to prevent:
    a. Compliance steer
    b. Jounce and rebound
    c. Toe changes
    d. Wheel hop

19. It is fairly common to find a Strut/SLA rear suspension on which type of vehicle?
    a. Front-wheel drive only
    b. Rear-wheel drive only
    c. Heavy trucks only
    d. Both front- and rear-wheel drive

20. Which type of rear suspension is used on all current Honda models?
    a. Full-floating
    b. Semi-trailing arm
    c. Semi-independent
    d. Strut/SLA

21. A typical application for a multi-link suspension would be a:
    a. FWD compact sedan
    b. 4WD sport utility vehicle
    c. RWD light truck
    d. RWD performance cars

22. A semi-independent suspension is used only at the:
    a. Front of a RWD vehicle
    b. Rear of a FWD vehicle
    c. Front of a FWD vehicle
    d. Rear of a RWD vehicle

23. A typical semi-independent rear suspension includes the following:
    a. Crossbeam
    b. Semi-trailing arm
    c. Roll bar
    d. Panhard rod

24. The shock absorbers may be angled forward to help brace the knuckle with which type of suspension?
    a. Short-long-arm
    b. Strut/short-long-arm
    c. Multi-link
    d. Semi-independent

25. A Hotchkiss drive is another name for which rear suspension configuration?
    a. Semi-floating axle with coil springs
    b. Solid axle with semi-elliptical leaf springs
    c. Beam axle with trailing arms and struts
    d. Driven axle with multi-links and struts

11

Drive Layout and Driveline Joints

OBJECTIVES

Upon completion and review of this chapter, you will be able to:

- Identify and define the different types of drive layouts.

- Identify the components and terms associated with front-wheel (FWD) and rear-wheel drive (RWD) drivelines and define their use.

- Identify the types of universal and constant-velocity joints and define their use.

KEY TERMS

all-wheel drive (AWD)
ball-and-cage constant
  velocity (CV) joint
birfield joint
constant velocity
  (CV) joint
cross-groove joint
double-Cardan joint
double-offset joint
fixed joint
fixed tripod joint
four-wheel drive
  (4WD)
front-wheel drive
  (FWD)
full-time four-wheel
  drive
inboard constant
  velocity (CV) joint

lead
outboard constant
  velocity (CV) joint
part-time four-wheel
  drive
plunging joint
plunging tripod joint
pull
rear-wheel drive
  (RWD)
Rzeppa joint
S-plan joint
torque
torque steer
triplan joint
tripod
tripod constant
  velocity (CV) joint
tulip

INTRODUCTION

While keeping the tires in contact with the road and ensuring a smooth ride are primary tasks of the suspension, there are other influences affecting tire traction and ride quality. The most notable of these other influences is drive layout. Automobiles are front-wheel drive (FWD), rear-wheel drive (RWD), four-wheel drive (4WD), or all-wheel drive (AWD), and each drive configuration has unique characteristics, advantages, and disadvantages (Figure 11-1).

Even though the driveline is not really part of the suspension, drivelines are briefly examined in this chapter because their function is related to how the suspension works. In addition, two types

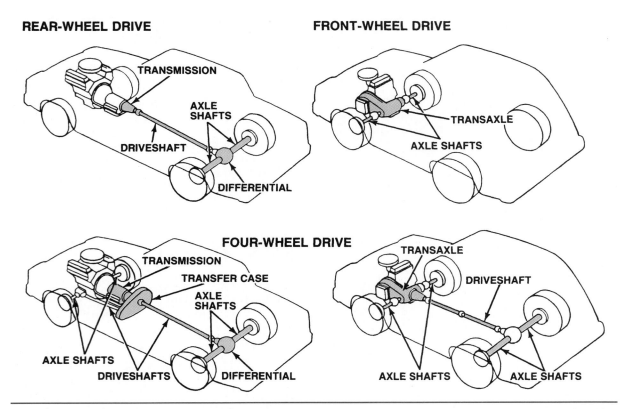

Figure 11-1. Each drive layout—rear-wheel drive (RWD), front-wheel drive (FWD), and four-wheel drive (4WD)—has unique advantages and drawbacks.

of driveline joints—universal joints (U-joints) and constant velocity (CV) joints—are detailed because these driveline components are often serviced during suspension repairs. This chapter is divided into four sections:

- Front-wheel drive
- Rear-wheel drive
- Four-wheel drive
- Driveline joints

In any driveline, the transmission transfers torque from the engine to a differential, or final drive, which drives the axle shafts. The axle shafts provide the power to the drive wheels. Four-wheel drivetrains include a transfer case and all-wheel drivetrains contain additional gearing to transmit power to both axles. Driveline joints link the driveline shafts to the other driveline components.

FRONT-WHEEL DRIVE

On most **front-wheel drive (FWD)** applications, the transmission and final drive are housed together in a single unit called a "transaxle" (Figure 11-2).

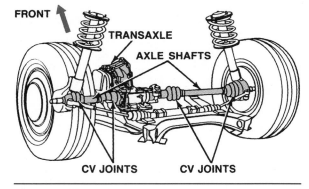

Figure 11-2. A FWD transaxle installs into the engine compartment between the front wheels and transmits torque to the wheels through the axle shafts.

Although most transaxles connect directly to the engine and drive the front wheels, a rear transaxle connected to the engine by a driveshaft is used in few high-performance applications. Also, some FWD transmissions have a separate final drive unit with the differential gears in a dedicated housing, rather than a true transaxle. Axle shafts transmit power from the final drive to the front

FRONT-WHEEL DRIVE

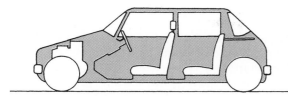

REAR-WHEEL DRIVE

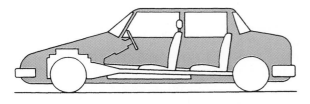

Figure 11-3. A FWD layout has more floor space and can be built shorter than a RWD one. However, a RWD vehicle can be built with a lower coefficient of drag, and the weight of its drivetrain is more evenly distributed.

wheels, and CV joints at each end of the axle shafts link them to the transaxle and the wheels.

Although FWD has recently become the favored driveline layout for most automobile manufacturers, this popularity has less to do with handling and economy than with other production concerns. The initial motivation for manufacturers switching to a FWD platform was to increase fleet fuel efficiency in order to meet government mandated corporate average fuel economy (CAFÉ) standards. Smaller, lighter vehicles get better fuel mileage than larger, heavier ones. When the transmission and final drive are both at the front of the chassis, no driveshaft is needed, there is no heavy rear differential, the rear suspension is lighter, and consequently the vehicle weighs less. In addition, most engines used with a FWD transaxle are placed transversely in the chassis, and a transverse engine does not stick out as far in front of the front wheels, so the vehicle can be built smaller overall with the same interior dimensions.

Space is another advantage of FWD (Figure 11-3). Since there is no front-to-rear driveshaft, the passenger compartment floor can be lower and does not have a hump for the transmission tunnel. Front-wheel drive vehicles generally have generous interior space for their size because of the transverse engine and lack of a driveshaft, but the front wheelwells often intrude into the floor area of the front seats. More trunk room is available because there is no rear differential taking up room, only the rear suspension.

For the purposes of this book, the most important characteristics of a FWD layout are the effects on ride, handling, and steering. The most noticeable factor in this area is that the weight of a FWD platform is concentrated on the front axle. This is very important to remember when raising a FWD vehicle on a lift. If the lift is not properly supporting the vehicle, the front end will tip forward when the wheels lift off the ground. Always check the appropriate service literature for proper lift points and techniques before raising a vehicle on a hoist

Power steering is almost a necessity on a FWD vehicle because so much of the sprung weight is concentrated on the front wheels. The added weight of a power steering system cancels out part of the weight savings of a FWD platform. A benefit of having most of the weight over the front wheels is an increase in traction compared to a design with less weight on each axle. More weight on the steered axle makes it easier to control the vehicle during a skid. Extra weight on the front axle also provides greater steering control when driving in snow, gravel, or other loose surfaces because the additional weight allows the tires to "bite" more deeply into the loose surface. In addition, the increased front weight is sprung weight, so the vehicle has less unsprung weight overall.

Less unsprung weight at the rear means a FWD vehicle is less likely to fishtail if the rear tires break loose during cornering on wet or icy pavement. The forward motion of the front wheels tends to pull the rear of the vehicle back into place. This FWD characteristic is known as "self-aligning." Another FWD characteristic is a natural tendency to "understeer." With understeer, the vehicle turns, or steers, less sharply than the steering wheel input demands should the front tires loose traction (Figure 11-4). In other words, an understeering vehicle "plows" straight ahead regardless of the direction in which the wheels are steered. If the front tires skid, lifting off the accelerator—the instinctive reaction of most drivers—helps maintain control of a FWD vehicle, rather than sending the vehicle spinning, which is typical with a RWD vehicle. Understeer and oversteer are also discussed in Chapter 3 of this *Classroom Manual*.

It is important to remember that these FWD characteristics—self-aligning and understeer—are strongest when the vehicle is unloaded. With passengers in the back seat, heavy baggage in the luggage compartment, or when towing a trailer, the increased rear weight counteracts the characteristics that normally result from a front-heavy

Torque Tube Drive

Torque tubes, which are large, rigid, tube-shaped driveshaft housings that fasten to the transmission with a large, spherical universal joint at one end and are bolted to the differential at the other end, were popular RWD drivetrain components through the 1950s. The strong rigid structure of a torque tube provides a simple method of controlling axle windup. As rotation of the rear wheels moves the rear axle housing forward, the differential housing transfers the forward motion to the torque tube, which places a forward thrust, rather than a lifting motion, on the front of the chassis. Today,

torque tubes are still valued on race cars and are also used on some high-performance production models.

For the average owner—and technician—the advantages of a torque tube are outweighed by the problems it causes in making the drivetrain elements so inaccessible, and therefore expensive, to repair. For example, to replace the clutch in a torque-tube drivetrain requires the removal of either the engine or the rear axle. An exposed driveshaft, which can be disconnected from the transmission relatively easily, makes things easier.

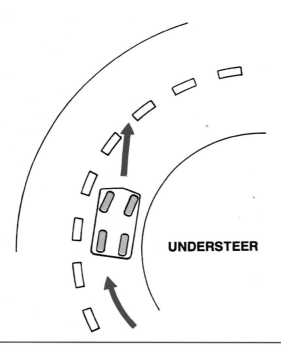

Figure 11-4. During an understeer condition the response to steering wheel input is reduced, so the vehicle tends to plow straight ahead even though the wheels are turned sharply.

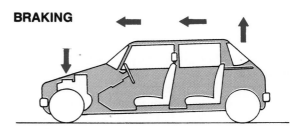

Figure 11-5. Vehicle weight shifts forward during braking, and since a FWD platform is already front-heavy, nearly all of the vehicle weight is on the front axle while it slows.

condition. There are much greater differences in handling between unloaded and loaded conditions in a FWD model than in a RWD vehicle because the weight distribution changes much more.

Weight distribution affects braking as well as steering. Braking always effectively shifts vehicle weight forward, and this tendency is exaggerated on a FWD layout (Figure 11-5). Therefore, FWD vehi-

cles usually have larger front brake discs and need more braking force at the front. Again, any load in the rear changes the dynamics quite a bit, so some FWD vehicles, such as the DaimlerChrysler minivans, use load-sensitive brake proportioning valves. These devices send more braking force to the front brake circuits when the vehicle is unloaded and more to the rear circuits when a heavy load compresses the rear suspension. Typically, these valves operate in response to vehicle height at the rear, which is why it is illegal to use load-leveling devices to lift the rear under heavy load when a vehicle has this type of proportioning valve.

Another effect of the concentration of weight on the front wheels in a FWD platform is that the front tires wear out faster than the rear tires. Following the factory-recommended tire rotation schedule is important to prevent uneven wear. Finally, the combination of the driveline with the wheels that steer the vehicle often creates a condition called "torque steer," which is discussed later in this chapter.

REAR-WHEEL DRIVE

On most **rear-wheel drive (RWD)** vehicles, the transmission and the engine are at the front of the chassis and transmit power through a driveshaft to a rear differential. Axle shafts transmit power from the differential to the rear wheels. The driveshaft usually has one or more U-joints or CV joints, while the axle shafts use driveline joints only if the vehicle has independent rear suspension (IRS). Most IRS systems use CV joints to link the axle shaft to the differential and wheel, but a few use U-joints. The front-engine, RWD powertrain layout is most common, but there are also several other less frequently used RWD layouts. These include rear-engine, mid-engine, and front-engine rear transaxle designs.

Front Engine

Until the mid-1980s nearly all domestic models used a front-engine RWD layout. Since then, FWD has become the common passenger car platform, but RWD is still popular on trucks. Most pickups, light trucks, and sports-utility vehicles use a RWD layout (Figure 11-6). Typically, 4WD versions are an adaptation of the base RWD platform.

A RWD layout provides some advantages in high-performance applications. With RWD, it is easy to mount the engine longitudinally and lower in the chassis, because it does not sit on top of or alongside a transaxle. This lower engine means that RWD allows a low hood profile and therefore a low coefficient of drag. Less drag raises top speed capability and increases fuel efficiency because there is less air resistance to vehicle movement. In addition, some manufacturers, such as BMW, install their engines at an angle for an even lower profile. Finally, the SLA suspension systems typically used with a RWD layout also contribute to a lower hood profile than the strut suspensions usually paired with a FWD layout, because the top mounting point of a SLA system is lower.

Another performance advantage to RWD is that a RWD vehicle tends to be more responsive than a FWD one. While the average driver may appreciate the characteristic resistance to changes in direction of FWD, race and enthusiast drivers prefer a RWD layout that *does* change direction quickly in response to steering input. The trick is not to let responsiveness become instability. However, this responsiveness can become a lia-

REAR-WHEEL DRIVE

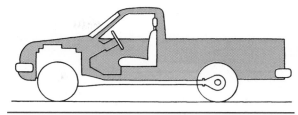

Figure 11-6. Trucks are still predominantly RWD, a layout that provides a sturdy rear axle, but suffers from a high proportion of unsprung weight at the rear when the truck is unloaded.

bility when roads are slippery, particularly if the vehicle has a solid rear axle. A solid drive axle not only puts more weight at the rear of the chassis, but also increases the unsprung weight in the rear suspension. As explained in Chapter 8 of this *Classroom Manual,* the tires lose traction more easily when there is a higher proportion of unsprung weight. Thus, the rear wheels are more likely to break loose on a slippery surface and the weight of the rear axle makes the rear end fishtail, or even causes a spinout and loss of control.

When the rear wheels lose traction on a turn, the condition is called "oversteer" because the vehicle turns more sharply than directed by steering wheel input (Figure 11-7). During an oversteer condition, the driver must keep the same pressure on the accelerator and steer into the skid. However, many drivers panic and do the opposite, which is why it is more common to lose control of a skidding RWD vehicle than a FWD one.

Finally, some performance engineers insist that combining the steering and the driving functions at the same pair of wheels is an inherently bad idea, and they point to problems such as torque steer and increased steering effort to prove their point.

Trucks have retained a RWD platform for a number of reasons. Although it is nice to have a small, compact rear suspension on models designed to transport passengers, the rear suspension of a truck needs to be strong in order to carry loads. A solid drive axle, which is commonly used at the rear of trucks, has the strength to support a heavy-duty suspension. When trucks and other heavy vehicles are unloaded, however, the rear-wheel traction is quite poor because there is less weight on the wheels. Tradition is another reason for RWD trucks. Truck buyers simply expect RWD, and therefore companies that sell trucks build them with that layout.

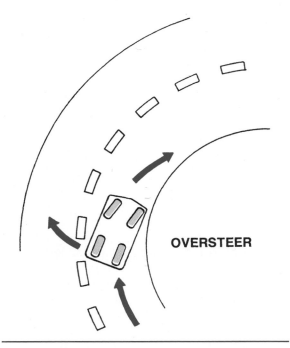

Figure 11-7. During an oversteer condition, the response to steering wheel input is increased, so the vehicle turns more sharply in the direction in which the wheels are aimed. As the rear end swings wide, the vehicle either fishtails or spins out of control, depending on the severity of the oversteer condition.

Rear Engine

On a rear-engine platform, the engine and transaxle are at the rear of the chassis, which places a great deal of weight on the rear wheels to provide good traction (Figure 11-8). During braking in a rear-engine vehicle, the vehicle weight shifts forward and is more evenly distributed between the axles, which provides more precise control. As with a front-engine FWD layout, the lack of a driveshaft in a rear-engine RWD model reduces overall weight. Unlike a FWD, power steering is not as necessary with a rear-engine RWD vehicle because the weight is not concentrated over the wheels that do the steering. In fact, the steering in a rear-engine car is very light, which makes the design prone to oversteer. Currently, the Porsche 911 is the only rear-engine model in production.

A drawback to the rear-engine layout is that it is difficult to cool the engine properly. To compensate for this lack of cooling, rear engines typically run on a richer air-fuel mixture, which lowers combustion temperature. As a result, a rear engine is less fuel-efficient and produces more harmful emissions than a similarly sized front engine. Difficulty in meeting emissions standards is one of the primary reasons that the Volkswagen Type I, the most familiar and successful rear-engine RWD vehicle, was taken out of production.

Mid-Engine

On a mid-engine platform the engine and transaxle are located just behind the front seats with most of their mass positioned ahead of the rear axle (Figure 11-9). For a driving enthusiast, this layout provides the best compromise between responsiveness and stability, which is why it is a popular race car design. However, a mid-engine layout is not a practical production alternative because most buyers want functional back seats and adequate trunk space, both of which are almost impossible to achieve with a mid-engine design. Like a rear-engine, a mid-engine is difficult to cool, and prone to overheat.

Due to design limitation, a mid-engine platform is generally found only on exotic and expensive performance-oriented models such as the Acura NSX, Ferrari 355, and Lamborghini Diablo. Two exceptions would be the Pontiac Fiero and Toyota MR2, which were both late-model, mass-produced vehicles built on a mid-engine platform.

Front-Engine Rear Transaxle

A front-engine rear transaxle platform is an unusual design generally found only on performance-oriented models. With this arrangement, a driveshaft or torque tube connects the engine at the front of the chassis to a rear transaxle. As with a FWD transaxle, the transmission and differential are combined in a single housing and drive axles connect the final drive gears to the wheels. Placing the transmission at the rear of the chassis improves handling characteristics by providing a more equal weight distribution between the front and rear axles.

In general, the front-engine rear transaxle layout has seen limited production. Porsche has used this layout since the mid-1970s for a number of models including the current 928 and 968. A front-engine and rear transaxle is also a feature of the 1998 Chevrolet Corvette.

Figure 11-8. The rear-engine of the Porsche 911 is positioned behind the transaxle, drive axles, and the rear wheels.

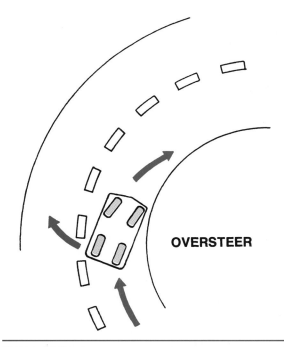

OVERSTEER

Figure 11-9. The powertrain, which includes the engine and transaxle, is positioned behind the seats and toward the front of the drive axles on a mid-engine layout.

FOUR-WHEEL DRIVE

On most **four-wheel drive (4WD)** trucks, the transmission transfers some of the engine torque to the rear differential and some to a transfer case.

The transfer case turns a driveshaft that transmits power to a front differential (Figure 11-10). The two differentials turn the axle shafts that drive the wheels. Virtually all 4WD vehicles are front-engine designs, but there are exceptions. The Porsche 911 Carrera 4 is a 4WD version of the rear-engine 911 (Figure 11-11). Another exception is the 4WD Toyota Previa van that has a mid-engine layout.

There are two basic methods of providing 4WD: **part-time four-wheel drive** and **full-time four-wheel drive** (Figure 11-12). Part-time 4WD systems allow the driver to manually switch from 2WD to 4WD as needed. A full-time 4WD system is always active and the driver never switches between 2WD and 4WD mode. However, this does not mean that torque is always transferred to all four wheels. Under normal conditions, the system operates in 2WD mode. If traction is lost and the tires begin to slip, electronic controls or a viscous clutch engage 4WD mode to increase traction.

The primary advantage of any 4WD system is an overall improvement in traction under difficult driving conditions, such as off-road; in dirt, sand, or other unstable surfaces; or on the road, when it is snow-covered, icy, or wet. In these situations, one or more drive wheels are likely to slip on the loose or slippery surface, but other drive wheels can move the vehicle if it has 4WD.

There are several drawbacks to 4WD that affect how the vehicle handles. Most of these result from the tendency of the two drive axles to rotate at slightly different speeds. In the situations for

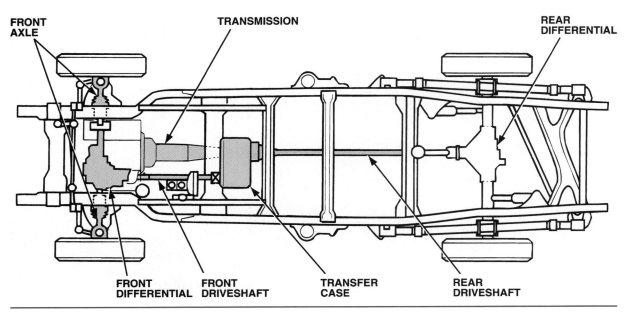

Figure 11-10.   On a typical 4WD truck, engine torque travels through the transmission to the rear driveshaft and a transfer case, which delivers some of the torque to the front axle through a separate driveshaft.

Figure 11-11.   The rear-engine Porsche 911 Carrera 4 uses an output shaft to transfer torque to a front differential to power the front wheels and provide 4WD.

which 4WD is designed—loose, slippery, or uneven surfaces—this tendency does not matter as much because the two axles have less effect on each other. However, when the vehicle is driven on a dry, smooth road surface, all four tires adhere strongly to the road and resist slipping. Therefore, to make up the speed difference, the transfer case gears begin to bind and the tires rub against the road, causing them to wear out quickly. That is why there must be some means— either driver-operated or mechanically or electronically controlled—to switch from 4WD to 2WD mode.

Weight in a 4WD vehicle is fairly evenly distributed because there is a differential or final drive at each axle. But the extra driveshafts, trans-

fer case, and differential add to overall weight. Therefore, 4WD systems do have a detrimental effect on fuel efficiency. In addition, the extra equipment adds to the initial cost of the vehicle, and the added complexity adds to the cost of certain repairs and maintenance as well. In short, 4WD is advantageous only if a driver uses it frequently enough to make the extra cost and fuel consumption worthwhile.

All-Wheel Drive

All-wheel drive (AWD) is similar to a full-time four-wheel drive system, but is typically used on a modified FWD platform with a transverse-mounted engine. An AWD driveline configuration usually combines the transfer case with the transaxle. An extra output shaft extends from the transaxle to a rear differential to drive the rear wheels (Figure 11-13). Both axles transfer torque to drive the vehicle at all times. A viscous coupling, center differential, or transfer clutch, which may be incorporated into the transaxle assembly or be a standalone unit, ensures that the front and rear axles can rotate at different speeds. A special clutch in the transfer case varies torque transfer between the axles of the *Shop Manual* depending upon the amount of available traction. See Chapter 11 for Driveline Component Service.

PART-TIME FOUR-WHEEL DRIVE

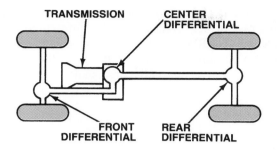

FULL-TIME COMPUTER-CONTROLLED FOUR-WHEEL DRIVE

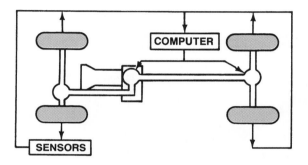

FULL-TIME FOUR-WHEEL DRIVE WITH VISCOUS CLUTCH

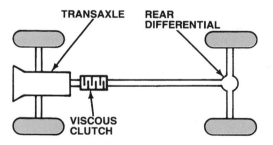

Figure 11-12. With a part-time 4WD system, the driver manually selects either the 2WD or 4WD mode. With a full-time 4WD system, a computer or a viscous clutch controls 4WD engagement based on driving conditions.

DRIVELINE JOINTS

An automotive driveline uses rotating shafts to transmit **torque**, or turning power, from one component to another. In a typical RWD layout, a driveshaft connects the transmission to the differential, and two axle shafts connect the differential to the wheel hubs. A FWD configuration eliminates the driveshaft, but retains the two axle shafts

between the differential gears and the wheel hubs. A 4WD system uses additional shafts to transfer torque to both axles and to propel all four wheels.

Driveline joints allow changes in angles between two rotating shafts. They connect driveshafts to a transmission or transfer case output shaft and a differential input shaft, and they link jointed axle shafts to stub shafts in the differential or final drive and in the wheel hub (Figure 11-14). There are two types of automotive driveline joints:

- Universal joint
- Constant velocity joints

In a front-to-rear driveshaft, these joints allow the front or rear suspension to compress and extend, moving the wheels at that suspension upward and downward in relation to the rest of the vehicle, without interfering with torque transfer from the transmission to the differential. Therefore, driveshafts are always jointed. Usually, the driveshaft has universal joints (U-joints), but some manufacturers use constant velocity (CV) joints.

Axle shafts may or may not use driveline joints, depending on whether the drive axle has an independent suspension. With an independent suspension, the axle shafts must be jointed to allow one wheel to travel vertically without affecting the other wheel. Most axle shafts use CV joints, but a few driven rear axle shafts have U-joints.

Universal Joints

A universal joint (U-joint) consists of two yokes—located at the ends of the two shafts it joins—and a crosspiece, which links the yokes (Figure 11-15). A U-joint is also known as a "Cardan joint," in reference to the inventor of the design. As mentioned earlier, U-joints are commonly used on driveshafts and used less frequently on axle shafts. The Chevrolet Corvette and some Jaguar models are two examples of vehicles that have axle shaft U-joints with an independent rear suspension.

Some U-joints use four yokes and two crosspieces. The proper name for this design is a **double-Cardan joint,** but it is also referred to as an "H-member" joint (Figure 11-16). An ordinary U-joint, with one crosspiece, can shudder and change the rate of shaft rotation speed if the angle between the shafts it connects becomes too sharp. The double-Cardan design alleviates this problem. The placement and type of U-joints used varies by application and by the overall length of the shaft required to span the distance between the transmission and differential. A vehicle with a short wheelbase may simply use two single-Cardan joints, one at either end of the driveshaft. A slightly longer driveshaft may connect to the transmission with a single-Cardan joint and to the differential with a double-Cardan joint. Long wheelbase models, such as trucks, often have a U-joint joining the front of the driveshaft to the transmission output shaft, a double-Cardan joint in the middle of the shaft, and another U-joint joining the rear of the driveshaft to the differential input shaft. Other RWD designs simply use three single-Cardan joints, one at the front, one in the middle, and one at the rear, on the driveshaft.

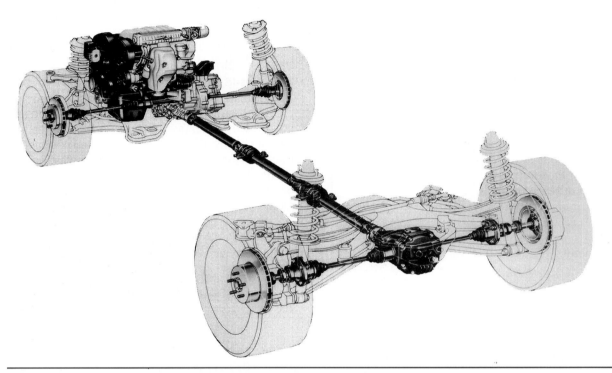

Figure 11-13. An additional gearset in the FWD transaxle powers the output shaft, which transfers torque to a rear differential to drive the rear wheels on this all-wheel drive system.

DRIVELINE JOINTS

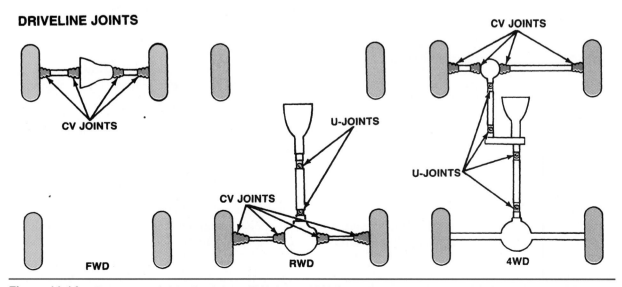

Figure 11-14. Two types of driveline joint—CV joint and U-joint—allow angular changes between rotating shafts. Typical locations for CV joints and U-joints are shown, but specific driveline layouts vary in detail.

When used on axle shafts, U-joints allow the wheels to travel vertically, but most applications do not provide a sufficient range of movement to allow the wheels to turn on a steering axis. However, many 4WD trucks do have U-joints on front axle shafts because the manufacturers do not consider steering "nibble" a problem in a truck. Another limitation of U-joints at the axle shaft is that they cannot plunge, or slide in and out, in relation to the differential the way that plunging CV joints can. Plunging joints are described later in this chapter. During vertical wheel travel, the arc of the axle shaft and the arc of the suspension components must be identical to avoid exerting opposing forces on the wheel. For this reason, a rear axle shaft with U-joints must be considered a part of the suspension (Figure 11-17). This complicates the task of designing the suspension and is one of the reasons most IRS drive axles use CV joints at the rear.

Constant Velocity Joints

Constant velocity (CV) joints are used on the front axle of FWD vehicles and on the front axle of 4WD vehicles with an independent front suspension (Figure 11-18). Most RWD and 4WD vehicles with an independent rear suspension also use CV joints on the rear axle as well (Figure 11-19). The name **constant velocity (CV) joint** derives from the fact that the device transmits torque between rotating shafts and allows the shafts to change angles without changing the rotational speed. As mentioned earlier, CV joints may be used on the driveshaft, but their most common application is on axle shafts.

In terms of their position on an axle shaft, there are two types of CV joint: inboard and outboard. The

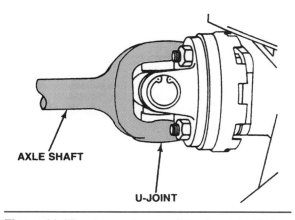

AXLE SHAFT

U-JOINT

Figure 11-17. Jaguar is one of the few manufacturers using U-joints on the rear axle shafts. Since U-joints do not plunge, the rear suspension must be designed to move in the same arc as the axle shaft.

DRIVESHAFT U-JOINT

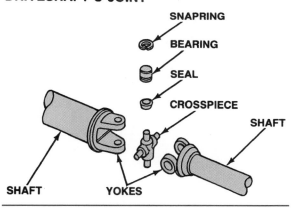

SNAPRING

BEARING

SEAL

CROSSPIECE

SHAFT

SHAFT

YOKES

Figure 11-15. The single-Cardan universal joint, commonly known as a U-joint, is often used on a driveshaft.

DOUBLE-CARDAN U-JOINT

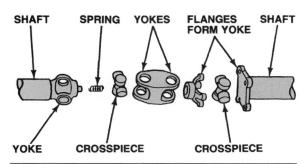

SHAFT   SPRING   YOKES   FLANGES FORM YOKE   SHAFT

YOKE   CROSSPIECE   CROSSPIECE

Figure 11-16. A double-Cardan U-joint contains two crosspieces to allow more flex and less shudder than a single-Cardan joint.

FRONT-WHEEL DRIVE

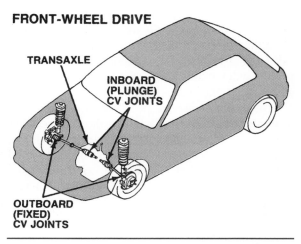

TRANSAXLE

INBOARD (PLUNGE) CV JOINTS

OUTBOARD (FIXED) CV JOINTS

Figure 11-18. Constant velocity joints link the front axle shafts to the wheels and to the final drive gears of the transaxle in FWD applications.

REAR-WHEEL DRIVE

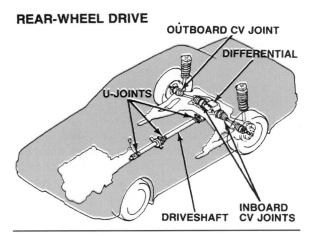

Figure 11-19. Universal joints handle the angle changes in most RWD driveshafts, while CV joints provide the flexibility and plunging action required of the rear axle shafts on an IRS system.

inboard constant velocity (CV) joint connects the inner end of the axle shaft to the differential side gears, while the **outboard constant velocity (CV) joint** attaches the outer end of the axle shaft to the stub shaft in the wheel hub.

On a front drive axle, the inboard joint is always a **plunging joint,** that is, the CV joint allows the axle shaft to move laterally, or in and out (Figure 11-20). This plunging action is necessary because the arc of the axle shaft travel and the arc of the suspension travel are not the same (Figure 11-21). A plunging joint is usually longer than a non-plunging one to provide room for this lateral motion (Figure 11-22). The outboard joint on a front axle does not plunge because it must be short enough to bend sharply along the steering axis of the wheels (Figure 11-23). A non-plunging CV joint is called a **fixed joint**.

When used on a rear axle, either the inboard or outboard CV joint, or both, may be plunging joints, since the wheels do not have to pivot sharply on a steering axis. Each of the outboard CV joints on a vehicle with an anti-lock brake system (ABS) usually has a toothed tone ring on its outside diameter. Together with the wheel speed sensor, the tone ring provides an electronic signal to the ABS control module that varies with wheel speed (Figure 11-24).

In addition to being plunging or fixed, CV joints can be further classified according to how they function and how they are constructed. Again, there are two basic types:

* Ball-and-cage
* Tripod

All ball-and-cage designs are variants of the original—Rzeppa—CV joint. Ball-and-cage variants include

CV JOINT PLUNGING ACTION

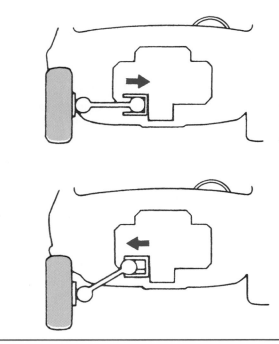

Figure 11-20. The plunging joint can move laterally, or slide in and out, as well as pivot vertically and horizontally to accommodate axle shaft movement.

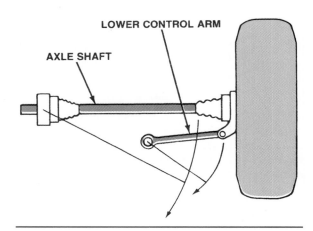

Figure 11-21. A plunging inner CV joint is necessary because the arc of the axle shaft travel and the arc of the suspension travel are not the same.

the Birfield, double-offset, and cross-groove designs. There are also variations of the basic tripod CV joint, such as the triplan joint developed by the GKN manufacturing company and the S-plan joint designed by General Motors.

Regardless of the design, all CV joints have an outer covering, or boot, to protect their inner working parts and ensure a reliable service life.

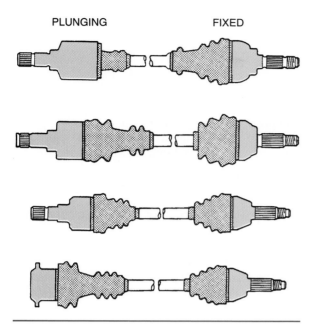

Figure 11-22. Typically, the plunging inner CV joint on an axle shaft has a longer housing than the fixed outer CV joint.

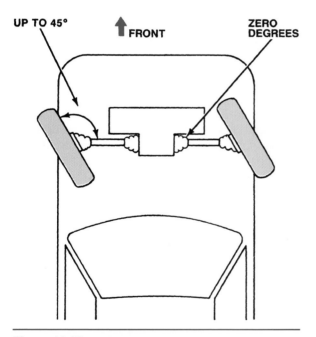

Figure 11-23. The outboard, or fixed, CV joint on the front axle must be able to pivot sharply while continuing to rotate as the wheels turn during cornering.

Constant Velocity Joint Boots

Constant velocity joints are protected by pleated boots, similar to those used on the inner tie rod ends of rack and pinion steering systems (Figure 11-25). These protective boots keep dirt and water from

Figure 11-24. A tone ring on the outboard CV joint and a wheel speed sensor provide a variable speed signal to the ABS control module.

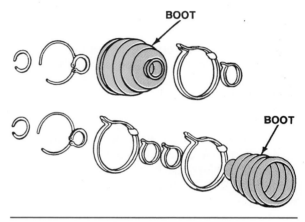

Figure 11-25. Constant velocity joint boots are rubber or plastic pleated covers that protect the joint from contamination and lubricant loss.

contaminating the grease in the CV joint, and also prevent the lubricant from leaking out of the joint. Clamps hold the boots in place.

Constant velocity boots may become torn, punctured, or loose, and very soon after that happens contamination or lack of lubrication can ruin the joint. Consequently, CV joint boots are designed to withstand as many potentially damaging substances and conditions as possible.

Most boots are made from either a neoprene synthetic rubber or a thermoplastic compound. Neoprene is a flexible material, while thermoplastic is stiff and must have folds designed into it to allow the boot to flex. Thermoplastic boots resist puncture damage well, but require special clamps to keep them in place. Neoprene and thermoplastic boots are usually tested for flexibility at temperatures ranging from 40°F to 250°F (5°C to 120°C).

Boots designed to resist extremely high temperatures, such as from a nearby catalytic converter,

A Brief History of CV Joints

The original fixed constant velocity (CV) joint—the Rzeppa joint—is named for Alfred Hans Rzeppa, who invented it in Detroit in the 1920s. Although an American invention, Rzeppa joints were not used by domestic manufacturers for many decades because in the United States—with ready supplies of cheap steel and gasoline—solid-rear-axle, RWD powertrains dominated the market well into the 1970s.

In Europe, where materials and gasoline were more expensive, small, economical, FWD models with independent front suspension became popular much earlier. In the 1950s, European manufacturers modified the Rzeppa design and invented other designs to suit their vehicles and to provide the plunging action that made front-wheel drive practical.

The plunging double-offset joint—a variation of the Rzeppa joint—was designed in England by the Hardy Spicer Company. A German company, Lobro—short for Lohr & Bromkamp—designed the plunging cross-groove joint. A French company, Glaenzer Spicer, departed completely from the Rzeppa design and invented the tripod joint, which can be constructed as either a plunging or fixed joint.

Today, the firms of Hardy Spicer and Glaenzer Spicer, and the Lobro Company, are all part of one organization, the GKN Group, which manufactures both original-equipment and replacement CV joints. Other CV joint manufacturers include ACI, Citroen, and SSG (Saginaw Design).

---

are called "high-temperature" boots and are either made of silicone or a substance called "Vamac." The flexibility of these boots is tested at temperatures up to 400°F (200°C). Silicone resists heat well, but is expensive and also porous. Porosity allows some of the lubricating grease to "weep" out of the boot under normal operating conditions. However, Vamac is not quite as heat-resistant as silicone, but it costs less and is not porous.

Boot materials are also selected for their ability to resist deterioration from ozone and other airborne contaminants, chemicals such as engine oil and coolant, and the grease used to lubricate CV joints. However, no one material can perfectly withstand all damage or deterioration, so design engineers choose the material best suited to a particular application.

Ball-and-Cage Constant Velocity Joints

A **ball-and-cage constant velocity (CV) joint** uses an inner race, six ball bearings, a ball cage, and an outer race (Figure 11-26). The inner and outer races have machined grooves in which the ball bearings ride. The balls are set 60 degrees apart around the circumference of the joint. The cage keeps the balls in alignment so that no matter what the angle between the shafts is, the balls always bisect—or cut in half—that angle. In effect, this characteristic halves the operating angle of the shafts, eliminating vibration and preventing

a change in the rate of rotation. There are four common types of ball-and-cage CV joint:

- Rzeppa
- Birfield
- Double-offset
- Cross-groove

Rzeppa and Birfield joints are fixed, while double-offset and cross-groove joints are plunging designs. All ball-and-cage CV joints are often referred to as "Rzeppa joints" in service publications, but that terminology is imprecise. True Rzeppa joints are the fixed type, and any plunging ball-and-cage joint must be either a double-offset or cross-groove joint.

Rzeppa Joint

The **Rzeppa joint,** which follows the basic ball-and-cage design just described, has a relatively short outer race, with straight grooves (Figure 11-27). A Rzeppa joint allows up to 50 degrees of movement between the axle shaft and the wheel stub shaft. This provides a slight margin of movement because the steering system typically requires no more than a 45-degree operating angle.

As the "windows" in the ball cage of a Rzeppa joint wear, excess play between the cage and balls causes a clicking sound during turning. Inboard joints do not make this sound because the turning of the front wheels does not affect their operation. The Rzeppa joint and the similar Birfield joint are found on the outboard front axle of most FWD vehicles.

BALL-AND-CAGE CV JOINT

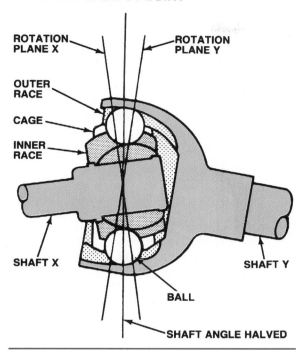

Figure 11-26. Each shaft rotates at a right angle to its plane of rotation and a ball-and-cage CV joint effectively divides the difference between the two angles in half.

RZEPPA CV JOINT

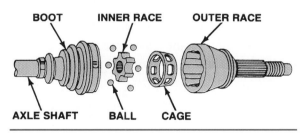

Figure 11-27. The Rzeppa joint is a fixed ball-and-cage design CV joint because the grooves in the outer race are not long enough to allow the joint to plunge.

Birfield Joint

Many manufacturers use a **Birfield joint** as the outboard CV joint of their FWD models (Figure 11-28). Although it carries a different brand name, the Birfield joint is a fixed, ball-and-cage CV joint very similar to the Rzeppa design. Birfield joints cannot be disassembled and must be replaced as a unit along with the shaft on which they are mounted.

Double-Offset Joint

Double-offset joints are a plunging design used at the inboard end of an axle shaft. The outer race

BIRFIELD CV JOINT

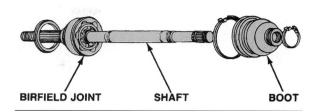

Figure 11-28. The Birfield joint is a fixed design similar to the Rzeppa joint, but the assembly is an integral part of the axle shaft and cannot be disassembled.

DOUBLE-OFFSET CV JOINT

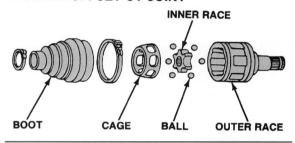

Figure 11-29. The double-offset joint resembles a Rzeppa joint with a longer outer race and grooves, which allows the joint to plunge.

and the ball grooves of a **double-offset joint** are longer than those in a Rzeppa joint (Figure 11-29). Longer grooves permit the balls to roll inward and outward inside the outer race, to allow the plunging action needed at the transaxle end of the axle shaft.

A double-offset joint provides 25 degrees of movement between the transaxle output shaft and the axle shaft and allows up to 2.38 inches (60 mm) of plunge. Double-offset joints are popular with a number of Japanese manufacturers, including Mazda, Mitsubishi, Nissan, and Subaru, and are also found on few domestic models.

Cross-Groove Joint

Cross-groove joints, which are shorter than double-offset joints, are a plunging design used at the inboard position. Rather than the long outer race with straight grooves of the double-offset joint, the **cross-groove joint** uses a shorter outer race with angled grooves (Figure 11-30). Angled grooves are machined into both the inner and outer races, so as the balls travel along the grooves the joint plunges (Figure 11-31).

A cross-groove joint provides up to 22 degrees of movement between the transaxle output shaft

CROSS-GROOVE CV JOINT

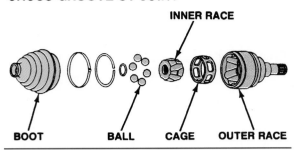

Figure 11-30. The cross-groove joint uses angled grooves on both the inner and outer races to provide plunging action.

CROSS-GROOVE

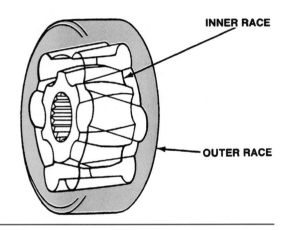

Figure 11-31. This cut-away drawing shows how the grooves in the two races relate to each other when the cross-groove joint is assembled.

and the axle shaft and allows 1.75 inches (45 mm) of plunge. Cross-groove joints are popular with German manufacturers and are also used on a few domestic and Japanese models. Porsche, BMW, and Mercedes all use cross-groove joints at both ends of the rear axle shafts on RWD models with independent rear-suspensions. Audi and Volkswagen use them on both front- and rear-axle applications. General Motors, Lexus, Mitsubishi, and Toyota also use cross-groove joints on certain models.

Tripod Constant Velocity Joints

A **tripod constant velocity (CV) joint,** which uses a three-legged "spider," or **tripod,** with a roller bearing on each of the three legs, can be ei-

ther a fixed or plunging type joint (Figure 11-32). The roller bearings ride on tracks, which are machined into the sides of a housing called the **tulip.** The shaft to which the tripod and rollers are attached can move at an angle to the shaft attached to the tulip (Figure 11-33). There are two tulip designs: open and closed. The roller tracks are openings in the sides of the tulip in an open design, while these tracks are machined grooves inside the tulip in a closed design. There are four common types of tripod joint:

- Fixed tripod
- Plunging
- Triplan
- S-plan

The term "tripod" has caused some confusion because it was adopted from the French language, so service literature may call these CV joints "tripot joints" or "tripode joints" although they are all the same design. Triplan and S-plan joints, however, are slightly different designs.

Fixed Tripod Joint

Like the Rzeppa joint, the **fixed tripod joint** is used at the outboard end of the axle shaft. In this design, splines at the center of the tripod connect it to one shaft, and a three-pronged steel retainer secures the tripod to the tulip. The tulip may be either integral to the second shaft or connected by splines (Figure 11-34). The three roller bearings, which assemble on the legs of the tripod, rotate in the tracks of the tulip to allow up to 45 degrees of movement between the axle shaft and the wheel stub shaft. Fixed tripod joints are rare, but are used by some French manufacturers, such as Renault.

Plunging Tripod Joint

A **plunging tripod joint** is used as an inboard joint. The tripod splines to the end of one shaft, but it is not fixed to the outer race (Figure 11-35). An open or closed tulip splines to, or is an integral part of, the second shaft. Because the tripod is not fixed, it can roll along the tracks in the tulip to provide plunge, as well as pivot to allow angle changes between the two shafts.

Plunging tripod joints typically allow up to 25 degrees of movement between the output shaft of the transaxle and the axle shaft and provide approximately 2.38 inches (60 mm) of plunge. Acura, DaimlerChrysler, Ford, General Motors, Honda, Saab, and Toyota use plunging tripods as the inboard joints on most of their FWD

TRIPOD CV JOINT

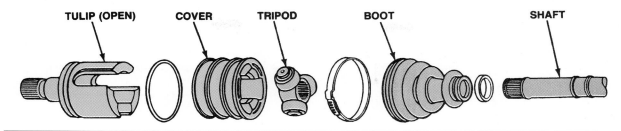

TULIP (OPEN)   COVER   TRIPOD   BOOT   SHAFT

Figure 11-32. A tripod CV joint uses a tripod with roller bearings and a tulip, rather than a ball-and-cage assembly, to allow directional changes and plunging action.

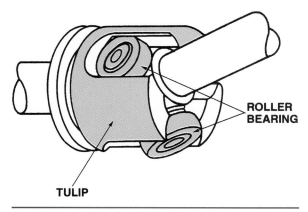

ROLLER BEARING

TULIP

Figure 11-33. The roller bearings on the tripod roll along the tracks in the tulip.

PLUNGING TRIPOD CV JOINT

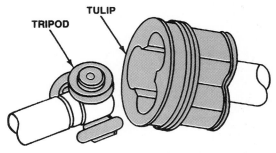

TRIPOD   TULIP

Figure 11-35. A plunging tripod joint has longer tracks on the tulip to allow the roller bearings to travel laterally and provide plunging action.

FIXED TRIPOD CV JOINT

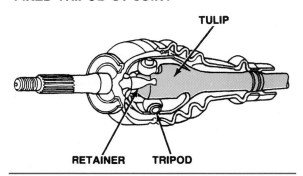

TULIP

RETAINER   TRIPOD

Figure 11-34. The fixed tripod joint uses a retainer to keep the tripod positioned in the tulip.

models. Mitsubishi and Nissan are among some other manufacturers using plunging tripods on a few of their models.

Triplan Joint
Ford developed the **triplan joint** to replace the plunging tripod joint for use on the Lincoln Con-

tinental. A triplan joint is basically the same as the tripod joint, but it uses needle bearings instead of roller bearings. The three needle bearing assemblies ride in tracks to keep the axle shafts from shuddering. The triplan joint cannot be disassembled for service (Figure 11-36).

S-Plan Joint
General Motors uses an **S-plan joint,** which is a variation of the tripod design, on some models. An S-plan joint is a plunging tripod in which the rollers are replaced with square blocks that contain needle bearings along the sides (Figure 11-37). The tripod legs can rotate in the center of the bearing block, and the bearings allow the tripod to move inward and outward in the tulip. Like the triplan joint, the S-plan joint is designed to reduce shudder.

Torque Steer

Some FWD vehicles with unequal-length axle shafts are prone to a steering problem known as **torque steer.** Torque steer causes the vehicle to

TRIPLAN JOINT

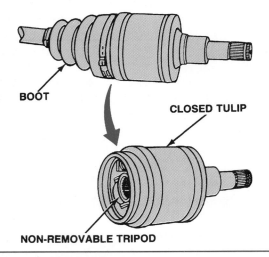

BOOT

CLOSED TULIP

NON-REMOVABLE TRIPOD

Figure 11-36. The Ford triplan joint, which cannot be disassembled for service, is similar to a plunging tripod joint, but it uses needle bearings to prevent shudder.

S-PLAN JOINT

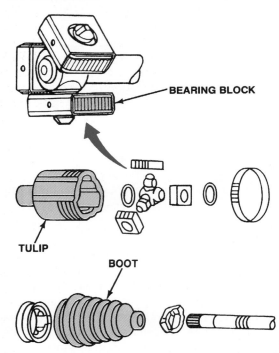

BEARING BLOCK

TULIP

BOOT

Figure 11-37. The General Motors S-plan joint is a plunging design that uses blocks containing needle bearings in place of roller bearings. This CV joint looks unusual, but the design effectively prevents shudder.

steer toward one side during hard acceleration at speed, and in the opposite direction during sudden deceleration (Figure 11-38). Typically, torque steer occurs when the driver suddenly accelerates or de-

TORQUE STEER

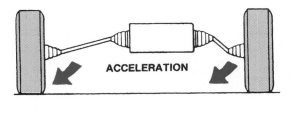

ACCELERATION

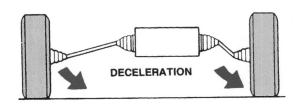

DECELERATION

Figure 11-38. Front-wheel drive systems using unequal-length axle shafts are prone to a condition called "torque steer" because of the unequal torque the axles transfer. The rest of the suspension, including the alignment geometry, is designed to compensate for this tendency.

celerates from a speed of about 40 mph (65 km/h) or above, and the condition disappears if the transmission is placed in neutral.

Automotive engineers agree that torque steer is related to the axle shafts and CV joints transferring torque to the wheels. Shifting into neutral eliminates the condition because it stops the transmission of torque through the axles. The tendency to steer in the opposite direction during deceleration results from engine braking applying an opposing force to the axle shafts and CV joints.

However, not all engineers agree on the exact cause of torque steer. Some blame the CV joint angles and some the difference in length between the axle shafts. Some engineers believe that either theory can be valid, depending on the particular vehicle.

CV Joint Angles

A popular theory is that torque steer is a result of unequal CV joint angles created by different axle shaft lengths. According to this theory, the angle of the axle shaft to the CV joint creates a twisting force at the outer CV joint. This twisting force tends to make the wheel toe in, but the steering linkage generally keeps the wheels straight.

As long as the angle of the axle shaft to the outer CV joint is the same on both sides of the vehicle, the resulting twisting forces are the same at each wheel and cancel each other out. With unequal-length axle shafts, the best way to keep the shaft-to-joint angles equal is to keep both shafts parallel to the ground. Some vehicles are designed so that the axle shafts are parallel to the ground when the vehicle is being driven at speed.

If one or both shafts are not parallel to the ground, the shaft-to-joint angles are not the same. Conditions that place the axle shafts at unequal angles include:

- Unequal ride height side-to-side
- Engine and transaxle installed at an incorrect angle
- Front sub-frame installed at an incorrect angle
- Worn engine or sub-frame mounts
- Heavy rear load that raises the front of the vehicle
- Collision damage

When the shaft-to-joint angles differ from side to side, the twisting forces developed at the outer CV joints differ as well. This creates a stronger tendency for one wheel to toe in. Sudden acceleration at high vehicle speeds increases the torque being transmitted through the axle shafts, the steering linkage gives in to the stronger torque applied to one steering arm, and the toed-in wheel leads the vehicle to produce a noticeable torque steer.

Axle Shaft Length

An alternate theory is that torque steer is a result of the longer axle shaft flexing slightly more than the shorter one, which makes the wheel on the longer shaft slower to respond to sudden changes of acceleration or deceleration. According to this theory, torque steer results either from unequal-length axle shafts or from unequal-length output shafts within the transaxle that connect the differential side gears to the inboard CV joints. If torque steer is a problem inherent to the use of different-length axle shafts, there is no cure for it except to avoid sudden acceleration or deceleration. However, many engineers believe that any difference in flexibility between the longer and shorter shafts would be so small that the effects would not be noticeable to the average driver.

Similar Conditions

It is important not to confuse torque steer with symptoms of "lead" or "pull." Lead and pull are terms used to describe conditions that are similar to torque steer, but occur at a constant speed—not just during acceleration or deceleration—and continue to occur with the transmission in neutral.

Lead, which causes the vehicle to steer toward one side if the driver lets go of the steering wheel, is a less noticeable condition than pull. **Pull** describes a driving condition in which the driver must actively steer toward one side in order to keep the vehicle moving straight ahead. Causes of lead or pull include:

- Unequal front tire inflation
- Unequal-diameter front tires
- Incorrect front wheel alignment
- Off-center belt on a belted radial front tire
- Dragging brake pads

Remember, these problems remain constant regardless of the amount of torque being transmitted through the axle shafts.

SUMMARY

Drive layout affects tire traction and ride quality, so it is related to the main functions of the suspension. There are four basic drive layouts: front-wheel drive (FWD), rear-wheel drive (RWD), four-wheel drive (4WD), and all-wheel drive (AWD). Most FWD vehicles have power steering, tend to understeer, and usually have good front-tire traction because of the concentration of weight above the front wheels. Rear-wheel drive vehicles usually tend to oversteer—especially when drivers try to correct skids—and often have poorer traction at the front tires than FWD models, but are generally more responsive and aerodynamic as well. Mid-engine and rear-engine vehicles have good handling characteristics, but design difficulties make these configurations rare. All RWD designs are free of torque steer. Four-wheel drive provides good overall traction on slippery or unstable driving surfaces, but designers must ensure that the axles do not drive at two different speeds on paved road surfaces. The term "all-wheel drive" is generally applied to a FWD model with a transverse engine and transaxle modified to provide full-time 4WD.

Two types of driveline connections, U-joints and CV joints, are used to allow angle changes in the driveshaft or axle shafts. Universal joints (U-joints) are most frequently used on the driveshafts of RWD and 4WD vehicles. A few models with IRS use U-joints on the rear axle shafts, and some 4WD trucks with independent front suspension use them on the front axle shafts as well. Constant velocity

(CV) joints are most often used on the front axle shafts of FWD or 4WD vehicles, but are sometimes found on rear axle shafts of RWD or 4WD vehicles with independent rear suspensions, and on the driveshafts of a few RWD vehicles. There are two basic types of CV joint construction: ball-and-cage and tripod. Rzeppa, double-offset, and cross-groove CV joints are ball-and-cage types. Tripod CV joints can be plunging tripod, fixed tripod, tri-plan, or S-plan joints.

Some FWD vehicles—usually those with un-equal-length axle shafts—exhibit a driving condition known as "torque steer." Torque steer causes the vehicle to steer to one side under sudden acceleration at speed, and to the opposite side under sudden deceleration. Some engineers believe that torque steer is a result of different axle shaft lengths, while others believe differing angles on the two outboard CV joints cause the condition.

Review Questions

For each of the following questions, choose the letter that represents the best possible answer.

1. Compared to a rear-wheel-drive vehicle, one with front-wheel drive tends to more readily:
   a. Fishtail
   b. Oversteer
   c. Understeer
   d. Spin

2. Technician A says that the weight distribution of a vehicle affects braking. Technician B says that the weight distribution of a vehicle affects steering. Who is correct?
   a. A only
   b. B only
   c. Both A and B
   d. Neither A nor B

3. A load-sensitive brake proportioning valve is generally used on:
   a. Front-wheel-drive vehicles
   b. Rear-wheel-drive vehicles
   c. Four-wheel-drive vehicles
   d. All-wheel-drive vehicles

4. Technician A says that a rear-engine vehicle is prone to understeer. Technician B says that a rear-engine design has inherent brake problems. Who is correct?
   a. A only
   b. B only
   c. Both A and B
   d. Neither A nor B

5. To allow the two drive axles of an all-wheel-drive vehicle to turn at slightly different speeds, all of the following devices may be used EXCEPT:
   a. Viscous coupling
   b. Center differential
   c. Transfer clutch
   d. Transfer case

6. The proper name for a universal joint, or U-joint, is:
   a. Cardan joint
   b. CV joint
   c. H-member
   d. Rzeppa joint

7. Technician A says that the inboard CV joint of a drive axle is always a non-plunging joint. Technician B says that a non-plunging joint is also called a fixed joint. Who is correct?
   a. A only
   b. B only
   c. Both A and B
   d. Neither A nor B

8. A double-Cardan U-joint uses:
   a. A ball and cage
   b. Two yokes and two crosspieces
   c. Four yokes and two crosspieces
   d. Four yokes and two tripods

9. Which of the following is NOT a ball-and-cage CV joint design?
   a. Birfield
   b. Double-offset
   c. Rzeppa
   d. S-plan

10. High-temperature CV-joint boots are often made of:
    a. Neoprene
    b. Silicone
    c. Teflon
    d. Thermoplastic

11. A ball-and-cage constant velocity joint uses:
    a. Three ball bearings set 120° apart
    b. Four ball bearings set 90° apart
    c. Six ball bearings set 60° apart
    d. Eight ball bearings set 45° apart

12. Which of the following is NOT a plunging type CV joint?
    a. Double-offset
    b. Cross-groove
    c. Birfield joint
    d. S-plan joint

13. How much movement between the axle shaft and the wheel stub shaft does a Rzeppa joint allow?
    a. 45 degrees
    b. 50 degrees
    c. 55 degrees
    d. 60 degrees

14. Cross-groove joints are typically used at the:
    a. Inboard position of the axle shaft
    b. Outboard position of the axle shaft
    c. Transmission end of the driveshaft
    d. Differential end of the driveshaft

15. Technician A says that a tripod CV joint is a non-plunging joint. Technician B says that a tripod CV joint is a fixed joint. Who is correct?
    a. A only
    b. B only
    c. Both A and B
    d. Neither A nor B

16. How much movement does a fixed tripod joint allow between the axle shaft and the stub shaft?
    a. 45 degrees
    b. 50 degrees
    c. 55 degrees
    d. 60 degrees

17. Which of the following joints uses needle bearings?
    a. Rzeppa
    b. Double-offset
    c. Triplan
    d. Tripod

18. Torque steer is thought to be caused by all of the following EXCEPT:
    a. Unequal-length axle shafts
    b. Unequal shaft-to-joint angles
    c. Unequal ride height
    d. Worn CV joint ball cages

19. Lead or pull can be caused by:
    a. Front tire over-inflation
    b. Unequal-diameter front tires
    c. Worn brake pads
    d. Unequal-length axle shafts

20. Which of the following CV joint designs is always a fixed joint?
    a. Rzeppa
    b. Double-offset
    c. Triplan
    d. Tripod

12

Electronically Controlled Suspension Systems

OBJECTIVES

Upon completion and review of this chapter, you will be able to:

- Describe the types of automotive computer input and output signals used in electronic suspension control systems.

- Identify the components of a typical electronically controlled automotive suspension system and explain system operation.

- Describe the function and basic operation of the electronic control modules (ECM/ECU) used in electronic suspension control systems.

- Define the components and explain the operation of the GM electronic suspension control (ESC) system.

- Describe the operation of air-adjustable shocks and automatic level control.

KEY TERMS

actuator	input
alternating current	lightemitting
amplitude	diode (LED)
analog	motor
armature	output
commutator	phototransistor
desiccant	pulse-width
digital	modulation
electromagnet	regenerative dryer
electronic control	switch
module (ECM)	transistor
frequency	trim height

INTRODUCTION

Since the mid-1980s, vehicle manufacturers have been introducing models with electronic suspension controls that provide a variable shock stiffness or spring rate. This chapter examines some of these systems, ranging from the simple load-leveling systems on some models to the more complex active suspension systems, such as those on the Infiniti Q45, the Lincoln Continental, and the Mitsubishi Galant.

The main advantage of electronic controls is that they let the suspension react differently to different conditions, so the driver does not have

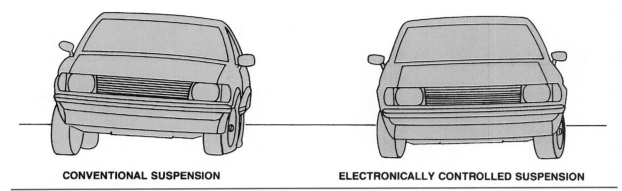

CONVENTIONAL SUSPENSION   **ELECTRONICALLY CONTROLLED SUSPENSION**

Figure 12-1. The electronically controlled suspension regulates body roll during cornering and other reactions to road forces better than a conventional system does.

to choose between performance and comfort. Instead, the system provides a firm suspension feel for fast cornering and quick acceleration and braking, along with a soft ride for cruising. Electronic suspensions can also counteract road forces and minimize their effect on the vehicle body (Figure 12-1).

Before studying specific electronic suspension systems, it is important to understand how the electronic components used for suspension controls function. This chapter begins with a brief discussion of electronic components, then continues with an analysis of the various electronic suspension systems in use. Electronic suspension systems can be grouped into five categories, according to the equipment they use:

• Electro magnetic speed dampening
• Rear load leveling
• Variable-rate air springs
• Variable shocks
• Air springs with variable shocks

Within each category, individual systems can have different purposes. Some respond to driver input, some to road conditions; others simply maintain a correct vehicle height. See Chapter 12 of the *Shop Manual* for Electronically Controlled Suspension Service.

ELECTRONIC SUSPENSION CONTROLS

All of the systems described in this chapter use some or all of the following electronic parts:

• Sensors
• Switches
• Electronic control modules
• Actuators

Sensors and switches provide **input** to the electronic control module (ECM), or system computer. The ECM, which may also be referred to as the electronic control unit (ECU), is a small computer that receives input in the form of electrical signals from the sensors and switches and provides **output** electrical signals to the system actuators (Figure 12-2). The electrical signal causes an **actuator** to perform some type of mechanical action.

Typical input signals on an electronically controlled suspension indicate ride height, vehicle speed, throttle position, or what switch position the driver has chosen by a console switch allowing a choice between certain suspension functions. The mechanical response of the actuator changes shock stiffness or spring rate.

Sensors

Sensors, which are the input devices that transmit signals to the electronic control module (ECM), monitor operating conditions and component functions. A sensor produces a variable electrical signal that describes the state, position, or operating status of the part it monitors. An electronically controlled suspension generally relies on sensors that provide signals indicating:

• Ride height
• Vehicle speed
• G-force
• Steering angle
• Throttle position

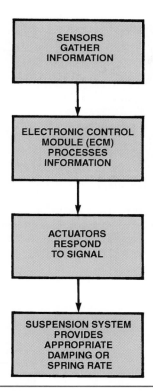

Figure 12-2. Input devices monitor conditions and provide information to the control module, which processes the information and operates the actuators to perform mechanical actions.

Most electronic suspensions use height and speed sensors and the use of other sensors varies according to how sophisticated the system is. Following is a brief discussion on the operation of frequently used sensors.

Ride Height Sensor

A height sensor senses the vertical relationship between a suspension component and the body. Its signal indicates to the ECM how high the frame or body is, or how compressed the suspension is. A number of sensor designs are used to determine ride height, but common practice is to use a photocell type of sensor. The ride height sensors Toyota uses in the Lexus LS400 with an electronically modulated air suspension serve as an example of this design (Figure 12-3).

On the Lexus and GM systems, four height sensors, one at each wheel, deliver an input signal to the ECM. All four sensors are similar and use a control link, lever, slotted disc, and four photo interrupters to transmit a signal. Each photo interrupter consists of a **lightemitting diode (LED)** and a **phototransistor,** which reacts to the LED.

HEIGHT SENSOR

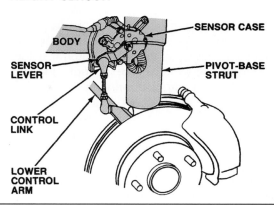

Figure 12-3. This Toyota height sensor, which bolts to the body and connects to the lower control arm through a control link and lever, produces an input signal voltage that varies with suspension compression and extension.

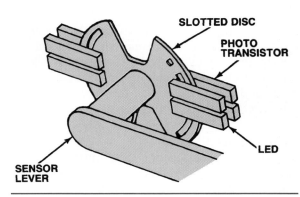

Figure 12-4. As suspension action moves the lever, it rotates the slotted disc to vary how much of the phototransistors are exposed to the LEDs, which varies the input signal. The ECM interprets the signals to determine body height.

The sensor assembly is enclosed in a flat, round case that fastens firmly to the vehicle body. The center of the disc is a pivot point for the disc and for the sensor lever. The outer end of the lever attaches to the control link, which is connected to the lower suspension control arm. Therefore, as the suspension compresses and extends, the control link moves the lever and rotates the slotted disc.

Inside the sensor, the LEDs and phototransistors are positioned opposite each other on each side of the slotted disc (Figure 12-4). When the system is activated, the ECM applies voltage to the LEDs, which causes them to illuminate. Light from an LED shining on the phototransistor causes the **transistor** to generate a voltage signal. Signals generated by the phototransistors are delivered to the ECM as an input that reflects ride height.

As suspension movement rotates the disc, the slots, or windows, on the disc either allow light from the LEDs to shine on the phototransistors or prevent it. The windows are positioned in such a manner that, in combination with the four LEDs and transistors, the sensor is capable of generating 16 different levels of voltage. This variable voltage, which is transmitted to the ECM as an input signal, directly corresponds to one of 16 possible positions of the suspension. This input signal tells the ECM the position of the suspension in relation to the body—in other words, the ride height, or how much the suspension is compressed. Whether the input voltage signal is increasing or decreasing allows the ECM to determine if the suspension is compressing or extending.

In addition, by processing the signals from the four height sensors, the ECM determines the relative position of the body to the suspension, or the attitude of the vehicle. Comparing front wheel input signals to those of the rear wheels determines the amount of pitch caused by forces of acceleration or deceleration. A side-to-side comparison allows the ECM to determine the amount of body roll generated by cornering force.

Vehicle Speed Sensor

The vehicle speed sensor (VSS) transmits a voltage signal to the ECM that varies in proportion to vehicle speed (Figure 12-5). Any of the following devices can produce a speed signal:

- Pickup coil
- Hall-effect switch
- Optical sensor
- Magnetic reed switch

The VSS generates a signal that increses in **frequency,** or how fast voltage switches, as vehicle speed increases. In addition to controlling the operation of the suspension, the VSS input signal may be used to operate the speedometer, control torque converter clutch operation, cut fuel supply during high speed operation to prevent engine damage, and as an input for electronic cruise control and antilock brake systems. Each of the four types of commonly used sensors is discussed in the following text.

Pickup Coil

Pickup coil sensors, which are also called variable reluctance sensors or permanent magnet generators, are voltage-generating sensors. The pickup

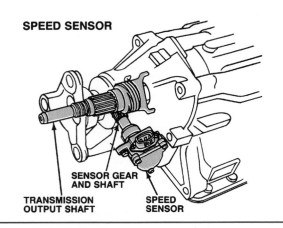

Figure 12-5. This Toyota vehicle speed sensor (VSS) is gear-driven by a transmission output shaft.

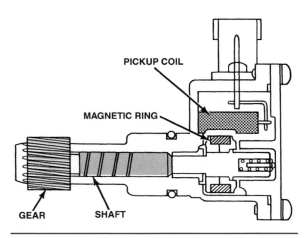

Figure 12-6. As the speedometer-driven gear shaft rotates, the rotating magnetic ring interacts with the pickup coil to create a speed signal voltage.

coil is wound around a permanent magnet and placed near a rotating trigger wheel. The trigger wheel is mounted on the transmission output shaft, differential ring gear, speedometer cable, or some other part whose rotational speed varies directly with vehicle speed (Figure 12-6). As the teeth on the trigger wheel pass by the magnet, the magnetic field expands and collapses to generate an **alternating current** (AC) voltage (Figure 12-7). As the speed of the vehicle increases, so does the frequency and **amplitude** of the output voltage signal.

Hall-Effect Switch

A Hall-effect switch generates a **digital** (on/off) signal that changes in response to the speed of a shutter wheel. The function and position of the shutter wheel is similar to that of the trigger wheel of a pickup coil sensor. A Hall-effect switch usually

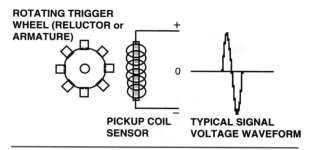

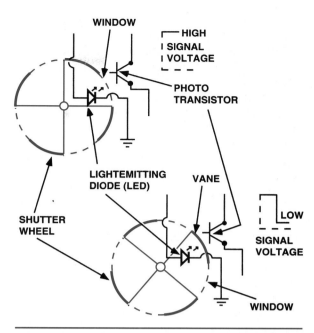

Figure 12-7. A pickup coil sensor uses the expanding and collapsing field of a permanent magnet coil created by a rotating trigger wheel to generate an alternating current signal.

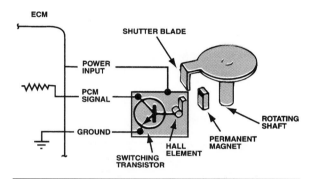

Figure 12-9. Windows rotating past an LED allow light to momentarily strike the phototransistor producing a speed-dependent, variable-frequency digital input signal.

Figure 12-8. A Hall-effect switch uses a semiconductor to generate a digital voltage signal whose frequency varies in proportion to rotational speed.

has three wires, unless it is a combination-type sensor, and all three circuits connect to the ECM. One circuit carries an input voltage to power up the element, a second circuit supplies a signal voltage, usually 5 or 12 volts, and the third wire provides a ground path. The ECM processes the signal voltage to determine vehicle speed (Figure 12-8). Current in the signal circuit is switched on and off to ground as the shutter blade rotates through the Hall-effect sensor. When a shutter vane is between the element and the magnet, the magnetic field is blocked and the signal voltage will be high. When the shutter blade is not between the element and the magnet, the magnetic field is generated across the element causing the signal voltage to go low. How quickly the signal voltage switches from high to low varies directly with shutter wheel rotation speed, which directly corresponds to vehicle speed.

Optical Sensor

The Lexus ride height sensor described earlier, which uses an LED and a phototransistor to generate a voltage signal, is an optical sensor. However, the sensor operation is slightly different

when used as a speed sensor. On a speed sensor, the disc generally has more than four windows and rotates at a speed that corresponds to vehicle speed. As the windows pass between the LED and the phototransistor, the voltage level switches from low to high producing a digital (on/off) voltage signal that is transmitted to the ECM. The speed of the signal switching directly corresponds to the speed of the vehicle (Figure 12-9).

Reed Switch

A reed switch uses a rotating permanent magnet with multiple poles to cycle a thin strip of metal, or a "reed," to generate a voltage signal. The reed is a small flexible piece of magnetically attractive sheet metal positioned between two contact points. The ECM applies a reference voltage to one contact point, the other contact provides a ground path, and the reed supplies the input voltage signal to the ECM (Figure 12-10). Alternating positive and negative poles of the magnet attract or repel the reed as they rotate past. This switches the reed between the two contact points sending a digital signal to the computer.

Most Toyota models have a reed switch built into the speedometer that functions as a vehicle speed sensor. The sensor produces a signal voltage that increases in frequency in proportion to the speed of the permanent magnet.

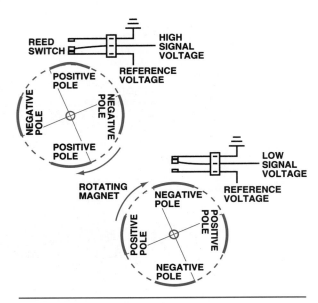

Figure 12-10. Changing magnetic polarity cycles a reed switch between contact points to produce a signal voltage.

G-Force Sensor

As explained in Chapter 3 of this *Classroom Manual,* the force of gravity that resists changes in speed or direction is known as G-force. In a moving vehicle, G-force pushes back during acceleration, forward during braking, and to one side or the other during cornering. Most electronic suspension systems derive acceleration and braking force information from sensors that monitor throttle position or brake pedal position. Some systems use an additional G-force sensor to measure how the vehicle is reacting to the force of gravity under cornering conditions.

Unlike most sensors, which generate a signal based on a mechanical action, a G-force sensor detects only force. To be effective, a G-force sensor must react only to that force and not be influenced by the mechanical movement of any part of the vehicle. As a result, a G-force sensor is a rather sophisticated device. The lateral G-sensor of the Mitsubishi Active Electronic Control Suspension (A-ECS) system serves as an example of this type of sensor. The sensor assembles into a case that mounts on the frame at the front of the vehicle (Figure 12-11).

The Mitsubishi lateral G-sensor is an electromagnetic device consisting of a movable core floating in silicone oil, a primary coil, and two secondary coils (Figure 12-12). The ECM applies a reference voltage to the primary coil in order to create a magnetic field around the core. The magnetic field of the primary coil generates voltage in

G-FORCE SENSOR

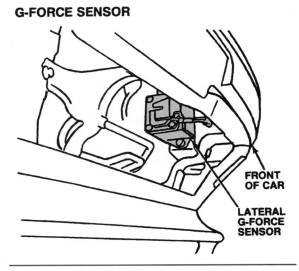

Figure 12-11. The Mitsubishi A-ECS lateral G-force sensor assembly mounts on a frame side member at the front of the chassis.

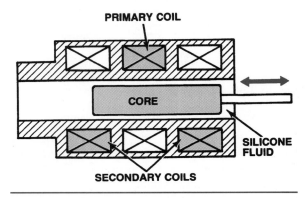

Figure 12-12. The core, which is located between the primary and secondary coils, floats in silicone fluid, so G-force can push it in either direction.

one or both of the secondary coils through induction (Figure 12-13). Voltage created in the secondary coils provides the input signal to the ECM, and signal strength depends upon the position of the core in relation to the coils.

The core can react to G-force and move toward either side—toward the primary coil or secondary coil—of the assembly because it floats in the silicone fluid. Secondary coil voltage varies as the distance between the core and coils changes. The ECM measures the secondary coil voltages to determine core position, and this indicates G-force strength and in what direction it is acting (Figure 12-14).

Steering Angle Sensor

The steering angle sensor is used to determine how far, and in what direction the steering wheel

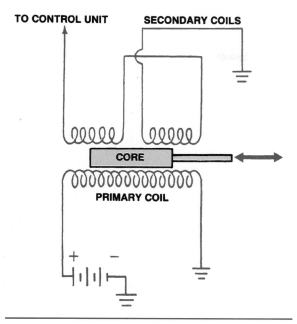

Figure 12-13. The position of the G-force sensor core determines how much voltage the secondary coils generate, which provides an input signal to the ECM.

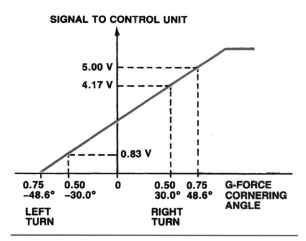

Figure 12-14. The signal voltage from the lateral G-force sensor allows the ECM to calculate how sharply and in what direction the vehicle is turning.

is turned. This sensor generally assembles onto the steering column and is often used by the variable-assist power steering system as well. Although a number of sensor designs are used, most are optical sensors that operate similarly to the ride height sensor described previously. The steering angle sensor of the Mitsubishi A-ECS system serves as an example.

Mitsubishi locates the steering angle sensor at the top of the steering column, just behind the steering wheel (Figure 12-15). The slotted disc fits onto and rotates with the steering shaft. An

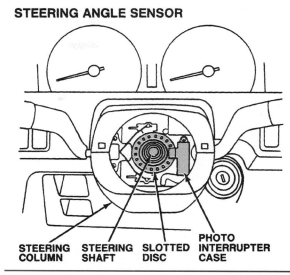

Figure 12-15. This Mitsubishi steering angle sensor, which assembles inside the steering column, uses a rotating slotted disc and a photo interrupter to generate input signals based on turning angle and speed.

opening on the photo interrupter case, which contains two LEDs and two phototransistors, fits over the disc and attaches to the column in a fixed position. As the steering wheel turns, the windows of the disc pass through the photo interrupter generating voltage in the phototransistors, which is transmitted to the ECM as an input signal. Each phototransistor transmits a unique signal pattern so the ECM can recognize which direction the steering wheel is turning. How quickly the signal switches between high and low voltage determines how fast the steering wheel is turning.

Throttle Position Sensor

The throttle position (TP) sensor is a potentiometer that transmits a voltage signal in proportion to the throttle opening. The TP sensor is generally part of the engine management system, but its signal is shared by a number of onboard computers. The ECM processes the TP sensor signal to determine the rate of acceleration. A potentiometer is simply a variable resistor that senses motion or position and transmits an **analog** voltage signal. A potentiometer has three terminals, or circuits:

- Reference voltage
- Signal voltage
- Ground

The computer applies a reference voltage, usually 5 volts, to the terminal at one end of the resistor, and the terminal at the opposite end of the resistor

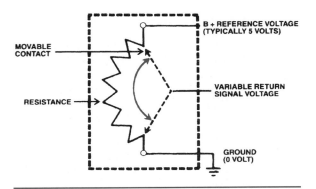

Figure 12-16. The throttle position (TP) sensor is a potentiometer that transmits a variable voltage signal based on the position of a movable wiper on a variable resistor.

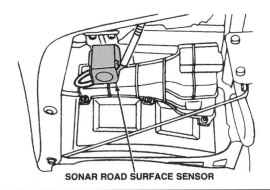

Figure 12-17. The Nissan Sonar System uses a road surface sensor to bounce supersonic waves off of the road ahead of the wheels, then processes the signal echo to determine pavement condition.

provides a ground path. The third terminal, which is located between the other two, attaches to a movable wiper that sweeps back and forth across the resistor. This is the terminal that sends the variable signal voltage back to the ECM (Figure 12-16). The wiper mechanically attaches to the device being sensed, in this case, the throttle plates.

Signal voltage from a potentiometer will be high or low, depending on whether the movable wiper is near the supply or ground end of the resistor. On most TP sensors signal voltage is low at closed throttle, approximately 0.5 to 1.1 volts. As the throttle opens, voltage gradually increases to approximately 4.75 volts at the wide-open position.

Miscellaneous Sensors

Some systems use additional sensors to provide further information to the ECM. For example, the Nissan Maxima and Infiniti M30 have a sonar system used to determine road surface conditions. This road surface sensor directs a supersonic wave against the road surface ahead of the vehicle and reads the signals that bounce back to sense bumps or dips before reaching them (Figure 12-17). Other systems use sensors to monitor pneumatic or hydraulic pressure in the supply circuits to the shocks or air springs.

Switches

A **switch** is like a sensor, only simpler. Instead of sending a variable voltage signal, it sends either a constant voltage signal or no signal at all. A basic electrical switch has two positions, open and closed (Figure 12-18). When the switch is open, current cannot pass through it. When it is closed, it provides a path for current. Some applications

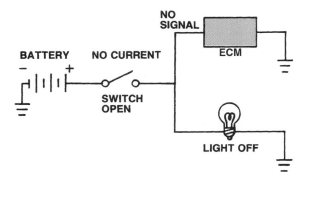

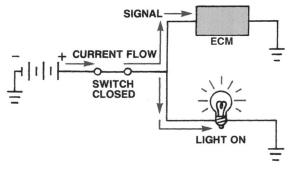

Figure 12-18. A switch, such as this brake light switch, is a simple device that opens or closes to allow or prevent current in a circuit or circuits.

use a three-position switch that has an open position and two closed positions. Each of the closed positions completes a different circuit. Common electronic suspension control switches include:

- Suspension control setting
- Brake light
- Door position
- Gear selector lever position

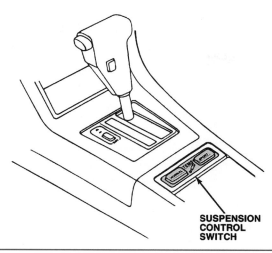

Figure 12-19. A switch typically allows the driver to select between "normal" and "sport" suspension operating modes.

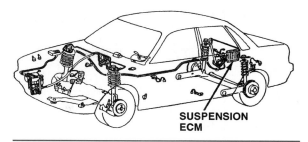

Figure 12-20. The ECM for the electronic suspension system is often mounted at the back of the vehicle and accessed through the trunk.

The suspension control setting switch allows the driver to choose a certain operating mode for the suspension (Figure 12-19). Typically, the switch offers a choice of a "normal-sport" or "soft-medium-firm" setting. In general, a "normal" or "soft" setting allows the ECM to automatically vary suspension operation between soft and firm, depending on road and driving conditions, while a "sport" or "firm" setting makes the ECM keep the suspension firm at all times. Some models use a three-position switch that gives the driver an additional choice of suspension setting.

A brake light switch closes when the driver steps on the brake pedal. The closed switch allows current through the brake light circuit to light the brake lamp bulbs. When the suspension control unit is part of the brake light circuit, it receives current whenever the driver applies the brakes. This signal affects how the ECM program works, and influences the signals it sends to the actuators.

Door position and gear selector lever position switches perform an override function to temporarily disable the suspension control system under certain conditions, for example, when a door is open or the transmission is in park or neutral. Be aware that a malfunction on any of these switch circuits can render the suspension control system inoperative.

Electronic Control Module

An **electronic control module (ECM),** also called an electronic control unit (ECU), is a small onboard computer that uses a microprocessor to interpret input signals and create output signals. Generally, each electronic control system uses its own computer, or ECM. That is, there is one ECM for the electronic suspension, another for electronically variable power steering—as discussed in Chapter 6 of this *Classroom Manual*—and still others for engine functions, fuel system operation, and passenger-compartment climate control.

Service manuals provide information on where each ECM is located, as well as where to hook up diagnostic tools and how to retrieve diagnostic trouble code (DTC) information (Figure 12-20). When the ECM receives erratic readings or feedback from sensors and actuators, it performs a self-diagnostic routine to determine what part or parts of the system are malfunctioning. Once it makes that determination, it stores the information in the form of a DTC, which can be retrieved with the right diagnostic tools. If the ECM itself malfunctions, it cannot be repaired and must be replaced.

Actuators

Each actuator in an electronically controlled suspension system receives output signals from the ECM and responds to these signals, or commands, by performing a mechanical action. Actuators are usually inductive devices, which operate on an electromagnetic field, and most are either a motor or some type of solenoid.

Electromagnets

A simple **electromagnet** consists of a soft iron core with a coil of wire, usually copper, wrapped around it (Figure 12-21). Electrical current traveling through the coiled wire creates a magnetic field around the core. All magnets are polarized; that is, they have a north, or positive, and a south,

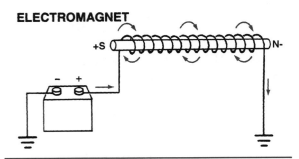

Figure 12-21. As current passes through a coil wrapped around an iron core, it creates a magnetic field around the core.

Figure 12-22. When magnets are near each other, like poles repel and opposite poles attract.

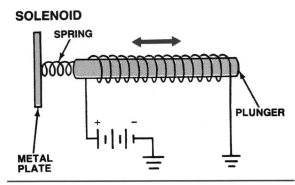

Figure 12-23. When current magnatizes the plunger in a solenoid, the magnetic field moves the plunger against spring force to open the valve. With no current, the spring pushes the plunger back to its original position to close the valve.

or negative, pole. When the opposite poles of two magnets are placed near each other—positive-to-negative—the magnets attract each other. Place the same poles together—positive-to-positive or negative-to-negative—and the magnets repel each other (Figure 12-22). Magnets also attract and are attracted to certain types of metals, especially iron and steel.

When an electromagnet has more than one coil, the stronger primary coil can induce voltage into the weaker secondary coil. This inductive transfer occurs even though there is no physical connection between the two coils. This is the principle by which the Mitsubishi lateral G-force sensor discussed earlier operates.

A number of automotive actuators are electromagnetic solenoids, but other types of electromagnetic devices are used in automotive applications as well. In fact, any motor or relay, as well as alternators and generators, use an electromagnetic field to perform their tasks.

Solenoids

In a solenoid, the core of the electromagnet also acts as a plunger to open and close a passage or to move a linkage. Solenoids are cylindrically shaped with a metal plate at one end and open at the other end to allow the plunger to move in and out. The electromagnetic coils are placed along the sides of the cylinder. A preload spring forces the plunger toward one end of the device when the solenoid is deenergized, or there is no current in the coil.

When the solenoid is energized, current passes through the coil and magnetizes the core. The magnetized core is attracted to the metal plate and the strength of the magnetic field overcomes spring force to pull the plunger inward (Figure 12-23). When the electrical current switches

off, the solenoid deenergizes and spring force returns the plunger to its rest position. In this way, a solenoid translates an electrical signal into a mechanical action.

The airflow control valve of the Mitsubishi A-ECS system provides an example of a solenoid used in an electronically controlled suspension (Figure 12-24). As the solenoid plunger extends and retracts, it opens and closes air passages between the system air-pressure tank and the air springs. The position of the plunger determines whether the springs receive more pressure, or whether pressure bleeds out of them. Increasing the pressure in the air springs lifts the body higher, and decreasing the pressure by bleeding air from the springs lowers the body.

Solenoids are digital devices. That is, they can be in only one of two states—either on or off. However, the ECM can vary the amount a solenoid opens by manipulating the output signal to the coil. If the signal is rapidly switched on and off, spring and magnetic forces do not have enough time to react and effectively move the plunger between the signal changes. This signal manipulation, known as **pulse-width modulation,** is often used to vary the effect of a solenoid in automotive applications. Pulse width is the amount of time the current is on compared to the amount of time it is off.

SOLENOID OFF

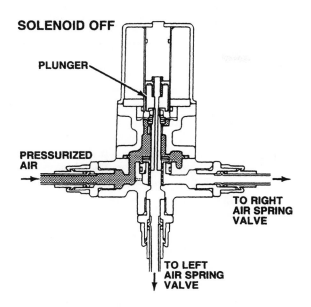

SOLENOID ON

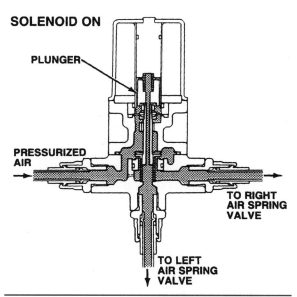

Figure 12-24. This air supply solenoid blocks pressurized air from the air spring valves when off. The plunger pulls upward to allow airflow to the air spring valves when the solenoid is energized.

Motors

If a current-carrying conductor is placed in a magnetic field, it tends to move from the stronger field area to the weaker field area. A **motor** uses this principle to convert electrical energy into mechanical movement. Electrical current is directed through the field coils on the motor frame to create a magnetic field within the frame. By applying an electrical current to the **armature,** which is in-

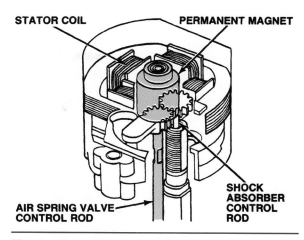

Figure 12-25. This Lexus actuator motor uses a permanent magnet and four stator coils to drive the air spring valve control rod directly, and the shock absorber control rod through a gear set.

side the motor frame, the armature rotates from a strong field area to a weaker field area. After a half-rotation, the **commutator** reverses the current traveling through the armature, causing it to travel another half-rotation. Armature movement can in turn move another part, such as a gear, pulley, or shaft, attached to it.

Actuator Motors

A number of motor designs are used in various applications on an electronic suspension control system to perform mechanical actions. The suspension control actuator of the Lexus LS400 serves as an example in the following discussion.

Located at the top mount of the air spring variable shock assembly of each wheel, the suspension control actuator moves a control rod that regulates air pressure to the spring, which determines ride height. The actuator is an electromagnetic device consisting of four stator coils and a "permanent magnet" core (Figure 12-25). Permanent magnet means the device is simply a magnet, not an electromagnet, so it is active and generates a magnetic field at all times. Electrical current is not needed to polarize a permanent magnet because the field is always present.

The ECM applies current to two stator coils at a time to create opposing magnetic fields around the core, which causes the core to rotate into a new position. Which coils are energized determines how far and in which direction the core rotates (Figure 12-26). By switching current from one pair of coils to the other, the ECM moves the

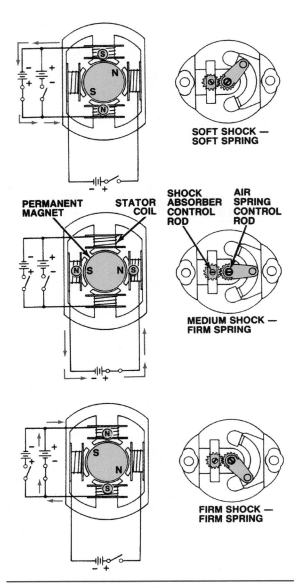

SOFT SHOCK — SOFT SPRING

PERMANENT MAGNET   STATOR COIL   SHOCK ABSORBER CONTROL ROD   AIR SPRING CONTROL ROD

MEDIUM SHOCK — FIRM SPRING

FIRM SHOCK — FIRM SPRING

Figure 12-26. The stator coils of the Lexus actuator are energized in three different ways, which moves the permanent magnet core into one of three positions, to position the shock absorber and air spring control rods.

core into a new position, and a third position is available by reversing the polarity of the coils.

A gear at the base of the permanent magnet connects to a rod that operates the air valve to the air spring. The gear also drives another gear, which operates the control rod of the variable shock absorber. Thus, the three positions of the suspension control actuator motor provide three shock absorber stiffness settings in addition to a variable air spring.

GM Electronic Suspension Control Description and Operation

The electronic suspension control (ESC) system (Figure 12-27), also known as the magneto-rheological real time damping (MRRTD) system, independently controls the fluid viscosity in each of the four shock absorbers in order to control the vehicle ride characteristics. The ESC system is capable of making these changes within milliseconds. GM uses this system on many of its luxury vehicles, including the Chevrolet Corvette and the Cadillac XLR. The ESC system consists of the following major components:

- ESC module (3)
- Four dampers contained in the two front struts (5 and 6) and the two rear shock absorbers (1 and 9)
- Four position sensors (2, 4, 7, and 8)
- ALC air compressor module (10)
- ELC relay (not shown)

The ESC system with rear automatic level control (ALC) controls damping forces in the front struts and rear shock absorbers in response to various road and driving conditions. The rear ALC portion of the system maintains a proper vehicle trim height under various vehicle load conditions. For more information on the ALC, refer to Automatic Level Control Description and Operation in Automatic Level Control. The ESC module receives the following inputs: wheel-to-body position, vehicle speed, and lift/dive. The ESC module evaluates these inputs and controls actuators in each of the dampers independently to provide varied levels of suspension control. The ESC controls the damping mode selection according to the following factors:

- The vehicle speed
- The chassis pitch input
- The steering position
- The body-to-wheel displacement

Electronic Suspension Control (ESC) Module

The ESC module (Figure 12-28), controls how firm or soft each shock or strut should be to provide the best ride. The ESC module is also used to control the vehicle's rear height. The ESC module is usually located on the right side of the rear seat

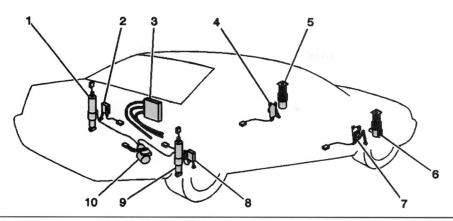

Figure 12-27. This diagram shows an electronic suspension control (ESC) system. (Courtesy of General Motors Corporation)

(1) ELECTRONIC SUSPENSION CONTROL (ESC) MODULE CONNECTOR C1
(2) ELECTRONIC SUSPENSION CONTROL (ESC) MODULE CONNECTOR C3
(3) ELECTRONIC SUSPENSION CONTROL (ESC) MODULE CONNECTOR C2
(4) ELECTRONIC SUSPENSION CONTROL (ESC) MODULE

Figure 12-28. This diagram shows the electronic suspension control (ESC) module. (Courtesy of General Motors Corporation)

back and is accessed through the trunk on four-door models. In the Corvette and XLR, however, it is located in the LH rear storage, as shown in (Figure 12-29).

The ESC module (Figure 12-29), provides electronic control logic and output drive for each shock absorber. The ESC module makes decisions due to road and driving conditions based on various inputs. The ESC module receives input information from

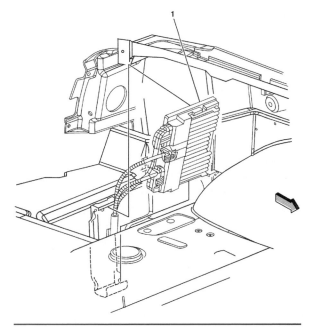

Figure 12-29. This ESC module location is found in a GM "Y" car. (Courtesy of General Motors Corporation)

sensors that are directly connected to the ESC module or from other systems through the serial data line. The ESC module uses these inputs in order to independently control the shock absorbers at each corner.

Electronic Suspension Control Position Sensors

The ESC position sensors (Figure 12-30) provide the ESC module with the body-to-wheel displacement input. These position sensors are 0- to-5 volt DC output devices that are used to measure

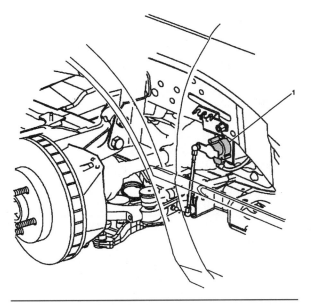

Figure 12-30. This diagram shows an ESC right front position sensor. (Courtesy of General Motors Corporation)

wheel-to-body movement/position. There are four position sensors on the vehicle, one per corner. The ESC module uses this and other inputs in order to control the stiffness of the shock absorber. If any body or wheel motion is detected, the ESC module will determine how soft or firm each shock absorber should be to provide the best ride. The ESC position sensors are mounted at each corner of the vehicle between the control arm and the body.

Electronic Suspension Control Shock Absorber or Strut

The ESC shock absorbers or dampers (Figure 12-31) are monotube type, which provide damping by increasing magnetic flux to magnetic particles to resist suspension movement. The ESC shock absorber has the capability of providing multiple modes or values of damping forces, in both compression and rebound direction. The damping forces are achieved by increasing or decreasing the magnetic flux to shock absorbers. The four suspension dampers, two front struts, and two rear shock absorbers each contain an integral actuator that is controlled by the ESC module. The actuator provides a wide range of damping forces between soft and firm levels. Damping is controlled by the amount of current supplied to the actuator via pulse width modulation. The front ESC actuator connector is located at the top of the shock absorber. The rear ESC actuator connector is at the top of the shock absorber. The rear shock absorbers have jumper harnesses for ease of mainte-

nance. Figure 12-32 shows the electrical connection to the damper.

Electronic Suspension Control Operation

The ESC system (Figure 12-33) uses the information from other systems in order to execute certain functions. The ESC system does not have a malfunction indicator lamp, but instead uses the instrument panel cluster (IPC) or driver information center (DIC) for the display functions. When the ESC system detects a malfunction that sets a diagnostic trouble code (DTC), the ESC system sends a message on the serial data line directly or through the PCM to the IPC or DIC, which will display one of the following messages:

- SHOCKS INOPERATIVE
- SERVICE RIDE CONTROL
- SERVICE SUSPENSION SYS
- SPEED LIMITED TO XXX
- MAXIMUM SPEED 80 mph (129 km/h)

The SHOCKS INOPERATIVE message will only be displayed if the ESC system detects a malfunction that sets a DTC and causes the ESC system to disable all four shock absorbers. The ESC system will send a message on the serial data line to the IPC to display this message. The SERVICE RIDE CONTROL message will only be displayed if the ESC system detects any malfunction that sets a DTC. The ESC system will send a message on the serial data line to the IPC to display this message.

The MAXIMUM SPEED message will only be displayed if the ESC system detects a malfunction that sets a DTC and causes the ESC system to disable all four shock absorbers. The ESC system will send a message on the serial data line to the PCM indicating that all four shock absorbers were disabled. The PCM then sends a message to the IPC to display this message.

The ESC module has the ability to store diagnostic trouble codes (DTCs) as current or history codes. Most ESC system malfunctions will display a message in the IPC and set a DTC. The message will remain ON until the RESET button is pressed on the driver information center (DIC). As long as the DTC is current, the message will be displayed after every ignition cycle and the RESET button must be pressed to bypass the message.

The ESC system uses an ignition cycling diagnostic approach in order to reduce the occurrence of false or intermittent DTCs that do not affect the functionality of the ESC system. This allows for the fail-soft actions to be taken whenever a malfunction condition is current, but requires the malfunction to be current for a certain number of

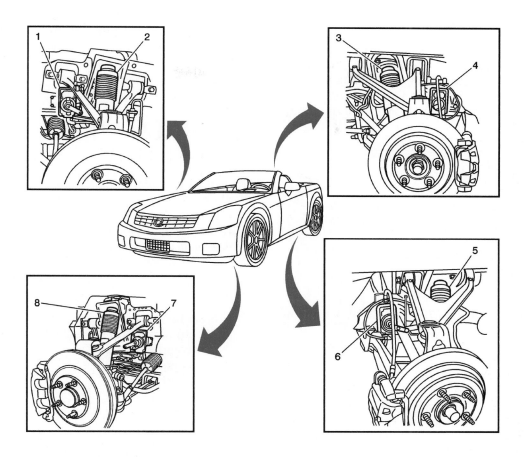

(1) SUSPENSION POSITION SENSOR - RIGHT FRONT
(2) SUSPENSION DAMPER - RIGHT FRONT
(3) SUSPENSION DAMPER - RIGHT REAR
(4) SUSPENSION POSITION SENSOR - RIGHT REAR
(5) SUSPENSION DAMPER - LEFT REAR
(6) SUSPENSION POSITION SENSOR - LEFT REAR
(7) SUSPENSION POSITION SENSOR - LEFT FRONT
(8) SUSPENSION DAMPER - LEFT FRONT

Figure 12-31. This diagram shows ESC front struts, rear shocks, and position sensors. (Courtesy of General Motors Corporation)

ignition cycles before the corresponding malfunction code and message will be stored or displayed.

If the ESC detects a malfunction, the ESC system defaults with a fail-soft action. A fail-soft action refers to any specific action the ESC system takes in order to compensate for a detected malfunction. A typical ESC fail-soft action would be if the ESC system detects a malfunction with a shock absorber; the ESC system will ignore this input and fail-soft to the TOUR ride setting.

It is possible for a suspension position sensor to become stuck. The ESC module would not detect this fault; therefore, a DTC would not be set and no message would be displayed by the IPC. The IPC or DIC will display one, both, or none,

depending on the fault that was encountered. The warning message(s) will continue to be displayed, until the fault(s) has been corrected. This fault is addressed under Symptoms—Electronic Suspension Control in the GM service information.

The SERVICE SUSPENSION SYS message will only display when a DTC is stored. The SPEED LIMITED to XXX will display a reduced speed when a malfunction occurs.

Vehicle Speed

The ESC module receives a vehicle speed input. It is obtained over the Class 2 serial communication bus. Vehicle speed is used to determine the amount of damper control necessary.

Lift/Dive

Lift/dive input is received from the PCM (power-train control module). When the ESC module receives an active lift/dive input, it will command a firm damping level on all four corners. The lift signal is calculated in the PCM based on throttle

position, transmission gear, vehicle speed, and brake switch status. The dive signal, also calculated in the PCM, is based upon the rate of change with the vehicle speed.

REAR LOAD LEVELING

Rear load leveling with air shocks is one of the earliest and simplest uses of electronic suspension control. A number of manufacturers, such as Ford and General Motors, offered this type of system, which adjusts the rear ride height to compensate for a heavy load, as an option on some models. The Ford system provides a typical example, and consists of:

- Rear height sensor
- Electronic control module
- Air compressor relay
- Air compressor
- Air dryer

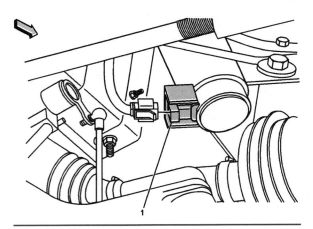

Figure 12-32. This diagram shows an ESC damper electrical connection. (Courtesy of General Motors Corporation)

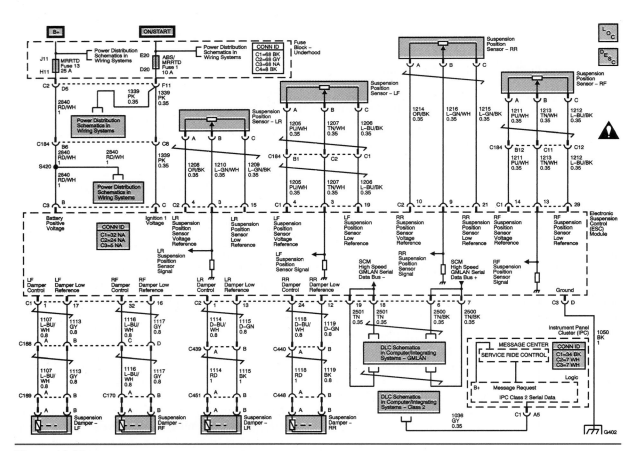

Figure 12-33. This diagram shows an ESC schematic. (Courtesy of General Motors Corporation)

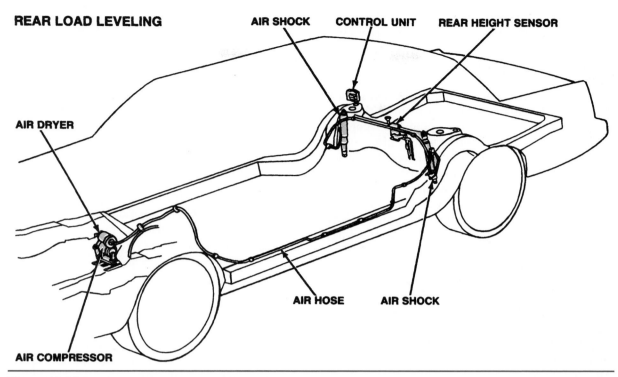

REAR LOAD LEVELING

AIR SHOCK   CONTROL UNIT   REAR HEIGHT SENSOR

AIR DRYER

AIR HOSE   AIR SHOCK

AIR COMPRESSOR

Figure 12-34. The rear height sensor on this Ford load leveling system signals the ECM when heavy loads compress the rear suspension, then the ECM activates the air compressor to increase the air pressure in the rear shocks.

- Air vent solenoid
- Air hoses
- Rear air shocks
- On/off switch

The rear height sensor and the ignition circuit provide input information to the ECM (Figure 12-34). A timer on the ignition circuit keeps the system active for 30 minutes after the ignition is switched off. The ignition switch must be in the "run" position for more than 10 seconds to reactivate the system after shutdown.

The height sensor monitors the distance between one of the rear suspension arms and the rear crossmember to determine **trim height.** If the trim height changes, the height sensor signal voltage increases or decreases to inform the ECM whether the suspension is compressing or extending. After the height sensor signal changes there is a 7- to 13-second delay before the ECM sends a command signal to the actuators. If the height sensor signal stops changing within that time, the system does not adjust the trim height. This strategy prevents the system from raising or lowering the rear of the vehicle in response to ordinary suspension travel.

To correct a low trim height, the ECM sends a signal to the air compressor relay, which starts the

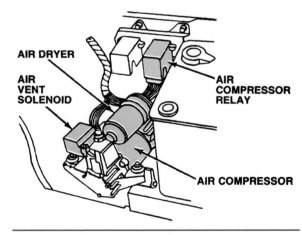

AIR DRYER

AIR VENT SOLENOID

AIR COMPRESSOR RELAY

AIR COMPRESSOR

Figure 12-35. To increase air pressure in the rear shocks, the ECM closes the air compressor relay, which applies power to the compressor motor.

air compressor motor (Figure 12-35). A dryer on the output side of the compressor contains silica gel **desiccant,** which removes moisture from the discharge air before it travels through the nylon air hoses to the air chamber of the rear shocks. Compressed air fills the air chambers, raising the rear of the vehicle. Once the height sensor signal to the

ECM reflects the correct trim height, the ECM de-energizes the relay to switch off the compressor.

To compensate for too high a trim height, the ECM activates the vent solenoid, which is on the compressor, to bleed air from the shocks. The vented air comes back through the hoses and dryer, which takes moisture back out of the desiccant, before venting. This helps prevent the desiccant from becoming saturated after a few uses. A drying system that conserves the desiccant in this way is called a **regenerative dryer**, and most air suspensions use one.

A minimum retention valve inside the dryer keeps system air pressure from dropping below a threshold in the 8 to 24 psi (55 to 165 kpa) range. A certain amount of air must be retained in the system so that the air chambers do not collapse during shock extension. Another preventive measure is that the ECM allows the air compressor to run for a maximum of two minutes and the vent solenoid for a maximum of one minute at a time. This prevents the system from constantly charging or venting in the event of a leak or failure.

The on/off switch, which is located in the trunk, allows the load-leveling system to be disabled to prevent unexpected movement when lifting or towing the vehicle (Figure 12-36). On some models, if the load leveling system is not switched off before lifting or jacking up the vehicle, system damage may result as the air chambers can overinflate and explode.

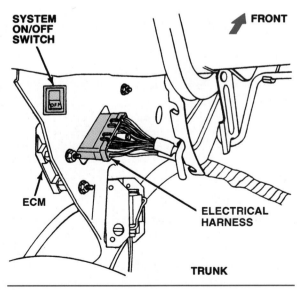

Figure 12-36. An on/off switch, located in the trunk near the ECM, disables the electronic suspension system for servicing or towing the vehicle.

Automatic Level Control Description and Operation

The RTD system is a bi-state real time damping system. The suspension control module controls the suspension damper solenoids and suspension position sensors, along with parts of the automatic level control (ALC) system and electronic variable orifice (EVO) power steering system.

The automatic level control system consists of the following:

- Suspension control module
- Compressor/leveling module
  - Air pressure sensor
  - Exhaust solenoid
- Compressor motor relay

The objective of the automatic level control system is to provide constant ride height at all load conditions. The suspension control module monitors body-to-wheel height, and vehicle speed. The suspension control module will use the rear body-to-wheel displacements and vehicle speed inputs to keep the rear trim height of the vehicle at its desired level.

VARIABLE-RATE AIR SPRINGS

The use of electronically controlled air springs with conventional shocks is mainly limited to larger luxury sedan applications. This option was available on some front-wheel-drive, Daimler-Chrysler models and the RWD Ford Crown Victoria, Mercury Grand Marquis, and Lincoln Mark VII. The Ford system has air springs only at the rear axle, while the DaimlerChrysler system adjusts the height of the air springs at all four wheels.

In an air spring system with ordinary shock absorbers, the main concern is trim height. The ECM varies air pressure in the springs in order to keep the vehicle at the proper height at all times. The Ford system used on the Lincoln Mark VII serves as an example of a variable-rate air spring system. The DaimlerChrysler system operates similarly, and all air-spring systems have much in common with the rear air-shock load-leveling system just discussed.

System Input

The Ford air suspension system uses three sensors and four switches as input devices:

- Left front height sensor
- Right front height sensor
- Rear height sensor
- Ignition switch
- Brake light switch
- Dome light switch
- On/off switch

The three height sensors transmit a signal to the ECM that reflects trim height at each axle (Figure 12-37). The ignition and brake light switches tell the ECM whether the ignition switch is on or off, and if the brake pedal is depressed. The dome light switch indicates whether any doors are open. The on/off switch disables the air spring system to avoid unexpected movement while towing or servicing the vehicle.

Electronic Control Module Operation

Should the ECM receive information from any of the height sensors indicating that the trim height is too high or too low, it energizes the actuators to add or bleed air from the air springs. The ECM can signal each of the front springs individually or the rear springs as a pair, but cannot raise or lower both axles at once. If both front and rear trim height is incorrect, the ECM adjusts the rear springs first, and then the front springs.

The system actuators can still operate for up to an hour after the ignition is switched off. If the front axle needs to be raised within that hour, the ECM can power the compressor for up to 30 seconds, and up to 15 seconds when the rear axle needs to be raised. To bleed pressure after shutdown and lower trim height, the ECM can activate the vent solenoid for up to 3 seconds for the front springs and 10 for the rear springs. The ECM does not lower the vehicle if the height sensor was indicating that the vehicle was high when the ignition was switched from "run" to "off." Once the ignition has been off for more than an hour, the ECM no longer operates the system.

Any time the ignition is switched to the "run" position, the ECM raises the vehicle, if necessary, within the first 45 seconds. If trim height is too high and the vehicle must be lowered, the ECM delays doing so for 45 seconds after the ignition is switched on. In addition, the ECM does not lower the vehicle if the dome light switch indicates a door is open, but will raise the vehicle, if necessary, with an open door. If the brake light switch indicates the driver is applying the brakes, control system operation is suspended, even if all the doors are shut. If the system is in the process of raising the rear of the car when the driver steps on the brake, the ECM finishes that command before disabling. If a door is open and the brakes are applied, the ECM lowers the suspension if needed, but does not raise it.

System Actuators

An air compressor with a regenerative dryer provides the air charge required to inflate the air

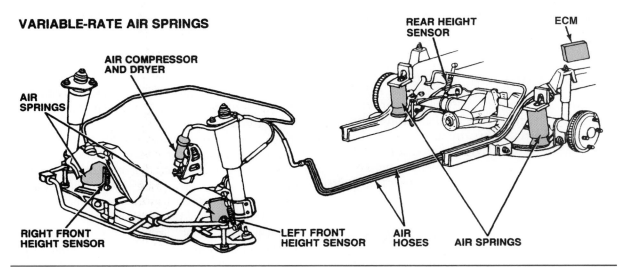

VARIABLE-RATE AIR SPRINGS

Figure 12-37. The Ford variable-rate air spring system uses three height sensors, two front and one rear, to monitor trim height and provide input signals to the ECM.

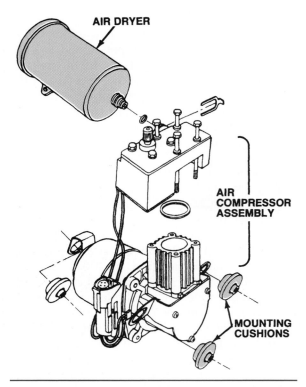

Figure 12-38. Mounting cushions isolate the air compressor from engine compartment vibrations and all air flowing to or from the springs passes through the regenerative dryer.

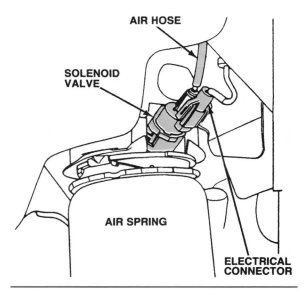

Figure 12-39. A solenoid valve at the top of each spring regulates airflow into or out of the air spring.

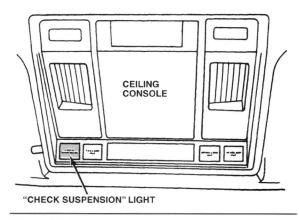

Figure 12-40. A warning lamp alerts the driver if the ECM detects an electronic suspension circuit malfunction or the on/off switch is off.

springs on the Ford air suspension system, and a vent solenoid is used to relieve air pressure and deflate the springs (Figure 12-38). By energizing the compressor relay, the ECM directs current to turn on the compressor motor when trim height needs to be raised. The ECM command to lower the vehicle is an electrical signal that opens the vent solenoid to bleed air pressure out of the system (Figure 12-39).

System Function Indicator

The Ford air suspension ECM also provides a signal to a warning lamp on the ceiling console in the passenger compartment (Figure 12-40). The ECM turns on this light, and records a DTC, if it senses that there is a problem in the system or if the system is disabled by the on/off switch.

VARIABLE SHOCKS

Of all electronic suspension control types, those using variable-shock valves are the most common. These systems have some advantages, the most significant of which is lower weight, over systems that use air shocks or air springs. Air systems require air compressors and dryers, which add considerably to the weight of the vehicle. Variable-shock systems, however, add only the weight of the electronic components and actuators.

A sampling of manufacturers that offer a variable-shock system includes DaimlerChrysler, Ford, General Motors, Nissan, and Toyota. Their systems include the DaimlerChrysler Electronically Controlled Suspension (ECS); Ford Automatic Ride Control (ARC) and Programmed Ride Control (PRC); General Motors Computer Command Ride (CCR), Selective Ride Control (SRC), and speed-dependent damping; Mazda Auto-Adjusting Suspension (AAS); Nissan Full-Active Suspension and

Looking Down the Road: Active Steering

Now that driving enthusiasts are becoming accustomed to the idea of active suspensions, automotive designers are preparing to spring a new idea on them—active steering. For example, engineers at Saab Automobile drew on their aircraft design knowledge to create a one-handed active steering system that eliminates the steering wheel! Based on the aeronautical "fly-by-wire" concept, this "drive-by-wire" system locates a stick control to one side of the driver. This location offers several advantages, including more freedom for engineers in designing an instrument panel for optimal safety during a collision. The driver rests an arm on the armrest of the seat, and the system uses this as a reference point for receiving road data. Saab

is working on active steering as a part of the European Prometheus project, whose goal is safer, cleaner, and more efficient traffic throughout Europe.

Sonar Suspension II; and Toyota Electronic Modulated Suspension (TEMS). Most of these systems respond to both driving conditions and the driver-selected position of the control switch. The General Motors SRC system, used on some Corvette models, responds only to a driver-operated switch.

The Toyota Electronic Modulated Suspension (TEMS) system of the Supra provides an example of a variable-shock system (Figure 12-41).

System Input

The Toyota TEMS system has a dedicated ECM that only operates the suspension controls. Three sensors and two or three switches provide input signals to the ECM:

- Steering angle sensor
- Throttle position sensor
- Vehicle speed sensor
- Control switch
- Brake light switch
- Neutral start switch

The throttle position (TP) sensor does not send information directly to the suspension ECM. Instead, the powertrain control module (PCM) that regulates engine operations relays the signal it receives from the TP sensor to the TEMS computer. Input device signals allow the ECM to determine:

- If the vehicle is cornering, and if so how sharply, and in what direction
- If the vehicle is accelerating

- How fast the vehicle is moving
- What shock firmness the driver prefers for cruising conditions
- If the driver is applying the brakes
- What transmission gear is selected

The ECM uses this information to determine how stiff the shocks should be and sends signals to that effect to the actuators (Figure 12-42).

Electronic Control Module Operation

The control switch allows the driver to choose between "normal" or "sport" operating mode (Figure 12-43). At the "normal" setting, the ECM maintains a soft shock setting under most conditions, while the shocks are kept at medium firmness most of the time when "sport" mode is selected. If vehicle speed exceeds 75 mph (120 km/h) with "normal" mode selected, the ECM automatically changes the shocks to medium firmness, then returns to a soft setting when speed drops below 62 mph (100 km/h).

The ECM automatically changes the shocks from soft or medium to a firm setting under the following conditions:

- Sudden cornering, indicated by the speed and steering sensors
- Sudden acceleration from speeds below 13 mph (20 km/h), indicated by the speed and throttle position sensors

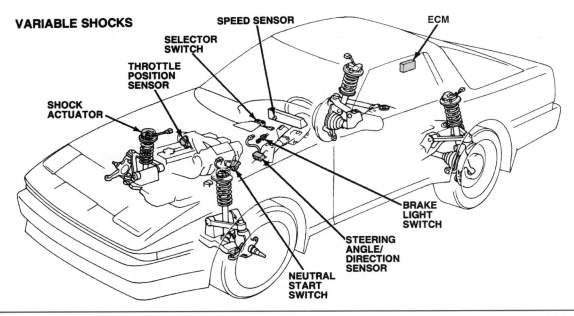

Figure 12-41. The Toyota Electronic Modulated Suspension (TEMS) components and their locations are fairly typical of an electronically controlled variable-shock system.

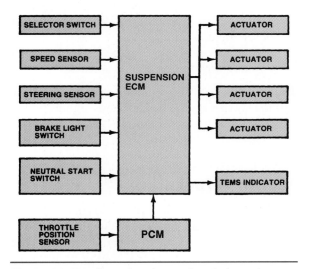

Figure 12-42. Based on input signals from the sensors and switches, the ECM calculates the best in shock stiffness for the present driving conditions, then transmits output signals to the actuators to obtain the desired setting.

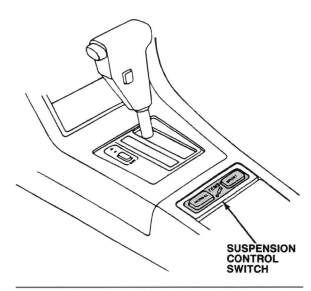

Figure 12-43. The Toyota TEMS control switch allows the driver to choose between "normal," which provides soft shock dampening, and "sport," which provides medium dampening under most circumstances.

- Braking from speeds above 36 mph (60 km/h), indicated by the speed sensor and brake light switch
- Shifting of the automatic transmission from neutral or park into any other gear, at speeds below 6 mph (10 km/h), indicated by the speed sensor and neutral start switch

The ECM switches the shocks from firm back to medium or soft under these conditions:

- Two or more seconds after cornering, depending on how sharply the steering wheel was turned
- Three seconds after acceleration, or when vehicle speed reaches 31 mph (50 km/h)
- Two seconds after the brake light switch goes off
- Five seconds after the automatic transmission is shifted out of neutral or park, or when vehicle speed reaches 9 mph (15 km/h)

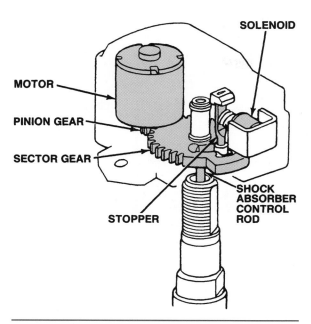

Figure 12-44. A TEMS shock absorber actuator uses a motor to drive a pinion gear, which turns the sector gear connected to the valve control rod. The solenoid determines the position of the stopper.

System Actuators

The TEMS actuators are located at the tops of the struts and are wired in parallel so they operate together (Figure 12-44). Each actuator assembly consists of:

- Motor and pinion gear
- Sector gear and stopper
- Solenoid
- Shock absorber control rod

When the TEMS control module energizes the actuator motor, it turns a small pinion gear at the base of the motor in one direction or another. The pinion gear turns the larger sector gear, which attaches to the shock absorber control rod along its axis. The stopper extends through a slot in the sector gear and determines where the sector gear comes to rest. This in turn determines the position of the control rod (Figure 12-45).

When ECM signals for soft damping, the motor and pinion gear turn the sector gear clockwise until one end of the slot comes up against the stopper. For medium damping, the sector gear turns counterclockwise until the opposite end of the slot hits the stopper. The ECM activates the solenoid when the sensors indicate firm damping is needed. The solenoid pulls the stopper in, which releases the gear so it rotates to a new position.

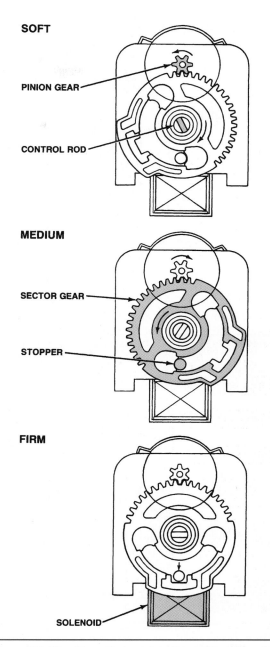

Figure 12-45. For soft damping, the motor drives the pinion gear counterclockwise. For medium damping the motor, sector gear, and control rod rotate clockwise. The solenoid pulls the stopper back to keep the sector gear and control rod centered for firm damping.

The shock absorber control rod, which extends into the center of the shock absorber piston rod, has three sets of orifices through which shock absorber fluid can flow (Figure 12-46). When the sector gear positions the control rod for soft damping, all three sets of orifices are open. This allows more fluid to flow through the piston, so the shock compresses and extends quickly. When

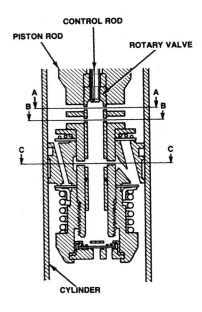

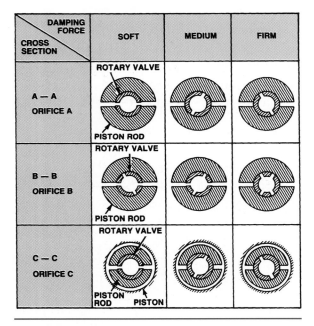

Figure 12-46.   With the control rod positioned for soft damping, orifices "A," "B," and "C" are all open; orifices "A" and "C" close for medium damping; and all three close for a firm shocks setting.

the sector gear moves the control rod for medium damping, the new position blocks two of the sets of orifices to restrict fluid flow. This makes it harder for the piston to move through the fluid, so shock compression and extension are slower. In the firm position, all the control rod orifices are blocked, so compression and extension are at their slowest rate.

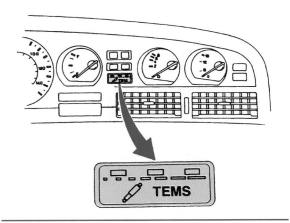

Figure 12-47.   One lamp lights on the dashboard indicator if the shocks are at a soft setting, two lamps light at a medium setting, and all three light when the shocks are firm. The lights flash if the ECM detects a problem in the system.

System Function Indicator

In addition to controlling the actuators, the ECM also provides an output signal to a set of TEMS indicator lamps on the instrument panel (Figure 12-47). The indicator lamp has three lights:

- The left light goes on when the shocks are at their soft setting
- The left and middle lights go on to indicate a medium setting
- All three lights go on when the shocks are at a firm setting

All three lights also go on for about two seconds when the ignition is switched on as a bulb check. If the ECM detects a TEMS circuit malfunction, a DTC is recorded and the indicator lights flash to alert the driver.

AIR SPRINGS WITH VARIABLE SHOCKS

Another more sophisticated type of electronic suspension controls combines adjustable air springs with variable-rate shock absorbers. These systems are typically found on luxury sedans, such as the Lincoln Continental and Mitsubishi Galant. The Mitsubishi Active Electronic Control Suspension (A-ECS), which uses coil springs to support the vehicle weight, small air springs to adjust trim height, and variable shock damping, serves as an example of this design (Figure 12-48).

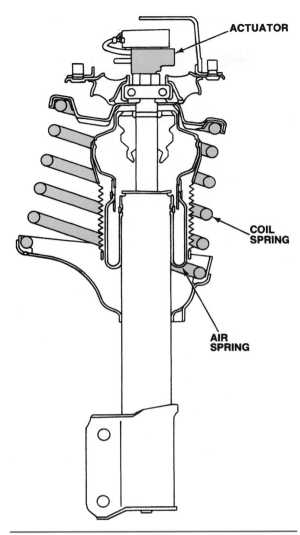

Figure 12-48. The struts of the Mitsubishi A-ECS system use a coil spring to support the vehicle weight, an air spring to adjust trim height, and variable-rate valving to regulate damping action.

System Input

The A-ECS control module receives information from a wide variety of sensors and switches, including the:

- Control mode selector switch
- Steering angle and direction sensor
- Lateral G-force sensor
- Throttle position sensor
- Vehicle speed sensor
- Brake light switch
- Front height sensor
- Rear height sensor
- Vehicle height selector switch
- Door open switch
- Backup light switch
- Headlight switch

In addition, internal pressure sensors and switches monitor air pressure in the system and provide feedback information to the ECM. Information from the input devices allows the A-ECS control unit to keep track of:

- What shock stiffness the driver prefers under most circumstances
- How far and in what direction the steering wheel is turning
- The strength of lateral G-forces acting on the vehicle during cornering
- The rate of acceleration
- The vehicle speed
- Whether the brake pedal is applied
- The vehicle trim level height
- The driver-selected trim level
- Whether any doors are open
- What gear the transmission is in
- Whether the headlights are on

The ECM processes this input information to determine what corrective action to take (Figure 12-49). Then, it transmits signals to the system actuators to maintain the appropriate damping and trim height for the present driving situation.

Electronic Control Module Operation

The A-CES features two driver-selected modes: ride height and shock absorber dampening rate. Two air spring ride height settings and three shock absorber operation modes are available (Figure 12-50).

The two air spring settings are "high" and "auto," and the "auto" setting is the normal position. In this mode the ECM determines and adjusts spring height in response to road conditions. The "high" setting, which adds air to the springs and lifts the vehicle body, is designed for driving on rough roads that require additional clearance for suspension compression and rebound.

The three driver-selectable shock stiffness settings are "sport," "auto," and "soft." With the "sport" mode selected, the ECM maintains shock absorber damping at the firmest setting at all times. The "auto" selection allows the ECM to adjust the shocks to a hard, medium, or auto soft setting in response to sensor and switch inputs. Depressing the "auto" button a second time while the system is

AIR SPRING WITH VARIABLE SHOCKS

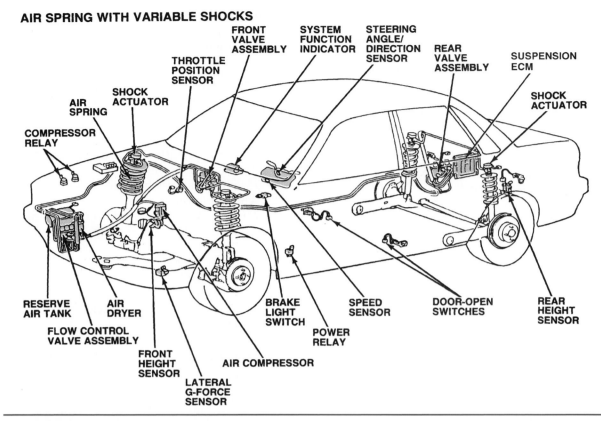

Figure 12-49. A variety of sensors monitor driving conditions, including speed, turning angle, and lateral G-forces, to provide ECM input data for the Mitsubishi A-ECS system.

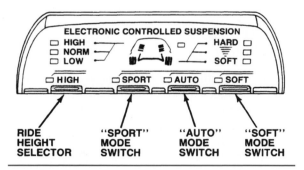

Figure 12-50. The driver-operated switches allow a choice between two spring rates and three shock stiffness settings.

operating in "auto" mode overrides input signals and the ECM maintains medium shock damping. With the "soft" mode selected, the ECM varies the shock settings between hard, medium, and manual soft, which is slightly softer than auto soft. Based on input sensor signals, the ECM adjusts the shock damping to control the following types of movement:

• Body roll
• Front-end dive

• Rear-end squat
• Pitching and bouncing

In addition to regulating shock damping, the system responds to vehicle speed and adjusts the air springs to maintain the correct trim level.

Antiroll Control

The A-ECS system monitors body roll through the steering angle and direction sensor and the lateral G-force sensor. When the input from these sensors indicates the vehicle is turning sharply, the ECM responds by adjusting the air springs to keep the body more level. As the body begins to lean into a corner, the ECM increases air pressure to the springs at the outside of the turn and vents pressure from the springs at the inside of the turn. This counteracts the tendency of the body to lean or roll during turns (Figure 12-51). This unequal spring pressure is maintained until sensors indicate that the vehicle has completed the turn and is once again driving straight ahead. At that point, the ECM gradually bleeds and adds air to the springs until they are once again balanced side-to-side.

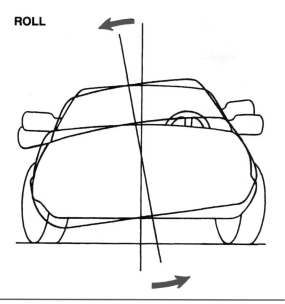

Figure 12-51. Antiroll control strategy adjusts pressure in the air springs side-to-side to reduce body roll during cornering.

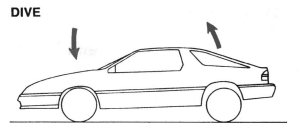

Figure 12-52. Antidive control strategy adjusts pressure in the air springs front-to-rear to reduce body dive caused by weight transfer during hard braking.

Figure 12-53. Antisquat control strategy adjusts pressure in the air springs front-to-rear to reduce body squat caused by weight transfer during rapid acceleration.

The ECM also changes the shock damping during turns by switching from manual soft to medium or from auto soft to hard as needed. However, if the height sensors indicate a rough road surface, such as gravel, the ECM maintains a medium shock setting, even if the system is operating in "auto" mode.

If the steering angle sensor indicates that the driver is "sawing," or moving the steering wheel quickly from one side to the other, the ECM does not adjust the spring settings. To keep adding and venting air on each side under these conditions would waste system energy and would not improve the handling.

Antidive Control

By processing signals from the vehicle speed sensor (VSS) and the brake light switch, the A-ECS control module calculates how much the body is likely to dive during hard braking (Figure 12-52).

To correct for dive, the ECM commands the front spring actuators to increase the air pressure in the front springs, while simultaneously bleeding air pressure from the rear springs. The ECM also adjusts shock absorber damping to a hard setting during quick stops as part of the antidive control strategy. When the input sensors indicate the antidive function is no longer needed, the ECM returns the springs and shocks to their original settings.

If the vehicle begins to accelerate after the brake is applied, as might happen on a downhill slope, the ECM vents air from all four springs.

Antisquat Control

When the throttle position (TP) sensor voltage signal indicates rapid or wide-open throttle acceleration, the ECM vents air from the front springs and increases pressure in the rear springs. If the throttle sensor signals wide-open throttle for more than one second, the ECM changes the shock setting to "hard." These strategies prevent "squat," as vehicle weight transfers toward the back of the vehicle and the rear suspension compresses (Figure 12-53). Once the TP signal stablizes, the ECM returns the spring air pressures and shock damping to their original levels.

The backup light switch circuit provides an ECM input to indicate if the transmission is in reverse when accelerating. With the vehicle moving in reverse, the ECM increases pressure in the front springs and vents air from the rear springs.

Pitching and Bouncing Control

The A-ECS system uses two height sensors, front and rear, to track suspension movement on an uneven, bumpy, "washboard" surface. When a height sensor indicates that the suspension is compressing, the ECM vents air from the springs at that axle to keep the body from moving up. As the suspension rebounds, the ECM routes air pressure to

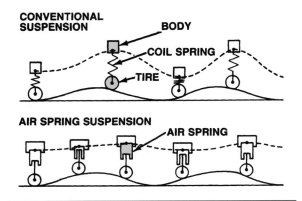

Figure 12-54. The sophisticated Mitsubishi actuators pump air into and out of the air springs as the wheels ride over bumps to keep the body more level than a conventional coil spring system.

fill the springs. Since the air springs effectively pump air out and in as the wheels go up and down, there is less body bounce, which reduces pitch (Figure 12-54). This prevents a rolling body motion when driving over repeated bumps.

If the sensors indicate that the body is pitching or bouncing, the ECM may switch the shock setting from manual soft to medium at any speed, but it changes from auto soft to hard only at speeds above 81 mph (130 km/h).

Speed-Responsive Damping

As mentioned earlier, the ECM keeps the shock setting at hard regardless of input from the speed sensor if the driver has selected "hard" mode. In "soft" mode, the ECM switches the shocks from manual soft to medium when vehicle speed reaches 80 mph (129 km/h), while in "auto" it switches from auto soft to medium at 61 mph (99 km/h). Deceleration ECM strategy switches the shocks from medium to manual soft at 73 mph (117 km/h) in "soft" mode, and back to auto soft at 40 mph (64 km/h) in "auto" mode.

Vehicle Height Adjustment

When the air spring selector is in "auto" mode, the ECM may select any of three vehicle height adjustments: high, normal, or low. Under most circumstances, the ECM strategy keeps the vehicle at its normal height. It raises the car in response to input from the height and speed sensors. If the height sensors signal a suspension movement of 1.6 inches (40 mm) or more twice within a two-second period, and vehicle speed is at least 25 mph (40 km/h), the ECM increases air pressure in all four springs to raise the trim height.

When the vibration or the speed decreases, the ECM adjusts spring pressure to maintain a normal trim height after a 12-second delay.

Input signals from the ride height sensors, VSS, and the headlight switch are used to determine ECM trim-lowering strategy. If the headlights are off when the VSS signal indicates a vehicle speed of 56 mph (90 km/h), air is bled from the front springs to lower the front of the vehicle. If vehicle speed remains between 56 and 61 mph (90 and 99 km/h) for 10 seconds, air is bled from the rear springs as well. The ECM lowers the rear immediately if vehicle speed reaches or exceeds 62 mph (100 km/h). Trim height returns to normal when vehicle speed decreases to 43 mph (70 km/h). With the headlights on, both front and rear springs lower at the same time, to keep the headlights aimed correctly.

As mentioned earlier, the driver can choose a "high" mode by pushing a console button. In response, the ECM sends more air to all four springs to raise the trim height. The driver-selected "high" mode is only available at vehicle speeds below 44 mph (71 km/h). Above that speed, the ECM overrides the selector switch and operates in "auto" mode.

All trim height change operations are suspended if sensor signals indicate sharp cornering, sudden braking, or sudden acceleration. To change the ride height under these conditions might make the handling unstable.

System Actuators

The damper actuators, which operate similarly to the damper actuators in the Toyota system discussed earlier in this chapter, are wired in parallel so that they all act together. Each actuator consists of a stepper motor that rotates a control rod inside the shock absorber piston rod to regulate fluid flow through the orifices and control shock stiffness (Figure 12-55).

There are two air spring actuators, or valve assemblies, one for each axle. The actuators are wired in series so that they can act independently of each other. Each valve assembly contains three solenoids that regulate airflow to the springs. A third actuator, the flow control valve assembly, distributes air pressure to the spring actuator valves. An air supply system provides the high-pressure air charge required to inflate the air springs (Figure 12-56). The air supply system consists of:

- Air compresser
- Dryer

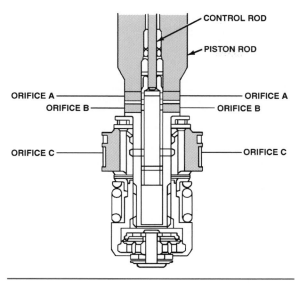

Figure 12-55. The control rod rotates inside the piston rod to vary the hydraulic fluid orifice openings on the Mitsubishi variable-rate shock absorbers.

- Reserve tank
- Flow control valve assembly
- Front valve assembly
- Rear valve assembly

The air compressor supplies pressurized air through a regenerative dryer to the reserve tank, and it vents system air through an exhaust valve. The exhaust air returns to the compressor through the dryer.

The reserve tank contains two sub-tanks: high-pressure and low-pressure. Tank pressure is maintained by a high-pressure switch, low-pressure switches, and a return pump. The high-pressure air tank stores system air, and the pressure switch signals the ECM if pressure falls below 108 psi (745 kPa). In response, the ECM starts the compressor motor to recharge the system. The compressor switches off once pressure in the tank reaches 135 psi (930 kPa).

The low-pressure sub-tank collects the air pressure vented from the springs when the ECM

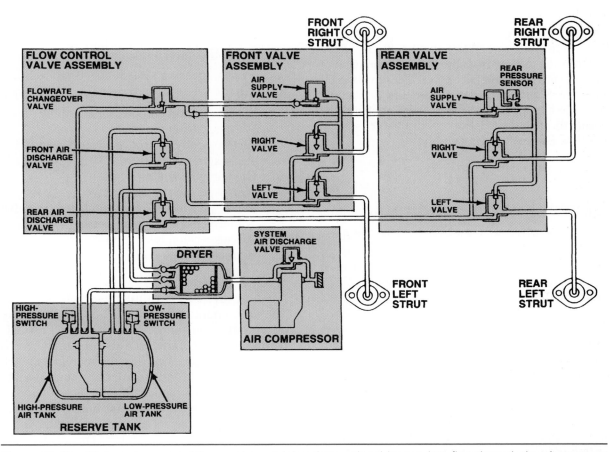

Figure 12-56. Three valve assemblies, each containing three solenoids, regulate flow through the air pressure control system to adjust the air springs.

is lowering them. The low-pressure switch sends an ECM input signal when pressure in this tank reaches 20 psi (140 kPa). In response, the ECM turns on the return pump, which transfers air from the low-pressure tank into the high-pressure tank. The pump switches off when pressure in the low-pressure tank is below 10 psi (70 kPa).

The flow control valve assembly contains three solenoid valves: the flowrate changeover valve, front air discharge valve, and rear air discharge valve. The flowrate changeover valve regulates airflow from the high-pressure tank to both the front and rear springs, through the front and rear valve assemblies. The front air discharge valve directs exhaust air from the front springs through the front valve assembly to the low-pressure tank and the exhaust valve on the compressor. The rear air discharge valve directs exhaust air from the rear springs through the rear valve assembly to the low-pressure tank and the exhaust valve.

The front valve assembly also contains three solenoid valves: the front air supply valve, front right valve, and front left valve. The rear valve assembly is basically the same, containing the rear air supply valve, rear right valve, and rear left valve. On both assemblies the air supply valve controls the airflow from the flowrate changeover valve to the right and left valves. These valves either direct pressurized air from the air supply valve to the air spring, or exhaust air from the spring through the front or rear discharge valve in the flow control valve assembly.

System Function Indicator

Since the Mitsubishi A-ECS has a number of functions and operational modes, it uses a number of lamps on a system indicator to inform the driver of the operating status of the system (Figure 12-57). A set of three lamps lets the driver know if the springs are at the "high," "norm," or "low" setting. Another set of three lamps informs the driver of the shock stiffness setting. A "high" lamp, located above the vehicle height selector switch, illuminates if the driver manually selects the "high" mode for the air springs. The control mode selector switches display "sport," "auto," or "soft" as a reminder of which shock operation mode is selected. Finally, a malfunction indicator lamp (MIL) illuminates if the ECM detects a malfunction in the A-ECS system.

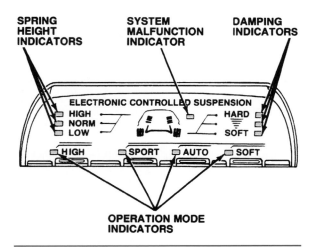

Figure 12-57. A dashboard indicator display informs the driver of A-ECS system operational status.

Hummer Air Suspension Description and Operation

The primary mission of the air suspension system for the rear suspension under loaded and unloaded conditions is:

- Keep vehicle visually level
- Maintain optimal ride height

The air suspension system consists of the following items:

- Air suspension compressor assembly
- Air suspension module
- Electronically controlled air suspension relay
- Air suspension sensors
- Ride height switch
- Air suspension exhaust valve
- Air suspension inflator switch and fill valve
- Air suspension pressure sensor
- Air suspension inlet valves
- Rear air springs

Air Compressor Assembly

The air compressor (Figure 12-58) is a positive displacement air pump, powered by a 12 V DC permanent magnet motor. A thermal limit switch protects the compressor. The thermal limit switch is normally closed and provides a ground signal to the air suspension module. If there is an overtemperature condition the thermal limit switch will open and signal the air suspension module to deactivate the compressor relay. The compressor will stop running and a DTC will set. Intake air for the compressor is drawn through an intake fil-

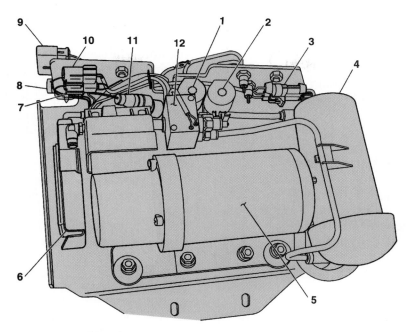

(1) AIR SUSPENSION INLET VALVE—LR
(2) AIR SUSPENSION INLET VALVE—RR
(3) COMPRESSOR CONNECTOR
(4) AIR SUSPENSION AIR DRYER
(5) AIR SUSPENSION COMPRESSOR
(6) AIR SUSPENSION MODULE
(7) AIR SUSPENSION EXHAUS CONNECTOR
(8) C450
(9) C451
(10) AIR SUSPENSION INLET VALVE CONNECTOR—LR/RR
(11) AIR SUSPENSION PRESSURE SENSOR
(12) AIR SUSPENSION EXHAUST VALVE

Figure 12-58. This diagram shows a Hummer air compressor assembly. (Courtesy of General Motors Corporation)

ter and line that is attached to the fuel filler pipe in the left rear wheel area. The air compressor assembly is mounted to a bracket that is located under the rear center of the vehicle. The compressor air dryer is mounted next to the air compressor. It contains a moisture-absorbing chemical that dries the compressed air before it is delivered to the rear air springs. Moisture is removed from the dryer and returned to the atmosphere when air is exhausted from the air springs during vehicle lowering.

Air Suspension Module

The air suspension module (Figure 12-58) will conduct several self-tests at every ignition activation, while other tests do not commence until wheel speed is detected at the wheel speed sensors. During a self-test, if any of the module components are found to be malfunctioning a DTC

will set and the corresponding telltale is activated. The telltale message that the air suspension module can display is SERVICE SUSPENSION SYSTEM. Each DTC consists of one current and one history DTC. History codes will be cleared after 100 consecutive malfunction-free ignition cycles or with a scan tool. The air suspension module communicates with other modules in the vehicle via class 2. There is a standby feature in the air suspension module whereby downward leveling is possible for 30 minutes after the ignition has been turned off. This allows the vehicle to level after a load has been removed. The leveling function will be disabled when any door or liftgate is open or when the inflator is being used. To prevent energizing the electronically controlled air suspension relay or air suspension inlet valves during normal ride motions, the air suspension module provides a calibrated delay before leveling the vehicle.

Air Suspension Exhaust Valve

The air suspension exhaust valve (Figure 12-58) is used to exhaust air from the air springs and lower the vehicle. The air suspension exhaust valve is mounted on the head of the compressor. The air suspension module controls the air suspension exhaust valve.

Air Suspension Pressure Sensor

The air suspension system uses the air pressure sensor to monitor system pressure. The air suspension module uses that signal to determine if there is a leak in the system and to maintain a minimum air pressure in the system.

Air Suspension Inlet Valves

The air suspension system has two inlet valves (Figure 12-58) one for the right air spring and one for the left air spring. The valves are mounted to the valve block with the air suspension pressure sensor and are located next to the compressor. The valves are activated and controlled independently by the air suspension module.

Air Suspension Sensors

The rear air suspension sensors (Figure 12-59) are potentiometers, which detect height changes at the rear of the vehicle. The sensors relay the height changes to the air suspension module. The sensors are mounted to the frame at the rear wheel area on the

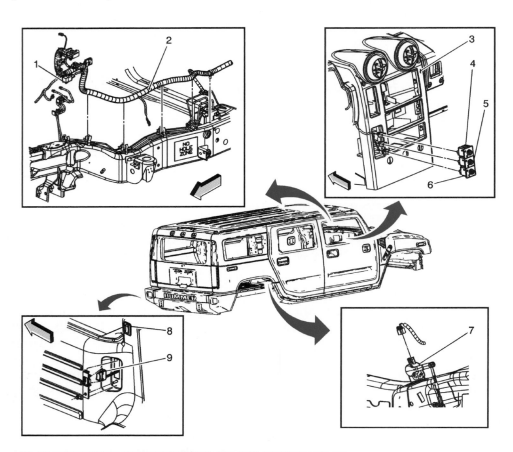

(1) ELECTRONICALLY CONTROLLED AIR SUSPENSION RELAY
(2) CHASSIS HARNESS
(3) I/P COMPARTMENT
(4) TRACTION CONTROL SWITCH
(5) TOW/HAUL SWITCH
(6) RIDE HEIGHT SWITCH
(7) AIR SUSPENSION SENSOR—LR
(8) DOOR LOCK SWITCH—REAR
(9) AIR SUSPENSION INFLATOR SWITCH

Figure 12-59. This diagram shows the Hummer air suspension sensors. (Courtesy of General Motors Corporation)

left and right sides. The activation arm is attached to the upper control arms of the rear suspension.

Ride Height Switch

Extended ride height is used to increase vehicle ground clearance. When the ERH switch (Figure 12-59) is activated the vehicle will raise two inches at the rear. The extended ride height will only occur if vehicle speed is less than 40 mph (64 km/h) with the liftgate and all doors closed as the engine is running. When the switch is activated the switch LED will flash while the vehicle is transitioning to extended ride height. When the vehicle reaches extended ride height, the switch LED will be on continuously. The vehicle will return to normal height when the switch is activated again and the switch LED will go off. The vehicle will automatically return to normal height if vehicle speed increases over 40 mph (64 km/h) and the switch LED will turn off.

Air Suspension Inflator Switch and Fill Valve

The inflator system (Figure 12-59) consists of an inflator hose to provide a means of inflating objects and a switch with an LED located in the rear compartment. The inflator will only function when the engine is running and the vehicle is in park. The switch LED will be illuminated with the inflator on. The inflator function will have priority over leveling functions.

Electronically Controlled Air Suspension Relay

The air suspension module controls the compressor by the use of a relay (Figure 12-60). The relay and wiring are protected with a 60-amp fuse. The air suspension module will only activate the compressor relay when the engine is running.

Rear Air Springs

The air springs (Figure 12-61) are mounted in the frame in the same location where the coil spring is mounted for a vehicle without air suspension. Support pieces are affixed to the axle for the air springs.

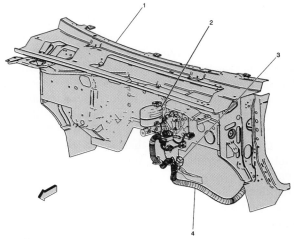

(1) DASH-UPPER PLENUM
(2) MASTER CYLINDER
(3) ELECTRONICALLY CONTROLLED AIR SUSPENSION RELAY
(4) CHASSIS HARNESS

Figure 12-60. This diagram shows a Hummer air suspension relay. (Courtesy of General Motors Corporation)

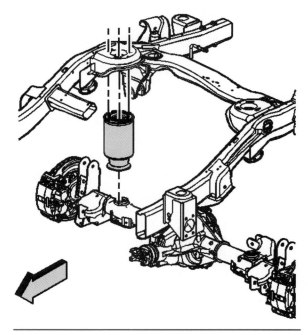

Figure 12-61. This diagram shows Hummer air springs. (Courtesy of General Motors Corporation)

SUMMARY

Electronically controlled suspension systems allow the suspension to react differently to different circumstances. Among the electronic controls used in such systems are sensors, switches, an electronic control module, and actuators. Sensors and switches provide input about the road condition and suspension operation to the ECM, which is a small computer. The ECM then sends electronic signals to the system actuators, which perform mechanical actions such as varying shock orifices or regulating airflow into and out of air springs. Motors and electromagnets are common types of actuators. A solenoid is a type of electromagnet.

Electronic suspensions can be divided into four groups according to how they function. Rear load-leveling systems use air shocks at the rear wheels to adjust the rear trim level under varying loads. Some suspensions have air springs, in which changing the air pressure changes the vehicle height in response to load changes. Most models with air springs have them at all four wheels, but some use air springs only at the rear. Some electronic systems use variable shocks, in which the shock absorber stiffness changes in response to various road conditions and driving maneu-vers. Often the driver can choose the stiffness. Finally, a few more sophisticated systems use both air springs and variable shocks at each wheel. In these systems both spring rate and shock stiffness change in response to changing conditions, driving techniques, and loads.

The GM electronic suspension control system controls damping forces in the front struts and rear shock absorbers in response to various road and driving conditions. The ESC shock absorbers or dampers are a monotube type and provide damping by increasing magnetic flux to magnetic particles inside the shock fluid to resist suspension movement. The ESC shock absorber has the capability of providing multiple modes or values of damping forces, in both compression and rebound direction. The rear automotive level control (ALC) portion of the system maintains a proper vehicle trim height under various vehicle load conditions. For more information on the ALC, refer to Automatic Level Control Description and Operation in Automatic Level Control. The ESC module receives the following inputs: wheel-to-body position, vehicle speed, and lift/dive. The ESC module evaluates these inputs and controls actuators in each of the dampers independently to provide varied levels of suspension control.

Review Questions

For each of the following questions, choose the letter that represents the best possible answer.

1. The sensors most frequently used in electronic suspension systems include those for:
   a. Acceleration and G-force
   b. Height and speed
   c. Height and steering angle
   d. Speed and acceleration

2. Technician A says that sensors and switches provide input signals to the actuators. Technician B says that sensors and switches provide input signals that the ECM uses to control actuators. Who is correct?
   a. A only
   b. B only
   c. Both A and B
   d. Neither A nor B

3. Photo interrupters, which contain an LED and a phototransistor, are typically used in:
   a. G-force sensors
   b. Throttle position sensors
   c. Steering angle sensors
   d. Actuators

4. Which of the following electrical devices transmits a variable voltage signal?
   a. Actuator
   b. Sensor
   c. Switch
   d. Relay

5. An electronic control module is a:
   a. CPU
   b. Computer solenoid
   c. Microprocessor
   d. Mini-computer

6. Technician A says that a solenoid is a special kind of permanent magnet. Technician B says that a solenoid contains a spring-loaded plunger. Who is correct?
   a. A only
   b. B only
   c. Both A and B
   d. Neither A nor B

7. Which component of an electric motor is used to reverse current?
   a. Armature
   b. Commutator
   c. Electromagnet
   d. Solenoid

8. An air shock drying system that uses exhaust air to remove moisture from its desiccant is called:
   a. An air dryer
   b. A double-desiccant system
   c. A regenerative dryer
   d. A silica gel dryer

9. To keep the air chambers from collapsing during shock extension in the Ford system, the pressure is always kept above:
   a. 4 psi (25 kPa)
   b. 8 psi (55 kPa)
   c. 15 psi (105 kPa)
   d. 24 psi (165 kPa)

10. If the ignition switch is turned off, the ECM on a Ford air spring system:
    a. Cannot operate
    b. Can operate the system for up to 5 minutes
    c. Can operate the system for up to 30 minutes
    d. Can operate the system for up to 45 minutes

11. Which of the following switches is NOT part of the Ford air suspension system?
    a. Brake light switch
    b. Dome light switch
    c. Ignition switch
    d. Trunk light switch

12. The most common type of electronically controlled suspension system uses:
    a. Air shocks
    b. Air springs
    c. Variable-rate air springs
    d. Variable shocks

13. Which of the following is NOT a variable-rate shock absorber system?
    a. DaimlerChrysler ECS
    b. Ford PRC
    c. General Motors SRC
    d. Mitsubishi A-ECS

14. The Toyota TEMS system automatically changes the shocks to a firm setting during:
    a. Braking from speeds above 25 mph
    b. Sudden acceleration from speeds below 10 mph
    c. Sudden cornering
    d. Wide-open throttle at cruise speeds

15. Technician A says that the Toyota TEMS actuators are located at the bottom of the struts. Technician B says that the TEMS actuators are wired in series so they always operate together. Who is correct?
    a. A only
    b. B only
    c. Both A and B
    d. Neither A nor B

16. To increase suspension damping, the Toyota TEMS actuators:
    a. Increase spring air pressure
    b. Decrease spring air pressure
    c. Close more hydraulic orifices
    d. Open more hydraulic orifices

17. On the Mitsubishi A-ECS system, the driver selected air spring settings are:
    a. "High" and "Low"
    b. "High," "Low," and "Auto"
    c. "High," "Low," and "Normal"
    d. "High" and "Auto"

18. If the throttle sensor in the A-ECS system signals wide-open throttle for more than one second, the shock absorber setting automatically changes to:
    a. Hard
    b. Medium
    c. Auto soft
    d. Manual soft

19. The flow control valve assembly of the Mitsubishi A-ECS system contains all of the following, EXCEPT:
    a. Flowrate changeover valve
    b. Front air discharge valve
    c. Rear air discharge valve
    d. High-pressure switch

20. Technician A says that the flow control valve assembly of the Mitsubishi A-ECS system contains three solenoid valves. Technician B says that the front valve assembly of the Mitsubishi A-ECS system contains three solenoid valves. Who is correct?
    a. A only
    b. B only
    c. Both A and B
    d. Neither A nor B

13

Wheels
and Tires

OBJECTIVES

Upon completion and review of this chapter, you will be able to:

- Explain automotive wheel rim design.
- Define the different types of automotive wheel bearings.
- Identify the basic characteristics of the automobile tire and explain the three basic types of passenger tire construction.
- Identify and explain the types of tire ratings, including tire size ratings and spare tires.
- Define the terms associated with vehicle vibrations.
- Define the terms "static balance," "dynamic balance," "tramping," and "radial force variation."
- Differentiate between dynamic and static wheel balance.

KEY TERMS

adhesion
aquaplaning
belted bias ply tire
bias ply tire
bolt circle
centrifugal force
coefficient of
  friction (Cf)
cycle
damping
directional tire
dynamic balance
hop
hydroplaning
inner tube
inner wheel bearing
knockoff wheel
lateral runout
match mounting
negative offset
pneumatic tire
positive offset
order
out of round
outer wheel bearing
radial load
radial ply tire
Radial runout

remote control door
  lock receiver
  (RCDLR)
resonance
responder
rim width
run-flat tires
self-sealing tires
self-supporting tires
sidewall
slip angle
speed rating
static balance
thrust load
thrust movement
tire
tire aspect ratio
tire beads
tire carcass
tire casing
tire contact patch
tire performance
  criteria (TPC)
tire placard
tire ply
tire pressure
  monitor (TPM)
tire section height

tire section width
tire tread
tramp
tubeless tire
undertread layer
wheel
wheel bearing endplay
wheel bearing preload
wheel backspacing

wheel balance
wheel diameter
wheel disc
wheel dish
wheel offset
wheel rim
wheel runout
wobble

INTRODUCTION

The wheel and tire assemblies of a vehicle serve a number of important purposes. It is the task of the wheels and tires to:

- Aim the vehicle, through both steering system input and alignment angles
- Bear the weight of the vehicle and transfer it to the ground
- Provide contact between the vehicle and the road
- Absorb small road shocks

In addition, the wheels and tires at the drive axle move the vehicle, and the tires ensure traction under varying road conditions. The first part of the wheel and tire function, aiming or steering the car, is dealt with in Chapters 4 through 7 of this *Classroom Manual,* which cover steering systems, and in Chapter 14, which covers wheel alignment.

This chapter, which addresses how wheels and tires are designed to carry out their purposes, begins with a study of wheels and the wheel bearings that allow rotation. This is followed by a brief discussion of brake friction assemblies, even though the brakes are not actually a part of the steering, suspension, or the wheel and tire assembly. Knowledge of brake construction and operation is important because brake service is frequently performed in the process of suspension, wheel, or alignment repair tasks. The chapter concludes with an examination of tire design and construction, and introduces some of the terminology of tire dynamics as well. See Chapter 13 in the *Shop Manual* for wheel and tire service

WHEELS

An automotive **wheel** consists of the disc that rotates on the axle or spindle and the rim onto which the tire mounts (Figure 13-1). Most automotive wheels are made of steel, although some are made

WHEEL

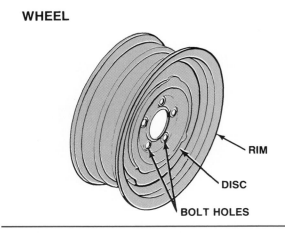

Figure 13-1. The wheel consists of the disc that attaches the assembly to the axle and the rim on which the tire mounts.

of magnesium, aluminum alloy, or even plastic. Magnesium wheels are expensive, and generally used only in racing. Aftermarket "mag" wheels, sold to enthusiasts, are named after magnesium alloy racing wheels, but most "mag" wheels are actually constructed of aluminum alloy. Aluminum alloy wheels are a popular original-equipment option on many models, and are also common aftermarket purchases. The first plastic, or polymer composite, original equipment wheel was developed by the Motor Wheel Corporation and introduced on the 1989 Shelby CSX, a limited-edition version of the Dodge Shadow. Other companies make composite wheels as well, and although gaining in popularity, their use is not yet widespread.

Wheel Disc

The **wheel disc,** also referred to as the "web," "center section," or "face," is the plate-like part of the wheel that bolts onto the hub. Typically, automotive wheel discs have either four or five bolt holes for securing the wheel to the hub. Some French wheels have only three bolt holes, while pickup trucks often have six and heavy trucks have ten or more. The disc may also have a larger center hole that fits around the spindle dust cap. However, not all wheels have this center hole.

Either lug nuts or lug bolts secure the wheel to the hub. If the wheel uses lug nuts, the hub has threaded studs that fit through holes in the wheel disc, and the lug nuts thread onto the studs. A lug bolt passes through a hole in the disc and fits into a threaded bore on the hub. Lug nuts are more

MATCHING-TAPER FASTENERS

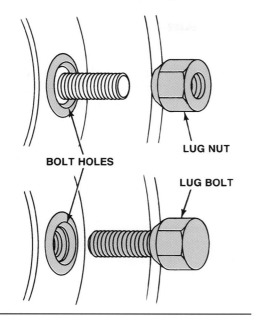

Figure 13-2. The inner flange of the lug nuts or lug bolts and the bolt holes of the wheel disc are usually tapered to center the wheel on the hub and provide a more secure fit.

common on domestic vehicles, while some import manufacturers, especially European ones, use lug bolts. Another fairly common European practice is to use lug nuts with a right-hand thread on one side of the vehicle and lug nuts with a left-hand thread on the other side.

The bolt holes on the wheel disc are tapered to match the taper on the face of the lug nuts or the flange of the lug bolts (Figure 13-2). The two tapers align and center the wheel as the nuts or bolts are tightened. The matching tapers also increase the clamping force that holds the wheel in place. Always make sure to install lug nuts with the tapered side facing the tapered hole in the wheel.

When mounting a wheel and tire assembly onto the hub, it is important to tighten the lug nuts or bolts to the torque value specified by the manufacturer. Nuts or bolts that are too loose may work free and fall off, making the wheel insecure or even allowing the wheel to come off the hub—with disastrous results. Lug nuts or bolts that are too tight also cause problems. Over tightening deforms the wheel disc mounting holes, strips threads, breaks studs, and may distort the brake disc or hub as well. Lug nuts and bolts should be hand-tightened to specified torque; *never* use an impact wrench to tighten them.

WHEEL RIM CONTOUR

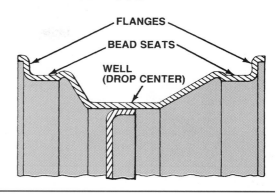

Figure 13-3. The wheel rim well provides a space for the tire beads to fit into during mounting; the bead seat provides a tire-to-wheel sealing surface; and the flange holds the beads in place.

Wheel Rim

The **wheel rim** encircles the disc and provides the tire mounting area. The rim is made from a length of contoured steel bent into a circle with the ends carefully welded and machined to provide a smooth joint. The rim is then welded to the disc to form a complete wheel. A wheel rim is contoured into three areas:

- Well, or drop center
- Bead seats
- Flanges

These contours allow tire mounting and secure the tire to the wheel (Figure 13-3). During tire mounting, the tire beads fit into the well. The tire beads move into the bead seats as the tire is inflated, and the flanges keep the beads in place.

Wheel Specifications

Automotive wheels are built to specifications, and certain terms are used to describe specific measurements or relationships between the parts of a wheel. Wheels are designed for particular vehicle application and manufacturing specifications include:

- Center hole diameter
- Bolt circle
- Wheel offset
- Wheel backspacing and dish
- Wheel diameter and rim width

A vehicle uses wheels in which the offset, dish, diameter, and rim width must be within certain

BOLT CIRCLE

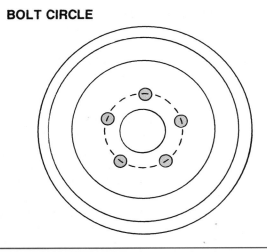

Figure 13-4. The bolt circle, which is an imaginary circle drawn through the centers of the lug bolt holes, is specified in terms of the number of holes and the diameter of the circle they form.

limits to accommodate the suspension, steering, and drivetrain characteristics, and to fit into the available space while providing safe handling.

Wheel specifications may be given in inches or millimeters. In fact, it is possible, although not common, for two vehicles of the same make and model to have different sets of dimensions—one in inches and one in millimeters—depending on the plant at which they were assembled. However, both the inch and metric wheel would use the same size tire.

Center Hole Diameter

Most wheels have a hole in the center through which the end of the spindle, covered by a dust cap, protrudes. However, some late-model wheels do not have a center hole. It is important when installing new wheels to make sure that there is a center hole if one is necessary and that the hole properly fits over the spindle and dust cap. To avoid problems, make sure the wheel meets the original equipment (OE) specifications for the vehicle on which it is being installed.

Bolt Circle

The **bolt circle** of a wheel refers to an imaginary circle drawn to connect the centers of all the lug bolt holes. Wheel manufacturers use a set of two numbers to indicate the bolt circle. The first number is how many bolt holes are in the wheel and the second number is the diameter of the bolt circle (Figure 13-4). For example, a 5–5½ bolt circle describes a set of five bolt holes that form a circle with a 5½-inch diameter.

The "Mag" Wheel

One of the most commonly installed aftermarket accessories is a set of "mag" wheels. Originally, the name "mag" was short for magnesium, the material the wheels were made of. Ted Halibrand began producing magnesium alloy wheels in 1947 for use on the Sprint cars he raced on the California dirt tracks. The wheels worked so well on the dirt track that by 1951 he was supplying them to teams running the Indianapolis 500. Soon after, other companies started producing magnesium wheels, and by the mid-1960s most race cars ran on magnesium alloy wheels.

Attracted to the style and image of the wheels, enthusiasts were replacing stock wheels with "mags" for street use by the early 1960s. Unfortunately, magnesium wheels had some drawbacks for street use. Magnesium is costly, and magnesium wheels have limited impact resistance and tend to oxidize and corrode rapidly unless advanced and expensive manufacturing techniques are followed. Another drawback to street use is the fact that wheels constructed of the wrong magnesium alloy are highly flammable!

Wheel manufacturers were eager to exploit the new market, but to overcome the drawbacks of magnesium they switched to an aluminum alloy for most street applications. However, the well-recognized "mag" name was still used for the newer aluminum wheels. Although these newer designs were heavier—magnesium is two-thirds the weight of aluminum—aluminum alloy is still lighter and less expensive than steel. Compared to magnesium wheels, aluminum alloy wheels are easier to work with from a manufacturing standpoint, have greater impact and corrosion resistance, and are not flammable.

Over the years, design improvements, new alloying elements, and surface coatings have improved magnesium wheels to the point that Honda offers real magnesium alloy wheels as an option on the Prelude—but only in Japan, for now.

Wheel Offset

When viewing the cross-section of a wheel, the **wheel offset** is the distance from the face of the wheel disc—the "vertical mounting plane"—to

WHEEL DIMENSIONS

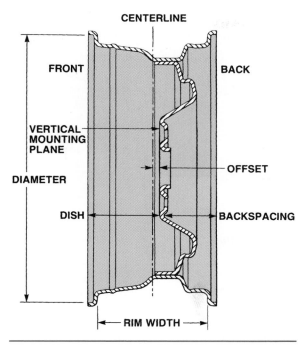

Figure 13-5. A number of dimensions determine whether a wheel will fit a particular application.

the rim centerline. If the mounting plane is farther inboard than the centerline, the wheel has **negative offset.** A wheel has **positive offset** if the vertical mounting plane is farther outboard than the centerline. Be aware that a few wheel manufacturers use exactly the opposite definitions for positive and negative offset. Keep this in mind when reading service literature or catalogs, and especially when ordering wheels (Figure 13-5).

On a wheel with extreme positive offset, the front, or outboard, side of the wheel disc is flush, or nearly flush, with the front side of the rim. Typically, wheels on a front-wheel-drive (FWD) vehicle have a considerable positive offset to allow clearance for CV joints, suspension parts, and brake system components behind the wheel disc.

Wheel Backspacing and Dish

Wheel backspacing, also called the "back side setting," is the distance from the back, or inboard, side of the wheel disc to the inner flange of the wheel rim. Two wheels with the same offset but different rim widths have different backspacing. Backspacing determines the complementary measurement, **wheel dish.** Dish is the distance from the outboard flange of the rim to the verti-

cal mounting plane. Like offset, backspacing and dish measurement specifications may be given in either inches or millimeters. Also similar to offset, backspacing and dish affect clearance for driveline, suspension, and brake parts.

Wheel Diameter and Rim Width

Wheel diameter is the distance across the center of the wheel between the edges of the wheel flange when viewed from the outboard side. Automobile wheel diameters most commonly range from 12 to 17 inches, or 305 to 432 millimeters. **Rim width** is the measurement across the inside of the wheel, from the inner edge of one flange to the other. Wheel rim width corresponds to tire width, which is explained later in this chapter.

Custom Wheels

Most optional or aftermarket wheels designed for street use are constructed of cast or forged aluminum alloy. Some custom wheels have an aluminum alloy wheel disc with a steel rim.

Enthusiasts value aluminum alloy wheels because they are lighter-weight and more attractive than stock steel wheels. Aluminum alloy wheels are often clear-coated to prevent oxidation or other damage, which gives them a different appearance from the baked-on paint finish commonly used on steel wheels. Special coated wheel weights must be used when balancing aluminum wheels to avoid damaging the wheel. Aluminum tends to form an electrolytic reaction with standard clip-on wheel weights. This reaction, which breaks down the finish coating, causes permanent damage to the wheel. Sometimes adhesive-backed weights are used to balance custom wheels that do not have a rim flange to clip regular weights to, or to enable placing weights in an unobtrusive location to avoid marring the aesthetics of a custom wheel.

Early custom wheels were often a spoke design commonly known as a "wire wheel." The spokes provide some degree of flexibility on a chassis with a very stiff suspension and also increase air circulation to cool the brakes. However, a spoke design is not really practical for modern tubeless tires, as each spoke makes a hole in the wheel flange through which air can escape. To prevent air leaks, manufacturers apply a sealant to the spoke holes, but adjusting the spokes can break the seal. The alternative is to use an inner tube.

Each spoke has an adjustment nipple, and the spokes are individually adjusted to keep the wheel round, balanced, and centered.

Wire spoke wheels generally use a single center nut, rather than several lug nuts or bolts, to mount the wheel on the spindle. A wheel mounted in this way is called a **knockoff wheel** and the large center nut is the "knockoff." The knockoff has two or more handles, or "ears," to make installing and removing it easier. A soft-faced hammer is used to loosen and tighten the knockoff. Originally designed for racing, knockoff wheels allowed quick wheel changes during pit stops. Some modern wheels still use knockoff wheels, but without spokes.

WHEEL BEARINGS

Many non-driven wheels use two wheel bearings—the **inner wheel bearing** and the **outer wheel bearing**—installed between the hub and the spindle or axle shaft (Figure 13-6). Like all bearings, the wheel bearings have the primary job of reducing friction between moving parts. In addition, the wheel bearings also bear the vehicle weight and transfer it to the wheels and tires. Wheel bearings consist of four main parts:

- Inner race
- Outer race
- Cage
- Rollers or balls

The rollers or balls eliminate friction by rolling between two surfaces, while the inner and outer races provide smooth surfaces for them to ride on, and a cage keeps the rollers or balls separated from each other and evenly spaced (Figure 13-7).

Lubrication is another important factor in the ability of a wheel bearing to reduce friction. Although some wheel bearings used on a driven solid rear axle are lubricated by gear oil in the axle housing, most wheel bearings are packed with grease during assembly. Wheel bearing grease performs several functions. It helps the rollers or balls move smoothly, dissipates heat from the bearing components, protects the wheel bearing from dirt and other contaminants, and helps prevent rust and corrosion. Seals keep the grease inside the wheel bearing. Lubricants and seals are discussed in Chapter 2 of this *Classroom Manual*.

Wheel bearings must support the vehicle weight under two types of load:

- Radial
- Thrust

WHEEL BEARINGS

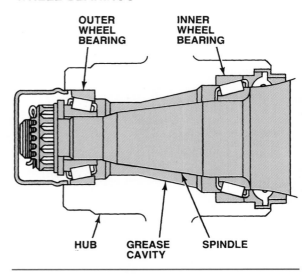

Figure 13-6. The wheel bearings reduce friction between the spindle and hub and also transfer the weight of the vehicle to the hub on a non-driven wheel.

WHEEL BEARING CONSTRUCTION

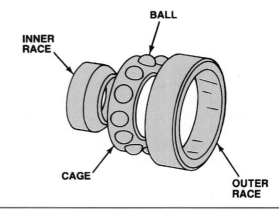

Figure 13-7. A cage keeps the balls of this ball bearing spaced apart as they ride between the inner and outer races.

The **radial load** is applied to the bearings at all times as the vehicle weight presses on the wheels, whereas a **thrust load** occurs only during cornering when chassis components exert a side force on the bearings (Figure 13-8). Wheel bearings must have load-carrying capacity in both directions. Wheel bearings at a drive axle should also be able to control the **thrust movement** of the axle shaft, in addition to bearing the thrust load. A wheel bearing that cannot control thrust movement develops excessive endplay.

Some wheel bearings, especially the roller type, are adjustable for endplay or preload.

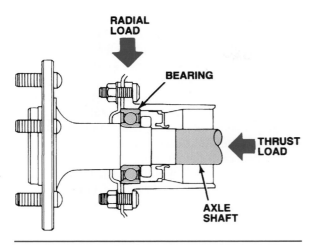

Figure 13-8. Radial load is the vehicle weight pressing on the wheels, and thrust load occurs as chassis components exert a side force during cornering.

Wheel bearing endplay is the amount the wheel can slide laterally, or in-and-out, on the spindle and is a result of clearance between the rollers or balls and the races. When specified, allowable wheel bearing endplay is very slight and measured in thousandths of an inch or hundredths of a millimeter. Too much endplay causes the wheel to wobble as it rotates and changes alignment angles. Too little endplay causes binding and overheating, which eventually causes the bearing to seize. **Wheel bearing preload** occurs when there is pressure, rather than clearance, between the rollers or balls and the races. Rear wheel bearings on a RWD solid rear axle may have preload specifications to hold the bearings in place against the outward force of the axle shaft and differential pinion gear. Preload increases friction and heat in the bearing because the parts are in contact with each other.

Wheel bearings are often categorized as being serviceable or non-serviceable. A serviceable wheel bearing can be removed, disassembled, cleaned, inspected, lubricated, and re-installed if found in good condition. A non-serviceable wheel bearing is permanently sealed and cannot be disassembled, inspected, or lubricated (Figure 13-9). Therefore, if a non-serviceable bearing fails, it must be replaced as a unit. A non-serviceable wheel bearing is usually referred to as a "sealed" bearing, and is often integrated into the hub assembly. In this case, the hub and bearing are replaced as a unit. With either type of bearing, if it has worn enough to damage the hub, the hub must also be replaced. The *Shop Manual* describes these procedures.

A number of different bearing designs are used as wheel bearings in modern automotive applica-

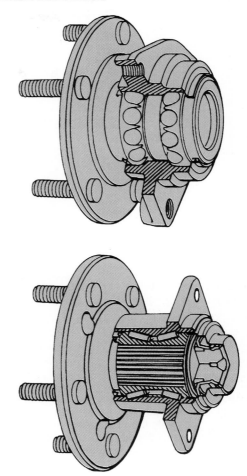

Figure 13-9. Many late-model wheel bearings are non-serviceable, or permanently sealed, so the entire assembly must be replaced if the bearing fails.

tions. Wheel bearings can be categorized by their construction into one of three types:

- Cylindrical roller bearings
- Tapered roller bearings
- Ball bearings

The main difference between these bearing classifications is in the type of rollers or balls used to reduce friction (Figure 13-10). Design differences affect the radial load and thrust load carrying abilities of the bearing.

Roller Bearings

Roller bearings have more surface area in contact with the races than a comparably sized ball bearing.

BEARINGS

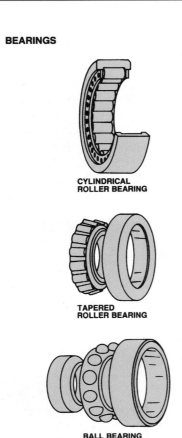

CYLINDRICAL ROLLER BEARING

TAPERED ROLLER BEARING

BALL BEARING

Figure 13-10. Roller bearings have more surface area in contact with the races and can withstand greater radial loads than ball bearings, but ball bearings are more effective at controlling thrust movement if the balls ride in a groove on the races.

This allows a roller bearing to support a greater radial load. In a roller bearing, the rollers can be either cylindrical or tapered.

A cylindrical roller bearing cannot control thrust movement of an axle shaft because the smooth cylinder offers no resistance to the lateral movement of the hub along the length of the spindle. A tapered roller bearing has cone-shaped rollers, with one end smaller than the other. These install with the tapered, or smaller, end of the inner bearing facing the tapered end of the outer bearing. This arrangement helps control thrust movement because the larger ends resist lateral movement of the hub on the spindle. Tapered roller wheel bearings are used on both driven and non-driven axles.

Ball Bearings

Both the radial and thrust load carrying capacity are less for a ball bearing than for a roller bearing because the surface area in contact with the races is smaller with a ball than with a roller. However,

ball bearings usually can control thrust movement of an axle shaft because the balls ride in grooves, rather than on a flat surface, on the inner and outer races. The groove walls resist the lateral movement of the wheel on the spindle. The most frequent use of ball bearings is at the rear wheels of RWD vehicles with a solid rear axle. These bearings install into the axle housing, and are often press-fitted to the axle shaft. Some FWD vehicles, especially older models, use ball bearings at the front wheels. Typically, these FWD designs are a sealed double ball bearing—both the inner and outer bearing are assembled together and a single cage contains the balls for both bearings. Most ball bearings are non-serviceable.

BRAKE FRICTION ASSEMBLIES

This text does not cover the hydraulic system that operates the brakes, but does briefly examine the brake friction assemblies found at the wheels. There are two reasons for a chassis technician to be familiar with brake friction assemblies. First, it is often necessary to disassemble the wheel brakes in the course of servicing suspension components. Second, whenever the wheels are removed and the brake friction assembly is exposed, the brakes should be carefully inspected to make sure the system can operate safely. Early detection of brake friction wear can prevent damage to the drum or rotor caused by a friction surface that is worn away.

Some brake shoe and pad linings contain asbestos, which is a health hazard. The *Shop Manual* describes safe methods of servicing brake friction assemblies.

Automobiles use two types of brake friction assemblies: drum brakes and disc brakes. Drum brakes are an older technology. Some older and antique models may have drum brakes at all four wheels, but most late-model vehicles use either disc brakes at the front wheels and drum brakes at the rear, or disc brakes at all four wheels. Disc brakes, which dissipate heat better than drum brakes, are less likely to lose braking ability under heavy or repeated braking.

Drum Brakes

The main parts of a drum brake friction assembly at a wheel are the:

- Brake drum
- Brake shoes
- Wheel cylinder

The wheel cylinder moves the brake shoes into contact with the drum to create friction and slow the rotation of the wheel (Figure 13-11). Bolts or clamps attach the wheel cylinder to a brake backing plate that mounts on the knuckle or axle housing. Springs and other brake hardware attach the brake shoes to the backing plate and each other to create tension and hold the assembly in place. The brake drum fits over the friction assembly, the wheel fits onto the drum, and the wheel lug bolts or nuts hold both the wheel and the brake drum in place.

As the driver depresses the brake pedal, the brake system uses hydraulic pressure to move a piston outward at each end of the wheel cylinder. This piston action forces the brake shoes against the drum, and the friction between the shoes and drum stops the wheel. The shoes are covered with a lining material that slowly wears away after repeated braking. If the lining wears completely away, the metal of the shoes contacts the metal drum and scratches, or scores, the drum. A machining process known as turning can restore the drum friction surface if the damage is minor; otherwise, the drum must be replaced.

DRUM BRAKE

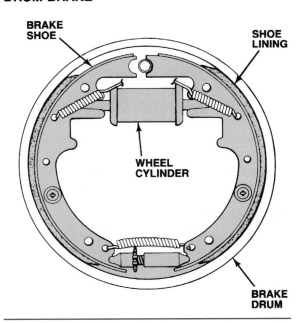

BRAKE
SHOE

SHOE
LINING

WHEEL
CYLINDER

BRAKE
DRUM

Figure 13-11. The brake drum rotates with the wheel and the wheel cylinder moves the shoes into contact with the drum to generate friction and slow it down when the brake pedal is depressed.

To avoid damage to the drum, simply replace the brake shoes before the lining wears out. When inspecting drum brakes, check the thickness of the lining material on the shoes. Manufacturers publish minimum thickness specifications, but as a general rule, the shoes need replacing when the friction material is worn to or below the thickness of the metal on the portion of the shoe it attaches to. Also check for signs of hydraulic fluid leakage at the wheel cylinders. Any detectable leakage indicates a need for service. Make sure all of the springs are intact and look for signs of wear, such as bends, nicks, looseness, and discoloration due to overheating.

Disc Brakes

The main parts of a disc brake assembly at a wheel are the:

- Disc, or rotor
- Caliper
- Brake pads

The rotor is a flat, circular metal disc that bolts onto, or is an integral part of, the hub. The caliper straddles the rotor and holds the brake pads, which install between the caliper and the front and back faces of the rotor (Figure 13-12). As the driver applies the brake pedal, hydraulic pressure pushes a piston or pistons out of the caliper to force the brake pads against the rotor. Friction between the pads and the rotor stops the wheel from rotating.

Like brake shoes, brake pads have a friction lining that slowly wears out as the brakes are applied. If the lining wears away, the rivets holding the lining in place, or the metal pad backing plate itself if the pad is adhesive-backed, scores the rotor. As with brake drums, turning a rotor can correct minor damage, but most often a damaged rotor must be replaced.

Early wear detection is the best way to prevent rotor damage. Inspect the brake pads for unusual wear patterns and measure the thickness of the friction material. Again, minimum thickness specifications are available, but as a rule of thumb, the thickness of the friction material should be greater than that of the metal backing plate. Look for signs of hydraulic fluid leakage, which indicates the caliper must be rebuilt or replaced. Also, check over the friction faces of the rotor for deep scratches and gouges, heat checks—which appear as a series of tiny hairline cracks—and discoloration caused by overheating. Any of these conditions indicates a need for brake service.

DISC BRAKE

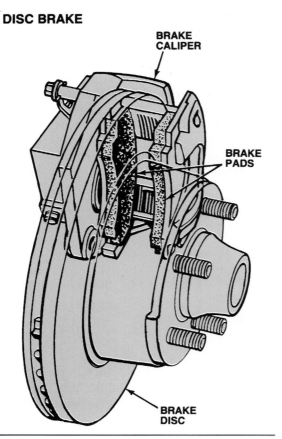

Figure 13-12. A caliper squeezes the brake pads against the two rotor faces to create friction and slow the rotation of the wheel on a disc brake assembly.

TIRES

The **tire** is a rubber cushion that mounts onto the wheel to provide traction and to absorb minor road shocks (Figure 13-13). On an automobile, the tire is always a **pneumatic tire,** meaning that it is filled with air. Early pneumatic tires used an **inner tube** filled with air and a stiff outer casing that held the tire shape and provided grip through the tread (Figure 13-14). In the 1940s, automotive tire manufacturers began switching to a **tubeless tire** design, which eliminates the inner tube and encases the air in a chamber formed by the tire carcass and the wheel rim (Figure 13-15). When selecting tires for a particular application, a number of factors must be considered, including:

- Tire construction
- Special-purpose tires
- Tire specifications
- Tire characteristics

Figure 13-13. Air in a tire helps cushion the vehicle against minor road shocks, and the tire tread grips the pavement to provide traction.

Tire Construction

Although a modern tubeless tire is a one-piece component, its structure can be divided into three sections:

- Carcass
- Casing
- Tread

The tire carcass is the foundation of the tire, the casing provides some stiffness to the structure, and the tread design determines traction (Figure 13-16).

Tire Carcass

A **tire carcass** consist of two elements (Figure 13-17):

- Plies
- Beads

A **tire ply** consists of cords of rayon, nylon, fiberglass, polyester, or steel arranged alongside each other and bonded together. The carcass is constructed of several plies, arranged so that the cords provide strength and flexibility. The way

TUBE-TYPE TIRE

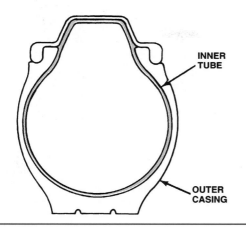

Figure 13-14. Early automotive tires were a tube-type design with an inner tube to contain the air and an outer casing to provide stiffness and shape the tire.

TUBELESS TIRE

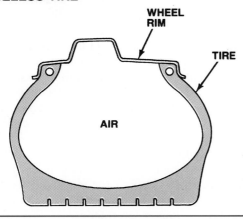

Figure 13-15. The tire casing and wheel rim form an air chamber on a tubeless tire, so there is no need for an inner tube.

that the plies are arranged determines the tire construction type.

The **tire beads** are strands of steel wire looped around the inner circumference of each sidewall to hold the tire on the wheel. When the tire is installed onto the wheel and inflated, the beads fit into the parts of the wheel rim called the "bead seats" to form an airtight seal.

The plies and beads are bonded together with rubber to form the carcass. An additional layer of fabric and hard rubber is bonded around the beads to protect them.

TIRE CONSTRUCTION

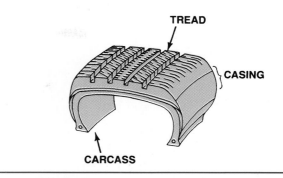

Figure 13-16. The carcass is the tire foundation, the casing gives the tire stiffness, and the tread adheres to the road to provide traction.

TIRE CARCASS

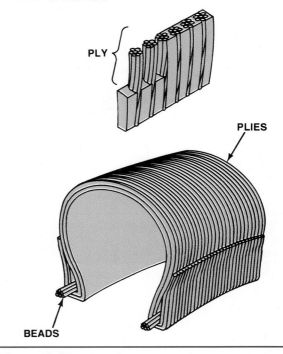

Figure 13-17. The tire carcass consists of the plies, which are made of cords bonded together, and the beads that secure the tire to the wheel rim.

Ply Patterns

There were three ways tire manufacturers arranged the plies when building tires (Figure 13-18). In past years there were three types of ply patterns: bias, belted bias, and radial. Only the radial ply pattern is now used in over-the-road vehicles.

PLY PATTERNS

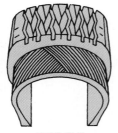

BIAS PLY

BELTED BIAS PLY

RADIAL PLY

Figure 13-18. The three methods of tire ply arrangement are bias, belted bias, and radial. Radial tires have replaced bias ply and belted bias as the standard tire design.

BIAS (BIAS BELTED) TIRES

On a **bias ply tire** (Figure 13-18) the first ply layer is positioned with the cords diagonal to the beads and a second layer is placed so its cords run across the cords of the first layer. Additional plies may be added in an alternating pattern for extra strength. A **belted bias ply tire** has the same carcass construction with the addition of two or more corded belts that run around the circumference of the tire.

The plies of a **radial ply tire** are laid with the cords at a 90-degree angle to the beads. This placement of the cords along the radius of the tire circle gives the design the name "radial ply." Two addi-

TIRE CASING

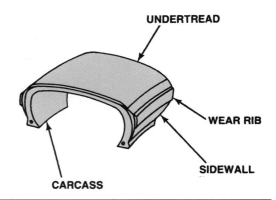

Figure 13-19. The elements of the tire casing—sidewall, undertread, and wear rib—are bonded onto the carcass. The sidewall and undertread add some stiffness to the structure, the undertread helps the tread bond to the tire, and the wear rib is optional.

tional belts, made of rayon, fiberglass, or steel, are placed between the radial plies and the tread.

For many years, all automotive tires were a bias ply construction. Radial tires began appearing on European models in the 1950s, and effectively took over the tire market in the 1970s. Belted bias ply tires were a compromise between the old and new technologies and were used as the industry made the transition from bias ply to radial. Belted bias ply tires provided a certain compromise between tire stiffness and flexibility throughout the tire carcass, but radial ply tires are considered superior. The radial plies provide a more flexible sidewall for improved road shock absorption, while the belts stiffen the tread for good road contact and traction.

Tire Casing

The **tire casing** consists of various layers of rubber bonded to the carcass (Figure 13-19). Layers bonded to the outer surface of each side form the **sidewall.** An optional strip of rubber, which is called the "wear rib," "curb guard," or "buffer strip," is bonded to the sidewall to protect it on some tires. The **undertread layer,** a ¹⁄₁₆-inch to ⅛-inch (2-mm to 3-mm) thick layer of rubber, fits across the outer circumference of the tire to help bond the carcass to the tread.

Tire Tread

The **tire tread** is the layer of rubber bonded around the outer circumference of the casing.

Tread rubber is a special compound designed for long wear and good traction. The rubber compound varies according to the intended purpose of the tire. Some tires have a tread design that delivers better traction when rolling in a particular direction. Such a tire is called a **directional tire,** and it must be installed on the correct side of the vehicle so that it will rotate in the proper direction when the vehicle is moving forward. Some models with directional tires use different sizes of tire from front to rear, so that each tire can be used only in one position. Typically, use of this type of tire is limited to exotic high-performance models, such as the Corvette ZR-1 or Porsche Turbo Carrera.

Grooves, Ribs, and Sipes

The pattern in the tread helps the tire grip the road when it is wet and exposes more surface area to the air for cooling when the road is dry. Tread patterns are designed to direct water on the pavement away from the rubber that contacts the road. Grooves around the circumference of the tire provide sideways stability on a wet road, and sideways grooves provide forward traction. Tires designed for highway use have a zigzag pattern for a good balance between the two.

The raised area between two grooves is called a "rib," while the small grooves molded into the tire ribs to give the tread more gripping edges are known as sipes (Figure 13-20). Sipes are smaller than the major tread grooves and may run at the same angle as the grooves or across the ribs. As the tread bends under pressure, the sipes open to expose extra gripping edges. Sipes also help the

tread force water from between the tire and pavement for better traction on wet roads.

Tread Patterns

Tire tread depth is the measurement from the top of the tread ribs to the bottom of the grooves. A new-tire tread depth is usually $\frac{9}{32}$ to $\frac{15}{32}$ of an inch (7 to 12 millimeters), but some truck tires have a deeper tread. Automotive tires have tread wear indicators, which are continuous bars that run across the entire tread and appear when the pattern is worn to the last $\frac{1}{16}$ of an inch (1.5 millimeters) (Figure 13-21). These inform the owner that the tire needs replacement.

Special-Purpose Tires

Tire designs may be modified if the tire is meant for a special purpose. Some widely used types of special-purpose tires are:

- Snow tires
- Rain tires
- Off-road tires
- Temporary spare tires

In addition, commercial trucks and mobile homes use tires designed especially for carrying heavy loads. Be aware that it is *never* safe to install those tires on passenger vehicles.

Snow Tires

Snow tires have wide, deep grooves and wide ribs (Figure 13-22). Although less rubber contacts the road with this design, the tread bites more deeply into soft snow and mud. Snow tires are designed for low-speed operation and poor traction condi-

TIRE TREAD

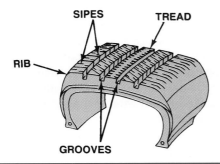

Figure 13-20. The tire tread runs around the circumference of the tire, and its pattern helps maintain traction. The ribs provide grip, while the grooves and sipes direct any water on the road away from the gripping surface of the tire.

WEAR INDICATORS

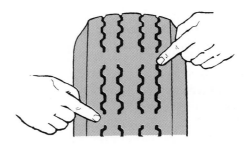

Figure 13-21. Tread wear indicators appear when the tread thickness wears to $\frac{1}{16}$ of an inch (1.5 mm) as a warning that the tire should be replaced.

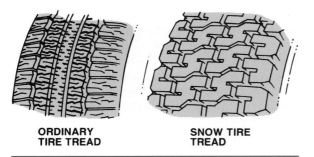

ORDINARY TIRE TREAD   **SNOW TIRE TREAD**

Figure 13-22. The thicker grooves and ribs that allow snow tires to grip better in snow and mud also detract from heat dissipation, so snow tires should not be used in warm weather for driving on dry pavement.

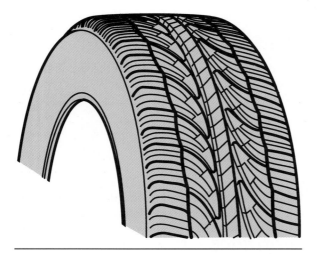

Figure 13-23. Rain tires have a tread designed to channel water on the pavement away from the contact patch to improve traction on wet pavement.

tions. The tread generates more heat at high speeds and may create high-speed vibrations, so snow tires should not be used for normal highway driving in warm weather.

Studded tires are snow tires with small metal studs embedded in the tread for better gripping on ice or hard-packed snow. Studs can damage the pavement, and they may actually provide less traction than non-studded tires, so some states prohibit or limit their use to certain areas.

Rain Tires
Rain tires have wide, deep grooves and a tread design that maximizes water displacement (Figure 13-23). These tires, which are designed for operation on wet pavement, often have a directional tread to more effectively channel water away from the contact patch. Like snow tires, a

Figure 13-24. Although designed to improve traction on loose surfaces, many off-road tires are purchased for their image and never leave the pavement.

rain tire generates more heat than a conventional tread design when driven on dry pavement.

Off-Road Tires
The use of off-road tires has grown dramatically over the last few years with the popularity of sport utility vehicles. Off-road tires have large ribs and deep grooves designed to dig into loose surfaces such as mud, gravel, and sand (Figure 13-24). Although common on sport utility vehicles that never leave the pavement, highway operation actually defeats the purpose of an off-road tire. Many off-road tires are purchased simply for appearance and image, rather than practicality. Traction is reduced and temperatures rise when an off-road tire is operated on paved surfaces, and the tires also generate an excessive amount of noise.

Space-Saver Spare Tires
Space-saver spare tires and their wheels are designed to reduce the amount of storage space they occupy in the vehicle and are intended for emergency use only. Space-saver spare tires are designed to get the vehicle to a service station, not for ordinary use. These tires have a minimal service life and the vehicle should be driven at a reduced speed when a space-saver spare is installed. Maximum operating speed and service life are generally embossed on the sidewall of the tire. Typically, operation should be limited to about 50 miles (80 kilometers) at speeds below 45 mph (70 km/h).

Run-Flat Tires

Technologies are currently being developed to help maintain vehicle mobility as a tire is punctured, which are known as **run-flat tires.** There are two types of run-flat tires: self-sealing and self-supporting tires. In the future we will see auxiliary supported systems for use as original equipment. Goodyear, pioneer of the run-flat tire, developed it for such cars as the Corvette and the Plymouth Prowler. These specialty two-seaters have humongous tires and no space to hold a spare tire.

Self-Sealing Tires

Self-sealing tires are designed to fix most punctures instantly and permanently. These tires feature standard tire construction except for an extra lining inside the tire under the tread area. This lining is coated with a puncture sealant which can permanently seal most punctures from nails, bolts, or screws up to ³⁄₁₆ of an inch in diameter. These tires provide a seal around the object when the tire is first punctured and then fill in the hole in the tread when the object is removed. Because these tires are designed to seal the tire immediately upon being punctured, most drivers will never even know that they experienced a puncture. Also, because these tires feature standard tire constructions, the traditional loss-of-air symptoms, which accompany a flat tire, remain to warn the driver if the tire is damaged beyond repair. Therefore, self-sealing tires do not require a low air pressure warning system. Examples include the Firestone FT70c Sealix, Uniroyal Tiger Paw with NailGard, Tiger Paw Royal Seal, and General Gen-Seal.

Self-Supporting Tires

Self-supporting tires feature a stiffer internal construction, which is capable of actually temporarily carrying the weight of the vehicle, even after the tire has lost all air pressure. These tires typically sandwich rubber between layers of heat resistant cord in the sidewall to help prevent the sidewalls from folding over on themselves. "Pinching" the sidewalls in the event of loss of air pressure gives the tires "self-supporting" capability. They also feature specialized beads, which allow the tire to firmly grip current original equipment and aftermarket wheels in the event of air loss. Because self-supporting tires are so good at masking the traditional loss-of-air symptoms, which accompany a flat tire, they require a tire pressure monitoring system to alert the driver about a loss of air

pressure. Without such a system, the driver may not notice underinflation and may inadvertently cause additional tire damage by failing to inflate or repair the tire at the first opportunity. Typically, self-supporting tires maintain vehicle mobility for 50 miles at speeds up to 55 mph. The Firestone Firehawk SZ50 EP RFT developed specifically for the Chevrolet Corvette C5, as well as the BF Goodrich Comp T/A ZR SSS, Dunlop SP Sport 9000 DSST, Firestone Firehawk SH30 RF, and Michelin ZP, are self-supporting run-flat tires.

Auxiliary Supported Run-Flat Systems

Auxiliary supported systems combine unique wheels and tires and are currently under development for use on future original-equipment vehicle applications. In these systems, when the tire loses pressure, it rests on a support ring attached to the wheel. The advantage to this type of system is that it will place most of the task of providing run-flat capability on the wheel (which doesn't "wear out" or need to be replaced), and minimizes the responsibility of the tire (which does wear out and requires replacement). Auxiliary supported systems can improve ride quality because their sidewall's stiffness can be equivalent to today's standard tires. The system currently in use is the Michelin PAX System. The disadvantage to auxiliary supported systems is that their unique wheels will not accept standard tires and that their lower volume will make this type of system more expensive.

TIRE SPECIFICATIONS

Tire specifications provide a reference for matching the right size and type of tire to each wheel and vehicle application. Tire size, dimension, design specifications, and details about the tire manufacturing are molded into the tire sidewall.

Tire Size and Dimensions

A tire must be the right size for the wheel it is mounted on, and two measurements determine this fit. First, the tire inner diameter must match the wheel diameter (Figure 13-25). For example, a 16-inch wheel requires a tire with a 16-inch inner diameter. Second, the width of the tire at the beads must match the wheel rim width (Figure 13-26). However, tire bead width and wheel rim width are not always an exact match. For example, a tire manufacturer may allow a 6-inch wide tire to be

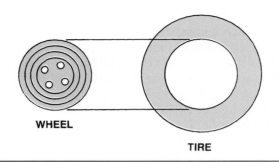

Figure 13-25. The tire inner diameter must match the outer diameter of the wheel on which it is mounted.

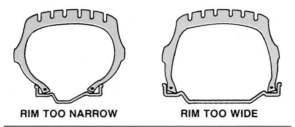

Figure 13-26. The width across the tire beads and the wheel rim width must be within an acceptable range specified by the manufacturer.

used on a 7-inch wide rim. Consult specifications from the manufacturer for the allowable range.

Some other tire dimensions to take into account are the section width, section height, and aspect ratio. The section width and height are both measurements of the tire cross section. The **tire section width** is the measurement across the width of the tire, from the outside of one sidewall to the other. The **tire section height** is the measurement from the top of the beads to the bottom of the tread. Both of these measurements indicate the dimensions of the tire when it is mounted on the wheel and inflated, but *without* a load on it. The **tire aspect ratio** is a comparison of the section height to the section width. To determine aspect ratio, divide the section height by the section width, then multiply by 100 to eliminate the decimal point (Figure 13-27).

The diameter, section width, and aspect ratio are all indicated in the sizing code on the tire sidewall, as explained in the following section.

Tire Sidewall Information

A great deal of information about a tire is molded into its sidewall (Figure 13-28). This information includes:

- Tire size code
- Uniform tire quality grading system (UTQGS) code

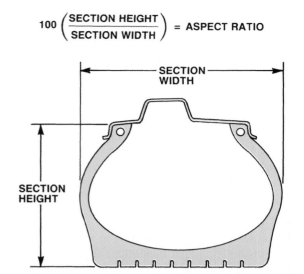

$$100 \left(\frac{\text{SECTION HEIGHT}}{\text{SECTION WIDTH}} \right) = \text{ASPECT RATIO}$$

Figure 13-27. To determine the aspect ratio, divide the section height by the section width, then multiply by 100 to eliminate the decimal point.

Figure 13-28. The Tire Industry Safety Council requires that a great deal of information appear on the tire sidewall.

- GM tire performance criteria (TPC)
- Load range
- Maximum load
- Maximum pressure
- Other designations

The Tire Industry Safety Council requires certain information to be on the tire sidewall as a benefit to the consumer and technician.

■ Tire Shaving

Many racing organizations require certain classes of cars to run on highway-approved tires with grooved tread. The drivers of such cars commonly shave the tire tread to a lower depth, using a tire truing machine.

In the tread of an ordinary, unshaved tire, the rubber blocks stand relatively tall and unsupported, and the tread flexes and squirms slightly during high-speed cornering. This flex, which slightly reduces stability and traction, hinders speed through the curve. The squirm of the unshaved tread also rapidly builds heat in the rubber. In fact, the tire will overheat and blister after just a few laps at racing speeds, causing large portions of rubber to pull away from the tread—a phenomenon racers call "chunking."

Tires shaved to a tread depth of approximately 3⁄32 of an inch (2.3 mm) are perfect for a dry race track. They resist flexing, improve cornering traction, and last much longer. The tire companies have caught on to this practice and some who cater to racers manufacture tires with tread already molded to the proper depth. However, when racers compete in the rain, they use unshaved tires, with a higher tread depth. Even race drivers go a little slower in the rain, so the tread flexes less, and the rain water keeps the tread cool. Also, the deeper grooves remove the water from under the tire more effectively, improving wet-weather traction.

To showcase their new street-performance tire, the Radial T/A, B. F. Goodrich joined forces with the International Motor Sports Association (IMSA) to create the Radial T/A Challenge Series in the mid-1970s. This new race series, which featured late-model sports sedans, required the cars to run on performance radial street tires. At first, the Radial T/A was the only IMSA-approved tire, but not for long. Not to be outdone by its rival, Goodyear soon introduced the Eagle GT tire, which IMSA approved for use in the now renamed Radial Challenge Series. This led to a fierce tire war between the two industrial giants waged on the race tracks of North America. It was rumored at the time that Goodyear was manufacturing the Eagle GT with a dual-rubber compound in order to gain a competitive edge. That is, the base of the tire was constructed of a soft compound, suitable for competition, covered by a hard-rubber compound designed for street use. Once the tread was shaved, the soft rubber was exposed and the Eagle GT street tire was effectively converted to a true competition tire. Whether true or not, the two tire manufacturers battled fiercely for several years, much to the delight of the race teams who were receiving free tires, before switching the focus of their attention on other aspects of motor sports.

Tire shaving is a trick for racers only. Unshaved tires last much longer on the street and provide better traction and safety in wet weather.

Tire Size Code

One of the most important pieces of information is the identification code. The format of how this information is presented has undergone several revisions since it was first introduced in the 1960s. The current size code, adopted in 1989, uses an alphanumeric series of characters. The tire-size code indicates:

- Type of vehicle for which the tire is designed
- Tire section width, in millimeters
- Tire aspect ratio
- Type of tire
- Wheel diameter, in inches
- Tire load index
- Tire speed rating

P-Metric Tire Sizes

Most P-metric tire sizes do not have exact corresponding alphanumeric tire sizes. Replacement tires should be of the same **tire performance criteria (TPC)** specification number including the same size, the same load range, and the same construction as those originally installed on the vehicle. Consult a tire dealer if you must replace the P-metric tire with other sizes. Tire companies can best recommend the closest match of alphanumeric to P-metric sizes within their own tire lines.

Many vehicles are equipped with steel belted all-season radial tires as standard equipment. These tires qualify as snow tires, with a higher-than-average rating for snow traction than the non-all-season radial tires previously used. Other performance areas, such as wet traction, rolling resistance, tread life, and air retention, are also improved. This is done by improvements in both tread design and tread compounds. These tires are identified by an "M + S" molded in the tire sidewall after the tire size. The suffix MS is also molded in the tire sidewall after the TPC specification number. The optional handling tires used on some vehicles now also have the MS marking after the tire size and the TPC specification number.

Example: P215/60R15 87H (Figure 13-29)

- **"P"** means this is a passenger car tire (as opposed to a tire made for a truck or other vehicle). P-metric is the U.S. version of a metric tire-sizing system.
- **"215"** Section Width: The width of the tire in millimeters from sidewall to sidewall. This measurement varies depending on the width of the rim to which the tire is fitted: larger on a wider rim, smaller on a narrow rim. The number on the side of the tire indicates the width measured with the tire fitted to the recommended rim width.
- **"60"** Aspect Ratio: The ratio of height to width; this tire's height is 60% of its width.
- **"R"** Construction: How the plies are constructed in the tire carcass. "R" means radial. "B" in place of the "R" means the tire is belted bias construction. "D" in place of the "R" means diagonal bias construction.
- **"15"** Rim Diameter: The diameter of the wheel in inches.
- **"87"** Load Index: This tire has an industry-standard maximum load of 1,201 lbs. Different

numbers correspond to different maximum loads. The maximum load is shown in lbs. (pounds) and in kg (kilograms), and maximum pressure in PSI (pounds per square inch) and in kPa (kilopascals). Kilograms and kilopascals are metric units of measurement (Figure 13-30).
- **"H"** Speed Rating: This tire has an industry-standard maximum service speed of 130 mph. Tires using an older European system carry the speed rating in the size description: 215/60HR15. Different letters correspond to different maximum service speeds (Figure 13-31).
- The letters **"DOT"** certify compliance with all applicable safety standards established by the U.S. Department of Transportation (DOT). Adjacent to this is a tire identification or serial number; a combination of numbers and letters with up to 11 digits.
- The sidewall also shows the type of cord and number of plies in the sidewall and under the tread.

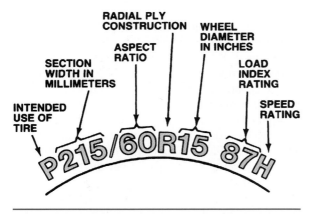

Figure 13-29. A standard, alphanumeric tire-size code structure has been used by the tire industry since 1989.

The speed and load rating are important considerations for both the technician and the vehicle owner. If the vehicle exceeds either maximum, the tire can disintegrate and cause an accident. A

tire that is not inflated properly becomes unsafe above the maximum ratings.

Some tires, especially those designed for older and antique vehicles, may be labeled using one of the previous coding systems (Figure 13-32). Typically, these are used on specialty tires designed to maintain the original appearance on vintage automobiles.

Uniform Tire Quality Grading System (UTQGS)

Except for snow tires, the DOT requires manufacturers to grade passenger car tires based on three performance factors; tread wear, traction, and temperature resistance.

Tread Wear

The tread wear grade is a comparative rating based on the wear rate of the tire when tested under controlled conditions on a specified government test course. For example, a tire graded 150 would wear one and a half (1½) times as well on

LOAD INDEX	LOAD	
75	853 LBS	(387 KG)
76	882 LBS	(400 KG)
77	908 LBS	(412 KG)
78	937 LBS	(425 KG)
79	963 LBS	(437 KG)
80	992 LBS	(450 KG)
81	1,019 LBS	(462 KG)
82	1,047 LBS	(475 KG)
83	1,074 LBS	(487 KG)
84	1,102 LBS	(500 KG)
85	1,135 LBS	(515 KG)
86	1,168 LBS	(530 KG)
87	1,201 LBS	(545 KG)
88	1,235 LBS	(560 KG)
89	1,279 LBS	(580 KG)
90	1,323 LBS	(600 KG)
91	1,358 LBS	(615 KG)
92	1,389 LBS	(630 KG)
93	1,433 LBS	(650 KG)
94	1,477 LBS	(670 KG)
95	1,521 LBS	(690 KG)
96	1,565 LBS	(710 KG)
97	1,609 LBS	(730 KG)
98	1,653 LBS	(750 KG)
99	1,709 LBS	(775 KG)
100	1,764 LBS	(800 KG)
101	1,819 LBS	(825 KG)
102	1,874 LBS	(850 KG)
103	1,929 LBS	(875 KG)
104	1,934 LBS	(900 KG)
105	2,039 LBS	(925 KG)
106	2,094 LBS	(950 KG)
107	2,149 LBS	(975 KG)
108	2,205 LBS	(1,000 KG)
109	2,271 LBS	(1,030 KG)
110	2,337 LBS	(1,060 KG)
111	2,403 LBS	(1,090 KG)
112	2,469 LBS	(1,120 KG)
113	2,535 LBS	(1,150 KG)
114	2,601 LBS	(1,180 KG)
115	2,679 LBS	(1,215 KG)

Figure 13-30. Each number in the load index rating system indicates the maximum load a tire can carry when inflated to its maximum pressure.

Speed Rating	Maximum Speed
Q	99 mph
S	112 mph
T	118 mph
U	124 mph
H	130 mph
V	149 mph
W	168 mph
Y	186 mph
Z	Above 149 mph

Figure 13-31. Each letter in the speed rating system represents a maximum speed at which a tire is designed to safely operate when inflated to its maximum pressure.

OLDER TIRE-SIZE SYSTEMS

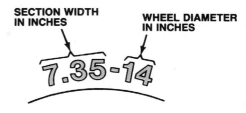

U.S. NUMERIC SYSTEM USED THROUGH LATE 1960s

SECTION WIDTH IN INCHES

WHEEL DIAMETER IN INCHES

7.35-14

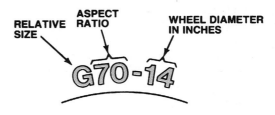

U.S. ALPHANUMERIC SYSTEM USED 1968-1976

RELATIVE SIZE

ASPECT RATIO

WHEEL DIAMETER IN INCHES

G70-14

EUROPEAN METRIC SYSTEM

SECTION WIDTH IN MILLIMETERS

RADIAL PLY CONSTRUCTION

WHEEL DIAMETER IN INCHES

185R14

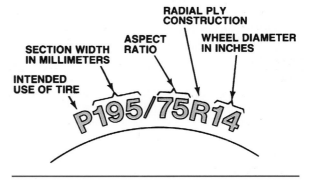

P-METRIC SYSTEM USED 1976-1989

SECTION WIDTH IN MILLIMETERS

INTENDED USE OF TIRE

ASPECT RATIO

RADIAL PLY CONSTRUCTION

WHEEL DIAMETER IN INCHES

P195/75R14

Figure 13-32. Through the years, the tire industry has used a number of coding systems to indicate tire size and profile, and the newer the system, the more tire information the code contains.

the government course as a tire graded 100. A tire graded 200 would wear twice as well on the government test track as one graded 100. The relative performance of tires depends upon the actual conditions of their use, however, and may depart significantly from the norm due to variations in driving habits, service practices, and differences in road characteristics and climate.

- More than 100—Better
- 100—Baseline
- Less than 100—Poorer

Traction

The traction grades from highest to lowest—AA, A, B, and C—represent the tire's ability to stop on wet pavement as measured under controlled conditions on specified government test surfaces of asphalt and concrete. The traction grade is based upon "straight ahead" braking tests; it does not indicate cornering ability. A tire marked "C" may have poor traction performance.

- AA—Highest traction
- A—High Traction
- B—Intermediate
- C—Acceptable

Temperature Resistance

The temperature grades represent the tire's resistance to the generation of heat when tested under controlled conditions on a specified indoor laboratory test wheel. Sustained high temperatures can cause the materials of the tire to degenerate and thus reduce tire life. Excessive temperatures can lead to tire failure. Federal law requires that all tires meet at least the minimal requirements of Grade C. The temperature grades are A (the highest), B, and C. Sustained high temperature can cause the tire's material to degenerate and reduce tire life, and excessive temperature can lead to sudden tire failure. Grade C corresponds to a level of performance which all passenger car tires must meet under the Federal Motor Vehicle Safety Standard No. 109. Grades A and B represent higher levels of performance on the laboratory test wheel than the minimum required by law.

- A—Best
- B—Intermediate
- C—Acceptable

Load Range and Speed Rating

While there is no industry-wide definition of load range (Figure 13-30), truck tires are frequently marked with ply ratings and equivalent load range. These markings are used to identify the load and inflation limits of that particular tire, when used in a specific type of service. The **speed rating** (Figure 13-31), is the maximum service speed of a passenger car tire. Light truck tires are not speed rated. The speed ratings of passenger car tires (Figure 13-31) show the rating indicators and their mile-per-hour equivalents. This rating system applies to all tire makers.

Load Range, Maximum Load, and Maximum Pressure

Some, but not all, tires have a letter designation that indicates load range, or tire strength. These range from "A" to "L," and a passenger car tire generally falls into the "B" load range. The maximum load and inflation pressure information are printed out plainly, instead of being in code. Typically, this designation follows this format: "MAX. LOAD 685 kg (1510 LBS.) • 240 kPa (35 PSI) MAX. PRESS." This tire is designed to carry up to 1,510 pounds when inflated to 35 psi. Never exceed either of these specifications.

Steel Belted All-Season Radial Tires

Many vehicles are equipped with steel belted all-season radial tires as standard equipment. These tires qualify as snow tires, with a higher-than-average rating for snow traction than the non-all season radial tires previously used.

Other Designations

Additional miscellaneous information is embossed on the sidewall of the tire. The name of the tire manufacturer and the brand name of the tire always appear on the sidewall. The word "radial" appears somewhere on every radial ply tire. On a mud and snow tire, "M/S," "M + S," or "M & S" is found on the sidewall. All tires carry a description of the ply materials and the number of plies. A typical example would be: "TREAD 2 PLIES POLYESTER CORD • 2 PLIES STEEL CORD • 2 PLIES NYLON CORD" and "SIDEWALL 2 PLIES POLYESTER CORD." The description "tubeless" or "tube-type" appears somewhere on the tire. A designation beginning with "DOT" indicates that the tire meets safety standards set by the Department of Transportation. The numbers and letters following the "DOT" are codes that indicate the manufacturer, tire size, manufacturing date, and other information. A directional tire has a mark or marks on the sidewall to indicate what direction the tire should rotate

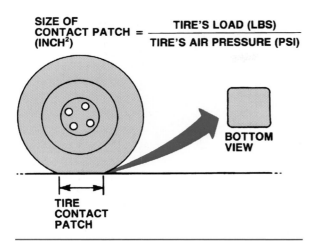

$$\text{SIZE OF CONTACT PATCH (INCH}^2) = \frac{\text{TIRE'S LOAD (LBS)}}{\text{TIRE'S AIR PRESSURE (PSI)}}$$

BOTTOM VIEW

TIRE CONTACT PATCH

Figure 13-33. The contact patch is the area of the tire that actually touches the pavement when under load.

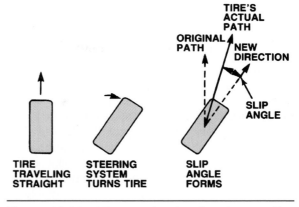

TIRE'S ACTUAL PATH

ORIGINAL PATH

NEW DIRECTION

SLIP ANGLE

TIRE TRAVELING STRAIGHT

STEERING SYSTEM TURNS TIRE

SLIP ANGLE FORMS

Figure 13-34. When a tire that has been rolling straight is steered in a new direction it forms a slip angle and travels in a path somewhere between the original direction and the steered direction while the vehicle corners.

when the vehicle moves forward, and also has a "directional pattern" marking somewhere on the tire.

Depending on the manufacturer, the sidewall may contain still more information about the tire than the items previously discussed.

Tire Characteristics

Certain technical terms are used to describe the way a tire behaves when it is moving over the pavement. These terms define the dynamic characteristics of a tire.

The first and most basic concept in tire dynamics is the "footprint," or **tire contact patch.** This is the part of the tire that actually touches the road surface (Figure 13-33). Theoretically, the size of the contact patch can be calculated by dividing the load on the tire in pounds by the inflation pressure in psi (pounds per square inch) of the tire. The result is the size of the contact patch in square inches. However, the shape of the tire also affects the contact patch size, so the formula is not completely accurate. As a tire rolls, the contact patch continually changes along the circumference of the tire.

Adhesion, which is the amount of grip between the contact patch and the road, is closely related to the contact patch. A tire has a finite amount of adhesion that keeps it in contact with the road, and some of this adhesion force is lost during acceleration, braking, and cornering. Tires deform slightly during these movements, making less adhesion available to keep the tires in contact with the road. For example, if a driver accelerates in a turn, the tires are more likely to lose their grip on the road

because both the cornering and acceleration forces use up some of the available adhesion force.

Tire adhesion divided by the weight the tire is supporting equals the **coefficient of friction (Cf)** of the tire. Various circumstances, such as braking, cornering, acceleration, and vehicle weight distribution, alter the Cf of the tires. A tire with a Cf of 1.0 exerts a gripping force equal to the weight it supports. Automotive tires commonly develop a Cf around 0.8 to 1.0 under ideal driving conditions. Modern racing tires are capable of developing a Cf of 1.5, which was once thought to be impossible since it means the tire adheres to the pavement with a force 50% greater than the weight it supports!

Whenever a rolling tire is deflected from a straight-ahead path, it develops a **slip angle,** which is the angle between the direction the tire is pointed and the direction that it actually moves. For example, as the driver turns the steering wheel to negotiate a corner, the steering system pulls the front wheel and most of the tire to a new angle. However, the contact patch does not follow the steered direction of the wheel because the force of adhesion is gripping the pavement (Figure 13-34). Therefore, the contact patch resists both the directional change and the centrifugal force generated by the turn. To allow for this resistance, the tire rubber around the contact patch deforms and as a result it slides along the road at an angle to the new direction, which creates the slip angle. The same thing happens to the rear tires as they slide at an angle to the new direction in which the vehicle is traveling. As the vehicle straightens out, each leading edge of the continually changing contact patch moves a little closer toward the direction the tire is aimed, until the slip angle virtually disappears.

When a driver accelerates or decelerates during a turn, the force of acceleration or deceleration—especially at the drive wheels—decreases the adhesion of the tire. At the same time, a portion of the gripping force of the tire is also being used to create a slip angle. If the amount of adhesion required by changing speed and that needed to form the slip angle for cornering add up to more adhesion than the tire is able to provide, the tire slips along the pavement causing the vehicle to skid. Skidding can also occur during straight-ahead driving if extreme deceleration or acceleration demands more adhesion than the tire is capable of providing.

Tire adhesion varies according to the rubber compound used in the tread and the tread design itself. It may seem as though the more adhesion, the better the tire, but there are limits to the advantages of a very "sticky," or "soft," tire. To take the idea to an absurd length, consider the fact that a tire with absolute adhesion could not move! While a sticky tire with a high level of adhesion may be good for racing because it allows extreme acceleration and high-speed cornering without a loss of traction, tires that provide high adhesion also tend to get hot, wear out relatively quickly, and are impractical for road use. Typically, the rubber compound of a street tire is a compromise that provides a balance between a cool-running, long-lasting tread and an adequate level of adhesion for most operating conditions.

A final tire operational term is **hydroplaning,** a condition that occurs when a tire is driving on a wet surface (Figure 13-35). Also known as **aquaplaning,** this condition results from water build-up forming into a wedge in front of a rolling tire. If vehicle speed is fast enough, the tire starts to ride up onto the wedge so that a portion of the contact patch is actually on the water surface instead of the pavement. The narrower a tire, the less likely it will hydroplane, because a wedge of water does not form as easily at the front of a narrow tire.

The **tire placard** (Figure 13-36) is used to display tire pressure and capacity information. It is permanently located on the edge of the driver's door. Refer to the placard to obtain the following:

- The maximum vehicle capacity weight
- The cold tire inflation pressures
- The tire sizes (original equipment tires)
- The tire speed ratings (original equipment tires)

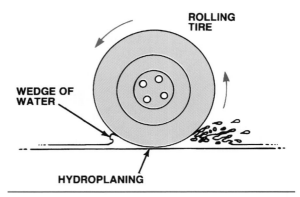

Figure 13-35. A tire rolling on a wet surface builds up a wedge of water in front of it, and if the tire rolls up onto the wedge it is hydroplaning, or driving on top of the water instead of the pavement.

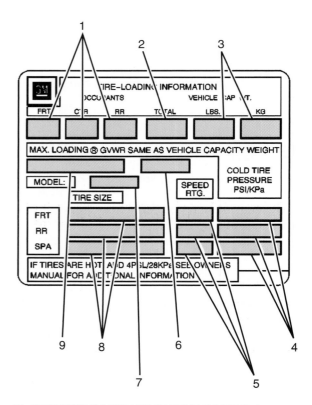

(1) **SPECIFIED OCCUPANT SEATING POSITIONS**
(2) **TOTAL OCCUPANT SEATING**
(3) **MAXIMUM VEHICLE CAPACITY WEIGHT**
(4) **TIRE PRESSURES, FRONT, REAR, AND SPARE**
(5) **TIRE SPEED RATING, FRONT, REAR, AND SPARE**
(6) **TIRE LABEL CODE**
(7) **ENGINEERING MODEL MINUS FIRST CHARACTER**
(8) **TIRE SIZES, FRONT, REAR, AND SPARE**
(9) **VEHICLE IDENTIFICATION NUMBER**

Figure 13-36. This diagram shows a remote control door lock receiver (RCDLR). (Courtesy of General Motors Corporation)

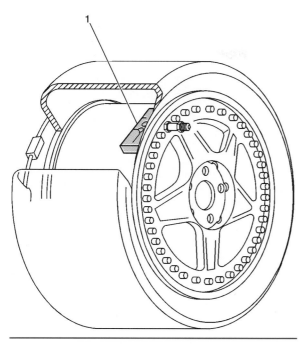

Figure 13-37. This diagram shows radio frequency transmitting pressure sensors inside each wheel/tire assembly. (Courtesy of General Motors Corporation)

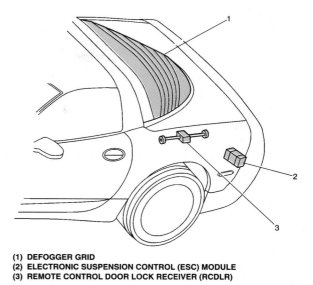

(1) DEFOGGER GRID
(2) ELECTRONIC SUSPENSION CONTROL (ESC) MODULE
(3) REMOTE CONTROL DOOR LOCK RECEIVER (RCDLR)

Figure 13-38. This diagram shows a remote control door lock receiver (RCDLR). (Courtesy of General Motors Corporation)

Tire Pressure Monitor Description and Operation

The **tire pressure monitor (TPM)** (Figure 13-37) system allows the driver to display all four-tire pressures on the driver information center (DIC) while the vehicle is being driven. The system uses the **remote control door lock receiver (RCDLR),** body control module (BCM), powertrain control module (PCM), four radio frequency transmitting pressure sensors inside each wheel/tire assembly, and a class 2 serial data circuit to perform the system functions.

When the vehicle is stationary for more than 20 minutes, the sensors go into power down mode. In this mode the sensors transmit tire pressure data once every 60 minutes, which minimizes sensor battery consumption. These batteries are not serviceable and require sensor replacement if low. As vehicle speed increases to 20 mph (32 km/h) the sensor's internal roll switches turn the sensors on and they will each begin to transmit a unique identification code and a radio frequency signal.

The RCDLR (Figure 13-38) receives and translates this data into tire location and tire pressure. The RCDLR sends this data to the DIC via a class 2 serial data circuit where the tire pressures are displayed. If the TPM system detects a tire pressure above 289 kPa (42 psi), the HIGH TIRE PRESSURE warning message is displayed. If the system senses a tire pressure between 34–172 kPa (5–25 psi), the LOW TIRE PRESSURE warning message is displayed. And if the system senses pressure below 34 kPa (5 psi), the FLAT TIRE warning message is displayed. After this message two chimes will sound, followed by the message MAX SPEED 55 MPH. The next message to appear is REDUCED HANDLING. The TPM system can also compensate for high and low altitudes using the PCM's barometric pressure sensor via a class 2 serial data circuit. The RCDLR has the ability to detect malfunctions within the TPM system. Any malfunctions detected will cause the DIC to display the SERVICE TIRE MONITOR warning message.

VEHICLE VIBRATIONS

The designs and engineering requirements of vehicles have undergone drastic changes over the last several years. Vehicles are stiffer and provide more isolation from road input than they did previously. The structures of today's stiffer vehicles are less susceptible to many of the vibrations, which could be present in vehicles of earlier designs. However, vibrations can still be detected in a more modern vehicle if a transfer path is created between a rotating component and the body of the vehicle.

There are not as many points of isolation from the road in many vehicles today. If a component produces a strong enough vibration, it may overcome the existing isolation, at which point the component needs to be repaired or replaced. The presence/absence of unwanted noise and vibration is linked to the customer's perception of the overall quality of the vehicle. Vibration is the repetitive motion of an object, back and forth, or up and down. The following components cause most vehicle vibrations:

- A rotating component
- The engine combustion process firing impulses

Rotating components will cause vibrations when excessive imbalance or runout is present. During vibration diagnosis, the amount of allowable imbalance or runout should be considered a TOLERANCE and not a SPECIFICATION. In other words, the less imbalance or runout, the better.

Rotating components will cause a vibration concern when they are not properly isolated from the passenger compartment: Engine firing pulses can be detected as a vibration if a motor mount is collapsed. A vibrating component operates at a consistent rate (km/h, mph, or rpm). Measure the rate of vibration in question. When the rate/speed is determined, relate the vibration to a component that operates at an equal rate/speed in order to pinpoint the source. Vibrations also tend to transmit through the body structure to other components. Therefore, just because the seat vibrates does not mean the source of vibration is in the seat. Vibrations consist of the following three elements:

- The source—the cause of the vibration.
- The transfer path—the path the vibration travels through the vehicle.
- The **responder**—the component where the vibration is felt.

In Figure 13-39, the source is the unbalanced tire. The transfer path is the route the vibrations travel through the vehicle's suspension system into the steering column. The responder is the steering wheel, which the customer reports as vibrating. Eliminating any one of these three elements will usually correct the condition. Decide, from the gathered information, which element makes the most sense to repair. Adding a brace to the steering column may keep the steering wheel from vibrating, but adding a brace is not a practi-

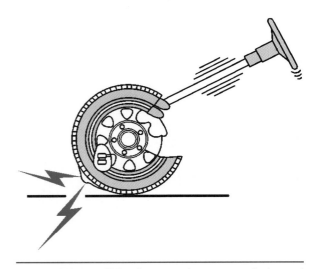

Figure 13-39. This diagram shows an unbalanced tire. (Courtesy of General Motors Corporation)

cal solution. The most direct and effective repair would be to properly balance the tire.

Vibration can also produce noise. As an example, consider a vehicle that has an exhaust pipe grounded to the frame. The source of the vibration is the engine firing impulses traveling through the exhaust. The transfer path is a grounded or bound-up exhaust hanger. The responder is the frame. The floor panel vibrates, acting as a large speaker, which produces noise. The best repair would be to eliminate the transfer path. Aligning the exhaust system and correcting the grounded condition at the frame would eliminate the transfer path.

Basic Vibration Terminology

The following are the two primary components of vibration diagnosis:

- The physical properties of objects
- The object's properties of conducting mechanical energy

The repetitive up-and-down or back-and-forth movement of a component causes most customer vibration complaints. The following are the common components that vibrate:

- The steering wheel
- The seat cushion
- The frame
- The IP

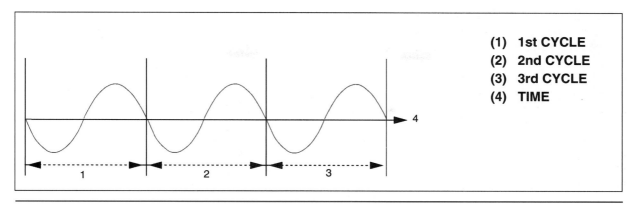

Figure 13-40. This diagram shows vibration cycles in powertrain components.

Vibration diagnosis involves the following simple outline:

1. Measure the repetitive motion and assign a value to the measurement in cycles per second or cycles per minute.
2. Relate the frequency back in terms of the rotational speed of a component that is operating at the same rate or speed.
3. Inspect and test the components for conditions that cause vibration.

Cycle

The term **cycle** means that it describes an action that begins and ends at the same point. A vibration is an example of an event that has repetitive cycles. See Figure 13-40. To observe the characteristics of a vibration, perform the following steps:

1. Clamp a yardstick to the edge of a table, as shown in (Figure 13-41).
2. Push down on the end of the yardstick and quickly release.
3. Observe the motion of the stick as it repeats its up and down motion. Notice that it cycles above and below a midpoint.
4. The speed of the repeating cycle is called the frequency, such as 10 seconds per second or 600 cycles per minute (10 × 60 seconds in a minute equals 600).

The distance that the end of the yardstick moves is called the amplitude and is the total distance the end of the stick moves from the top of its travel to the bottom.

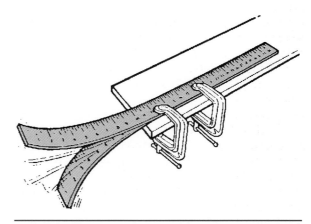

Figure 13-41. This diagram shows a vibration experiment.

Clamping the yardstick with a different distance overhanging the table, results in a change in frequency.

Frequency

Frequency is the rate at which an event occurs in a given amount of time. See (Figure 13-42). Another term that is used when describing a vibration is the period of time. Cycles per second are expressed in hertz. One hertz is one cycle per second.

Amplitude

As described earlier, the amplitude is the maximum value of the periodically occurring event. See Figure 13-43.

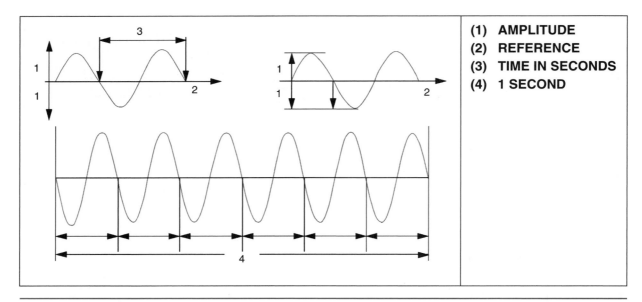

Figure 13-42. This diagram shows frequency wave forms.

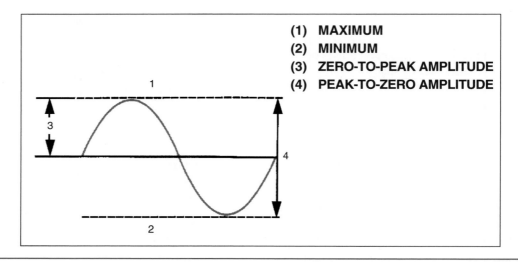

Figure 13-43. This diagram identifies amplitude.

The amplitude is often referred to as the magnitude of the vibration. A severe vibration or disturbance would have greater amplitude than a minor vibration or disturbance. Amplitude is measured by the actual distance of movement of the vibration. For example, an out-of-balance wheel would have a greater amplitude when the vehicle is being driven at 50 mph (80 km/h) compared to 25 mph (40 km/h).

Free Vibration
Free vibration is the continued vibration in the absence of any outside force. In the yardstick exam-

ple, the yardstick continued to vibrate even after the end was released.

Forced Vibration
Forced vibration is when an object is vibrating continuously as a result of an outside force.

Centrifugal Force

A spinning object with an imbalance generates a centrifugal force (Figure 13-44). Performing the

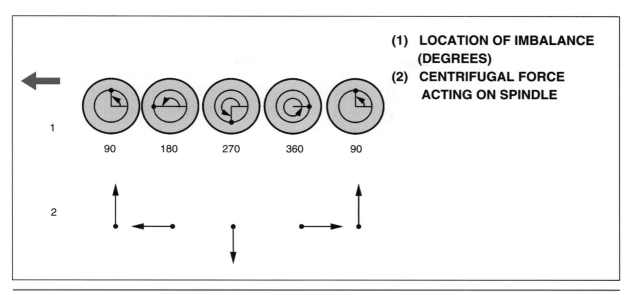

(1) **LOCATION OF IMBALANCE (DEGREES)**
(2) **CENTRIFUGAL FORCE ACTING ON SPINDLE**

1

90   180   270   360   90

2

Figure 13-44. This diagram displays centrifugal force.

following steps will help to demonstrate centrifugal force:

1. Tie a nut to a string.
2. Hold the string. The nut hangs vertically due to gravity.
3. Spin the string. The nut will spin in a circle.

Centrifugal force is trying to make the nut fly outward, causing the pull you feel on your hand. An unbalanced tire follows the same example, as the nut is the imbalance in the tire, and the string is the tire, wheel, and suspension assembly. As the vehicle speed increases, the disturbing force of the unbalanced tire can be felt in the steering wheel, the seat, and the floor. This disturbance will be repetitive (Hz) and the amplitude will increase. At higher speeds, both the frequency and the amplitude will increase. As the tire revolves, the imbalance, or the centrifugal force, will alternately lift the tire up and force the tire downward, along with the spindle, once for each revolution of the tire.

Natural or Resonant Frequency

The natural frequency is the frequency at which an object tends to vibrate (Figure 13-45). Bells, guitar strings, and tuning forks are all examples of objects that tend to vibrate at specific frequencies when excited by an external force.

Suspension systems, and even engines within the mounts, have a tendency to vibrate at certain

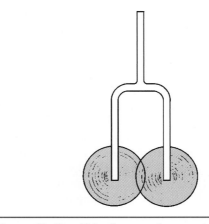

Figure 13-45. This diagram shows natural frequency.

frequencies. This is why some vibration complaints occur only at specific vehicle speeds or engine rpm. The stiffness and the natural frequency of a material have a relationship. Generally, the stiffer the material, the higher the natural frequency of the vibrating item. The opposite is also true. The softer a material, the lower the natural frequency. Conversely, the greater the mass, the lower the natural frequency.

Resonance

All objects have natural frequencies. The natural frequency of a typical automotive front suspension, typically in the 10–15 Hz range, is the result

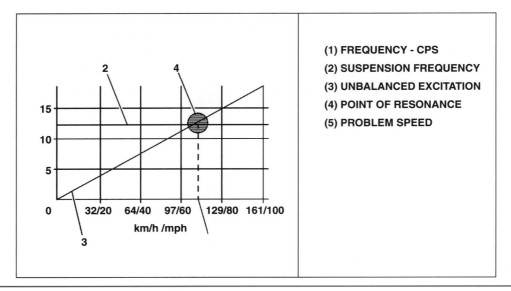

Figure 13-46. Resonance causes suspension to vibrate.

of the suspension design. The suspension's natural frequency is the same at all vehicle speeds. As the tire speed increases along with the vehicle speed, the disturbance created by the tire increases in frequency. Eventually, the frequency of the unbalanced tire will intersect with the natural frequency of the suspension. This causes the suspension to vibrate. The intersecting point is called the **resonance** (Figure 13-46).

The amplitude of a vibration will be greatest at the point of resonance. While the vibration may be felt above and below the problem speed, the vibration may be felt the most at the point of resonance.

Damping

Damping is the ability of an object or material to dissipate or absorb vibration. The automotive shock absorber is a good example (Figure 13–47). The function of the shock absorber is to absorb or dampen the oscillations of the suspension system.

Beating (Phasing)

Two separate disturbances that are relatively close together in frequency will lead to a condition called beating, or phasing. A beating vibration condition will increase in intensity or amplitude in a repetitive fashion as the vehicle travels at a steady speed. This beating vibration can produce the familiar droning noise heard in some vehicles (Figure 13-48). *Beating* occurs when two vibrating forces are added to each other's amplitude. However, two vibrating forces

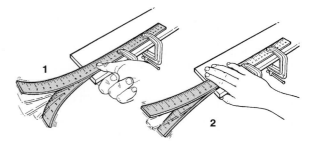

(1) LOW DAMPING
(2) HIGH DAMPING

Figure 13-47. Damping is the ability to dissipate or absorb vibration.

can also subtract from each other's amplitude. The adding and subtracting of amplitudes in similar frequencies is called beating. In many cases, eliminating either one of the disturbances can correct the condition.

Order

Order refers to how many times an event occurs during one revolution of a rotating component. For example, a tire with one high spot would create a disturbance once for every revolution of the tire. This is called first-order vibration, as shown in Figure 13-49.

An oval-shaped tire with two high spots would create a disturbance twice for every revolution. This is called second-order vibration, as shown in Figure 13-50. Three high spots would be third-

1 + 2 = 3

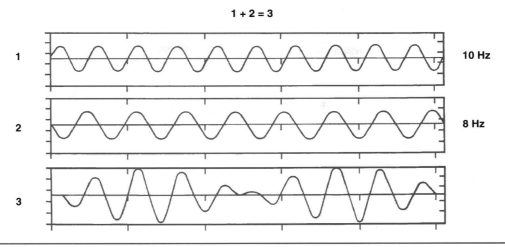

Figure 13-48. Beating (phasing) wave forms occur when two vibrating forces are added to each other's amplitude.

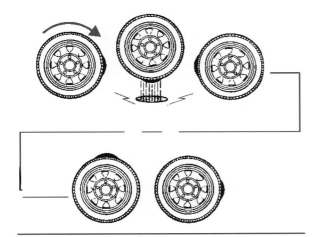

Figure 13-49. This diagram shows first-order vibration.

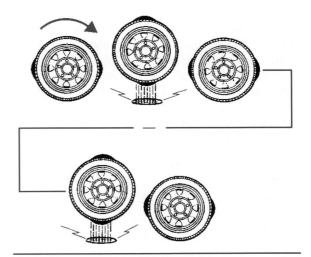

Figure 13-50. This diagram shows second-order vibration.

order, and so forth. Two first-order vibrations may add or subtract from the overall amplitude of the disturbance, but that is all. Two first-order vibrations do not equal a second-order. Due to centrifugal force, an unbalanced component will always create at least a first-order vibration.

WHEEL RUNOUT AND BALANCE

Runout and balance are not actually wheel alignment measurements, because suspension condition or position does not affect them. They are determined only by wheel and tire condition. However, runout and balance should be checked and corrected before performing a wheel alignment be-

cause they affect handling and tire wear. A wheel with runout or one that is out of balance causes a vehicle to handle poorly and wears the tire out quickly, even if the alignment angles are correct.

Wheel runout is a measure of the movement of a wheel and tire assembly around its axis. **Wheel balance** indicates the weight distribution of a wheel and tire along its circumference.

Runout

The perfect runout measurement is zero because any measurable runout is a result of imperfect wheel or tire rotation. There are two types of runout:

- Radial
- Lateral

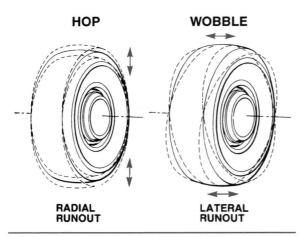

HOP   WOBBLE

RADIAL   LATERAL
RUNOUT   RUNOUT

Figure 13-51. Radial runout—top-to-bottom move-ment—causes wheel hop; lateral runout—side-to-side motion—causes wobble, and both cause tire wear.

Radial runout produces a vertical deviation, while lateral runout causes horizontal movement (Figure 13-51). Runout is measured in fractions of an inch or fractions of millimeters. Although severe runout is often visually apparent, accurate measurements are made with a runout gauge. A runout gauge, which is a type of dial indicator, precisely measures the amount of runout.

Radial Runout

Radial runout is seen from the side of the vehi-cle as the wheel and tire assembly rotates on its hub. A wheel with radial runout does not rotate in a true circle. The driving problem radial runout causes is called **hop** or **tramp** because the tire hops off the ground and makes a tramping noise as it lands. Sometimes a wheel or tire with radial runout is described as **out of round,** because its rotation pattern is not a circle. Wheel radial runout is measured at the wheel rim bead seat, and total wheel and tire assembly radial runout is measured at the tire tread (Figure 13-52).

Lateral Runout

Lateral runout is seen from the front of the vehicle as the wheel and tire assembly rotates on its hub. A wheel with lateral runout does not rotate in one ver-tical plane, which causes the assembly to **wobble.** Wheel lateral runout is measured at the wheel rim flange, and total wheel and tire lateral runout is mea-sured at the tire sidewall (Figure 13-53).

Runout Tolerances

No wheel and tire assembly can rotate perfectly. As a rule of thumb, about 0.030 inch (0.760 mm)

RADIAL RUNOUT

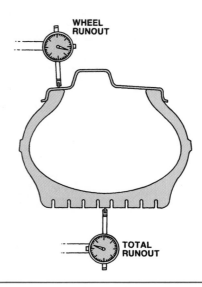

WHEEL
RUNOUT

TOTAL
RUNOUT

Figure 13-52. Radial runout is measured at points that indicate whether the wheel and tire move up-and-down as they rotate. Measuring at two points helps pinpoint whether the wheel or the tire has runout.

LATERAL RUNOUT

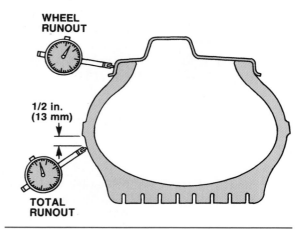

WHEEL
RUNOUT

1/2 in.
(13 mm)

TOTAL
RUNOUT

Figure 13-53. Lateral runout is measured at points that indicate whether the wheel and tire move side-to-side as they rotate. Total lateral runout is measured an inch below the tire wear rib.

of runout, either radial or lateral, is acceptable. This amount of runout may be perceptible to an extremely sensitive driver, while 0.060 inch (1.525 mm) is noticeable to most drivers, and 0.090 inch (2.285 mm) to virtually every driver. However, every manufacturer specifies maxi-mum allowable runout measurements for each model, taking into account tire size and type, and vehicle weight. Total runout should be measured

RADIAL RUNOUT

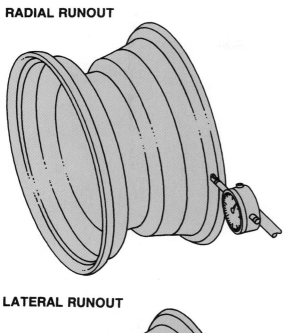

LATERAL RUNOUT

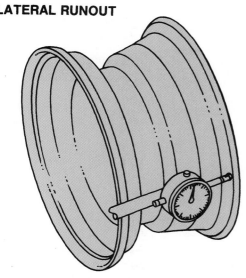

Figure 13-54. The most accurate method of measuring wheel runout is to dismount the tire and take dial indicator readings on the inside of the wheel rim.

on warm tires, which have been driven long enough to eliminate any flat spots on the tread and bulges in the sidewall caused by standing. The most accurate wheel runout measurements are obtained by dismounting the tire and measuring inside the wheel rim (Figure 13-54).

Causes of Runout

In addition to detracting from handling, excessive runout accelerates tire wear. Therefore, if runout exceeds specifications, it is important to locate and eliminate the cause. Assuming that the tire and the wheel are both the proper size and that the

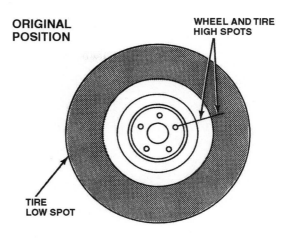

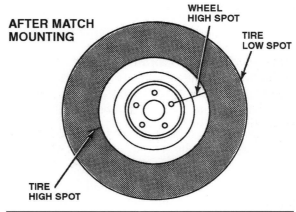

Figure 13-55. To match mount a wheel and tire, mount the tire with its highest point of runout opposite the highest point of wheel runout.

tire is correctly inflated, several things can cause radial or lateral runout, including:

- An incorrectly mounted tire
- Uneven tread wear
- A bent wheel rim
- Imbalance

If wheel runout is acceptable, but total runout is excessive, the problem is in the tire. If both wheel and total runout are excessive, the cause is probably a faulty wheel or a lack of balance. Occasionally, a bent wheel rim can be straightened, but most often it must be replaced. In some cases, it is possible to compensate for runout by **match mounting** the tire to the wheel. Match mounting means mounting the tire so that its point of highest runout is located at the point of lowest wheel runout (Figure 13-55). As wheel and tire technology and manufacturing methods improve, match mounting is becoming less necessary. However, match mounting is still a good idea when a wheel and tire have irregularities.

CHECKING LUG STUD RUNOUT

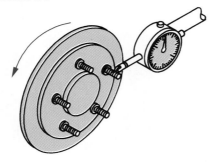

Figure 13-56. With the dial indicator attached to the vehicle frame, the plunger lightly resting on a stud, and the dial face zeroed, slowly rotate the wheel and watch for variations as each stud brushes the dial indicator.

Causes of Radial Runout

In addition to the previously noted conditions, which may cause either radial or lateral runout, radial runout may be the result of:

- Off-centered lug bolts, or bolt runout
- Hub or spindle runout
- Tire sidewall stiffness variations

The distance of each lug bolt or stud from the center of the wheel should not vary by more than 0.015 inch (0.380 mm) when measured with a dial indicator (Figure 13-56). Sometimes it is possible to compensate for variation by mounting the tire and wheel with its lowest point of runout near the lug bolt or stud with the highest runout. However, if lug bolt or stud runout is excessive, the hub or axle must be replaced. If the hub is out of round, the wheel will have runout only when it is mounted on the hub (Figure 13-57).

Weak spots in the tire sidewall cause the tire to bulge at that point when the vehicle weight rests on the wheels. The bulge changes the measurement from the wheel axis to the ground, which is simply another description of radial runout. A tire with a weak, bulging, or distorted sidewall should be replaced (Figure 13-58). Slight indentations are normal and are caused by the tires being stacked on top of each other during shipping and storage.

"Tire truer" machines, which "true" a tire by trimming the tread to remove high spots, are available for correcting radial runout (Figure 13-59). However, tire truing is not a recommended practice. This procedure has several drawbacks:

- Not all tires have spare rubber in the tread.
- Trimming the tread shortens tire life.

CHECKING HUB RUNOUT

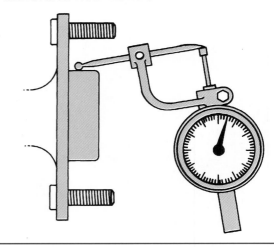

Figure 13-57. If the wheel hub is out of round, the wheel and tire exhibit runout, but only when mounted on the hub.

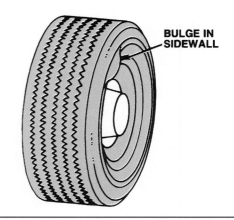

BULGE IN SIDEWALL

Figure 13-58. Distortions or bulges in the tire sidewall indicate a weak spot that may eventually blow out.

- The runout problem may recur later.
- Less tread reduces tire safety, especially on wet roads.

Replacement is the only sure cure for an out-of-round tire.

Causes of Lateral Runout

In addition to the tire or wheel problems mentioned earlier that cause either type of runout, lateral runout may result from:

- Hub damage
- Wheel mounting flange damage

The face of the hub or mounting flange should have less than 0.010-inch (0.255-mm) of runout

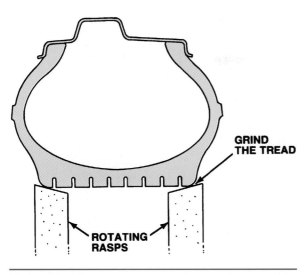

GRIND
THE TREAD

ROTATING
RASPS

Figure 13-59. A tire truer makes a tire round by grinding off any irregularities in the tread, but this is not a recommended procedure.

when measured with a dial indicator (Figure 13-60). Remove the wheel and carefully inspect for debris on the face of the mounting flange and the flange contact area of the wheel. Anything that prevents the wheel from completely seating on the flange face causes lateral runout. If the mounting surfaces are clean, it is sometimes possible to compensate for mounting flange runout by positioning the lowest point of tire and wheel runout near the flange high spot. However, in most cases a distorted mounting flange must be replaced.

Balance

A wheel and tire assembly is in **static balance** if its weight is evenly distributed around its hub. It is in **dynamic balance** if its weight is evenly distributed from side-to-side. Wheel imbalance, whether static or dynamic, causes unstable steering, poor ride quality, and rapid tire wear (Figure 13-61).

Static Balance

When a wheel and tire assembly that lacks static balance hangs freely on the spindle, it rotates until the heavy spot is at the bottom because gravity pulls the heavy spot down as far as possible (Figure 13-62). If the wheel and tire is balanced, gravity affects it equally at all points, so it does not spin if hung freely.

**CHECKING MOUNTING
FLANGE RUNOUT**

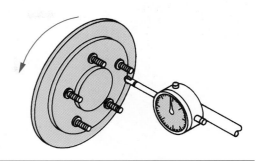

Figure 13-60. As the wheel flange rotates, the dial indicator registers the amount of surface variation. If there is too much variation, it affects the tire and wheel, causing lateral runout.

**STATIC IMBALANCE
HOP**

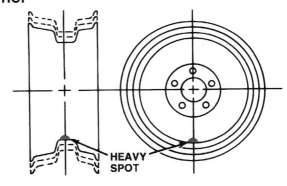

HEAVY
SPOT

**DYNAMIC IMBALANCE
WOBBLE**

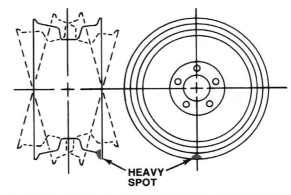

HEAVY
SPOT

Figure 13-61. Wheel imbalance is a result of uneven weight distribution. Static imbalance, uneven weight around the circumference, causes the wheel to hop, while a dynamic imbalance, uneven side-to-side weight, produces a wobble.

STATIC IMBALANCE

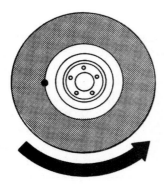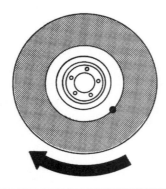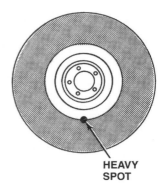

HEAVY
SPOT

Figure 13-62. The heavy spot of a tire hanging freely on its axis makes the tire rotate until the heavy part comes to rest at the bottom. If the tire were statically balanced, it would remain still.

Dynamic Balance

When a wheel and tire assembly that lacks dynamic balance rotates on the spindle, it wobbles because centrifugal force is stronger at the heavy spot and forces that side out. If the assembly is balanced, centrifugal force affects it equally at all points, and it does not wobble as it rotates.

Correcting Imbalance

Balancing a wheel and tire assembly involves placing the wheel and tire on a balancer, locating the heavy spot, and attaching a balancing weight to the wheel rim at a point opposite the heavy spot to counteract its effect (Figure 13-63). Most shops use dynamic balancers that pinpoint both static and dynamic imbalance. It is possible to do static balancing alone, using a bubble balancer. This is an older technology that is seldom used anymore because this method does not include checking for or correcting dynamic balance. Correct static balance and dynamic balance are both necessary to minimize tire wear.

Wheel Balancing Weights

A wheel balancing weight is made of soft lead, with either a steel clip or an adhesive to attach it to the wheel rim. Weights are generally supplied in ¼-ounce (7-gram) increments (Figure 13-64). Clip-on weights are lightly hammered onto the wheel rim. Adhesive weights have a paper cover over the adhesive, which is peeled off to attach the weight to the wheel. Adhesive weights are often a several-ounce strip that is incrementally scored into ¼-ounce (7-gram) sections, which al-

Figure 13-63. A wheel balancer pinpoints where weight is needed to compensate for an imbalance. Attaching the correct weight to the wheel rim restores balance.

lows the technician to cut off the required amount of weight (Figure 13-65). In general, adhesive weights tend to be less true than clip-on weights, so they may not actually weigh the same amount as indicated on them. Adhesive is also a less secure attachment method and these weights have a tendency to come loose and fall off of the wheel over a period of time. Typically, adhesive wheel weights are used to balance aluminum-alloy wheels, which might develop an electrolytic reaction to a steel clip.

Whenever the balancer indicates that several weights are required, it is best to consider whether some can be combined to produce the same effect with less total weight added. Attach-

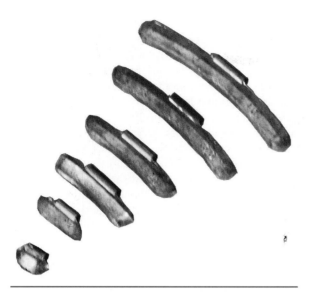

Figure 13-64. Clip-on wheel weights typically range in size from ¼ ounce (7 grams) to 4 ounces (112 grams).

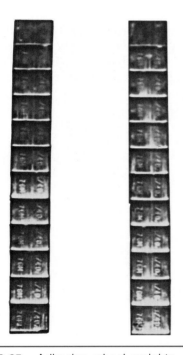

Figure 13-65. Adhesive wheel weights, generally used to balance alloy wheels, are supplied as a strip graduated in ¼-ounce (7-gram) increments.

ing too many individual weights to the wheel causes the weights to counteract each other. A computerized wheel balancer electronically calculates the most efficient weight placement to make wheel balancing quick and easy. As a rule, no more than six ounces (170 grams) should be added to the weight of the wheel and tire.

SUMMARY

The wheel consists of a disc and rim that are welded together. The disc bolts to the hub and the tire mounts on the rim. Specifications indicating the size and dimensions of the wheels are used to select the proper wheels for different vehicle applications. Most original-equipment wheels are made of steel, while many aftermarket custom wheels are made of an aluminum alloy. Older vehicles may have wire spoke wheels, which provide extra flexibility and cooling for drum brakes.

The wheel bearings allow the wheel to rotate on the axle shaft or spindle with reduced friction. Wheel bearings withstand thrust loads and radial loads, and also control thrust movement. Some wheel bearings are adjustable for endplay or preload. The three types of wheel bearings are cylindrical roller, tapered roller, and ball bearings. Some wheel bearings can be disassembled for service, while others are non-serviceable, sealed units.

Although not considered a part of the suspension or steering, the brake friction assembly often requires disassembly and reassembly during chassis repairs. The two types of brake assemblies are drum brakes and disc brakes.

The rubber tire mounts onto the wheel and is filled with air, which provides a cushion against minor road shocks and traction. Older tires used an inner tube, but modern tires are tubeless. Tires are constructed in three main sections: the carcass, which is the foundation of the structure; the casing, which provides stiffness; and the tread, which provides traction. The carcass design determines whether a tire is bias, belted bias, or radial ply. Most tires used since the 1970s are radial ply designs. Snow tires, rain tires, off-road tires, and space-saver spare tires are types of special-purpose tires. Specifications indicating the size, design, and dimensions of the tire are used to match tires to wheels. Information molded onto the tire sidewall reveals a great deal about the construction and capabilities of a tire.

Wheel runout and balance are not alignment measurements, but they should be correct before a wheel alignment is performed. Runout is the measure of the movement of a wheel and tire assembly around its axis, and balance indicates the weight distribution of a wheel and tire assembly along its circumference.

Run-flat tires help maintain vehicle mobility as a tire is punctured. There are two types of run-flat tires: self-sealing and self-supporting tires. The tire performance criteria (TPC) specification number matches the size, load range, and construction to those originally installed on the vehicle. Many vehicles are equipped with steel belted all-season radial tires as standard equipment. These tires qualify as snow tires, with a higher-than-average rating for snow traction than the non-all season radial tires previously used. The tire placard is used to display tire pressure and capacity information.

The tire pressure monitor (TPM) system allows the driver to monitor and display all tire pressures on the vehicle driver information center (DIC) while the vehicle is being driven. The system uses the remote control door lock receiver (RCDLR), BCM, PCM/ECM, (4) radio frequency transmitting pressure sensors inside each wheel/tire assembly, and a class 2 serial data circuit to perform the system functions.

Rotating components will cause vibrations when excessive imbalance or runout is present. During vibration diagnosis, the amount of allowable imbalance or runout should be considered a TOLERANCE and not a SPECIFICATION. In other words, the less imbalance or runout, the better.

Rotating components will cause a vibration concern when they not properly isolated from the passenger compartment. A vibrating component operates at a consistent rate (km/h, mph, or rpm).

When the rate/speed is determined, relate the vibration to a component that operates at an equal rate/speed in order to pinpoint the source. Vibrations also tend to transmit through the body structure to other components. Therefore, just because the seat vibrates does not mean the source of vibration is in the seat. Vibrations consist of the following three elements: source—the cause of the vibration; transfer path—the path the vibration travels through the vehicle; and the responder—the component where the vibration is felt.

Tires have handling characteristics that determine how well they grip the road at any given moment. Adhesion is the amount of grip a tire has. The coefficient of friction (Cf) of a tire is the amount of friction between it and the pavement. Slip angles occur whenever a tire slides in a different direction than the way it is aimed. Tires have only a certain amount of adhesion to use during driving, cornering, accelerating, and decelerating. Any combination of these forces divides up the available adhesion among them. Hydroplaning, or aquaplaning, occurs when a tire on a wet surface drives onto a wedge of water that forms in front of it. Hydroplaning causes the tread to lose contact with the pavement.

Review Questions

For each of the following questions, choose the letter that represents the best possible answer.

1. Technician A says that most automotive wheels are made of steel. Technician B says that magnesium wheels are a common aftermarket option. Who is right?
   a. A only
   b. B only
   c. Both A and B
   d. Neither A nor B

2. Technician A says that European manufacturers frequently use lug nuts, rather than bolts, to secure the wheels to the hub. Technician B says that it is important to install lug nuts with the flat side toward the wheel. Who is right?
   a. A only
   b. B only
   c. Both A and B
   d. Neither A nor B

3. Before the tire is inflated, its beads fit into which part of the wheel?
   a. Drop center
   b. Bead seats
   c. Flanges
   d. Disc

4. Technician A says that the bolt circle specification indicates the diameter of the lug bolts used to secure the tire. Technician B says that not all modern wheels have a center hole. Who is right?
   a. A only
   b. B only
   c. Both A and B
   d. Neither A nor B

5. Which of the following statements is NOT true of a wheel with an extreme positive offset?
   a. The wheel disc is nearly flush with the front of the rim.
   b. It is likely to be used on a RWD vehicle.
   c. It allows a lot of room for suspension and brake system components.
   d. The vertical mounting plane is farther outboard than the wheel centerline.

6. Aluminum alloy wheels commonly:
   a. Have a baked-on paint finish
   b. Are lightweight
   c. Require clip-on wheel weights
   d. Are standard original equipment

7. Knockoff wheels are secured to the axle with:
   a. One nut
   b. Two nuts
   c. Three nuts
   d. Four nuts

8. Most wheel bearings are lubricated with:
   a. ATF
   b. Bearing oil
   c. Gear oil
   d. Grease

9. Excessive wheel bearing endplay can result from too much:
   a. Thrust movement
   b. Radial movement
   c. Bearing preload
   d. Axle shaft preload

10. When used as wheel bearings, most ball bearings are:
    a. At the rear of FWD vehicles
    b. At the front of RWD vehicles
    c. Non-serviceable
    d. On the non-driven axle

11. Drum brakes:
    a. Use friction pads
    b. Are usually on the rear wheels only
    c. Are a relatively new technology
    d. Use a rotor

12. Which of the following does NOT describe the typical modern automotive tire?
    a. Tube-type
    b. Pneumatic
    c. Radial
    d. UTQGS rated

13. A tire wear indicator is found:
    a. In the undertread
    b. In the tread
    c. In the carcass
    d. On the sidewall

14. Technician A says that a space-saver spare tire weighs less than an ordinary tire. Technician B says that a space-saver spare should be used for as short a time as possible. Who is right?
    a. A only
    b. B only
    c. Both A and B
    d. Neither A nor B

15. Technician A says the tire inner diameter must match the wheel diameter exactly. Technician B says the width of the tire at the beads must match the wheel rim width exactly. Who is right?
    a. A only
    b. B only
    c. Both A and B
    d. Neither A nor B

16. If a tire size code reads "P213/70R14 82H," the tire's:
    a. Maximum inflation pressure is 70 kPa
    b. Design is belted bias
    c. Aspect ratio is 82
    d. Section width is 213 mm

17. The size of the tire contact patch is NOT influenced by:
    a. Weight on the tire
    b. Pressure in the tire
    c. Tire shape
    d. Tire inner diameter

18. A tire develops the greatest slip angle during:
    a. Cornering
    b. Braking
    c. Acceleration
    d. Straight-ahead driving

19. Tires with a high rate of adhesion tend to:
    a. Lose traction during acceleration
    b. Maintain traction during cornering
    c. Last for many miles
    d. Stay cool during use

20. Tires are likely to hydroplane on:
    a. Dry pavement
    b. Icy pavement
    c. Wet pavement
    d. Snowy pavement

21. Technician A says that a wheel and tire assembly with radial runout does not rotate in a true circle. Technician B says that lateral runout causes the wheel and tire assembly to "wobble" as it rotates. Who is right?
    a. A only
    b. B only
    c. Both A and B
    d. Neither A nor B

22. An acceptable level of wheel and tire runout, which may be perceptible to an extremely sensitive driver, is typically less than:
    a. 0.010 inch (0.250 mm)
    b. 0.015 inch (0.380 mm)
    c. 0.020 inch (0.510 mm)
    d. 0.030 inch (0.760 mm)

23. Technician A says that an incorrectly mounted tire may cause radial runout. Technician B says that uneven tread wear may cause lateral runout. Who is right?
    a. A only
    b. B only
    c. Both A and B
    d. Neither A nor B

24. Technician A says that a bent hub may cause lateral runout. Technician B says that a bent wheel mounting flange may cause lateral runout. Who is right?
    a. A only
    b. B only
    c. Both A and B
    d. Neither A nor B

25. Technician A says that a wheel and tire assembly is in static balance when its weight is evenly distributed around its hub. Technician B says that a lack of static balance causes shimmy, but does NOT cause tire wear. Who is right?
    a. A only
    b. B only
    c. Both A and B
    d. Neither A nor B

26. A wheel and tire assembly is in dynamic balance when:
    a. Its weight is evenly distributed around its hub
    b. Its weight is evenly distributed side-to-side
    c. It does not vibrate at speeds greater than 60 mph (100 km/h)
    d. It has no radial or lateral runout

14

Wheel Alignment Fundamentals

OBJECTIVES

Upon completion and review of this chapter, you will be able to:

- Identify the terms "caster," "camber," "thrust angle," and "toe" (turning radius), and define them in relation to steering geometry and wheel alignment.

- Explain the following steering geometry terms: "steering axis inclination," "scrub radius," "toe-out on turns" (Ackerman Angle), "thrust angle," and "setback."

- Explain the difference between a two-wheel and a four-wheel alignment.

KEY TERMS

Camber
camber roll
Caster
caster trail
diagonal wipe
directional control
  angle
dog-tracking
four-wheel alignment
geometric centerline
geometric centerline
  alignment
included angle
road crown
scrub radius
setback
shimmy

Steering axis
  inclination (SAI)
steering geometry
thrust alignment
thrust angle
thrust line
thrust line alignment
tire wear angle
toe
toe change
toe-in
toe-out
toe-out on turns
turning center
turning radius
two-wheel alignment
wheel alignment

INTRODUCTION

Proper **wheel alignment** positions the suspension to keep the wheels and tires traveling in a straight line as the vehicle is driven (Figure 14-1). Wheel alignment angles are based on the "steering geometry," which is used to determine whether chassis parts are positioned for proper handling and minimum tire wear.

Correct wheel balance along with zero tire and wheel runout promote the same results as proper wheel alignment and also ensure that the wheel and tire assembly does not wobble or bounce as it rolls down the road.

This chapter examines these suspension aspects that keep the vehicle traveling straight, the

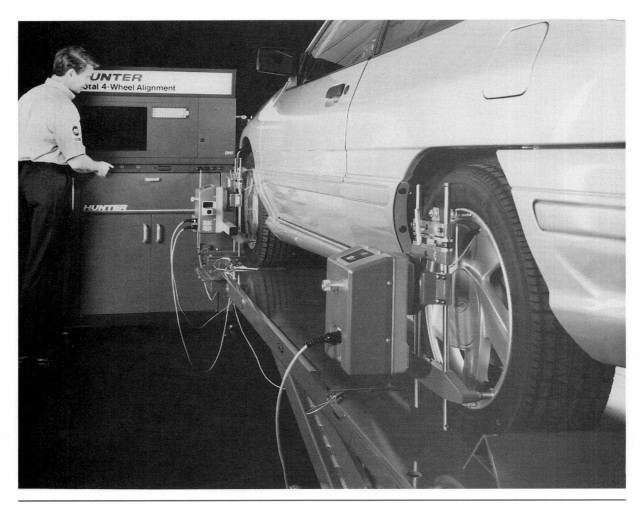

Figure 14-1. Wheel alignment angles are measured and adjusted for optimal handling and minimal tire wear. (Courtesy of Hunter Engineering)

steering accurate, and provide a comfortable ride. The text discusses:

- Steering geometry
- Wheel alignment

Wheel runout and balance are checked before measuring steering geometry angles. After checking steering geometry, the wheel alignment angles are corrected to factory specifications. There are two wheel alignment techniques: two-wheel and four-wheel. A two-wheel alignment corrects angles at the front wheels only, while a four-wheel alignment corrects them at all four wheels.

STEERING GEOMETRY

Wheel alignment involves determining the correct angles between suspension and steering parts, wheels, and the road surface. Because align-

ment deals with angles and affects steering, the method of describing alignment measurements is called **steering geometry** (Figure 14-2). There are five steering geometry angles:

- Camber
- Caster
- Toe
- Steering axis inclination (SAI)
- Toe-out on turns

A typical alignment involves checking and adjusting camber and toe at the rear wheels; checking and adjusting camber, caster, and toe at the front wheels; and checking SAI and toe-out on turns at the front wheels.

There are two more steering geometry angles that are not specific to each wheel but measure the spatial relationship among all four wheels. These angles are:

- Thrust angle
- Setback

STEERING GEOMETRY ANGLES

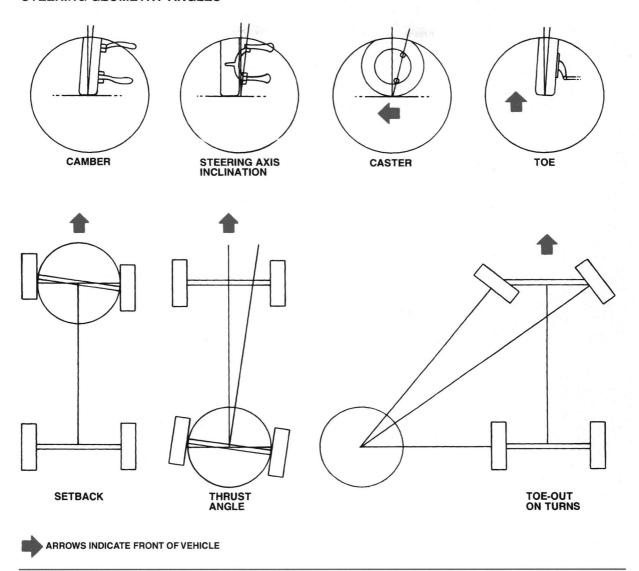

CAMBER

STEERING AXIS
INCLINATION

CASTER

TOE

SETBACK

THRUST
ANGLE

TOE-OUT
ON TURNS

ARROWS INDICATE FRONT OF VEHICLE

Figure 14-2. All alignment measurements can be made in degrees of a circle, which is why the science of measuring them is called "steering geometry." Toe and setback can also be measured in linear units, generally inches or millimeters.

In addition to the spatial relationships described by thrust angle and setback, there is also axle setback. This occurs when one axle is pushed or knocked sideways, as in a collision.

All steering geometry angles can be measured in degrees of a circle (°), and measurements smaller than one degree are given in minutes ('). As with time, where 60 minutes equal one hour, each degree of a circle consists of 60 minutes. Although all angles can be measured in degrees, toe and setback may also be measured linearly, or in terms of distance. Linear toe and setback specifications may be provided as fractions of an inch or millimeters.

Alignment angle measurements and specifications may be either negative or positive numbers. Positive specifications or measurements have either a plus (+) sign or no symbol in front of them, while negative specifications or measurements are proceeded by a minus (−). Whether negative or positive, alignment specifications and readings usually include fractions or decimals. The fractions are based on the number four, going from fourths, or quarters, to eighths, sixteenths, thirty-seconds, and occasionally sixty-fourths. The decimals are simply the decimal equivalents of the fractions.

The degrees, minutes, and seconds system of measurement is currently used in Europe. In North America, most modern alignment equipment uses decimal degrees. Decimal degrees permit measuring alignment angles up to the precision of $\frac{1}{100}$ (0.01) of a degree.

Steering geometry angles are adjusted while the vehicle is at rest, but road forces and drag change the angles once the vehicle is moving. Therefore, manufacturers specify adjustment angles that change to an optimal setting while the vehicle is moving. For example, zero camber and toe are ideal alignment angles to prevent tire wear, but specifications for these angles are usually above or below zero in the hope that they will reach zero when the vehicle is being driven.

The five traditional alignment angles can be classified as either tire wear angles, directional control angles, or both. A **tire wear angle** helps prevent tire wear when correct and accelerates tire wear when incorrect. Of the five traditional alignment angles, the ones affecting tire wear are:

- Camber
- Toe
- Toe-out on turns

See Chapter 14 of the *Shop Manual* for the four-wheel alignment procedures.

A **directional control angle** affects steering and handling, and all five of the traditional alignment angles are directional control angles. Usually, setback and thrust angle are not discussed within these categories. Their importance is the effect they have on other alignment angles.

Front-wheel caster, camber, and toe, and rear-wheel camber and toe are usually adjustable. Adjustment methods, which are described in the *Shop Manual,* vary by application (Figure 14-3). Although the suspension is designed to allow some adjustments, others require the installation of aftermarket devices. Steering axis inclination (SAI) and toe-out on turns are non-adjustable angles, although camber adjustment can affect SAI. Typically, when SAI and toe-out on turns are out of specification there is damage within the suspension or steering system that requires the repair or replacement of the damaged parts. Thrust angle and setback are reference angles, indicating the relationship of the rear wheels to the chassis and of the wheels on the same axle to each other. Both are non-adjustable angles that generally indicate damaged components when out of specification.

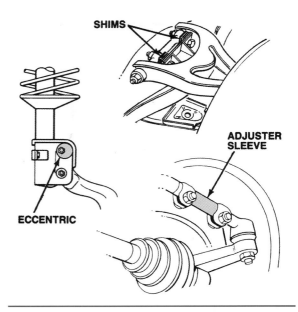

Figure 14-3. Some common alignment adjustment methods include rotating an eccentric cam, removing and installing shims, and turning an adjustment sleeve.

Adjustable suspension angles compensate for normal suspension wear. For instance, as coil springs settle, camber decreases. Adjusting the camber returns the wheels to their original angle without replacing the springs. Thus, alignment prevents the need for more extensive suspension repair. However, this is true only as long as the wear is slight. When spring sag becomes excessive, the springs must be replaced before camber can be adjusted correctly.

Camber

Camber is the inward or outward tilt of a wheel as viewed from the front of the vehicle (Figure 14-4). Specifically, it is the angle between the centerline of the wheel and tire and a true vertical line that is perpendicular to a level surface (Figure 14-5). A wheel has zero camber when it is perfectly straight up and down, so that the wheel centerline and the vertical line are the same. If the top of the wheel leans outward, away from the body, the wheel has positive camber. If the wheel leans inward at the top, it has negative camber. Camber is measurable on both the front and rear wheels.

Correct camber keeps the tire tread in good contact with the road. Zero camber while driving is the ideal position for this purpose, but wheels and tires seldom maintain zero camber under actual driving conditions.

CAMBER

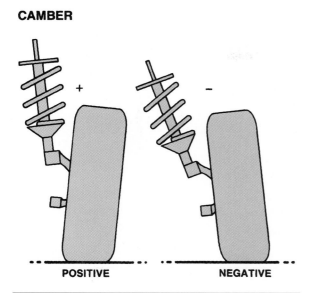

Figure 14-4. A wheel has camber if it leans inward or outward when viewed from the front.

Effects of Camber

Camber is a tire wear angle. Too much positive camber causes the outside edge of the tire to wear out faster, while too much negative camber increases wear on the inside edge. Camber is also a directional control angle. If camber is unequal side-to-side, the vehicle pulls toward the side with more positive camber.

The reason incorrect camber causes both tire wear and steering pull is that a cambered tire rolls like a cone. That is, the wheel rolls as if one side of the tire had a larger diameter than the other side (Figure 14-6). The tread on the smaller side is forced under the tire, which makes the tire wear faster on that side. At the same time, the larger side of the tire must travel farther with each revolution of the wheel, so the vehicle pulls toward the smaller side.

Any excessive camber, whether positive or negative, accelerates wheel bearing wear because vehicle weight is not distributed in the way the bearings were designed to support it. Positive camber places extra weight on the inner wheel bearing, and negative camber increases the load on the outer wheel bearing.

Influences on Camber

Once a vehicle is being driven, a number of factors begin to affect camber. These include:

- Uneven loading
- Body roll during turns

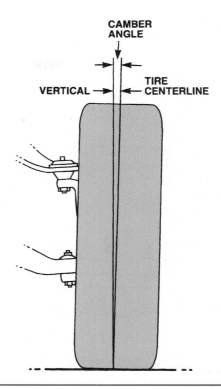

Figure 14-5. The angle between a true vertical line and the centerline of the wheel and tire is the camber angle.

- Road crown
- Rough road surface
- Suspension wear
- Suspension damage
- Tire size
- Caster

Some of these factors cause long-term or permanent changes in camber, while the effects of others is only temporary.

Uneven cargo or passenger loading can cause body tilt (Figure 14-7). The driver frequently is the only person in the vehicle, and manufacturers may assume that there will usually be more weight on the left side when they set camber specifications. A heavy driver or passenger, or one who is over 280 pounds (130 kilograms), has a greater effect on camber.

Another type of body tilt is roll during cornering. Centrifugal force shifts the weight of the vehicle toward the outside of the turn, and the body tilts as a result. This places more weight on the wheel and tire at the outside of the turn while reducing weight on the inside wheel and tire. In response to body roll, camber decreases at the outside wheel and increases at the inside one

CAMBER WEAR

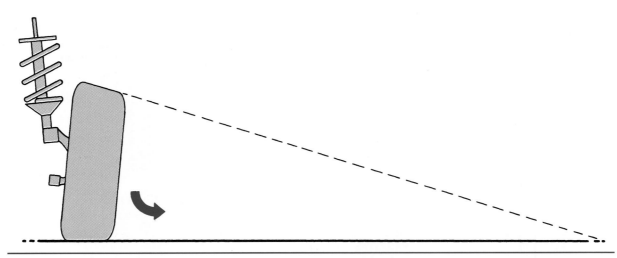

Figure 14-6. A cambered tire rolls like a cone, which causes the vehicle to pull toward the side with more positive camber and wears out the shoulder on that side of the tire.

(Figure 14-7). The faster the cornering speed, the greater the effects on camber, which is why high-speed cornering wears out the edges of tires.

Most roads are built higher at the middle than at the sides to prevent water from accumulating on the surface. This slope is called **road crown.** Road crown tends to cause positive camber at the right wheel and negative camber at the left (Figure 14-8). In urban areas, where most streets have a high road crown to promote drainage, experienced alignment technicians may adjust camber toward the negative end of the specified range at the right wheel and make the left wheel more positive to compensate for the local conditions. However, this difference in camber settings from side-to-side, which is called "cross camber," should never exceed one-half of a degree.

Inequalities in the road surface can cause temporary camber changes (Figure 14-9). As explained in Chapter 9 of this *Classroom Manual,* short-long-arm (SLA), MacPherson strut, and strut/short-long-arm (strut/SLA) suspensions produce "camber change" when they compress. That is, the suspension draws the top of the wheel and tire inward to decrease camber during jounce.

Suspension wear is yet another factor. Over time, as springs settle and begin to sag, and other suspension parts wear and fatigue, wheels tend to develop negative camber (Figure 14-10). Road hazards and minor mishaps, such as driving into a hole in the road or striking a curb, may bend suspension

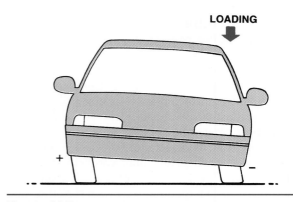

Figure 14-7. Body tilt, whether caused by uneven loading or roll during turns, changes camber.

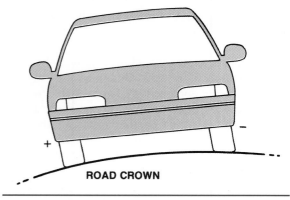

Figure 14-8. Road crown changes camber, but alignment specifications may already take this into account. Always keep the side-to-side settings within the specified range when making adjustments.

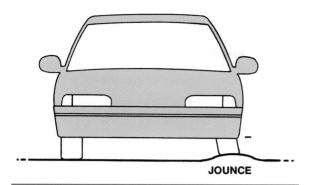

Figure 14-9. With a SLA, strut, or strut/SLA front suspension, camber temporarily decreases as a wheel rides over a bump.

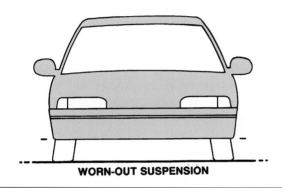

Figure 14-10. Sagging springs, worn ball joints, and other suspension damage due to age decrease camber.

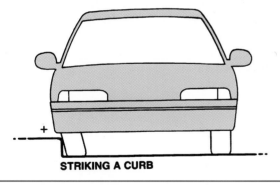

Figure 14-11. Striking a tire against a curb can damage the suspension and cause positive camber.

parts in ways that cause permanent positive camber (Figure 14-11). Installing new tires of a different size after an alignment also changes the camber.

In addition, the caster angle may produce a change in the camber angle when the wheels are turned to one side or the other. This condition is known as "camber roll."

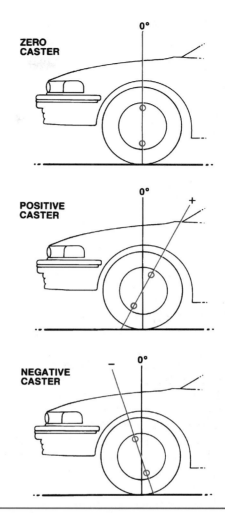

Figure 14-12. With positive caster, a line drawn through the steering axis intersects the ground in front of the tire contact patch. With negative caster, the line intersects the ground behind the contact patch.

Caster

Caster, which is the forward or backward angle of the steering axis as viewed from the side of the vehicle, is a directional stability angle. The caster angle is the difference between a line drawn through the steering axis and a vertical line drawn through the center of the wheel and tire (Figure 14-12). The steering axis runs through the upper and lower ball joints of SLA and strut/SLA suspensions, through the upper strut mount and lower ball joint on a strut suspension, and along the centerline of the kingpin on a kingpin suspension.

Caster and SAI, which are described later in this chapter, both measure steering axis tilt, but caster is seen from the side of the vehicle and SAI

I Want to Study Cars, Not Geometry!

Alignment angles are given as negative or positive numbers, and these numbers can be confusing at first glance. A negative number can look larger than a positive number, but a negative number is always less because it is less than zero. Remember that as an angle becomes more positive it *increases,* and as it becomes more negative it *decreases.* For example, if a vehicle has a caster specification of ¾ (0.75°) and right front wheel caster measures −$\frac{7}{32}$° (−1.22°), *increase* caster by 1$\frac{31}{32}$° (1.97°) at that wheel to correct. If the camber specification is −2¼° (−2.25°) and caster at the right front wheel measures 1⅝° (1.63°), *decrease* camber by 3⅞° (3.88°) to correct.

Also remember that an angle can increase while still remaining in negative numbers, and decrease while remaining positive. Adjusting the camber of a wheel from −1¾° (−1.75°) to −1° *increases* camber by ¾° (0.75°). Adjusting from 1$\frac{13}{16}$° (1.81°) to ⅞° (0.88°) *decreases* camber by $\frac{15}{16}$° (.93°). Always read alignment specifications and calculate alignment adjustments carefully to see if they need to increase or decrease.

from the front. These angles are generally measured only on the front wheels because rear wheels do not have a steering axis, except on vehicles with four-wheel steering (4WS).

If the steering axis leans toward the rear of the vehicle from the top, the wheel has positive caster, and the wheel has negative caster if the steering axis tilts toward the front of the vehicle. If the caster line is vertical, the wheel has a zero caster angle. Most front wheels have some means of adjusting caster.

Effects of Caster

A high positive caster usually increases the levels of:

- Straight-ahead stability
- Steering effort required
- Steering wheel return, or return-to-center force

Wheels with high positive caster tend to travel straight, resist turning, and return to their straight-ahead position as soon as possible. Generally, the straight-ahead stability and steering wheel return associated with high caster are considered good qualities, while the increased steering effort required is considered a problem. Also, increased caster often increases the amount of road shock that the driver and passengers feel because it in effect aims the bumps at the passenger compartment.

Decreasing caster decreases steering stability when the vehicle is traveling straight ahead and decreases the tendency of the steering wheel to re-center after a turn. However, there is little resistance to changing direction, so steering effort is light. On late-model vehicles, negative caster specifications are rare, but a number of large, heavy models produced during the 1960s and 1970s were designed to operate with negative caster. Negative caster was specified because the amount of weight on the wheels made steering these vehicles extremely difficult when caster was positive. Many older vehicles without power steering used negative caster, and models with power steering used positive caster.

Uneven caster between the two front wheels causes the vehicle to pull toward the side with less caster. This is because that wheel is more easily deflected outward by road forces, Figure 14-13. Caster between the two wheels on an axle should be equal, or vary by less than ¼-degree. Even though caster is not a tire wear angle, instability from incorrect caster may cause wheels to **shimmy,** or shake side-to-side, which results in cup wear on the tires.

Caster, rather than camber, is often used to compensate for road crown, since caster is not a

UNEQUAL CASTER

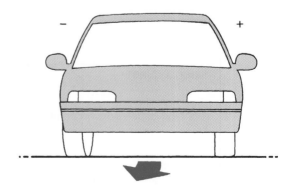

Figure 14-13. Caster is a directional stability angle; the less caster a wheel has, the less stable it is. A vehicle tends to pull toward the side with the least amount of caster when that wheel is deflected from a straight-ahead path.

tire wear angle. Compensating for road crown is not necessary in all regions and should only be considered for vehicles driven primarily on local roads that have a high crown.

Caster Trail

One reason that high positive caster increases the required steering effort is because it increases the **caster trail** as well. Caster trail is the distance between where the caster line intersects the ground and the center point of the tire contact patch (Figure 14-14).

With positive caster, the caster trail increases the turning resistance of the wheel, which requires more steering effort. However, with negative caster, the caster trail does not have this effect and the steering effort remains unchanged. To illustrate, imagine the casters on a toolbox that is being moved across the floor (Figure 14-15). The steering axis is vertical, although not through the hub of the wheel. If the wheel is ahead of the steering axis, the resistance of the floor opposes the wheel, which is easily deflected by anything in its path. This causes the wheel to wobble and makes the toolbox unstable as it moves. The natural tendency of the caster assembly is to rotate on the steering axis so that the wheel trails behind the axis, which gives it a positive caster angle. With positive caster, the resistance of the floor keeps the wheel in position. In other words, the caster trail resists changes in direction and the toolbox remains stable as it moves.

To circumvent the problem of high steering effort created by an increased caster trail due to a high positive caster, some manufacturers increase the caster angle without altering the caster trail. To do this, the lower point of the steering axis is shifted toward the rear so that the caster angle is at or behind the centerline of the wheel. This permits a high positive caster angle, but the distance from where the caster line intersects the ground to the center of the wheel, or the caster trail, remains small (Figure 14-16).

Camber Roll

Unless it is zero, which rarely occurs, caster affects camber during cornering to create a condition known as **camber roll.** With positive caster, the backward tilt of the steering axis causes the spindle on the outside wheel to move up as the front wheels turn on the steering axis, while the spindle on the inside wheel moves down. This produces a camber

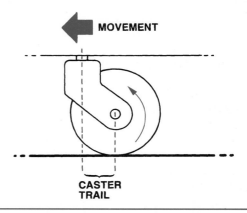

Figure 14-15. Resistance of the floor to the casters on a toolbox being moved places the wheel contact point behind the steering axis, or pivot point, to give the wheel positive caster. The resistance of the floor in the caster trail stabilizes the wheel.

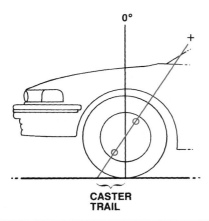

Figure 14-14. Caster trail is the distance between the point where the caster line intersects the ground and the center of the tire contact patch.

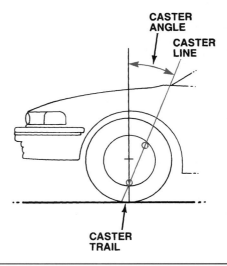

Figure 14-16. Moving the caster line behind the center of the wheel increases the caster angle without increasing the caster trail.

CAMBER ROLL

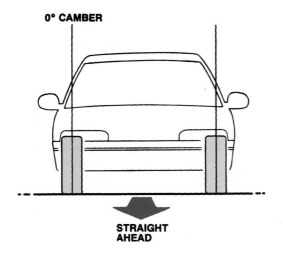

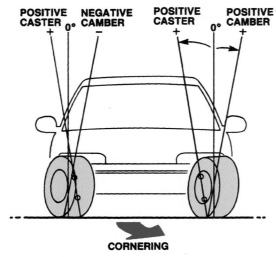

Figure 14-17. Because the wheel steers on the caster line, the wheel tilts to one side while cornering if the caster line is tilted. A tilted wheel has camber, so caster causes camber roll during turns.

decrease at the outside wheel and an increase in camber at the inside wheel (Figure 14-17). The higher the caster, the more it affects camber during turns. Negative caster affects camber in the opposite direction.

Unless the steering axis is vertical, which is highly unlikely, a wheel has camber during turns due to camber roll, even if the camber reading is zero when the wheel is straight ahead. Camber roll causes wear on both edges of the tires because the camber is positive when the vehicle steers in one direction and negative when steering in the opposite direction. Be aware: Tires that are underinflated produce the same tread wear pat-

tern. Check for proper tire inflation before blaming camber roll for a tread wear problem.

Influences on Caster

Caster does not change as easily as camber. However, there are some things that will affect caster and even cause it to change. These include:

- Raising or lowering the front or rear of the vehicle
- Braking force
- Road shock
- Bent or damaged suspension parts

Raising or lowering the front or rear of the vehicle changes caster because the modification repositions the steering knuckles (Figure 14-18). If the vehicle is lowered at the rear, caster increases by the degree that the frame is tilted. Caster decreases similarly when the front of the vehicle is lowered. Braking force affects caster because as the vehicle slows, inertia transfers weight toward the front. This weight transfer lowers the front end during braking, which decreases caster.

Road shock moves the wheels up and down, toward the body and away from it. This motion can affect the positions of the ball joints in relation to each other, or the lower ball joint in relation to a strut, and consequently alters caster.

Bent or damaged suspension parts can permanently alter the steering knuckle position. Any suspension damage must be repaired before caster can be checked and corrected.

Toe

A tire has been traditionally referred to as if it were a foot, and following this convention the front edge of the tire is the "toe," the rear edge is the "heel," and the tire contact patch is the "footprint." Therefore, a measurement taken between the front edges of the tires on the same axle is called **toe.** If the wheels and tires point straight ahead, toe is zero. Tires on the same axle pointing toward each other have **toe-in,** and those pointing away from each other have **toe-out** (Figure 14-19). Toe-in is also known as positive toe, while toe-out may be referred to as negative toe.

As mentioned earlier, toe can be measured in degrees of a circle, or linearly in inches or millimeters. Measuring toe angle in degrees is generally considered the more accurate method. The reason for this is that a linear measurement is actually a degree measurement converted to inches

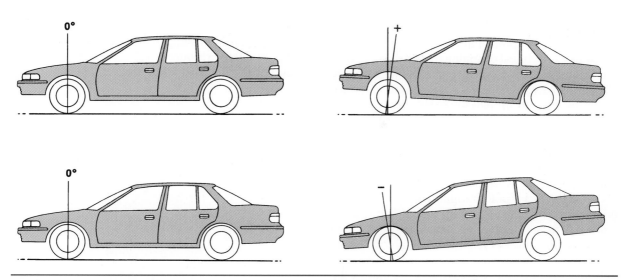

Figure 14-18. Lowering the rear of a vehicle increases front wheel caster, while lowering the front end decreases caster.

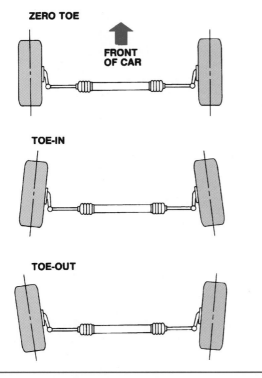

Figure 14-19. Tires point straight ahead with a zero toe angle, toward each other with toe-in, and away from each other with toe-out.

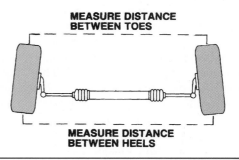

Figure 14-20. Linear toe measures the total toe, or the difference in the distance between the front center of the tires and the distance from center-to-center at the rear of the tires.

standard, the toe reading will be inaccurate unless the alignment equipment being used allows the operator to specify a non-standard tire diameter. Measuring the toe angle in degrees, wherein tire diameter is irrelevant, is therefore more accurate. In addition, a linear measurement represents the total toe, or the combined toe for both wheels. Total toe measured linearly is the difference in the distance between the front centers of the tires and that of the rear centers (Figure 14-20). However, a degree measurement can be taken for each individual wheel, which allows toe angles to be adjusted equally from side-to-side.

Keep in mind, changes in camber always produce a change in toe. This means that all the factors that affect camber, such as vehicle load and worn suspension components, also affect toe. Caster changes affect toe as well. Therefore, it is important to correct camber and caster angles before making toe adjustments.

or millimeters using a mathematical formula. However, this formula is based on the assumption that the diameter of the tires is 28.265 inches, a standard defined by the Society of Automotive Engineers (SAE). So, for example, if the tire diameter is actually 32 inches, rather than the SAE

Effects of Toe

Toe is the most important tire wear angle, and a zero toe setting is the ideal condition to prevent wear during driving. When a wheel is not pointed straight ahead, the tire scuffs sideways along the road surface as it rolls forward. If total toe is incorrect by three-quarters of an inch (20 mm), half the tire tread can wear off within 2,000 miles (3,200 kilometers) (Figure 14-21). Be aware, extensive city driving can produce unusual tire wear that is often mistakenly blamed on an incorrect toe angle. This type of wear is due to the fact that tight right-hand cornering requires a much sharper turning angle than a more gradual left-hand cornering. Regular tire rotation evens out this type of wear pattern to help alleviate the problem. Toe is also a directional control angle. Whether toe-in or toe-out, incorrect toe causes the vehicle to wander and the wheels to shimmy.

Tire tread wear caused by excessive toe is easy to detect on bias-ply tires because their stiff construction tends to produce a feathered wear pattern (Figure 14-22). However, excessive toe wear on radial tires is difficult to tell from camber wear. If a wheel is toed-in, the tire wear is concentrated on the outside edge, as it would be with high positive camber. Toe-out causes wear on the inner edge of the tire, similar to that of high negative camber. Unlike camber wear, toe wear tends to be the same on both tires of the same axle because the drag of the road surface tends to equalize toe side-to-side, even if one wheel has more toe than the other.

Excessive toe on the rear wheels of a FWD vehicle produces a unique tire wear pattern called **diagonal wipe** (Figure 14-23). Toe makes the tires scuff along the road while the vehicle is moving,

**TOE WEAR ON
BIAS PLY TIRE**

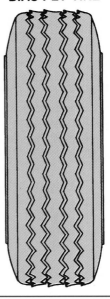

Figure 14-22. Excessive toe produces a feather-edged wear pattern on bias-ply tires. If the sharp edges point toward the inside, the wheel is toed-in, and if they point toward the outside, the wheel is toed-out.

TOE WEAR

Figure 14-21. Incorrect toe causes a shoulder wear pattern, similar to that of incorrect camber, but toe wear tends to be more severe than camber wear.

**DIAGONAL
WIPE**

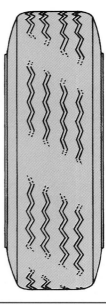

Figure 14-23. The rear tires on a FWD vehicle wear in a pattern called "diagonal wipe" if the toe angle is incorrect.

and the rear tires drag for a little while, then hop because there is little weight to keep them firmly planted on the road. After the tires alternately drag and hop for some distance, they begin to wear in stripes running diagonally across the tread.

Toe Change

Even when toe is correct with the vehicle standing on a level surface, toe change can occur as the suspension travels up and down. Toe change is measured by checking toe at 1-inch (25-mm) increments of suspension travel, from complete extension, or jounce, to complete compression, or rebound. Ideally, toe change should be zero. Excessive toe change indicates a problem with the tie rod; either one of the tie rod ends is at the wrong height, or the tie rod is the wrong length (Figure 14-24).

Toe change can be charted on a graph. The best graph pattern is a straight vertical line, which reflects zero toe change, throughout suspension jounce and rebound. A sharp curve of toe-in or toe-

out during suspension travel indicates that the tie rod is the wrong length (Figure 14-25). A diagonal line from severe toe-in or toe-out at rebound to severe opposite toe during jounce indicates that the outer tie rod end is at the wrong height relative to the inner tie rod end (Figure 14-26). To correct, one end or the other must be brought into specifications. Note that it is possible for a wheel to have zero toe at ride height and still have severe toe change.

Recall that incorrect toe can cause shimmy. Toe change causes the same handling problems as incorrect toe, except the symptoms occur only during suspension travel. Toe change is sometimes called "bump steer," as described in Chapter 5 of this *Classroom Manual,* because it affects steering over bumpy surfaces. Another term applied to toe change is "roll steer," because body roll that occurs during turns produces suspension travel and consequently results in toe change.

Steering Axis Inclination (SAI)

Steering axis inclination (SAI) is the angle between the steering axis and a vertical line at the wheel centerline as viewed from the front of the vehicle (Figure 14-27). On a SLA or strut/SLA suspension, the steering axis is an imaginary line running through the centers of the upper and lower ball joints. On a strut suspension, the line runs through the top of the strut, at the pivot, and the lower ball joint. On a kingpin suspension, the

TOE CHANGE

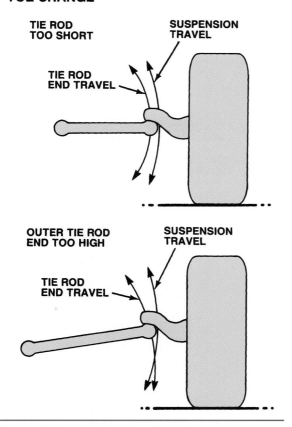

Figure 14-24. Toe change during bounce is caused by a difference between suspension travel and the travel of the outer tie rod end. Steering arm position affects toe because it extends along the side of the wheel.

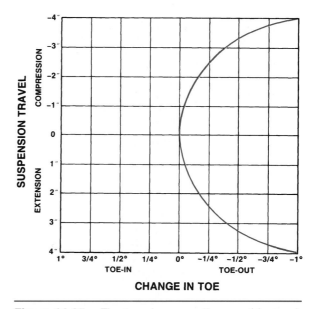

Figure 14-25. The toe change pattern on this graph indicates that the tie rod is the wrong length. This pattern would indicate the tie rod is too short if the steering arm extends toward the rear of the vehicle.

line runs through the kingpin axis and may be called "kingpin inclination (KPI)." The "ball joint inclination (BJI)" and "kingpin inclination (KPI)" are both alternative names for SAI.

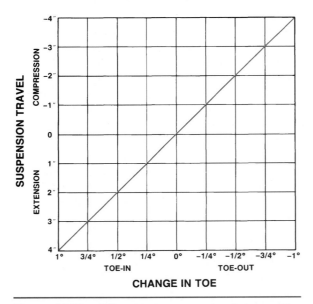

Figure 14-26. If the steering arm extends toward the rear of the vehicle, the toe change pattern on this graph indicates that the outer tie rod end is higher than the inner tie rod end, and either or both may be at the wrong height.

As mentioned earlier, SAI and caster measure the same line, only from different viewpoints. Therefore, SAI and caster are somewhat similar in their effects, and both are important directional control angles.

SAI Measurements

Like all alignment angles, SAI is measured in degrees. A strut suspension has a high SAI, while SLA and strut/SLA suspensions with a low knuckle have less SAI.

Although SAI is typically not individually adjustable, camber adjustments that require repositioning the top of the strut on a strut suspension simultaneously affect camber and SAI. Measuring the SAI angle is also a method of verifying suspected suspension damage. The SAI measurement indicates the position of the ball joints, or ball joint and strut, and the steering knuckle and spindle. On a kingpin suspension, SAI indicates the position of the kingpin, steering knuckle, and spindle. If any of these parts are bent, SAI will be out of specification. The only way to correct SAI is to replace the defective parts.

Another alignment angle related to SAI is the **included angle.** The included angle is the SAI angle plus or minus the camber angle (Figure 14-28). With positive camber, add the camber angle to the SAI to determine the included angle, and subtract

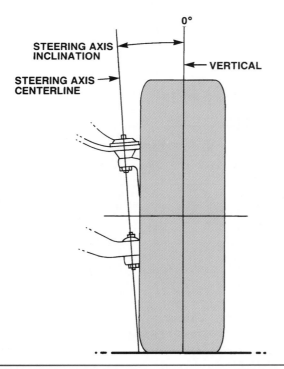

Figure 14-27. Steering axis inclination is the difference between the steering axis and a vertical line through the center of the wheel when viewed from the front.

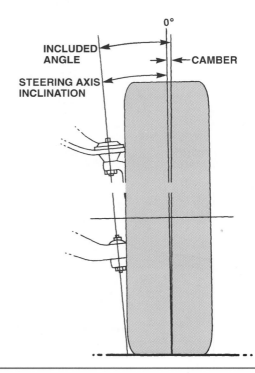

Figure 14-28. The included angle is the SAI angle plus the camber angle.

a negative camber angle from the SAI to calculate the included angle. Included angle analysis is useful in diagnosing bent suspension components.

Effects of SAI

Steering axis inclination is a critical alignment for strut suspensions because the strut serves a dual purpose—suspension arm and shock absorber. Also, since the upper strut mount attaches to a fender well, the strut cannot be tilted back very far, and the amount of caster provided in these suspensions is limited. However, the strut can be tilted inward to some degree to increase the SAI, which helps compensate for a small caster angle. On a FWD vehicle with a strut suspension, SAI is much more important than caster in ensuring steering stability.

To help return the wheels to their straight-ahead position after cornering, the SAI angle puts the spindle at an angle when the wheels are turned either to the left or right. This angle makes the spindle arc downward, which works with gravity to place a downward force on the wheel and tire (Figure 14-29).

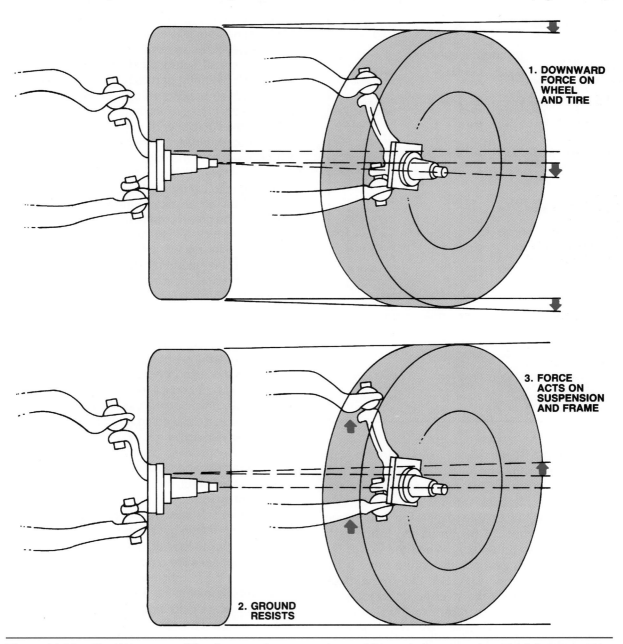

1. DOWNWARD FORCE ON WHEEL AND TIRE

3. FORCE ACTS ON SUSPENSION AND FRAME

2. GROUND RESISTS

Figure 14-29. The SAI exerts a lifting force on the suspension and frame during cornering, which is opposed by the force of gravity. The force of gravity opposes SAI to straighten the wheels and return the suspension to a neutral position once the turn is complete.

DIAGNOSING SAI, CAMBER, AND INCLUDED ANGLE

SAI	CAMBER	INCLUDED ANGLE	DIAGNOSIS
SLA AND STRUT/SLA SUSPENSIONS			
Correct	Less than specs	Less than specs	Bent steering knuckle or spindle
Less than specs	Greater than specs	Correct	Bent lower control arm
Less than specs	Greater than specs	Greater than specs	Bent lower control arm and steering knuckle or spindle
Greater than specs	Less than specs	Correct	Bent upper control arm
STRUT SUSPENSIONS			
Correct	Less than specs	Less than specs	Bent spindle and/or strut
Correct	Greater than specs	Greater than specs	Bent spindle and/or strut
Less than specs	Greater than specs	Correct	Bent control arm or strut tower out at top
Less than specs	Greater than specs	Greater than specs	Bent control arm or strut tower out at top, also bent spindle and/or strut
Less than specs	Less than specs	Less than specs	Strut tower out at top and bent spindle and/or bent strut or control arm
Greater than specs	Less than specs	Correct	Strut tower in at top
Greater than specs	Greater than specs	Greater than specs	Strut tower in at top and bent spindle and/or strut
KINGPIN TWIN I-BEAM SUSPENSION			
Correct	Greater than specs	Greater than specs	Bent spindle
Less than specs	Greater than specs	Correct	Bent I-beam
Less than specs	Greater than specs	Greater than specs	Bent I-beam and spindle
Greater than specs	Less than specs	Correct	Bent I-beam

However, the wheel and tire cannot move downward because the tire is on the ground, which creates resistance. This resistance returns the downward force back through the spindle and steering knuckle to the suspension and frame causing the wheel to lift up on the frame as it turns on the steering axis. When the driver releases the steering wheel, the lifting force is removed. Now, gravity forces the frame back down, which causes the steering knuckle, spindle, wheel, and tire to return to their straight-ahead position. Because of SAI, gravity straightens the wheels after a turn, so the driver does not have to.

Scrub Radius— Positive or Negative?

When a manufacturer designs a new vehicle, starting with a clean sheet of paper, the engineers can design almost any suspension geometry imaginable. Why do they choose a negative scrub radius over a positive one, or vice versa? It depends upon the intended use of the vehicle and how the engineers want the vehicle to operate. Either a negative or a positive scrub radius is a "good" design as long as the suspension works along with it. However, each type of scrub radius makes a vehicle handle differently, particularly under braking.

When braking on a surface where one side of the chassis has better traction than the other, the vehicle tends to pull toward the side with better grip. An example might be a road that is wet near the edge but dry near the center. A vehicle driving on this road would have good traction at the left tires, but the right tires would be on a slick surface. If the driver brakes, the greater traction on the left tends to pull the vehicle left. In this situation, the scrub radius determines what the driver feels through the steering wheel and how the steering wheel must be turned to keep the vehicle moving in a straight path.

Under the same road conditions, a vehicle with positive scrub radius pulls to the left and steers slightly to the left as well. The driver feels the steering wheel tug to the left and must steer to the right in order to keep the vehicle traveling in a straight line. The steering system "tells" the driver about the road surface and what the vehicle is doing and requires the driver to play an active role in keeping the vehicle stable. Sports cars commonly have positive scrub radius, and designers in favor of it say that positive scrub radius increases driving enjoyment by increasing driver involvement.

A vehicle with negative scrub radius reacts differently. In our example, the vehicle still tends to pull to the left, but the negative scrub radius opposes the change. The driver feels a slight tug to the right in the steering wheel, but the vehicle maintains a straight path without corrective steering input from the driver. Designers who endorse a negative scrub radius cite the safety benefits of this self-correction.

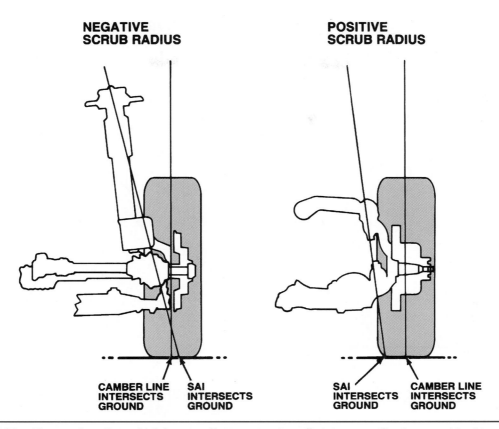

NEGATIVE SCRUB RADIUS

POSITIVE SCRUB RADIUS

CAMBER LINE INTERSECTS GROUND

SAI INTERSECTS GROUND

SAI INTERSECTS GROUND

CAMBER LINE INTERSECTS GROUND

Figure 14-30. The scrub radius, which has an effect on steering effort, toe specifications, and braking stability, is the distance between where the SAI and camber lines intersect the ground.

SAI and Scrub Radius

The distance between the points where the SAI line and the centerline of the tire, or camber line, intersect the ground is the **scrub radius** (Figure 14-30). Scrub radius, which is also known as "steering offset," is a factor in determining steering effort. If the SAI line intersects the ground inside the camber line, the tire has a positive scrub radius. If the SAI line crosses over the camber line and intersects the ground at the outside, the tire has a negative scrub radius. If the lines intersect the ground at the same place, the tire has a zero scrub radius. Most SLA and strut/SLA suspensions have a positive scrub radius, while most strut suspensions have a negative scrub radius. The scrub radius in a strut/SLA suspension with a long knuckle is smaller than on most SLA designs.

Scrub Radius Effects

The size of the scrub radius affects how easy or difficult it is to turn the wheels and tires. If the scrub radius is large, a large part of the tire contact patch has to scrub across the ground as the wheels steer into a turn. This increases the steering effort

required and also increases tire wear. A smaller scrub radius reduces steering effort and minimizes tire wear during cornering. In strut/SLA suspensions with a long knuckle and small SAI angle, the scrub radius is very small (Figure 14-31).

Whether the scrub radius is positive or negative helps determine the toe specifications. A scrub radius can create a drag on the tire during straight-ahead driving, and this drag makes the wheel tend to pivot on the steering axis. Drag created by a positive scrub radius, which is outboard of the axis, makes the wheel tend to toe-out. Manufacturers often specify a slight amount of toe-in for wheels with a positive scrub radius to compensate for this tendency. Conversely, a tire with a negative scrub radius tends to toe-in during straight-ahead driving because the drag is inboard of the steering axis. A slight toe-out specification compensates for the drag of a negative scrub radius.

Scrub radius also affects braking stability, especially if braking force is unequal from side-to-side. If the brakes on one wheel apply with more force than the brakes at the other wheel, the wheel with greater braking force tends to pull outward. Because

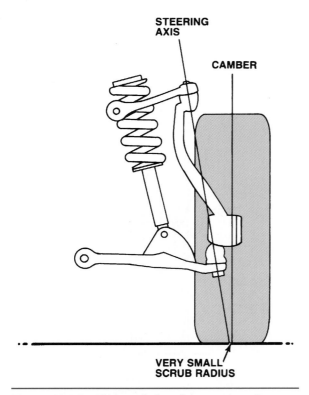

Figure 14-31. The small size of the scrub radius on a strut/SLA suspension minimizes its effects on handling.

a positive scrub radius also tends to aim a wheel outward, the braking force and the positive scrub radius combine to pull the vehicle toward one side. A tire with a negative scrub radius, however, opposes the outward force of a grabbing brake. Therefore, a vehicle with a negative scrub radius has greater directional stability when braking forces are uneven. A disadvantage of wide aftermarket wheels is that the additional width of the tire increases the scrub radius, and the more positive scrub radius thus decreases braking stability.

Toe-Out on Turns

When a vehicle is driven around a corner, the front wheel at the inside of the curve must turn at a greater angle than the front wheel at the outside. This requires that the wheels be toed-out during turns. **Toe-out on turns** allows the outside wheel to travel in a larger arc than the inside wheel.

As explained in Chapter 5 of this *Classroom Manual,* toe-out on turns is designed into the steering system by angling the steering arms inward toward the center of the rear axle (Figure 14-32).

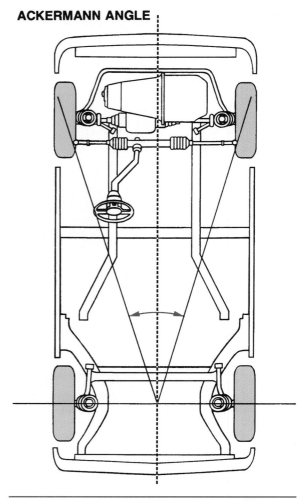

Figure 14-32. The Ackermann angle is formed by imaginary lines drawn from the midpoint of the rear axle through the steering arms.

With this design, which is known as the "Ackermann angle," the arc of the steering arm is smaller as it moves toward the wheel than it is as it moves away from the wheel. As a result, wheel movement is less in one direction than in the other.

Because toe-out on turns is designed into the construction of the steering arms, if one or both of the arms becomes misaligned or bent, the Ackermann angle changes. The only way to correct toe-out on turns is to replace the defective part or parts.

Toe-out on turns is designed in relation to the wheelbase of the vehicle. Wheelbase is the distance from the center of the front axle to the center of the rear axle. Taking this measurement into consideration, the Ackermann angle is used to plot the toe-out on turns during suspension design. Theoretically, the centerlines of both front wheels should intersect the centerline of the rear wheels at

ACKERMANN EFFECT

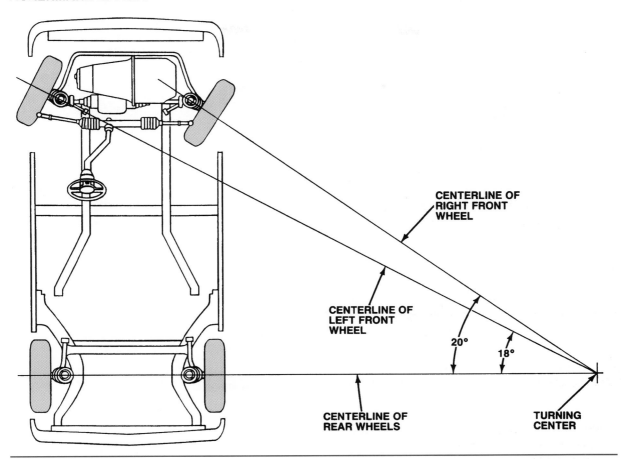

Figure 14-33. Theoretically, the Ackermann effect, which is caused by the Ackermann angle, places the turning center in line with the rear axle.

the same point during a turn (Figure 14-33). The point where all the centerlines intersect is the **turning center.**

Under actual driving conditions, centrifugal force acts on the vehicle to some extent, depending on vehicle speed and mass, and all four tires slip toward the outside of the turn. The actual turning center, therefore, is ahead of the centerline of the rear wheels (Figure 14-34). The distance from the turning center to the outside wheels is the **turning radius.** Because the angle of toe-out on turns determines the turning radius, the angle itself is sometimes referred to as the "turning radius."

With a four-wheel steering system, the turning radius is much smaller when the rear wheels steer opposite the front wheels (Figure 14-35). Four-wheel-steering systems and their modes of operation are described in detail in Chapter 7 of this *Classroom Manual.*

The ordinary slippage that occurs during cornering, along with camber roll—as explained earlier—causes some wear on both the inside and outside edges of the tires. This wear pattern is similar to that caused by low tire inflation pressure. Slippage and tire wear increase during high-speed cornering, but this type of wear is kept to a minimum under normal driving conditions.

When toe-out on turns is out of specification, the tire scuffs and squeals as the vehicle is driven around corners. Tire wear increases as a result of the scuffing, and the vehicle develops an increased tendency toward side-slip.

Thrust Angle

The angle between the thrust line and the geometric centerline is the **thrust angle** (Figure 14-36). The **thrust line** is a line that bisects, or cuts in half,

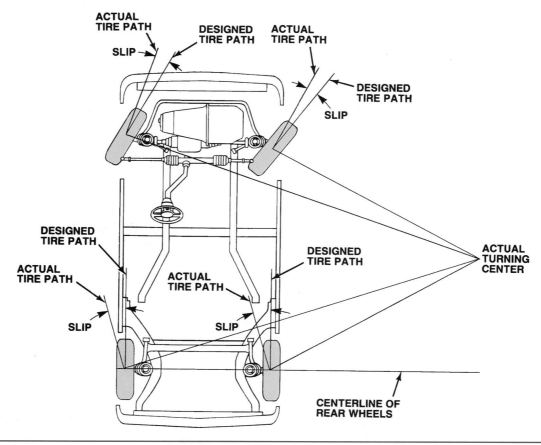

Figure 14-34. In reality, the tires slip across the pavement during cornering. However, toe-out on turns allows the outer wheel to travel in a wider arc than the inner wheel, which minimizes tire slip.

the total toe of the rear wheels. The **geometric centerline** of the vehicle is a line that bisects the front and rear axles.

The thrust angle is important because the rear wheels determine the position of the front wheels during straight-ahead driving. This is true whether the vehicle is front-wheel drive or rear-wheel drive. When traveling straight ahead, the rear wheels "steer" the vehicle and the front wheels align themselves accordingly. In other words, the vehicle tends to travel along the thrust line.

Ideally, the thrust line and the geometric centerline are the same, which occurs when the toe angle is the same at each rear wheel. In this case, the thrust angle is zero, and the rear wheels steer the vehicle straight ahead. If the front wheels are aligned to the centerline and there is no thrust angle, the rear wheels follow in the tracks of the front wheels—a condition called tracking. However, if the front wheels are aligned to the centerline and there *is* a

thrust angle, the rear wheels steer the rear axle along the thrust line, causing the following problems:

- Crooked steering wheel
- Camber and toe change at the front wheels
- Tire wear
- Pull

If it is not possible to eliminate the thrust angle, the front wheels may be aligned to the thrust line, rather than to the geometric centerline. When the front wheels are aligned to a thrust angle, all four wheels drive straight down the road but the rear wheels do not track the front wheels. Instead, they travel in a parallel line to the front wheels, but offset slightly toward one side. This causes the vehicle body to travel at an angle to the road—called **dog-tracking.** Dog-tracking may look odd in extreme cases, but it does eliminate the handling and tire wear problems of a thrust angle. Extreme

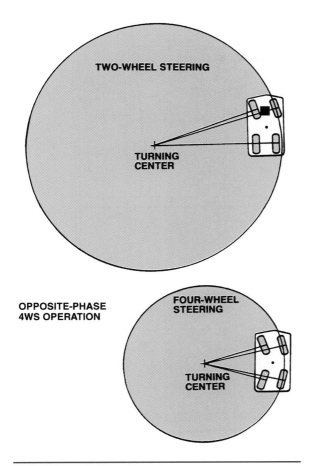

OPPOSITE-PHASE 4WS OPERATION

Figure 14-35. When the rear wheels turn in the opposite direction of the front wheels, the turning radius is much smaller.

cases of dog-tracking may affect the aerodynamics of the vehicle in straight-ahead driving.

The thrust angle is sometimes referred to as the "track angle" because it relates to how the rear wheels track the front wheels.

Setback

The term **setback** refers to one wheel on an axle being positioned farther back in the chassis than the other (Figure 14-37). Setback can be measured either linearly, in inches or millimeters, or in degrees. If the right wheel is farther back than the left one, the axle has positive setback. If the left wheel is farther back, the axle has negative setback. Usually, about one inch (25 mm) or 0.5 degree (30 minutes) is the maximum setback allowable in either direction. Severe setback is usually the result of a collision moving one wheel farther back. Even within acceptable limits, set-

back can cause steering wheel misalignment. Uneven caster can cause setback at the front axle.

TYPES OF WHEEL ALIGNMENT

Wheel alignment procedures can be broken into four categories:

- Geometric centerline alignment
- Thrust line alignment
- Two-wheel alignment
- Four-wheel alignment

From early automotive history to the 1980s, a two-wheel alignment was considered an adequate procedure for restoring good handling and preventing tire wear. This practice followed the assumption that if the front wheels were straightened out, the rear wheels had nothing better to do than follow right behind. Moreover, the typical rear suspension was not particularly sophisticated. A rigid rear axle did not allow fine adjustments that would result in delicate handling improvements.

Through the 1980s, manufacturers competed to produce ever more refined and exactly controlled suspensions, and precise handling became a selling point. As a result, drivers became more knowledgeable about steering characteristics and more insistent upon good handling. Also, specialized suspension systems became common at both the front and rear axles, to the extent that independent rear suspension, once found only on imported luxury and sport models, became a standard feature on the majority of late-model vehicles.

Knowledgeable drivers and complex suspensions brought with them the need for more precise, accurate alignment techniques. Today, camber and toe adjustments can be made at the rear wheels of most vehicles with an independent rear suspension, and a four-wheel alignment is now a routine procedure. Even vehicles with non-independent, non-adjustable rear suspensions can benefit from a thrust alignment, which takes into account the position of the rear wheels (Figure 14-38).

Before aligning the wheels, a pre-alignment inspection is performed to eliminate problems such as mismatched tires, sagging springs, incorrect engine cradle alignment, or severely bent or damaged suspension or steering parts that can interfere with correcting alignment. If any of these problems are present, they must be corrected before performing the alignment. If these problems

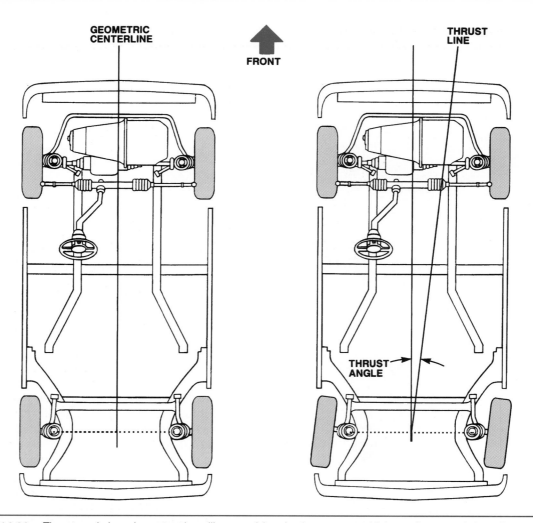

GEOMETRIC CENTERLINE

FRONT

THRUST LINE

THRUST ANGLE

Figure 14-36. Thrust angle is an important handling consideration because a vehicle tends to travel along the thrust line.

Aligning the Model A

A mechanic performing a front-wheel alignment on a Model A Ford in the 1930s had the same goals in mind as a present-day technician aligning the front wheels of a modern vehicle—correct tracking, handling, and minimum tire wear. As with a modern Ford Taurus, the Model A performed best when the caster, camber, and toe were set to factory specifications. However, the procedures for an alignment were somewhat different than they are today, primarily because of the solid-beam front axle of the Model A. This axle was made of tempered alloy steel and was extremely strong. It had to be, because it and the radius rods leading back to the frame were all that kept the front wheels in alignment.

To set camber to the specified seven degrees, the front axle—while still attached to the vehicle—was clamped into a jig, then bent into the correct shape using bottle or hydraulic jacks. Camber could not be changed without also affecting the steering axis inclination. To adjust caster, the jacks were moved to the radius rods that connected the axle to the center of the frame. Bending the center of the radius rods down increased caster, while bending them up decreased it. Specifications called for five degrees of caster.

The Model A required about 1/16 to 1/8 inch of toe-in, and toe could be adjusted without the use of jacks. The beam-axle front suspension had ball pivots at the ends of the steering arms, which were linked together by a single tie rod with ball plug sockets threaded on each end. Toe adjustments were made by detaching the tie rod from the ball pivots, threading the ball plug sockets in or out the necessary distance, then re-attaching the tie rod.

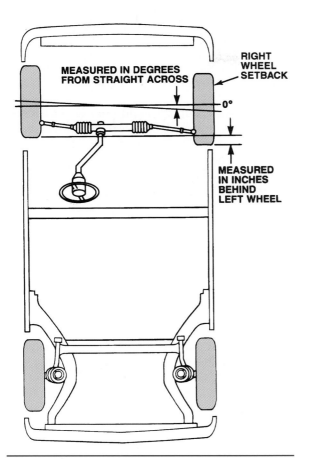

Figure 14-37. Setback causes steering wheel misalignment, and when a vehicle with setback travels straight ahead, the steering wheel is cocked to one side to match the angle of the steering linkage.

THRUST ALIGNMENT

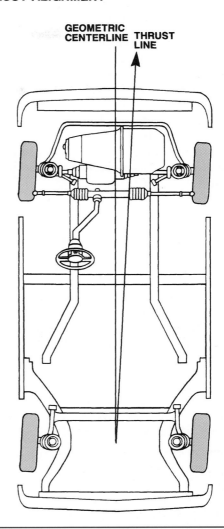

Figure 14-38. In a thrust alignment, which is performed when rear toe cannot be brought within specifications, the front wheels are aligned to the thrust line, rather than the geometric centerline.

are not corrected, alignment angles generally cannot be brought to specifications.

A vehicle ride height measurement should be considered essential in every pre-alignment inspection. The springs are vital suspension components that help determine alignment angles such as caster and camber. If the springs are sagging, or the vehicle leans from side-to-side or front-to-rear, they must be replaced before the wheels can be accurately aligned. On vehicles with a torsion bar suspension, adjusting the torsion bars generally brings the ride height to within specifications.

The vehicle should also be inspected for frame damage prior to performing a wheel alignment, especially if there is evidence of prior collision damage. It is difficult and often futile to align a vehicle with frame damage using traditional alignment methods. Extensive alignment adjustments and aftermarket alignment parts should

never be used to compensate for damaged suspension components. Always replace bent or damaged suspension components before proceeding with a wheel alignment. If the frame is damaged, refer the vehicle to a qualified frame repair shop before attempting an alignment.

A simple pre-alignment check that is often overlooked is tire inflation. A surprising number of driving problems can be corrected with proper tire inflation, and maintaining correct inflation lengthens the life of the tires. Pre-alignment checks and procedures are described in more detail in the *Shop Manual*.

Geometric Centerline Alignment

The **geometric centerline alignment** method uses the centerline of the vehicle as the reference for setting front and rear toe. This method was used for many years when most vehicles were rear-wheel drive and used a non-adjustable rear suspension. Using the geometric centerline method is no longer recommended by vehicle manufacturers but could be used if the rear toe is known to be parallel to the center of the vehicle.

Thrust Line Alignment

The thrust line is the imaginary line that bisects the total rear toe setting. A **thrust line alignment** is performed by adjusting the front toe parallel to the rear toe, and not parallel to the geometric centerline of the vehicle. By performing a thrust line alignment, the steering wheel will be straight while the vehicle is being driven on a straight road.

Two-Wheel Alignment

A **two-wheel alignment** is performed on only the front wheels, which are aligned to the vehicle centerline. Front wheel camber, caster, and toe are measured and, whenever possible, adjusted. Unless the manufacturer specifies otherwise, either caster or camber is aligned first. Frequently, the same mechanism adjusts both caster and camber simultaneously. Consult an alignment manual or service manual for the location of adjustment mechanisms and exact instructions on how to make adjustments. Some typical methods include:

- Adding or removing shims
- Turning an eccentric cam
- Repositioning a mounting bolt in a slotted hole

This is by no means an inclusive list. Alignment methods are described in detail in the *Shop Manual.*

On some MacPherson strut suspensions, caster is not adjustable because the steering knuckle is an integral part of the strut. However, caster should be checked, even when it is non-adjustable, to make sure it is even side-to-side. On a strut suspension, incorrect or uneven caster indicates a damaged suspension part, possibly the strut itself, or a control arm. Replacing the damaged part or parts should restore caster.

Caster and camber should both be rechecked after one is adjusted because they affect each other. In fact, most alignment equipment derives caster by measuring camber roll as the front wheels turn equal amounts in each direction from the straight-ahead position.

The camber and caster adjustments tend to change the toe angle, so toe is not set until the other two adjustments are complete. Front toe adjustments are made at the tie rods, by turning a threaded portion of the rod or by turning an adjustment nut until toe is correct. Chapter 5 of this *Classroom Manual* describes tie rod designs in detail, and the *Shop Manual* provides specific adjustment procedures.

Neither SAI nor toe-out on turns is adjustable, but both should be checked to ensure that the suspension is in good repair. Incorrect toe-out on turns indicates a problem with the steering arms. If either of these two angles is out of specification, inspect the suspension and replace all damaged parts.

Four-Wheel Alignment

In a **four-wheel alignment,** rear wheel alignment is checked and, if possible, corrected before the front wheels are aligned. A four-wheel alignment requires four-wheel alignment equipment. It is impossible to correctly align the rear wheels using equipment designed to align the front wheels only.

The rear wheel toe setting determines the thrust angle. After both rear wheels have the toe set, then the front wheel toe settings are set to be parallel to the thrust line. If everything is perfect, the thrust line will be the same as the geometric center line of the vehicle. However, some variation is possible and the alignment equipment readings should fall within specifications to be sure that the vehicle tracks properly and the steering wheel will be straight.

On rear suspensions with adjustable camber and toe, setting toe correctly eliminates the thrust angle. Therefore, front wheel toe can be set in reference to the vehicle centerline. Adjusting rear camber is also important for correct handling because if excessive camber causes pull at one rear wheel, it will affect overall vehicle steering. When rear wheel alignment is as correct as possible, the front wheels are aligned as in a two-wheel alignment.

The reason for adjusting the rear wheels first is to make it possible to perform a thrust angle alignment if rear toe is not adjustable, as in the case of a vehicle with a solid rear axle. In a **thrust alignment,** front toe is set with reference to the thrust line rather than the vehicle centerline. If the thrust angle is zero, front wheel toe can be set to the vehicle centerline (Figure 14-39).

Setback is another four-wheel alignment concern. If one wheel is set back beyond the specified allowance, the vehicle needs suspension and steering linkage repair to position the wheel correctly before a proper alignment can be performed.

FOUR-WHEEL ALIGNMENT

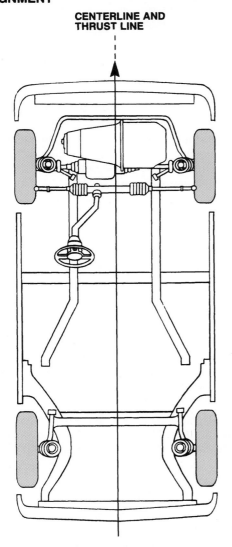

CENTERLINE AND THRUST LINE

Figure 14-39. There is no thrust angle on a four-wheel alignment because all four wheels are aligned to the geometric centerline.

WHEEL ALIGNMENT EQUIPMENT

There are many different ways to measure the alignment angles on a vehicle. The most common way is the use of an alignment machine or rack. The equipment used for checking alignment angles has evolved from string and measuring tapes to today's computerized machines (Figure 14-40), which are most commonly used in current shops. A typical computerized system gives information on a CRT screen to guide the technician step-by-step through the alignment process after the vehicle is compensated for wheel runout. When compensation is complete, alignment measurements are instantly displayed. Also displayed are the specifications for that vehicle. In addition to the normal alignment specifications, the CRT may display asymmetric tolerances, different left- and

Figure 14-40. This technician is using computer alignment equipment. (Courtesy of Hunter Engineering)

Figure 14-41. This photo shows typical computerized alignment equipment components. (Courtesy of Hunter Engineering)

right-side specifications, and cross specifications (difference allowed between left and right side). Graphics and text on the screen show the technician where and how to make adjustments.

As adjustments are made on the vehicle, the technician can observe the center block slide toward the target. When the block aligns with the target, the adjustment is within half the specified tolerance. Other alignment equipment often used are turning radius gauges, caster-camber gauges, optical toe gauges, and tram gauges.

You can use the following process for a typical four-wheel alignment:

1. Select vehicle make and model.
2. Vehicle specifications can be easily selected two ways:
   • Scroll through the specifications list.
   • Enter the vehicle identification number (VIN).
3. Measure angles: After compensation, camber, toe, and thrust line measurements are displayed. Caster, SAI, and IA are displayed following caster steer.
4. Adjust the vehicle.

A patented bar graph shows the amount and direction of adjustment required. As you make adjustments, the arrow moves across the bar graph. The bar graph changes from red to green as the alignment adjustment comes within specification.

1. Four high-resolution digital video cameras (one per target) continuously monitor tar-

gets at each wheel. Cameras are mounted up high, out of harm's way (Figure 14-41).
2. Optional handheld LED remote indicators provide complete control while performing rolling compensation and making vehicle adjustments (Figure 14-41).
3. Sensors provide the same high-speed screen updates as conventional sensors (Figure 14-41).
4. Alignment targets require:
   • No calibration
   • No electronics
   • No cables
   • No batteries
5. Sensors can be used with existing Hunter 811 Series alignment equipment using WinAlign® software (7.0 or higher required).

SUMMARY

Wheel alignment is a procedure for positioning wheels and tires so they travel in a straight line as the vehicle is driven down the road. A calculating system called "steering geometry" is used to check and correct alignment.

There are five traditional steering geometry angles: caster, camber, toe, toe-out on turns, and steering axis inclination (SAI). All alignment angles are measured in degrees (°) of a circle or degrees and fractions of degrees, although it is possible to measure toe linearly, or in inches or millimeters. However, measuring toe in degrees is a more accurate method. Alignment angles measured in degrees use negative or positive numbers to indicate the direction of the angle.

Caster is the angle between a vertical line drawn through the center of the wheel and the steering axis line as viewed from the side of the vehicle. Caster trail is the distance between the points at which these two lines intersect the ground. Camber is the angle between a true vertical line, perpendicular to the ground, and a line drawn through the center of the tire when viewed from the front of the vehicle. Toe is the angle between the geometric centerline of the vehicle and a line drawn through the center of the tire as viewed from above. Toe-out on turns is the difference in toe at each front wheel during a turn. Steering axis inclination is the angle between a vertical line and a line drawn through the steering axis when viewed from the front. The included angle is the sum of the SAI and camber measurements of a wheel. The distance from the point at which the SAI line intersects the ground to the center of the tire contact patch is the scrub radius.

Caster, SAI, and toe-out on turns are typically measurable only at the front wheels. The only ex-ceptions are vehicles with 4WS. Tire wear angles affect how quickly tires wear out. Camber, toe, and toe-out on turns are tire wear angles. Directional control angles affect how the vehicle handles, and all five traditional angles are directional control angles.

Two other angles are the thrust angle and setback. The thrust angle is the angle between the geometric centerline of the vehicle and a line bisecting rear toe. Setback is the angle between the vehicle centerline and the line formed by the front or rear axle.

Camber, caster, and toe are adjustable angles. Toe-out on turns, SAI, thrust angle, and setback measurements indicate suspension or steering component damage.

A two-wheel alignment measures front-wheel alignment and aligns the front wheels with reference to the geometric centerline. A four-wheel alignment measures the alignment of all four wheels. If possible, the thrust angle is eliminated and all four wheels are aligned with reference to the centerline. If the thrust angle cannot be eliminated, a "thrust alignment," which aligns the front wheels to the thrust line rather than the centerline, is performed.

Review Questions

For each of the following questions, choose the letter that represents the best possible answer.

1. Caster is measured in which of the following:
   a. Centimeters
   b. Millimeters
   c. Degrees
   d. Both A and B

2. Some vehicles use a steering damper to reduce large amounts of which of these items:
   a. Positive caster
   b. Negative caster
   c. Positive camber
   d. Negative camber

3. When the front wheels are parallel to each other, the toe is which of these items:
   a. Negative
   b. Positive
   c. Zero
   d. Toed out

4. Positive camber improves all of these items, EXCEPT:
   a. Road isolation
   b. Ride quality
   c. Directional stability
   d. Turning radius

5. Front steering geometry and four-wheel alignment is being discussed. Technician A says that the camber is positive when the top of the wheel is tilted in. Technician B says caster is negative when the steering knuckle and wheel is tilted backward. Who is right?
   a. A only
   b. B only
   c. Both A and B
   d. Neither A nor B

6. While discussing front wheel camber, Technician A says if a front wheel has a positive camber angle, the camber line is tilted inward from the true vertical centerline of the wheel and tire. Technician B says if the camber is equal on both wheels, the vehicle tends to go straight. Who is right?
   a. A only
   b. B only
   c. Both A and B
   d. Neither A nor B

7. Which of the following is NOT a steering geometry term?
   a. Camber
   b. Toe
   c. Caster axis inclination
   d. Thrust angle

8. Which of the following alignment angles have the most effect on tire wear?
   a. Camber, toe, and toe-out on turns
   b. Caster, camber, and steering axis inclination
   c. Setback, camber, and caster axis inclination
   d. Caster, camber, and setback

9. Technician A says that camber and toe are usually non-adjustable angles. Technician B says that steering axis inclination and toe-out on turns are usually non-adjustable angles. Who is right?
   a. A only
   b. B only
   c. Both A and B
   d. Neither A nor B

10. Technician A says that if camber is unequal side-to-side, the vehicle pulls toward the side with more positive camber. Technician B says that if caster is unequal side-to-side, the vehicle pulls toward the side with more positive caster. Who is right?
    a. A only
    b. B only
    c. Both A and B
    d. Neither A nor B

11. Which alignment angle defines the inward or outward tilt of the top of the tire when viewed from the front of the vehicle?
    a. Toe
    b. Caster
    c. Camber
    d. Thrust

12. As viewed from the front of the vehicle, a tire that is straight up and down, or perpendicular to the road, has:
    a. Zero toe
    b. Zero caster
    c. Zero camber
    d. Zero SAI

13. Technician A says that caster is the forward or backward tilt of the steering axis as viewed from the side of the vehicle. Technician B says that the thrust line is the inward or outward tilt of the tire as viewed from above the vehicle. Who is right?
    a. A only
    b. B only
    c. Both A and B
    d. Neither A nor B

14. Technician A says that the caster angle affects the directional stability of the vehicle. Technician B says that if the steering axis tilts toward the front of the vehicle from the top, the wheel has negative caster. Who is right?
    a. A only
    b. B only
    c. Both A and B
    d. Neither A nor B

15. When both caster and toe are out of specification, the vehicle will pull toward the side with:
    a. Less caster
    b. More caster
    c. Less toe
    d. More toe

16. When the wheels with positive caster are steered into a corner:
    a. Camber decreases at the outside tire
    b. Camber increases at the outside tire
    c. Caster decreases at the outside tire
    d. Caster increases at the outside tire

17. The linear total toe measurement is the:
    a. Difference between the toe measurement and the tire contact patch
    b. Addition of the heel measurement and the scrub radius
    c. Difference between the tire toe and heel measurements
    d. Addition of the tire toe and heel measurements

18. Throughout suspension movement, toe change should ideally be:
    a. Less than 1/16 inch (1.6 mm)
    b. Less than 1/8 inch (3.2 mm)
    c. More than 1/16 inch (1.6 mm)
    d. Zero

19. As viewed from the front of the vehicle, the steering axis inclination is the angle between:
    a. The steering axis and total camber
    b. The steering axis and total caster
    c. The steering axis and a vertical line
    d. The steering axis and a horizontal line

20. Technician A says that the Ackermann angle allows the inside tire to travel in a smaller arc than the outside tire during turns. Technician B says that the steering arms are angled in toward the center of the rear axle to produce the Ackermann angle. Who is right?
    a. A only
    b. B only
    c. Both A and B
    d. Neither A nor B

Glossary

A-Arm Suspension: Another name for a SLA suspension.

Ackermann Angle: The angle formed by imaginary lines drawn through the steering arms when those lines form a "V," whose point intersects the center of the rear axle.

Ackermann Effect: Toe-out on turns resulting from using Ackermann steering geometry. The effect of the Ackermann angle is to reduce scuffing by having both front wheels circle around the same turning center.

Actuator: A device that receives an electrically coded command from an electronic control module and responds by performing a mechanical action.

Adhesion: Gripping power. For an automotive tire, adhesion is the amount of grip between the contact patch and the road.

Aerodynamics: The study of the effect of airflow on a moving object.

Air Bag: A large nylon bag, compactly stored in the steering wheel or dashboard, that inflates in a fraction of a second during a head-on collision to protect the driver or passenger from impact with the steering wheel and dashboard.

Air Bag Module: The part of a steering wheel that contains the air bag, ignitor, flammable-gas canister, and sodium azide pellets. Also called an "inflator module."

Air Shock Absorber: A heavy-duty shock absorber stiffened by the addition of an air chamber at the top of the cylinder.

Air Spring: A spring made of a closed rubber chamber filled with air.

All-Wheel Drive (AWD): A full-time four-wheel drive system typically found on a FWD platform with a transverse engine modified to transfer torque to both axles. This configuration usually combines the transfer case with the transaxle, which drives an extra output shaft that connects to a rear differential to power the rear wheels.

Alternating Current: The movement of electrical current through a conductor first in one direction, then in the opposite direction.

Amplitude: The strength of an electrical signal determined by the difference between the lowest and highest voltage levels.

Analog: A voltage signal or processing function that can vary infinitely between a minimum and maximum level.

Antiroll Bar: A transverse suspension link that transfers some of the load on one wheel to the opposite wheel on the same axle in order to minimize body roll during cornering. Also called an "antisway bar," "sway bar," or "stabilizer bar."

Aquaplaning: Another name for hydroplaning.

Armature: A current-carrying conductor inside a motor, which reacts to the magnetic field generated by the field coils by moving to a weaker area of the field. Armature movement provides mechanical energy for work.

Axial Play: Movement along, or parallel to, the axis of a shaft. Axial play is measured in fractions of inches or millimeters.

Axis: A line on which an object rotates.

Axle: The rod on which a wheel or wheels rotate. Depending on the suspension design, an automotive axle may or may not directly link the two wheels.

Axle Windup: In a rear, driven axle, the reaction of the axle housing against axle shaft rotation, in which the axle housing tries to rotate in the opposite direction. Axle windup creates a lifting force on the driveshaft.

Ball Joint: A type of coupling, whose two main parts are a ball and socket, that allows continuous angle changes between the two components it joins together.

Ball Nut: A part of a recirculating ball steering gear that has a groove cut inside it corresponding to the groove on the worm gear, creating a tunnel through which steel balls roll to move the ball nut and sector gear.

Ball-and-Cage Constant Velocity (CV) Joint: A CV joint that consists of an inner race, six ball bearings—

which are set 60 degrees apart—a ball cage, and an outer race.

Bar Mount: A shock absorber mounting bar that extends across the top or bottom of the shock and has slots for attaching it to the frame or suspension with bolts or studs.

Bayonet Mount: A shock absorber mounting stud that extends straight out from the top or bottom of the shock.

Beam Axle: A bar or tube running from one wheel to the other on a non-drive axle.

Bearing: A component that reduces friction between two parts that move relative to each other. A bearing may be either a smooth surface between two parts, or a caged device of balls or rollers.

Belted Bias Ply Tire: A bias ply tire with one or more corded belts running around the circumference of the tire.

Bevel Gear: A gear with teeth cut at an angle on its outer surface. Bevel gears often transmit motion between two shafts at an angle to one another.

Bias Ply Tire: A tire in which the carcass is formed of plies with their cords running diagonally to each other.

Birfield Joint: A fixed, ball-and-cage CV joint that is one assembly with the shaft on which it is mounted.

Bolt Circle: The circle formed by the lug bolt holes of a wheel disc. Bolt circle is specified by the number of bolt holes and the diameter of the circle they form.

Boot: A protective cover, pleated to allow compression and expansion, made of rubber or plastic. Also called a "bellows."

Bounce: In a suspension, the cycle of jounce followed by rebound, or compression and extension.

Bump Steer: A steering condition in which a tie rod resists steering arm movement during suspension travel and either jerks the steering arm inward or pushes it outward, effectively steering the wheel in a direction not intended by the driver.

Bump Stop: A rubber cushion that prevents metal-to-metal contact when the suspension compresses or prohibits excessive travel when the suspension extends.

Bushing: A rubber or metal cylinder that allows relative movement between the two parts it joins together.

Cam and Lever Steering Gear: A type of standard steering gear, no longer in common use, that uses a cam as the input gear and a pivoting lever as the output gear.

Camber: The angle between the centerline of the tire and a vertical line perpendicular to a level surface. More simply, camber is the tilt of a wheel and tire assembly, viewed from the front of the vehicle.

Camber Change: The increase in negative camber during jounce that occurs in SLA, strut, and SLA/strut suspensions. This camber change decreases tire scuff during bumps.

Camber Roll: The amount of camber change that occurs when wheels are steered to either side and pivot on the steering axis. Caster determines camber roll.

Caster: The angle between the steering axis and a vertical line perpendicular to a level surface, viewed from the side. More simply, caster is the forward or backward tilt of the steering axis.

Caster Trail: The distance between where the caster line intersects the ground and the center of the tire contact patch.

Center Link: The part of a parallelogram steering linkage that transmits movement from the pitman arm to the tie rods.

Center of Gravity (CG): The point in an object around which the weight of the object is evenly distributed.

Center Point Steering Linkage: A steering linkage configuration consisting of a pitman arm, drag link or drag link and bellcrank, intermediate steering arm, and two tie rods. The tie rods meet at the center of the linkage and are connected to the intermediate steering arm, which the drag link connects to the pitman arm. Also called "equal arm steering linkage."

Centrifugal Force: That force which tends to keep moving objects traveling in a straight line, when a moving vehicle is forced to make a turn, centrifugal force attempts to keep it moving in a straight line, if the vehicle is turning at too high a speed, centrifugal force will be greater than the frictional force between the tires and the road and the vehicle will slide off the road. It is the reciprocal of centripetal force, which is the true force.

Chapman Strut Suspension: A type of MacPherson strut system used at the rear axle. The term "Chapman strut" is commonly used in Britain in reference to the designer who first used rear MacPherson struts.

Chassis: The part of an automobile structure consisting of the steering system, the suspension system, and the wheels and tires.

Check Ball: A type of hydraulic valve consisting of a ball that seals an orifice when it is seated and can be unseated to open the orifice.

Clearance: The space between mechanical parts that permits movement between them.

Clockspring Contact: A tightly coiled metal strip that allows steering wheel rotation while maintaining electrical contact between the electrical wiring in the steering wheel and the wiring harness in the steering column.

Coefficient of Friction (Cf): A measurement of friction between two surfaces. For an automotive tire, the coefficient of friction indicates the adhesion between the contact patch and the road surface.

Coil Spring: A spring made of a length of steel alloy wire wound into a coil.

Coil-over Shock Absorber: A heavy-duty shock absorber stiffened by the addition of a coil spring around the cylinder.

Column Cover: The cover encasing the section of the steering column that extends into the passenger compartment to conceal the wiring for jacket-mounted switches.

Column Jacket: The part of the steering column that encases and protects the steering shaft and serves as the mounting point for a number of driver-operated devices.

Commutator: A device that changes the direction of electrical current. In many motors, the commutator is a conductive ring that is split into two or more pieces. Brushes carry current to and from the commutator, and the direction of the current reverses as the commutator rotates.

Compliance Steer: A rear toe change that results from suspension links and bushings deforming due to cornering force. Engineers design suspension bushings to predictably distort under particular circumstances to provide compliance steer.

Compression Rod: A strut rod that extends from a frame mounting point forward to the control arm. Also called a "leading strut rod" because the control arm leads the rod.

Compression-Loaded Ball Joint: A load-carrying suspension ball joint in which the force exerted by the arm works with the force exerted by the knuckle to push the ball into the socket and seat the joint.

Consistency: Firmness or texture; the consistency of an automotive grease is mainly a factor of how thick it is.

Constant Velocity (CV) Joint: A shaft coupling, consisting either of a ball and cage assembly or a tripod and tulip, that allows changes in the angle between two rotating shafts without affecting the rate of rotation.

Constant-Rate Spring: A spring that continues to compress at the same rate as more weight is applied to it.

Control Arm: A suspension link that attaches to the knuckle or wheel flange at one end and pivots on a frame member at the opposite end.

Control Valve: The valve in a power steering system that controls the application of pressurized fluid against the power piston.

Cross Steering Linkage: A single-tie-rod steering linkage in which the drag link reaches from the pitman arm on one side of the vehicle to the tie rod end on the opposite side.

Cross-Groove Joint: A plunging, ball-and-cage CV joint that uses angled grooves in the inner and outer races to allow plunge.

Crossmember: A lateral, or transverse, steel rail in the automobile frame, running from one side member to the other.

Cycle: A sequence of changes of state after which the system is in its original state again. A series of events or operations, which have a tendency to repeat in the same order.

Damping: The ability of an object or material to dissipate or absorb vibration.

Damping Force: The total resistance, compression, and extension, of a shock absorber. Also called "control force."

Dead Axle: A solid, non-drive axle. Dead axles can be used at either the front or rear of a vehicle, but they are more common at the rear.

Desiccant: A drying agent, consisting of a substance that attracts moisture to itself and so removes moisture from another element.

Diagonal Wipe: A tire wear pattern, which usually occurs on the rear tires of a front-wheel-drive vehicle, that appears as diagonal stripes across the tread and results from excessive toe.

Digital: A voltage signal or processing function with only two levels: on/off or high/low.

Direct-Acting Shock Absorber: A shock absorber that attaches directly to the frame and suspension of the vehicle.

Directional Control Angle: A wheel alignment angle that affects the steering and handling of the vehicle.

Directional Tire: A tire tread pattern that provides the greatest amount of traction when rotating in one particular direction. A directional tire should not be switched from one side of the vehicle to the other.

Dive: Forward tilting of the vehicle body caused by deceleration forces pushing down on the front of the vehicle, effectively rotating the body around the lateral horizontal axis.

Dog-Tracking: A condition in which the rear wheels of a vehicle follow a path parallel to the path of the front wheels.

Double-Cardan Joint: A shaft coupling, consisting of two sets of yokes with two crosspieces joining them together, that allows changes in the angle between two rotating shafts with minimal effect on the rate of rotation.

Double-Offset Joint: A plunging, ball-and-cage CV joint that uses long grooves in the outer race to allow plunge.

Double-Wishbone Suspension: Another name for a SLA suspension or for a strut/SLA suspension.

Downforce: Air pressure on top of a vehicle, pushing it downward.

Drag Link: A steering linkage part that connects the pitman arm to another linkage component. A drag link is used in steering configurations in which the pitman arm is indirectly connected to the rest of the linkage.

Drive Axle: An axle that transmits torque from the differential gears to the wheels.

Dropping Point: The temperature at which a grease sample forms a drop that falls off the sample.

Dynamic Balance: The state of a wheel and tire assembly if its weight is evenly distributed side-to-side.

Electric Power Steering (EPS): A power steering system that uses an electric motor to reduce the amount of effort needed to steer the vehicle.

Electromagnet: A soft iron core wrapped in a coil of conductive material, usually copper wire. When current passes through the conductive coil, it magnetizes the core and creates a magnetic field around the assembly.

Electronic Control Module (ECM): In an automotive electronic system, a small onboard computer that processes information received from sensors and sends signals to various actuators so they operate in response to the driving conditions.

Electronic Suspension Control (ESC) System: The Electronic Suspension Control (ESC) system, also known as the Magneto-Rheological Real Time Damping (MR-RTD) system, independently controls the fluid viscosity in each of the four shock absorbers in order

to control the vehicle ride characteristics. The ESC system is capable of making these changes within milliseconds.

Endplay: Axial play, when measured at the end of a shaft.

EPS Motor: Electric power steering electric motor.

Equal-Arm Suspension: A suspension system, obsolete for many years, that uses two control arms of equal length, upper and lower, at each wheel. Also called "parallelogram suspension."

ESC Damper: The ESC shock absorbers or dampers are monotube type, which provide damping by increasing magnetic flux to magnetic particles to resist suspension movement. The ESC shock absorber has the capability of providing multiple modes or values of damping forces, in both compression and rebound direction.

ESC Module: The ESC module is used to control how firm or soft each shock or strut should be to provide the best ride. The ESC module is also used to control the vehicle's rear height.

ESC Position Sensors: The ESC position sensors provide the ESC module with the body to wheel displacement input. These position sensors are 0 to 5 volt DC output devices that are used to measure wheel-to-body movement/position.

Fail-Safe System: Any component or group of components that enables a vehicle to operate safely in the event that one of its systems, such as a hydraulic or an electronic system, malfunctions.

Fixed Joint: A CV joint that does not allow plunging movement of a shaft, but does allow a sharper angle between the shafts. A fixed joint is always used at the outboard end of a front axle shaft and can be used

at the inboard end or outboard end of a rear axle shaft.

Fixed Tripod Joint: A tripod CV joint in which the tripod is fixed to the tulip in such a way as to prevent plunging action of the joint.

Flat Ride Tuning: Varying the natural frequency between the front and rear suspensions in order to prevent pitch.

Flexible Coupling: A shaft coupling, made of rubber or fabric reinforced rubber and a solid safety connection, that allows changes in the angle between two rotating shafts.

Flow Control Valve: Alternate name for a modulator valve.

Fluid: A liquid substance. In an automotive hydraulic system, fluids transfer pressure from one surface to another. Automotive fluids also frequently have the secondary purpose of lubricating and cooling moving parts.

Force: A push or pull acting on an object, usually measured in pounds or newtons.

Four-Wheel Alignment: A wheel alignment procedure performed on all four wheels of a vehicle; rear wheels first, then front wheels.

Four-Wheel Drive (4WD): An automotive drive layout in which all four wheels provide the power to move the vehicle.

Four-Wheel Steering (4WS): A type of steering system that can operate all four wheels when the driver turns the steering wheel.

Frame: Supporting structure; in an automobile, the frame is made of two steel side members and a number of crossmembers that support the body, engine, and drivetrain.

Frequency: In electronics, the number of periodic voltage oscillations that occur within a given amount of time, usually expressed as cycles per second, or hertz.

Friction: The resistance to motion of two moving objects or surfaces in contact with each other. Friction generates heat and causes wear in metal components.

Front-Wheel Drive (FWD): An automotive drive layout in which the front wheels provide the power to move the vehicle.

Full-Floating Axle: A solid, driven axle in which the wheel bearings and hub ride on the axle housing, and the wheel attaches to the axle shaft through a flange at that end of the shaft.

Full-Time Four-Wheel Drive (4WD): A 4WD system in which the driver cannot disengage the 4WD function. Full-time 4WD systems generally use some type of limited-slip coupling or computer controls to vary the torque between the front and rear axles, to keep the wheels turning at equal speeds.

G: A unit of measurement for G-forces. One G equals the force of gravity on an object.

Gas-filled Shock Absorber: A hydraulic shock absorber in which the air in the reserve tube is replaced by pressurized gas.

Gear Lash: A lack of mesh between two gears, resulting in a lag between when one gear moves and when it engages the other.

Gear Mesh Preload: The resistance that the sector gear or roller of a standard steering gear exerts against worm gear movement, or the force that is required to move the worm gear against that resistance.

Gear Oil: A petroleum-based oil of the proper viscosity and chemical composition for use in a gearbox. Gear oils cling to gear surfaces to reduce friction and heat generated by the moving gears.

Gear Pump: A pump that uses the meshing of two gears inside the pump body to produce fluid flow. The meshing of the rotating gears creates fluid chambers of varying volumes.

Geometric Centerline: An imaginary line that bisects the front and rear axles of a vehicle.

Geometric Centerline Alignment: An alignment that is made using the centerline of the vehicle as a guide. It is used as a reference for front wheel toe; the toe on each front wheel is adjusted to specifications using the geometric centerline as a reference. This type of wheel alignment has been used for many years. It may provide a satisfactory wheel alignment if the rear wheels are properly positioned and the thrust line is at the vehicle centerline.

G-Force: The force of gravity on an object, which resists changes in speed or direction.

Grease: A thick, non-pourable lubricant, usually made of oil thickened with a soap. Automotive greases are usually petroleum-based and contain additives related to their intended use.

Haltenberger Steering Linkage: A steering linkage configuration consisting of a pitman arm, drag link, and tie rod. The drag link connects the pitman arm to the passenger side steering arm, and the tie rod connects the drag link to the driver side steering arm.

Heavy-Duty Shock Absorber: An extra-stiff hydraulic shock absorber.

Hop: A ride problem that results from radial runout and occurs when a tire repeatedly loses contact with the pavement, then lands again harshly.

Horn Circuit: An electrical circuit, wired in series or through a relay,

that provides current to operate the horn when the driver pushes the horn button.

Hotchkiss Drive: A solid, rear, driven axle with a leaf spring suspension.

Hydraulic Shock Absorber: A shock absorber that damps the oscillation of the suspension spring through hydraulic resistance. Typically, this term refers to the most basic hydraulic shock design.

Hydraulics: The study of liquids and their use to transmit force and motion.

Hydroplaning: A driving condition that occurs when a tire driving on a wet surface builds up a wedge of water in front of it and then drives up onto the wedge, losing contact with the road surface.

I-Beam: A solid, metal axle whose cross-section looks like the capital letter I.

I-Beam Suspension: A suspension system that uses an I-beam axle and usually includes semi-elliptical leaf springs. I-beam suspensions generally are used only on heavy duty, RWD trucks.

Idler Arm: The part of a parallelogram steering linkage that helps the pitman arm to support the center link. The idler arm allows center link movement but does not transmit any movement.

Inboard Constant Velocity (CV) Joint: The CV joint that joins an axle shaft to the transaxle, differential, or transfer case. In a front axle, the inboard CV joint is always a plunging joint.

Included Angle: The steering axis inclination angle plus or minus the camber angle.

Independent Suspension: A suspension design that allows each wheel on an axle to travel vertically without affecting the opposite wheel.

Inertia: The tendency of an object to remain at rest if it is at rest and to remain in motion in the same direction if it is in motion.

Inner Tube: An air-tight rubber tube that fits inside the tire casing and contains air of a tube-type tire.

Inner Wheel Bearing: Of the two bearings between the wheel hub and the spindle or axle shaft, the bearing that is further inboard.

Input: Information that an electronic control module receives and uses to carry out its program. In an automotive electronic system, input comes from sensors and switches throughout the vehicle.

Input Gear: The gear that provides input motion to, or drives, the rest of the gears in a gear system.

Instant Center: The point around which a wheel and tire assembly pivots during suspension travel.

Integral Power Steering System: A power steering system in which the control valve and the power piston are incorporated into the steering gear construction.

Integral Reservoir: A power steering fluid reservoir that is part of the construction of the power steering pump.

Integral-Stud Mount: A shock absorber mounting stud that extends at a right angle from the top or bottom of the shock.

Interleaf Friction: Resistance created by the leaves of a leaf spring sliding against each other as the spring compresses and extends.

Internal Gear: A gear with teeth cut on its inner circumference. Also known as a ring gear.

Jounce: Suspension compression, occurring when the wheel and tire travel over a bump, or pressure is applied to the top of the suspension.

Kickback: Vibrations and road shocks transmitted through the steering system that the driver can feel at the steering wheel.

Kingpin: A metal cylinder used in the steering knuckle of some beam axles that allows the knuckle to pivot when the steering linkage moves the steering arm.

Knockoff Wheel: A wheel secured to the hub by a single center nut.

Knuckle: A metal casting that supports the wheel, joins the suspension to the wheel, and provides pivot points between them. At a non-drive axle, the knuckle includes the wheel spindle.

Lateral Horizontal Axis: An imaginary line that runs from side-to-side on a vehicle and intersects the center of gravity, around which the car body rotates, or pitches, during acceleration or deceleration.

Lateral Runout: The type of wheel runout that occurs when a wheel and tire do not rotate in a single plane.

Lead: A driving condition in which the vehicle steers to one side if the driver lets go of the steering wheel.

Leaf Spring: A spring made of one or more long, thin strips of spring-steel alloy or plastic composite material.

Leaf Spring Suspension: A suspension system that uses two semi-elliptical leaf springs to secure the axle to the frame. Leaf spring suspensions are typically used on the rear axle of trucks.

Lever Arms: The two short sections of an antiroll bar that extend forward or backward from the end mounting points to the center section of the bar.

Lever Shock Absorber: A shock absorber that attaches directly to the frame, but indirectly, through a lever, to the suspension of the vehicle.

Lift: A condition in which air pressure under a vehicle lifts some of the weight of the vehicle off the wheels.

Light-Emitting Diode (LED): A gallium-arsenide diode that emits energy as light. Current can pass through a diode in only one direction, and an LED turns the current passing through it into light. In an automotive electronic system, a light-emitting diode may be used as a dashboard indicator or as a sensor.

Link: A joining piece. A suspension link is any of the metal rods or arms that are part of the linkage that connects the frame and the wheels.

Live Axle: Alternate name for a solid, drive axle.

Load-Carrying Ball Joint: A ball joint that links a suspension arm to a knuckle and transfers sprung weight from the arm to the wheel.

Long-and-Short-Arm Steering Linkage: A steering linkage configuration consisting of a pitman arm and two tie rods. The tie rods connect directly to the pitman arm at the steering gear. Also called "compensated pitman steering linkage."

Longitudinal Axis: An imaginary line that runs the length of a vehicle front to rear and intersects the front and rear roll centers around which the car body rotates, or rolls, during cornering.

Lower Control Arm: In a SLA or strut/SLA suspension, the lower and longer of the control arms linking the knuckle to the frame. Front suspensions use only one lower control arm, but rear suspensions may use more than one.

MacPherson Strut: A strut that is solidly mounted to the knuckle and includes the suspension spring as part of its construction.

MacPherson Strut Suspension: A strut suspension in which a coil spring is integral to each strut and the strut base mounts rigidly to the knuckle.

MAGNASTEER II®: The GM trademark Variable Effort Steering (VES) system that varies the amount of effort required to steer the vehicle as vehicle speed changes or lateral acceleration occurs.

Magnetic rotary actuator: An electromagnetic actuator that adjusts the amount of power steering assist to achieve a given level of effort to steer the vehicle.

Match Mounting: A method for minimizing runout of a wheel and tire assembly that consists of mounting the tire with its point of highest runout at the point of lowest wheel runout.

Memory Steer: Steering pull caused by installing rubber bonded socket joints without centering the steering system. The joints try to return to their original position, as if they "remembered" it.

Modified Strut: A strut that is solidly mounted to the knuckle but does not include the suspension spring as part of its construction.

Modified Strut Suspension: A strut suspension in which the springs are mounted on the lower control arm, and the strut base mounts rigidly to the knuckle. Modified strut suspensions are more common at the rear than the front.

Modulator Valve: The valve in a power steering pump that controls fluid flow into the pressure hose.

Monoleaf Spring: A leaf spring using only one leaf. Monoleaf springs are usually made of plastic composite material.

Monotube Shock Absorber: A hydraulic shock absorber that uses only one tube, the pressure tube, along with two pistons.

Motor: A machine that converts electrical energy to mechanical energy.

Multi-Link Suspension: A generic term, generally applied to unique suspension designs that do not fit into common categories. Multi-link suspensions are generally used at the rear of performance vehicles.

Natural Frequency: The rate at which the frame and body of a vehicle bounce when there are no shock absorbers installed on the suspension. Also called "suspension frequency" or "wheel frequency."

Negative Offset: A characteristic of a wheel in which the face of the wheel disc is behind, or further inboard than, the rim centerline.

Non-Load-Carrying Ball Joint: A ball joint that links a suspension arm to a knuckle but does not transfer sprung weight from the arm to the wheel. Also called a "follower joint."

Oil: A thick, viscous, but pourable lubricant. Automotive oils are usually petroleum-based and contain additives related to their intended use.

Opposite-Phase Operation: An operational mode of some four-wheel-steering systems, in which the rear wheels steer in the opposite direction of the front wheels.

Order: Refers to how many times an event occurs during one revolution of a rotatintg component.

Orifice: A small opening that regulates fluid pressure and flow. An orifice can be a restriction in a fluid line or a hole between two fluid chambers.

Out of Round: A term used to describe a wheel or tire with radial runout, because it is not perfectly circular.

Outboard Constant Velocity (CV) Joint: The CV joint that joins an axle shaft to the stub axle at the wheel. In a front axle, the outboard CV joint is always a fixed joint.

Outer Wheel Bearing: Of the two bearings between the wheel hub and the spindle or axle shaft, the bearing that is further outboard.

Output: Electrically coded commands that an electronic control module sends to an actuator or actuators. In an automotive electronic system, the output causes a change in some aspect of the vehicle operation.

Output Gear: The final gear in a gear system, which transmits motion to another component.

Oversteer: A driving condition, resulting from greater slip angles at the rear tires than the front, in which the vehicle turns more sharply than steering system input demands.

Overturning Moment: The tendency of a vehicle to overturn during cornering. The greater the tendency becomes, the closer the vehicle is to its overturning moment.

Panhard Rod: A transverse link, used in rear suspensions, joined to the frame at one end and to a beam axle or axle housing at the other end.

Parallelism: A condition of a parallelogram steering linkage in which the center link is parallel to a level surface.

Parallelogram Steering Linkage: A steering linkage configuration consisting of a pitman arm, an idler arm, a center link, and two tie rods. The pitman arm, idler arm, and center link form three sides of a parallelogram.

Part-Time Four-Wheel Drive (4WD): A 4WD system in which the driver can manually disengage one axle from the drivetrain, to provide two-wheel drive.

Pascal's Law: The principle that pressure on a confined fluid is transmitted equally in all directions and acts with equal force on equal areas.

Passive Restraint System: An automatic method of restraining the occupants of a vehicle, to help prevent injury in the event of a head-on collision. The two most common passive restraint devices are automatic shoulder belts and air bags.

Phase-Reverse Operation: An operational mode of some four-wheel-steering systems, in which the rear wheels steer first in the opposite direction of the front wheels, then in the same direction.

Phototransistor: A transistor, also known as a photocell, that reacts to light by producing an electronic signal. In an automotive electronic system, a phototransistor may be used as a sensor.

Pig-Tail Spring End: The end of a coil spring that is cut off, then bent into a smaller, tighter coil than the rest.

Pinion Bearing Preload: The resistance that the bearings in a rack and pinion steering gear exert against the pinion gear and shaft, or the force that is required to overcome that resistance.

Pinion Gear: A smaller gear that meshes with a larger gear wheel or toothed rack.

Pinion Torque: The force required to move the pinion of a rack and pinion steering gear against the resistance exerted by the rack.

Pitch: Forward and rearward tilting of a vehicle body that occurs when acceleration or deceleration forces push down on the front or rear of the chassis effectively rotating the body around the lateral horizontal axis.

Pitman Arm: The part of some steering linkages that joins the linkage to the steering gear sector shaft and transmits movement from the steering gear to the linkage. Pitman arms are used in parallelogram and some other linkage configurations.

Pivot-Base Strut: A strut that mounts on a pivot bushing affixed to a suspension component, usually the lower control arm.

Platform: The flat surface, usually made of metal, that forms the floor, underbody, and lower side panels of a unit-body vehicle. Frequently, manufacturers build several different models on the same platforms.

Play: The distance that a mechanical part can move without encountering another part.

Plunging Joint: A CV joint that allows plunging, or in-and-out, movement of a shaft. A plunging joint is always used at the inboard end of a front axle shaft and can be used at the inboard end or the outboard end of a rear axle shaft.

Plunging Tripod Joint: A tripod CV joint in which the tripod is not fixed to the tulip, so that the joint can provide plunging action.

Pneumatic Tire: A tire filled with pressurized air. All automotive tires are pneumatic.

Polar Moment of Inertia: The tendency of a vehicle to maintain the same speed and direction. A high polar moment of inertia provides straight-ahead stability; a low polar moment of inertia provides more control during cornering and other changes in direction.

Positive Offset: A characteristic of a wheel in which the face of the wheel disc is in front of, or further outboard than, the rim centerline.

Pour Point: The temperature at which a fluid becomes liquid enough to pour.

Pour Point Depressants: Additives that lower the pour point of a fluid. A lower pour point enables a fluid to remain liquid, instead of becoming stiff, at colder temperatures.

Power Piston: The hydraulically operated piston in a power steering system that helps move the output member of the steering gear when pressure is applied to one side of it.

Power Steering Control Module (PSCM): A computer that is part of the EPS assembly, which uses a combination of torque sensor inputs, vehicle speed, calculated system temperature, and the tuning profile to determine the amount of steering assist.

Power Steering Fluid: The petroleum-based hydraulic fluid used in automotive power steering systems. Power steering fluid contains additives that raise its boiling point, lower its pour point, and make it compatible with the seals and components in a specific power steering system.

Power-Assisted Steering: A boost added to steering system operation so that the driver can turn the steering wheel with less effort.

Powertrain Control Module (PCM): In an automotive electronic system, a small onboard computer that processes information received from sensors and sends signals to various actuators to regulate their operation in response to the driving conditions.

Preload: The resistance one mechanical part exerts against the movement of another part, or the force that is required to overcome that resistance. Preload is measured in inch-pounds, foot-pounds, or Newton-meters.

Pressure: Force applied to a specific area, usually measured in pounds per square inch or kilopascals.

Pressure Hose: The strongly constructed, reinforced-rubber hose in a power steering system that carries fluid under pressure from the pump to the steering gear. In a linkage power steering system, the pressure hose links the pump to the power cylinder.

Pressure Relief Valve: A valve in any hydraulic component that opens to bleed excess pressure when fluid pressure is excessively high. In a power steering system, a pressure relief valve may be used in the pump and the steering gear.

Pressure Switch: An electronic switch on a power steering pump that signals the powertrain control module (PCM) when high pump pressure is placing an excessive load on the engine. In response, the PCM increases engine idle speed to prevent stalling.

Pull: A driving condition in which the driver must actively steer toward one side in order to keep the vehicle moving straight.

Pulse-Width Modulation: The continuous on/off cycling of a solenoid a fixed number of times per second.

Quadrasteer™: The GM trademark name for its four-wheel steering system.

Rack: A gear made of a straight bar with teeth cut into it.

Rack and Pinion Steering Gear: A type of steering gear that uses a pinion as the input gear and a rack as the output gear.

Rack and Pinion Steering Linkage: A term used to refer to the two tie rods that transmit movement from a rack and pinion steering gear to the steering arms.

Radial Load: A load resting on the circumference of a circular component. Wheel bearings carry a radial load because the weight of the vehicle rests on them.

Radial Ply Tire: A tire in which the carcass is formed of plies with their cords at a 90-degree angle to the beads. Most automotive tires manufactured since the 1970s are radials.

Radial Runout: The type of wheel runout that occurs when a wheel and tire do not rotate in a perfect circle around the hub.

Radius Arm: A sturdy suspension link that braces a twin I-beam, or sometimes an axle housing, against the frame.

Rear Power Cylinder: A name used for the unit that steers the rear wheels in a four-wheel-steering system when the unit acts as a rear steering gear but uses hydraulics instead of gearing.

Rear Steering Gear: A type of steering gear designed to steer the rear wheels in a four-wheel-steering system.

Rear-Wheel Drive (RWD): An automotive drive layout in which the rear wheels provide the power to move the vehicle.

Rear Wheel Position Sensor: A variable position resistor that reports the position of the rear wheels to the rear wheel steering control computer.

Rear Wheel Steering Control Module: A computer that controls all aspects of the 4-wheel steering system.

Rear Wheel Steering Mode Switch: Located in the instrument panel, it allows the driver the option of selecting 2-wheel steering, 4-wheel steering, or 4-wheel steering tow modes of operation. The mode switch has indicators that show which mode the rear wheel steering system is in.

Rear Wheel Steering Motor: A stepper motor located on the rear axle that will operate the rear wheel steering rack and pinion, which performs the rear wheel steering.

Rebound: Suspension extension that occurs when the compressing force is removed and the suspension springs release their stored energy.

Recirculating Ball Steering Gear: A type of standard steering gear that uses a worm gear as the input gear and a sector gear as the output gear

and links them indirectly with a ball nut and a series of steel balls.

Regenerative Dryer: In an air-pressurizing system, a dryer that removes moisture from the air as it is drawn into the system, and returns moisture to the air as it is vented from the system. The desiccant in a regenerative dryer lasts longer because it does not become saturated.

Relay Circuit: An electrical circuit in which closing a switch in a low-voltage series circuit triggers current flow through a separate, higher-voltage circuit.

Remote Reservoir: A power steering fluid reservoir that is separate and remotely mounted from the power steering pump. A suction hose connects a remote reservoir to the pump.

Resilience: The ability of an object to return quickly to its original shape after being twisted or compressed.

Resonance: The natural frequency of a typical automotive front suspension is in the 10-15 Hz range. This natural frequency is the result of the suspension design. The suspension's natural frequency is the same at all vehicle speeds. As the tire speed increases along with the variable speed, the disturbance created by the tire increases in frequency. Eventually, the frequency of the unbalanced tire will intersect with the natural frequency of the suspension. This causes the suspension to vibrate. The intersecting point is called the resonance.

Responder: The component where the vibration is felt.

Return Hose: The reinforced-rubber hose in a power steering system that carries fluid from the steering gear to the fluid reservoir.

Rim Width: The distance across the inside of the wheel rim from the inner edge of one flange to the other.

Ring Mount: A shock absorber mount that consists of a bushing enclosed by a ring at the top or bottom of the shock through which a bolt or stud can fit.

Road Crown: The downward slope of a road from its center to its edge.

Roll: The sideways tilting of a vehicle body that occurs when G-force pushes the center of gravity outward to effectively rotate the body around the longitudinal axis.

Roll Axis: Another name for the longitudinal axis.

Roll Center: A point located along the longitudinal axis around which a section of the vehicle rotates during cornering.

Roller Pump: A pump that uses a rotor and rollers inside an elliptic cam ring to produce fluid flow. The action of the rollers creates fluid chambers of varying volumes.

Rotary Control Valve: A type of power steering control valve that operates by rotating one part of it within the other. Also called a torsion bar control valve.

Rubber Bonded Socket (RBS) Tie Rod End: A type of ball joint used in some Ford steering linkages, consisting of a rubber-encased ball stud and a socket.

Run Flat Tires: These are tires that can maintain vehicle mobility as they are punctured.

Rzeppa Joint: A fixed, ball-and-cage CV joint.

Same-Phase Operation: An operational mode of a four-wheel-steering system, in which the rear wheels steer in the same direction as the front wheels.

Scrub Radius: The distance between the points where the steering axis and the centerline of the tire intersect the ground, viewed from the front.

Sector Gear: A gear with teeth cut along only a section of its circumference.

Sector Shaft Endplay: The axial, or end-to-end, movement of the sector shaft in a standard steering gear.

Self-Sealing Tires: Designed to fix most punctures instantly and permanently, these tires feature standard tire construction with the exception of an extra lining inside the tire under the tread area that's coated with a puncture sealant which can permanently seal most punctures from nails, bolts, or screws up to $\frac{3}{16}$ of an inch in diameter.

Self-Supporting Tires: With a stiffer internal construction, which is capable of actually temporarily carrying the weight of the vehicle, even after the tire has lost all air pressure, these tires typically sandwich rubber between layers of heat resistant cord in the sidewall to help prevent the sidewalls from folding over on themselves and "pinching" their sidewalls in the event of loss of air pressure to give the tires "self-supporting" capability.

Semi-Elliptical Leaf Spring: A leaf spring installed so that when viewed from the side, it looks like half an ellipse.

Semi-Floating Axle: A solid, driven axle in which the wheel bearings mount onto the axle shaft or fit inside the axle housing, the brake drum or rotor mounts onto the end of the axle shaft, and the wheel mounts onto the brake drum.

Semi-Independent Suspension: A suspension system in which a crossbeam and a pair of trailing arms indirectly link the rear wheels of a non-driven axle.

Semi-Trailing Arm: A control arm that extends back from a crossmember to the axle housing or a knuckle at an angle to the vehicle centerline.

Semi-Trailing Arm Suspension: A rear suspension system that uses one or more pairs of semi-trailing arms with coil springs or struts.

Sensor: A device that provides an electric signal to an electronic control module to indicate a certain physical condition. In an automotive electronic system, sensors monitor such conditions as vehicle speed, throttle opening, or steering angle.

Series Circuit: An electrical circuit in which electricity has only one path that it can follow when the circuit is complete.

Serpentine Belt: One drive belt that transmits power to all engine-driven accessories. Also called a "V-ribbed" or "poly-V" belt.

Setback: A condition in which one wheel of an axle is located further back in the chassis than the opposite wheel.

Shift Lock Actuator: The ignition lock cylinder control actuator system's purpose is to prevent putting the automatic transmission into gear without applying the service brakes.

Shimmy: Side-to-side movement of the wheels that transfers across the axle and into the passenger compartment.

Shock Absorber: A cushioning device that provides friction to damp the oscillation of a suspension spring. Also called a "damper."

Shock Absorber Ratio: The proportion of shock absorber resistance during extension to the resistance during compression.

Short-Long-Arm (SLA) Suspension: A suspension system that uses at each wheel: a shorter upper arm, a longer lower arm, and a coil spring, torsion bar, or a transverse leaf spring. Short-long-arm suspensions have been widely used on a variety of vehicles.

Side Member: One of two longitudinal steel rails that run along the sides of the underbody of an automobile and are a part of its frame.

Sidewall: The part of the tire casing that stiffens the sides of the tire.

Single-Tie-Rod Steering Linkage: A steering linkage configuration consisting of a pitman arm, drag link, and tie rod. The drag link connects the pitman arm to the tie rod, and the tie rod connects the two steering arms.

Slip Angle: The angle between the direction the tire is aimed and the direction that it actually moves.

Slip Yoke: Two pieces of a shaft, splined together, that can slide axially to allow variation in shaft length.

Slipper Pump: A pump that uses a rotor and spring-loaded slippers inside an elliptic cam ring to produce fluid flow. The action of the slippers creates fluid chambers of varying volumes.

Soap: An additive, formed through a chemical reaction between a base and fatty acids. Soaps make oil thicken into grease. Common bases of soaps in automotive greases are lithium and aluminum.

Solenoid: An electromagnet whose magnetic field operates a rod or shuttle. Typically, the rod or shuttle is extended when the field is weak and retracted when the field is strong.

Solid Axle: A physical link between two wheels that permits one wheel to move vertically without affecting the other wheel. A solid axle in an automobile may be a beam or a differential and axle shafts.

Source: The cause of the vibration.

S-Plan Joint: A type of plunging tripod joint that replaces the tripod roller bearings with bearing blocks to keep the shafts from shuddering.

Speed Rating: An industry-standard maximum service speed for tires.

Tires using an older European system carry the speed rating in the size description: 215/60HR15. Different letters correspond to different maximum service speeds.

Spool Control Valve: A type of power steering control valve that operates by sliding back and forth in a machined bore.

Spool Valve: A hydraulic valve, consisting of lands and valleys, that resembles a spool for thread. The lands seal orifices and the valleys open them.

Spring: A cushioning device that compresses to absorb the force of movement between two parts and then returns to its original shape. Automotive suspensions use four common types of spring: leaf spring, coil spring, torsion bar, and air spring.

Spring Frequency: The rate at which a spring oscillates after it is released from compression or extension.

Spring Rate: The strength or stiffness of a spring, in terms of how much weight it takes to compress the spring a certain amount. Also called "deflection rate."

Sprung Weight: Out of the total weight of a vehicle, the weight that is supported by the suspension springs.

Square Spring End: The end of a coil spring that is cut off, then bent to be square with the spring coils.

Squat: Rearward tilting of the vehicle body caused by acceleration forces pushing down on the rear of the car.

Standard Ball Joint: The type of ball joint most commonly used in steering and suspension systems, typically consisting of a ball stud, socket, wear surface or bearing, preload spring, and dust cover.

Standard Steering Gear: The type of steering gear that was most commonly used from the early years of the automotive industry until the

1980s. The term refers to a number of non-rack and pinion steering gear designs.

Static Balance: The state of a wheel and tire assembly if its weight is evenly distributed around the hub.

Static Load: The load that is continually applied to a spring installed in a suspension.

Static Weight Distribution: The proportion of total vehicle weight resting on each tire when the vehicle is at rest.

Steering Arm: An arm, extending either forward or backward from the steering knuckle that links the wheel to the steering linkage.

Steering Axis: The axis on which the steering knuckle pivots. The steering axis runs through the kingpin, through the centers of the upper and lower ball joints, or through the top pivoting point of the strut and the center of the lower ball joint.

Steering Axis Inclination (SAI): The angle between the steering axis and a vertical line perpendicular to a level surface, viewed from the front. More simply, steering axis inclination is the inward or outward tilt of the steering axis.

Steering Column: The part of the steering system that links the steering wheel to the steering gear. The steering column consists of the steering shaft, column jacket, and column cover. U.S. Federal law requires that the steering column be collapsible.

Steering Column Locking Motor: The steering column lock control module (SCLCM) controls the steering wheel theft deterrent lock function, which allows the column to be electronically locked. The SCLCM controls the column lock motor using an internal lock relay, an internal unlock relay, and an internal lock enable relay.

Steering Damper: A shock absorber that damps steering linkage movement to reduce kickback and shimmy.

Steering Gear: The part of the steering system that changes the rotary movement of the steering shaft to lateral movement of the steering linkage. Also called a "steering gearbox."

Steering Gear Input Shaft: A short shaft linking the steering shaft to the input gear of the steering gear. Usually, a U-joint or flexible coupling joins this shaft to the steering shaft.

Steering Gear Ratio: The number of degrees that the input gear of a steering gearbox must turn in order to turn the output gear one degree. The steering gear ratio is the major determining factor of the overall steering ratio.

Steering Geometry: A method of measuring wheel alignment using angles measured in degrees of a circle.

Steering Knuckle: A knuckle that includes a steering arm to link the wheel to the steering linkage.

Steering Limit Valve: A valve, used in some power steering gears, that drains some pressure away from the power piston at the extremes of piston movement to reduce power assist as the steering wheel approaches complete stop.

Steering Linkage: The assembly of steering system components that transmits movement from the steering gear to the wheels.

Steering Ratio: The number of degrees of rotation a steering wheel must move in order to move the road wheels one degree. High ratios are slower ratios, and low ratios are faster ratios.

Steering Shaft: The shaft inside the steering column that provides the direct mechanical link between the steering wheel and the steering gear.

Steering System: The automotive system that aims the vehicle. The major parts are the steering wheel, steering shaft, steering gear, and steering linkage.

Steering Wheel: The part of the steering system that the driver uses to steer the vehicle.

Steering Wheel Freeplay: The amount the steering wheel can be turned, using light pressure, before it meets resistance. It is an indicator of steering system responsiveness.

Steering Wheel Position Sensor (SWPS): A variable position resistor that reports the position of the steering wheel to the rear wheel steering control computer.

Stepper Motor: A motor that operates in incremental steps, from de-energized to fully energized.

Stiffness: The resistance level of any suspension cushioning device, either a spring or shock absorber.

Stress Raiser: A flaw in the metal of a coil spring or torsion bar that creates extra stress on the metal, which causes it to bend more easily at that point.

Strut: A sturdy shock absorber that is also a structural component of the suspension.

Strut Rod: A suspension link that braces a lower control arm against the frame to prevent front-to-rear movement.

Strut Suspension: A suspension system that uses at each wheel: a strut whose base rigidly mounts to the knuckle, a lower control arm or arms, and a coil spring, which can be either integral to the strut or a separate component.

Strut/Short-Long-Arm (Strut/SLA) Suspension: A suspension that uses upper and lower control arms and a pivot-base strut at each wheel. As in a SLA suspen-sion, the upper control arm or arms are shorter than the lower control arm or arms. Usually the pivoting strut base mounts on a lower control arm.

Stub Axle: A wheel spindle extending from a knuckle or suspension arm that supports one wheel. A stub axle is used at each wheel of a non-drive axle with independent or semi-independent suspension.

Sub-Frame: A small frame, which is separate from the unit-body platform, that installs onto a unit-body to support the engine or the rear differential.

Supplemental Inflatable Restraint (SIR) System: Another name for an air bag.

Suspension System: The automotive system that supports the body and powertrain, and transfers vehicle weight to the wheels and tires. The major parts are the frame, axle, control arms and other links, cushioning devices, and wheel knuckle.

Switch: A device within an electrical circuit that can stop current by moving a pair of contacts away from each other, or provide a path for current by placing the contacts in touch with each other. When the contacts are not touching, the switch is "open" and disrupts the current path. When the contacts do touch, the switch is "closed" and current can pass through it.

Tangential Spring End: The end of a coil spring that is cut off mid-coil and left in the coil shape.

Tapered-End Spring: A coil spring with the end of the wire ground flat.

Tension Rod: A strut rod that extends from a frame mounting point rearward to the lower control arm. Also called a "trailing strut rod" because the control arm trails the rod.

Tension-Loaded Ball Joint: A load-carrying suspension ball joint in which the force exerted by the arm opposes that exerted by the knuckle. The opposing forces seat the ball in the socket of the joint.

Three-Quarter-Floating Axle: A solid, driven axle in which bearings are mounted in a hub on the brake drum or rotor. The brake assembly mounts onto the axle housing, splines connect the axle shaft to the hub, and the wheel attaches to the hub and brake assembly.

Thrust Alignment: A wheel alignment procedure that aligns the front wheels to the thrust line, rather than to the vehicle centerline, which is performed when a thrust angle cannot be eliminated from the vehicles.

Thrust Angle: The angle between the thrust line and the geometric centerline of a vehicle.

Thrust Line: An imaginary line that extends forward from the center point of the rear axle and bisects, or cuts in half, the total toe of the rear wheels.

Thrust Line Alignment: A four-wheel alignment based on the thrust line of the vehicle. The thrust line created by the rear wheels is used as a reference for front wheel toe adjustment. When the front wheel toe is adjusted with a thrust line reference and this line is not at the geometric centerline, neither the front nor rear wheels are parallel to the geometric centerline. Under this condition, none of the four wheels is facing straight ahead when the vehicle is driven straight ahead. This action results in excessive feathered wear on all four tire treads. This type of alignment assures a centered steering wheel when the vehicle is driven straight ahead.

Thrust Load: A load transferred along the length of a shaft. Wheel bearings carry a radial load during cornering, as centrifugal force ap-

plies a side load along the axle shaft or spindle.

Thrust Movement: Movement along the length of a shaft. Wheel bearings must contain thrust movement during cornering, as centrifugal force tries to move the axle shaft or spindle outward.

Tie Rods: The parts of a steering linkage that transmit movement to the steering arms. Most tie rods consist of an inner tie rod end and an outer tie rod end, and sometimes an adjusting sleeve or rod.

Tilt Mechanism: A device that allows the driver to adjust the angle of the steering wheel relative to the steering column.

Tire: The rubber cushion that mounts on the wheel to provide traction and to absorb minor road shocks.

Tire Aspect Ratio: The tire section height divided by the tire section width, then multiplied by 100.

Tire Beads: Steel wire strands looped around the inner circumference of each tire sidewall that hold the tire on the wheel.

Tire Carcass: The foundation of the tire, consisting of plies forming the basic shape of the tire and beads around the inner circumference of each side of the tire that secure and seal the tire to the wheel.

Tire Casing: Layers of rubber bonded to the tire carcass to give it stiffness.

Tire Contact Patch: The part of the tire that touches the ground. Also called the "footprint."

Tire Performance Criteria (TPC): This is a specification number molded into the sidewall. This number represents performance standards for traction, endurance, dimensions, noise, handling, and rolling resistance. Other performance areas, such as wet traction,

rolling resistance, tread life, and air retention, are also included. These tires are identified by an M + S molded in the tire sidewall after the tire size. The suffix MS is also molded in the tire sidewall after the TPC specification number. The optional handling tires used on some vehicles now also have the MS marking after the tire size and the TPC specification number.

Tire Placard: This is a label used to display tire pressure and capacity information. It is permanently located on the edge of the driver's door. Refer to the placard to obtain the following: maximum vehicle capacity weight, cold tire inflation pressures, tire sizes (original equipment tires), and tire speed ratings (original equipment tires).

Tire Ply: Rayon, nylon, fiberglass, polyester, or steel cords arranged alongside each other and bonded together to form the material used to construct a tire carcass.

Tire Pressure Monitor (TPM): This is a system that allows the driver to display all 4-tire pressures on the Driver Information Center (DIC) while the vehicle is being driven.

Tire Section Height: The height of the tire cross section from the top of the beads to the bottom of the tread.

Tire Section Width: The width of the tire cross section from the outside of one sidewall to the other.

Tire Tread: The layer of rubber bonded around the outer circumference of the tire casing that has a pattern molded into it to help the tire grip the road.

Tire Wear Angle: A wheel alignment angle that affects the rate at which tires wear out.

Toe: The angle between the direction a wheel is aimed and a line parallel to the centerline of the vehicle. When measured linearly, toe is the distance between the leading edges of the tires subtracted from the distance between the trailing edges.

Toe Change: A change in the direction a tire is aimed that results from suspension compression or extension. Tie rod height and length affect toe change, which is essentially the same condition as bump steer.

Toe-In: A description of the toe angle when the leading edges of the two tires on the same axle point toward each other. Also called "positive toe."

Toe-Out: A description of the toe angle when the leading edges of the two tires on the same axle point away from each other. Also called "negative toe."

Toe-Out on Turns: The tendency for the outside wheel to travel in a larger arc than the inside wheel as the vehicle is driven around a corner. Toe-out on turns is a result of the Ackermann angle.

Tolerance: The acceptable clearance between any two mechanical parts.

Torque: Turning force; force that produces rotation.

Torque Arm: A large suspension link, used with a RWD powertrain, that parallels the driveshaft and bolts to the differential at one end and the transmission at the other. A torque arm distributes the force of axle windup along its length.

Torque-Sensor: A sensor that determines the amount of steering assist on an electric power steering system (EPS).

Torque Steer: A driving condition in which the vehicle steers to one side during hard acceleration from high speed and in the opposite direction during sudden deceleration. Front-wheel-drive vehicles with unequal-length axle shafts are prone to torque steer.

Torsion: Twisting action, particularly as applied to turning one end of a rod while the other end is kept from turning.

Torsion Bar: A spring made of a length of steel alloy rod.

Track Rod: Another name for a Panhard rod.

Track Width: The distance between the centers of the contact patches of the two tires on the same axle.

Tracking: The natural tendency of the rear wheels on a vehicle in motion to follow in the tracks of the front wheels.

Trail Angle: The angle at which the axis of the bushings in a semi-trailing arm intersects the vehicle centerline.

Trailing: A descriptive word for any suspension component that extends back from a crossmember and is parallel to the vehicle centerline.

Trailing Arm: A control arm that runs parallel to the vehicle centerline and extends back from a crossmember to the axle housing or a knuckle.

Trailing Arm Suspension: A rear suspension system, usually used with a solid axle, that uses one or more pairs of trailing arms with springs or struts to position the axle. A trailing arm suspension usually includes a Panhard rod or a central control arm.

Tramp: Another name for hop.

Transfer Path: The path the vibration travels through the vehicle.

Transistor: An electronic device, made of a semiconductor material, that controls the path of electrical current. A transistor is a three-terminal device used for signal amplification, switching, and detection.

Triangulation: The use of a three-point connection between the frame and wheel. A triangular suspension structure effectively braces the wheel against road forces from all directions, but still allows the wheel to move vertically and pivot on the steering axis.

Trim Height: In general, the height of a vehicle body. Manufacturers specify measuring trim height either from the center of each wheel or from a level ground surface to a specific point on the body.

Triplan Joint: A type of plunging tripod joint that uses needle bearings to keep the shafts from shuddering.

Tripod: The part of a tripod CV joint that has three arms, each with a roller joint, that allows tulip rotation, and that can roll up and down the tracks in the housing, or tulip. Also called a "spider."

Tripod Constant Velocity (CV) Joint: A CV joint that consists of a tripod and tulip.

Tubeless Tire: A type of tire that uses no inner tube but in which the air chamber is formed by the tire carcass and the wheel rim. Most automotive tires manufactured since the 1940s are tubeless.

Tulip: The housing of a tripod CV joint, which has three tracks for the tripod to travel in.

Turning Center: The imaginary point around which a vehicle rotates during cornering.

Turning Radius: The distance from the turning center to the outside wheels during cornering. Sometimes this term is used to refer to toe-out on turns, since that angle determines the turning radius.

Twin I-Beam Axle: Two I-beams, each fastened to a knuckle at one end and to the frame at the other end.

Twin I-Beam Suspension: A suspension system that uses two I-beams and usually includes radius arms and coil springs. Twin I-beam suspensions generally are used only in certain Ford RWD trucks.

Two-Wheel Alignment: A wheel alignment procedure performed only on the front wheels of a vehicle.

Two-Wheel Steering (2WS): A type of steering system that operates only the front wheels when the driver turns the steering wheel.

Uncompressed Length: The length or height of a spring with no load applied to it. Also called "free length."

Understeer: A driving condition, resulting from greater slip angles at the front tires than the rear, in which the vehicle turns less sharply than steering system input demands.

Undertread Layer: The part of the tire casing that stiffens the circumference of the tire and helps bond the tread to the carcass.

Unequal-Arm Suspension: Another name for a SLA suspension.

Unit-Body Construction: A method of building an automotive frame and body so that the frame is integral to the body and consists of strong, reinforced body panel sections.

Universal Joint (U-Joint): A shaft coupling, consisting of two yokes with a steel crosspiece joining them together, that allows changes in the angle between two rotating shafts. Also called a "Cardan joint."

Unsprung Weight: Out of the total weight of a vehicle, the weight that is not supported by the suspension springs.

Upper Control Arm: In a SLA or strut/SLA suspension, the higher and shorter of the control arms linking the knuckle to the frame. Front suspensions use only one upper control arm, but rear suspensions may use more than one.

Vane Pump: A pump that uses a slotted rotor and sliding vanes inside

an elliptic cam ring to produce fluid flow. The sliding of the vanes creates fluid chambers of varying volumes.

Variable Effort Steering: A steering system where the steering assist is in proportion to the amount of steering effort required.

Variable Shock Absorber: A shock absorber whose resistance can be changed either manually or automatically.

Variable Steering Ratio: A steering ratio that is high, or slow, during the first degrees of steering wheel movement and decreases, or becomes faster, the further the steering wheel is turned.

Variable-Assist Power Steering System: A type of power steering system that provides more assist at low speeds and for sharp cornering, and less at high speeds and for wider turns. A variable system may be hydraulically or electronically controlled.

Variable-Rate Spring: A spring that compresses more slowly as more weight is applied to it.

V-Belt: A drive belt with a V-shaped cross section that transmits power to one or two engine-driven accessories.

Vertical Axis: An imaginary line that runs from top-to-bottom of a vehicle and intersects the center of gravity, around which the body rotates, or yaws, after the vehicle changes direction.

Viscosity: The resistance to flow of an oil or fluid. The more viscous a fluid or oil is, the thicker it is, and the higher its resistance to flow.

Weight Transfer: The movement of the center of gravity in an object that results from external forces.

Wheel: The component, consisting of a disc and rim, onto which the tire mounts and which rotates on the axle or spindle.

Wheel Alignment: The positioning of the wheels of a vehicle in relation to each other and to the vehicle structure.

Wheel Backspacing: The distance between the back, or inboard, side of the wheel disc and the inner wheel rim flange. Also called "back side setting."

Wheel Balance: The weight distribution of a wheel and tire. A wheel and tire are out of balance if their weight is not evenly distributed around the hub and side-to-side.

Wheel Bearing Endplay: The amount that a wheel can slide axially, or in-and-out, along the length of the spindle.

Wheel Bearing Preload: The amount of pressure between the rollers or balls and the races of the wheel bearings.

Wheel Diameter: The distance across the center of the wheel between the outer edges of the wheel rim flange.

Wheel Disc: The flat, round part of a wheel that bolts onto the hub.

Wheel Dish: The distance between the face, or outboard side, of the wheel disc and the outer wheel rim flange.

Wheel Offset: The distance between the face of the wheel disc and the rim centerline.

Wheel Rate: The amount a suspension spring compresses as compared to the force applied to the wheel and tire.

Wheel Rim: The part of the wheel that encircles the wheel disc and retains the tire. The rim consists of the well, bead seats, and flanges.

Wheel Runout: Imperfect movement of a wheel and tire assembly around its axis. A wheel and tire have runout if they do not rotate in a perfect circle around the hub and in a single plane.

Wheelbase: The distance from the centerline of the front axle to the centerline of the rear axle.

Wobble: A ride problem that results from lateral runout and occurs when the top of a rolling tire constantly moves in and out.

Worm and Roller Steering Gear: A type of standard steering gear that uses a worm gear as the input gear and a roller as the output gear.

Worm and Sector Steering Gear: A type of standard steering gear, no longer in common use, that uses a worm gear as the input gear and a sector gear as the output gear. The two gears are in direct mesh.

Worm Bearing Preload: The resistance that the thrust bearings in a standard steering gear exert against worm gear movement, or the force required to move the worm gear against that resistance.

Worm Endplay: The axial, or end-to-end, movement of the worm gear in a standard steering gear.

Worm Gear: A gear that is shaped like a shaft with gear teeth cut as a continuous spiral around its outer surface. A worm gear changes the axis of rotation when it turns another gear.

Yaw: Swaying movement of the vehicle body that occurs when road forces push the front or the rear of the car to one side, effectively rotating the body around the vertical axis.

Index